The
a
Dell.

ig Little Books. Ron
ow up to be a comic-
Co. of Connecticut
comic books that will
ed Funnies on Parade,
given away as a
Chicago, the Humor
k-and-white comic
e Dan.

William
rs Al
ey
ces a
itles,
ted Tales,
d Crime
Crime,
or titles
ly.

1934 *Eastern Color decides to sell comic books on the stands. They launch* Famous Funnies, *which contains sixty-four full-color pages, costs a dime, and includes reprints of such strips as* Mutt & Jeff, Joe Palooka, *and, after the third issue,* Buck Rogers. *The magazine proves to be a success.* ■ *At the very end of the year, impecunious ex-cavalryman, army critic, and pulp-fiction writer Major Malcolm Wheeler-Nicholson brings forth a tabloid-size comic book featuring all original material.* New Fun *is published by his National Allied Publishing, Inc., which will eventually become, after the major is tossed out, DC Comics.*

1935 *Late this year Major Nicholson rechristens his pioneering magazine* More Fun Comics *and reduces it to the half-tabloid size invented by* Famous Funnies. *He introduces* New Comics, *his second original material title. The major continues in shaky financial shape. His early, underpaid contributors include Sheldon Mayer, Creig Flessel, and Jerry Siegel and Joe Shuster.*

1936 *More reprint titles.* Popular Comics *from Dell,* Tip Top Comics *from United Feature,* King Comics *from David McKay. On the original front a pair of Nicholson alums start* The Comics Magazine *(soon changed to* Funny Pages*). They follow that with* Funny Picture Stories *and* Detective Picture Stories, *the first all-detective comic.*

1937 *Original stuff continues.* ■ *Entrepreneur Harry "A" Chesler introduces* Star Comics *and* Star Ranger Comics, *an early Western.* ■ *Everett "Busy" Arnold starts* Feature Funnies, *the cornerstone of his Quality line.* ■ *Major Nicholson, in partnership with Harry Donenfeld and Jack Liebowitz, introduces* Detective Comics.

1938 *The Golden Age commences when Jerry Siegel and Joe Shuster's* Superman *debuts in Detective Comics, Inc.'s* Action Comics #1, *and the concept of superheroes is introduced.* ■ *Pulp-publisher Fiction House starts the oversized* Jumbo Comics, *which introduces Sheena, Queen of the Jungle.*

1951 *Martin Goodman abandons such company names as Timely Comics and hangs the Atlas logo on all his comic books.*

1952 *Kurtzman invents* Mad *for EC, featuring such artists as Jack Davis, Wally Wood, and Will Elder.*

1953 *Fawcett shuts down its comic-book division and Billy Batson ceases shouting, "Shazam!" and turning into Captain Marvel.* ■ *3-D comic books are, all too briefly, a big hit.*

1954 *Continued proliferation of crime and horror comics causes proliferation of public criticism.* ■ *Fredric Wertham's* Seduction of the Innocent *links comic-book reading with juvenile delinquency and sexual perversion. The Senate Committee on Juvenile Delinquency holds hearings on comic books, parents and community leaders toss offending comics on bonfires in various parts of the country, and publishers feel obliged to set up the Comics Code Authority to self-police themselves. Even so, many companies collapse and hard times follow for most of the survivors.*

COMIC BOOK ENCYCLOPEDIA

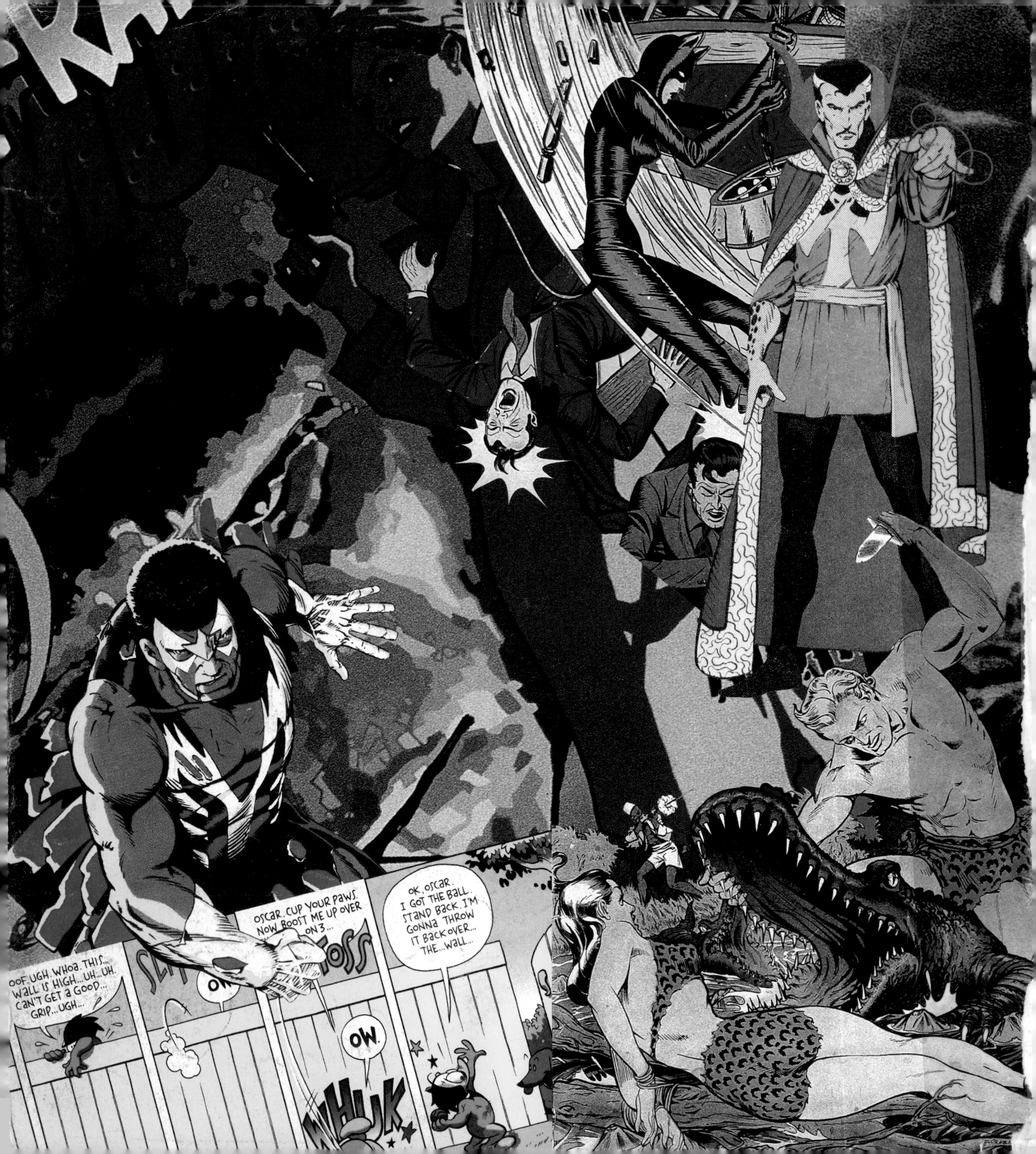
OOF. UGH. WHOA. THIS... WALL IS HIGH... UH... UH. CAN'T GET A GOOD... GRIP... UGH...
OSCAR. CUP YOUR PAWS. NOW BOOST ME UP OVER ON 3...
OW.
WHUK
OK, OSCAR. I GOT THE BALL. STAND BACK. I'M GONNA THROW IT BACK OVER... THE... WALL...

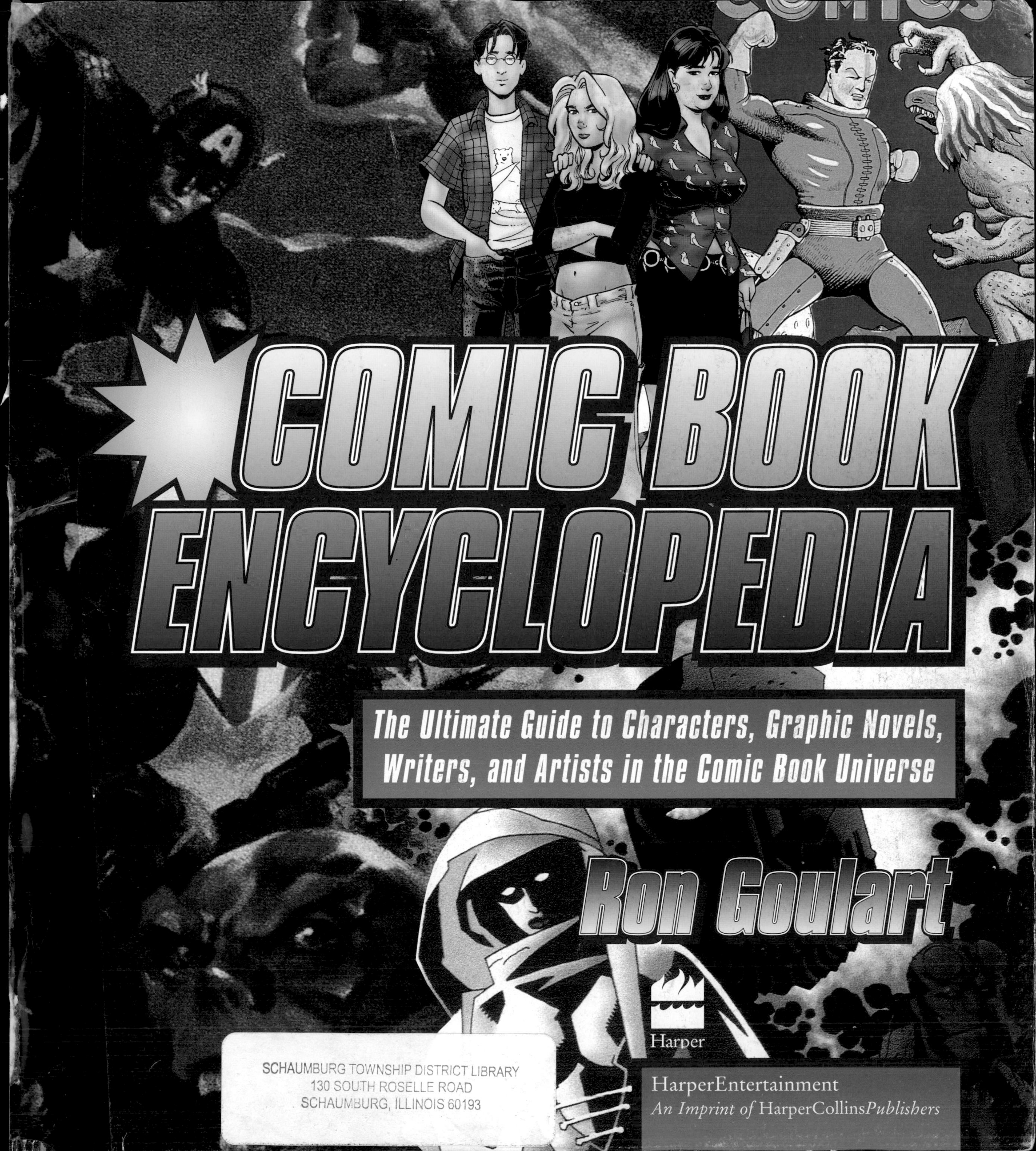

COMIC BOOK ENCYCLOPEDIA

The Ultimate Guide to Characters, Graphic Novels, Writers, and Artists in the Comic Book Universe

Ron Goulart

Harper

HarperEntertainment
An Imprint of HarperCollins*Publishers*

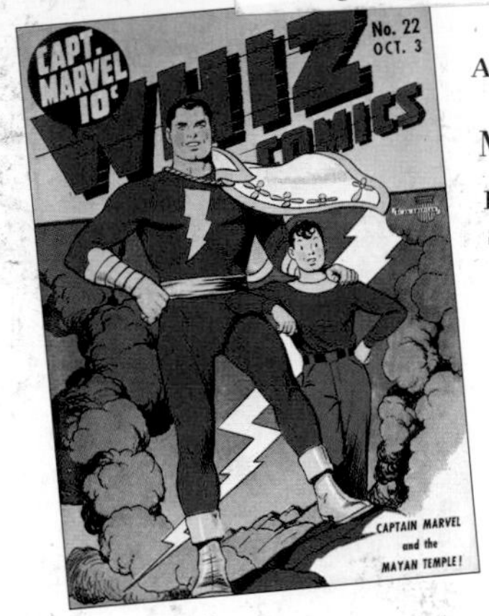
CAPT. MARVEL 10¢
WHIZ COMICS
No. 22
OCT. 3
CAPTAIN MARVEL and the MAYAN TEMPLE!

ACKNOWLEDGMENTS

Many thanks to all those who came out of the woodwork to help make this the best comic book encyclopedia ever: Will Eisner, Terry Moore, Denis Kitchen, Robert Crumb, Walter Calmette (and Felix the Cat), Carol Platt (and Marvel Comics), Ellie Frazetta (and her legendary husband, Frank Frazetta), Frank Cho, Mike Mignola, Michel Bareau (and Tintin), Maggie Thompson (editor of *Comic Buyer's Guide*), Valerie Ingram (and Archie comics), and Stuart Wells for his countless slides and scans.

HarperCollins books may be purchased for educational, business, or sales promotional use. For information please write: Special Markets Department, HarperCollins Publishers Inc., 10 East 53rd Street, New York, NY 10022.

FIRST EDITION

Designed by Joel Avirom and Jason Snyder
Design assistant: Meghan Day Healey

Printed on acid-free paper

Library of Congress Cataloging-in-Publication Data

Goulart, Ron, 1933-
Comic book encyclopedia : the ultimate guide to characters, graphic novels, writers, and artists in the comic book universe / Ron Goulart.—1st ed.
p. cm.
ISBN 0-06-053816-3 (hardcover)
1. Comic books, strips, etc.—Encyclopedias. I. Title.
PN6707.G68 2004
741.5'03—dc22 2004042541

04 05 06 07 08 TP/❖ 10 9 8 7 6 5 4 3 2 1

LETTER FROM THE EDITOR:

I LOVE COMIC BOOKS. As a kid, they taught me how to read. Not only were the dialogue boxes easy to absorb, but comic companies would bold the big words for some reason, which I would then look up and learn. So although people stared at me funny, reading on the train, comics were essential to my youth, and still are today—because they've continued to grow, and evolve.

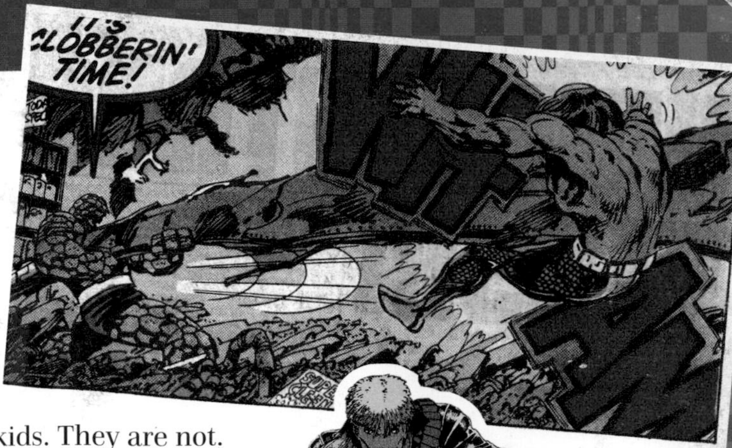
IT'S CLOBBERIN' TIME!

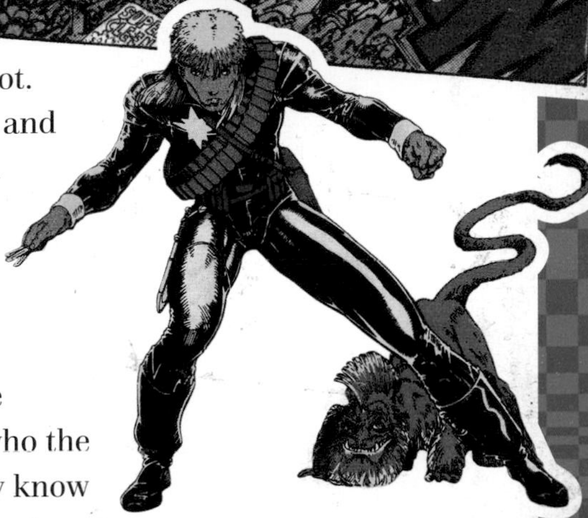

Comics get a bum rap because people think they're just for kids. They are not. They are the artistic expression of our most prevalent thoughts, feelings, and ideas, and in much the same way that our favorite novels use words to depict mood, style, and depth, comics rely on both words and art. At their best, they can create a visual world on par with even our most beloved books (pick up a copy of *Understanding Comics* by Scott McCloud if you're interested in the fundamentals).

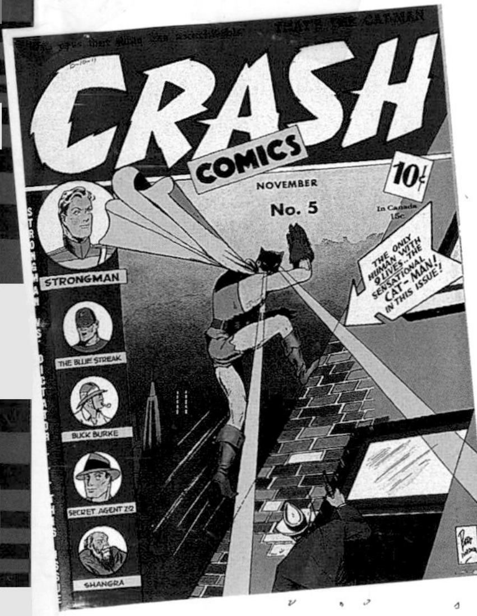
CRASH
COMICS
NOVEMBER
No. 5
10¢
STRONGMAN

But there are millions of individual comics and thousands of graphic novels lying around, and if you're interested in the subject—like how things got started, who the players are, and what to read—how would you possibly know where to begin? *Comic Book Encyclopedia* makes that easier, with a quick-reference time line, fun, encyclopedic entries on everything from Archie to Zorro, and an index to boot, so that anything you want to know can be found.

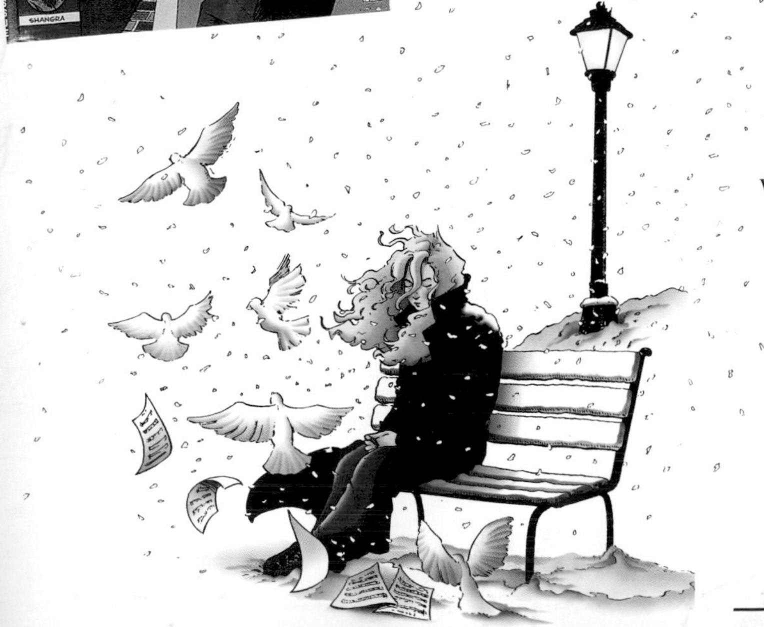

Best of all, this book offers a bunch of graphic novels to read, from tried-and-true superhero favorites (*Daredevil: Born Again, Superman for All Seasons, Batman: Dark Knight, The Incredible Hulk: Volume 1*) to more intellectual fare (*The Watchman, Astro City, Sandman*) poignant oddities (*Maus, Creature Tech, Jimmy Corrigan*), reality-based escapes (*Strangers in Paradise, Blankets, Sin City*), and crime (*Goldfish, Colère Noire*).

All in all, the book gives you everything you'd ever want to know about comics, and for me, the best part was that I got to work with comic-book legend Ron Goulart, who has proven beyond a shadow of a doubt that he's the best comic historian alive and that this book is the greatest thing out there—bar none.

Enjoy.

All best,

Josh Behar
Senior Editor
HarperCollins*Publishers*

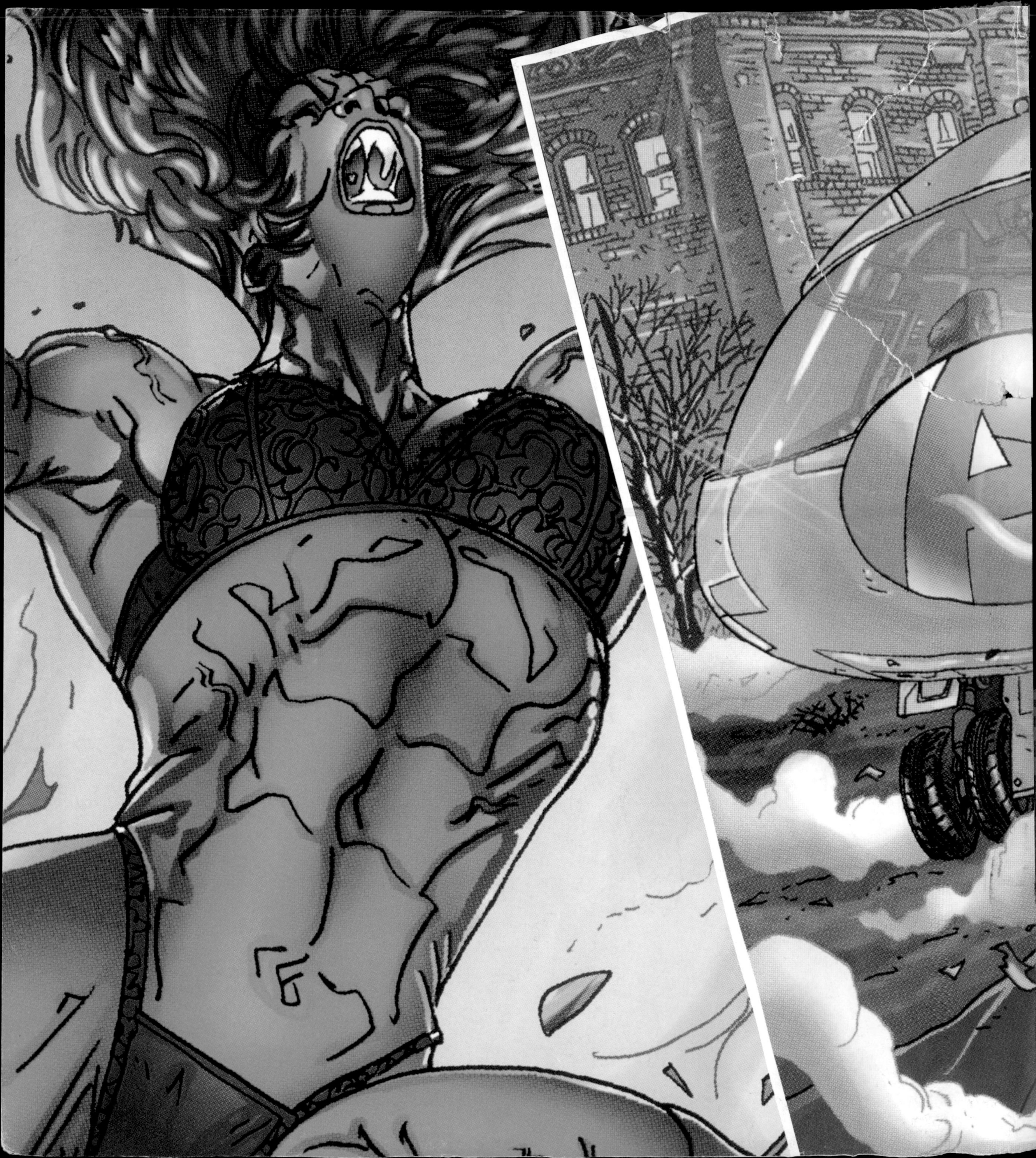

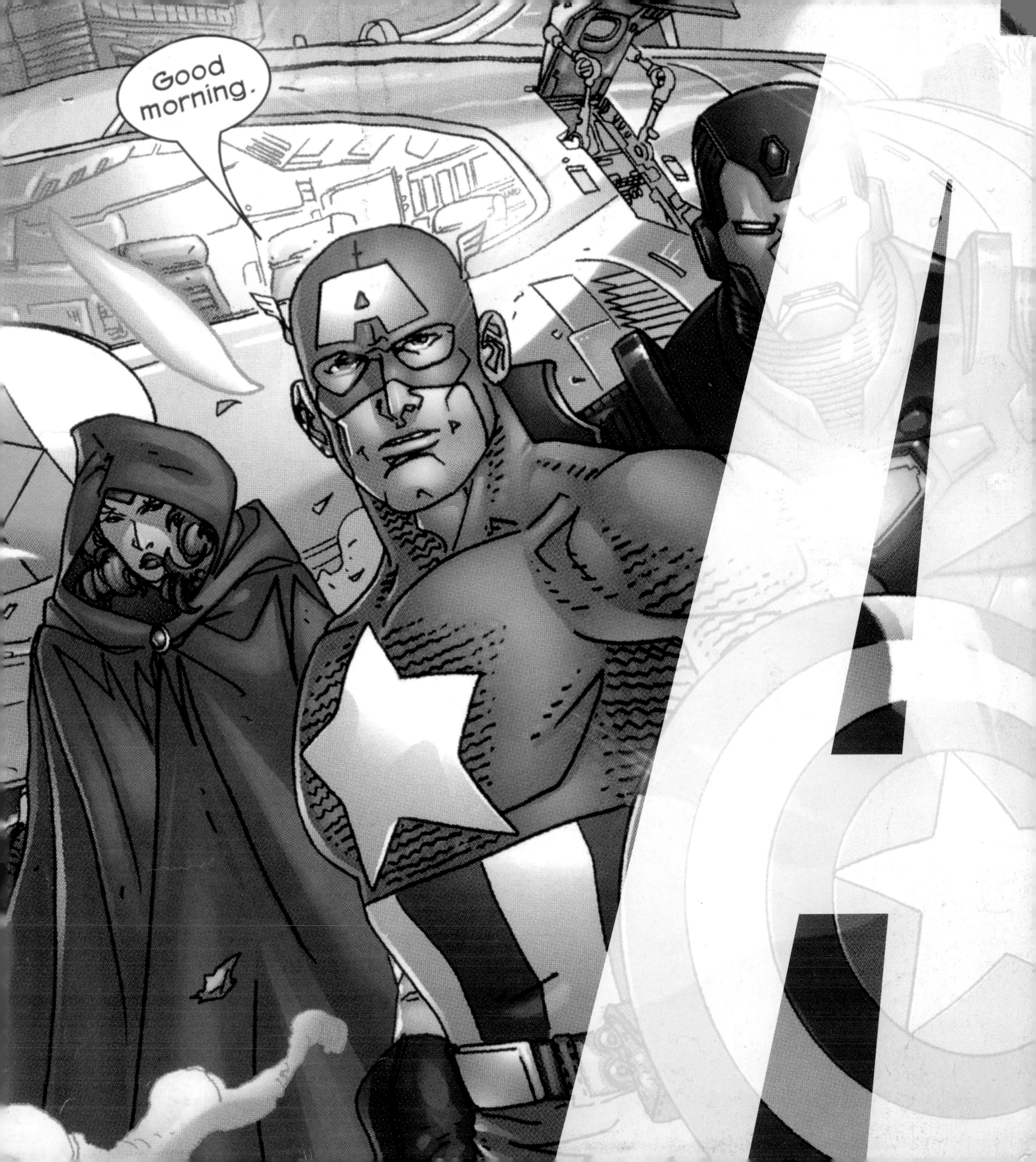
Good morning.

A-1 COMICS

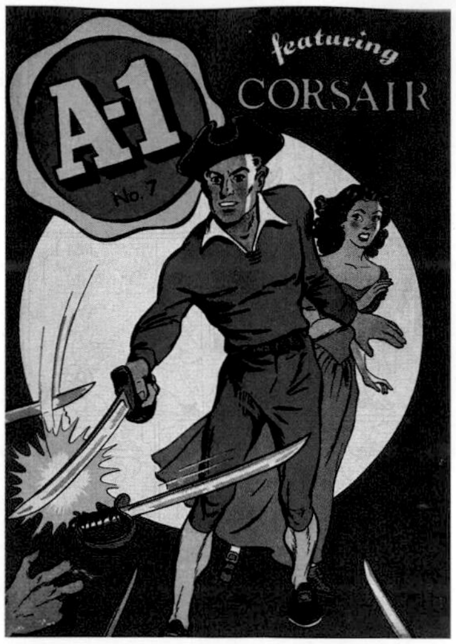
featuring
CORSAIR
A-1
No. 7

■ This was an umbrella under which Vincent Sullivan's Magazine Enterprises tried out a variety of characters and titles. Begun in 1944, the early numbers of *A-1* consisted of issues reprinting such newspaper strips as *Kerry Drake*, *Texas Slim*, and *Teena*. Among the original *A-1* titles that succeeded and went out on their own were *Tim Holt* and *The Ghost Rider*. Sullivan also devoted issues to *Thun'da*, *Cave Girl*, and *Strongman*. Titles that didn't thrive included *Dick Powell Adventurer! Fibber McGee and Molly*, and *Jimmy Durante Comics*.

The final issue of *A-1*, published in 1955, was devoted to Bob Powell's *Strongman*.

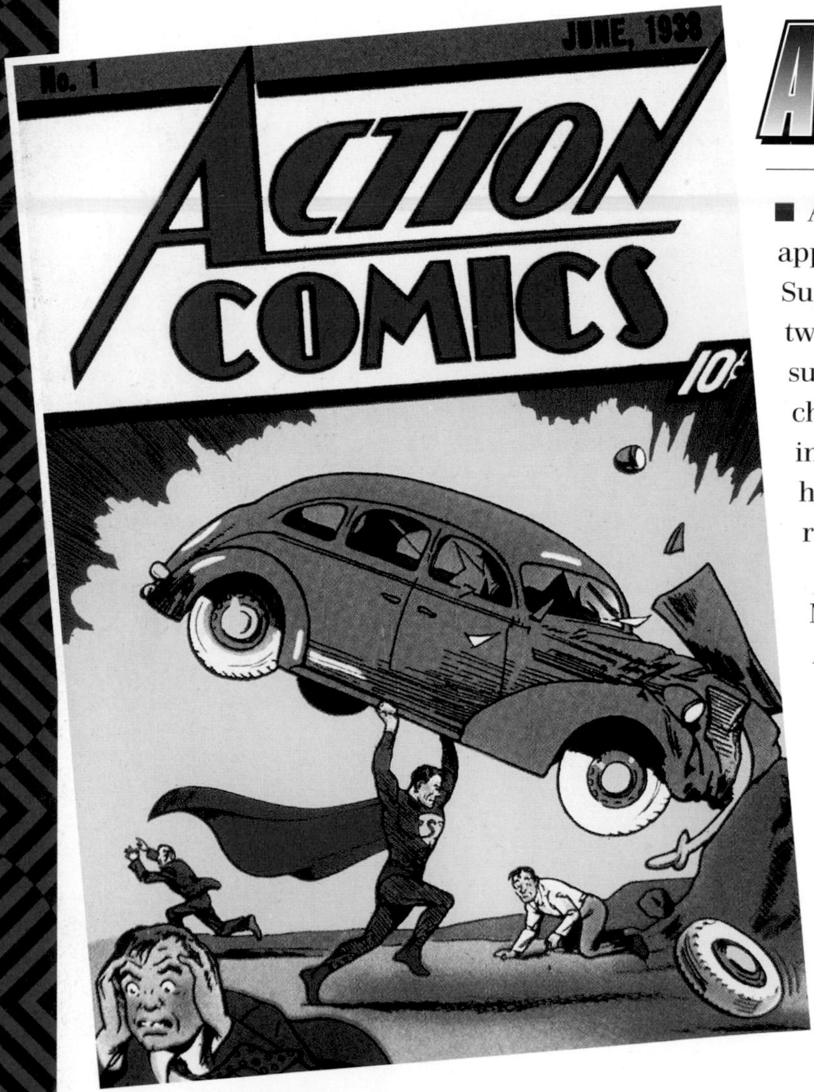
No. 1
JUNE, 1938
ACTION
COMICS
10¢

ACTION COMICS

■ An extremely influential magazine, DC's *Action Comics* first appeared on the stands in the spring of 1938. It introduced Superman, the most important comic book character of the twentieth century. The first of his kind, he inspired the superhero boom of the late thirties and early forties that changed the small-time funny-book business into a major industry. Before another year was out, the sales of *Action* had grown impressively. And other publishers began to realize that costumed heroes sold comics.

The last title contemplated by founding publisher Major Malcolm Wheeler-Nicholson before he left the company, *Action* was edited by Vincent Sullivan. He gave the starring position to Jerry Siegel and Joe Shuster's *Superman*. The new book introduced quite a few other characters. Most notable, as well as most durable, of the bunch was master magician Zatara, drawn by Fred Guardineer and written, from the second issue on, by Gardner Fox. In addition to fighting crime and mischief with white magic, Zatara found time to sire Zatanna. Also found in early issues were Tex Thomson by Bernard Baily, Pep Morgan, also by Guardineer, and Scoop Scanlon by Bill Ely.

Over the next few years additional characters came and went. Bert Christman's *Three Aces* joined up in the fall of 1939, later drawn by Chad Grothkopf. The urban cowboy known as the Vigilante by Mort Meskin arrived in the spring of 1941. Tex Thomson became Mr. America and later Americommando. Congo Bill started trekking through the pages of *Action* in 1941, as well. Fred Ray was the artist. *Tommy Tomorrow* was added in 1947, an early effort by Curt Swan. In 1950 the lineup narrowed down to Superman, Congo Bill, the Vigilante, and Tommy Tomorrow.

Later *Action* residents included the Legion of Super Heroes, Supergirl, the Human Target, Green Arrow, the Secret Six, Blackhawk, and Phantom Lady. These latter three put in time during 1988, when the magazine became *Action Comics Weekly*. Before a year was out, *Action* was again a monthly. And thus, as it passed the eight-hundred-issue mark, it has remained.

ADAM STRANGE

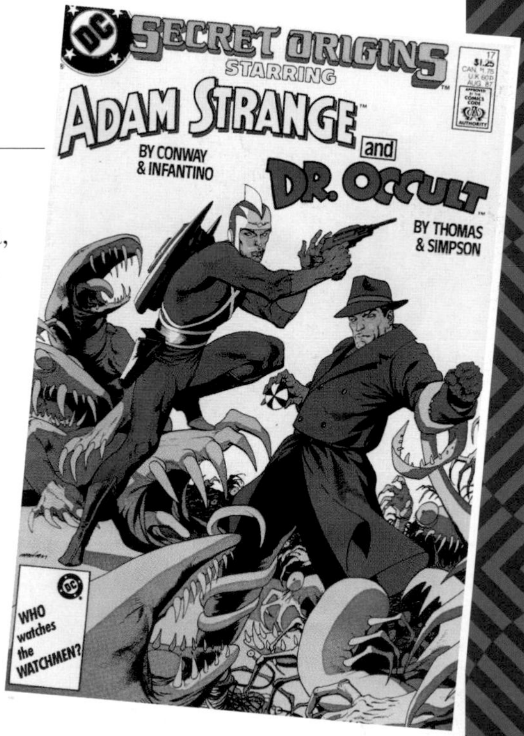
SECRET ORIGINS
STARRING
ADAM STRANGE
and
DR. OCCULT
BY CONWAY & INFANTINO
BY THOMAS & SIMPSON
WHO watches the WATCHMEN?

■ Commencing in 1937, writer Gardner F. Fox went on a spree of creating comic-book characters that were both popular and enduring. They included the Sandman, the Flash, Hawkman, the Justice Society, and Dr. Fate. Still at it in the late 1950s, Fox invented Adam Strange. This pulp-style sci-fi hero was introduced in DC's *Showcase* #17 late in 1958 and appeared in the next two 1959 bimonthly issues, in a series titled *Adventures on Other Worlds.* With #53 of *Mystery in Space* (August 1959), he was installed as a regular and became the magazine's cover boy. He remained in the book until #102 (October 1965). The first artist was the Toth-influenced Mike Sekowsky, but Carmine Infantino took over for most of the *Mystery* run.

Inspired by Edgar Rice Burroughs's John Carter of Mars, who'd journeyed to Mars by mystical means and fallen in love with a lovely princess with the unlovely name of Dejah Thoris, Fox had archeologist Adam Strange whisk up to the far-off planet Rann (pronounced Ron) by way of something called the Zeta Beam. On Rann, decked out in a bright-red spaceman outfit acquired in transit, Adam fell in love with a lovely local girl with the lovely name of Alanna. He also became entangled, exactly like John Carter, in a series of violent political intrigues.

Unfortunately for his courtship of Alanna, the Zeta Beam would wear off and he'd go zipping back home to Earth. Eventually he figured out when the beam would make its next pickup and managed to be there so that he'd be transported once more to Rann. His romance with Alanna was frequently interrupted, but it progressed and there were always plenty of battles and intrigues to occupy his spare time while a tourist.

Adam Strange's last space adventure occurred in 1990 in a three-part DC miniseries titled *Adam Strange: Man of Two Worlds.* Written by Richard Brunning and drawn by Andy Kubert, this version returned him to Rann and Alanna. He became a father, but since this was the nineties, a bleak period for many comic characters, Alanna was eventually killed.

ADAMS, ARTHUR (1963-)

■ A self-taught artist who taught himself well, Adams became a fan favorite and frequent poll winner soon after he made his Marvel debut in 1985. His style, which has matured over the years, is complex and meticulous while also being lively and compelling. And he knows how to tell a story.

His first job with Marvel was the six-issue limited series *Longshot*. Since there wasn't a fixed deadline, Adams has said, "I think it took eight months for the first issue." He'd been given the assignment in 1984 and *Longshot* didn't begin appearing until the summer of 1985. The magazine sold fairly well and also generated considerable reader response for Adams's work. He next was given established Marvel characters to draw, including X-Men and Spider-Man. He soon became one of the most popular young artists in the business. In the early 1990s, he drew a trio of *Fantastic Four* issues.

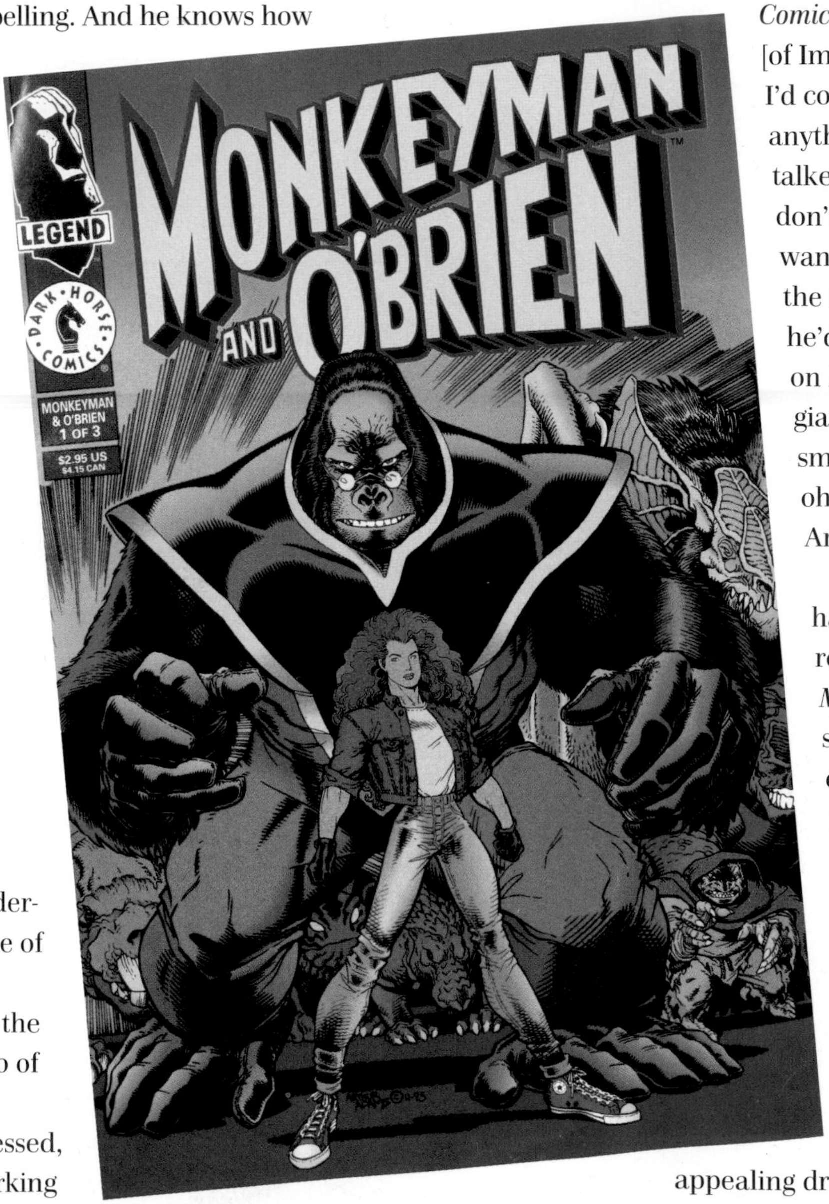
MONKEYMAN AND O'BRIEN
LEGEND
DARK HORSE COMICS
MONKEYMAN & O'BRIEN 1 OF 3
$2.95 US
$4.15 CAN

As the nineties progressed, Adams branched out, working as well for Dark Horse and Image. A longtime fan of movie monsters, he was happy to draw covers and do scripts and breakdowns for Dark Horse's *Godzilla*. In 1993 he penciled an ambitious forty-eight-page graphic novel version of Universal's *Creature from the Black Lagoon*. Then came his magnum opus, *Monkeyman & O'Brien*. According to a recent interview in *Comic Book Artist*, "Erik Larsen [of Image] called and asked if I'd considered making up anything of my own . . . So I talked to him and said, 'Oh, I don't know what the hell I'd want to do.'" After considering the matter, Adams decided he'd like to try a variation on *King Kong*—"So I had the giant scientist ape, and this smart woman, realizing, oh, my God, I just made up Angel and the Ape."

Admittedly slow, Adams has never settled into a regular schedule for *Monkeyman & O'Brien*. A smattering of handsomely drawn issues appeared in 1996 and others have appeared at irregular intervals since. The characters also appeared briefly in comic-strip form in *Dark Horse Extra*.

In the new century Arthur Adams has been doing some of his most appealing drawing for *Tom Strong's Terrific Tales*. His *Jonni Future*, written by Steve Moore, is a fantasy about a very attractive young woman and her adventures in time and dimension.

ADAMS, NEAL (1941–)

■ An influential and innovative artist, Adams did the majority of his comic-book work after he'd drawn the successful newspaper strip *Ben Casey* in the early 1960s. By the late 1960s, he was working for DC. Adams drew *Deadman* in *Strange Adventures*, upgraded *Batman* and rescued him from his TV-induced camp phase and, working with writer Denny O'Neil on *Green Lantern/Green Arrow*, epitomized the relevancy phase that comics went through in the early 1970s. He also drew *X-Men* and *The Avengers* for Marvel.

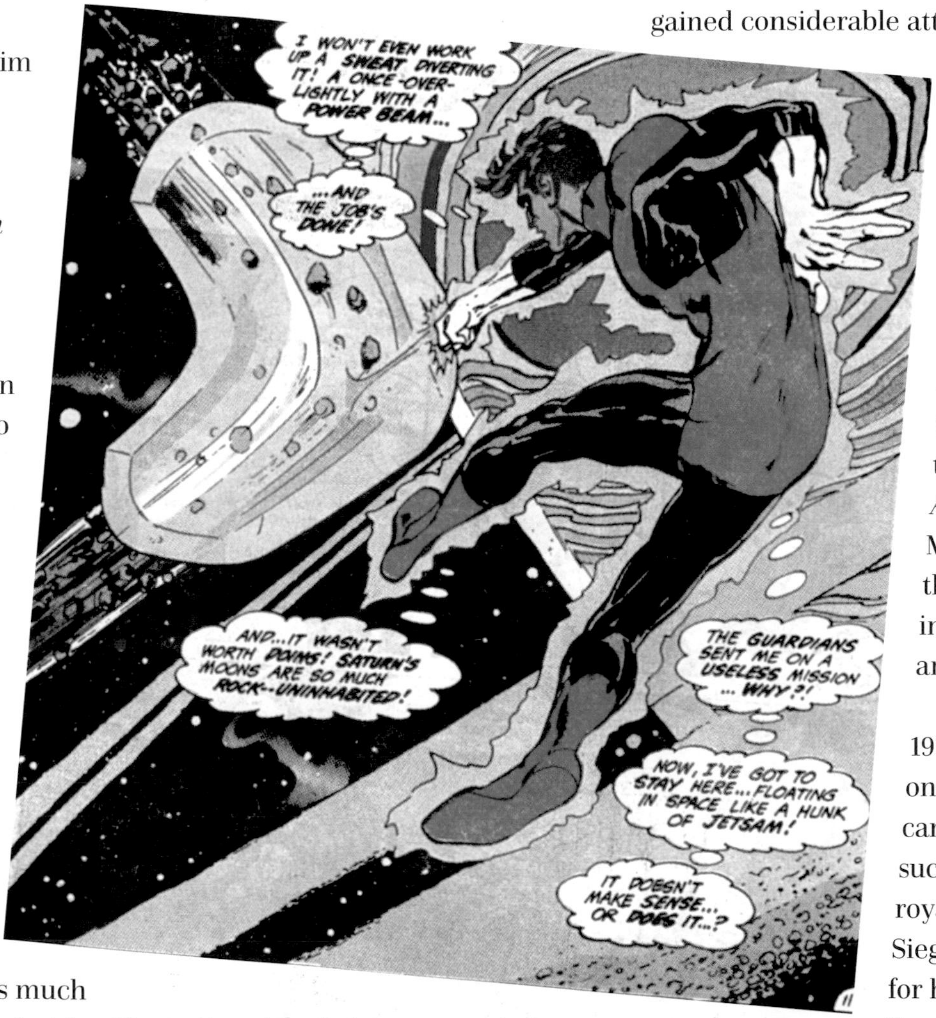
I WON'T EVEN WORK UP A SWEAT DIVERTING IT! A ONCE-OVER-LIGHTLY WITH A POWER BEAM...
...AND THE JOB'S DONE!
AND...IT WASN'T WORTH DOING! SATURN'S MOONS ARE SO MUCH ROCK--UNINHABITED!
THE GUARDIANS SENT ME ON A USELESS MISSION ... WHY?!
NOW, I'VE GOT TO STAY HERE...FLOATING IN SPACE LIKE A HUNK OF JETSAM!
IT DOESN'T MAKE SENSE... OR DOES IT...?

Neal Adams had worked for the Johnstone and Cushing art service while still in his teens. They produced cartoon and comic-strip ads, and one of their star performers was Stan Drake. The young Adams was much influenced by Drake's sketchy, illustrative style. Later he assisted Drake on *The Heart of Juliet Jones* newspaper strip. The work he did for comic books went beyond the house styles of DC and Marvel, bringing in a slick advertising look as well as a touch of gritty realism.

His *Deadman*, while causing fan enthusiasm and colleague admiration, did not prove to be a viable hero initially. The social awareness issues of *GL/GA*, dealing with such problems as drug abuse and racism and broadening the range of what comic books could do, gained considerable attention in the media. The magazine itself, though, was canceled early in 1972. Adams drew his modernized and somewhat sophisticated version of Batman about this same time, also managing to work on *The Avengers* over at Marvel. His take on the Dark Knight influenced several artists who followed.

In the middle 1970s Adams was also one of those who campaigned for and succeeded in getting royalties for Jerry Siegel and Joe Shuster for having created *Superman*. Adams started producing his own comics in the 1980s, including *Echo of Future Past*. He has been far less active in comic books for the past two decades, and his Continuity Associates has concentrated on advertising and animatics.

ADVENTURE COMICS

■ In business for nearly a half a century, DC's *Adventure* showcased a wide variety of characters over the years. These included Superboy, Starman, Hour-Man, Supergirl, the Legion of Super Heroes, Manhunter, and two versions of Sandman. The second of Major Malcolm Wheeler-Nicholson's pioneering original material comic books, it was titled *New Comics* when it began late in 1935. With the twelfth issue (January 1937) the title was modified to *New Adventure Comics* and from the thirty-second (November 1938) the title became simply *Adventure Comics.* By this time Major Nicholson was no longer in charge and Detective Comics, Inc. ran the show.

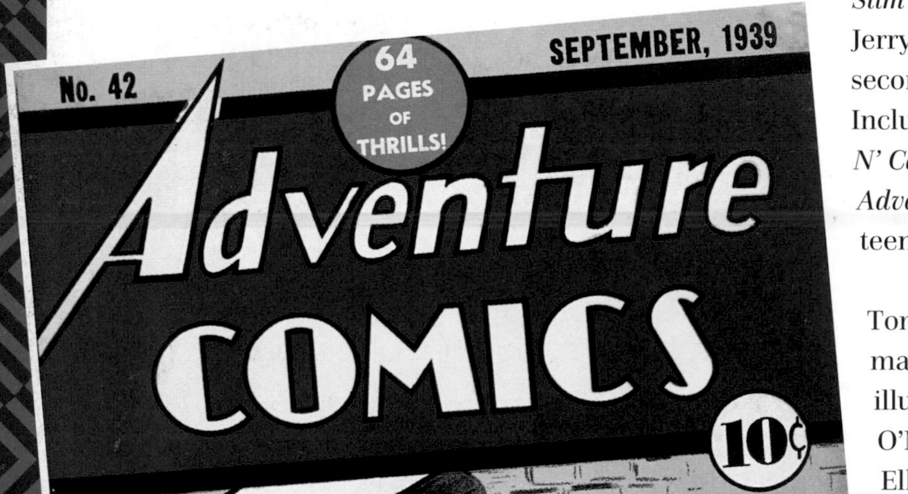
No. 42
64 PAGES OF THRILLS!
SEPTEMBER, 1939
Adventure
COMICS
10¢
Another thrilling episode of THE SANDMAN in this issue!

In the early days the magazine was a collection of mostly one- and two-page features, both humor and adventure, the majority of them laid out in Sunday page format. On the adventurous side were *Castaway Island, Slim and Tex, Captain Quick,* and *Dale Daring.* Work by Jerry Siegel and Joe Shuster began appearing in the second issue with their G-man serial *Federal Men.* Included in the funny stuff were *Dickie Duck, Sagebrush N' Cactus, J. Worthington Blimp,* and *The Strange Adventures of Mr. Weed.* These last two were by a talented teenage Brooklyn cartoonist named Sheldon Mayer.

The roster of artists in the early years also included Tom Hickey, an art school recruit, Creig Flessel, a pulp-magazine illustrator, H. C. Kiefer, a European-trained illustrator, and Russell Cole, Munson Paddock, and Leo O'Mealia, all veteran newspaper cartoonists. Whit Ellsworth and Vin Sullivan, who took turns drawing the early humorous covers, also acted as associate editors.

With the twelfth issue the magazine began to transform itself. Humor all but vanished from the covers, replaced by action and violence and now drawn by Flessel. The interior was overhauled as well. While almost all the adventure strips were still to be continued, they now took up four to eight pages. After Major Nicholson departed in the spring of 1938, several new serious features were added—*Anchors Aweigh!, Captain Desmo, Tod Hunter,* and *Rusty and His Pals* by a pre-Batman Bob Kane.

And after the final name change, even more adventurers showed up. There was Cotton Carver, a world explorer who ended up venturing into a fantasy empire at the center of the Earth. Gardner Fox, a confirmed disciple of Edgar Rice

Burroughs, was the writer. The artists included Ogden Whitney and Jack Lehti. The original Sandman, the crimebuster with the gas mask and the green business suit, made his debut in #40 (July 1939). Bert Christman was the first artist; Fox helped with the scripts. Some months later in #48, Hour-Man usurped Sandman's star position and Bernard Baily's time-limited superman was also featured on most of the *Adventure* covers. But then Starman arrived. He was auspiciously launched in #61, getting the cover and the leadoff position. Starman, whose abilities derived from the radiated starlight he collected by way of his gravity rod, was the joint effort of Fox and former sports cartoonist Jack Burnley.

The Shining Knight came on stage in #66, nicely drawn by Flessel. Wearing golden armor and mounted on a winged horse, the knight had been frozen for several centuries. Thawed, he became a sort of Connecticut Yankee in reverse. In issue #69 (December 1941), the Sandman got an updated look—yellow tunic and tights, purple cowl, cape, and boots—and a boy companion named Sandy. Chad Grothkopf was the artist who handled the transition story, and Paul Norris drew the next two. Then the formidable team of Joe Simon and Jack Kirby took over, and Sandman became the uncontested champ for the next several years.

In 1946, Superboy, who originated the year before in *More Fun Comics*, moved over to *Adventure* to assume the featured spot. In the late 1950s, the Legion of Super Heroes, with such members as Cosmic Boy, Saturn Girl, and Lightning Lad, was first seen. Supergirl entered in the 1960s. *Adventure* continued, digest-size in its final days, until the early 1980s.

ADVENTURES INTO THE UNKNOWN

■ Introduced in the fall of 1948, the American Comics Group's *Adventures into the Unknown* was the first regularly issued horror comic book. Despite the setbacks and collapses most of the later rivals suffered in the early 1950s, it thrived until the summer of 1967. This was chiefly due to that fact that the magazine served up a relatively restrained and polite type of supernatural material. *Unknown* was especially fond of witches, werewolves, sorcerers, and all sorts and conditions of ghosts.

While the editor Richard Hughes was a prolific writer, many of the early yarns were written by an assistant editor named Norman Fruman. "Richard rarely wrote the supernaturals," Fruman says in Michael Vance's history of ACG. "They, by all odds, were the most difficult ones to write. I wrote the supernaturals and the science fictions." Ogden Whitney drew a great many of the horror tales and provided numerous covers throughout the magazine's lifetime. Among the many other regular artists were Al Williamson, Paul Reinman, Charles Sultan, and the exceptional and virtually unsung Emil Gershwin.

By the time *Unknown* was well into its second decade, superheroes were back in favor and selling again. Somewhat reluctantly, Richard Hughes added a superhero to the lineup. Nemesis, written by Hughes under his pen name of Shane O'Shea and drawn by Pete Costanza, was introduced in #154 (August 1967). Rather a silly-looking fellow, he wore black-and-blue striped shorts, a red tunic with an hourglass insignia, a blue hood, and several other pieces of nonmatching haberdashery. His origin, pretty much borrowed from that of DC's Spectre, explained that he was a dead law officer who came back to Earth to fight crime. The sand ran out of Nemesis's hourglass sixteen issues later. Four issues after that *Adventures into the Unknown* followed him into the unknown.

AIR FIGHTERS COMICS

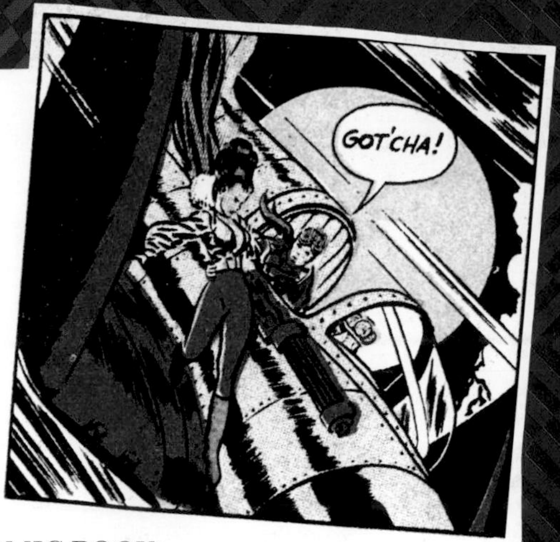
GOT'CHA!

■ After its first issue appeared late in 1941, *Air Fighters* was grounded for a full year. Then Hillman Periodicals, with some help from artist/writer Charles Biro, tried again and this time had better luck. The magazine, its title changed to *Airboy Comics* in 1945, stayed aloft until 1953.

It was Airboy, a blond youth who flew a very unusual plane, who kept the magazine popular, with some help from a walking vegetable patch called the Heap and a new line of characters that Biro and others had come up with. These included the Iron Ace, Sky Wolf, the Bald Eagle, and the Black Angel, an aviatrix who wore an exceedingly tight costume. The unsuccessful first issue, packaged by the usually dependable Funnies, Inc., had attempted to succeed with such bland characters as the Black Commander, Flying Cadet Jack Dale, and Mack Duff—Junior Mechanic. In addition to a livelier batch of characters, the second issue boasted a typical Biro cover, full of action, blood, and lettering. In the foreground was a Japanese pilot sitting in his cockpit and bleeding from the mouth. Behind him in the distance readers saw Airboy in this bird-winged airplane sending machine-gun bullets at yet another Japanese Zero as it burst into flames. There were also several patches of large colored copy on the cover proclaiming such things as "NEW!" "GREATEST COMIC BOOK YET!!"; "NOTHING LIKE IT!!"; and "Who Is AIRBOY."

Inside, Airboy's origin was laid out. He was an orphan who, dressed in red-and-blue flying togs, used an experimental wing-flapping plane called Birdie to combat the Nazis and the Japanese. The plane was the gift of the kindly monks who'd raised the lad and, instead of producing liqueurs, built eccentric aircraft. Airboy's most formidable opponent was a striking, dark-haired girl pilot called Valkyrie. Although she was said to have a heart "as black as the Devil's," she eventually became fond of Airboy, reformed, and teamed with him to fight against the Nazis. Biro never drew anything inside the magazine, and Fred Kida was the best of the Airboy artists, his specialty being Valkyrie and her Airmaidens. Later artists included Dan Barry and Ernie Schroeder, who spent several years with the boy aviator.

ALL-AMERICAN COMICS

■ M. C. Gaines did not have faith in superheroes. Even though he had been in on the discovery of *Superman*, the publisher didn't believe that comic-book buyers would be interested in more of the same. Late in 1938, he'd made an agreement to produce a series of comic books that would carry the DC colophon. The first two titles were *Movie Comics*, which soon failed, and *All-American Comics*, which was to have a long and successful life. When, however, *All-American* #1 (April 1939) appeared, there was not a single superhero to be found within. In fact, half of its sixty-four pages were devoted to newspaper strip reprints. Since Gaines's earlier experience had been with *Famous Funnies* and then *Popular Comics* and *The Funnies*, reprint titles all, he defined a comic book as something that included funny paper reruns. Although Sheldon Mayer, the young editor, believed otherwise, it took him quite a while to convince his boss. And they never did get rid of the *Mutt & Jeff* reprints.

The early issues included reprints of strips that had already appeared in *Famous* and *Popular*, including

Skippy, *Reg'lar Fellers*, and Gaines's apparent favorite *Mutt & Jeff*. Among the features created expressly for *All-American* were *Red, White and Blue*, about a saboteur-bashing trio consisting of a soldier, a sailor, and a marine, Jon L. Blummer's *Hop Harrigan*, dealing with a young aviator, and *Adventures into the Unknown*, adapted from the juvenile fantasy novels of Carl H. Claudy. Mayer brought his Scribbly the boy cartoonist over from *The Funnies*. In the eighth issue began *Gary Concord, the Ultra-Man*, a science-fiction epic about Concord, the High Moderator of the United States of North America in the year 2239 A.D., who was struggling to bring peace to a war-torn world. The fact that the credit was to Don Shelby has led to speculation that, since it was an anagram of By Sheldon, Mayer wrote it. He strongly denied this in later years, assuring questioners that Jon Blummer both wrote and drew the feature.

Finally, in the sixteenth issue (July 1940), a superhero called the Green Lantern was introduced. Mart Nodell was the artist and Bill Finger, the uncredited cocreator of *Batman*, the writer. By the following year Irwin Hasen was ghosting many of the *Green Lantern* stories and also drawing a series of striking covers for *All-American*.

Once GL arrived in the magazine, other costumed heroes started moving in. The Atom arrived in #19 (October 1940), followed by Dr. Mid-nite in #25 (May 1941) and Sargon the Sorcerer in #26. This magician strip was drawn by Howard Purcell and written by John Wentworth, who was also writing *Red, White and Blue*. Sargon was John Sargent, who inherited the ancient Ruby of Life and discovered that it granted him magic powers. When in his Sargon mode, he wore the ruby in his yellow turban. *All-American* had by this time dropped all its reprints save *Mutt & Jeff*. Gaines also started a separate *Mutt & Jeff* comic book in 1939, and Mayer drew the covers for several years.

During the years of World War II, with many artists in the service, Mayer hired new cartoonists. The exceptional Joe Gallagher drew *The Atom* and *Red, White and Blue*. Paul Reinman became the regular *Green Lantern* artist and was the first to draw the popular villain Solomon Grundy. In its one-hundredth issue (August 1948) a new cowboy hero, using the name Johnny Thunder and drawn by Alex Toth, pushed GL out of the spotlight. In #103 it was rechristened *All-American Western*, and all the other earlier characters, including Mutt & Jeff, were gone. As trends in comics continued to change, the magazine next became *All-American Men of War* in 1952 and as such remained on view until the summer of 1966.

In 1999, DC used the title *All-American Comics* for a one-shot that was part of their *The Justice Society Returns!* series.

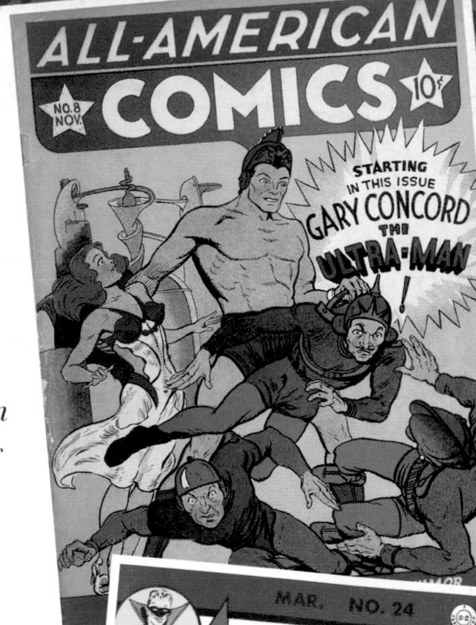
ALL-AMERICAN
COMICS
NO. 8 NOV.
10¢
STARTING IN THIS ISSUE
GARY CONCORD
THE
ULTRA-MAN
!

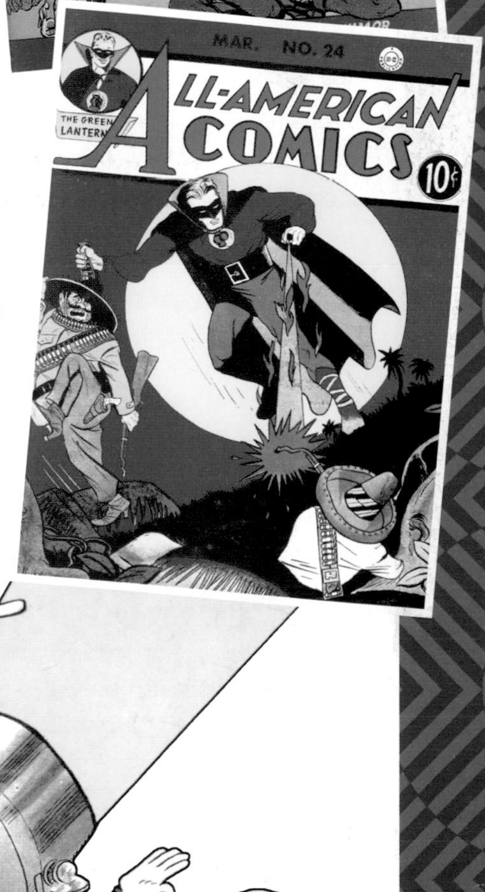
MAR.
NO. 24
ALL-AMERICAN
COMICS
10¢
THE GREEN LANTERN

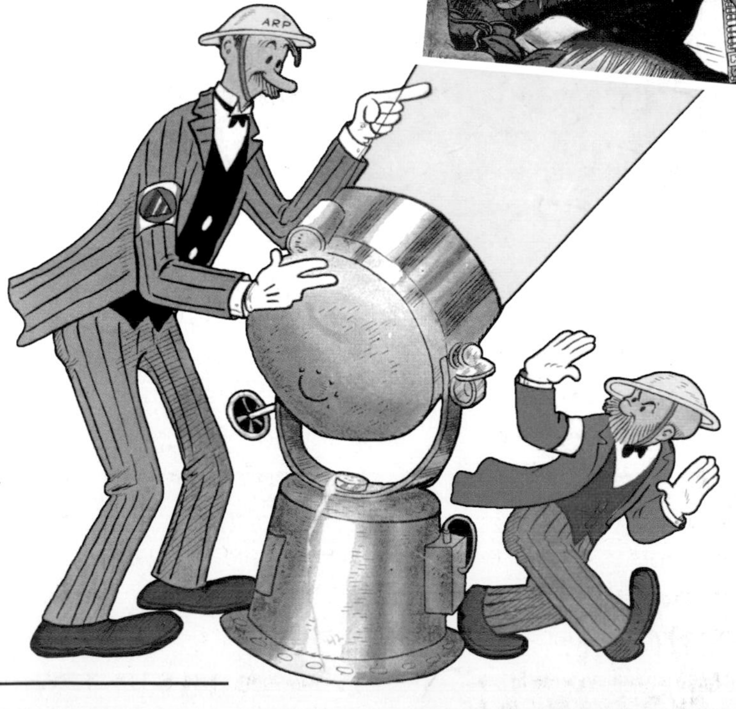
ARP

No.14
NOV... DEC.
ALL FUNNY COMICS
Ten Cents
MY DIET SAYS I CAN HAVE ONLY ONE SANDWICH FOR LUNCH!

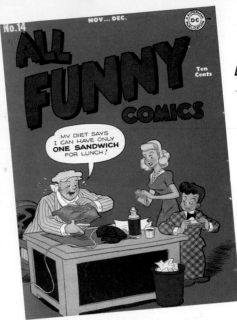

ALL FUNNY COMICS

■ DC's earliest title devoted exclusively to humor, it dealt with funny people and not funny animals. *All Funny* began as a wartime quarterly late in 1943, offering a mix of established features that included *Genius Jones* and *Penniless Palmer* and new ones such as *Two-Gun Percy*, *Hamilton & Egbert*, and *Buzzy*. Written and drawn by George Storm, *Buzzy* centered around a teenage lad who attempted to play the trumpet. Taking advantage of the growing interest in teen titles, DC promoted Buzzy to a book of his own the next year.

Among the other contributors were Stan Kaye, Howard Sherman, Henry Boltinoff, and newspaper veterans Paul Fung, Jimmy Thompson, and Tom McNamara. The magazine, by then a bimonthly, ended with its twenty-third issue in the spring of 1948.

ALL STAR COMICS

■ The idea of issuing a comic book with new adventures of popular heroes from all the existing DC titles had already been tried in *New York World's Fair Comics*. The innovation that *All Star* introduced was having them team up to work together. This happened in the third issue (Winter 1940), when the resident heroes joined together to form a crime-fighting group called the Justice Society of America. In the fourth issue, the JSA all worked on the same case. This first hero team in comic books was the joint invention of editor Sheldon Mayer and writer Gardner F. Fox.

Mayer, who edited *All Star* from the outset, also created its star-spangled logo and laid out the first two covers. Although Fox wrote all the chapters, each hero was drawn, in the early days, by his regular artist. The opening and closing chapters wherein all the members gathered at headquarters were drawn initially by regular *Flash* artist E. E. Hibbard. The original members of the Justice Society were the Green Lantern, the Spectre, Hawkman, Hour-Man, Sandman, Dr. Fate, the Flash, and the Atom. Johnny Thunder, accompanied by his thunderbolt, crashed the meetings until he was finally initiated in #6 (August-September 1941). He provided comic relief, something Mayer was partial to.

A bonus story in the bimonthly eighth issue introduced Wonder Woman, who was then set up in *Sensation Comics*, DC's newest monthly. The boys in the band admitted her back into *All Star* in the eleventh issue, but being a sexist bunch, had her work as recording secretary and not a full-fledged JSA member. The Flash and the Green Lantern, when they achieved their own magazines, dropped from active membership. Newcomers and replacements included Starman, Dr. Mid-Nite, and Wildcat. Black Canary, who replaced Johnny Thunder in *Flash Comics*, also replaced him in the Justice Society in 1948.

When the JSA got together, they defended America against spies, traveled to the other planets, fed the starving of Europe, and defeated—sometimes only temporarily—such master criminals as the Brain Wave, the Psycho-Pirate, Degaton, Solomon Grundy, and Vandal Savage.

Later, some of the villains, mimicking their betters, appeared as the Injustice Society.

Other artists who drew covers and the opening and closing chapters were Jack Burnley, Joe Gallagher, and Martin Naydel. Alex Toth, Joe Kubert, and Irwin Hasen were later contributors. While the scripts continued to be by Fox, the team of Arthur Peddy and Bernard Sachs took to drawing entire issues. The original run ended with #57 early in 1951. As an indication of how comics were changing, the magazine was converted to *All Star Western* and continued for another ten years.

All Star Comics, with various rosters of JSA members, was briefly revived in 1974 and 1999. The Justice Society has continued to pop up elsewhere over the years.

ALL STAR SQUADRON

■ See JUSTICE SOCIETY OF AMERICA.

ALPHA FLIGHT

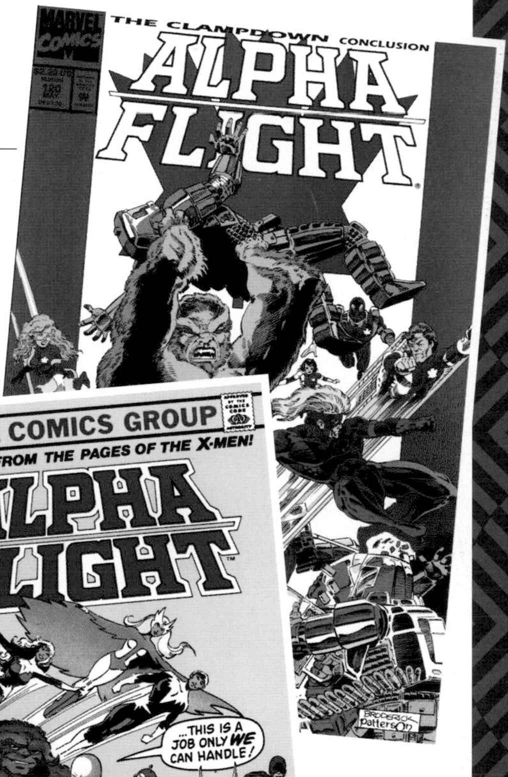
MARVEL COMICS
THE CLAMPDOWN CONCLUSION
ALPHA FLIGHT

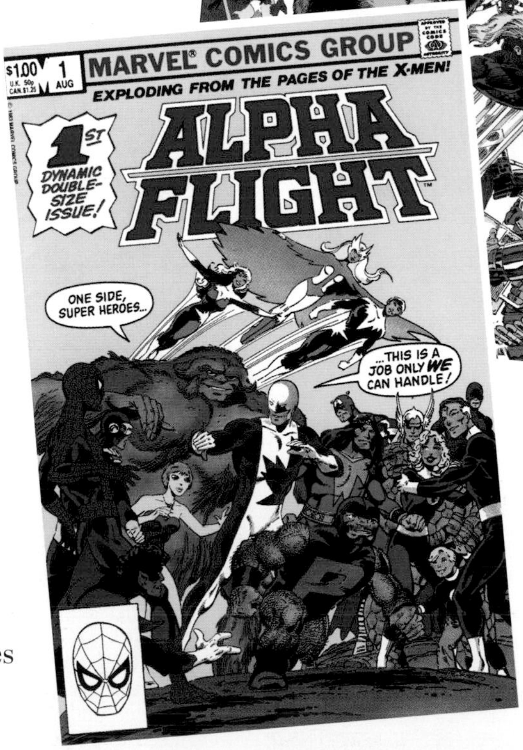
$1.00
1 AUG
MARVEL COMICS GROUP
EXPLODING FROM THE PAGES OF THE X-MEN!
ALPHA FLIGHT
1ST DYNAMIC DOUBLE-SIZE ISSUE!
ONE SIDE, SUPER HEROES...
...THIS IS A JOB ONLY WE CAN HANDLE!

■ Another lovely bunch of mutants, Marvel introduced them in the summer of 1983. The gang gathered together in *Alpha Flight* were all Canadians, created by John Byrne, who'd grown up in Canada.

The saga as it unfolded over the years, with a changing crew of artists and writers, made the intricate complexities of the *X-Men* continuities seem simple and crystal-clear by comparison. The early cast included Vindicator, Shaman, Snowbird, Aurora, the Guardian, and nonmutant Canadian Prime Minister Trudeau. In addition to Walter Langkowski, who turned into the Canadian version of Bigfoot known as Sasquatch, the real Sasquatch also showed up later on. One of the mutants was able to turn into both an owl and a polar bear, and another, Northstar, admitted he was gay during the heat of battle. This garnered him considerable publicity at the time. Another of the male mutants became a lady named Wanda for a while. The Guardian became the Vindicator and vice-versa, and in addition, the Guardian and the Vindicator were married. Another mutant died and came back as a dwarf.

The stories, dealing with the group's battles with such modest villains as the Master of the World, moved back and forth in time and were rich with flashbacks and footnotes. A typical note would say something like "This takes place before last month's issue." The original flight lasted for 130 issues before ending in 1994. A new series ran from 1997 to 1999.

AMAZING FANTASY

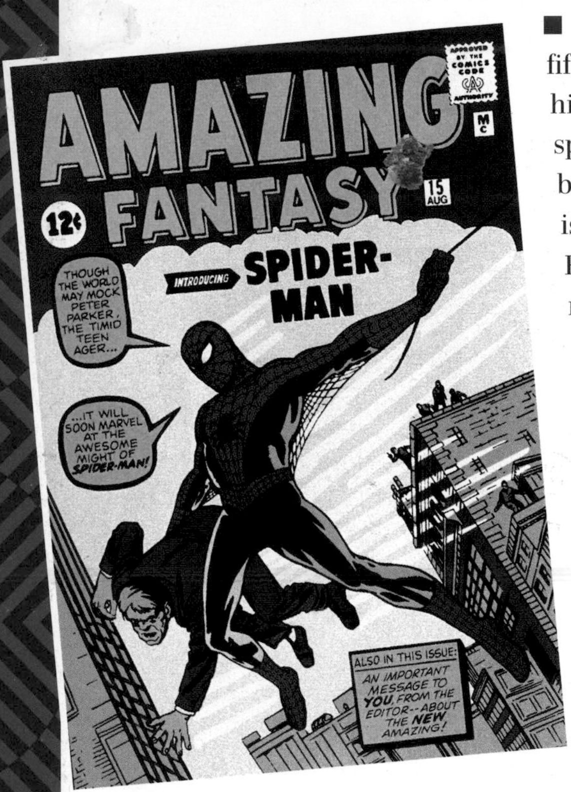
APPROVED BY THE COMICS CODE AUTHORITY
AMAZING
MC
12¢
FANTASY
15 AUG
INTRODUCING
SPIDER-MAN
THOUGH THE WORLD MAY MOCK PETER PARKER, THE TIMID TEEN AGER...
...IT WILL SOON MARVEL AT THE AWESOME MIGHT OF SPIDER-MAN!
ALSO IN THIS ISSUE: AN IMPORTANT MESSAGE TO YOU FROM THE EDITOR--ABOUT THE NEW AMAZING!

■ After changing its name twice, *Amazing Fantasy* suspended operations. That fifteenth and final issue (August 1962) guaranteed the magazine a place in comics history, however, since it was the birthplace of Spider-Man. Starting up in the spring of 1961 under the title *Amazing Adventures*, it had dealt in the usual Marvel brand of fantasy and sci-fi. Among the monsters prowling the initial half dozen issues were Manoo, Sserpo, and Monsteroso, this latter billed as "the MOST FEARFUL creature of all time!" Scripts were chiefly the work of Stan Lee, the main artists were Jack Kirby, in charge of the Monster-of-the-Month, and Steve Ditko. With the seventh issue, the title was switched to *Amazing Adult Fantasy* and the book promised "spine-tingling, supernatural thrillers for the more mature reader!" One of the creatures provided for the mature reader was a huge chap called Tim Boo Ba.

For the fifteenth issue the title was shortened to just plain *Amazing Fantasy*. On the cover, as drawn by Kirby, Spider-Man was seen for the first time. In the eleven-page story inside, written by Lee and illustrated by Ditko, readers met Peter Parker, Aunt May (quite a bit plumper back then), and, of course, Spidey. At the yarn's end, Lee said, "And so a legend is born and a new name is added to the roster of those who make the world of fantasy the most exciting realm of all!" Early the next year, the first issue of *The Amazing Spider-Man* was released.

AMAZING-MAN COMICS

■ The leading character in the magazine was Aman the Amazing-Man, written and drawn by Bill Everett. Aman was indeed an amazing fellow. On the cover of the initial issue, #5 (September 1939), he was seen chained hand and foot, lying in a Houdini position while chomping at the neck of a large, nasty-looking cobra. This definitely was not standard superhero behavior at the time. In addition to Aman, the new Centaur publication included such characters as the Iron Skull, the Shark, Mighty Man, and Minimidget.

Amazing-Man's origin began "25 years ago, in the mountains of Tibet, [when] the Council of Seven selected an orphan of superb physical structure, and each did his part to develop in the child all the qualities of one who would dominate the world of men by his great, strength, knowledge and courage . . . His friend Nika, the young chemist, endowed him with the power to make himself disappear in a cloud of green vapor, and extracted from him the promise to always be good and kind and generous." Aman had to pass a sort of obstacle course of tests before being considered ready to journey to the United States to combat criminals and evildoers. These included not only the tussle with the cobra but a tug-of-war with a bull elephant. His costume consisted of blue shorts and boots and a small shield embossed with the letter "A" strapped to his bare chest. This apparently stood for Amazing and not adulterer.

Carl Burgos, still a few months off from creating the Human Torch, contributed the Iron Skull. A nose-less android in a business suit, the Skull fought crime in the future, the distant 1970s. The Shark was a Sub-Mariner type, drawn by Lew Glanzman. Minimidget was a doll-sized gangbuster who was teamed up with an equally small lady named Ritty. Mighty Man could shrink, grow, and change shape, a couple of years before Plastic Man came up with the idea. From #12 through #21, Frank Thomas produced *Dr. Hypno* (originally *Dr. Psycho*). Hypno had the ability to project his mind into that of any animal, catching criminals while inhabiting the body of everything from a monkey to an elephant. For the final two issues Basil Wolverton did one of his serious space operas, *Meteor Martin.*

In #23 (August 1941) Amazing-Man at last took on a boy sidekick. Instead of being called Amazing Boy, he was known simply as Tommy. The magazine ended three issues later.

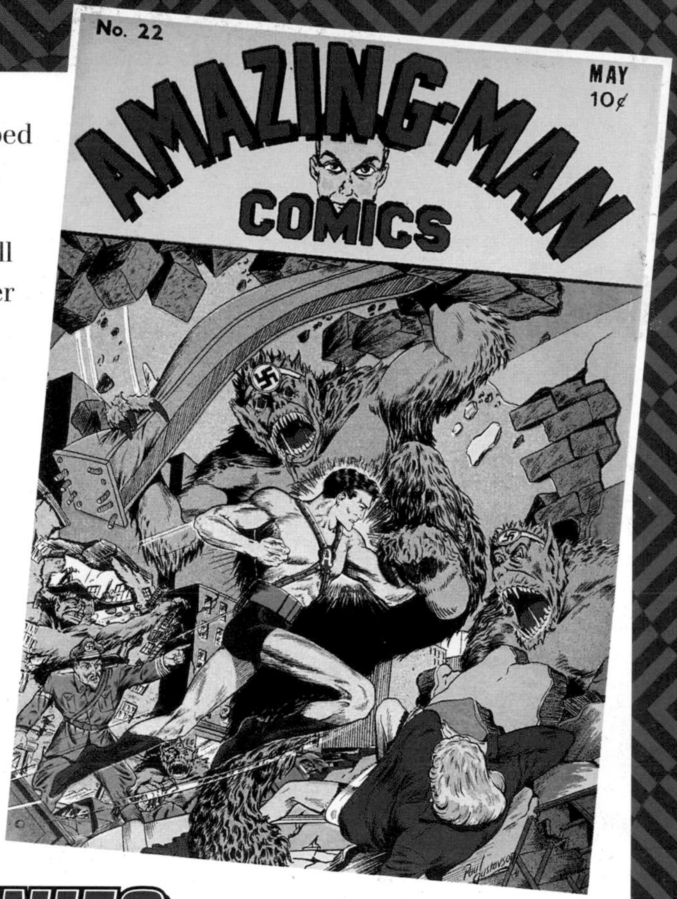
No. 22
MAY
10¢
AMAZING-MAN
COMICS

AMAZING MYSTERY FUNNIES

■ Published by the recently formed 1930s publisher, Centaur Publications, Inc., the magazine represented an earlier gathering of many of those who would later put together *Marvel Mystery Comics.* Lloyd Jacquet, the editor, would eventually found the Funnies, Inc. shop. The artists who worked for *Amazing Mystery* during its two-year run included Bill Everett, Carl Burgos, and Paul Gustavson, who went on to draw Sub-Mariner, the Human Torch, and the Angel.

Everett's sci-fi epic *Skyrocket Steele* began in the second issue (September 1938), Burgos's sci-fi epic *Air-Sub DX* began in the seventh (February 1939), and Gustavson's *Fantom of the Fair*, concerning a costumed crimefighter who fought crime at the New York World's Fair, began in the eleventh (July 1939). Among the other features were *Daredevil Barry Finn* by Tarpe Mills, *Space Patrol* by Basil Wolverton, and *Speed Centaur* by Malcolm Kildale. This latter offered one of the more unusual heroes in comics, since Speed was half man and half horse. In one adventure he donned a disguise and appeared as a complete horse.

Though *Amazing Mystery Funnies* ended in the summer of 1940, many of its alumni went on to better things.

AMERICAN FLAGG

■ See CHAYKIN, HOWARD.

AMETHYST, PRINCESS OF GEMWORLD

■ A fantasy showing the influence of both *The Wizard of Oz* and Tolkein, *Amethyst* was introduced by DC early in 1983. It was created by writers Dan Mishkin and Gary Cohn (who also invented Blue Devil) in collaboration with artist Ernie Colon. The first series ran for twelve issues, ending early the next year.

THE PUNISHMENT IS NOT ENOUGH.
MY GEMWORLD HAS BEEN WOUNDED TO THE HEART.
THE SCARS ARE MINE!!
AS WILL BE THE RECKONING!

DC
AMETHYST
PRINCESS OF GEMWORLD
75¢
8
DEC 83

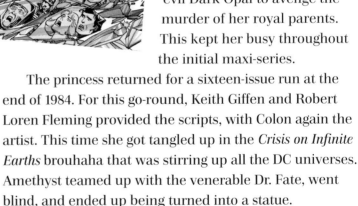

In the everyday America of the eighties, blonde Amy Winston had just become a teenager. But when she crossed over into the parallel universe of Gemworld, she was the full-grown Princess Amethyst. A fairy-tale locale full of places and people named after gems, Gemworld had such locations as Sardonyx, Ruby, and, of course, an Emerald City. There were also Lady Turquoise, Lord White Opal, and Lady Amber, plus all sorts of gemstones and jewels underfoot. Amethyst found herself being courted by Prince Topaz and battling the evil Dark Opal to avenge the murder of her royal parents. This kept her busy throughout the initial maxi-series.

The princess returned for a sixteen-issue run at the end of 1984. For this go-round, Keith Giffen and Robert Loren Fleming provided the scripts, with Colon again the artist. This time she got tangled up in the *Crisis on Infinite Earths* brouhaha that was stirring up all the DC universes. Amethyst teamed up with the venerable Dr. Fate, went blind, and ended up being turned into a statue.

Late in 1987, she was revived, met Prince Topaz all over again, battled evil as personified by a possessed chap named Mordru, and got turned into a statue once more all in four issues. Amethyst looked her best during this brief return, since the estimable Spanish artist Esteban Maroto took care of the artwork. Mindy Newell, who had a slight problem keeping her *thee*'s and *thou*'s straight, was responsible for the convoluted scripts.

ANDERSON, MURPHY (1926-)

■ One of his specialties has always been science fiction. His earliest professional work was drawing *Star Pirate* and *Life on Other Planets* for Fiction House's *Planet Comics* in 1944. A fan of *Buck Rogers* since childhood, Anderson was given the opportunity to draw the daily strip in 1947. He stayed with it for two years, then quit, but was persuaded to draw Buck's twenty-fifth-century adventures again for a year in 1958. For Ziff Davis's brief fling with comic books, he worked on *Amazing Adventures* and *Lars of Mars*.

Signing up with DC in the early 1950s, Anderson went on to draw such sci-fi features as *Captain Comet*, *The Atomic Knights*, and *John Carter of Mars*. Anderson's style changed some over the years, but always remained attractive, visually appealing, and easily recognizable. He was also an excellent inker and worked with Carmine Infantino on *Adam Strange* and with Gil Kane on both *The Green Lantern* and *The Atom*.

Murphy Anderson took over the production of the Army's *PS Magazine* after Will Eisner left it. Having formed Murphy Anderson Visual Concepts, he withdrew pretty much from comic books to concentrate on commercial art and producing color separations. His cartooning work in recent years has consisted mostly of re-creations of old comic-book covers (his own and others'), which can be seen on such magazines as *Alter Ego* and the 2003 edition of the *Comic Book Price Guide*.

ANDRU, ROSS (1927–1993)

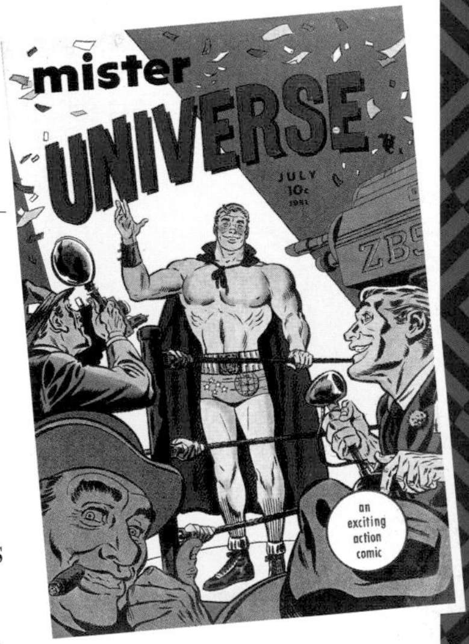
mister
UNIVERSE
JULY
10¢
an exciting action comic

■ A leading exponent of the DC house style of the sixties (as exemplified by Mike Sekowsky, etc.), Andru penciled *Wonder Woman* from 1958 to 1967 and *Metal Men* from 1962 to 1968. In the seventies he worked for Marvel on such heroes as *Spider-Man*. His partner at DC was Mike Esposito, who inked all his work for that publisher.

Andru had studied at the Cartoonists and Illustrators School in Manhattan, which was cofounded by Burne Hogarth. His first professional cartooning job was penciling, without credit, Hogarth's Sunday *Tarzan* page. He teamed up with Mike Esposito in the early fifties to turn out *Mr. Universe*, a nicely done adventure comic book about a world-traveling wrestler. It lasted only five issues. The two also produced an unsuccessful newspaper soap-opera strip titled *Martha Hart*. By the late fifties they were employed by DC. Andru and Esposito became the first artists to draw *Wonder Woman* after cocreator H. G. Peter was put out to pasture in 1958. In addition to *Wonder Woman* and *Metal Men*, the team also drew *Sea Devils*, *Rip Hunter*, and *Suicide Squad*.

Andru, without Esposito, moved over to Marvel in 1972. While his main assignment was penciling *Spider-Man*, he also turned out pages for *Dr. Strange*, *The Fantastic Four*, and *X-Men*. Comics historian Michael Vance has said of Andru that "[his] pencils were clean, bold and technically beyond criticism." Will Jacobs and Gerald Jones, in *Comic Book Heroes*, said, "Andru generally produced forceful and dramatic work."

Andru returned to DC in the eighties. Early in the next decade, shortly before his death, he teamed again with Esposito on a *Zen Intergalactic Ninja* mini-series published by Archie Comics.

ANDY PANDA

■ See NEW FUNNIES.

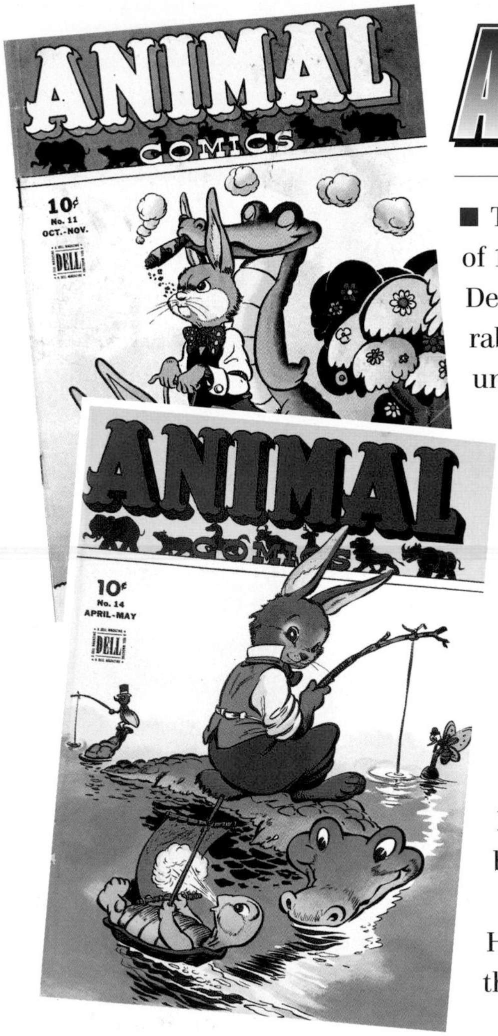
ANIMAL
COMICS
10¢
No. 11
OCT.-NOV.
DELL
ANIMAL
COMICS
10¢
No. 14
APRIL-MAY
DELL

ANIMAL COMICS

■ The undisputed star of *Animal Comics* was Pogo, born in the magazine at the end of 1941. He was the creation of erstwhile Disney animator Walt Kelly. The editor of Dell's kid-oriented magazine was Oskar Lebeck, who also included the venerable rabbit gentleman Uncle Wiggily in his lineup of animals. *Animal Comics* lasted until 1947 and its thirtieth issue.

Uncle Wiggily was added in the second issue. He'd been a rabbit since 1910, when author Howard R. Garis invented him for a daily bedtime-story column for newspaper syndication. In spite of his longevity and reputation, Wiggily didn't manage to outshine Pogo. Even when Uncle Wiggily was featured on a cover, members of the swamp gang were almost always there, too.

Kelly's possum debuted in the very first issue in a story titled "Albert Takes the Cake." Pogo was rather seedy looking at the offset, unfortunately resembling a real possum. And as the title indicates, he was upstaged by the cunning and voracious Albert the Alligator. After a year or so, Pogo had become a more attractive character and was also able to hold his own against Albert. Kelly was progressing as well, concocting audacious tales that blended burlesque, nonsense, and an occasional touch of cannibalism.

Among the other characters in the book were Cilly Goose, Hector the Henpecked Rooster, and a sheep by the name of Blackie. Kelly sometimes drew them as well.

ANT-MAN

■ While other superheroes were thinking big, Henry Pym was thinking small. Up until Ant-Man's arrival, *Tales to Astonish* was just another showcase for fantasy and horror tales and such Stan Lee–Jack Kirby monsters as Moomba, Vandoom, Trull, and the Creature from Krogarr. In fact, in Pym's first appearance in #27 (January 1962) he displayed no intention of ever becoming a mini-crimefighter.

Possibly influenced by the special effects in the 1957 movie *The Incredible Shrinking Man*, scientist Pym invented a green fluid that could shrink anything and, to be on the safe side, another green fluid that could cause the shrunken object to grow back to its original size. Pym considered these inventions "a boon to mankind!" To test the stuff, he splashed a bit of the shrinking fluid on himself. In seconds he was the size of an ant. Finding himself in his backyard, Pym wandered into an anthill and had considerable trouble with the residents until he discovered he could use judo on the most belligerent ants. Back in his lab, he used the other fluid to get back to his regular size. Tossing both fluids out, he vowed, "They're far too dangerous to ever be used by any human again!" He also promised himself never again "to knowingly step upon an ant hill."

However, by *Tales to Astonish* #35 (September 1962) the demand for new superheroes had increased. Thinking better of his serums, Pym reinvented them. He designed a costume of "steel mesh consisting of unstable molecules which stretch and contract as his body does." He also whipped up a cybernetic helmet that allowed him to communicate with ants. As fate would have it, just as

the young scientist had donned his costume for a tryout, communist agents broke into his laboratory to steal the top-secret "gas to make people immune to radioactivity" that Pym and his assistants were also working on. Returning to the anthill as Ant-Man, he recruited a large quantity of ants and defeated the spies.

The creative team behind Ant-Man consisted of Stan Lee, who thought up the character, his brother Larry Lieber, who wrote the scripts, Jack Kirby, who penciled, and Dick Ayers, who inked. Kirby was soon replaced by the dependable Don Heck. In #44 Ant-Man acquired a tiny female associate known as the Wasp. Then in #49, perhaps tired of risking getting stepped on or swatted, Pym used his growth serum to turn himself into Giant Man. Later he became Goliath and then Yellow Jacket. In each of his alter egos he was accepted for membership in the Avengers.

An entirely different chap, Scott Lang, assumed the Ant-Man role in the later 1970s. He still makes occasional appearances in Marvel titles.

APARO, JIM *(1932-)*

■ When he began drawing for Charlton Comics in the late 1960s, Jim Aparo was still an art director at a Connecticut advertising agency. Moonlighting for editor Dick Giordano, he drew such second-string characters as Nightshade, Wander, Tiffany Sinn, Thane of Bagarth, and Miss Bikini Luv. He worked his way up to Charlton's version of Lee Falk's *The Phantom*, his favorite assignment with the company.

Giordano, hired to edit at DC, invited him to work for them as well. By now a full-time cartoonist, Aparo drew

Aquaman, The Spectre, Deadman, The Phantom Stranger, and stories for both *House of Secrets* and *House of Mystery*. He worked on *Batman* from the early 1970s to the early 1990s. Aparo also illustrated numerous Batman team-ups—pairing the Dark Knight with everybody from the Teen Titans to the Joker—in DC's *The Brave and the Bold* and *Batman and the Outsiders*, a title he'd cocreated.

Aparo works in an appealing style that shows he's learned from his two favorite newspaper strip artists, Alex Raymond and Milton Caniff.

AQUAMAN

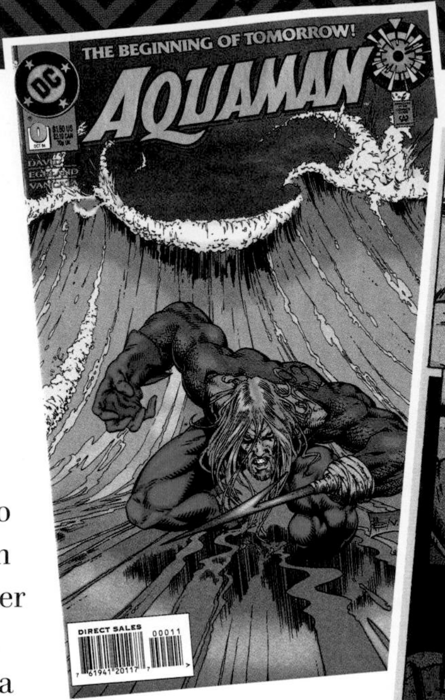
THE BEGINNING OF TOMORROW!
AQUAMAN
DIRECT SALES

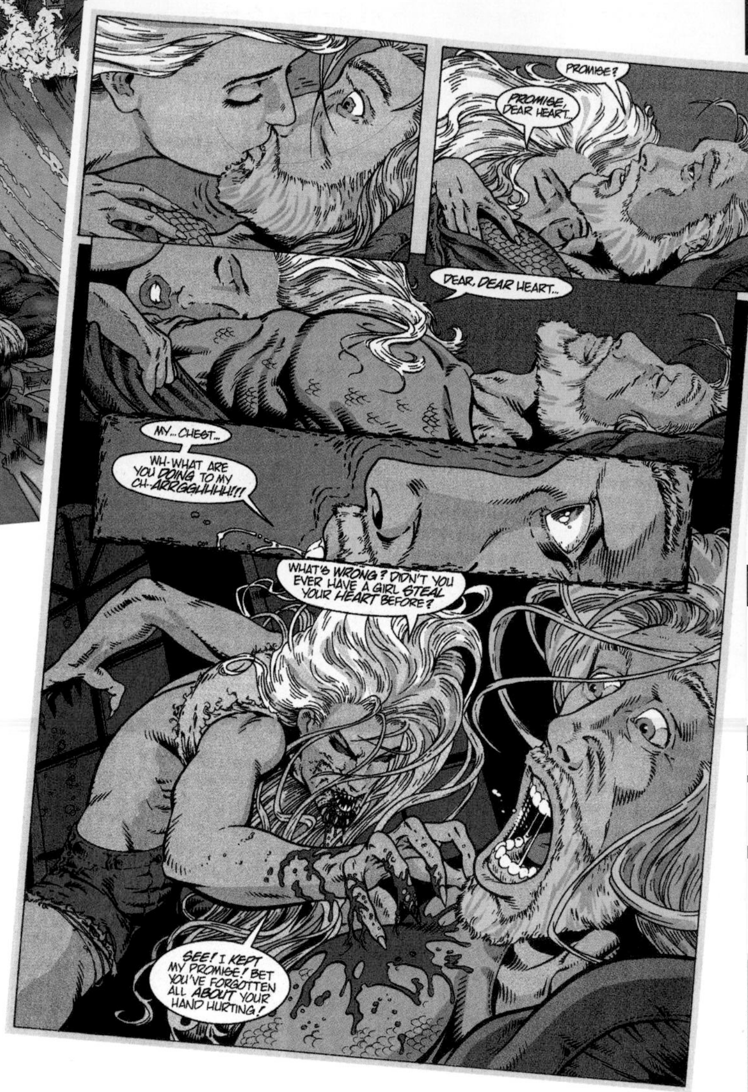
PROMISE?
PROMISE, DEAR HEART.
DEAR, DEAR HEART...
WHAT'S WRONG? DIDN'T YOU EVER HAVE A GIRL STEAL YOUR HEART BEFORE?
SEE! I KEPT MY PROMISE! BET YOU'VE FORGOTTEN ALL ABOUT YOUR HAND HURTING!

■ An underwater hero for over three-score years, he has yet to become waterlogged. And though Aquaman has sunk from sight now and then, he has always managed to resurface. He first swam into view in DC's *More Fun Comics* #73 (November 1941). Unlike Sub-Mariner, he was a fully-clothed aquatic hero, wearing a tunic of golden chain mail and sea-green tights and gloves. Aquaman was the collaborative creation of editor Mort Weisinger and artist Paul Norris.

In the original story Aquaman explained to a curious sea captain that he was the son of a noted scientist who'd discovered the ruins of an ancient city, possibly Atlantis, in the ocean's depths. After moving them into a watertight undersea home, his father used the ancient books and records to teach his son how to breathe underwater, develop great strength, and swim with tremendous speed. For good measure, Aquaman learned how to communicate with fish and other aquatic creatures. When in trouble, he could summon the denizens of the deep to help him.

At maturity, Aquaman decided "there is much evil in the upperworld" and that he must leave the sea periodically to punish evildoers. Over the years his origin has been revised several times. A later version stated that he was the result of a union between his lighthouse-keeper father and a woman from Atlantis (this sounds as though it was inspired by the old sea chantey "The Eddystone Light," popularized by Burl Ives, about a lighthouse-keeper who slept with a mermaid one stormy night). More recent accounts maintain that Aquaman himself is a native of the fabled undersea kingdom and was abandoned as a child.

The feature continued in its modest way in *More Fun* until early in 1946. Then the sovereign of the sea moved into *Adventure Comics* for an extended stay. Manly Wade Wellman and Otto Binder were the chief scripters in the 1940s and both Louis Cazeneuve and John Daly provided artwork. Early in 1960, when Ramona Fradon was the artist, Aquaman finally got a sidekick. Garth was an outcast from Atlantis, which was no longer a defunct location. Upon teaming up he became known as Aqualad (Aqua-boy for his first appearance).

In 1962, after nearly twenty years at sea, Aquaman was given his own magazine. It was in the *Aquaman* comic book that his hitherto placid life took on most of its complexities. He married an undersea queen named Mera, fathered a son who was named, inevitably, Aquababy, and was for a time the king of Atlantis. He also discovered that he had an evil half-brother Orm, also known as Ocean Master. This comic book, with scripts by George Kashden and Steve Skeates and art by Nick Cardy and then Jim Aparo, sank in the early 1970s.

The title has been revived several times since. In a later return a caption explained that Aquaman "has never known peace. His half-brother is his greatest enemy. His only son is dead. Murdered by yet another enemy. His wife tried to kill him, then abandoned him." Because of his dense body structure, the undersea hero is able to "withstand great pressure and change in temperature." Due to that helpful density, he tips the scales at a hefty 325 pounds.

The Aquaman of the 1990s was, understandably, a much grumpier fellow, as well as much hairier. He sported impressively long hair, a moustache and a beard, and a frequent snarl. In the *Aquaman* book that started up in 1994, written by Peter David, he lost a hand and replaced it with a hook. That series ended with its seventy-fifth issue (January 2001). Early in 2003 yet another series commenced. Clean-shaven and short-haired once again, Aquaman is on a roving assignment from the Lady of the Lake that involves him with assorted mythological creatures while working at cleaning up water pollution.

ARAGONES, SERGIO *(1937–)*

■ A man who has turned doodling into a fine art, and a very profitable art as well, Aragones first came to prominence in the early 1960s through the pages of *Mad.* Or rather in the margins of those pages, where his tiny doodled figures were to be seen circumnavigating the page in such a lively way that they often seemed much funnier than the material they were framing. Aragones soon moved up from marginal notes and in the early 1980s created *Groo.*

Born in Spain and raised in Mexico, he migrated to America in 1962. "When I found out how much cartoonists made in the United States," he has explained, "that was that." He was soon gainfully employed at *Mad.* By 1967 Aragones had added DC to his client list. Besides being a frequent contributor to *Plop,* he had a hand in the scripting of *Angel and the Ape* and *Bat Lash.*

An outgoing and amusing fellow, one who studied mime as well as architecture in school, he's also had a show-biz career, having appeared, for example, on television in the final season of *Laugh-In.*

In addition to the long-lasting barbarian spoof, *Groo,* which is scripted by his friend Mark Evanier, Aragones has in recent years turned out a variety of other projects. One such, put forth in 1999, was *Fan Boy.* Written by Evanier, the miniseries kidded a typical obsessive comics fan and had Aragones working in tandem with such serious artists as Gil Kane, Dick Sprang, and Mike Grell. *Mad* editor Nick Meglin has said of Sergio Aragones, "He never loses sight of the fact that he is a humorist, an attitude that, perhaps more than any other single fact, is responsible for his great success."

ARCHIE

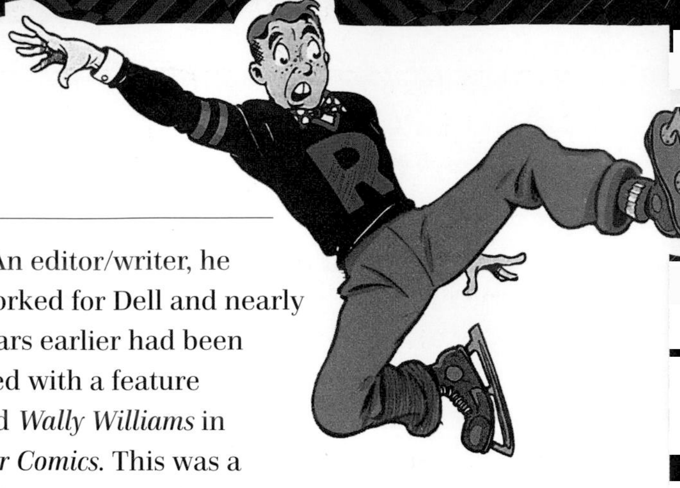

■ Now in his second century as a teenager, Archie first appeared in publisher MLJ's *Pep Comics* #22 (May 1941). The magazine was then an enclave of serious-minded heroes such as the Shield and the Hangman, but the intrusive freckled, redheaded Archie would eventually change all that. He was created, with some input from others, by cartoonist Bob Montana. Archie, along with Jughead, Betty, Veronica, and Reggie, has been attending Riverdale High for over sixty years.

Teenagers were coming into their own in the early 1940s, both as a target for manufacturers and a source of inspiration for entertainment. Henry Aldrich, the well-meaning but bumbling teen who was the prime inspiration for Archie, had first appeared in 1938 in Clifford Goodrich's Broadway play, *What a Life*. Henry had jumped to radio and then into movies. MLJ decided that a comic-book version of Henry Aldrich and the various other wacky teens who were proliferating in the media would appeal not only to teenage readers but to kids who were eager but had yet to reach their teens. Archie Andrews led the same sort of problem-ridden life as Henry Aldrich, Andy Hardy, and the rest and got entangled with the same sort of pretty girls.

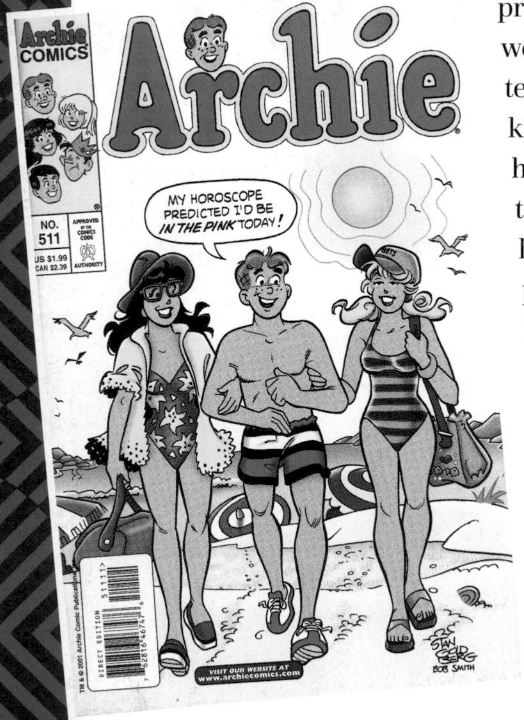
Archie COMICS
Archie
MY HOROSCOPE PREDICTED I'D BE IN THE PINK TODAY!
NO. 511
US $1.99
CAN $2.39
VISIT OUR WEBSITE AT www.archiecomics.com
BOB SMITH

Usually unsung when credit for developing *Archie* is handed out is Vic Bloom, who wrote the script for the first story. An editor/writer, he also worked for Dell and nearly two years earlier had been involved with a feature entitled *Wally Williams* in *Popular Comics.* This was a light adventure strip that dealt mostly with high school athletics. Interestingly enough, Wally attended Riverview High, had a best friend named Jughead, and a blonde girlfriend named Betty. His mentor was his gray-haired Gramps. In Bloom's introductory script for *Archie*, Betty and Jughead figured again and Riverview became Riverdale. Archie, who looked only about thirteen at the offset, had a full set of parents but turned for advice to his live-in Gramps. In *Pep* and *Jackpot*, where he was also appearing, Archie quickly grew into an older teenager and acquired a jalopy. Both Gramps and Bloom were soon gone.

The increasingly popular Archie got a magazine of his own in 1942. By that time most of the other regulars, including the slinky, dark-haired Veronica Lodge, the principal Mr. Weatherbee, and the all-purpose teacher Miss Grundy, were all in place. Eventually Archie took over *Pep Comics*, ousting all the serious characters. In the spring of 1946, MLJ officially became Archie Comic Publications. Over the years the Archie titles had multiplied and have included *Archie's Joke Book*, *Archie's Girls Betty and Veronica*, *Archie's Pal Jughead*, *Archie Comics Digest*, *Archie's Madhouse*, *Archie's Pals 'N' Gals*, *Jughead's Jokes*, *Betty & Veronica Summer Fun*, and *Little Archie.* In recent years the Archie comic books have been in digest format.

In addition to Montana, a small army of other cartoonists has drawn the Archie material, including Harry Sahle, Bill Vigoda, Al Fagaly, Tom Moore, Harry Lucey, George Frese, and Dan DeCarlo.

ARMSTRONG, ROGER (1917-)

■ Long a successful watercolor painter and art teacher in Southern California, in his youth Armstrong drew for the *Looney Tunes and Merrie Melodies* comic book. He was responsible for *Mary Jane and Sniffles, Elmer Fudd,* and *Porky Pig*, starting in the early 1940s. He also drew the *Bugs Bunny* Sunday newspaper page in the middle 1940s, as well as handling many of Bugs's comic-book appearances later in that decade.

Armstrong, who was fast, dependable, and good, also drew a string of comic strips from the forties to the eighties. In addition to *Bugs Bunny*, he put in time on *Ella Cinders, Little Lulu, Napoleon, The Flintstones*, and *Scamp*. Before turning full-time to landscape painting and instructing, he drew such later comic books as *Super Goof* and *Funky Phantom.*

THE ARROW

■ Here he was, the first costumed hero to show up in comic books after Superman and his publisher paid little initial attention to him. The Arrow arrived late in Centaur's *Funny Pages*, not getting there until #21 (September 1938), and he wasn't showcased on the cover until a year later. He did somewhat better thereafter, being featured on seven of the next dozen. Then, in the fall of 1940, *Funny Pages* closed up shop. In those early days, heroes in colorful costumes, no matter how clunky, were what sold comic books. The Centaur folks were late in realizing this basic economic notion. They did, however, manage to keep the Arrow alive for one more year by way of three erratically published issues of *The Arrow* magazine.

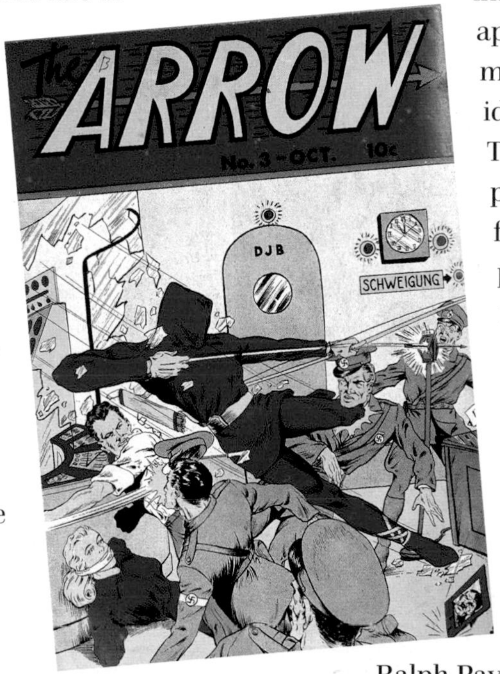
The ARROW
No. 3 - OCT. 10¢
DJB
SCHWEIGUNG

Paul Gustavson, until recently specializing in humor features, was the artist on *The Arrow*. Since there were then no rules about hero haberdashery, the early Arrow wore what looked like a suit of baggy red pajamas and a cowl that hid his face completely. Over time, Gustavson's illustrational style improved and the Arrow's costume and appearance improved as well. A real mystery man, the archer had no civilian identity until the very end of the run. Though never billed as having psychic powers, he possessed an uncanny knack for knowing where crimes were taking place. He'd show up, let fly a few arrows from his bow, and vanish. At times he also exhibited impressive strength, ripping doors off their hinges, etc. One of his specialties seemed to be rescuing pretty blonde young women.

Toward the end, the Arrow was recruited by a U.S. intelligence agency. Readers then learned that he was a good-looking blond fellow named Ralph Payne. On his final outing, the Arrow, in a new costume that masked only part of his face, slipped into Germany to fight the Nazis. Bob Lubbers drew that last adventure.

ASHE, EDD (1908–1986)

■ The son of a noted book and magazine illustrator, Edd Ashe, Jr., was himself a painter and a muralist. For over thirty years, from the late 1930s to the early 1970s, he was also a prolific comic-book artist. A talented if often hurried cartoonist, he drew a range of characters that included the Wizard, the Saint, the Blue Beetle, the Flame, Commando Yank, Don Winslow, the Human Torch, and Mike Shayne.

Working first out of the Chesler shop, Ashe contributed to such early MLJ titles as *Top-Notch* and *Zip*. For Lev Gleason's *Silver Streak Comics* he drew the Saint, and for the Fox line he created considerable covers as well as interior art. When Carl Burgos left the Human Torch in the early years of World War II, Ashe took over the drawing. By this time he was working out of Funnies, Inc. He drew *The Commando Yank* in *Wow* and entire issues of *Don Winslow*, both chores for Fawcett. Later on, he worked on everything from funny animals to private eyes for Dell. Ashe's final comic-book employer was Charlton.

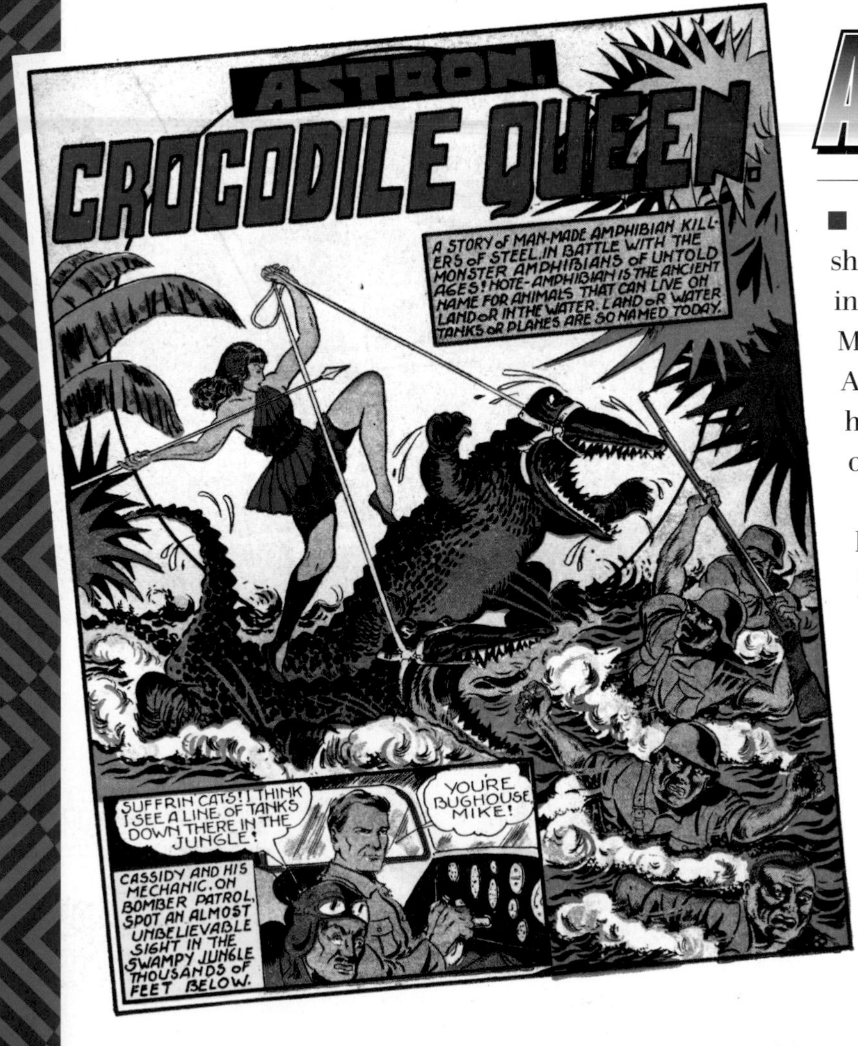
ASTRON
CROCODILE QUEEN
A STORY of MAN-MADE AMPHIBIAN KILLERS of STEEL IN BATTLE WITH THE MONSTER AMPHIBIANS of UNTOLD AGES! NOTE- AMPHIBIAN IS THE ANCIENT NAME FOR ANIMALS THAT CAN LIVE ON LAND or IN THE WATER. LAND or WATER TANKS or PLANES ARE SO NAMED TODAY.
SUFFRIN CATS! I THINK I SEE A LINE OF TANKS DOWN THERE IN THE JUNGLE!
YOU'RE BUGHOUSE, MIKE!
CASSIDY AND HIS MECHANIC, ON BOMBER PATROL, SPOT AN ALMOST UNBELIEVABLE SIGHT IN THE SWAMPY JUNGLE THOUSANDS of FEET BELOW.

ASTRON

■ A formidable woman, also known as the Crocodile Queen, she first appeared in the fifth issue of *Doc Savage Magazine* in 1941. Written and drawn by newspaper veteran Charles M. Payne, who'd been a professional since the 1890s, Astron's adventures offered a slightly wacky mix of fantasy, horror, World War II intrigue, romance, and a whole lot of crocodiles.

Astron, aided by a large herd of crocodiles who did her bidding, dwelled in a remote valley in a remote jungle. She guarded, with considerable help from her crocs, the Mystic Light that granted eternal life to all who bathed in its glow. What with an evil ancient sorceress who commanded an army of gorillas, covetous Nazis, and other ne'er-do-wells, the blond spear-wielding Astron led an active life. There were also two American aviators who'd crash-landed in her kingdom. The magazine ceased in late 1943.

THE ATOM: I

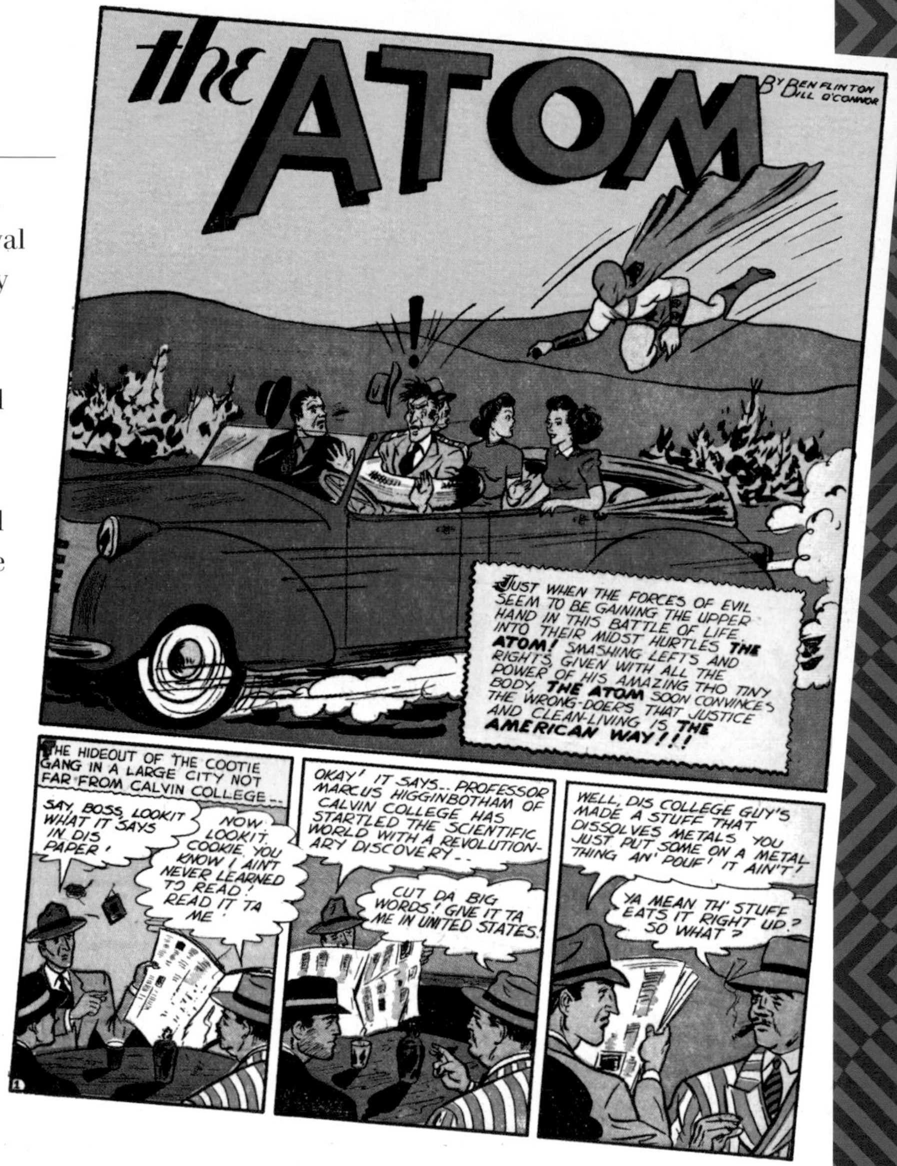
the ATOM
BY BEN FLINTON BILL O'CONNOR
JUST WHEN THE FORCES OF EVIL SEEM TO BE GAINING THE UPPER HAND IN THIS BATTLE OF LIFE, INTO THEIR MIDST HURTLES THE ATOM! SMASHING LEFTS AND RIGHTS, GIVEN WITH ALL THE POWER OF HIS AMAZING THO TINY BODY, THE ATOM SOON CONVINCES THE WRONG-DOERS THAT JUSTICE AND CLEAN-LIVING IS THE AMERICAN WAY!!!
THE HIDEOUT OF THE COOTIE GANG IN A LARGE CITY NOT FAR FROM CALVIN COLLEGE--
SAY, BOSS, LOOKIT WHAT IT SAYS IN DIS PAPER!
NOW, LOOKIT, COOKIE, YOU KNOW I AIN'T NEVER LEARNED TO READ! READ IT TA ME!
OKAY! IT SAYS... PROFESSOR MARCUS HIGGINBOTHAM OF CALVIN COLLEGE HAS STARTLED THE SCIENTIFIC WORLD WITH A REVOLUTIONARY DISCOVERY--
CUT DA BIG WORDS! GIVE IT TA ME IN UNITED STATES!
WELL, DIS COLLEGE GUY'S MADE A STUFF THAT DISSOLVES METALS. YOU JUST PUT SOME ON A METAL THING AN' POUF! IT AIN'T!
YA MEAN TH' STUFF EATS IT RIGHT UP? SO WHAT?

■ The original Atom took up residence in *All-American Comics* #19 (October 1940), three months after the arrival of the Green Lantern. He was initially called the Mighty Atom, a name possibly borrowed from that of a real-life, diminutive strongman of the day. Unlike the later hero with this name, he had no superpowers and owed his abilities to diet and exercise. This Atom was a redheaded college student named Al Pratt, who stood just over five feet tall. His school chums "constantly kid him about his small size" and have nicknamed him the Atom. Vowing to do something about his ninety-seven-pound weakling status, Pratt underwent physical fitness training with a down-on-his-luck trainer he met. He turned into a muscleman, one who "now has tremendous strength in one so small." Pratt adopted a secret costumed identity as the Atom and began a career of crimefighting. Since nobody treated his civilian self with any respect even after he became the Atom, Pratt was one of the more anguished heroes of the 1940s.

Writer Bill O'Connor and artist Ben Flinton created the character. They'd earlier been in partnership with cartoonist Leonard Sansone, who would create the popular Army panel *The Wolf* during World War II. As FOS they'd produced a minor feature called *The Phantom Sub* for *Blue Bolt*. Without Sansone their work was just passable. When Flinton and O'Connor followed Sansone into the service, Joe Gallagher became the artist. He didn't take a lyrical approach to drawing adventure material, favoring a gritty, cartoony look. Gallagher's Atom stories were rich with the props and locations of the meaner edge of big-city life—ashcans and alleys, street cleaners, pushcarts, junk wagons, tenements and shanties, pool halls, junkyards, mom-and-pop grocery stores, lampposts, and fire hydrants. He stayed with the character for several years, also drawing him as a member of the Justice Society in *All Star Comics*.

The Atom moved from *All-American* to *Flash Comics* in 1947. He acquired a new, flashier costume in 1948 and took a leave from comics the following year. Toward the end of his first run he picked up "atomic" strength to become a true superhero. He has returned on various occasions ever since, for such things as JSA-JLA team-ups, to serve on the All Star Squadron, and to do assorted guest turns. He has even managed to appear with the other hero who bears the name.

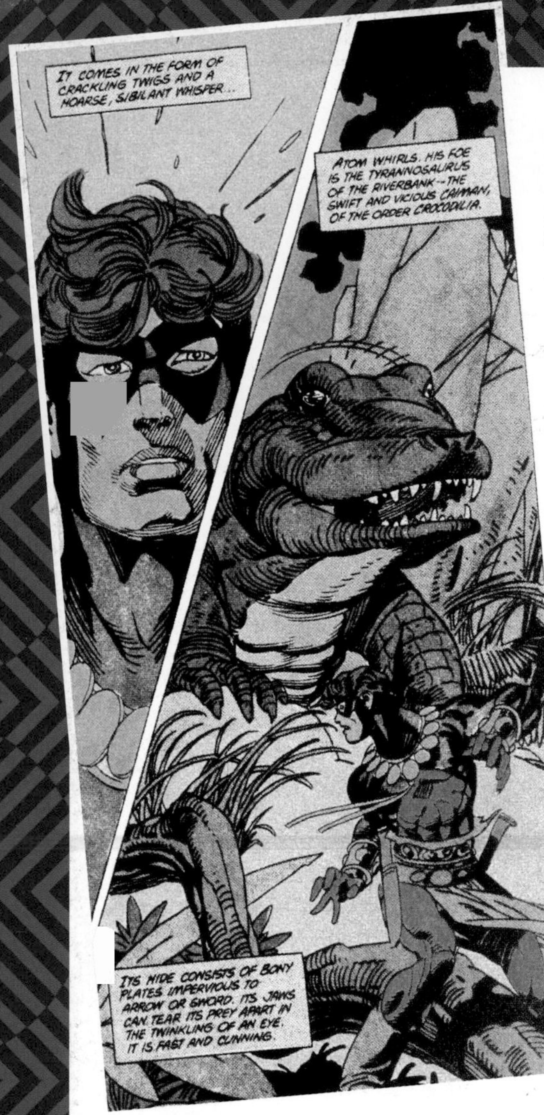
IT COMES IN THE FORM OF CRACKLING TWIGS AND A HOARSE, SIBILANT WHISPER...
ATOM WHIRLS. HIS FOE IS THE TYRANNOSAURUS OF THE RIVERBANK--THE SWIFT AND VICIOUS CAIMAN, OF THE ORDER CROCODILIA.
ITS HIDE CONSISTS OF BONY PLATES IMPERVIOUS TO ARROW OR SWORD. ITS JAWS CAN TEAR ITS PREY APART IN THE TWINKLING OF AN EYE. IT IS FAST AND CUNNING.

THE ATOM: II

■ A brand-new Atom, completely different from his namesake, debuted in DC's *Showcase* #34 (October 1961). Borrowing from Doll Man, the tiny superhero of the 1940s, editor Julius Schwartz and writer Gardner Fox created a fellow who could shrink at will. Gil Kane, an admirer of Doll Man's original artist Lou Fine, got the job of drawing the dinky do-gooder.

"I always felt the Atom of the 1940s was misnamed," Schwartz once said. "He was simply called the Atom because he was a short fellow. I got the idea of having him a regular six-footer able to reduce himself to any size he wanted to. It just struck us as we were groping around for a theme that wasn't being done by any superheroes." They gave their hero the civilian name of Ray Palmer, in honor of the longtime editor of *Amazing Stories*. That Palmer was extremely short may also have had something to do with it.

The Atom moved into his own magazine in the spring of 1962. It was retitled *The Atom & Hawkman* in 1968 and continued under that name until it folded the following year. Among the subsequent revivals were *Sword of the Atom* by Gil Kane and writer Jan Strnad, involving the tiny hero in sword-and-sorcery adventures in a world where everyone is six inches tall. He was also in a short-lived series *Power of the Atom* and in one of the DC Tangent series in 1997.

ATOMAN

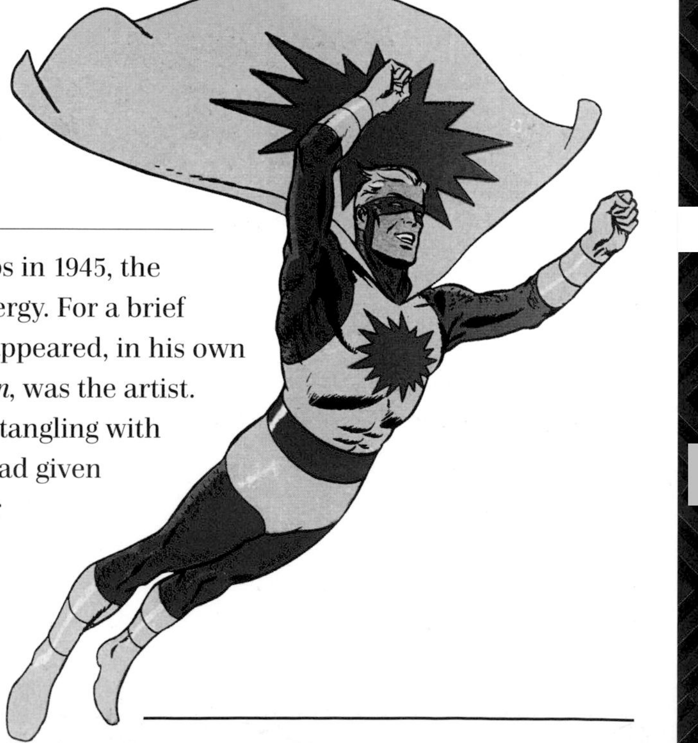

■ In the optimistic days after the dropping of the first atomic bombs in 1945, the majority of the American public was enthusiastic about nuclear energy. For a brief period superheroes with atomic powers came into being. Atoman appeared, in his own magazine, early in 1946. Jerry Robinson, fresh from ghosting *Batman*, was the artist.

Barry Dane, a scientist at the Atomic Institute, discovered after tangling with spies that "I am radio active." Working with radium and uranium had given him "atomic strength!" Stitching up a crimson-and-gold costume for himself, he went forth to "bring about a new age of peace, security and happiness for all." Unfortunately, the *Atoman* magazine fizzled out after its second issue.

THE ATOMIC KNIGHTS

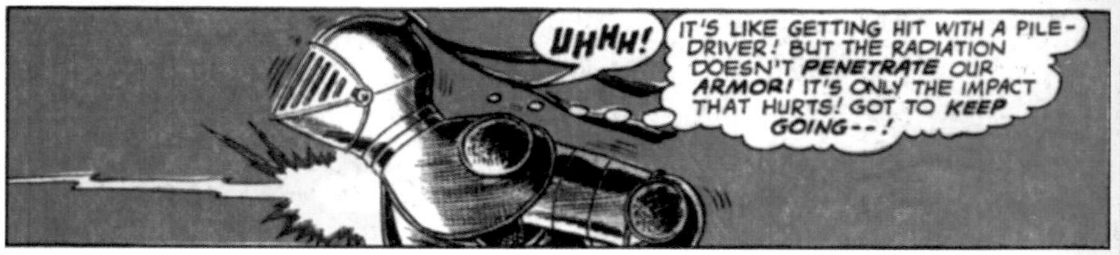
UHHH!
IT'S LIKE GETTING HIT WITH A PILE-DRIVER! BUT THE RADIATION DOESN'T PENETRATE OUR ARMOR! IT'S ONLY THE IMPACT THAT HURTS! GOT TO KEEP GOING--!

■ By the 1960s, the public attitude toward things atomic had changed. The proliferation of nuclear weapons and the Cold War converted optimism to fear. A common science-fiction scenario in books and movies showed a small group of survivors coping with a world devastated by nuclear war. *The Atomic Knights*, DC's major contribution to that genre, first appeared in *Strange Adventures* #117 (June 1960).

Set in the then-distant 1980s, it dealt with a half dozen survivors—five men and a woman—who donned ancient suits of armor that they'd discovered provided protection against radiation and surviving weaponry. The series ran to fifteen installments, appearing every three issues. By the time it ended in #160 (January 1964), the Knights had defeated the rogues who'd tried to rule the survivors, turned back an alien invasion, and converted their Midwest hometown into a green paradise.

Scripts were by John Broome and art by Murphy Anderson, who once said that the toughest part of the job was having to draw six separate and distinct suits of armor each time.

AUTRY, GENE (1907–1998)

■ Singing movie cowboy and multimillionaire, Gene Autry was also a comic-book hero from the early forties to the middle fifties.

Though born in Texas, he was not exactly at home on horseback. He could, however, play a guitar and sing Western tunes, and in 1928 he started singing on the radio. By the middle thirties, Autry was starring in a series of B-Westerns for Republic Pictures. In 1940, he came in fourth in the annual poll of the top-ten box-office stars—behind Mickey Rooney, Spencer Tracy, and Clark Gable, but ahead of Tyrone Power, James Cagney, and Bing Crosby.

Both *Popular Comics* and *Crackajack Funnies* had included short adaptations of his movies now and then in the late 1930s, but it wasn't until the last day of 1941 that a full-fledged *Gene Autry Comics* reached the newsstands. The first ten issues were published by Fawcett and represented their initial attempt at a cowboy title. Till Goodin, an authentic cowboy artist, provided the artwork. He'd been drawing the *Gene Autry Rides!* newspaper strip.

Dell took over the title with the eleventh issue in 1943, keeping it going until 1954. Jesse Marsh, equally at home on the range as he was in Tarzan's jungle, drew many of the issues and was followed by Russ Manning.

The Gene Autry of the comics was the same shrewd, amiable fellow he was on the screen, although he rarely stopped to sing. Riding his reliable horse, Champion, he battled rustlers, bushwhackers, claim jumpers, bank robbers, and all the other standard villains of the fictional West. From 1950 to 1955 there was also a Dell comic devoted to Gene's horse.

THE AVENGERS

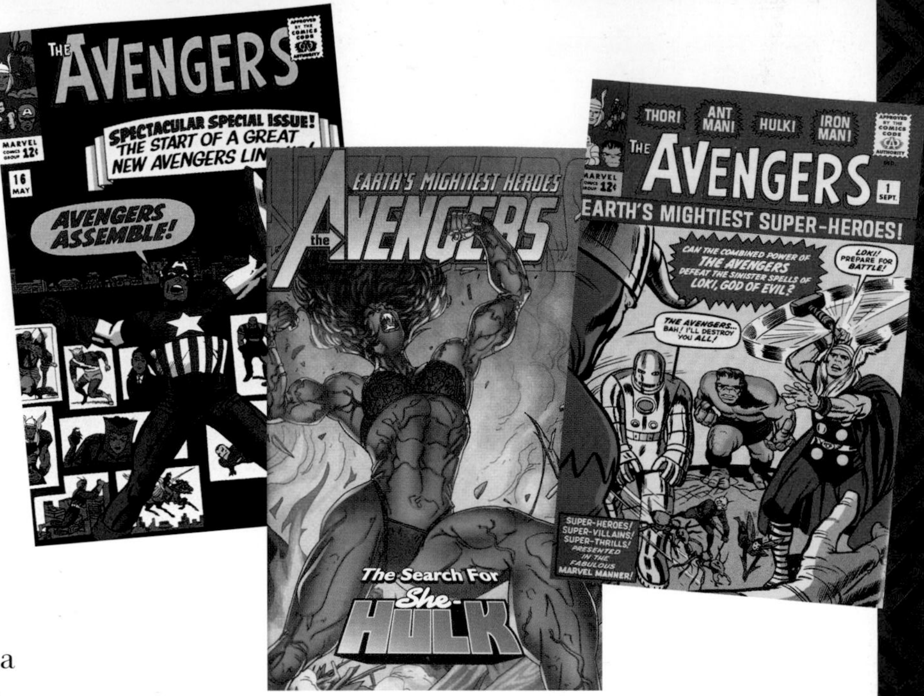
THE AVENGERS
SPECTACULAR SPECIAL ISSUE!
16 MAY
AVENGERS ASSEMBLE!
EARTH'S MIGHTIEST HEROES
the AVENGERS
The Search For She-HULK
THOR! ANT MAN! HULK! IRON MAN!
THE AVENGERS
1 SEPT.
EARTH'S MIGHTIEST SUPER-HEROES!
CAN THE COMBINED POWER OF THE AVENGERS DEFEAT THE SINISTER SPELLS OF LOKI, GOD OF EVIL?
LOKI! PREPARE FOR BATTLE!
THE AVENGERS... BAH! I'LL DESTROY YOU ALL!
SUPER-HEROES! SUPER-VILLAINS! SUPER-THRILLS! PRESENTED IN THE FABULOUS MARVEL MANNER!

■ As the team spirit spread through comics in the early 1960s, a gang of Marvel characters got together and decided to call themselves the Avengers. Perhaps one of them had been over to Great Britain recently and caught *The Avengers* show on the telly. The original members of the new Marvel group were the Hulk, Thor, Iron Man, Ant-Man, and the Wasp. The plot for "The Coming of the Avengers" was cooked up by Stan Lee and Jack Kirby, scripted by Lee and drawn by Kirby. The premier issue of *The Avengers* had a cover date of September 1963.

Touted as a "book-length super-epic" that featured "some of the Earth's greatest super-heroes!" the introductory episode had the superfolks gathering from hither and yon to overcome Loki, the Norse god of evil who'd already frequently troubled Thor. After dispatching Loki, they decided to work as a team. It was the Wasp, the one female in the bunch, who came up with the name Avengers in the final panel. The Hulk observes, "I pity the guy who tries to beat us!" Thor, magic hammer held high, declares, "We'll NEVER be beaten! For we are . . . THE AVENGERS!"

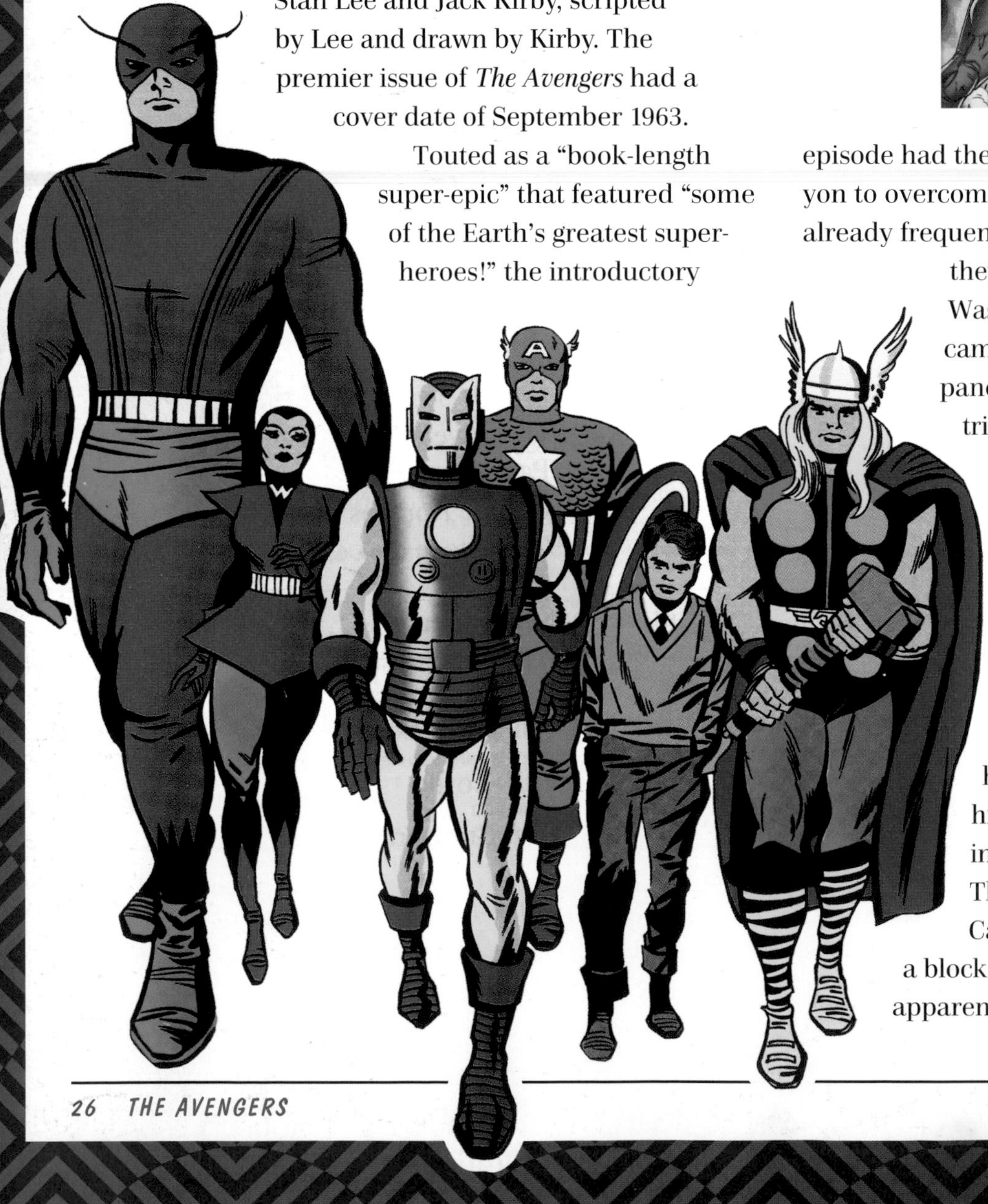

By the second issue Ant-Man, who'd grown tired of being teenie-weenie, had turned himself into the towering Giant Man, thus revising the Avengers roll call. Over the next two issues a couple of early Marvel heroes returned. This time, however, the Sub-Mariner was in one of his surly moods and did a turn as a villain in "one of the great battles of all time!!" Then in #4 (March 1964) the superpatriot Captain America was found floating inside a block of ice in the Atlantic, where he'd apparently been languishing for twenty years.

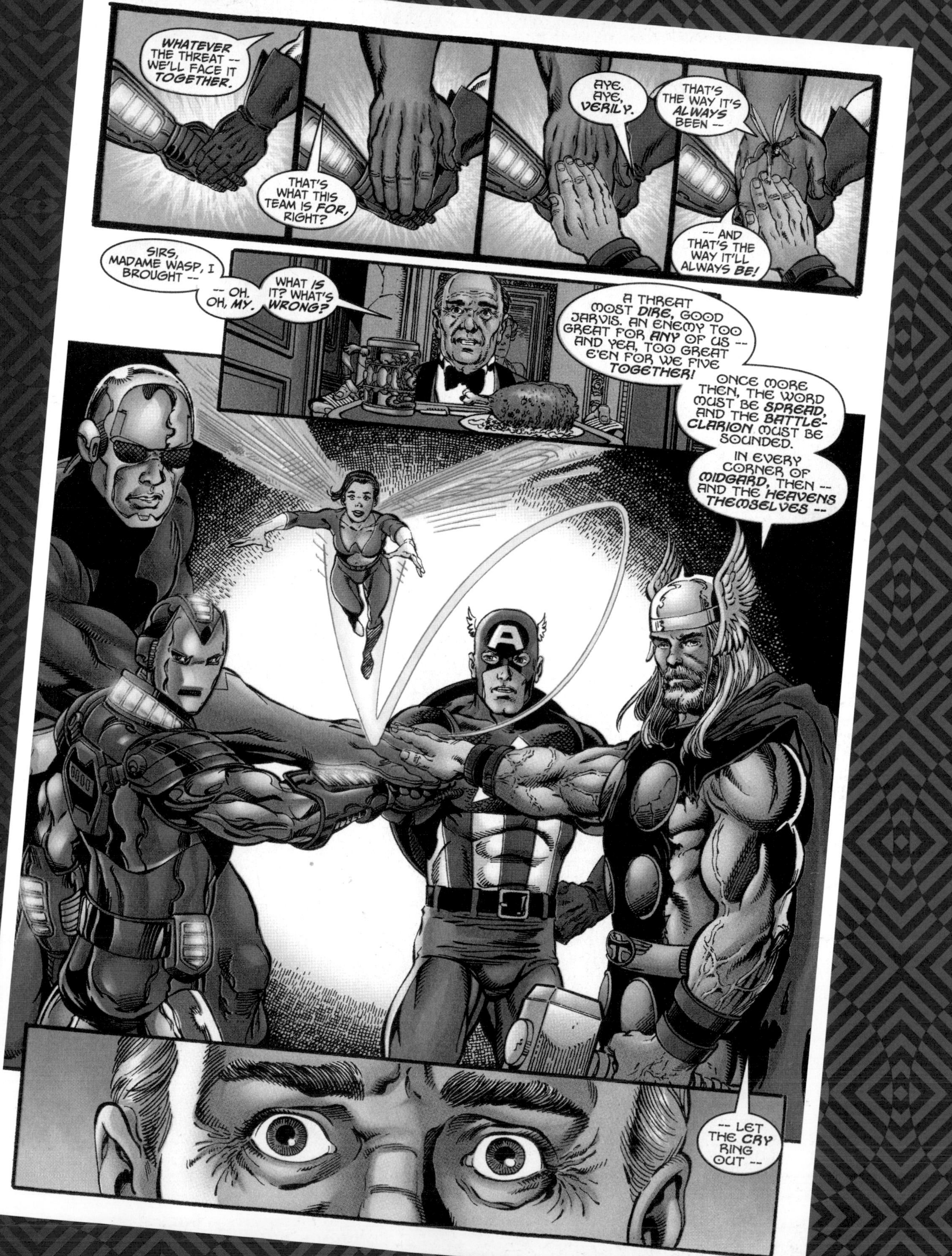

WHATEVER THE THREAT -- WE'LL FACE IT TOGETHER.
THAT'S WHAT THIS TEAM IS FOR, RIGHT?
AYE. AYE, VERILY.
THAT'S THE WAY IT'S ALWAYS BEEN --
-- AND THAT'S THE WAY IT'LL ALWAYS BE!
SIRS, MADAME WASP, I BROUGHT --
-- OH. OH, MY.
WHAT IS IT? WHAT'S WRONG?
A THREAT MOST DIRE, GOOD JARVIS. AN ENEMY TOO GREAT FOR ANY OF US -- AND YEA, TOO GREAT E'EN FOR WE FIVE TOGETHER!
ONCE MORE THEN, THE WORD MUST BE SPREAD, AND THE BATTLE-CLARION MUST BE SOUNDED.
IN EVERY CORNER OF MIDGARD, THEN -- AND THE HEAVENS THEMSELVES --
-- LET THE CRY RING OUT --

Eventually thawed out, he joined the Avengers, even though he was a bit fuzzy on current events. This represented Cap's Silver Age return.

The Avengers, who bickered like most Marvel hero groups, proved a popular saleable bunch. Over the next few years there was a considerable fluctuation in the basic membership. In 1965, for example, Hawkeye, Quicksilver, and the Scarlet Witch joined on. Later on Hercules, the Vision, Goliath, and Yellow Jacket were added. These last two were other manifestations of Ant-Man. Among the guest stars were Spider-Man, the Fantastic Four, and Wonder Man. On the list of major villains were the Living Laser, the Red Skull, Diablo, the Red Guardian, the Mandarin, the Executioner, Magneto, and Klaw.

The creative team changed as well. Other early pencilers included Don Heck, John Buscema, Gene Colan, and Neal Adams. George Roussos, Dick Ayers, and Joe Sinnott all served as inkers. Roy Thomas, who wrote a great many scripts, eventually also became editor in the summer of 1972. The original series reached 402 issues, ending in 1996. The makeup of the gang continued to fluctuate. Hellcat, the Falcon, the Beast, and She-Hulk all were members. Some later artists and writers were John Byrne, Joe Staton, and Walt Simonson.

In 1984 the Avengers set up a branch office that resulted in *West Coast Avengers.* Among the members were Hawkeye and Iron Man. At the end of the eighties, John Byrne assumed the scripting and drawing. With #48 (September 1989) the title was switched to *Avengers West Coast,* and as such the magazine continued until #102 (January 1994).

A second series of *The Avengers* commenced in 1996. Among the members were Captain America, Hawkeye, Thor, and the Vision. Jim Valentino wrote the scripts; Rob Liefeld did the drawing on the first issue. This version continued for thirteen issues. Early in 1998, *The Avengers* started all over again and continues to this day. Kurt Busiek was the initial writer, George Perez the artist. And the rallying cry, "Avengers assemble!" is still heard in the land.

 **AYERS, DICK** *(1927-)*

■ A dependable artist with an easily recognizable style, Ayers has been in comics since 1947. He was the cocreator of the original Ghost Rider and has also drawn the Human Torch, Sgt. Fury, the Hulk, Captain America, and Ka-Zar. He also inked a good deal of Jack Kirby's Marvel work.

Another student of Burne Hogarth's Cartoonists and Illustrators School, Ayers's first comic-book work was ghosting Jerry Siegel and Joe Shuster's *Funnyman* for the short Magazine Enterprises run. He next worked directly for Vincent Sullivan's ME, drawing the ever shorter run of *Jimmy Durante.* He moved on to serious Westerns, first with the Calico Kid and then the Kid's popular successor the Ghost Rider. The luminous Rider was in the Tim Holt comic before starring in a title of his own. Ayers, who was fond of the dual-identity cowboy, drew all fourteen issues of ME's *Ghost Rider*, plus all of the mystery man's appearances in such other ME titles as *Best of the West.*

Ayers worked for Marvel as well, starting in the early 1950s. He was the artist who drew the Human Torch's first and unsuccessful comeback try for *Young Men Comics* in 1953. Ayers remained with Marvel for decades, penciling a wide range of characters, including their revival of the original Ghost Rider. He inked Jack Kirby's pencils on *The Hulk, The Fantastic Four, The Avengers, The Rawhide Kid, X-Men,* etc. In the 1990s he drew another phosphorescent cowboy, the Haunted Horseman, for Bill Black's Paragon Publications.

Active today, Ayers has a website displaying the slogan, "Still producing at his drawing board!!"

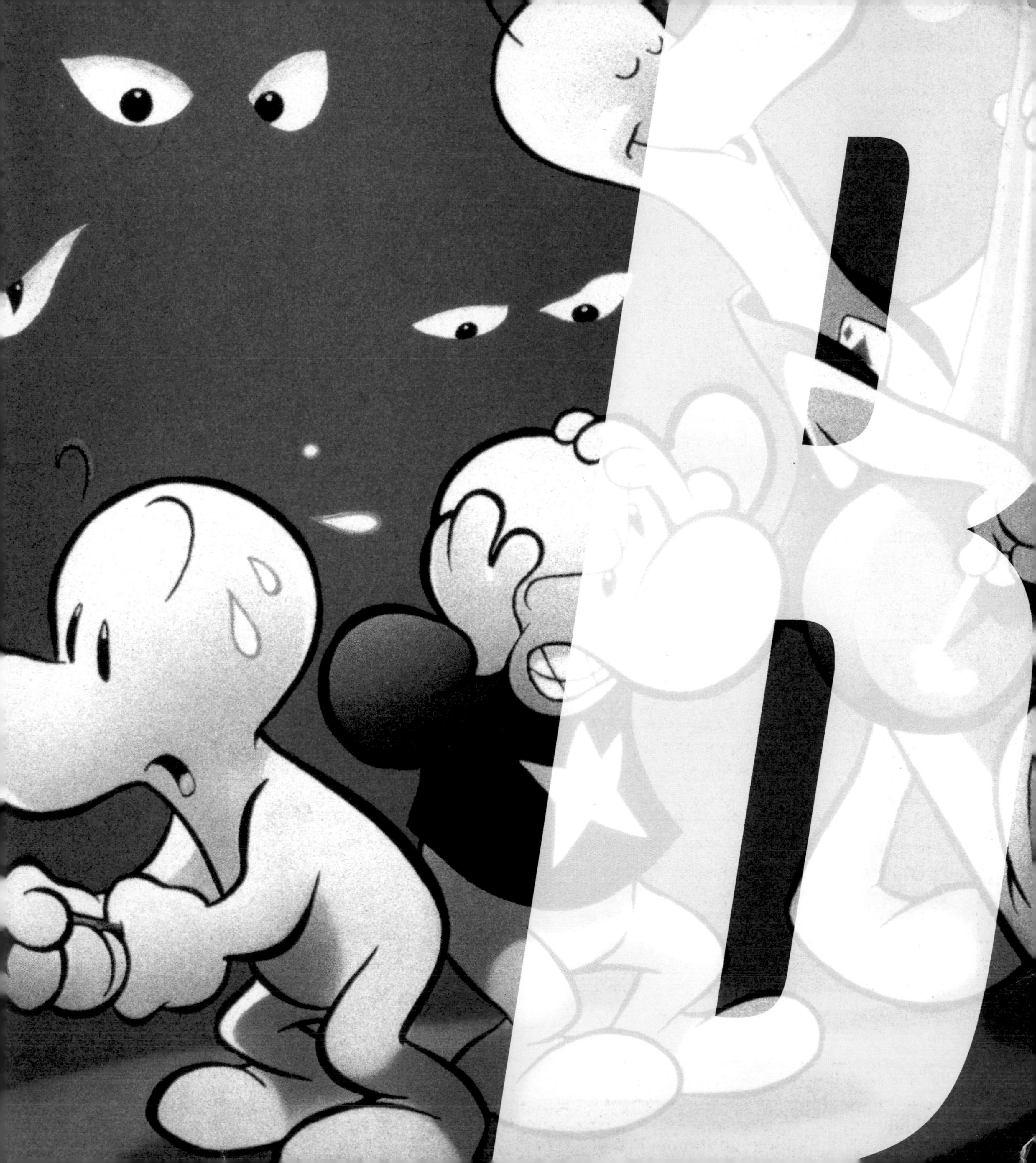

BABE

■ See ROGERS, BOODY.

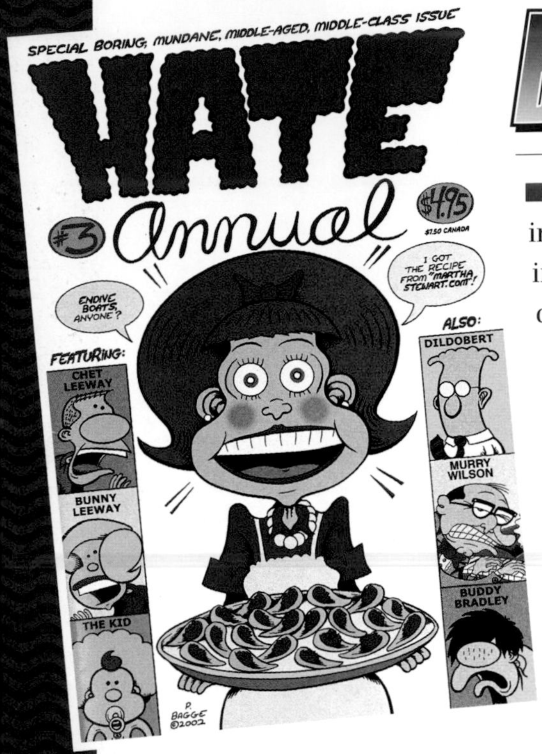
SPECIAL BORING, MUNDANE, MIDDLE-AGED, MIDDLE-CLASS ISSUE
HATE
#3 Annual
$4.95
$7.50 CANADA
ENDIVE BOATS, ANYONE?
I GOT THE RECIPE FROM "MARTHA STEWART.COM"!
FEATURING:
CHET LEEWAY
BUNNY LEEWAY
THE KID
ALSO:
DILDOBERT
MURRY WILSON
BUDDY BRADLEY
P. BAGGE ©2002

BAGGE, PETER

(1958–)

■ A master of the grotesque school of cartooning, Bagge (pronounced bag) has worked in both underground and aboveground comics. His own *Neat Stuff* and *Hate* have been independent successes, and in 2003 he created but did not draw *Sweat Shop* for DC. It deals with a bunch of hapless comics artists.

The majority of Bagge's characters are unhappy, maladjusted, and trapped in middle-class ruts. They are, the lot of them, ugly, have poor postures, and do double-takes that wouldn't be out of place in a Tex Avery animated cartoon. Bagge draws with the intensity and distortion of a graffiti artist.

A onetime editor of Robert Crumb's *Weirdo*, he started *Neat Stuff* to gather together a variety of his graphic fulminations in a single place. *Hate*, begun in 1990, is published by Fantagraphics and features Bagge's best-known loser Buddy Bradley. The 2002 edition of the *Hate Annual* proclaimed itself a "special boring, mundane, middle-age, middle-class issue." In addition to Buddy and his home decorating–obsessed wife, it also featured a parody entitled "Dildobert Joins the Al-Queda."

BAILY, BERNARD

(1916–1996)

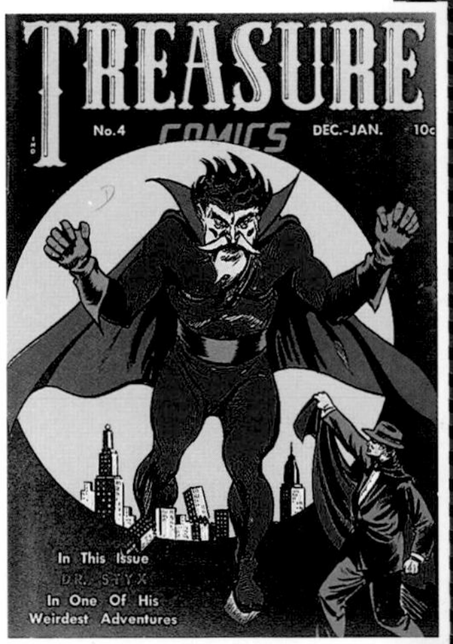
TREASURE
COMICS
No.4
DEC.-JAN.
10c
In This Issue
DR. STYX
In One Of His
Weirdest Adventures

■ A graduate of the Eisner-Iger shop, Baily started working for DC in 1938. A self-taught artist, he drew such early features as *Tex Thomson* and *The Buccaneer*. Then late in 1939, Jerry Siegel came up with the Spectre. "The look of the character I created, the script he wrote," Baily once explained. "I worked in the office for a while, then started working at home. Siegel did the writing on the Spectre the whole time." The ghostly superhero became the leading hero in *More Fun Comics* until the Green Arrow came along. Baily also drew the sixty-minute superhero Hour-Man in *Adventure Comics* from his entrance in #48 (March 1940) to his exit after #83 (February 1943).

In the middle 1940s Baily left DC to open his own shop. Among his employees were newspaper veteran C. A. Voight, a young Gil Kane, and a young Frank Frazetta. Baily put together the contents for such Prize Group titles as *Prize Comics* and *Treasure Comics*, also drawing a ghostbreaker character called Dr. Styx for the latter. He published some very short-lived comics of his own, among them *Spook Comics* and an unauthorized *Cisco Kid*. Returning to DC in the early 1950s with a new style, he contributed to their fantasy titles.

BAILEY, RAY (1913–1975)

■ Versatile, having assisted on the slapstick newspaper strip *Moon Mullins* and the illustrative adventure strip *Terry and the Pirates*, Bailey used his straight illustration style on his comic-book work. Most of that came after he'd drawn three newspaper adventure strips of his own: *Vesta West*, *Bruce Gentry*, and *Tom Corbett, Space Cadet*.

Drawing for a variety of comic publishers from the middle 1950s to the late 1960s, using his personal variation of the Milton Caniff style, Bailey worked on *The Gray Ghost*, *Ripcord*, *Mandrake*, *Buck Rogers*, *Steve Canyon*, and *Undersea Agent*. Falling on hard times caused by personal problems, he ended his days living in a hotel room on the edge of San Francisco's Tenderloin District.

BAKER, MATT (c. 1919–c. 1963)

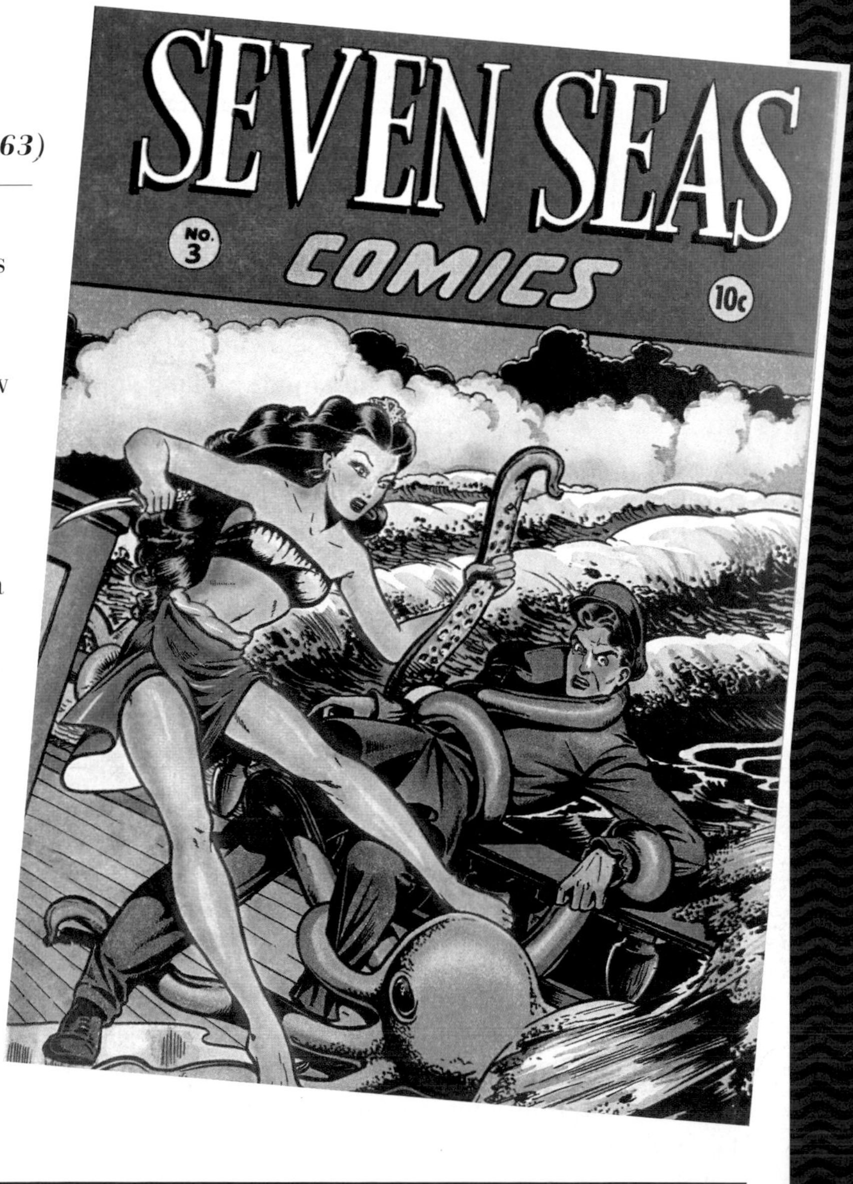
SEVEN SEAS
NO. 3
COMICS
10¢

■ A highly skilled depicter of pretty women, Baker's most famous character was the Phantom Lady. His specialty was what came to be called Good Girl Art and his cover for *Phantom Lady* #17 (April 1948) became one of the most widely reprinted comic-book covers of all time. It also drew the wrath of Dr. Fredric Wertham, who reprinted it in his *Seduction of the Innocent* with the caption "Sexual stimulation by combining 'headlights' with the sadist's dream of tying up a woman."

Far from being a sadist, Baker was a gifted artist with a distinctive style that several lesser artists at the time tried to imitate. One of the few African-Americans in comics, he went to work for the Jerry Iger shop in 1944. For Fiction House, Baker drew *Tiger Girl*, *Carmilla*, and *Sky Girl*. He also drew *South Sea Girl* and *Flamingo* for other markets. And when the Iger shop was providing art for *Classic Comics*, Baker drew the adaptation of *Lorna Doone*.

After comic books were forced to turn away from their cheesecake preoccupation in the middle 1950s, Baker turned to drawing Westerns, romance, and even *Lassie*. According to some rumors, he died of a heart attack brought on by overwork. There is still some disagreement as to when he was born and when he died.

BAT LASH

■ An unusual Western hero, he flourished briefly in the late 1960s. Bat Lash was the product of a creative team that included Sergio Aragones, Denny O'Neil, and Nick Cardy. Gil Kane also had a hand in the creation of the character. He mentioned that one of *his* sources of inspiration was the amoral cowpoke portrayed by James Coburn in the 1967 Paramount picture, *Waterhole* #3.

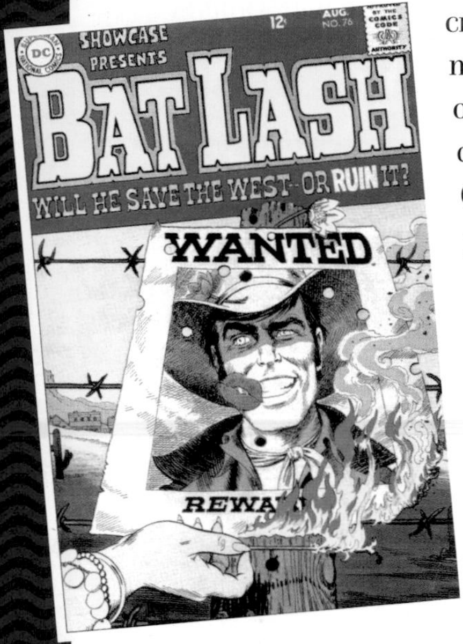
SHOWCASE PRESENTS
12¢
AUG. NO. 76
BAT LASH
WILL HE SAVE THE WEST—OR RUIN IT?
WANTED

A womanizer, a con man who didn't play fair, and a borderline outlaw, Bat first appeared in DC's *Showcase* #76 (August 1968). There he was on the cover, grinning out of a WANTED poster and wearing a small flower in the hatband of his Stetson. The first issue of Bat's own magazine was released two months later.

The scripts were by O'Neil and Aragones. Cardy, who drew the covers and the interior *Bat Lash* stories, used a somewhat lighter style than the one he used on such completely serious efforts as *Aquaman* and *Congo Bill*, a style well suited to the tone and attitudes of the stories. Writing in the *Comics Buyer's Guide* some thirty years later, columnist Mark Evanier described Bat as "an unheroic hero who roamed the West in his unique way: mercenary and inclined to eschew gunfights. He had an eye for fine foods and finer ladies . . . It is amazingly well-remembered for a comic book that was deemed a flop almost three decades ago."

Bat Lash made it only to its seventh issue in the autumn of 1969. "The market just fizzled out," said Cardy in a 1999 interview, "and the book was just not selling well enough. It's a shame because I think it was very good work."

BATMAN

■ Batman has been on duty in the moonlit streets of Gotham City for over three-score years. The creation of artist Bob Kane and writer Bill Finger, the Dark Knight was first seen in *Detective Comics* #27 (May 1939). Although this was a joint creative effort, Finger never received a credit for his writing.

Living up to its name, *Detective* featured nothing but detectives in its first two years, private eyes like Slam Bradley, official lawmen such as Speed Saunders and Steve Malone, and a

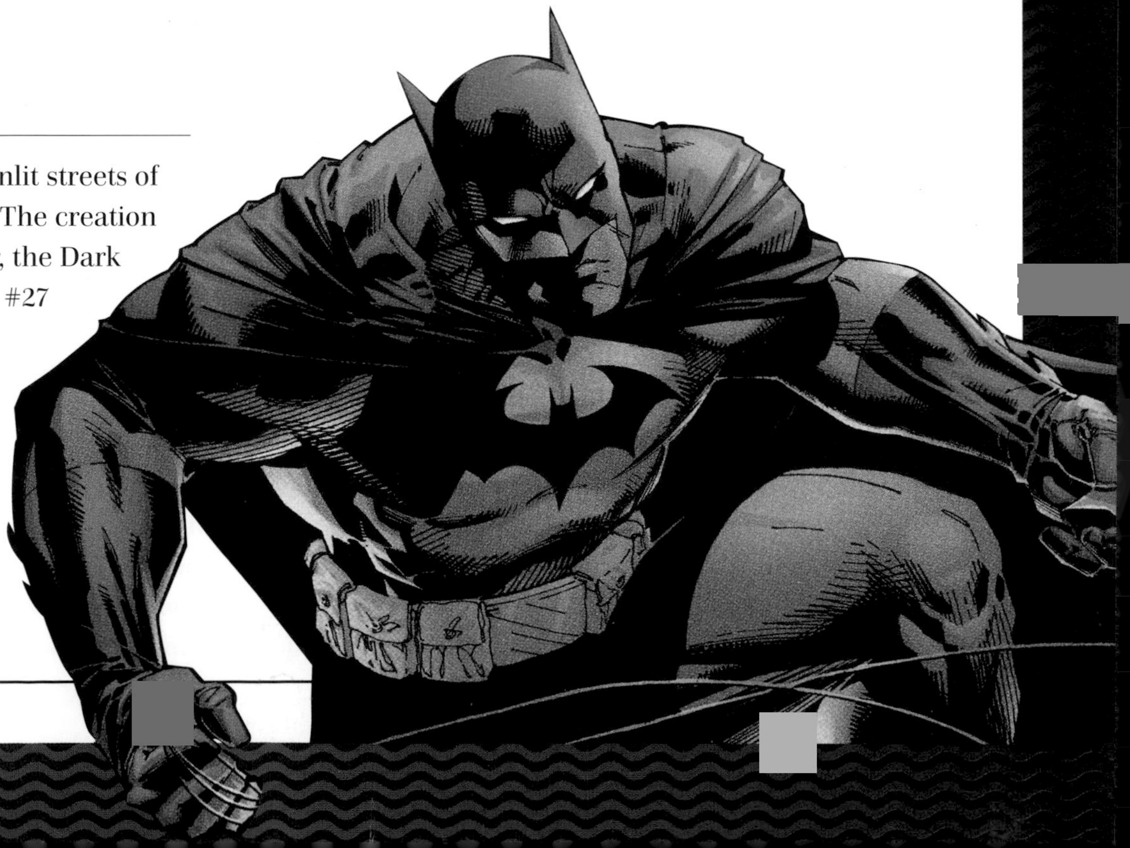

BY THE TIME THE DENSE SMOKE CLEARS...
THE RIDDLER WILL GET AWAY— AND I CAN'T FOLLOW HIM, KNOWING EAGLE WILL SUFFOCATE INSIDE THAT PUZZLE!

NOW BATMAN MATCHES HIS WITS AGAINST A HIGHLY COMPLEX PUZZLE, WITH A LIFE AT STAKE IF HE FAILS!
I'LL NEVER FIND THE SECRET OF THIS PUZZLE IN TIME TO SAVE HIM!

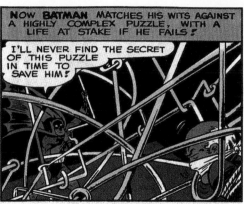

cloaked and masked mystery man known as the Crimson Avenger. Batman, therefore, when joining the magazine was expected to carry on in that tradition. And he did for the most part, rarely forgetting that he was basically a detective. True, he dressed in a rather flamboyant fashion, but so did many of the pulp heroes who inspired his creators, folks like the Shadow and the Spider.

No. 68
The BATMAN
Detective COMICS
OCT.
10¢
BEWARE TWO-FACE! IS HE ONE MAN OR TWO? SEE "THE MAN WHO LED A DOUBLE LIFE!"

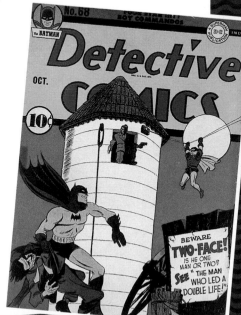

Bill Finger once admitted, "My first script was a take-off on a Shadow story . . . I patterned my style of writing Batman after the Shadow. Also after the Warner Bros. movies, the gangster movies." Kane added that another source of inspiration was a 1928 movie called *The Bat*, "in which the villain wore a bat-like costume which was quite awesome." Originally *The Bat* was a highly successful Broadway play by Avery Hopwood and Mary Roberts Rinehart. It was filmed again in 1931 as *The Bat Whispers*, with tough-guy actor Chester Morris starring. Basically an old dark-house mystery, it has to do with stolen money, secret rooms and passages, and a crazed killer who dresses up like a bat and gives his victims advance warning that he is going to strike.

In civilian life Batman was Bruce Wayne, "a bored socialite." When night fell, however, playboy Wayne became "powerful and awesome" and "a weird menace to all crime." Unlike his more sedate contemporaries in the private-eye line, Batman didn't wait for cases to come to him. He prowled the city looking for trouble. He always found it, dropping down on burglaries, kidnappings, murders, and worse. Although not above wisecracking while tangling with half a dozen gunmen, Batman was a pretty grim vigilante in his early days. Besides his gadget-laden utility belt, he carried a .45 automatic and was not shy about using it. A trained athlete and acrobat, he was capable of breaking a man's neck with one well-placed kick. Over the first months of the feature, Kane and Finger—with some help from Gardner Fox, who wrote several of the early scripts—gradually toned Batman down, filled in details, and introduced not only a batmobile but a batplane as well.

DC
Detective Comics
STARRING
BATMAN
1935
50 DC
1985

The earliest version of his origin appeared in *Detective* #33. In just two pages it was explained that young Bruce Wayne had witnessed the slaying of both his parents by a stickup man. The boy vowed that he'd "avenge their deaths by spending the rest of my life warring on all criminals." After years of dedicated work and study, the young man emerged a brilliant scientist and a top athlete. While musing one evening that he must have a persona that would "strike terror in their hearts," he was visited by a large bat that flew in the open window—"It's an omen. I shall be a BAT!" And thus was born "this

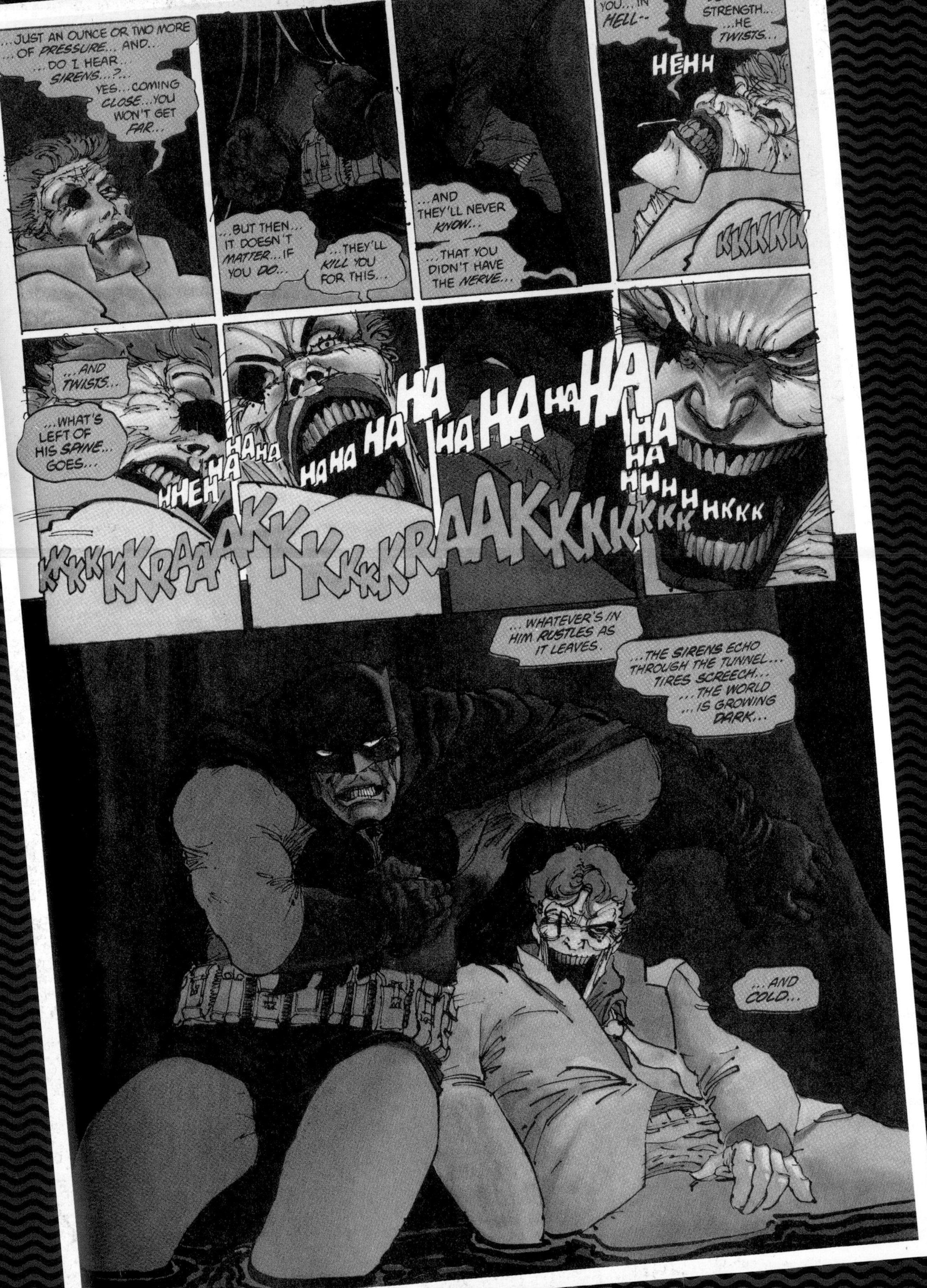
...JUST AN OUNCE OR TWO MORE OF PRESSURE... AND...
...DO I HEAR... SIRENS...?..
YES...COMING CLOSE...YOU WON'T GET FAR...
...BUT THEN... IT DOESN'T MATTER...IF YOU DO...
...THEY'LL KILL YOU FOR THIS...
...AND THEY'LL NEVER KNOW...
...THAT YOU DIDN'T HAVE THE NERVE...
I'LL... SEE YOU... IN HELL--
WITH A DEVIL'S STRENGTH... ...HE TWISTS...
HEHH
KKKKKK
...AND TWISTS...
...WHAT'S LEFT OF HIS SPINE... GOES...
HHEH HA HA HA
HA HA HA HA
HA HA HA HA HA HA
HA HA HHHH H HKKK
KKKKKRAAAKKKKKKRAAKKKKK
...WHATEVER'S IN HIM RUSTLES AS IT LEAVES.
...THE SIRENS ECHO THROUGH THE TUNNEL... TIRES SCREECH... ...THE WORLD ...IS GROWING DARK...
...AND COLD...

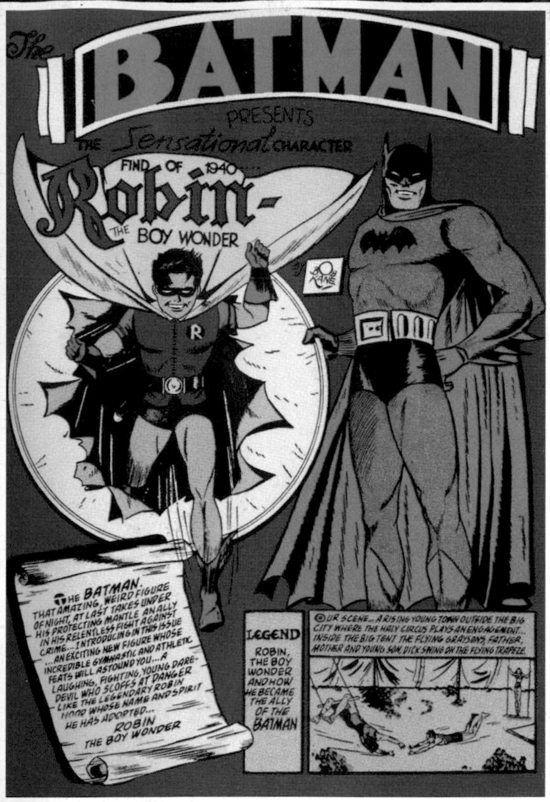
The BATMAN
PRESENTS THE Sensational CHARACTER FIND OF 1940....
Robin- THE BOY WONDER
THE BATMAN. THAT AMAZING, WEIRD FIGURE OF NIGHT, AT LAST TAKES UNDER HIS PROTECTING MANTLE AN ALLY IN HIS RELENTLESS FIGHT AGAINST CRIME... INTRODUCING IN THIS ISSUE ...AN EXCITING NEW FIGURE WHOSE INCREDIBLE GYMNASTIC AND ATHLETIC FEATS WILL ASTOUND YOU... A LAUGHING, FIGHTING, YOUNG DARE-DEVIL WHO SCOFFS AT DANGER LIKE THE LEGENDARY ROBIN HOOD WHOSE NAME AND SPIRIT HE HAS ADOPTED... ROBIN THE BOY WONDER
LEGEND
ROBIN, THE BOY WONDER AND HOW HE BECAME THE ALLY OF THE BATMAN
OUR SCENE... A RISING YOUNG TOWN OUTSIDE THE BIG CITY WHERE THE HALY CIRCUS PLAYS AN ENGAGEMENT... INSIDE THE BIG TENT THE FLYING GRAYSONS, FATHER, MOTHER AND YOUNG SON, DICK SWING ON THE FLYING TRAPEZE

avenger of evil, *The Batman!*" This short, simple narrative has been modified, expanded, and reworked many times over the years.

Robin was added in *Detective* #38 (April 1940). The Boy Wonder was actually Dick Grayson, a circus acrobat who worked with his mother and father as part of the Flying Graysons trapeze act. After his parents were killed in an accident rigged by gangsters, Dick was befriended by Batman and became his protégé. He moved into the socialite's mansion and underwent a training program—"And thus Dick Grayson, by the hand of fate, is transformed into that astonishing phenomenon, that young Robin Hood of today, ROBIN THE BOY WONDER!" Robin started a trend, and during the months that followed many other established heroes took on a boy sidekick.

Batman and Robin encountered some of the best and most appealing villains in comic books. Topping the list was the Joker, who has been plaguing the caped crusader ever since the first issue of *Batman* in 1940. The white-faced, purple-suited criminal mastermind was inventive and audacious. He almost always challenged the team by announcing that he was contemplating a crime and daring them, much in the style of the movie Bat, to stop him. Among the many other colorful foes introduced in the early years were the Penguin, the Scarecrow, Two-Face, the Cavalier, and Clayface. The most important woman in Batman's early life was a cunning jewel thief known as the Cat. Later on she changed her name to Catwoman and, because of his mixed feelings about her, Batman never quite succeeded in bringing her to justice.

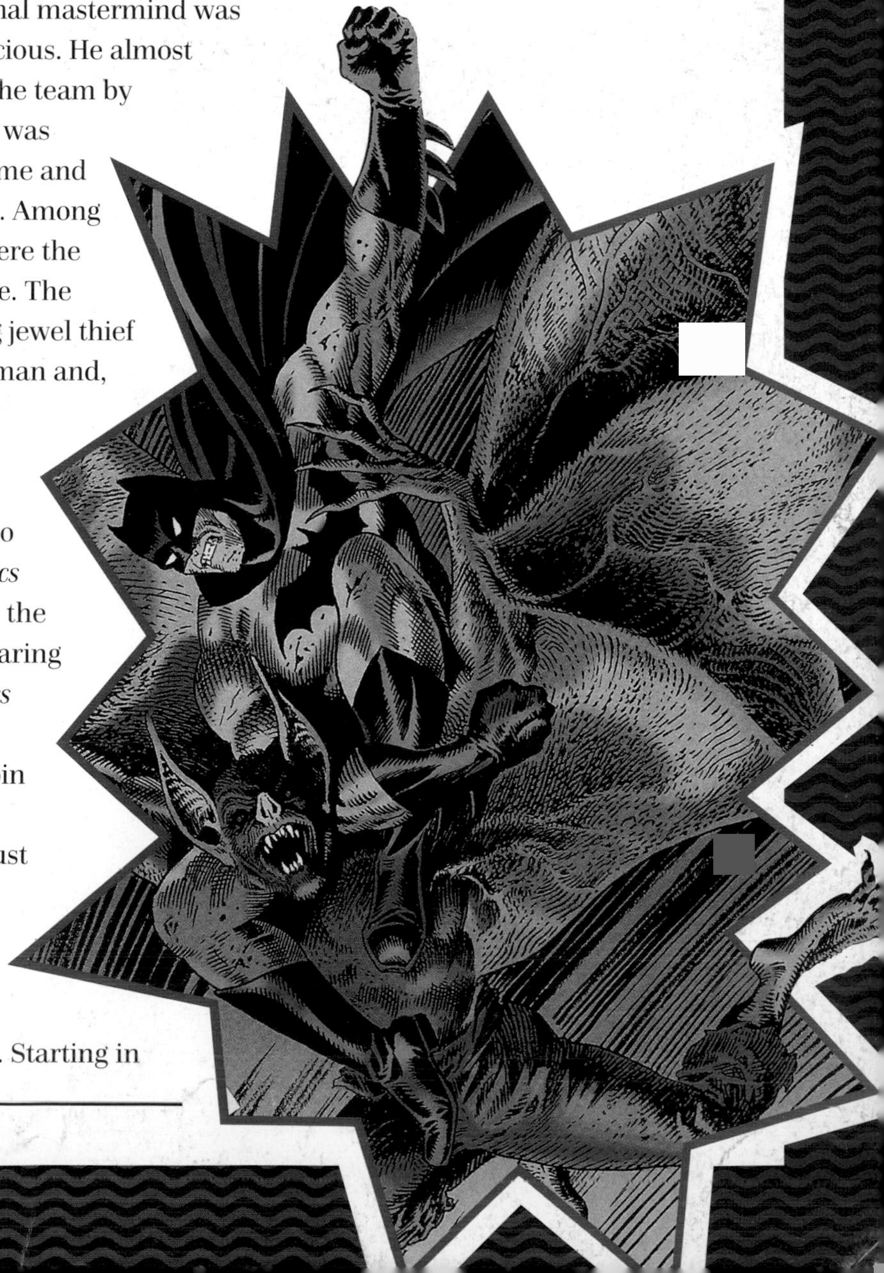

Batman, given his own magazine in 1940, was the first DC hero so honored after Superman. Batman and Robin also showed up in the 1940 edition of *New York World's Fair Comics* and thereafter were in its successor *World's Finest Comics*. In the middle 1940s, Robin added to his workload and began appearing in solo adventures as well. Beginning in *Star Spangled Comics* #65 (February 1947), a *Robin* feature led off each issue, replacing the Newsboy Legion. Jim Mooney drew these. Robin remained there until the magazine was converted into *Star Spangled War Stories* in 1952. In *World's Finest* #71 (July–August 1954), Batman and Robin entered into a partnership with Superman and began working as a trio in that magazine. Longtime *Batman* ghost Dick Sprang drew the feature.

Working without Robin, Batman embarked on a seemingly endless series of team-ups with other characters. Starting in

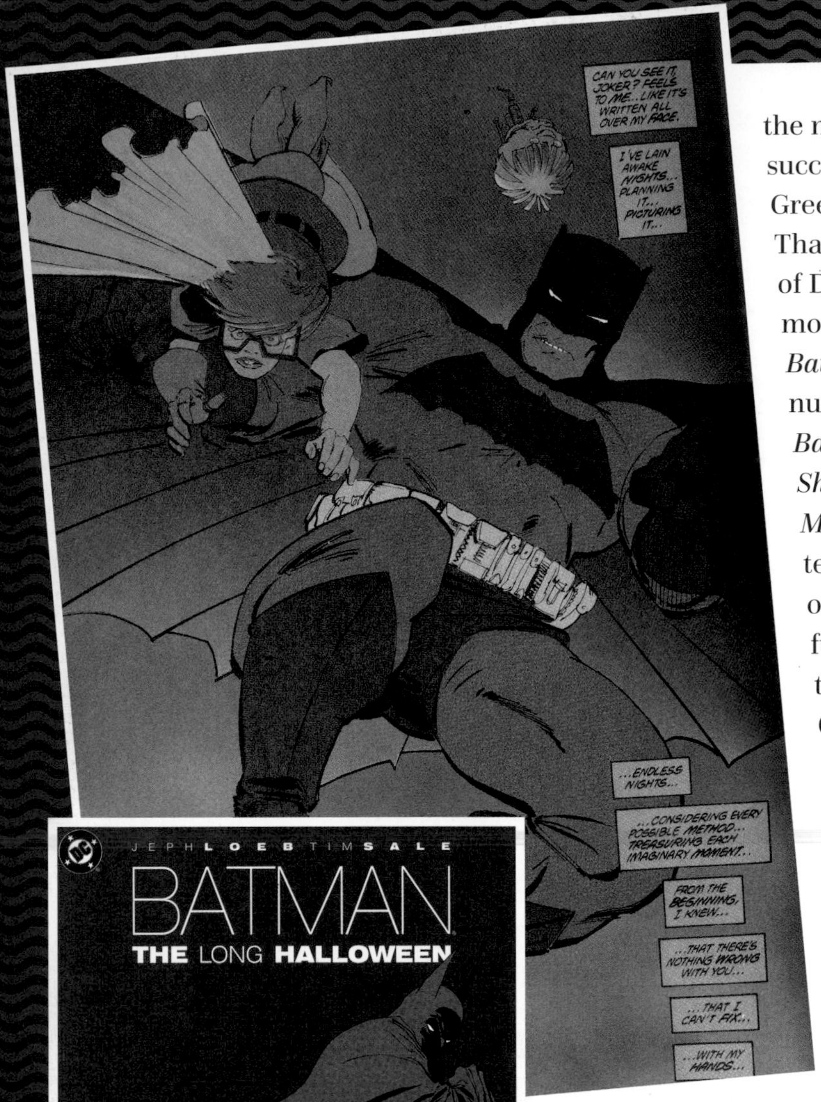
CAN YOU SEE IT, JOKER? FEELS TO ME...LIKE IT'S WRITTEN ALL OVER MY FACE.
I'VE LAIN AWAKE NIGHTS... PLANNING IT... PICTURING IT...
...ENDLESS NIGHTS...
...CONSIDERING EVERY POSSIBLE METHOD... TREASURING EACH IMAGINARY MOMENT...
FROM THE BEGINNING, I KNEW...
...THAT THERE'S NOTHING WRONG WITH YOU...
...THAT I CAN'T FIX...
...WITH MY HANDS...

the middle 1960s in *The Brave and the Bold*, he appeared with a succession of partners that included the Flash, Aquaman, the Green Arrow, Deadman, the Teen Titans, Sgt. Rock, and Wildcat. That continued into the early 1980s. Batman has proven to be one of DC's most extendable characters. He now appears in several monthly titles, including *Detective Comics, Batman Adventures, Batman*, and *Legends of the Dark Knight*. He has been featured in numerous graphic novels, miniseries and one-shots, such as *Batman: The Killing Joke, Batman: Hollywood Knight, Batman: Shadow of the Bat, Batman: The Long Halloween, Batman: No Man's Land*, and *Batman: The Golden Streets of Gotham*. Various teams of writers and artists have been able to provide variations of the contemporary Batman. Alternate Batmen have functioned in gas-lit Victorian London, the future, the era of the French Revolution, and nineteenth-century Gotham City. Characters associated with him, such as Robin, Batgirl, Harley Quinn, and Catwoman, all have magazines of their own. Even the mean-minded Joker has starred in books of his own.

When Dick Grayson eventually outgrew the part of Boy Wonder, he became a completely different crimefighter known as Nightwing. In 1983 a youth named Jason Todd was trained by Bruce Wayne to take over as Robin. Five years later, as the result of a nationwide phone poll, this new Robin was allowed to die, done in by the Joker. In 1989 yet another Robin was introduced, this time a lad named Tim Drake. In Frank Miller's 1986 innovative Dark Knight series, set in a gritty world some years hence, Robin was portrayed by a red-haired girl named Carrie Kelly.

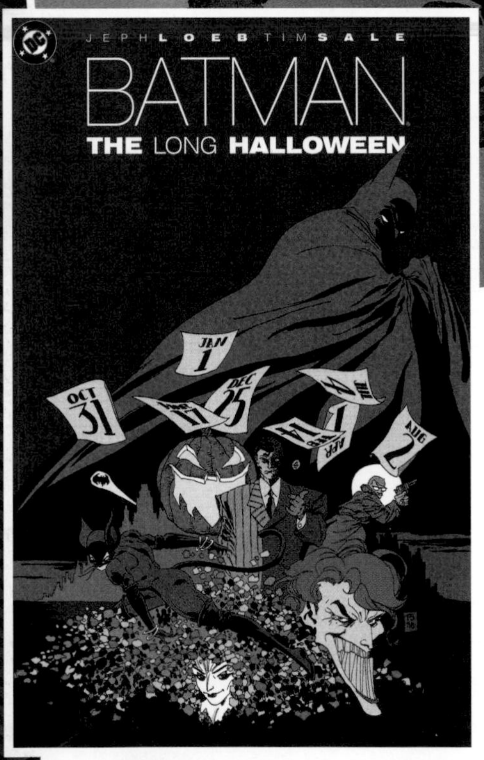
JEPH LOEB TIM SALE
BATMAN
THE LONG HALLOWEEN
JAN 1
OCT 31
DEC 25
AUG 2

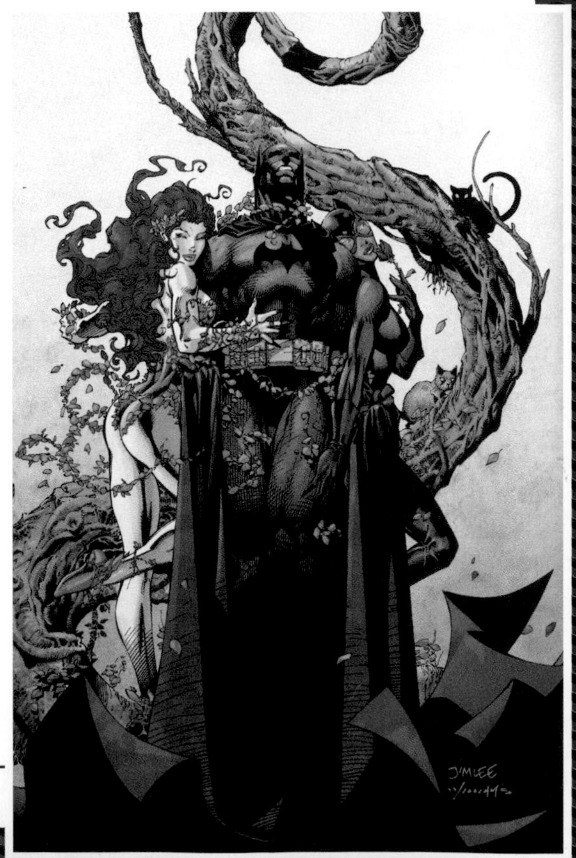
JIM LEE

Among the multitude of artists and writers who've worked on *Batman* are Jerry Robinson, George Roussos, Jack Burnley, Charles Paris, Jeph Loeb, Tim Sale, Denny O'Neil, Neal Adams, Dick Giordano, Gil Kane, Cliff Chiang, Sheldon Moldoff, Lew Schwartz, Fred Ray, Jan Van Meter, Brian Bolland, and Jose Garcia-Lopez.

ARCHIE ADVENTURE SERIES
TALES CALCULATED TO DRIVE YOU
BATS
12¢
SON, ARE YOU STILL READING THAT FLYING SAUCER TRASH !?

BATS

■ Invented by writer George Gladir and gag cartoonist Orlando Busino, *Tales Calculated to Drive You Bats* was published by the Archie folks and reached the newsstand late in 1961. Although its title indicates a nod to EC's *Tales Calculated to Drive You MAD*, the magazine was aimed at a slightly younger audience and was devoted exclusively to fairly polite horror spoofs.

Busino, already established as a gag cartoonist for such mass circulation magazines as *The Saturday Evening Post*, drew in a catchy, uncluttered style and also displayed his skill for inventive lettering on the *Bats* pages. Gladir's chief character was a bald mad scientist named Igor, whose sidekick was a talking bat named Freddie. In one sequence the bat noticed that a restaurant was offering a *Freddie Special* and persuaded Igor to order one. The waiter informed them that "The Freddie Special is ham & corn." Which also sums up Gladir's philosophy of humor.

By the time *Bats* folded late in 1962, after seven issues, Busino had left, never to return to comic books. Gladir stayed on, soon creating Sabrina the Teen-age Witch.

BECK, C. C. *(1910–1989)*

MAY • 1940
NUMBER 4
WHIZ COMICS
10¢
CAPTAIN MARVEL CRASHES THROUGH

WHIZ COMICS
10¢
CAPTAIN MARVEL Crushes the TIGER-SHARK!

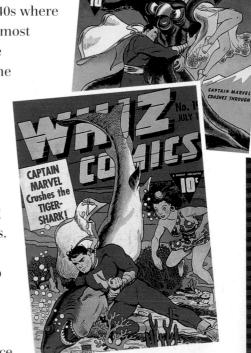

■ An admitted curmudgeon and an artist who never thought much of comic books, Charles Clarence Beck was cocreator of the most popular superhero of the 1940s. Captain Marvel, introduced in Fawcett's *Whiz Comics* late in 1939, reached a point by the middle 1940s where he was outselling DC's Superman and relegating him to the position of the second most popular superhero of the 1940s. Comparing his hero to the Man of Steel, Beck once explained that "Captain Marvel *looked* somewhat like Superman, but in character he was very different, and of course none of the big shots ever read it, so they were happy in their ignorance. They put it out and the public grabbed it right away, because it was different. And it was good."

After studying art at the Chicago Academy of Fine Art, Beck eventually got a job in the art department of Fawcett Publications, while they were still located in Minnesota. Versatile, he worked on everything from *Captain Billy's Whiz Bang* to *Motion Picture*. When Fawcett moved to New York City, Beck went along and the big shots picked him to draw Captain Marvel when they branched out into comic books. Beck's comic-book style was forceful, direct, and well thought out. "The basis I go on," he once explained, "is never put in a single line that isn't necessary. Don't try to show off." Though he always said it was the stories that made the character a hit, it was Beck's style that contributed equally to making *Captain Marvel* a best-seller.

When *Captain Marvel Adventures* was added, Beck got help from former pulp illustrator Pete Costanza. In the later 1940s, he and Costanza set up a shop to produce work for Fawcett and also advertising features like *Captain Tootsie.* Beck remained with the captain until Fawcett quit comics in 1953. In the late 1960s, he returned to comics for a very short spell to draw the brief run of *Fatman.* In the early 1970s, DC reintroduced Captain Marvel in a book titled *Shazam.* Beck was brought back to draw the revived hero. However, he quit after ten issues. "The original stories were exciting, varied, professionally handled," he said. "DC's were dull, boring, childish." Beck, living in Florida, never returned to comics, although he did paint many re-creations of his old *Whiz* and *Captain Marvel Adventures* covers.

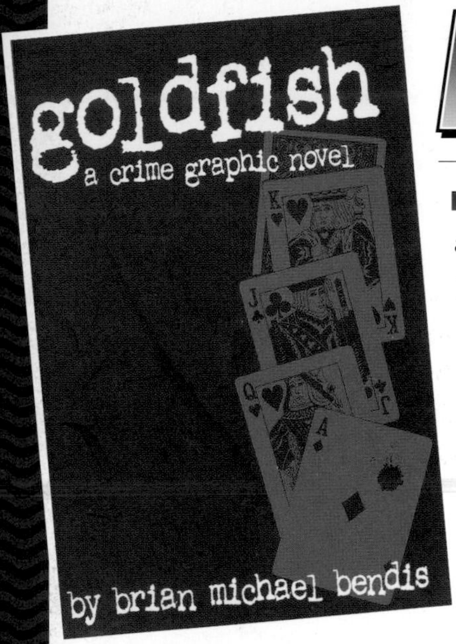
goldfish
a crime graphic novel
by brian michael bendis

BENDIS, BRIAN MICHAEL (1967-)

■ Both a cartoonist and a writer, it was as a writer that Bendis garnered reader attention and critical acclaim in recent years, particularly as the new century got going. A notable practitioner of the comic-book noir, he created *Powers* and has been scripting a very gritty version of *Daredevil* since 2000.

Bendis wrote and drew *AKA Goldfish* in the middle 1990s and followed that with *Jinx,* both dark private-eye stuff. In 1999 he won an Eisner Award for his scripting on *Torso,* and in 2000, working with artist Michael Avon Oeming, he introduced the popular *Powers,* about everyday cops who work in a world that also has superheroes. After coming to Marvel's attention, he's written, in addition to *Daredevil,* a six-issue run of *Elektra* and *The Ultimate Spider-Man.* Bendis has said that he tries to write only comics that he himself would buy.

BERG, DAVE (1921-2002)

■ Best remembered for the polite suburban satires he wrote and drew for *Mad* for several decades, Berg had an earlier and much more varied career in comic books. In the 1940s, with time out for military service during World War II, and the early 1950s he drew everything from the original Captain Marvel to quirky humorous fantasies.

He started working in the Will Eisner shop in 1940, initially doing backgrounds for *The Spirit.* When Jack Cole gave up *The Death Patrol* in *Military Comics,* Berg took it over. He turned out very inventive cartoony pages for what was at that time a sort of parody of the magazine's *Blackhawk.* For Quality's *Uncle Sam* he did a couple of funny fillers in verse, including one about superheroes going on strike. Over at Fawcett, in addition to now and then doing a Captain Marvel episode for *Whiz Comics,* Dave Berg also produced *Sir Butch* and *Spooks,* both strange humorous fantasies drawn in a lively style.

In the postwar years, Berg still moved back and forth between adventure and comedy. He drew the gung-ho *Combat Kelly* for Marvel and an updated *Alice in Wonderland* for Ziff Davis. In 1956 he began drawing his *The Lighter Side of . . .* for *Mad.* This feature, although drawn in a bland, subdued style, became popular, leading to several paperback reprint books. Berg kept at it until the end of his professional career.

BEST COMICS

10¢
BEST COMICS
NO. 2
FEATURING ADVENTURES OF THE RED MASK

BEST
10¢ COMICS
NO.4
FEATURING ADVENTURES OF THE RED MASK

■ Publisher Ned Pines's maiden venture into comic books in 1939 resulted in the odd-shaped and short-lived *Best Comics*. Whereas every other comic book on the stands favored a vertical format, *Best* used a horizontal format. While to the majority of readers the contents may have appeared original, all the strips were recycled from a ready-print Sunday tabloid section that had been distributed, none too successfully, by the Syndicated Features Corp. back in 1936.

The features, because of their source, were laid out like Sunday pages. The only costumed hero was a dull chap known as the Red Mask, whose disguise consisted of a red mask. Newspaper veteran Ray McGill drew a pretty-girl page titled *Peggy Wow*, newspaper veteran Loy Byrnes drew *Silly Willie* (using the anagram pen name Roy B. Nyles), and Kin Platt, soon to move on to superheroes, contributed a kid page called *Happy*. Being also a publisher of pulp fiction, Pines included text stories about the Masked Rider and Chab of the Jungle amidst the funnies.

Best Comics went through four issues from September to December of 1939, then ceased. Whether it was a flop or simply ran out of old Sunday pages is difficult to determine. Pines had much better luck with his next comic book, *Thrilling Comics*, which appeared just as *Best* was making its exit.

BIG LITTLE BOOKS

■ An alternative way of packaging comics material, the Big Little Book format was introduced in 1932. Based in Racine, Wisconsin, the Whitman Division of Western Publishing produced the small, chubby volumes. Each book was roughly 4" by 4" and 1½" thick. The bright covers were of cardboard and the interior pages between 240 and 320 were of pulp paper, supposedly leftover from other publishing ventures. Samuel E. Lowe guided the Whitman division, which was devoted to providing cheap kids' books to chain stores and five-and-dimes across the country, and is credited with inventing the format.

JACK ARMSTRONG
AND THE
IVORY TREASURE
THE BIG LITTLE BOOK
BASED ON THE FAMOUS RADIO SERIES

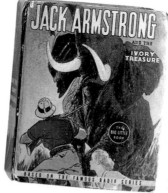

Each book alternated a page of text with a picture page. The very first BLB was *The Adventures of Dick Tracy, Detective*. The artwork was taken from Chester Gould's newspaper strip, modified by removing all captions and word balloons. Using the continuity as a guide, a writer converted it into a novel. Other early reprint titles included *Mickey Mouse, Little Orphan Annie, Buck Rogers, 25th Century AD*, and *Captain Easy, Soldier of Fortune.*

Whitman also turned out original stories for the Big Little Book series. Westerns were a popular category; and movie, fictional, and historical cowboys starred—Buck Jones, Tom Mix, Billy the Kid, the Lone Ranger, Buffalo Bill, Gene Autry, Roy Rogers, etc. Radio heroes such as Jack Armstrong, Jimmie Allen, the Green Hornet, and Mr. District Attorney were novelized. There were also characters created especially for Big Little Books. Maximo the Amazing Superman and the Ghost Avenger both came along in the early 1940s after superheroes had begun dominating comic books. There were adventuresome girls such as Kay Darcy and Peggy Brown, explorers like Hal Hardy, who hung out in the Lost Land of the Giants, racing car drivers, daredevil pilots, and G-Men.

Because Racine was close to Chicago, some newspaper cartoonists in the Windy City illustrated BLBs. Ken Ernst drew for several, as did Milt Youngren, Henry E. Vallely, and Erwin L. Hess. Russ Winterbotham wrote a great many of the original novels.

In 1938, by that time imitated by other publishers of low-priced fiction, Whitman changed the line name to Better Little Books. Though the books were never serious competition for comic books, they did offer an interesting occasional alternative. The first wave ended in the late 1940s. Western Publishing revived the format several times over the years, usually producing only pale imitations of the stuff of the 1930s and 1940s.

BIG SHOT COMICS

■ Publishers entering into the comic-book business in the early forties realized the importance of hiring a good editor. In this case, the Columbia Comic Corporation hired Vincent Sullivan away from DC, where he'd been in charge of *Action Comics* and *Detective Comics* and had been responsible for acquiring *Superman* and *Batman*. Like some of its predecessors, *Big Shot Comics* was a blend of original material and newspaper strip reprints and remained so throughout its entire run. The first issue, dated May 1940, offered brand-new characters like Skyman, the Face, and Marvelo along with newspaper reruns such as *Dixie Dugan*, *Joe Palooka*, and *Charlie Chan*.

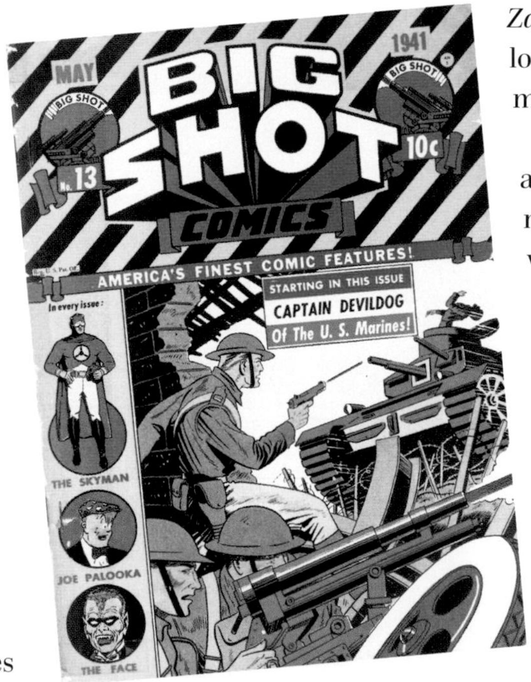
MAY
1941
BIG SHOT
No. 13
10¢
BIG SHOT
COMICS
AMERICA'S FINEST COMIC FEATURES!
STARTING IN THIS ISSUE
CAPTAIN DEVILDOG
Of The U. S. Marines!
In every issue:
THE SKYMAN
JOE PALOOKA
THE FACE

The Columbia Comic Corporation was headed by Charles McAdam, who was also the head of the McNaught Syndicate. Another partner was Frank Markey, a McNaught executive who also ran a small syndicate of his own on the side and had been a partner in the company that had launched *Feature Funnies* a few years earlier. Sullivan brought several DC contributors with him. Ogden Whitney, who'd drawn *Sandman*, drew *Skyman*; Mart Bailey, who'd drawn *Slam Bradley*, drew *The Face*; Fred Guardineer, who'd drawn *Zatara*, drew *Marvelo*; and Creig Flessel, longtime DC cover artist, contributed the majority of covers for several years.

The fourteenth issue (June 1941) added reprints of Boody Rogers newspaper strip *Sparky Watts*. Markey, who'd been syndicating this superhero spoof, was responsible for adding it to the lineup. After the original strips ran out, original material replaced it, and when Rogers returned from World War II service, he took over. Sparky Watts, his blond mock hero, became one of the stars of *Big Shot*, branching out into ten issues of his own title. The Skyman, a costumed crimefighter who flew about in a super-plane of his own invention, and the Face, who wore a gruesome mask while fighting crime, were the other two most popular characters.

Big Shot reached #104 before closing up shop in 1949. By that time Sullivan had long since left to start his own Magazine Enterprises company.

BINDER, JACK (1902–1988)

■ A competent journeyman artist and brother of writer Otto Binder, he got into comics in 1937. After managing the Harry "A" Chesler shop, Binder started a shop of his own in a remodeled barn in New Jersey. On his own he created the original Daredevil and the lesser-known Captain Battle, and he drew Mary Marvel for several years. He ended his comics career in the early 1950s drawing the Gabby Hayes title. His shop, which operated from 1940 to 1943, turned out some of the sloppiest, most abysmal assembly-line art ever seen in comic books.

BINDER, OTTO (1911–1974)

■ An impressively productive writer in the 1940s and early 1950s, and also possessed of a sense of humor, Otto Binder turned out over five hundred scripts for Fawcett's *Captain Marvel* alone. He was the cocreator of Mary Marvel, as well as her DC twin Supergirl. In addition, Binder wrote scripts for the Marvel Family as well as Hoppy the Marvel Bunny. The list of other characters he scripted includes the Shadow, Captain America, Miss America (another Mary Marvel imitator), the Young Allies, the Shield, the Black Hood, Hangman, Robotman, Superman, and Blue Bolt. In the 1960s he created *Mighty Samson* for Dell.

In the 1930s, under the pen name Eando Binder, he wrote science fiction for such pulps as *Thrilling Wonder* and *Amazing Stories*. It was for the pulps that he created Adam Link, a robot who inspired many a robotman.

BIRO, CHARLES (1911–1972)

MORE CHILLS AND THRILLS THAN EVER!
December
No. 6-10¢
DAREDEVIL
"The Greatest Name in Comics"
12 SMASH FEATURES
BIRO

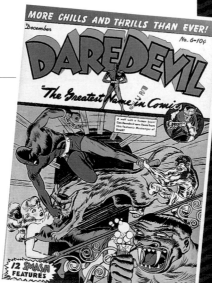

■ What Biro lacked in drawing ability he made up in audacity and inventiveness. The techniques he developed in the early 1940s to promote comic books and lure readers into grabbing them off the racks became standards of the industry. One of his great admirers was Stan Lee, who used Biro techniques to push Marvel to the front in the 1960s. Biro realized early on that a comic-book cover was a very effective advertising medium and he was never modest about touting the benefits of the magazines with which he was associated. He was also one of the earliest editors to talk directly to his readers.

Although Charles Biro is remembered for the violence of much of his work, especially on his covers for *Crime Does Not Pay*, he started in the late 1930s working at the Harry "A" Chesler shop drawing cute fillers with titles like *Goobyland*, *Land O' Nod*, and *Topsy Turvy*. At that point he specialized in drawing cute little toddlers wearing drop-seat pajamas. While he was the supervisor of the Chesler shop, he was in charge of providing material for the new MLJ titles. Biro switched to a somewhat crude, anatomically fuzzy adventure style for the occasion. The most successful character he drew for MLJ was the superhero *Steel Sterling*, the star of *Zip Comics*. Biro next went to work for the Lev Gleason outfit, taking over the original Daredevil when the boomerang-tossing hero got a comic book of his own. From the first issue the new title bore the slogan, "The Greatest Name in Comics." The covers also touted contests to be found within. Biro was next involved in inventing *Boy Comics*. After that came *Crime Does Not Pay*.

Biro edited that one with his old Chesler shop mate Bob Wood. Biro drew the covers for this one, but no interior art. His covers were brightly colored, mixing violence, bloodshed, and often sexy women. The backlash against crime comics in the 1950s was a serious blow to his career. Biro kept working on a sanitized *Daredevil* and *Boy Comics*, also returning to his beginnings in comics with *Uncle Charlie's Fables*. By 1962 he was out of the field, working as a graphic artist for NBC.

BISSETTE, STEVE

■ See SWAMP THING.

BLACK ANGEL

■ See AIR FIGHTERS COMICS.

BLACK CANARY

■ Being the Black Canary is a family tradition. The senior Black Canary was first seen in DC's *Flash Comics* #86 (August 1947). She also became a member of the Justice Society of America. The first version of the character was created by writer Robert Kanigher and artist Carmine Infantino. She originally appeared as a mystery woman guest in *Johnny Thunder*, where she was billed as "the most fascinating crook of all time." The hapless Johnny fell in love with her, little realizing that she would replace him from #92 onward.

By that time readers learned that she was actually dark-haired Dinah Drake, operator of a florist shop. By donning a long blonde wig, a low-cut satin costume, and black net stockings, she now became not a crook but a crimebuster. In the outfit she looked very much like a high-class cocktail waitress. In her *The Great Woman Super Heroes*, Trina Robbins comments that "her blonde wig, fishnet tights, and tight bolero jacket made up one of the more impractical getups in comics." Teamed with the Black

Canary, though originally unaware of her dual identity, was a tough private eye with the untough name of Larry Lance.

The Canary remained in *Flash* until its final issue (February 1949). She started guesting in *All Star* in #38 and was installed as a full-fledged member of the JSA in #41, replacing the unfortunate Johnny Thunder. She held on until the last issue in 1951. The Black Canary returned in *Justice League of America* #21, and in the early 1960s was eventually initiated into the JLA. Superman referred to her as the "prettiest member of the group." She met the Green Arrow at one of the group's meetings and he became, according to official DC history, "her lover and business partner."

From the late 1960s she appeared with the archer in many of his magazine appearances. "By now, the passage of time and the pressures of continuity have caused an amoeba-like split in the persona of our hero," editor Mike Gold pointed out in the 1991–1992 *Black Canary* miniseries. "It was determined that the Black Canary of the post–World War II period was the mother of the present Black Canary. . . . The older version died several years ago." The current Canary's father was private eye Larry Lance.

She has continued to appear now and then in miniseries. In the one-shot that introduced the *Birds of Prey* title in 1996, she wore a more sensible getup that didn't include either wig or fishnets. However, by the time *Birds of Prey* became a monthly series, the net stockings were back.

THE BLACK CAT: I

■ Although she possessed no superpowers, she was a very effective female crimebuster. Much more attractive than Wonder Woman, she was an expert at jujitsu, an accomplished motorcyclist, and, in her civilian identity, a major motion picture actress. The Black Cat was first seen in 1941.

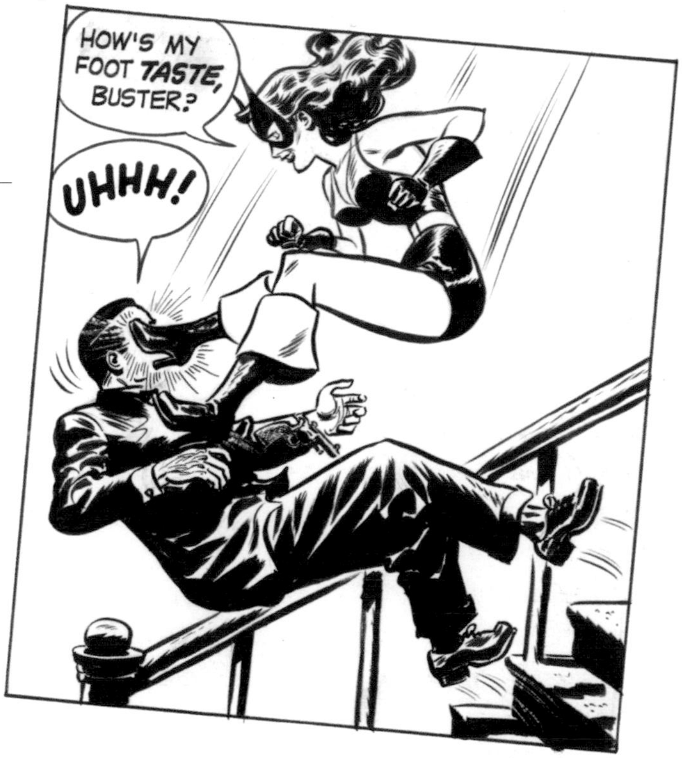
HOW'S MY FOOT TASTE, BUSTER?
UHHH!

During the summer of that year, Harvey Publications, already turning out digest-sized cartoon magazines such as *Army & Navy Jokes*, introduced *Pocket Comics*, a digest-sized comic book that offered one hundred pages, counting covers, for a dime. The most successful character in the new magazine proved to be the Black Cat, drawn by Al Gabriele.

Like the Phantom Lady and Lady Luck, she was yet another upper-class woman who put on a costume to combat crime. Like many of her playboy counterparts in the hero profession, Linda Turner, Hollywood star and America's sweetheart, "was bored with her ultra-sophisticated life." She decided to become the Black Cat "to expose fifth columnists," which is what spies and saboteurs were called in those days. As Batman's costume notions were inspired by a bat, Linda got her idea for an outfit after watching her pet cat Toby. Readers watched her designing and constructing the costume and a caption announced "two days later Linda dons a dynamic disguise." She had two basic reasons for donning the skimpy costume—"I'll have my thrills and do my duty to my country."

The redheaded actress suspected that the director of her current film was slipping Nazi propaganda into it. As she discovered, once she started investigating as the Black Cat, he was also inserting “special code scenes” so that “agents all over the country must see the picture to get their instructions.” In just twelve digest-sized pages, Linda not only exposed a nest of Hollywood-based spies but also broke into the studio by night to edit all the coded scenes out of the film. Apparently nobody, except for certain secret agents around the country, ever noticed that anything was missing. During her maiden adventure, the Black Cat met Los Angeles newspaperman Rick Horne. A handsome, though not especially perceptive, fellow, he appeared in every *Black Cat* story thereafter and never realized that Linda Turner and the Black Cat were one and the same. Thinking they were two different women, he courted them both.

After its fourth issue (January 1942) *Pocket* ceased to be. Three months later, the Black Cat moved into *Speed Comics*, which had just undergone a brief spell as a digest. She went on to catch a wide range of spies, gangsters, crooks, murderers, and con men. In addition to the handsome Horne, the other regulars were Tim Turner, Linda’s gray-haired father and a former cowboy star, and C. B. DePille, a flamboyant director who always wore a beret and dark glasses. Her dad was aware of her dual role, but Rick never did catch on, which may explain why her nickname for the newsman was “Stupid.” Toward the end of her run, she acquired a boy companion, a former circus acrobat known as the Black Kitten.

Several artists drew the feature after Gabriele, including the team of Pierce Rice and Arturo Cazeneuve, Joe Kubert, Bob Powell, and Jill Elgin, the only woman to draw *The Black Cat.* Soon after the Black Cat was given her own magazine in 1946, Lee Elias became the chief artist. A first-rate illustrator in the Milton Caniff tradition, Elias gave the feature a new, slicker look and amused himself by slipping real Hollywood personalities into the stories.

The changes that took place in *The Black Cat* comic book are indicative of those going on in the comic-book business in the decade following the end of World War II. Early in 1949, the title was changed to *Black Cat Western* and Linda had adventures exclusively in cowboy locales. At the end of the year, after only four Wild West issues, it was back to just plain *Black Cat.* With #30 (August 1951), the name became *Black Cat Mystery.* Getting in on yet another trend, Harvey converted to horror. Corpses, monsters, stranglers, and exploding skulls became standard fare on the covers. Then, early in 1955, as the Comics Code was coming into effect, the magazine once again became *Black Cat Western* and Linda Turner, in reprints, was back. That lasted for just three issues. Then came toned-down horror under the title *Black Cat Mystic.* The magazine sputtered out in 1958.

Harvey revived *Black Cat* briefly in the early 1960s, publishing three issues of a reprint book. In the late 1980s, Alfred Harvey began a sporadic series of reprints, mostly in black-and-white.

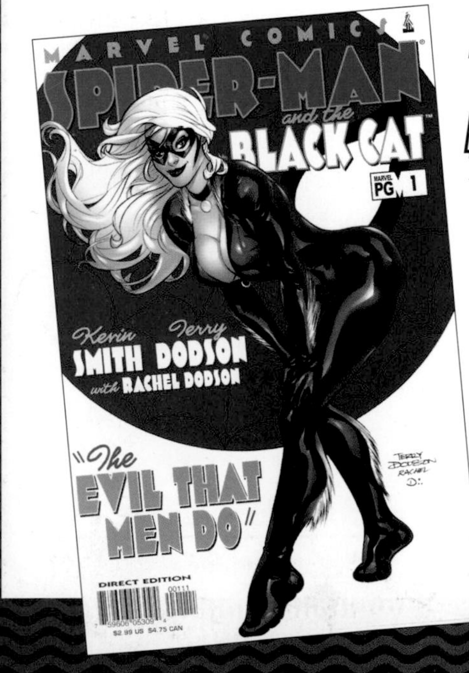
MARVEL COMICS
SPIDER-MAN and the BLACK CAT
PG 1
Kevin Terry
SMITH DODSON
with RACHEL DODSON
"The EVIL THAT MEN DO"
DIRECT EDITION

THE BLACK CAT: II

■ Believing firmly that you can’t keep a good name down, Marvel has made it a policy to revive character names that have fallen by the wayside. Following in the paw prints of DC’s Catwoman, Marvel’s Black Cat (aka Felicia Hardy) began her criminal career as a jewel thief. That occurred in *Amazing Spider-Man* #194 (July 1979). Eventually semi-reformed, she’s been romantically involved with Spidey over the years.

THE BLACK CONDOR

■ Another feral child who grew up to be a hero, Richard Grey was raised not by apes or tigers but by birds. Proving that nurture is more important than nature, he learned to fly and became the Black Condor. Drawn by Lou Fine, the Condor first appeared in *Crack Comics* #1 in the spring of 1940.

He was the child of an archeologist who was on an expedition "across the bleak steppes of Outer Mongolia" with his wife, infant son, and crew. The baby was orphaned when Yakki raiders attacked the camp, leaving everyone else dead. A giant condor swooped down, carrying little Richard off to her nest, where she raised him with her offspring. Growing up with condors, the boy eventually learned to fly from "studying the movements of wings, the body motions, air currents, balance and levitation." Growing into maturity "the man who can fly like a bird" one day encountered an old hermit. The old fellow taught Richard to read, write, and speak English. He becomes the Black Condor, vowing "to use my gift of flight toward aiding men."

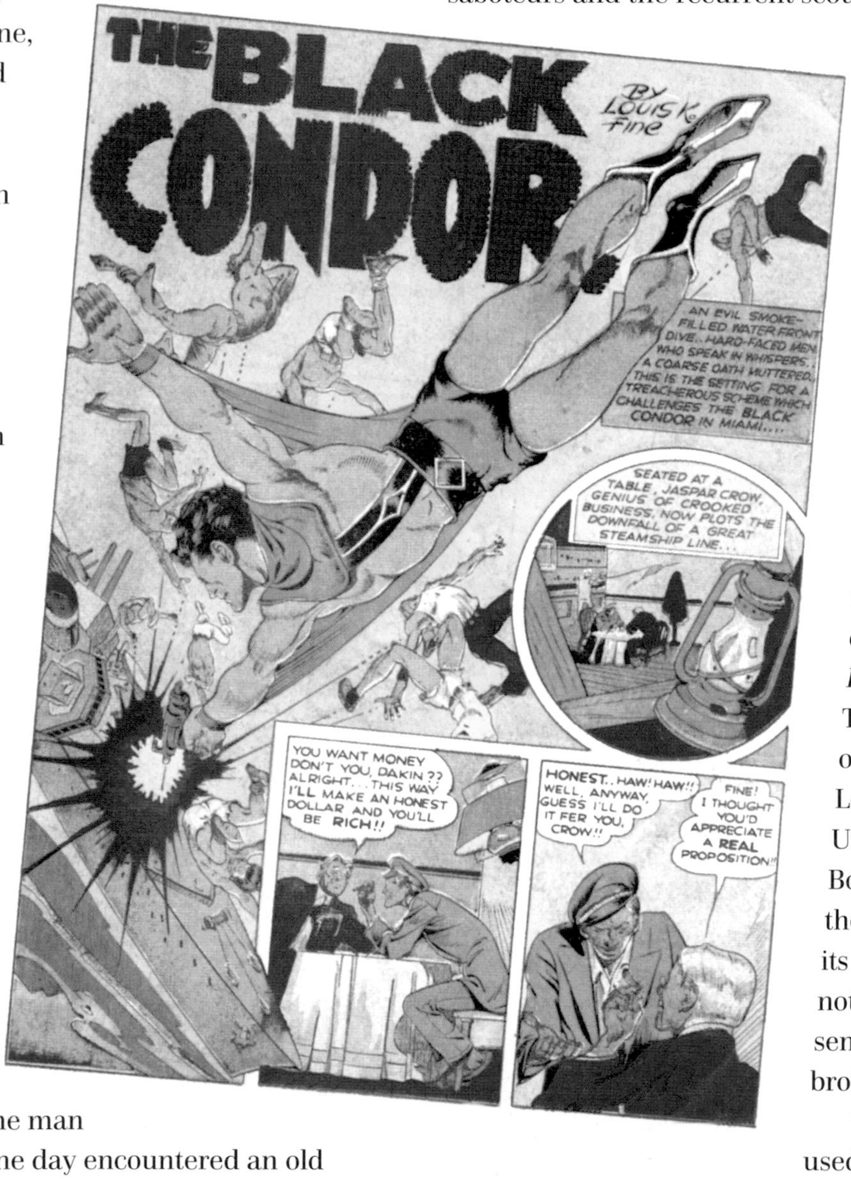
THE BLACK CONDOR
BY LOUIS K. FINE
AN EVIL SMOKE-FILLED WATER FRONT DIVE.. HARD-FACED MEN WHO SPEAK IN WHISPERS.. A COARSE OATH MUTTERED.. THIS IS THE SETTING FOR A TREACHEROUS SCHEME WHICH CHALLENGES THE BLACK CONDOR IN MIAMI....
SEATED AT A TABLE, JASPAR CROW, GENIUS OF CROOKED BUSINESS, NOW PLOTS THE DOWNFALL OF A GREAT STEAMSHIP LINE...
YOU WANT MONEY DON'T YOU, DAKIN?? ALRIGHT... THIS WAY I'LL MAKE AN HONEST DOLLAR AND YOU'LL BE RICH!!
HONEST.. HAW! HAW!! WELL, ANYWAY, GUESS I'LL DO IT FER YOU, CROW!!
FINE! I THOUGHT YOU'D APPRECIATE A REAL PROPOSITION!!

Coming to America, the Condor took over the identity of murdered senator Tom Wright, of whom he is the exact double. Thereafter he fought spies and saboteurs and the recurrent scoundrel Jasper Crow, a nasty tycoon who was "high lord of underhanded business." Fine remained with the Condor until the summer of 1942. The bird-man left *Crack* after #31 (October 1943). Drawn also by John Cassone, Charles Sultan, and on covers by Gill Fox.

DC, who assimilated many of the Quality characters, brought forth *Freedom Fighters* in 1976. This title featured a sort of poor man's Justice League that numbered Uncle Sam, the Human Bomb, Phantom Lady, and the Black Condor among its members. Apparently not in sync with seventies sensibilities, the group broke up after fifteen issues.

Trying again in 1992, DC used the name on a brand-new technologically created Black Condor. Written by Brian Augustyn and drawn by Rags Morales, this stayed aloft for roughly a year.

BLACK DIAMOND WESTERN

■ Brought to you by the folks who gave you *Crime Does Not Pay*, the magazine began life as *Desperado* in 1948 and offered "All True Wild West" crime stories. With the ninth issue (March 1949), it toned down and became *Black Diamond Western.*

Edited by Charles Biro and Bob Wood, it still ran some true crime Western yarns, but now starred a masked do-gooder known as the Black Diamond. An unusual cowboy hero, he wore both a mask and a lawman's badge. A sort of phantom U.S. Marshall, the Black Diamond roamed the pre–Civil War Old West righting wrongs. His sidekick was a burly fellow named Bumper, who parted his hair in the middle and sported a handlebar moustache. The original artist was William Overgard, and later artists included Dick Rockwell. Both men, at different times, ghosted Milton Caniff's *Steve Canyon* newspaper strip.

The book survived until 1956 and its sixtieth issue. From 1949 to 1951 Basil Wolverton contributed a far-from-serious filler entitled *Bingbang Buster and His Horse Hedy.*

THE BLACK DWARF

■ He was unquestionably the strangest of all the many strange characters who filled Harry "A" Chesler publications. The Black Dwarf surfaced briefly in the middle 1940s in two of Chesler's unsuccessful titles, first in *Spotlight Comics* and then in *Red Seal Comics.*

He gave the impression, when rigged out in his voluminous black robe, flowing black cape, and wide-brim black hat, that he was, at best, not quite five feet high. Yet captions assured readers that he was in reality "Shorty Wilson, former All-American gridiron star." To combat big-city crime, the Dwarf recruited a "squad of ex-crooks." His most frequent associates were a slim, dark-haired young woman known as Arsenic, possibly in reference to her former specialty, and a broken-nosed safecracker called Nitro.

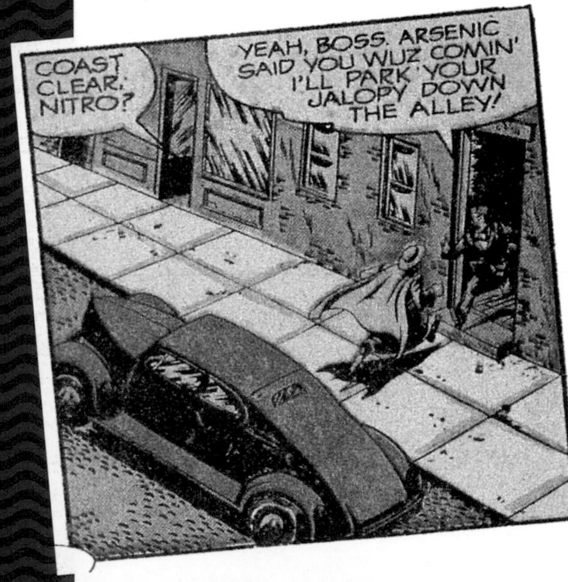
COAST CLEAR, NITRO?
YEAH, BOSS. ARSENIC SAID YOU WUZ COMIN' I'LL PARK YOUR JALOPY DOWN THE ALLEY!

The chief contributing factor to the overall strangeness of the feature was not the bizarre appearance of the hero or the rambling and often incoherent mystery plots, but rather the unparalleled artwork of Paul Gattuso. All his people were thin, angular, and endowed with extremely wide shoulders. Gattuso favored long shots, preferably from high above, often showing his characters from behind. Actions usually unfolded in gloomy nighttime city streets lined with oddly tilting apartment buildings and tenements.

After gracing three issues of *Spotlight* as the star of the book and eight of *Red Seal*, the Black Dwarf left comics. Gattuso held on a bit longer, gaining a certain fame by having a crime panel of his displayed in *Seduction of the Innocent.*

THE BLACK HOOD

Featuring THE BLACK HOOD
TOP-NOTCH comics
NO.17 JULY
10¢
THE WIZARD WITH ROY THE SUPER-BOY
Al.Camy

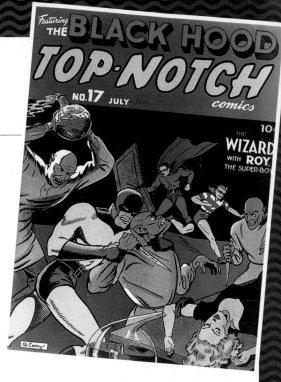

■ The black hood that the original Black Hood wore outlived him by several decades. His first go-round as a phantom vigilante got under way in MLJ's *Top-Notch Comics* #9 (October 1940). *The Black Hood* was the joint creation of editor/writer Harry Shorten and artist Al Cammarata, who used the pen name Al Camy. The masked man remained in *Top-Notch* until #44 (February 1944) and in his own magazine until the spring of 1946.

Like many another avengers of the forties, he was a policeman who suited up to fight crime in his own way. In Kip Burland's case, he didn't have much choice. Framed by a green-faced criminal mastermind called the Skull, Burland was kicked off the force to await trial as a jewel thief. But, while trying to track down the Skull on his own, the young cop was slugged, taken for a ride, shot, and tossed in the woods to die by the Skull's minions. What happened next was recapped in a caption in #10: "Saved from death by a hermit, Kip Burland has sworn to spend his life to tracking down society's greatest enemy, a super-killer known only as the Skull! Trained in science and criminology, and with tremendous physical powers, Kip has become the Black Hood, a man of mystery." As the Hood, Kip wore a black hood, black shorts, and black boots, along with a yellow tunic and tights. There was an advantage to this getup, explained the kindly old hermit: "With the name and costume of the Black Hood you are now a man of mystery. . . . Only mystery can strike terror into the hearts of criminals!"

After several more issues, Kip succeeded in sending the Skull to the electric chair. The magazine was converted to *Top-Notch LAUGH* with #28 (July 1942) and by #30 the Black Hood was the only serious character among the likes of Pokey Oakey, Senor Siesta, Suzie, and Gloomy Gus. He probably felt like a clergyman stranded in a boardinghouse full of carnival performers, but he stuck to his guns until #44 (February 1944). And he went on for another two years in his own quarterly. In his final days, drawn by Irv Novick, he shed his costume to work in civvies as a hard-boiled private eye doing business as the Black Hood Detective Agency.

The Black Hood has been brought back several times in the ensuing years. He returned for a while in the middle 1960s as part of the Mighty Crusaders and also starred in a few issues of *Mighty Comics.* In 1983 Archie Comics brought him back again in their Red Circle line of comics. This time around he was a motorcycle-riding Hood complete with black leather jacket. And the Kip Burland who donned the hood was a cousin of the earlier Kip. The Black Hood identity and hood were passed down from generation to generation: "It is only a piece of cloth . . . a piece of material sewn into the form of a HOOD. . . . It has no extraordinary powers or properties. . . . Yet over the long years of its history, it has been worn by men who risked their lives to help others. . . . Each adding to the heritage of this simple piece of cloth." Apparently somebody in the Burland clan had read the *Phantom* newspaper strip and liked the idea of passing a costume and identity along. Both Gray Morrow and Dan Spiegle illustrated his short-lived new career, with Alex Toth contributing covers.

DC licensed the character in 1991 to make him part of their Impact line. In the unsuccessful twelve-issue run, the black hood was passed around as assorted wearers came to bad ends. This was also the end of the Black Hood.

BLACK MAGIC

■ A horror title that managed to survive the purge of the early 1950s, the bimonthly *Black Magic* remained on the newsstands from 1950 through 1961. Part of the Prize Group, it was packaged by Joe Simon and Jack Kirby. Like the romance titles the team was also producing, the stories in this magazine were alleged to be true. "True amazing accounts of the strangest stories every told" was how a cover blurb put it each issue.

While the tales were grim and grotesque, they avoided the stabbings, beheadings, dismemberments, acid throwing, and moldering corpses to be found in many competing horror comics. Simon and Kirby drew the covers and usually the lead-off story. Other contributors included Mort Meskin, George Roussos, Bob Powell, Steve Ditko, Bill Draut, and Leonard Starr.

In his autobiography, Joe Simon recounted that *Black Magic* was one of the comics singled out by the senate investigation that helped eventually bring down William Gaines' EC horror titles and those of other publishers. According to Simon, their publisher never suggested any changes to the content of *Black Magic* and "we continued to produce it in the same old way."

Black Magic was born again briefly in 1973 when DC reprinted nine issues before giving up.

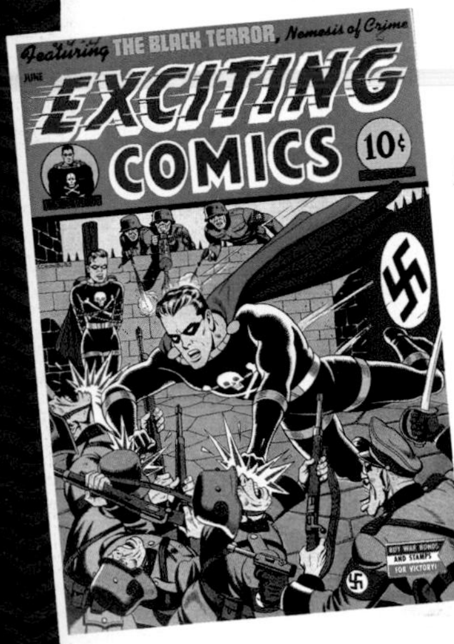
THE BLACK TERROR
EXCITING
COMICS
10¢

THE BLACK TERROR

■ Some superheroes have unique and fascinating powers, some have highly individual and quirky personalities, and others have to get by on little more than a nice costume. The Black Terror was one of these latter. His costume was jet-black with a touch of gold trim and an ominous white skull and crossbones emblazoned across the chest. It's also probable that the Punisher got the idea for his outfit from him. The origin story also shed some light on the question of where supermen got their outfits. After developing superpowers, the Terror sends his boy sidekick to the local costume shop.

The Black Terror and his boy companion Tim were first seen in *Exciting Comics* #9 (May 1941) and survived until the summer of 1949. The Terror was cocreated by prolific writer/editor Richard Hughes and artist Elmer Wexler. An early caption explained the hero's origin this way: "Dabbling in formic ethers, Bob Benton, a timid young druggist, chances on a source of mighty powers! With the help of young Tim Roland, he secretly employs his great strength as *THE BLACK TERROR* . . . Nemesis of Evil!" Despite his abilities, Tim never lost sight of the fact that he was a kid. Many was the time he traveled to the scene of a crime on his bicycle.

Wexler's work on the feature was excellent, but after he went into the service many third-rate artists filled in. The Black Terror, however, almost always looked great on the covers of the magazine and on his own *Black Terror* comic book, since the exemplary Alex Schomburg drew most of them. After the war, things improved considerably as artists such as George Tuska, Ruben Moreira, and the exceptional team of Mort Meskin and Jerry Robinson took turns with the character. The Black Terror left comics in 1949. An independent version of the character appeared briefly in 1989 and 1990.

BLACKHAWK

■ An old soldier who refused to fade away, Blackhawk has been leading his paramilitary crew into battle for over three-score years. A product of the Will Eisner shop, he first went into battle in *Military Comics* #1 (August 1941), published as part of Everett "Busy" Arnold's Quality line. Eisner, also editor of the new title, was cocreator of *Blackhawk*. Charles Cuidera provided the finished art.

"[I wanted] a super-guerilla," Eisner once explained. "I liked the idea of a group having an island of its own, outcasts from every nation. I had a fascination with the Foreign Legion then." The leader of the group was a Polish aviator whose sister and brother were killed in a Nazi bombing raid. He escaped from his country and emerged several months later as Blackhawk. He and his band of flying comrades were based on a mysterious island. Eventually the team, all of whom dressed in dark blue uniforms and visored caps, included Olaf, Hendrickson, Andre, Stanislaus, and Chuck. Chop-Chop, a broad caricature of an English-mangling Chinese, served as both cook and mascot. Over the years he would change more than any of the other Blackhawks.

Eisner drew the first two covers and wrote and laid out the first ten stories. Cuidera did the rest. The continuities were somewhat more naturalistic than much comic-book fare of the time, touching on the realities of the war in Europe and even allowing some characters to die. With the twelfth issue, Reed Crandall, with a little help from Alex Kotzky, took over the drawing. Crandall was an exceptional craftsman and seemed to relish drawing the nasty Axis villains and the sultry ladies who were required. He was also very good at depicting the many weapons, planes, gadgets, engines of destruction, and exotic locales required. He remained the chief artist for several years.

OUT OF THE CLEAR BLUE SKIES OVER BLACKHAWK ISLAND SOARS A BLONDE BOMBER WITH A SUNDAY PUNCH, A STREAMLINED FUSELAGE AND A SPEED OF 500 PER! --SHE'S THE LATEST THING IN THE AIR!
DON'T MISS HER!
BLACKHAWK

Quality added a *Blackhawk* title in 1944 and kept it going until late in 1956. After the end of Word War II, *Military* converted its name to *Modern Comics*. In both magazines, the postwar Blackhawks went after a variety of international villains. Among the other artists and writers were Bill Ward, William Woolfolk, and Manly Wade Wellman.

When Busy Arnold quit the comic-book business, he licensed several of his characters to DC. Although they didn't continue *Modern*, DC did pick up *Blackhawk* with #108 (January 1957). The artist was Dick Dillin, who'd also worked on the character at Quality. Cuidera returned as well to lend a hand. As the number of science-fiction stories

increased, monsters and robots were more frequently seen on the covers. Toward the end of the Quality run, Chop-Chop had become less of a caricature. The process continued at DC, although he continued to dress in Chinese fashion and not in a uniform.

In 1967, succumbing to superhero mania, DC turned the Blackhawks into superpowered, costumed heroes. That phase lasted for twelve issues. Then the Blackhawks became themselves again, but after only two more issues the magazine shut down late in 1968. There had been talk that Crandall would return, but that had never happened. Pat Boyette drew the final stories.

Early in 1976, DC tried again and came out with *Blackhawk* #244—"Back from the DEAD! The Greatest Fighting Team in the WORLD!" The stories, still set in the contemporary world, featured the old gang. Chop-Chop, however, was now named Chopper. No longer a caricature, he was a martial arts expert, spoke standard English, and wore the same uniform as his fellow Blackhawks. Steve Skeates was the writer, George Evans the artist.

That revival lasted exactly a year, then the gang was gone again until 1983. This time around, Blackhawk and his group were back in their natural habitat, the World War II years. Chop-Chop was now known as Wu Cheng. With Mark Evanier scripting and Dan Spiegle drawing, the Blackhawks sounded and looked better than they had in quite a while. Despite that, this revival lasted only a little over two years. In 1987, Howard Chaykin did a three-issue miniseries featuring a solo Blackhawk in a postwar adventure aimed at mature readers.

The next year Blackhawk showed up in the short-lived *Action Comics Weekly*. In 1989 the Blackhawks were back in their own monthly again, written by Martin Pasko and drawn by Rick Burchett. Set in 1947 and "suggested for mature readers," the new *Blackhawk* made it through sixteen issues before expiring in the summer of 1990. Blackhawk and his original *Military* crew can currently be seen in reprint form in DC's hardcover Archives Editions series.

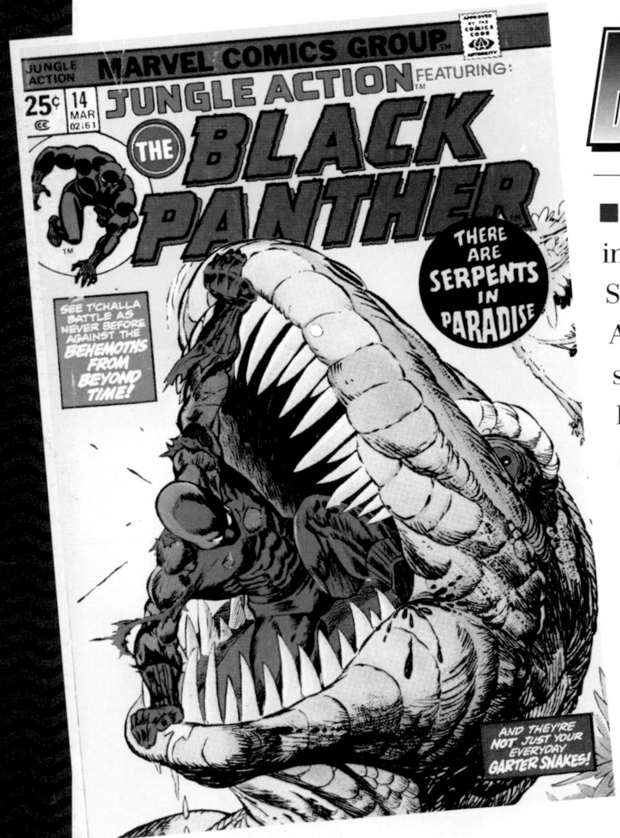
MARVEL COMICS GROUP
JUNGLE ACTION
25¢
14 MAR 02161
JUNGLE ACTION FEATURING:
THE BLACK PANTHER
THERE ARE SERPENTS IN PARADISE
SEE T'CHALLA BATTLE AS NEVER BEFORE AGAINST THE BEHEMOTHS FROM BEYOND TIME!
AND THEY'RE NOT JUST YOUR EVERYDAY GARTER SNAKES!

BLACK PANTHER

■ An African king who doubles as a superhero, he was introduced as a bit player in Marvel's *Fantastic Four* #52 (July 1966), thought up by Stan Lee and Jack Kirby. Seeming to have an affinity for the number 52, the Black Panther joined the Avengers in the fifty-second issue of their magazine in 1968. Next he became a solo hero, moving into *Jungle Action* in the sixth issue (September 1973). Rich Buckler was the first artist, Don McGregor the writer. *The Comic Book Heroes* says that McGregor "set about the task . . . with remarkable energy and serious intent." The next artist to work with him was Billy Graham. Eventually the Black Panther ceased commuting between his native Wakanda and America to remain an expatriate.

Finally in 1977, Marvel introduced a *Black Panther* title, with the first dozen issues written and drawn by the ubiquitous Jack Kirby. That ended in 1979. But a *Black Panther* returned in 1998 and is still being published. The latest user of the name is a policeman named Kevin Cole, who found the bullet-proof costume in an alley and decided to don it to do occasional vigilante work on the mean streets.

BLAZING COMICS

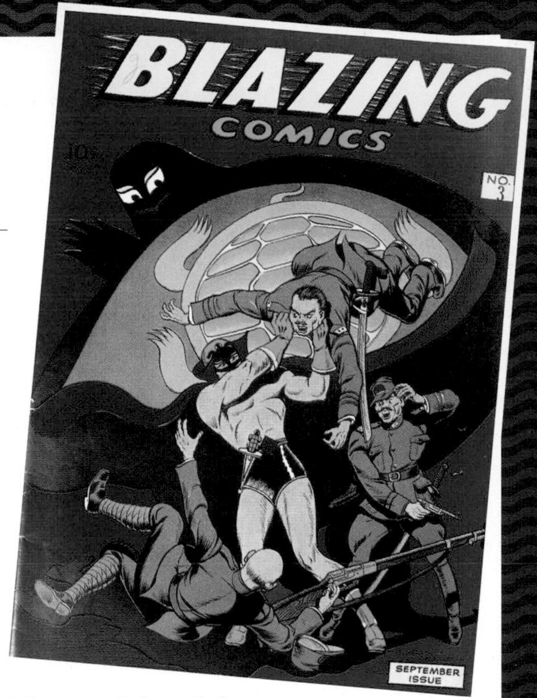
BLAZING
COMICS
NO. 3
SEPTEMBER ISSUE

■ Though produced by the Funnies, Inc., the same shop that had provided art and editorial for *Marvel Mystery*, this book was not a winner. First appearing in the spring of 1944, *Blazing Comics* expired after only five issues. It did manage, however, to give the world one of the most unusual costumed heroes of the World War II years—the Green Turtle. Drawn, and probably written, by an artist named Chu Hing, the feature had the Turtle aiding the Chinese in guerrilla warfare against the Japanese invaders. A true mystery man, he wore a green cowl and a cloak that had an enormous turtle design emblazoned on it. Since readers rarely saw the hero's face—not because of the half-mask he wore, but because he usually kept his back to the camera—it's possible that Chu Hing intended him to be Chinese, even though the colorist endowed him with a pinkish skin. The Turtle, who was aided by a sidekick called Burma Boy, flew a turtle-shaped rocket plane. *Blazing* also offered a magician detective known as Mr. Ree, a jungle girl named Jun-Gal, and an Native American fighter pilot called Red Hawk. There was also the swashbuckling Black Buccaneer, rendered by a youthful Leonard Starr.

BLONDE PHANTOM

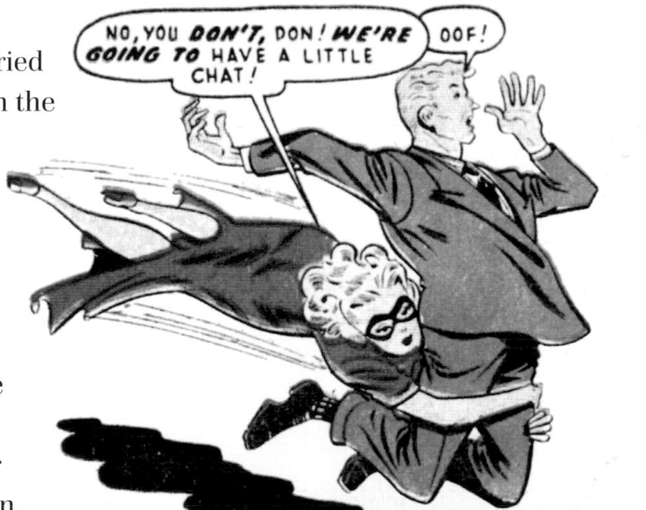
NO, YOU DON'T, DON! WE'RE GOING TO HAVE A LITTLE CHAT!
OOF!

■ Much like an aging movie actress, she went from being a star to being a supporting player. She began as one of the women Marvel tried to thrust into stardom to increase their number of female readers in the postwar 1940s. Venus, Sun Girl, and Namora were the others. The prolific Otto Binder was the original scriptwriter, and Syd Shores was the chief artist. The Blonde Phantom was first seen in *All Select Comics* #11 (Fall 1946), and with the next issue the magazine changed its name to hers.

In the civilian world, she was Louise Grant, mild-mannered secretary to private detective Mark Mason. Around the office Louise dressed conservatively, wore harlequin glasses, and had her hair pulled back into a bun. To become the Blonde Phantom, she let her hair down, changed into a low-cut, bare-midriff scarlet evening gown, and traded her specs for a black domino mask.

Although Louise had a crush on her dapper, pipe-smoking boss, she didn't have a very high opinion of his sleuthing abilities. In many instances she became the Phantom in order to clean up a case that Mason was bungling. The title survived through its twenty-second issue (March 1949). Then it was converted into *Lovers*, a magazine with even more potential appeal to a female audience. America's Lovely Lady of Adventure also appeared briefly in *Marvel Mystery*, *Sub-Mariner*, and *All Winners*.

Somewhere along the way she apparently married her boss. In 1989 Marvel revived Louise Mason, but this time only as a secretary. Older, plumper, but still blond, she became the secretary of Jennifer Walters, the She-Hulk. John Bryne was the one who resurrected her. She kept her office job throughout the five-year run of *The Sensational She-Hulk*.

BLONDIE

■ Still a very popular newspaper strip today, *Blondie* began in September of 1930. Chic Young, who'd drawn several other strips about flighty flappers, began this one as the mixture as before. But after a while, Blondie Boopadoop married Dagwood Bumstead, and in 1934 they had a son, whom they called Baby Dumpling. By this time *Blondie* was well on the way to becoming an enormously popular family humor strip. *Blondie* entered comic books in the middle 1930s, when Sunday page reprints became one of the features in David McKay's *Ace Comics*. When McKay started *Magic Comics* in 1939, the *Blondie* dailies, now in full color, were included along with reprints of *Mandrake*, *Secret Agent X-9*, and assorted other King Features strips. Over a dozen entire books of the Chic Young strip—showcasing the work of such ghost artists as Alex Raymond, Ray McGill, and Jim Raymond—were issued by McKay from the 1930s to the 1940s. Later a *Blondie* comic book promising that "all the comics are new and original" got going. Passed eventually from McKay to Harvey Publications, it continued with original material until 1976. The artist from the 1950s to the 1970s was Paul Fung, Jr.

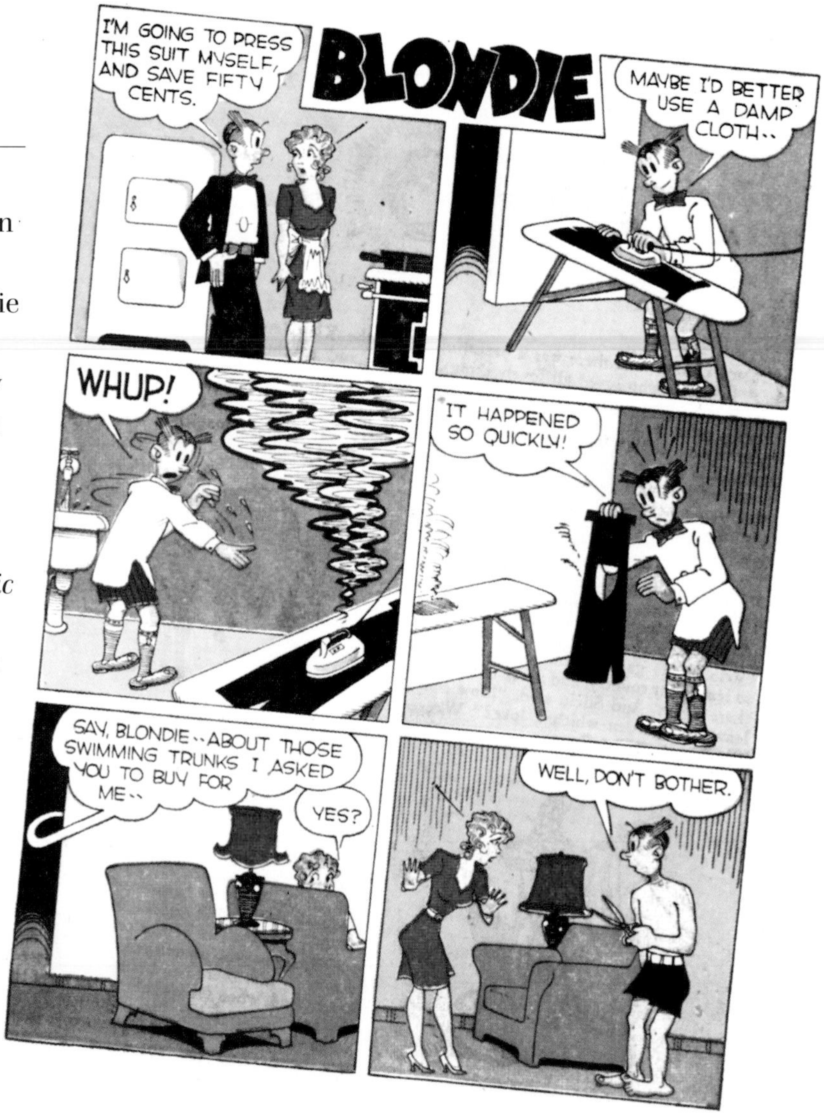

I'M GOING TO PRESS THIS SUIT MYSELF, AND SAVE FIFTY CENTS.
BLONDIE
MAYBE I'D BETTER USE A DAMP CLOTH..
WHUP!
IT HAPPENED SO QUICKLY!
SAY, BLONDIE..ABOUT THOSE SWIMMING TRUNKS I ASKED YOU TO BUY FOR ME..
YES?
WELL, DON'T BOTHER.

THE BLUE BEETLE

THE BLUE BEETLE
COAST TO COAST
Thrilling Drama of the Avenging Gang Smasher
Twice-a-Week
On Your Favorite Radio Station
CONSULT YOUR LOCAL NEWSPAPER, OR BETTER CALL YOUR FAVORITE LOCAL STATION, FOR THE SCHEDULE OF THIS SUPER-THRILLER. IF IT IS NOT SCHEDULED IN YOUR LOCALITY, ASK YOUR FAVORITE LOCAL STATION TO HAVE THE BLUE BEETLE ON THE AIR.

THE BLUE BEETLE
10¢
FEB.
FEATURING
THE BLUE BEETLE
IN
"CLAWS OF THE CAT!"
AND 3 OTHER SENSATIONAL ACTION THRILLERS
Plus
A SMASHING NEW FEATURE
THE GLADIATOR
AND DAVY, THE WISHMASTER

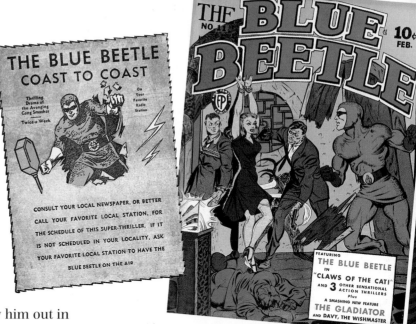

■ Nearly unsinkable, he was one of the more popular of the insect-inspired early comic-book characters. Not equal to the Green Hornet, but head and shoulders above the likes of the Red Bee and the Silver Scorpion, he was a costumed hero who was revived and reactivated several times over the years. He had his humble beginning in Victor Fox's *Mystery Men Comics* #1 (August 1939) and was the creation of an artist calling himself Charles Nicholas, probably Will Eisner. The Blue Beetle's initial run ended around 1950. Charlton brought him back in 1955 and again in the middle 1960s. In 1986 DC revived him yet again to try him out in a title of his own that lasted just short of two years. He was again on view in their *Justice League International*, where he hung out for a few more years.

The Blue Beetle started out toward the back of *Mystery Men*, appearing in short four-page adventures. In everyday life the Beetle was an impatient rookie cop named Dan Garrett, who was "given super-energy by Vitamin 2X." His chain-mail costume, by the way, made him "almost invulnerable." Whenever he wanted to be supercharged, he dropped into the local pharmacy run by his mentor Dr. Franz for a dose of 2X. Once empowered, he would rush around for eight or ten pages, cracking skulls and wisecracking as he hunted down such villains as the Wart, Scrag, Mr. Downhill, Countess Belladona, and a crazed scientist known as Doc.

BLUE BEETLE
WHAT HAPPENS WHEN DAN GARRET, ALIAS THE FIGHTING BLUE BEETLE, IS CALLED IN TO COMBAT FIENDISH EVIL-DOERS WHO IN-FLICT SAVAGE DEATH UPON INNOCENT VICTIMS? THE THUGS HAVE TAUNT-INGLY DEFIED ORDINARY METHODS OF LAW EN-FORCEMENT! CAN THE BLUE BEETLE OVER-COME THEM?

The Blue Beetle soon became Fox's most popular character. He moved into the front of *Mystery Men* and was showcased on every cover. He got a second magazine all his own and was also a star of an anthology, *Big 3*. The Nicholas byline remained, but a great many others drew the Beetle's adventures. These included Larry Antonette, Sam Cooper, Louis Cazeneuve, and Al Carreño. He was portrayed on covers by such artists as Lou Fine, Joe Simon, Edd Ashe, and Ramona Patenaude. Jack Kirby drew a short-lived daily newspaper strip. And there was also a

short-lived radio serial starring Frank Lovejoy, later a movie and television actor.

Blue Beetle's knack for survival was first demonstrated late in 1941, when for financial reasons Fox abruptly suspended operations and halted publication of all his titles. The *Blue Beetle* comic book, however, was continued by Holyoke Publishing, who'd been Fox's printer. Holyoke took over the magazine with #12 (June 1942), and in its first two issues used up all the Fox backlog of material. With #14, the Beetle was given a boy companion, a blond lad named Sparkington J. Northrup. He wore a simplified version of the hero's costume and called himself Sparky. He then became Spunky and after the nineteenth issue he retired and Dan Garrett went solo again. Later, when the Blue Beetle worked as a secret agent in Europe, Spunky returned, though in mufti. During his Holyoke phase, the Beetle had no evident superpowers and didn't make use of his vitamin supplement.

In the spring of 1944, Victor Fox returned to comics, launching new titles, reviving old ones, and taking back *Blue Beetle*. The Beetle had all his old powers back, plus the ability to fly. Jerry Iger's shop took over packaging the magazine in 1946, and artist Jack Kamen became one of the major contributors. The sex and violence content rose, and from #52, true crime stories were added. The final issue was #60 (August 1950) and had the slogan "True Crime Stories" prominently displayed on the cover.

Charlton brought back the character in 1955, first in reprints and then in original stories. The revival lasted four issues. Again in 1964 the publisher gave it another try. Dan Garrett was still the Blue Beetle, but now he became a superhero by way of a magic phrase said over a sacred scarab found in an Egyptian tomb. This revised version lasted for ten issues. Finally, in 1967 Charlton introduced a brand-new Blue Beetle in the person of Ted Kord, who also was converted into a superhero by way of a magic scarab. Steve Ditko was the artist on that five-issue run.

DC acquired Blue Beetle, along with other Charlton properties, in 1986. As written by Len Wein and drawn by Paris Cullins and Dell Barras, the Beetle was Ted Kord again. In the DC version, however, Kord had taken over the role after Dan Garrett was killed. A bit more successful, this incarnation of the Blue Beetle kept afloat for twenty-four issues. The Beetle also worked as a member of the Justice League into the early 1990s.

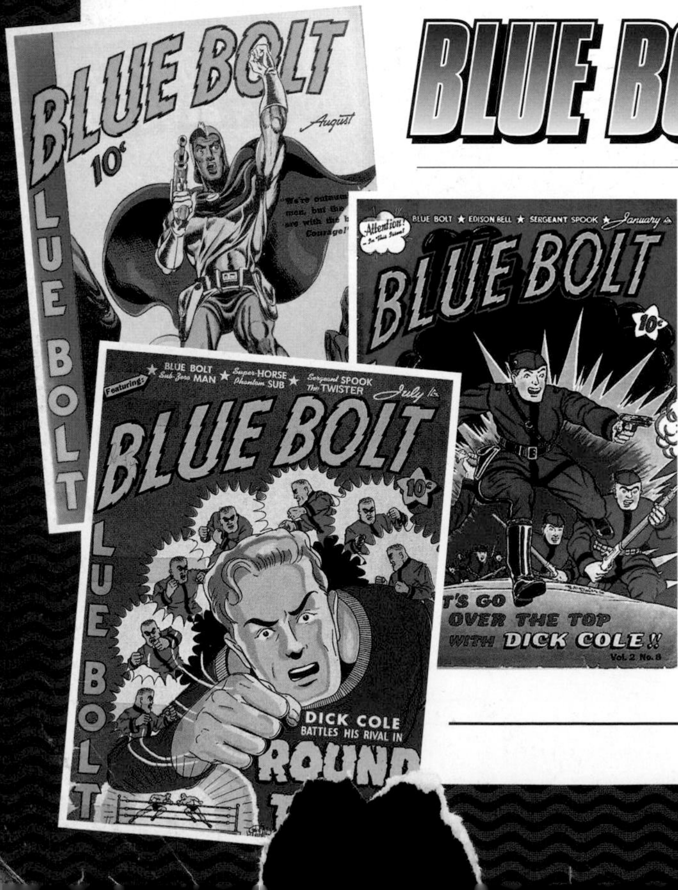
BLUE BOLT
August
10¢
BLUE BOLT
BLUE BOLT ★ EDISON BELL ★ SERGEANT SPOOK ★ January
BLUE BOLT
10¢
IT'S GO OVER THE TOP WITH DICK COLE!!
BLUE BOLT
10¢
DICK COLE BATTLES HIS RIVAL IN
BLUE BOLT

BLUE BOLT COMICS

■ Hiding behind the name Novelty Press, the Curtis Publishing Company, proprietors of *The Saturday Evening Post*, issued their second comic book in the spring of 1940. As they had done with their earlier *Target Comics*, Novelty relied on Lloyd Jacquet's Funnies, Inc., to provide the content. The lineup included superhero Blue Bolt, wonder boy Dick Cole, Venusian visitor Sub-Zero Man, a ghost known as Sergeant Spook, a boy inventor Edison Bell, and a super submarine known as the Phantom Sub. Newspaper veteran Jack A. Warren contributed a humor feature about two ne'er-do-wells who were eventually known as Krisko and Jasper.

The Blue Bolt was an erstwhile football hero who, after being struck by lightning, ended up in a lost kingdom beneath the earth.

After being given a booster shot of artificial lightning, he turned into the blue-clad, helmeted Blue Bolt. Although not an exceptional character, he's important for marking the first collaboration between Jack Kirby and Joe Simon, one of the most successful and prolific teams of the 1940s. Simon wrote and drew the first story, with Kirby taking over the penciling in the second issue. At the end of a year the team abandoned the feature and the Blue Bolt returned to the outer world again. He eventually gave up being a superman and joined the Air Corps. George Mandel was the next artist, followed by Tom Gill. Later on Wayne Boring, longtime *Superman* artist, drew the postwar civilian Blue Bolt under the pen name of Jack Harmon.

Dick Cole, who'd been scientifically raised to possess "amazing mental and physical powers," was a cadet at Farr Military Academy (the school song was "We'll Always Be Near to Farr"). Many of the crimes and conspiracies he tackled grew out of academy problems. Bob Davis created the feature. After his accidental death in 1942, his assistant Al Fagaly took over and did a lackluster job. Sub-Zero Man had the ability, apparently picked up on Venus, to freeze people on the spot with a beam from his forefinger. Larry Antonette, Bill Everett, and then John Daly drew his frigid escapades. Sergeant Spook was a murdered policeman who came back to haunt crooks and evildoers. Edison Bell invented things and also gave tips on how to build simple toys and devices at home.

The *Blue Bolt* magazine, toned down and sedate after World War II, held on until the summer of 1949. Bought out by Star Publications, it continued using nothing but reprints from earlier issues and fronted by the intricate, bright-colored covers of L. B. Cole. With the 111th issue late in 1951, it was turned into *Blue Bolt Weird.* By 1953 it was known as *Ghostly Weird Stories.*

BLUE DEVIL

DC
DANNY AND SHARON'S First Date!
75¢ 7 DEC 84
BLUE DEVIL
PLUS! OUR BEST NEW SUPER-VILLAIN YET AND A 1959 PINK CADILLAC IN PERFECT CONDITION!

"WALK RIGHT OVER," HUH? THAT'S NOT SUCH A BAD IDEA!
I THINK I'LL GIVE IT A TRY!
KRAK

■ Taken over by his costume and turned into a reluctant superhero, Blue Devil flourished in his own DC title from the spring of 1984 to the fall of 1986. A mock hero whose freewheeling adventures spoofed the preoccupations and pretensions of his more serious superhuman colleagues, Blue Devil was the creation of a quartet that consisted of writers Gary Cohn and Dan Mishkin and artists Paris Cullins and Gary Martin. Alan Gold edited the magazine during its relatively short life.

Hollywood stuntman Dan Cassidy was also a crackerjack special effects expert. His best special effect thus far was the Blue Devil suit he designed for a movie to be called *Blue Devil: The Movie.* However, when he donned the costume, which came equipped with an impressive pair of steer-like horns, he happened to get mixed up with a certified demon while on location. During an impressive donnybrook with the monster, which was named Nebiros, Dan was zapped by it. He found

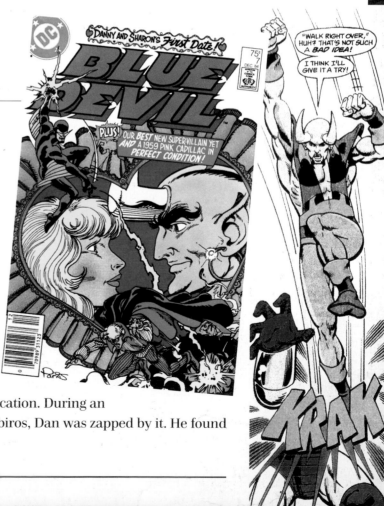

that he and the suit were now one. The blue latex had fused with his skin and the various built-in gadgets were now part of him. He had become a living, breathing Blue Devil, a sort of unhappy Six Million Dollar Man.

The rest of the lightly satirical series was chiefly concerned with the kvetching stuntman's efforts to shed the suit. In addition to a cast that included Sharon Scott, a somewhat light-witted blond actress who was Dan's girlfriend (and also one of the two folks who inadvertently unleashed the demon), Maria Bloom, his producer, her young nephew Gopher, who later became Devil Kid, a self-appointed boy wonder, Blue Devil got mixed up with such established DC characters as Zatanna, Starman, Superman, Firestorm, the Phantom Stranger, Wonder Woman, the Trickster, and the Creeper. He also, reluctantly, challenged such Marvelesque villains as Shockwave and Metallo.

Cohn and Mishkin wrote all the scripts, but various artists illustrated them. Gil Kane drew one guest issue, Ernie Colon and Alan Kupperberg put in longer hitches. *Blue Devil* amused quite a few readers, though apparently not enough to keep the book alive. It ended with the thirty-first issue (December 1986). Blue Devil never did get out of that suit.

BLUE RIBBON COMICS

■ The autumn leaves were starting to turn to gold in 1939 when three gentlemen with experience in the pulp-magazine business branched out into comic books. Their names were Morris (sometimes Maurice) Coyne, Louis Silberkleit, and John Goldwater, and they named their new comics company after the initials of their first names. MLJ's first title was *Blue Ribbon Comics*, on the stands sometime in September. Their pulp company had been called Blue Ribbon Magazines, Inc. Initially having no facility for creating comics, MLJ turned to the Harry "A" Chesler shop for the contents of their premier title. This accounts for the stodgy look of most of the features in the early issues of *Blue Ribbon*. In a time when superheroes were busting out all over, Chesler picked a wonder dog to be the leading character. Rang-A-Tang, even smarter than Rin-Tin-Tin, was eventually pushed to the back of the book by a spectral superhero dubbed Mr. Justice. Very similar to DC's Spectre, Mr. Justice was drawn by Harry Lucey and first materialized in #9 (February 1941).

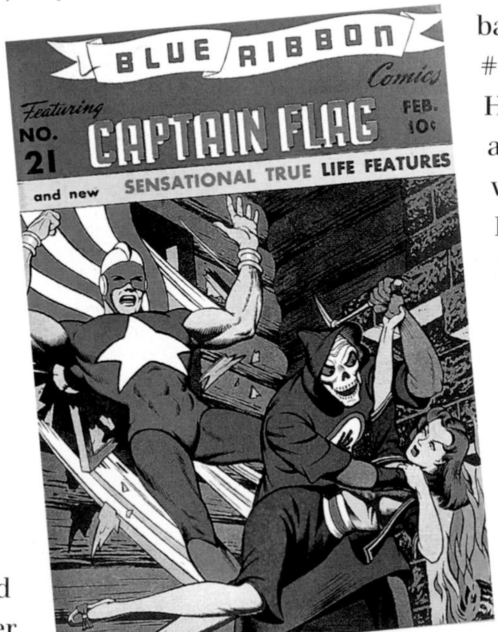
BLUE RIBBON
Comics
Featuring
NO. 21
FEB. 10¢
CAPTAIN FLAG
and new
SENSATIONAL TRUE LIFE FEATURES

Prior to his advent the magazine had severed its relationship with Chesler and added a batch of new characters. That began in #4. These included the Fox, Doc Strong, Hercules, and Ty-Gor. Corporal Collins, a leftover, was drawn by Charles Biro, who now went to work directly for MLJ. Irwin Hasen was the first artist on the Fox, and George Storm drew the early adventures of the feral jungle boy raised by tigers. In #16 (September 1941) Captain Flag, yet another superpatriot, joined up, drawn by Lin Streeter. *Blue Ribbon* never did as well as MLJ's other monthlies, *Top-Notch*, *Pep*, and *Zip*, perhaps because it never included a teenage character like Archie. It closed its doors after the twenty-second issue in the bleak winter of 1942. The MLJ partners would later change the name of their company to Archie Comics.

BOLLAND, BRIAN

(1951–)

■ One of the best and brightest of cover artists, his covers have graced numerous DC comic books since the early 1980s. Notably they have fronted many an issue of *Wonder Woman* and *Animal Man*. Bolland's major achievements in interior art are *Camelot 3000* and *Batman: The Killing Joke*. For English comics the Britain-based artist did a large amount of work for *2000 A.D.* and *Judge Dredd*.

A man who admits to being meticulous about his work and also to owning two hundred Frank Zappa records, Bolland broke into professional comics in the middle 1970s with the British weekly comic *2000 A.D.* For this title, he worked in black-and-white and developed into a first-rate inker. Coming to the attention of DC in 1990, in part through the offices of his friend, artist Joe Staton, he drew his first cover for them on *Green Lantern* #127. That led to an invitation to draw the twelve-issue *Camelot 3000*, written by Mike Barr.

In recent years Bolland has been using a computer to produce his artwork. "At the moment I use Adobe Photoshop almost exclusively," he explained in a recent *Comicology* interview. "There are two drawbacks to working this way . . . It's difficult to draw something that's upside-down. . . . The second drawback, the major one, is that there's no longer any artwork to exhibit or sell."

BOLTINOFF, HENRY

(1914 – 2001)

■ The king of the one-page humor features, he produced hundreds of them, mostly for DC Comics, from the early 1940s until the early 1970s. Boltinoff also drew longer comic-book features, including a couple of serious ones early on, plus gag cartoons, newspaper strips, and panels. A newspaper cartoonist in the 1930s, he moved into comic books in 1940. After a brief spell in the Bert Whitman shop, he freelanced and sold the majority of his stuff to editor Whit Ellsworth for all the Detective Comics, Inc., titles. Boltinoff sold to Fawcett comics as well and later to the Harvey titles.

Among the multitude of characters he created were Jerry the Jitterbug, Private Pete, Clancy the Cop (later Casey the Cop), Chief Hot Foot, Shorty, and Cora the Carhop. In the first five issues of *World's Finest* Boltinoff drew one of his few straight adventure strips, *Young Doc Davis*. In the middle 1940s, he drew *Dover & Clover*, a six-page feature about dim-witted twin detectives. This ran in *More Fun*, *All Funny*, and *Detective* at various times.

Boltinoff had a lively, uncluttered cartoon style, well suited to the funny fillers he specialized in. Besides his comic-book work, he turned out the *Nubbin* newspaper strip for several years, as well as the panel *Stoker the Broker* and the puzzle feature *Hocus Focus*. He never retired from cartooning.

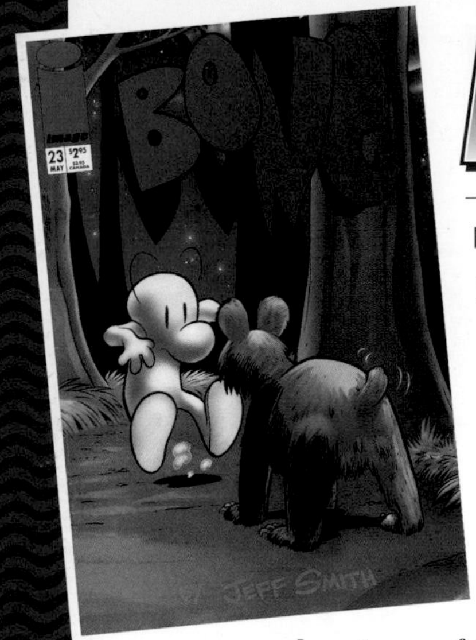
23
MAY
JEFF SMITH

BONE

■ A shining example of the possibilities of independent publishing, *Bone* was first seen in the late spring of 1991. Written and drawn by Jeff Smith and published by his Ohio-based Cartoon Books outfit, the black-and-white comic book deals with the adventures of the three Bone cousins. They are Fone Bone, Phoney Bone, and Smiley Bone, who, run out of their native Boneville, end up hiding out in a rustic valley and getting involved with the locals—including a young woman named Thorn and her feisty Gran'ma—and a variety of fantasy creatures, including a dragon and evil, giant rat creatures.

The Bone boys are not humans, although most of their friends are. They're more like funny animals, or rather generic funny animals. Fone Bone, the nice one, somewhat resembles a no-frills Pogo. Smith has said that he first drew the Bone cousins while in grade school, after having encountered Walt Kelly's *Prehysterical Pogo*. "I quickly understood, even in the fourth grade, that this was something that you didn't have to be embarrassed about. This was adult and intelligent." Carl Barks' *Uncle Scrooge* was another early influence, and when Smith finally came to produce a comic book of his own, he turned out a publication that mixed humor, adventure, and fantasy, showing the influence of both his artist/writer idols.

Within a relatively short time *Bone* caught on. Fans liked Smith's inventive and effective drawing and the funny, adventuresome, and sometimes romantic storylines. Comic shops increased orders, awards started coming his way, and within a year the early issues were going into second, third, and fourth printings. With an eye for merchandising, Smith added Bone T-shirts, miniature statues of his characters, posters, trading cards, and trade paperback reprints. Cartoon Books has thrived, now publishing other titles in addition to *Bone*, and Smith heads his own modest publishing empire. In 2003 he concluded the Bone saga and moved on to other things.

BORING, WAYNE *(1916–1986)*

■ He drew *Superman* for over thirty years, and his version of the Man of Steel has influenced every artist who came after him. Boring started assisting and ghosting for Joe Shuster in 1937. That was in Cleveland in the office that Siegel and Shuster had set up. According to him, "it was the smallest office in Cleveland." When Superman's creators lost control of their character late in the 1940s, Boring remained with DC. He drew both the comic-book adventures and the newspaper strip. By the early 1950s, he was allowed to sign his work.

He'd been employed as an assistant on the newspaper strip *Big Chief Wahoo* when he answered an ad in *Writer's Digest* and got the job with Siegel and Shuster. Before *Superman* was sold to DC's *Action Comics* in 1938, he worked on their other creations, notably *Federal Men* and *Slam Bradley*. As soon as *Superman* got rolling, Boring ghosted stories in the *Superman* magazine as well as sequences of the newspaper strip.

By the early 1940s, Wayne Boring had developed a distinctive style of his own. James Steranko once observed that "Boring salvaged the Man of Steel by transforming him into a massive muscled virile exuberance. His expressive faces and tight, incisive rendering brought new life into Superman's tired hulk." Despite all he did for the looks of Superman—and of Lois Lane—Boring was abruptly fired by editor Mort Weisinger in 1968.

While he'd worked at DC, Boring had done a bit of moonlighting for Novelty Press. He drew *Blue Bolt* in the magazine of that name and private eye Tony Gayle in *Young King Cole*. While his style was easily recognizable, he signed the alias Jack Harmon, which was derived from his father's first two names. In later years he worked on such newspaper strips as *Davy Jones*, *Rip Kirby*, and *Prince Valiant*. For Hal Foster's Arthurian opus Boring drew backgrounds. Resettling in Florida in his final years, he did little artwork and was employed as a security guard at the time of his death.

BOY COMICS

■ *Boy Comics*—"Two Years in the Making!"—was another audacious publication from the same group, publisher Lev Gleason and editors Charles Biro and Bob Wood, who were about to unleash *Crime Does Not Pay* upon the world. *Boy*, which began with issue #3 in the spring of 1942, promised "A boy hero in every strip!" Only the villains were adults.

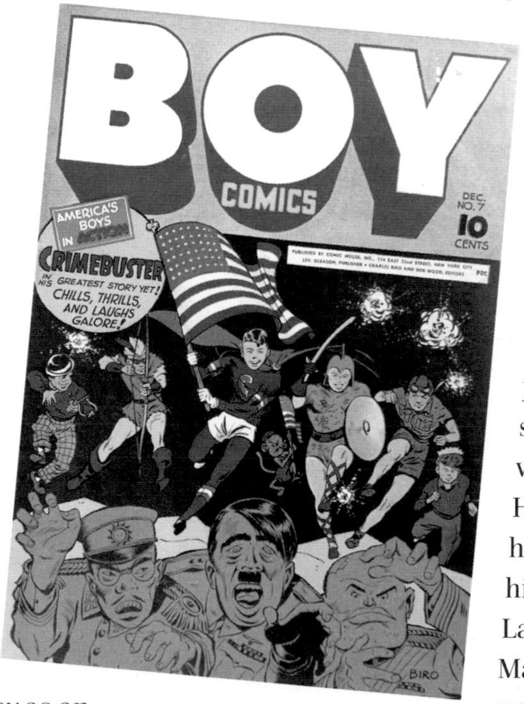
BOY
COMICS
DEC. NO. 7
10 CENTS
AMERICA'S BOYS IN ACTION
CRIMEBUSTER
IN HIS GREATEST STORY YET!
CHILLS, THRILLS, AND LAUGHS GALORE!
BIRO

The major young hero was Crimebuster, who turned his school hockey uniform into a costume. Biro originally drew his adventures. CB encountered an abundance of grown-up violence, bloodshed, and sex. His most frequent opponent was Iron Jaw, the vicious Nazi who'd killed CB's parents. The lower portion of Iron Jaw's face had been replaced with a wicked-looking pair of metal choppers. Another outré antagonist was the nasty He-She, half man and half woman. Biro used the covers of *Boy* as an important advertising medium, giving away a free monkey for the winning name for Crimebuster's monkey, touting the interior stories with blurbs like "IRON JAW RETURNS! A reptile will not die for a long time, even if cut into many pieces! So it is with the most deadly villain of all time!" and "First Torture, Then DEATH! With 130,000,000 lives at stake—Can CRIMEBUSTER Squash This Foul Jap Treachery?"

Among the other kid characters were Young Robin Hood, a boy pilot named Swoop Storm, and Dick Briefer's time-hopping street kid Yankee Longago.

Boy toned down considerably in the post–WWII years, with Charles Biro concentrating on such social problems as civic corruption and juvenile delinquency. The wordy scripts, although credited to Biro, were usually written by Virginia Hubbell. In Crimebuster's final years, he changed into civvies and went by his everyday name of Chuck Chandler. Later artists on CB included Norman Maurer, a boy himself when he started working at Gleason, Carl Hubbell, William Overgard, Dan Barry, and Joe Kubert. For many years Biro insisted that his hero's head be clipped from stats he'd prepared and pasted on each artist's drawings. *Boy Comics* continued until 1956.

THE BOY COMMANDOS

■ One of Joe Simon and Jack Kirby's most enduring youth groups, they were in comics from 1942 through 1949. After being introduced in *Detective Comics* #64 (June 1942), the Commandos next began appearing in a title of their own late that same year. This was Simon and Kirby's fourth feature for DC since leaving Timely.

A mixed bunch, the Boy Commandos consisted of Alfy, a plump British lad, Jan, a native of Holland who sported Dutch boy bob, Andre, a good-looking fellow from France, and Brooklyn, a streetwise American kid who wore a green turtleneck sweater and a bright red derby and carried a machine gun in a violin case. The mentor of the group was Captain Rip Carter, who commanded an outfit of adult commandos that had no qualms about letting the boys tag along on missions behind enemy lines in war-torn Europe. The battle cry of the group was, "The Commandos Are Coming!"

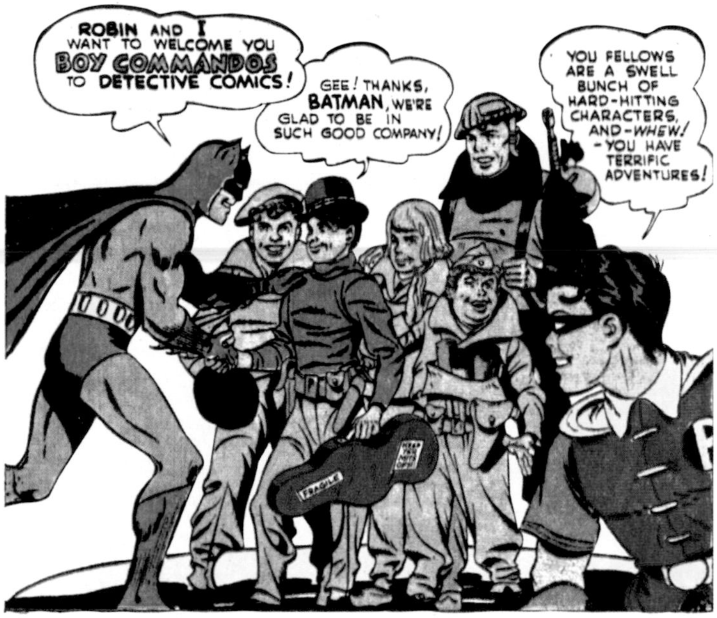
ROBIN AND I WANT TO WELCOME YOU BOY COMMANDOS TO DETECTIVE COMICS!
GEE! THANKS, BATMAN, WE'RE GLAD TO BE IN SUCH GOOD COMPANY!
YOU FELLOWS ARE A SWELL BUNCH OF HARD-HITTING CHARACTERS, AND-WHEW! -YOU HAVE TERRIFIC ADVENTURES!

After both Kirby and Simon entered the service, their names continued to appear on the feature. However, their ghost was Louis Cazeneuve, at his sloppiest, who made no effort to imitate their vigorous and flamboyant style. After the war the partners returned briefly to *The Boy Commandos*, a somewhat different group, though. Alfy and Jan were dropped and a kid named Tex was added, later to be replaced by a boy detective named Percy. When Simon and Kirby moved on again, Curt Swan became the regular artist. The Commandos specialized in international intrigue in their last years and even made a visit to Atlantis before retiring in 1949. DC published two issues of reprints of the early wartime stuff in 1973.

BOYETTE, PAT *(1923-2000)*

■ Former actor, TV anchorman, and low-budget movie director, Boyette switched careers again in the middle 1960s. Also an artist, he went to work for Charlton Comics. An avowed Texan, he stayed home in San Antonio and worked through the mail for the Connecticut-based publisher. "Although Charlton was not known for paying big fees," he once admitted, "it gave me an opportunity that the other companies didn't offer and that was the freedom to experiment, to do as I wanted, to make changes, to be happy."

During his nearly two decades with the company, Boyette produced an impressive amount of work for such titles as *Ghostly Tales*, *Billy the Kid*, *Flash Gordon*, *Fightin' Marines*, *The Phantom*, and *Peacemaker*, whose description was "A Man Who Loves Peace So Much That He Is Willing TO FIGHT FOR IT!"

When Charlton editor Dick Giordano moved to DC, he invited Boyette to work for them. He drew two issues of *Blackhawk* before returning to Charlton—"DC at the time demanded a regimentation that I wasn't readily eager to adhere to."

Boyette, while he did now and then work in a cartoony style, usually drew in an attractive illustrative style. His favorites were Roy Crane, Milton Caniff, and his friend Alex Toth, whose work he felt was "a perfect marriage of the attitudes of Caniff and the attitudes of Roy Crane." Boyette, who drew also for the Warren black-and-white titles, even published a few comic books of his own. At one point he went so far as to draw a revived Spencer Spook.

THE BRAVE AND THE BOLD

■ In the beginning, it was devoted to swashbuckling adventure tales in historic settings. The first issue of DC's *The Brave and the Bold*, with a cover date of August-September 1955, introduced a trio of sword-wielding heroes—the Viking Prince, the Golden Gladiator, and the Silent Knight, no relation to the Christmas hymn. With its twenty-fifth issue in the summer of 1959, the magazine was converted into a tryout area for such Silver Age heroes as the Teen Titans, the Justice League, Metamorpho, and a renovated Hawkman.

Combat specialist Robert Kanigher provided the scripts. Joe Kubert drew *The Viking Prince*, Irv Novick *The Silent Knight*, and Russ Heath *The Golden Gladiator*. Robin Hood was added to the lineup for a few issues from #5 on. By #16 the Prince and the Knight had *B&B* to themselves. Issues #23 and #24 were given over entirely to Kubert's Viking.

The next trio of issues tried out another Kanigher brainstorm, *Suicide Squad*. Issue #28 (March 1960) introduced the Justice League, an updated version of the old Justice Society written by Gardner Fox. After three issues of them and three of Cave Carson, a new, improved Hawkman by Fox and Kubert had a three-issue tryout. Hawkman and Hawkgirl tried out again in three more issues a bit further along. Then the Teen Titans, Metamorpho, and a revised Starman also auditioned before the magazine switched to a staging ground for a long series of Batman team-ups. Before the steam went out of the concept, the Dark Knight worked in tandem with the Atom, Wonder Woman, Deadman, Green Arrow, Plastic Man, Sgt. Rock, Black Canary, Aquaman, Adam Strange, Blackhawk, and a host of others, including himself (in both his Earth One and Earth Two modes). After the two-hundredth issue (July 1983), the magazine turned into *Batman and the Outsiders*. The talented Nick Cardy illustrated several of the early team-ups and also contributed a dozen covers.

DC used the title again in 1991 and 1992 for a six-issue series that included the Green Arrow and the Question.

BRIEFER, DICK (1915–1982)

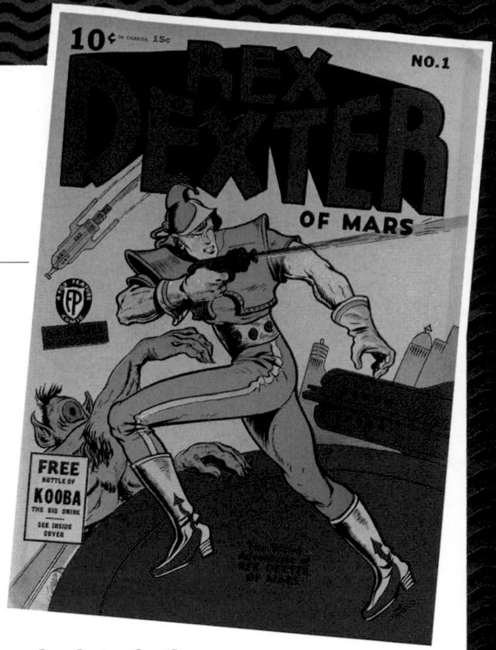
10¢
NO.1
REX DEXTER
OF MARS
FREE
KOOBA

■ He devoted half of his nearly thirty years to drawing the Frankenstein monster. A man with a sense of humor, Briefer had the most success with his comedy version of *Frankenstein.* But he began and ended his association with the creature drawing serious, sometimes gruesome stories about him. All the versions were done for the Prize Group. Briefer, who held liberal views, also did a feature about an Indian called *Real American* #1, and he used a historical swashbuckler called the Pirate Prince to criticize slavery. For good measure, he drew *Pinky Rankin,* a comic strip for *The Daily Worker.*

Briefer's earliest work appeared in *Wow* in 1936. Joining the Eisner-Iger shop, he drew for both *Jumbo Comics* and *Planet Comics.* He created *Rex Dexter of Mars* for the Fox line and his version of *Frankenstein* for *Prize Comics.* In the Briefer version the monster was called Frankenstein. Gradually he converted the feature to a slapstick spoof of horror movies and a lot of other aspects of contemporary society.

He left comics in the middle 1950s, moving to Florida. After working in advertising he spent his final years as a portrait painter.

BROOME, JOHN (1913–1999)

■ A writer important to the renaissance of superheroes in the late 1950s and early 1960s, Broome first got into comic books in 1942. After a brief career writing pulp science fiction, with future DC editor Julius Schwartz as his agent, Broome started selling scripts to Fawcett Publications for such characters as Lance O'Casey in *Whiz Comics.* After World War II, with the help of Schwartz, he went to work for DC. He turned out scripts for *All-American Comics, All Star,* and *Strange Adventures* (where he used the pen name Edgar Ray Merritt). When the Silver Age got rolling, Broome was for several years the major scriptwriter on both the new Flash and the new Green Lantern.

Comics historian Mike Benton points out in *Superhero Comics of the Silver Age* that Broome "fashioned much of the modern Green Lantern mythos." Broome also added Kid Flash to *The Flash.* Benton points out that "Broome's forte was super villains and the Flash had perhaps the most imaginative rogue's gallery of any of the DC superheroes."

Broome also created the Plastic Man simulacrum Elongated Man and the Atomic Knights. In addition he wrote scripts for *Batman, Star Hawkins,* and *Rex the Wonder Dog.* He scripted the *Superman* newspaper strip for awhile and the sparsely syndicated *Nero Wolfe* strip. Being freelance allowed Broome and his wife to live outside of Manhattan, and for some years they resided in Paris. Writer Mike Barr, who interviewed Broome at the 1998 San Diego comics convention, was impressed by his "grace, his good humor and even, in certain aspects, his serenity." That was the only comics convention Broome ever attended, and he died a few months later.

BUCK ROGERS

■ The interplanetary hero who first brought the benefits of pulp science fiction to comics, he was introduced in a novelette in *Amazing Stories*, written by Philip Nowlan in 1928. In January of the next year a daily *Buck Rogers* newspaper strip began, and in 1930 a full-color Sunday page was added. Nowlan provided the scripts and Dick Calkins drew the daily version. Russell Keaton, a much better artist than Calkins, ghosted the Sundays. In the autumn of 1934, the *Buck Rogers* pages were added to the selection of reprints to be found in the pioneering *Famous Funnies*. With the exception of a hiatus in the early 1950s, Buck and his associates—Doc Huer, Wilma, Buddy, Killer Kane, etc.—remained in the magazine for over twenty years. In addition, there were several complete *Buck Rogers* comics, using both reprint and original material. And Buck, over the years, branched out into radio, movies, and television. And people still refer to science fiction as "that Buck Rogers stuff."

BUGS BUNNY

■ See LOONEY TUNES AND MERRIE MELODIES.

BULLETMAN

■ See NICKEL COMICS.

BURGOS, CARL *(1917–1984)*

■ While not a major artist, he created one of the major superheroes. It was late in 1939, while working for the Funnies, Inc. shop, that Burgos invented the first Human Torch. Introduced in the first issue of *Marvel Comics*, the Torch became one of the three most popular characters publisher Martin Goodman had in the 1940s. The others were Sub-Mariner and Captain America. A primitive rather than a skilled draftsman, Burgos nevertheless had a forceful style and he was good at staging the scenes of conflict and chaos that the flaming activities of his protagonist required. Aware of his limitations, Burgos was proud of the fact that he never swiped. "If they wanted Raymond or Caniff," he once said, "they could look at Raymond and Caniff. The miserable drawing was all mine, but I was having fun."

Burgos entered comics in 1938, after working in an engraving plant. He was first employed in the Harry "A" Chesler shop. Next he joined the Funnies, Inc., shop, drawing *The Iron Skull* for *Amazing-Man Comics*, *The White Streak* for *Target Comics*, and *The Human Torch* for *Marvel Mystery Comics*. Burgos had a fondness for androids and all three of these characters were androids.

He went into the army in 1942. When he returned, although he again worked for Timely, he never quite fit in with the new look that comics had acquired in his absence. In 1966 he created a dreadful *Captain Marvel* of his own, a fellow who could do things like detach his fist in order to sock somebody across the street. In his final years he worked for Harris Publications in New York City.

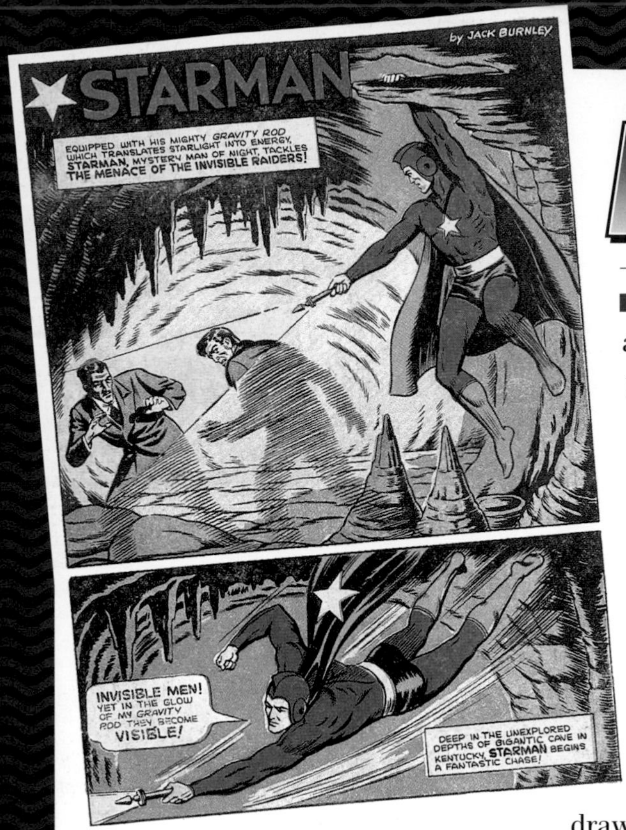
by JACK BURNLEY
STARMAN
EQUIPPED WITH HIS MIGHTY GRAVITY ROD WHICH TRANSLATES STARLIGHT INTO ENERGY, STARMAN, MYSTERY MAN OF NIGHT, TACKLES THE MENACE OF THE INVISIBLE RAIDERS!
INVISIBLE MEN! YET IN THE GLOW OF MY GRAVITY ROD THEY BECOME VISIBLE!
DEEP IN THE UNEXPLORED DEPTHS OF GIGANTIC CAVE IN KENTUCKY, STARMAN BEGINS A FANTASTIC CHASE!

BURNLEY, JACK (1911–)

■ A self-taught artist and an excellent illustrator, Burnley was drawing a nationally syndicated sports panel while still in his teens. His earliest published comic-book work consisted of sports fillers for McKay's *King Comics.* In 1940 he signed on with DC, ghosting both *Superman* and *Batman.* Jack Burnley was the first artist to draw both these characters. He was also the first to draw them together, on the cover of the 1940 edition of *New York World's Fair Comics.* The following year he was given his own superhero to draw. Despite an impressive launching and Burnley's impressive artwork, his *Starman* never became the hit that DC was obviously hoping for.

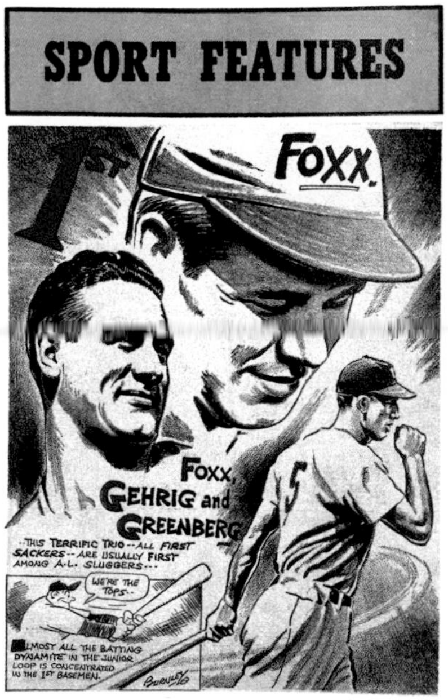
SPORT FEATURES
FOXX
FOXX, GEHRIG and GREENBERG
THIS TERRIFIC TRIO--ALL FIRST SACKERS--ARE USUALLY FIRST AMONG A.L. SLUGGERS---
WE'RE THE TOPS
ALMOST ALL THE BATTING DYNAMITE IN THE JUNIOR LOOP IS CONCENTRATED IN THE 1ST BASEMEN.

Because of his long experience drawing athletes, his superheroes were more realistically drawn and better muscled than those of many of his contemporaries. At the invitation of editor Sheldon Mayer, Burnley drew several of the introductory chapters in *All Star Comics,* as well as some of the covers. In a recent interview in *Alter Ego,* Burnley complained that drawing so many superheroes at once for *All Star* was "too much hard work." He decided, "I'm not going to do any more of them." Never that enamored of the comic-book field, he left it in 1947 to return to newspaper sports cartooning.

BUSCEMA, JOHN (1927–2002)

■ A fan favorite throughout his career and the major exponent of the Marvel house style of the 1960s and 1970s, he first worked for them in the late 1940s. Buscema drew crime, cowboy, and romance stories before moving to Whitman–Gold Key to draw such things as *Roy Rogers.* After also working for Quality, St. John, Ziff Davis, and Charlton, Buscema returned to Marvel.

Primarily a penciler, he drew most of Marvel's major characters, including Captain America, X-Men, Ghost Rider, the Avengers, and Conan. He took over the barbarian in 1973. "I love the character," he once said. "I love the stories." By this time he had developed a style that incorporated elements of Jack Kirby, John Romita, and Gil Kane. This amalgam became popular and was the dominant style at Marvel for several years. In 1978 Buscema solidified his claim to the style by producing a book titled *How to Draw Comics the Marvel Way.*

BUSIEK, KURT (1960-)

■ A comic-book scripter for over twenty years, Kurt Busiek is currently among the most popular. One of the main sources of his popularity is the independent *Astro City*, which he created in 1995. It was first published by Image Comics, then by Homage Comics. Brent Anderson is the artist, with Alex Ross providing covers and character designs. Quite a few superheroes inhabit Astro City, including the All-American, Slugger, the Tarnished Angel, and Starwoman. The series asks the question, as one fanzine put it, "What would real-life people be like if they lived in a comic book world where comic book logic applies?" Busiek also writes scripts for the more conventional *Avengers.*

BYRNE, JOHN (1950-)

■ In his more than a quarter of a century as a popular comic-book artist, John Byrne has drawn, and in some cases written, updated, and occasionally drastically modified, a great many major characters. These include the Fantastic Four, Superman, Ghost Rider, X-Men, Daredevil, Spider-Man, the Hulk, the She-Hulk, and Captain America. He has also created such features as *Alpha Flight* and *Next Men.* One of his recent projects was DC's 2003 twelve-part series, *Generations 3.* Featuring both Batman and Superman, as well as assorted other heroes, it follows them across several centuries. It was written, penciled, inked, and lettered by Byrne.

Born in England and reared in Canada, Byrne did his first professional work for Charlton in 1974 on *Space: 1999.* He next moved to Marvel. After being in the business for over a decade, he decided his style needed renovating. "How could I draw if I didn't draw like Neal [Adams]?" he asked himself, referring to one of his idols and influences. The new style he developed was much looser, more touched with humor, and easily recognizable as being by nobody else but John Byrne.

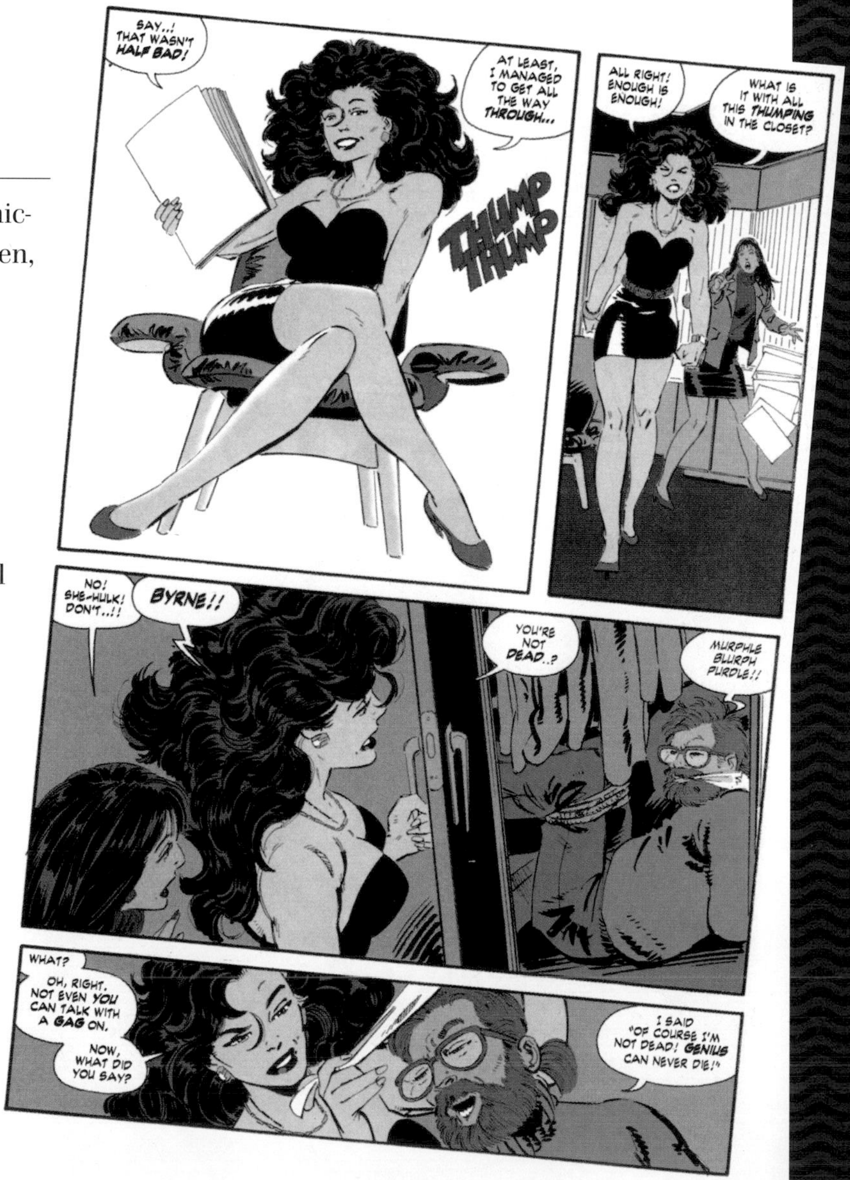
SAY...! THAT WASN'T HALF BAD!
AT LEAST, I MANAGED TO GET ALL THE WAY THROUGH...
THUMP THUMP
ALL RIGHT! ENOUGH IS ENOUGH!
WHAT IS IT WITH ALL THIS THUMPING IN THE CLOSET?
NO! SHE-HULK! DON'T...!!
BYRNE!!
YOU'RE NOT DEAD..?
MURPHLE BLURPH PURDLE!!
WHAT?
OH, RIGHT. NOT EVEN YOU CAN TALK WITH A GAG ON.
NOW, WHAT DID YOU SAY?
I SAID "OF COURSE I'M NOT DEAD! GENIUS CAN NEVER DIE!"

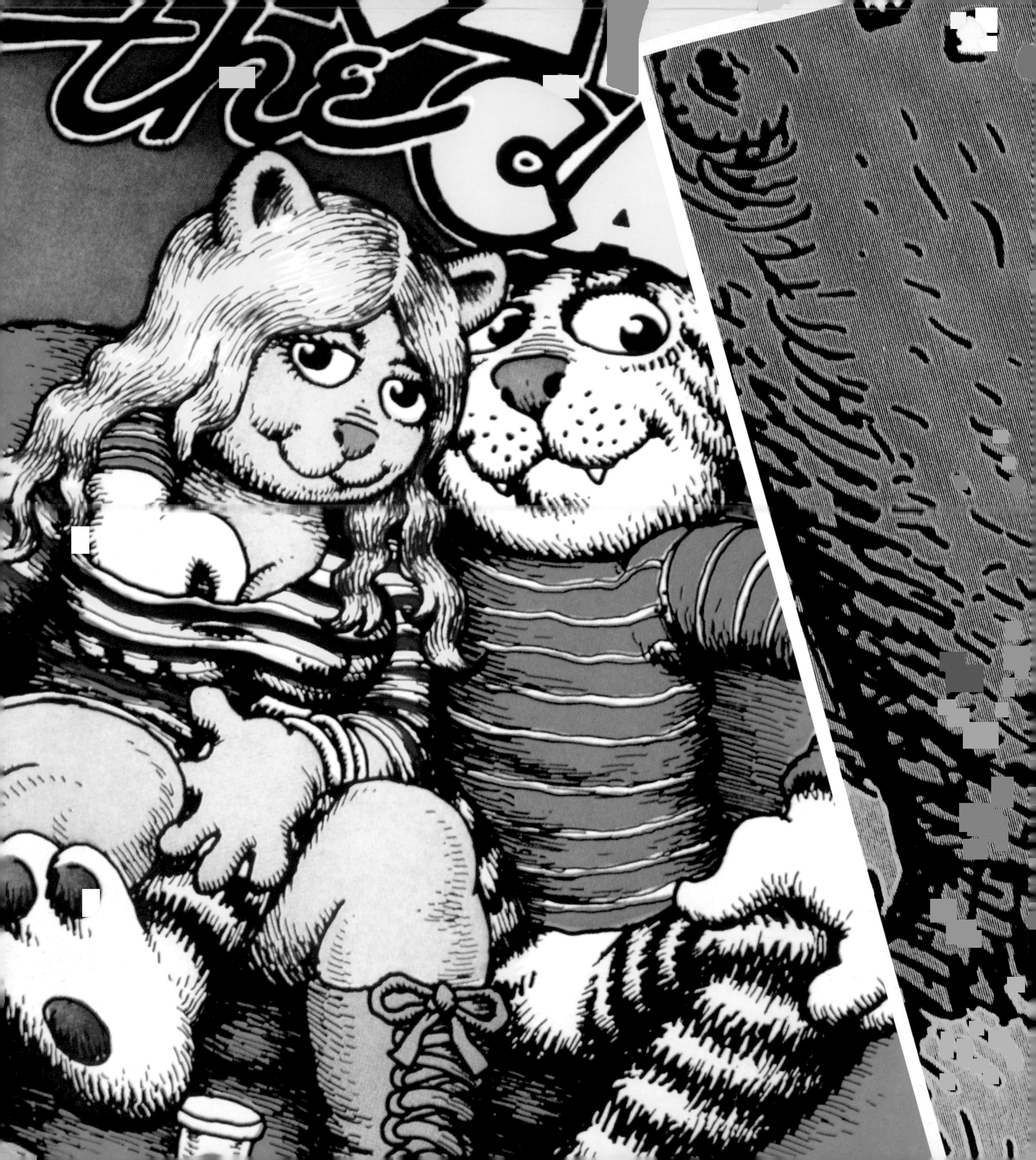
the

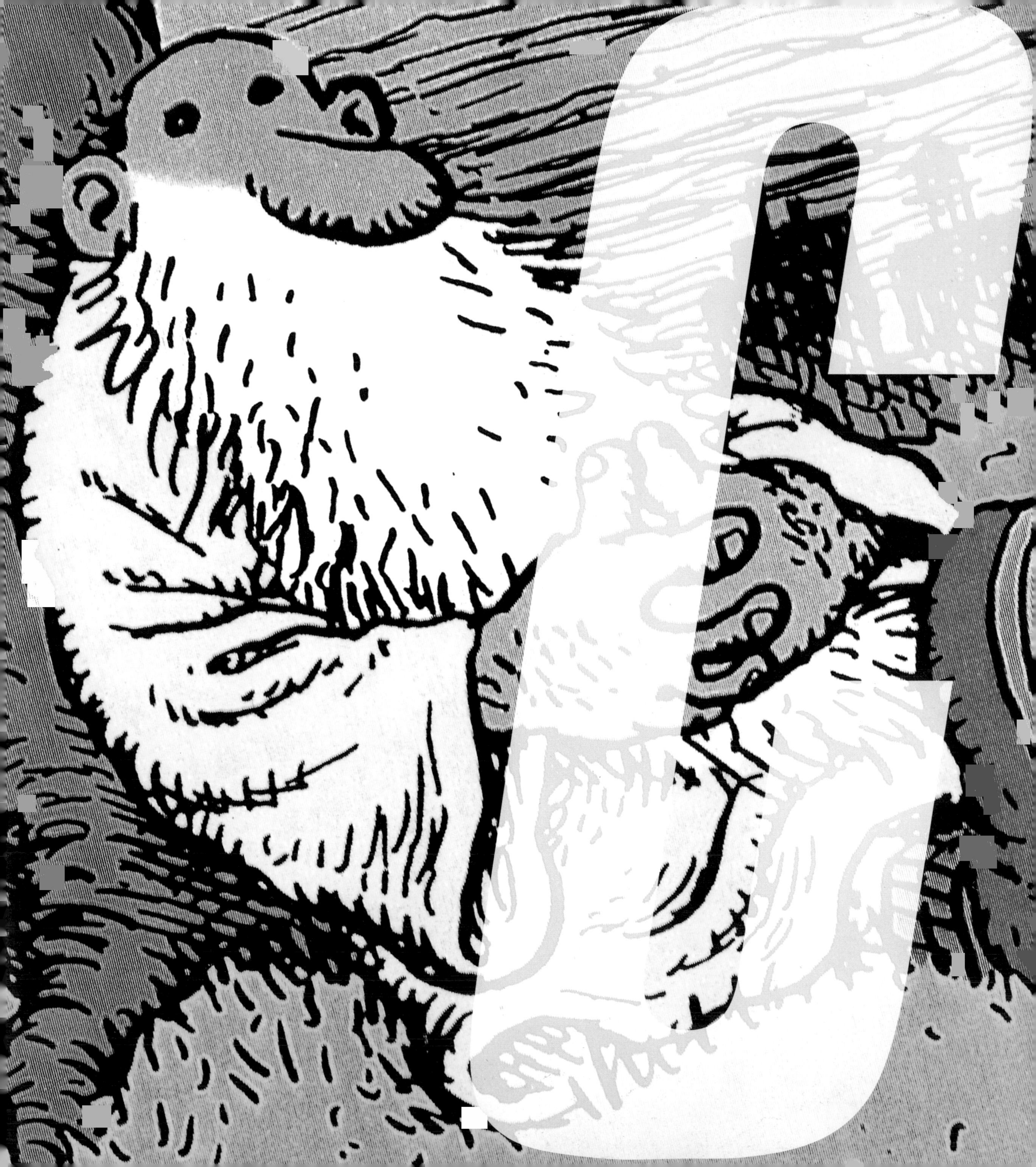

CAMPBELL, J. SCOTT

■ See DANGER GIRL.

CANDY

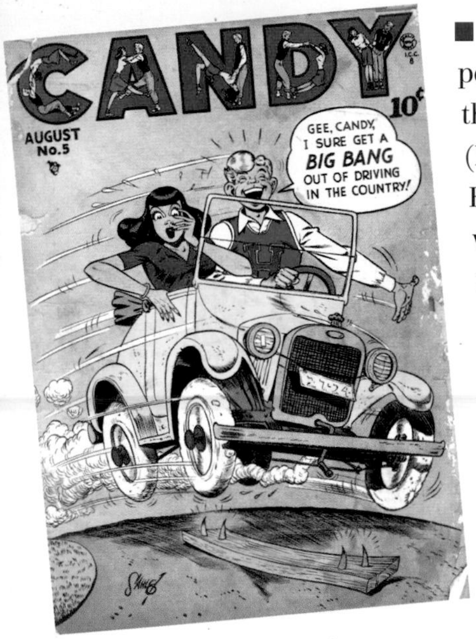
CANDY
AUGUST No.5
10¢
GEE, CANDY, I SURE GET A BIG BANG OUT OF DRIVING IN THE COUNTRY!

■ To ensure that their new teen feature had the same saleable look as the increasingly popular *Archie*, Quality hired Harry Sahle to draw *Candy*. Sahle had been working on the *Archie* comic book since early in 1943. Candy was introduced in *Police Comics* #39 (December 1944), previously an all-male enclave shared by the likes of the Spirit, the Human Bomb, and Plastic Man. At the same time that the perky brunette teenager was invading *Police*, a *Candy* daily newspaper strip, also drawn by Sahle, was getting under way. Writer Ed Groggin provided the scripts for both versions.

Candy was closer to Betty than Veronica, with a touch of Junior Miss and Corliss Archer. She was given to pinup poses and outfits, which endeared her to the magazine's adolescent readers. Candy, who had the usual set of doting but perplexed parents and a cute, manageable boyfriend named Ted, filled her conversations with up-to-the-minute expressions such as "All reet" and "But definitely."

She left *Police Comics* in 1950 at the same time the Spirit and Plastic Man were given their walking papers. The separate *Candy* magazine, begun in 1947, continued on until 1956. By then the newspaper strip was long gone.

CAPTAIN 3-D

■ A hard-luck hero, he appeared only once at the tail end of 1953 before oblivion set in. The only issue of *Captain 3-D* was a failure, losing publisher Alfred Harvey at least a quarter of a million dollars. The captain, who had a big 3D across the chest of his costume, was a casualty of the all-too-brief boom in three-dimensional comics in 1953.

The lone issue was put together by the Joe Simon and Jack Kirby shop. Mort Meskin penciled the Captain 3-D story, with Kirby doing some of the inking. According to Simon, Harvey ended up not only with low sales and a warehouse full of red-and-green 3-D glasses, but a threatened lawsuit from William Gaines, who claimed that the process used had been swiped from him.

CAPTAIN AMERICA

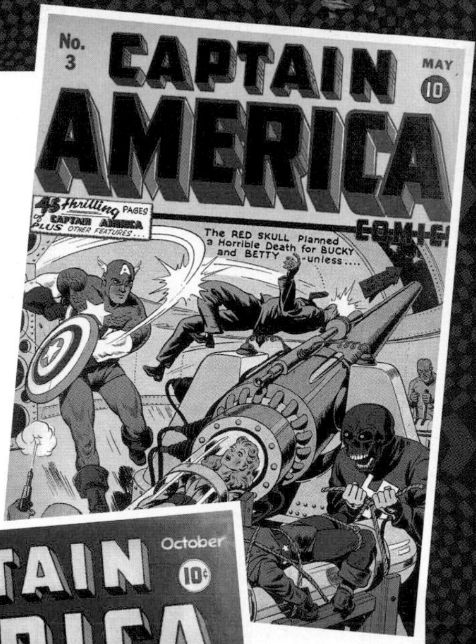
No. 3
CAPTAIN AMERICA
MAY
10¢
45 Thrilling Pages of CAPTAIN AMERICA PLUS OTHER FEATURES...
The RED SKULL Planned a Horrible Death for BUCKY and BETTY ...unless....

■ A living testimonial to the effectiveness of cryogenics, the 1940s superpatriot returned to comics in the 1960s after having been frozen in an Atlantic iceberg for twenty years. Or so younger Marvel readers were led to believe. Actually the comic-book comings and goings of the nation's most famous superpatriot were somewhat more complicated than that. He was created for Timely by Joe Simon and Jack Kirby. On the cover of the first issue of *Captain America Comics*, dated March 1941, he was seen in all his red, white, and blue glory socking Adolf Hitler. Until the advent of Captain America, characters who got whole comic books of their own first had to have a successful tryout elsewhere—Superman in *Action Comics*, Captain Marvel in *Whiz Comics*, the Human Torch in *Marvel Mystery Comics*. Simon and Kirby's star-spangled defender was an exception.

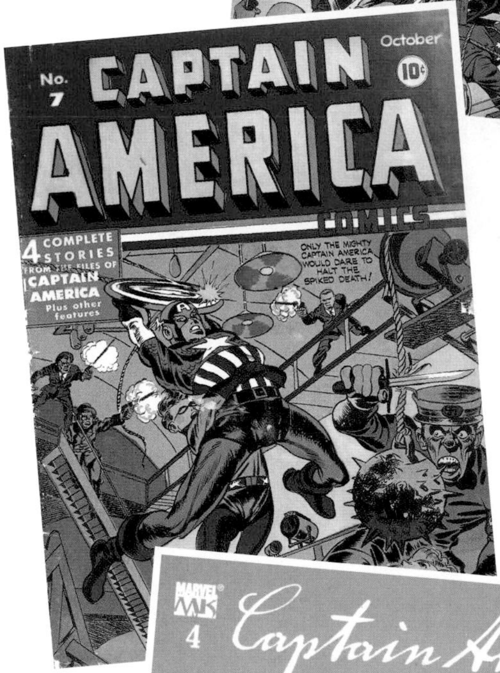
No. 7
CAPTAIN AMERICA
October
10¢
4 COMPLETE STORIES FROM THE FILES OF CAPTAIN AMERICA Plus other features
ONLY THE MIGHTY CAPTAIN AMERICA WOULD DARE TO HALT THE SPIKED DEATH!

The original story showed blond Steve Rogers trying to enlist in the army but being turned down "because of his unfit condition." It isn't clear in that introductory episode whether he willingly took an experimental injection from the noted scientist Professor Reinstein or whether he was forced into it, but he did go along with the doctor's scheme to create a super soldier. The "strange seething liquid" worked like a magical Charles Atlas course, turning Steve from a ninety-seven-pound weakling into a superhuman. Reinstein had envisioned a "corps of super-agents whose mental and physical ability will make them a terror to spies and saboteurs!" But the prof was gunned down by a Gestapo agent after creating just one superman, who then took the name Captain America.

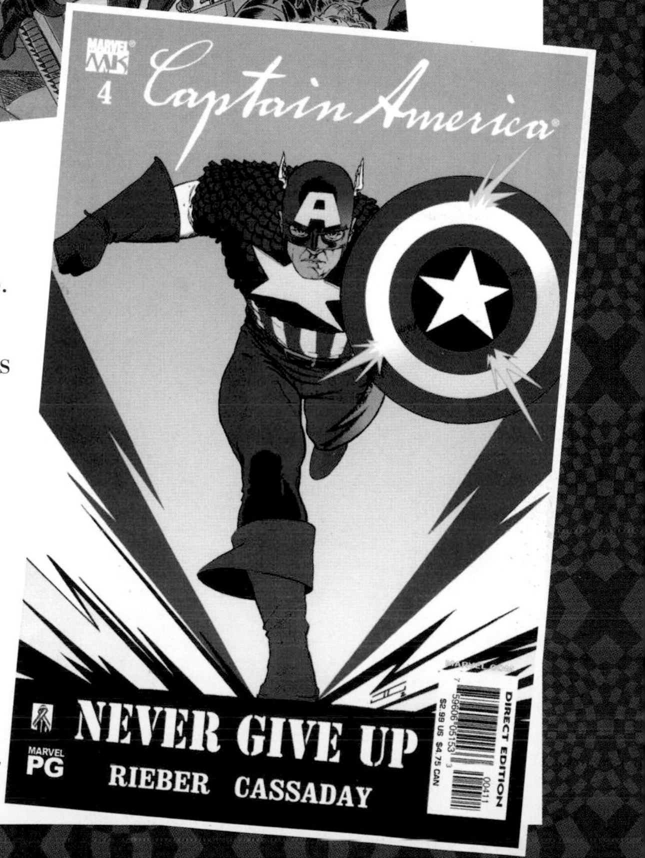
MARVEL MK
4
Captain America
NEVER GIVE UP
RIEBER CASSADAY
MARVEL PG
DIRECT EDITION

It would seem that carrying on a double life while a private in the United States Army would be extremely difficult, but that was what Rogers tried to do. He pulled it off and even met Bucky Barnes, a fearless youngster described as "the mascot of the regiment." The two teamed up against the "vicious elements who seek to overthrow the U.S. Government!" Chief among those vicious elements was the Red Skull, a Nazi agent who wore a crimson death's-head mask and was to Cap and Bucky what the Joker was to Batman and Robin. First surfacing in the initial issue, he returned twice more in the first year, then came back to plague them numerous times over the years.

When not battling enemies of democracy, the duo ran into some rather spooky foes, including a phantom hound, Oriental zombies, the Hunchback of Hollywood, the Black Talon, and the Black Witch. One of the decent characters introduced early on was Betty Ross, "a special investigator for the

U.S. government," whose cases often put her in need of rescue. When Simon and Kirby went over to DC after the tenth issue, the Captain and his boy companion were taken over by such artists as Al Avison, Syd Shores, and Al Gabriele, all of whom had assisted on the earlier issues.

If you don't believe --

Captain America and Bucky flourished during the World War II years, appearing not only in their own magazine but in *All Winners*, *U.S.A.*, and *All Select*. Bucky moonlighted as part of the Young Allies. In 1946, Steve Rogers and Bucky became civilians, and it was revealed that Rogers had been a schoolteacher. He went back to his old profession, working at the Lee School in Manhattan, and Bucky resided with him as his ward. They now specialized in fighting homegrown criminals and racketeers.

It's enough to hold it, soldier --
Hold the Dream.

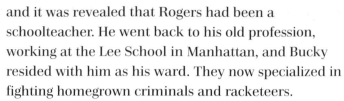

Captain America also became part of *Marvel Comics*, starting with #80 (January 1947). As part of the postwar effort to add more women characters, Bucky was retired in 1948—after having been wounded—and replaced by a costumed lady called Golden Girl. She was Cap's old government agent friend, now calling herself by the more patriotic name of Betsy Ross. The two remained together until late in 1949. *Marvel Comics* turned into *Marvel Tales*, a horror comic, in the spring of 1949. The *Captain America* book survived until late that same year and was titled *Captain America's Weird Tales* its final two issues.

In the middle 1950s Stan Lee tried to revive some of the retired superheroes. The Human Torch, Sub-Mariner, and Captain America appeared in individual stories in the revised *Young Men*, starting with #24 (December 1953), and then each was given a title of his own. *Captain America* #76 picked up the old numbering and was dated May 1954. Teamed again with Bucky, and drawn by John Romita, the superpatriot now performed as a dedicated cold warrior and was billed as "Captain America . . . Commie Smasher!" In some of the stories Steve Rogers was a professor at the Lee School, while in others he was once again in the army. The rejuvenated hero specialized in Russian plots. The Captain and Bucky tackled such dangers as an electricity-charged monster named Electro, who was green and had a red hammer and sickle on his chest and a scheme to blow up the United Nations headquarters. After thwarting that one, Captain America remarked to Bucky, "Americans play not to win, but for the sake of good sportsmanship and fair play . . . which Nazis and Reds know nothing about at all!" While seemingly in tune with many of the prevailing political ideals of the period, Captain America failed to capture the hearts and minds of comic-book readers, and his magazine collapsed after just three issues.

Eventually the Silver Age revival came along, and

when Captain America returned—without Bucky—he fared considerably better. He's been on the scene ever since. It was the old, original Cap who showed up in *The Avengers* #4 early in 1964 to join the team. The cover announced "Captain America Lives Again!" Inside, resorting to revisionist history, it was revealed that as a result of a long-ago battle with a villain known as Baron Zemo, Bucky was killed and the Captain ended up being frozen in an Artic chunk of ice for twenty years. Beginning with #58 (October 1964) Cap also started sharing *Tales of Suspense* with Iron Man. In 1968, with #100, the magazine became *Captain America*—"Cap in his own magazine at last!" Jack Kirby had returned to draw his superpatriot, and he continued to do so in the new title. Stan Lee wrote the scripts. In 1971 Cap got a new temporary sidekick in the person of the Black Falcon.

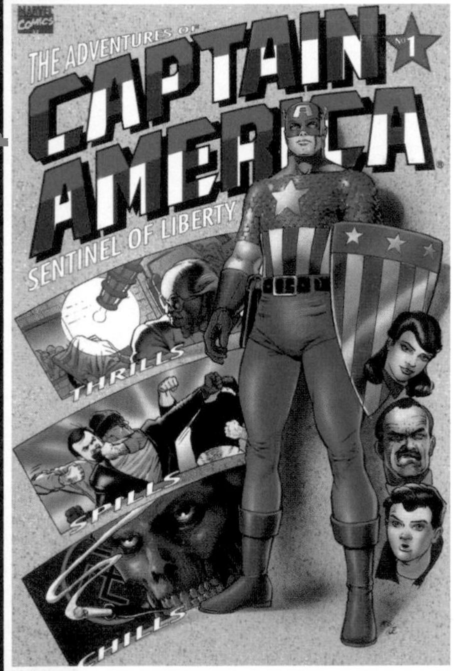
THE ADVENTURES OF
CAPTAIN AMERICA
No 1
SENTINEL OF LIBERTY
THRILLS
SPILLS
CHILLS

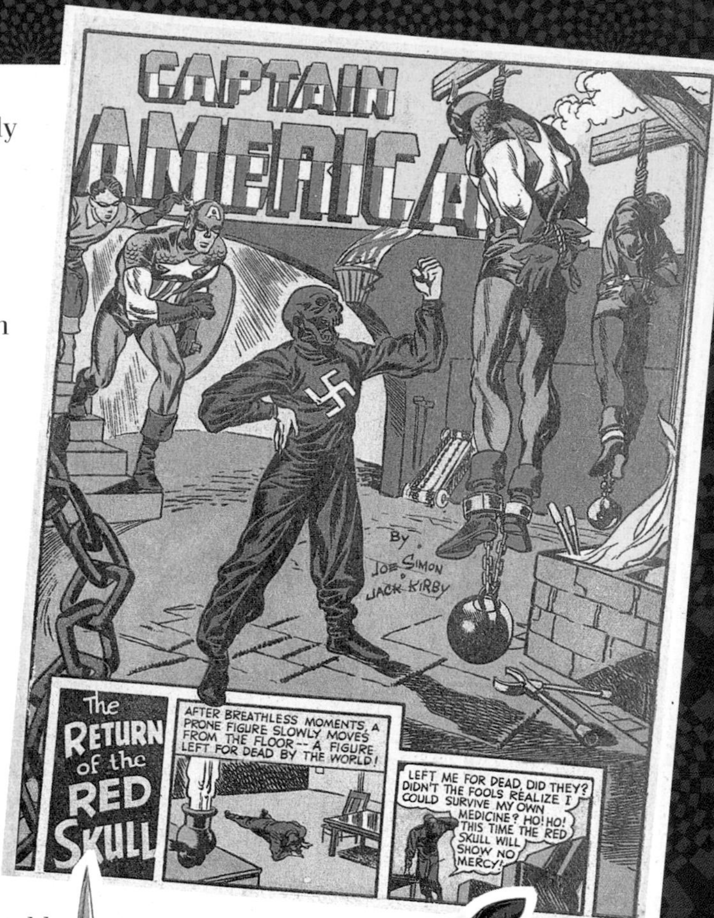
CAPTAIN AMERICA
BY JOE SIMON & JACK KIRBY
The RETURN of the RED SKULL
AFTER BREATHLESS MOMENTS, A PRONE FIGURE SLOWLY MOVES FROM THE FLOOR -- A FIGURE LEFT FOR DEAD BY THE WORLD!
LEFT ME FOR DEAD, DID THEY? DIDN'T THE FOOLS REALIZE I COULD SURVIVE MY OWN MEDICINE? HO! HO! THIS TIME THE RED SKULL WILL SHOW NO MERCY!

Over the years, the 1940s Captain America, along with Bucky, has reappeared now and then. The contemporary Captain America has also continued to flourish. Like many another mythical figure, the story of his origin and early days has been told, retold, and revised many times. It has also been explained that the right-wing Red baiter of the 1950s wasn't Cap but an imposter. Among the many artists and writers who've worked on the legend are Gil Kane, Steve Englehart, Roy Thomas, John Byrne, Mark Waid, Steve Gerber, Sal Buscema, Mike Zeck, Frank Robbins, Kevin Maguire, Howard Chaykin, and most recently Jae Lee.

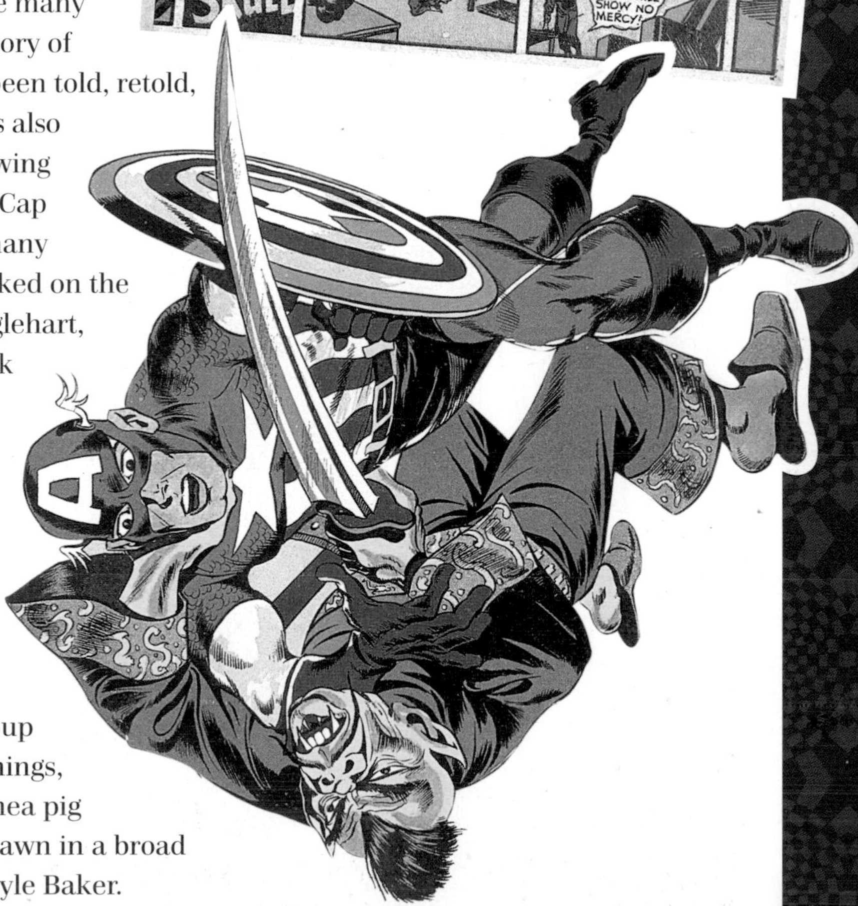

Captain America was still available in several forms as the twenty-first century got going. Late in 2002, amidst a flutter of publicity, Marvel introduced a miniseries titled *Truth: Red, White & Black*. Set in the early 1940s, it explored the idea that the super soldier serum that turned Steve Rogers into Captain America was first tested on a group of African-American soldiers. This resulted, among other things, into one of the men, Isaiah Bradley, becoming a sort of guinea pig Captain America. Scripted by Robert Morales, *Truth* was drawn in a broad cartoony style, one that wasn't especially appropriate, by Kyle Baker.

CAPTAIN MARVEL: I

■ More popular in the 1940s than Superman and considerably more amusing, Captain Marvel was introduced in the first issue of Fawcett's *Whiz Comics* early in 1940. Created by editor/writer Bill Parker and artist C. C. Beck, he thrived for over a decade and it took a lawsuit to put him out of business.

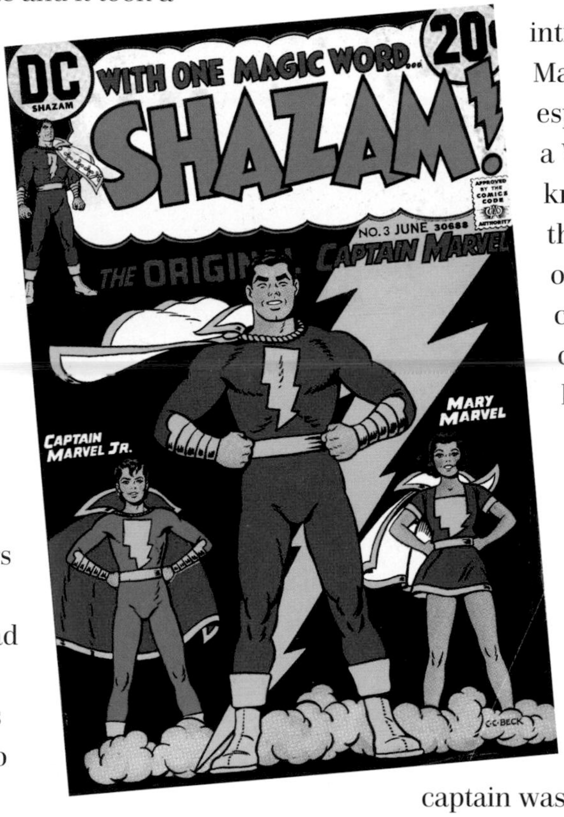
DC
SHAZAM
WITH ONE MAGIC WORD...
SHAZAM!
NO. 3 JUNE 30688
CAPTAIN MARVEL
CAPTAIN MARVEL JR.
MARY MARVEL
C.C. BECK

Late in 1939, Roscoe K. Fawcett sent out a promotion piece to magazine distributors across the country. It announced the impending debut of *Whiz Comics*, which would star Captain Marvel, "another character sensation in the comic field!" Until then the Fawcett organization had been known for such magazines as *Mechanix Illustrated*, *Motion Picture*, *Real Life Story*, and *Captain Billy's Whiz-Bang*. Now they were promising wholesalers a comic book, one that was "here to stay." The forthcoming title would lead the parade and bring "permanent profits." Many comic-book publishers would make similar claims and fail to live up to them, but in the case of Fawcett, all the advance hyperbole proved to be true.

The original name of the superhero was to be Captain Thunder, and he was going to be the leader of a group of heroes. But the group notion and the name were discarded. Parker came up with a variation on the dual identity theme. Captain Marvel was really a teenager named Billy Batson. By uttering the magic word "Shazam!" (revealed to him by a mysterious ancient wizard in a long-forgotten section of subway), Billy could transform himself to the red-clad Captain Marvel, the World's Mightiest Mortal. Despite the fact that the captain was invincible, it was Billy who quietly dominated the stories. Captain Marvel was the one who tangled with the villains, but he always returned to his true identity of Billy by again shouting, "Shazam!"

A batch of other characters were introduced in *Whiz* along with Captain Marvel. These included a costumed espionage agent called Spy Smasher, a Western bow-and-arrow expert known as the Golden Arrow, and Ibis the Invincible, a magician who had once lived in ancient Egypt and came back to life to fight twentieth-century evil, including the Devil himself, with his powerful Ibistick.

There was a great visual appeal to the early adventures of Captain Marvel, provided by Beck's simple, effective drawings, which had clarity and excellent design. He based the captain's face on that of movie star Fred MacMurray and the costume on that of a typical soldier in light opera. The captain was fortunate enough to have Sivana, billed as the World's Maddest Scientist, as his frequent opponent. The small, bald, bespectacled evil genius, who wore the same sort of white medical jacket as the neighborhood druggist Beck modeled him after, appeared in the first story and recurred with gratifying frequency. It often seemed that IQ point for IQ point, he was probably smarter than Cap, whom he was fond of calling the Big Red Cheese. Captain Marvel's early career was complicated by Beautia, Sivana's blonde and good-natured daughter. The young lady had a crush on him and he found himself looking on her with favor.

As the demand for Captain Marvel stories increased—the character was also soon appearing in *Captain Marvel Adventures* and *America's Greatest Comics* in addition to *Whiz*—Fawcett went to outside artists and then had Beck set up a shop of his own. Among the outsiders were Joe Simon and Jack Kirby, George Tuska, and the Jack Binder shop. Employed by Beck were Pete Costanza, Kurt Schafenberger, Dave Berg, and Marc Swayze. Otto Binder joined the team to do scripts in the second year. He was responsible for several hundred scripts, including just about all those dealing with time travel, space travel, and other sci-fi staples. He also invented the popular Mr. Tawny, the talking tiger.

Whiz Comics was selling nearly half a million copies a month before its first year was out. By 1943, *Captain Marvel Adventures* sold about a million copies per issue, and in 1946 the figure approached a million and a half. And that was the year when the magazine was appearing every two weeks. Life was not exactly a bed of roses for the Big Red Cheese, however, because in 1941 DC had taken legal action against Fawcett. It was their contention that Captain Marvel was so close to Superman that he represented an infringement of copyright. The lawsuits were fought throughout the 1940s and into the 1950s. Finally, when the ultimate ruling went against them, Fawcett ceased publishing Captain Marvel in any shape or form. The final issue of *Whiz* was dated June 1953, the last *Captain Marvel Adventures* November 1952.

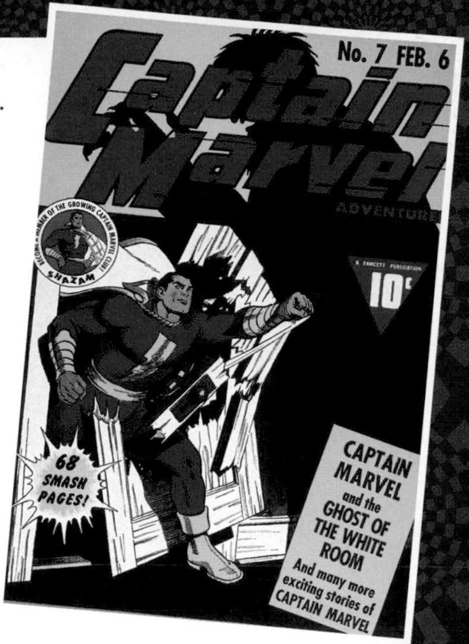
No. 7 FEB. 6
Captain Marvel
ADVENTURES
SHAZAM
10¢
68 SMASH PAGES!
CAPTAIN MARVEL and the GHOST OF THE WHITE ROOM
And many more exciting stories of CAPTAIN MARVEL

Detective Comics, Inc., who'd put him out of business in the first place, arranged for the return of Captain Marvel in 1973. They even hired C. C. Beck to draw the new comic books. It was called *Shazam!* because in the interim Marvel Comics had introduced a completely different Captain Marvel of its own and trademarked the name. Beck, unhappy with the scripts and the working conditions, did not long remain with the resurrection project. The magazine limped along until 1978, having inspired a relatively successful kids' television show.

DC has continued to revive Captain Marvel now and then, having him drawn in a more realistic, serious, and contemporary fashion. But he's never sold the way he did in his heyday in the 1940s. In the 1990s, DC got one of their best artists, Jerry Ordway, to write and draw *The Power of Shazam!* That lasted until 1999.

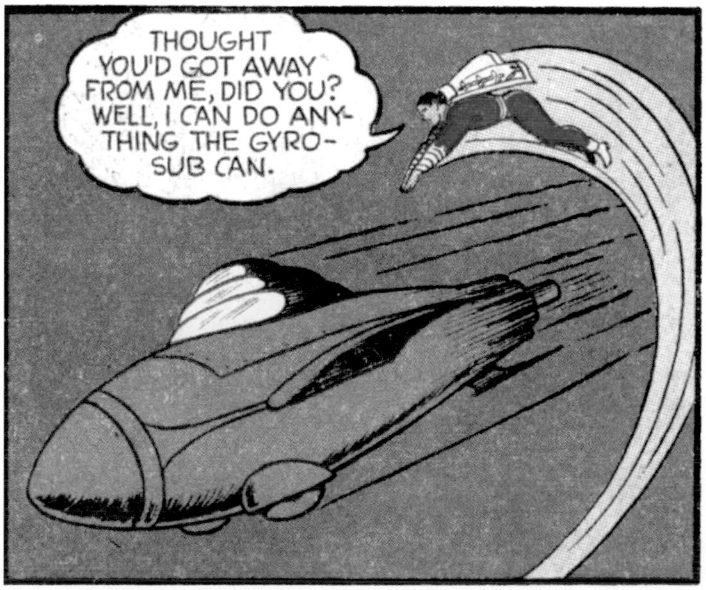
THOUGHT YOU'D GOT AWAY FROM ME, DID YOU? WELL, I CAN DO ANYTHING THE GYRO-SUB CAN.

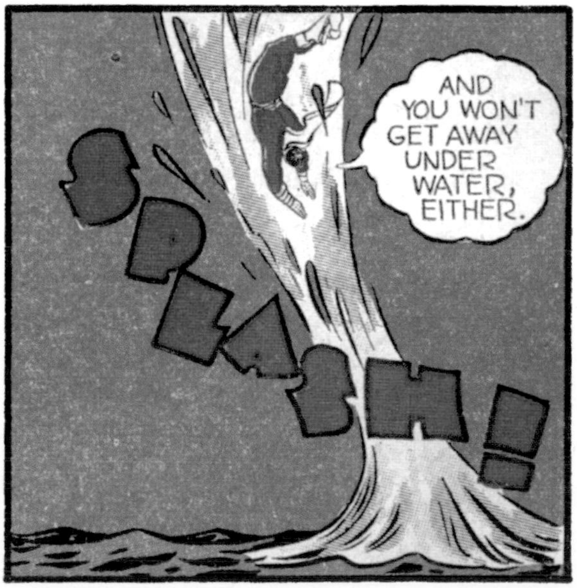
AND YOU WON'T GET AWAY UNDER WATER, EITHER.
SPLASH!

MARVEL
PSR 19 54
DAVID   LOPRESTI   SOTOMAYOR
CAPTAIN MARVEL®

7 59606 05396 4
$2.99 US $4.25 CAN
19

CAPTAIN MARVEL: II

■ Apparently being named Captain Marvel is not in itself a guarantee of success. Maybe you also need access to a magic word along the lines of "Shazam!" Undaunted, Marvel appropriated the name, and late in 1967 introduced their own Captain Marvel in *Marvel Super Heroes* #12. He was then given a title of his own. The impressively productive Stan Lee wrote the scripts about this super-powered alien who relocated on earth. Gene Colan was the artist. Marvel's Marvel, even after a costume change and the acquiring of the Hulk's sometime sidekick Rick Jones as his sidekick, was no match for the Big Red Cheese. As Internet comics historian Don Markstein has pointed out, "The character didn't make a great hit with readers." One of the problems was, as Markstein put it, that "Marvel didn't quite know what to do with him."

The captain survived through sixty-two issues of his magazine before he was canceled in 1979. Other artists on that first run included Gil Kane and John Buscema. Brought back in one-shots and minis in the 1980s and 1990s, this Captain Marvel was given another chance and launched in a new title in 2000. Still ongoing, it's written by Peter David.

CAPTAIN MARVEL, JR.

■ Fawcett Publications had introduced the enormously successful Captain Marvel early in 1940. The following year they began adding Marvels. This innovative notion eventually spread to other publishers, resulting in Superboy, Supergirl, and assorted other kith and kin of superheroes. In *Whiz Comics* #21 the three Lieutenant Marvels made the first of their occasional appearances. Then in *Whiz* #25 (December 1941) Captain Marvel, Jr. was introduced. Never as successful as his brawnier namesake, Junior enjoyed a long and lucrative career that lasted initially until 1953. By the time the Marvels

started multiplying, DC had apparently realized the impossibility of suing every superhero who wore a cape and had the ability to fly.

Captain Marvel, Jr.'s coming was preceded by the arrival of the man who would be his primary antagonist over the next year or so. Captain Nazi, "World Enemy No. 1," showed up in *Master* #21. He was Hitler's own personal superhero, a vicious fellow in a green-and-yellow costume with a swastika on the chest and epaulets on the shoulders. He wore his blond hair in a buzz cut and his face was "marked with a Heidelberg dueling scar." In his maiden visit to the United States, he was matched against Bulletman, but Captain Marvel dropped over from *Whiz* to lend a hand. Captain Nazi, managing to escape at the end of the story, left a note warning he'd be looking up Cap next month in *Whiz*.

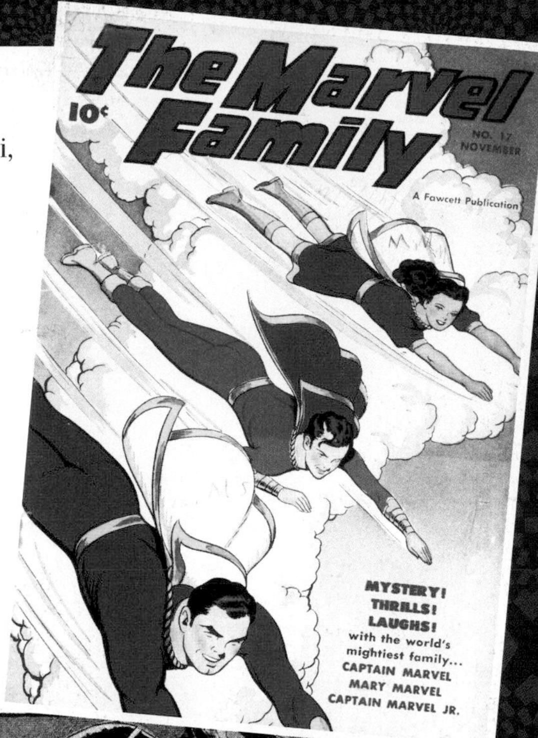
The Marvel Family
10¢
NO. 17
NOVEMBER
A Fawcett Publication
MYSTERY!
THRILLS!
LAUGHS!
with the world's mightiest family...
CAPTAIN MARVEL
MARY MARVEL
CAPTAIN MARVEL JR.

One of the side effects of that encounter was that young Freddy Freeman was crippled and left for dead by the German superman. Captain Marvel, however, carried Freddy to his old mentor Shazam, and the bearded wizard saved his life by granting him the ability to turn into a superhero at will. Freddy had to say "Captain Marvel!" to turn into Captain Marvel, Jr. Unlike Billy Batson, he wasn't converted into an adult, but into a super-teen. His costume was similar to that of the senior hero, but it was blue instead of red. In his civilian identity, the crippled Freddy worked as a streetcorner newsboy.

Captain Marvel, Jr., went to *Master* in the next issue to aid Bulletman in his return match with Captain Nazi. In #23 the young hero was given a spot of his own and became the star of the magazine. He battled the German superhero through eight different issues in 1942, in both American and European locales. After that, the villain faded away. Other early villains were Mr. Macabre and Captain Nippon. Later, the blue-clad superboy frequently tangled with Sivana, Jr., the nasty offspring of the senior Marvel's favorite foe.

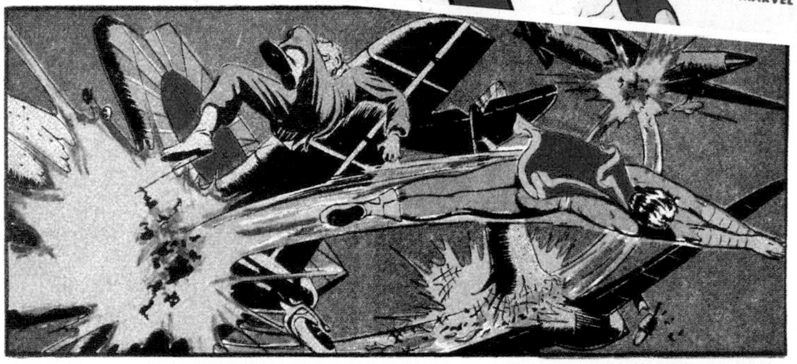

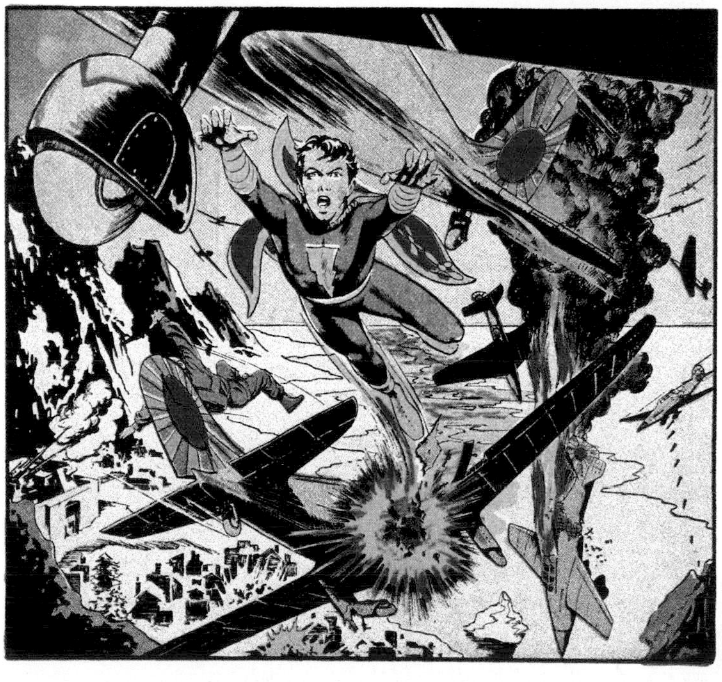

The initial artist, and also the first to draw the vile Captain Nazi, was Mac Raboy, who also did the *Master* covers for several years. An exceptional artist, he was notoriously slow and often had help. In some stories, entire pages are by other hands and some consist mostly of Photostats of earlier Raboy drawings. In Captain Marvel, Jr.'s own comic book, which started late in 1942, Al Carreño was the chief artist. Raboy drew the covers for this monthly, too. Further along, Bud Thompson, who'd previously drawn a newspaper panel about Hollywood stars that was written by one of the Fawcett brothers, became the artist for both magazines. Among the scriptwriters were Ed Herron, Bill Woolfolk, and Otto Binder.

Fawcett started *The Marvel Family* late in 1945. In this eventual monthly, the two captains and Mary Marvel, along with the spurious Uncle Marvel, joined together to form a sort of nepotistic Justice Society. The eighty-ninth and final issue was dated January 1954 and marked the final appearance of Junior in that era.

DC has revived him several times since.

CAPTAIN MIDNIGHT

■ At first Captain Midnight was heard and not seen, which may explain why there was never any agreement as to what he looked like. He began his media career as a radio hero in 1939 on a fifteen-minute five-times-a-week kids' radio show broadcast out of Chicago. By 1940 the show was being listened to all across the country on the Mutual network and was sponsored by Ovaltine, the chocolaty drink mix that had up to then been advertising by way of a *Little Orphan Annie* show.

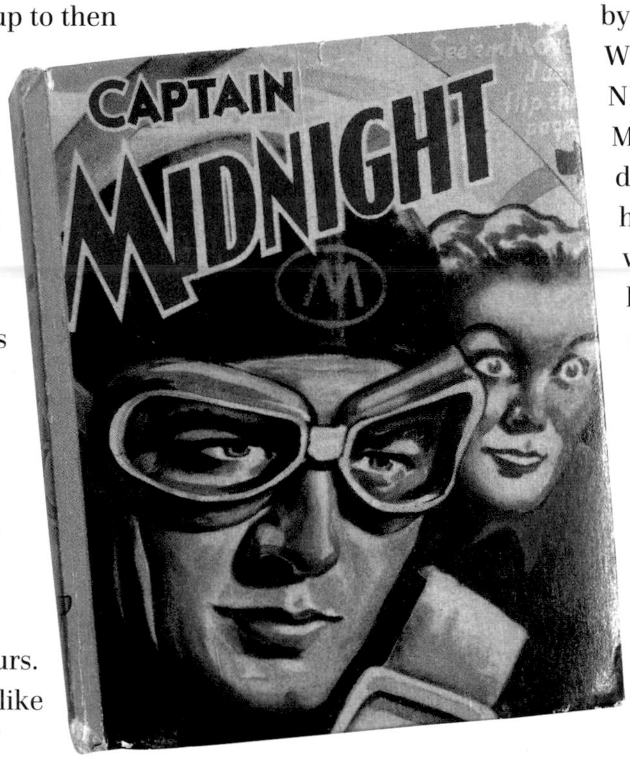
CAPTAIN
MIDNIGHT

A daredevil flying ace in World War II, the captain now headed an organization called the Secret Squadron. It was made up of pilots who were "hardy, adventuresome fellows who laughed at danger." His private air force, managed for him by a war buddy named Major Barry Steel, operated with the complete approval of the U.S. government and was initially devoted to combating spies, subversives, and saboteurs. The idea that an organization like the Secret Squadron was itself subversive and illegal apparently never occurred to Midnight and his colleagues.

Captain Midnight had two teenage wards, Chuck Ramsey and Joyce Ryan, who were both members of the Secret Squadron. A mechanic named Ichabod M. Mudd, usually called Ikky, provided airplane repairs as well as comic relief. On the radio show the major nemesis was a criminal mastermind named Ivan Shark. His daughter was even nastier than he was, as one might expect of a young woman christened Fury Shark. The Sharks recurred many times over the years to annoy the captain and his crew with their evil schemes.

As Captain Midnight's popularity grew, the character branched out into other areas. In 1941 he, the Secret Squadron, and the Shark family began appearing in both comic books and Big Little Books. The first BLB, entitled *Captain Midnight and the Secret Squadron*, was illustrated by Irwin L. Hess and written by Russ Winterbotham, who worked for the NEA newspaper syndicate. Hess drew Midnight as a mature fellow who dressed all in black, from airplane helmet to boots. His tunic had a winged clock across its chest. The hands of the clock, obviously, were set at midnight. Hess also drew a *Captain Midnight* newspaper strip that ran from 1942 to 1945.

Dell added a *Captain Midnight* story—ranging in length from six to ten pages—to each issue of *The Funnies*, starting with #57 (July 1941). Dan Gormley, who also drew funny animals, was the artist. His captain was more rugged-looking than Hess's and in these comic book excursions Captain Midnight wore a tan jacket with the midnight symbol emblazoned on its chest, plus an airplane helmet, riding pants, and boots. The character remained in *The Funnies* until the sixty-fourth issue, then was nudged out when the magazine, seeking a younger audience, became *New Funnies*. Gormley and the Secret Squadron moved briefly to *Popular Comics*.

In the autumn of 1942, Fawcett licensed the character and returned him to the newsstands in a complete book of his own. The captain, of course, retained that winged clock on his tunic. Midnight's real name was Albright, a fact not often mentioned on radio or in the earlier comic-book version. At his new home, however, he had, like many a costumed crimefighter, a dual identity. He was Captain Albright when in civvies and Captain Midnight when he suited up in his crimson costume. He was also able, because of a remarkable invention known as the gliderchute, to fly through the air without benefit of a plane.

The early artwork was provided by the Jack Binder sweatshop, the least inspired of any of the packagers of the era. It was bland and uninspired, the only exception being the series of exceptional covers provided intermittently by Mac Raboy. Later on, Leonard Frank undertook most of the interior art and the look of the magazine improved. After World War II Dan Barry worked on the feature. By that time the members of the Secret Squadron were all wearing uniforms and looking like rejects from a Blackhawk story. In the autumn of 1948, after the captain and his crew had been dabbling increasingly in science fiction adventures, the magazine changed its name to *Sweethearts* and commenced dispensing romance. The radio show ended the following year.

CAPTAIN TOOTSIE

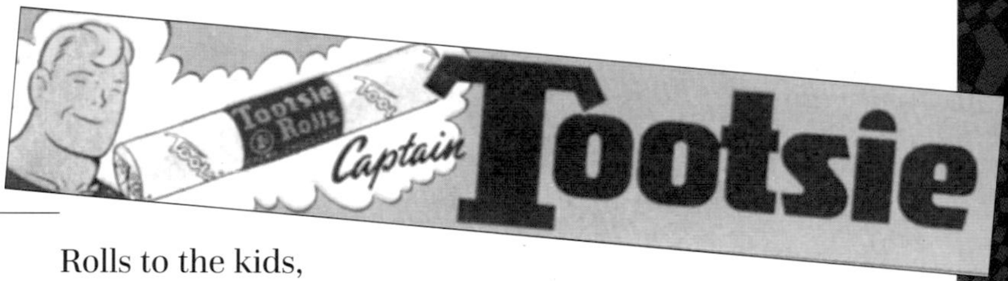

Tootsie Rolls
Captain Tootsie

■ An early example of the use of superheroes in advertising. As his name implies, the captain was a superhero dedicated to selling candy, and he was created directly for use in comic-book-format advertisements. He accomplished his huckstering of Tootsie Rolls in the 1940s and early 1950s in one-page ads for comic books and Sunday funnies sections. *Captain Tootsie* was drawn by C. C. Beck at the same time he was drawing the adventures of Captain Marvel. He had some help from artist Pete Costanza and editor/writer Rod Reed, both of whom also worked on the Marvel saga.

Captain Tootsie was pretty much a blond version of the *Whiz Comics* hero. The ads, done for the McCann-Erickson ad agency, began appearing in the middle 1940s, chiefly in Fawcett and DC comic books. The first in the series pitted the captain against Dr. Narsty, who was a full-grown version of Captain Marvel's favorite foe, the pint-sized Sivana. Tootsie palled around with a kid gang known as the Secret Legion. Rollo was the leader, and whenever Dr. Narsty or the Red Terror or a dangerous logjam showed up, he'd toot his Tootsie-Tooter, producing a "toootsieee!" sound. The blond captain would appear in a jiffy to clear up the problem. He'd then pass out Tootsie Rolls to the kids, explaining that they "will give you all EXTRA ENERGY for any job!" Obviously any confection containing chocolate and sugar would provide the promised "energy rush."

Beck and Costanza, who'd set up a studio in 1941, worked on Captain Tootsie for several years. When they dropped the ad strip in the late 1940s, a lesser artist took over. In 1950 Toby Press, a company owned by Al Capp and his two brothers, put out two issues of a *Captain Tootsie* comic book. Beck and Costanza had nothing to do with this.

Other huckster heroes found in comic books of the period included *Volto from Mars*, who sold "swell-tasting whole-grain Grape-Nuts Flakes" in one-pagers drawn by Frank Robbins and then Al Plastino; *The Adventures of "R.C." and Quickie*, drawn by Creig Flessel to sell Royal Crown Cola; the ninety-seven-pound weakling who tried Charles Atlas's Dynamic Tension and became a muscleman; *"Pepsi" the Pep*, drawn by Mal Eaton and later Graham Hunter; and *The Adventures of Sam Spade*, drawn by Lou Fine and plugging Wildroot Cream-Oil Hair Tonic, the sponsor of the CBS radio show of the same name.

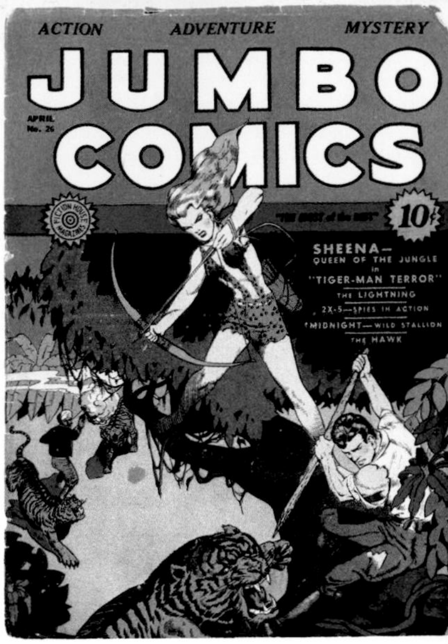
ACTION
ADVENTURE
MYSTERY
JUMBO COMICS
10¢
SHEENA—
QUEEN OF THE JUNGLE
"TIGER-MAN TERROR"
THE LIGHTNING
2X-5—SPIES IN ACTION
MIDNIGHT—WILD STALLION
THE HAWK

CARDY, NICK (1920–)

■ Still active as the twenty-first century commenced, Cardy drew his first comic-book pages in 1939. As Nick Viscardi, he wrote and drew the weekly four-page *Lady Luck* stories in *The Spirit* Sunday inserts. And for Fiction House, the home of Good Girl Art, he illustrated the adventures of such glamour girls as Senorita Rio, Jane Martin, and Camilla. By the time he returned from World War II service, he was signing himself Nick Cardy. In the middle 1950s he was working for DC and entering the most productive and impressive period of his career. Cardy had been good at the start, but unlike some of his colleagues he continued to improve.

Cardy drew *Rip Hunter*, *Congo Bill*, and *Tomahawk*, then revitalized *Aquaman*. By this time his style had developed even further and he was turning out some of the best illustrative stuff in comic books. In addition, Cardy was proving to be a first-rate and inventive cover artist. In discussing his approach to drawing a cover, Cardy once explained, "A cover is on the stands with maybe fifty other covers . . . so it's got to be interesting. So that's my practice on covers: very simple because that will jump out at you." He also illustrated most of the assorted Batman team-ups of the 1970s. But his major assignment was begun in 1965 with *The Teen Titans*.

Cardy has also done movie posters and commercial art. Still working at illustration, he now and then does a comic-book job. Recently he drew a cover for the fantasy title *Telos*.

CARLSON, GEORGE (1887–1962)

■ For a few years in the 1940s the veteran cartoonist, illustrator, and puzzlemaker George Carlson worked in comic books. It's for his contribution to *Jingle Jangle Comics*, a magazine seemingly aimed at very young readers, for which he's chiefly remembered. That and the fact that he did the dust jacket for *Gone With the Wind*.

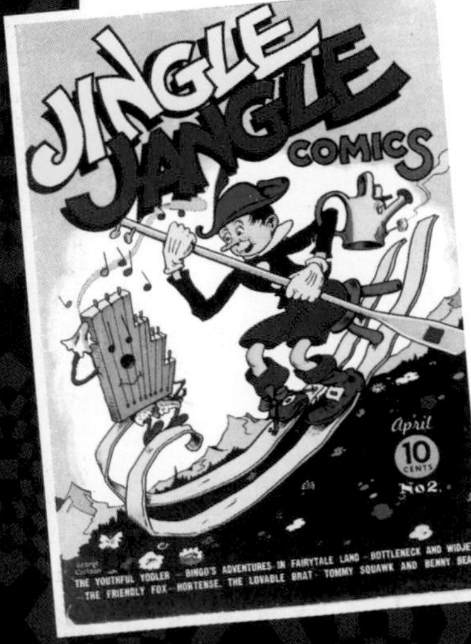
JINGLE JANGLE
COMICS
April
10 CENTS
No2.

The professional career of George Leonard Carlson began before World War I, and he sold gag cartoons to such humor magazines as *Judge*. He also turned out riddle and puzzle books for kids and was a regular contributor to *John Martin's Magazine*, a popular children's periodical. Carlson illustrated some of the Uncle Wiggily storybooks and produced several how-to books on cartooning. From the 1920s through the 1940s, he loaned Gene Byrnes a hand on his very successful *Reg'lar Fellers* newspaper strip, often ghosting it.

He had long been working on an idea for something he called *Jingle Jangle Tales*. Carlson tried selling it as both a Sunday comic page and a children's book, but with no success. Finally in 1942, Steve Douglas, editor of the pioneering *Famous Funnies*, bought it as a feature for a forthcoming new comic book. Douglas named the magazine *Jingle Jangle Comics* and *Jingle Jangle Tales* was the leadoff feature. Carlson also contributed a feature about a rather lamebrained fellow known as the Pie-Face Prince of Old Pretzleburg.

In his middle fifties, Carlson was apparently inspired to transcend the somewhat staid stuff he'd done earlier. Both his features blended burlesque, fantasy, and wordplay into a highly individual type of nonsense. He took a streetwise approach to fairy tales, obviously aware that he was dealing not only with the kids who were buying the comic book but also with the grown-ups who'd be reading the tales to them.

Jingle Jangle Comics, which remained a bimonthly, ended its run with the forty-second issue in 1949. Carlson returned to book illustration. In the years since, his comic-book work has gathered a small but loyal following. In a 1970 paean to him, Harlan Ellison wrote, "What he did was miraculous and happens only once in a particular art-form." The 1981 *A Smithsonian Book of Comic-Book Comics*, which included work by Jack Cole, Joe Shuster, Basil Wolverton, Carl Barks, Walt Kelly, and Will Eisner, reprinted two of Carlson's *Jingle Jangle Tales* and one adventure of the Pie-Face Prince. Coeditor Martin Williams said, "The achievement of his work in *Jingle Jangle Comics* is like Herriman's *Krazy Kat.*" He added that "what is called for next is a book collection of Carlson's best comic work–a book all to himself." That never happened.

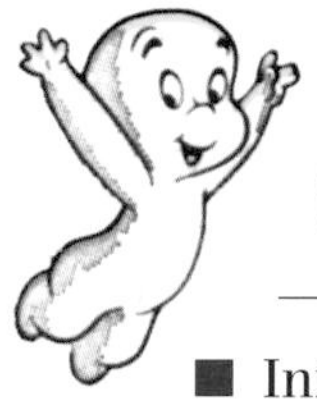

CASPER THE FRIENDLY GHOST

■ Initially more mild-mannered than even Clark Kent, Casper first materialized in comic books in 1949. He was introduced to the world in 1945 in an animated cartoon titled "The Friendly Ghost." The timid little spook was the joint creation of Sy Reit and Joe Oriolo, employees of Paramount's East Coast animation division at the time. The kid ghost didn't have a name at the outset and didn't get one until St. John Publications christened him for the first issue of their *Casper the Friendly Ghost* (September 1949). The Harvey organization took over the character in 1952 and did much better with him.

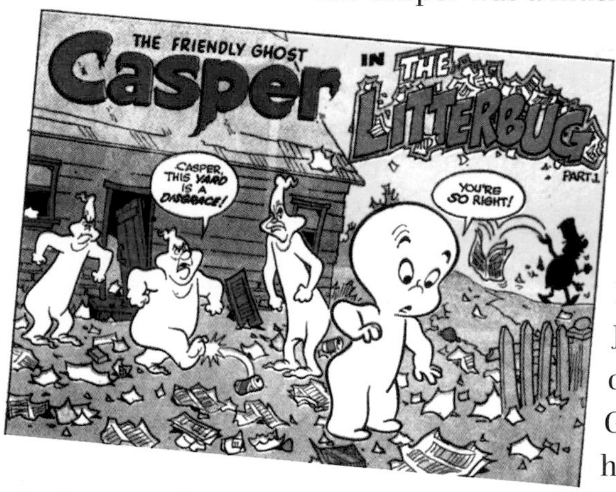
THE FRIENDLY GHOST
Casper
IN
THE LITTERBUG
PART 1
CASPER, THIS YARD IS A DISGRACE!
YOU'RE SO RIGHT!

Sid Jacobson became the editor with the second issue. The early stories were written and drawn by men who'd worked in the animation studio. Then the talented Warren Kremer became the regular artist. In a recent interview in *Comic Book Artist*, he explained, "Sid wanted somebody to draw *Casper* and he asked me. I said, 'I think I could do it' He said, 'Well, give it a shot.' So I started to draw." Kremer, who'd been doing adventure and horror stuff, got the job and was the main Casper artist for thirty-some years. He drew not only the majority of interior stories but also most of the covers. His Casper was a much more appealing and outgoing character. In appearance he looks somewhat like a thumbnail for Kremer's Richie Rich.

Very popular with young readers, as well as Warren Kremer fans, Casper continued under the Harvey banner into the 1990s. Jacobson and Kremer added such characters as Spooky, Wendy the Good Little Witch, and Casper's horse, Nightmare. The first two were spun off into series of their own. Casper himself was featured in over two dozen different Harvey titles, including several digests.

The personable spirit appeared in over fifty animated cartoons as well as on television shows. He was the star of a big-budget feature film in 1995. Marvel also published a limited run of a *Casper* title.

THE CAT-MAN

■ Like Tarzan, he was raised in the jungle by wild animals. In David Merryweather's case the animals were tigers and the jungle was in India. After his parents were killed by "jungle wild men" and he was left for dead, young David was "nurtured by a tigress." When he finally returned to civilization as an adult, he found himself "endowed with the attributes of the cat family." This meant that as Cat-Man he could "climb the steepest cliffs, see in the dark, scale trees and building. . . . And most important of all, he was endowed with nine lives."

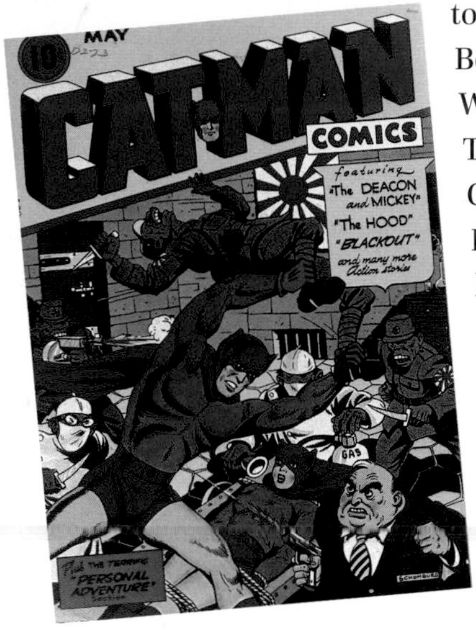
MAY
CAT-MAN
COMICS
featuring
"The DEACON and MICKEY"
"The HOOD"
"BLACKOUT"
and many more action stories
GAS
"PERSONAL ADVENTURE"

Introduced in *Crash Comics* #4 (September 1940), the Cat-Man proceeded to lose a life per issue. Fortunately for him the magazine lasted only one more issue. When he returned the next year in his own *Cat-Man Comics*, his speedometer had been set back and he had nine lives to use up again. Originally a product of the Bert Whitman shop, *Cat-Man* was drawn by Whitman and then by a young Irwin Hasen. The chief artist in the new magazine was Charles Quinlan, followed by Bob Fujitani. Fairly early on it was realized that if Cat-Man lost a life an issue, there'd be a blank spot around issue #10 and that gimmick was forgotten. Merryweather joined the army in 1941 and also became the guardian of a tough little blonde girl of ten or eleven. She became his costumed sidekick Kitten and by the middle 1940s had blossomed into a teenager. The magazine ceased after its thirty-second issue in 1946. The last round of covers were by that inventive believer in basic colors, L. B. Cole.

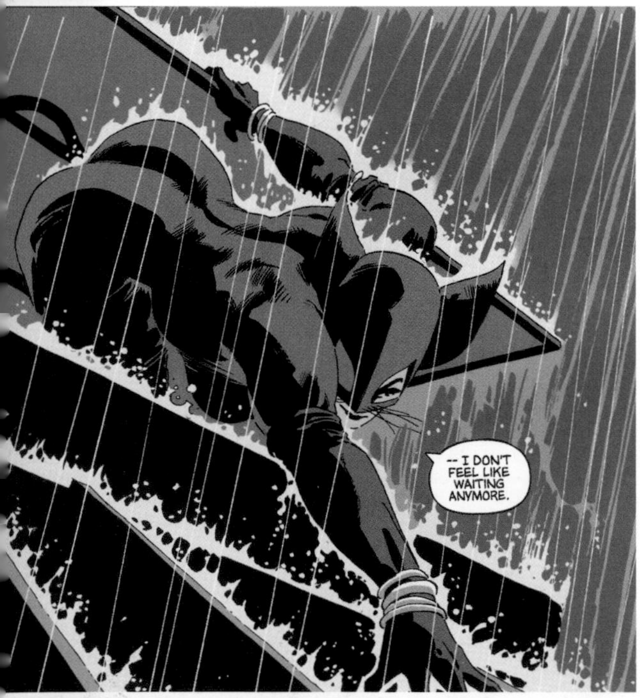
-- I DON'T FEEL LIKE WAITING ANYMORE.

CATWOMAN

■ A character with a lifespan nearly matching that of Batman, she began her career in *Batman* #1 early in 1940 and is still going strong, albeit much changed from her jewel-thief days. She challenged the Dark Knight in *Detective Comics*, *Batman,* and just about every other magazine he ever hung out in. Since the late 1980s, she has had three separate magazines of her own. For over sixty years one thing has remained constant, she is still *the* woman in Batman's life. In fact, in one of DC's now defunct parallel worlds she and Batman were the parents of a young girl who grew up to become the Huntress.

In that first issue of *Batman*, Selina Kyle met Batman on a yacht while she was attempting to swipe an emerald necklace worth a half million dollars. Disguised as a little old lady, Catwoman (known simply as the Cat in her maiden voyage) succeeded in swiping the necklace. Batman intervened,

DON'T.
WE'VE DONE THIS DANCE FOR A LONG TIME. TOO LONG.
AREN'T YOU AT *ALL* CURIOUS?

unmasked her, and retrieved it. While he returns to shore with her in a motor launch, he allows her to escape. Robin is not pleased. In fact, throughout the years he acts as the voice of conscience whenever Selina is around, a sort of oversized Jiminy Cricket. Batman remarks, "Lovely girl! . . . What eyes! . . . Maybe we'll bump into her again sometime." This he most certainly did. In various costumes and with varying attitudes toward crime, Catwoman has recurred innumerable times since that first fateful meeting. Sometimes she's been relatively sedate; sometimes she looks and acts like a dominatrix, complete with whip. The camp television show of the 1960s made frequent use of her.

DC
BRUBAKER
COOKE
ALLRED
Cat woman
1
dccomics.com
DIRECT SALES
$2.50 US $4.25 CAN

Catwoman entered a pinup phase early in 1989 when DC introduced a new *Catwoman* title. Now a full-figured woman in a skin-tight purple costume and black hip boots, she slinked around Gotham City mixing burglary with altruism. Jim Balent, who was not exactly first-rate at drawing buildings, automobiles, weapons, ordinary people, or even Batman, seemed to have only one artistic area in which he excelled and that was drawing Catwoman's large bosom. Popular with pinup fans, the series lasted for ninety-four issues and ended in 2001.

Fortunately, Selina was introduced to writer Ed Brubaker, and this changed her life for the better. Brubaker completely revised the Catwoman's world, adding noir elements and using a much more realistic and sophisticated approach to storytelling. Selina Kyle became slim, wore a new, more practical costume, and was seen as much in her private life as she was prowling housetops. Several talented artists have drawn the new *Catwoman* series, which began late in 2001. Among them Darwyn Cooke and Mike Allred, Brad Rader, Cameron Stewart, and Javier Pulido. In her new life, Catwoman is on relatively good terms with Batman and has also had a long-running affair with weather-beaten private eye, Slam Bradley. That recently ended, but the magazine continues. And Catwoman will be joining the many comic-book properties being translated into movie stars.

One thing I'll never get used to about the past is that it's never really over...
...Just when you think that your history is done-- locked away, forgotten...
RELENTLESS PART TWO
ED BRUBAKER WRITER
ARTIST
COLORIST
SEAN KONOT LETTERER
JG JONES AND PAUL MOUNTS COVER ARTISTS
NACHIE CASTRO ASSISTANT EDITOR
MATT IDELSON EDITOR
And I've spent so much of my life escaping in one way or another, it's hard to accept that there are traps even I get caught in from time to time.
But here it is-- This week two people from my past, who I thought I'd never see again, have both shown up in the East End...
TMP
One of them, Sylvia Sinclair, is partially responsible for who I am today, whether she knows it or not...
And I have to admit, I'm actually glad to see her again.
The other, though...
... I don't honestly know how I feel about.

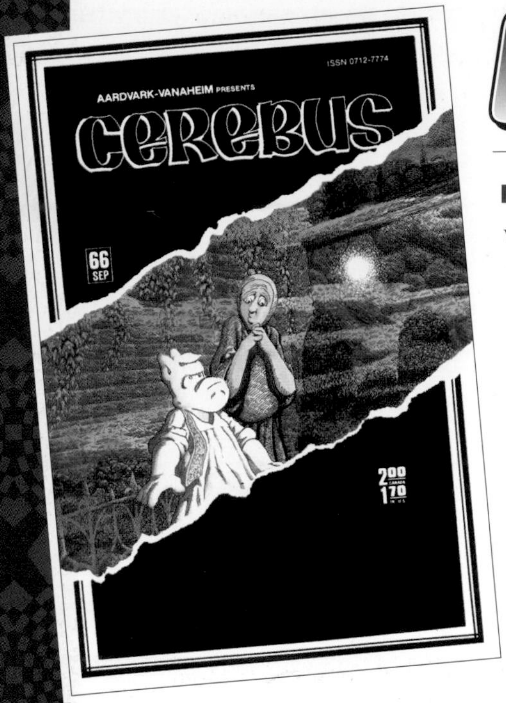
ISSN 0712-7774
AARDVARK-VANAHEIM PRESENTS
CEREBUS
66
SEP

CEREBUS

■ The most successful aardvark in comics, he's been around since 1977. Created, written, and drawn by Dave Sim, who is obsessed not only with aardvarks but Groucho Marx, *Cerebus the Aardvark* has been published from the beginning by Sim's own Aardvark-Vanneheim outfit. Begun as a sort of spoof of Conan and all the other comic-book barbarians, Cerebus—whose name is derived from a misspelling of Cerberus, the three-headed dog who guards the gates of hell—has branched out to offer satire on politics, popular culture, and society in general and espouse what some critics consider a misogynist point of view.

When he began *Cerebus*, Sim announced that he intended to produce three hundred issues and something like six thousand pages about his aardvark. After working on the saga for a quarter of a century, he expected to reach his goal sometime in 2004. In addition to regular issues, Sim has also published fat *Cerebus* reprint collections.

CHADWICK, PAUL

■ See CONCRETE.

CHALLENGERS OF THE UNKNOWN

■ Jack Kirby usually had good luck with teams, going as far back as the Boy Commandos. This grown-up team of heroes was created for DC and made its debut in *Showcase* #6 (February 1957). They moved into their own comic book in 1958 and continued to challenge the unknown, with time out for a few extended leaves over the next several decades. Since they had no special powers, they had to rely on their wits and diversified abilities to wage their campaign against odd and unusual villainy.

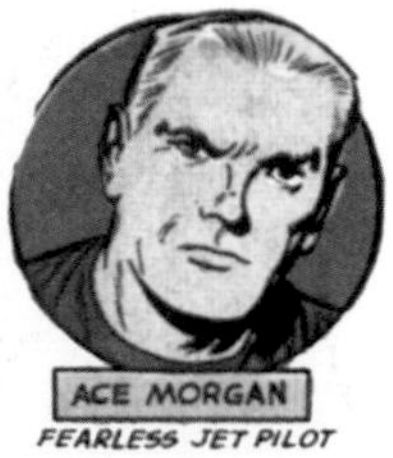
ACE MORGAN
FEARLESS JET PILOT

The group consisted of Ace Morgan, fearless jet pilot; Prof Haley, master deep-sea diver; Red Ryan, famed mountain climber; and Rocky Davis, Olympic wrestling champ—"Four strangers who escaped death when their plane crashed on the way to a ceremony honoring them for individual acts of heroism." As the copy further explained, "Knowing that they were living on borrowed time, the four men banded together to form . . . a group dedicated to exploring things that other men dare not." The Challs decked themselves out in purple jumpsuits when in their team phase. During the early years, they were joined by June Robbins, "a young adventuress and computer expert," who worked alongside them but was never an official member. The team faced an unsettling succession of unusual challenges. One issue they'd be captured by aliens who'd stick them in a space

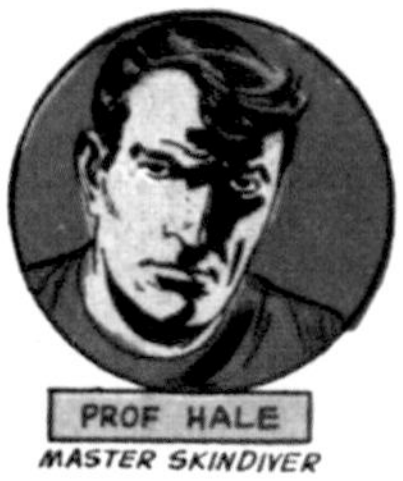
PROF HALE
MASTER SKINDIVER

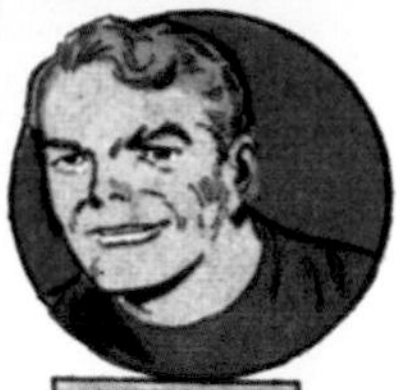

RED RYAN
MOUNTAIN CLIMBER

circus, the next they'd travel back in time and get dragooned into helping build the pyramids.

Ever restless, Kirby abandoned the Challengers after the eighth issue of their magazine. On Kirby's last five issues, Wally Wood served as inker. Various scripters followed and Bob Brown provided the artwork after Kirby's departure.

The title continued until 1969, returning again in 1973 and 1979. During one phase the Challs took to appearing in red-and-gold costumes that made them look more like superheroes. Later they returned to their purple togs, but added an hourglass symbol on the tunic. The team was revived by DC for an eight-issue run in 1991. Writer Jeph Loeb and artist Tim Sale, in their first collaboration, produced the feature. The Challengers name was assigned to a new bunch for an eighteen-issue run that commenced in 1997.

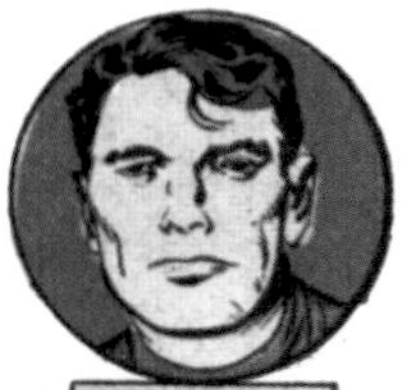

ROCKY DAVIS
OLYMPIC WRESTLING CHAMPION

CHARLIE CHAN

■ The epigrammatic Oriental sleuth appeared in comic books of one kind and another from 1939 to 1966. Before he ever set foot in a comic book, Charlie Chan had appeared in six novels, nearly a dozen movies, and a radio show. Created by Earl Derr Biggers, the Hawaiian detective began life in 1925, when the first Charlie Chan novel was serialized in *The Saturday Evening Post.* In 1931, after several false starts, a new movie Chan in the person of Warner Oland reached the screen. Swedish actor Oland, who'd played everything from Al Jolson's father in *The Jazz Singer* to Fu Manchu, proved a very popular Charlie Chan, and 20th Century Fox began a series of films. When Oland died in 1938, he was replaced by Sidney Toler.

Alfred Andriola, with considerable help, turned *Charlie Chan* into a newspaper strip for the McNaught Syndicate in 1938. His Chan looked like Oland, and he added the #1 Son character, who had been invented for the movies and played by Keye Luke. The following year *Feature Funnies*, owned in part by McNaught, commenced running reprints of the Andriola strip. When *Big Shot Comics* began in 1940, Chan and Son moved there to remain until 1947, long after the strip had stopped appearing in newspapers.

The next year, the Prize Group started an original material *Charlie Chan* comic book. Joe Simon and Jack Kirby drew the covers and Carmine Infantino drew most of the interior yarns. Charles Raab, who'd assisted on the strip, also drew some. This Chan title lasted for five issues. Charlton revived it in the middle 1950s, adding Chan's chauffeur Birmingham, played in the later low-budget Monogram Chans by black comedian Mantan Moreland.

DC joined the parade in 1958 with *The New Adventures of Charlie Chan*, drawn by Gil Kane and Sid Greene. This Charlie was slimmer, in order to match J. Carrol Naish, who was playing him on a syndicated TV series of the same name. Chan was plump again in the two issues of *Charlie Chan* drawn by Frank Springer that Dell tried in the middle 1960s. That constituted his last bow.

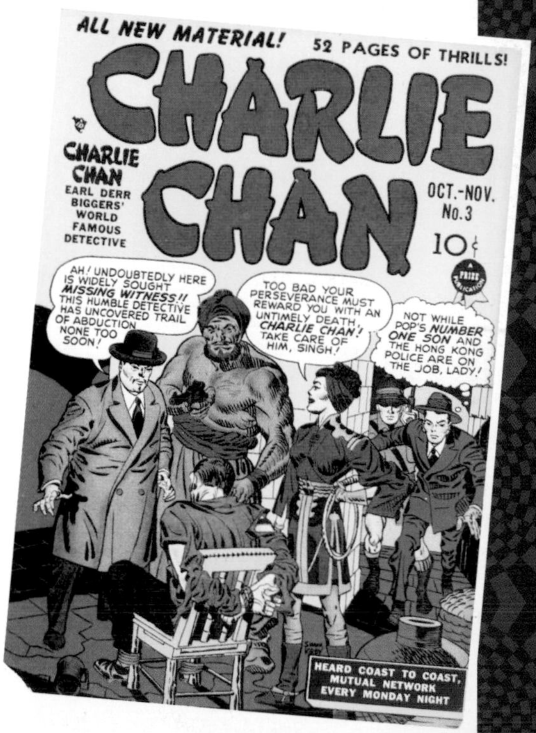
ALL NEW MATERIAL!
52 PAGES OF THRILLS!
CHARLIE CHAN
CHARLIE CHAN
EARL DERR BIGGERS' WORLD FAMOUS DETECTIVE
OCT.-NOV. No.3
10¢
AH! UNDOUBTEDLY HERE IS WIDELY SOUGHT MISSING WITNESS!! THIS HUMBLE DETECTIVE HAS UNCOVERED TRAIL OF ABDUCTION NONE TOO SOON!
TOO BAD YOUR PERSEVERANCE MUST REWARD YOU WITH AN UNTIMELY DEATH, CHARLIE CHAN! TAKE CARE OF HIM, SINGH!
NOT WHILE POP'S NUMBER ONE SON AND THE HONG KONG POLICE ARE ON THE JOB, LADY!
HEARD COAST TO COAST, MUTUAL NETWORK EVERY MONDAY NIGHT

CHAYKIN, HOWARD (1950–)

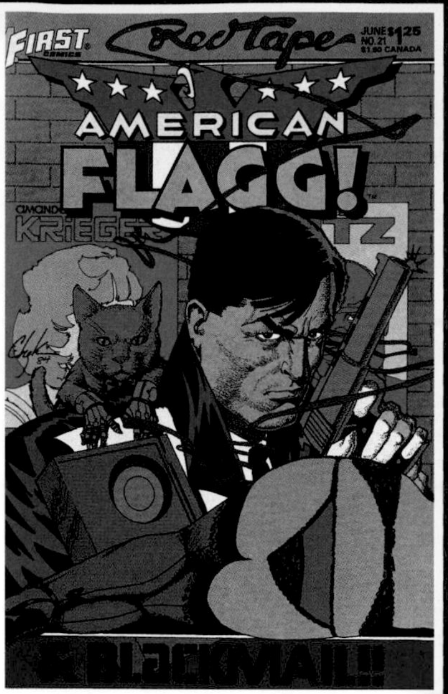
FIRST
JUNE $1.25
NO. 21
$1.60 CANADA
AMERICAN
FLAGG!
BLACKMAIL!!

■ During his apprentice years Chaykin served as an assistant to Gil Kane, Wally Wood, and Gray Morrow and learned something from each of them. By 1972 he was on his own, starting out at Marvel to draw *Star Wars.* He moved to DC to draw the short-lived *Sword of Sorcery.* Restless and independent, he tried a variety of other projects, creating a character called Cody Starbuck and also turning out one of the earliest American graphic novels when he adapted Alfred Bester's *The Stars My Destination.*

In 1983 Chaykin made his first great leap forward, writing and drawing *American Flagg!* for First Comics. An attractive blend of political satire and science fiction, it chronicled the adventures of Reuben Flagg, a futuristic lawman, his talking cat Raul, and quite a few pretty, and sometimes nasty, women.

He's also moved in and out of Hollywood scriptwriting over the years. And he wrote and drew *Power & Glory* for Malibu Comics in the early 1990s, wrote and drew the mature audience *Black Kiss,* and did a relatively grown-up version of *Blackhawk.* In recent years Chaykin has written both *American Century* and a Vertigo update of *Angel and the Ape.* His drawing ability continues to develop, and he has one of the most distinctive styles in comics. He once summed up his feelings about comic books by saying, "I love the idea of comics, but I'm not very interested in superheroes."

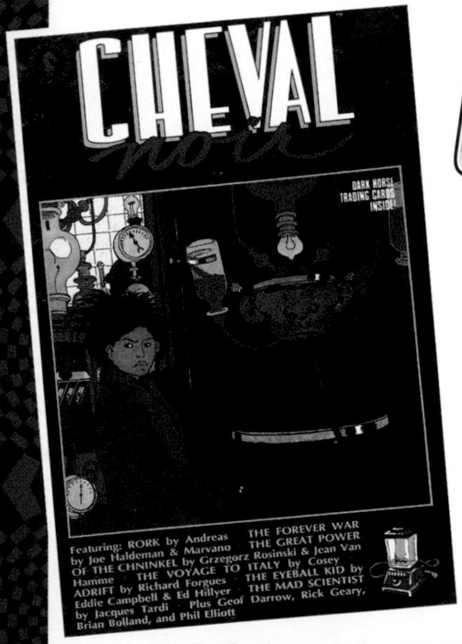
CHEVAL
DARK HORSE TRADING CARDS INSIDE!
Featuring: RORK by Andreas · THE FOREVER WAR by Joe Haldeman & Marvano · THE GREAT POWER OF THE CHNINKEL by Grzegorz Rosinski & Jean Van Hamme · THE VOYAGE TO ITALY by Cosey · ADRIFT by Richard Forgues · THE EYEBALL KID by Eddie Campbell & Ed Hillyer · THE MAD SCIENTIST by Jacques Tardi · Plus Geof Darrow, Rick Geary, Brian Bolland, and Phil Elliott

CHEVAL NOIR

■ A noble experiment on the part of Dark Horse Comics, this black-and-white title reprinted English translations of notable European comic-book features along with some off-trail American stuff. The first issue appeared in the summer of 1989 and included work by Phillipe Druillet, Jacques Tardi, and Francois Schuiten. The cover was by Dave Stevens.

Later issues featured such artists as Moebius, Daniel Torres, Eddie Campbell, Rick Geary, and Mike Kaluta. Several of Tardi's excellent graphic novels about early twentieth-century journalist/detective Adele Blanc-Sec were serialized in *Cheval Noir,* as was one of Moebius's Lt. Blueberry titles. In the second issue publisher/editor Mike Richardson told readers, "You probably won't see too many costume heroes running around in these pages. . . . No Batman or Wolverine. Don't worry, though; after reading the stories presented in *Cheval Noir* we don't think you'll miss them too much. In fact, we think you'll enjoy the change."

The magazine showcased some of the best overseas material for over four years. After the fiftieth issue (January 1994), it ceased publication. Then editor Jennie Bricker promised, "*Cheval Noir* will rise again!" But that never happened.

CHO, FRANK (1971–)

An excellent cartoonist and illustrator, Cho has said more than once, "I like drawing sexy women." He's also admitted, "Anything with monkeys I'm a fan of." Both of these interests are on display in his *Liberty Meadows.*

Cho's road to success was a relatively smooth one. Born in South Korea, he moved with his parents to the United States when he was six. While attending the University of Maryland, he created a comic strip titled *University 2* for the school paper. After he graduated in 1996, he continued the feature for Creators Syndicate under the title *Liberty Meadows.* The following year Frank Cho formed the Insights Studio Group to reprint the strip in a black-and-white comic-book form. Although the strip recently ended, the *Liberty Meadows* comic book continues.

The foremost and most popular character in the strip is the dark-haired Brandy, who meets Cho's definition of a sexy woman. She's employed at an animal sanctuary named Liberty Meadows and associates not only with humans but a crew of talking animals. These include a cigarette-smoking pig named Dean and a straw hat–wearing frog named Leslie. Among the humans is a smitten young fellow named Frank, who is not a portrait of the artist. When Cho himself does appear, it is in the form of an articulate monkey. Cho also draws all the covers, which often bear a resemblance to the artwork featured on pinup calendars in the remote past.

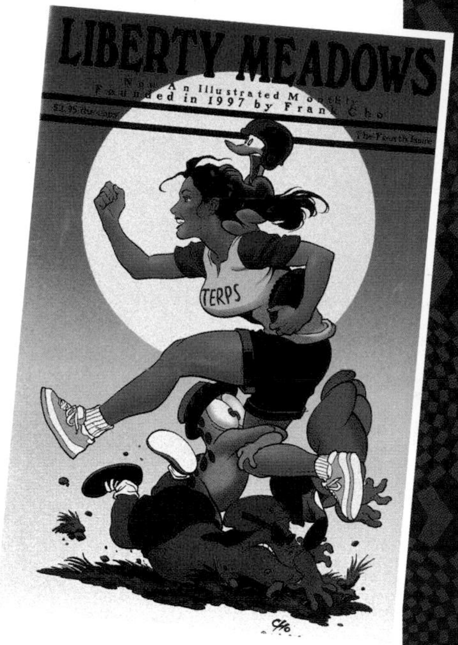
LIBERTY MEADOWS
TERPS

CHRISTMAN, BERT (1915–1942)

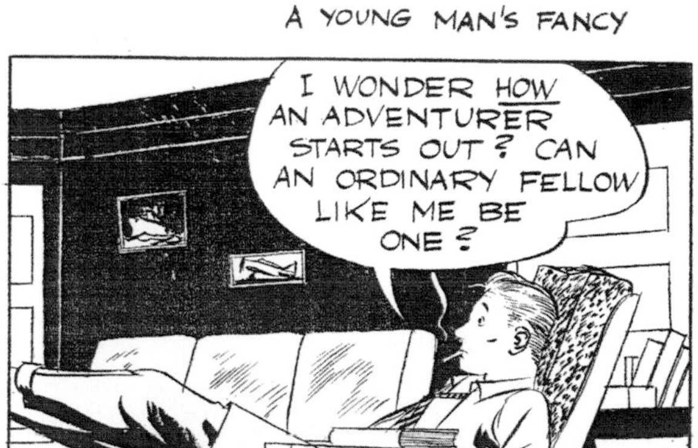
A YOUNG MAN'S FANCY
I WONDER HOW AN ADVENTURER STARTS OUT? CAN AN ORDINARY FELLOW LIKE ME BE ONE?
BERT CHRISTMAN

The first artist to draw the original Sandman, Christman illustrated the debut story in the 1939 issue of DC's *New York World's Fair Comics* and then four subsequent stories in *Adventure Comics*, beginning in #40 (July 1939). Although the prolific Gardner Fox is credited with writing the scripts, it's obvious that Christman had considerable input. The two young men shared the pen name Larry Dean.

Christman gets a few lines in most histories of comic books and comic strips. Usually, however, not for his drawing ability but because he was a war hero, a Flying Tigers volunteer who was killed over Burma in the second month of World War II. He was about twenty when he went to New York City from his hometown of Fort Collins, Colorado, in the middle 1930s. Although he majored in mechanical engineering at Colorado State, his longtime ambition was to be a cartoonist. His other great interest was aviation. He arrived in

Manhattan in the summer of 1936. After working for a small publishing outfit, Christman was hired by the Associated Press for their art bullpen. When Noel Sickles quit *Scorchy Smith*, an airplane adventure strip, Christman took it over. He was also able to sell stuff to some of the original-material comic books that had started up. He contributed to *Detective Picture Stories*, *Funny Pages*, and *Keen Detective Funnies*. His first work for DC was a one-shot titled "The Lucky Ring" in *Adventure* #33 (December 1938). Because of his training on *Scorchy* and the influence of Sickles, the young artist was now turning out work that was considerably more sophisticated than that usually on display in comic books, utilizing layouts and shots that weren't common then.

For *Action Comics* he began *The Three Aces* in #18 (November 1939). An out-and-out flying feature, it dealt with "three winged soldiers-of-fortune, who pledge themselves to a new kind of adventure. They roam the globe, working for peace and sanity." He signed the pen name Christopher to this one.

Peace and sanity weren't in strong supply in the late 1930s and, as the United States drew closer to entering World War II, Christman joined the navy as a flying cadet. By the summer of 1938, he was in Pensacola and eventually he served in the scouting squadron of the aircraft carrier *Ranger*. Eventually he joined the American Volunteer Group. As idealistic as the Three Aces, he told one of his sisters at the time, "People of the United States don't know the meaning of patriotism yet, but they will. It takes a severe shock to jolt them." The AVG, better known as the Flying Tigers, was assembled by U.S. Colonel Claire Chenault to help the Chinese defend the Burma Road. Christman soon saw action against the Japanese.

Just when he turned out *The Sandman* and *The Three Aces* isn't clear. Judging by the dates that he enlisted and was sent to Pensacola, it's evident he was already in the navy when both these features appeared. The obvious conclusion is that he did the DC work while on leave or in whatever spare time a navy cadet might have.

Though Christman was slightly wounded in combat in 1942, his enthusiasm remained high. He wrote to his former AP editor that, "When 'this' is over I'm sure I'll be content again to sit at a drawing board and pen my experiences and those of my friends in an authentic aviation strip." He was killed on his third combat mission over Burma, machine-gunned by a Japanese plane after he bailed out of his P-40.

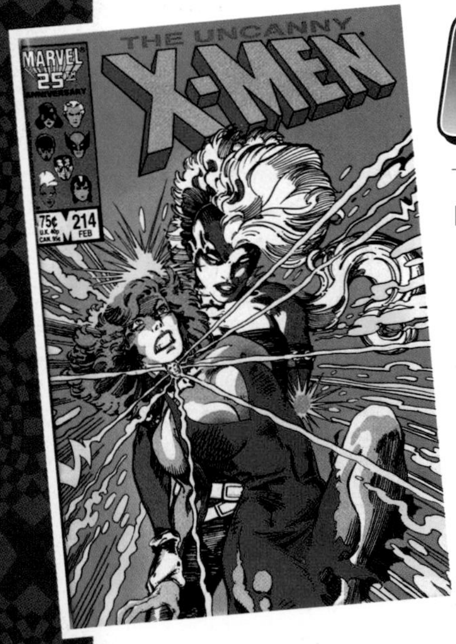
THE UNCANNY
X-MEN
MARVEL
214

CLAREMONT, CHRIS (c. 1953-)

■ He wrote the script for the best-selling comic book of all time, and that's only one of his many accomplishments. British-born, Claremont started working for comics in the early 1970s. He rapidly became one of the most inventive and most popular writers in the field. For a long spell he was Marvel's resident mutant expert, putting in seventeen years writing *Uncanny X-Men* and cocreating titles like *New Mutants*. He also wrote scripts for *Wolverine*, *Excalibur*, and *Captain Britain*. Moving away from Marvel, Claremont wrote for DC and Dark Horse, among others. He returned to Marvel to write the new *X-Men* #1 in 1991, with the extremely popular Jim Lee doing the artwork. The book, issued with four different covers, sold over 8 million–odd copies. That's a figure that's not likely to be equaled. Claremont, who's also written science fiction and fantasy novels, is currently scripting *The Fantastic Four*.

CLASSIC COMICS/CLASSICS ILLUSTRATED

■ The idea of adapting famous, and public domain, works of fiction to comic books is nearly as old as original-material comics. The pioneering Major Malcolm Wheeler-Nicholson included episodes of *A Tale of Two Cities*, *Ivanhoe*, *She*, and *Treasure Island* in his *More Fun* and *New Comics* in the middle 1930s. In the summer of 1941, *Target Comics* started running another version of *Treasure Island.* A few months later *Classic Comics* appeared on the nation's newsstands.

Albert Kanter had been a real estate broker, a traveling salesman, and a manufacturer of toy telegraph sets. In 1941 he was doing business in Manhattan as Elliot Publishing. Later publicity releases explained that Kanter had been impressed by the "furor in newspaper editorials and from Parent-Teacher organizations about the terrible effect that so-called 'horror' and 'blood and thunder' comics were having on juvenile minds." He thereupon conceived, so the story went, that notion of adapting literary classics to comic-book format. Mayer Kaplan, who worked as a bookkeeper and later as an editor for Kanter, once said, "I think it was purely a brilliant business decision. Comics were taking hold . . . I'm sure Albert Kanter had looked at it and said, 'What can we do in this format—which is growing like wildfire—that is different from what anyone else is doing?'" What Kanter did, after taking on two partners to provide additional financing, was to start publishing *Classic Comics.*

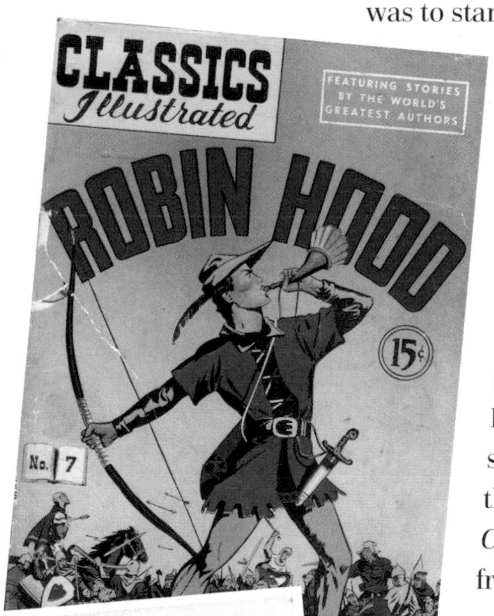
CLASSICS
Illustrated
FEATURING STORIES BY THE WORLD'S GREATEST AUTHORS
ROBIN HOOD
15¢
No. 7

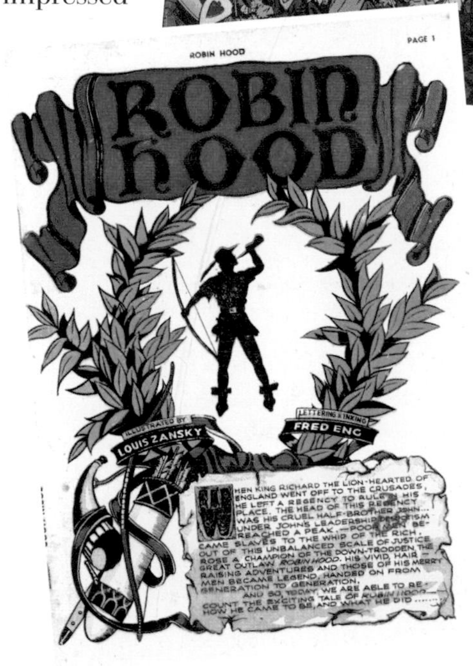
ROBIN HOOD
PAGE 1
ROBIN HOOD
LOUIS ZANSKY
FRED ENG

Left out of the latter day accounts of the magazine's birth is Lloyd Jacquet and his Funnies, Inc., shop. They'd been packaging *Target Comics* and producing the adaptations of *Treasure Island* and later *Gulliver's Travels* and *The Last of the Mohicans.* It seems quite probable that Jacquet pitched Kanter the idea of doing something similar. At any rate, just about all the artists who drew for *Classic Comics* during its first years were from Jacquet's shop.

The first title was *The Three Musketeers*, drawn by Malcolm Kildale. The initial print run was 200,000 copies, a relatively modest one for that period. Funnies, Inc., didn't provide its best artists—no doubt because Kanter was not paying top rates. Men like Kildale, Allen Simon, and Louis Zansky were second-rate at best, and, when rushing as they obviously were here, the results were far from compelling. The scripts, which Kaplan said were by Evelyn Goodman, "art director, secretary, script director," were not impressive. *Huckleberry Finn*, for example, was told in the third person in the *Classic Comics* version. *Ivanhoe*, *A Tale of Two Cities*, and *Moby Dick* also suffered.

Even so, the line caught on, possibly because kids discovered they could base book reports on the adaptations, as bad as they were, and thus save considerable reading time. The overall look improved in the middle 1940s, when Jerry Iger's shop took over production. The first title Iger packaged was *Oliver Twist*, #23 in the series and originally published in the summer of 1945. Artists such as Bob Webb and Matt Baker, who'd been drawing somewhat sexier material in the pages of *Jumbo Comics*, *Fight Comics*, etc., now started drawing *Two Years Before the Mast*, *Frankenstein*, and *Lorna Doone*. Henry Kiefer and Alex Blum, two of the busiest hacks in the 1940s, also drew many adaptations. Iger's partner Ruth Roche wrote most of the scripts. In the middle 1950s, Iger ended his association with the series and from then on Kanter relied on freelancers, including such former EC regulars as Joe Orlando, George Evans, and Graham Ingels.

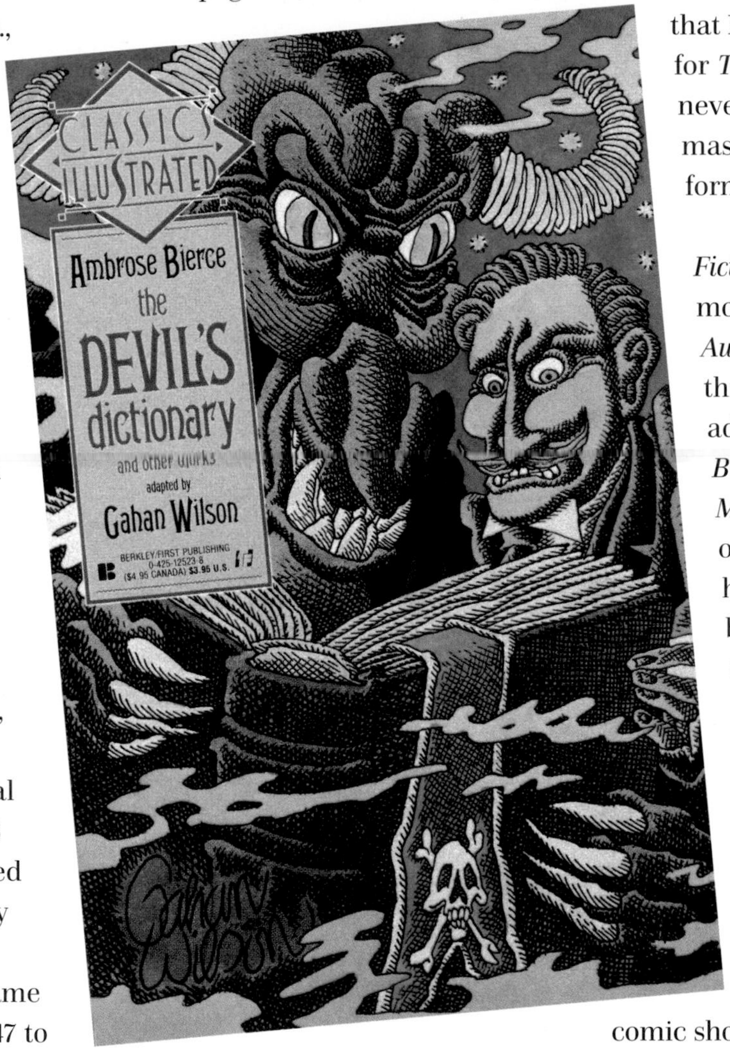
CLASSICS ILLUSTRATED
Ambrose Bierce
the
DEVIL'S
dictionary
and other works
adapted by
Gahan Wilson
BERKLEY/FIRST PUBLISHING
Gahan Wilson

Unlike other comic books, these were kept in print, and each title went through several editions. An account in a 1946 issue of *Publishers Weekly* stated that by that time the company had sold "about one hundred million of its 28 titles." The name of the line was changed in 1947 to *Classics Illustrated*, when the adaptation of *The Last Days of Pompeii* was issued. Under the new logo, classics were issued regularly until 1962.

Kanter never had much competition. Dell tried its own line of adaptations in 1942. Called *Famous Stories*, the series lasted only two issues, doing the ever popular *Treasure Island* and *Tom Sawyer*. In 1946 Jacquet attempted to set up the Bookomic Book Club, which would offer "REAL BOOKS in the modern cartoon-strip technique . . . done by fine artists . . . beautifully bound for permanence." His comic-book ads offered a complimentary copy of *Masterpieces Illustrated*, a sampler of things to come. This freebie recycled the three serialized adaptations that Harold DeLay had drawn for *Target Comics*. The club never materialized, and no masterpieces in cartoon-strip format were ever issued.

Later in the 1940s, *Fast Fiction*, later calling itself the more stately *Stories by Famous Authors*, began. It made it through thirteen issues, doing adaptations of such works as *Beau Geste*, *Scaramouche*, and *Macbeth*. Kiefer worked for this outfit, too. In the 1970s Marvel had a brief fling with good books and did three dozen *Classic Comics* of its own.

Late in 1989, a partnership between First Comics, Berkley Books, and the Classics Media Group launched a new series of *Classics Illustrated*. These were in the trade paperback format and sold for $3.95 in comic shops and bookstores. The early adaptations included *Great Expectations*, *The Scarlet Letter*, *Moby Dick*, and, of course, *Treasure Island*. A great deal better looking than most that had previously appeared under the *Classics Illustrated* umbrella, these comics boasted artwork by Bill Sienkiewicz, Dan Spiegle, Rick Geary, Kyle Baker, and Gahan Wilson. The line did not succeed, however, and by 1991 had ceased publication.

CLOAK AND DAGGER

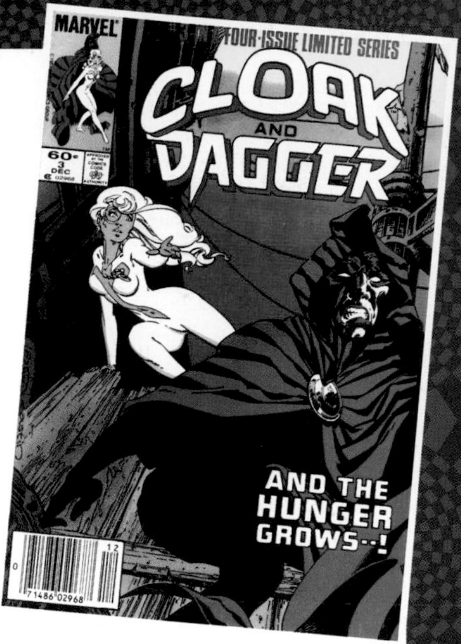
MARVEL
FOUR-ISSUE LIMITED SERIES
CLOAK AND DAGGER
60¢
3
DEC
AND THE HUNGER GROWS--!

■ A comic book that combined mutant fantasy with mean-streets reality, Marvel's *Cloak and Dagger* first appeared in 1983 as a four-part series. Its two resident superheroes were Tyrone Johnson (Cloak) and Tandy Bowen (Dagger). Both runaway teens and homeless street kids, they first bumped into each other in Manhattan and, because of one of those strange accidents that seem continually to befall comic-book characters, they became a team of oddly empowered vigilantes. Bill Mantlo was the initial writer, Rick Leonardi the first artist.

Kidnapped by crooked pharmacists, the African-American Tyrone and the blond Tandy were used as guinea pigs in the secret testing of a new illegal synthetic narcotic. The stuff had a few flaws and killed all the other homeless runaways who had taken part in the experiment. But Tandy and Tyrone were converted into instant mutants. Tyrone became a shadowy figure radiating darkness—he also seemed to carry a portable black hole around inside his cloak and could stuff evildoers into it to send them off into a distant, dark dimension.

Tandy became a source of light and developed the ability to hurl damaging daggers of intense electricity at her opponents. As Cloak and Dagger, they joined forces on a rather puritanical crusade against porn shops, wealthy wastrels, and such. Marvel brought them back in assorted limited series through the 1980s and into the 1990s, including a run under the snappy title *The Mutant Misadventures of Cloak and Dagger*. The duo returned again at the end of 2003.

THE CLOCK

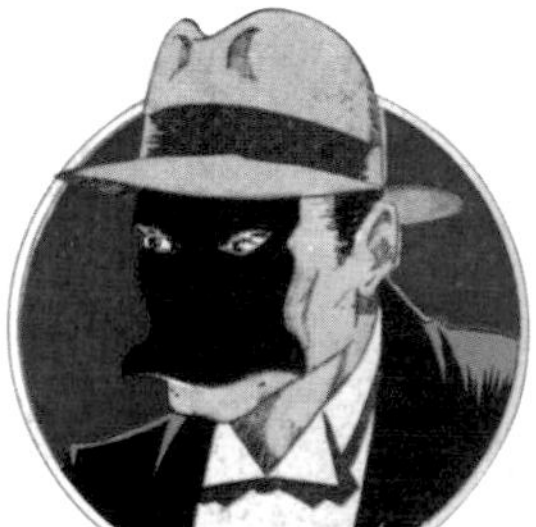

■ The first original masked hero to appear in comic books, the Clock's crimefighting costume consisted of a tuxedo, a gray fedora, and a black silken mask that covered his entire face. Sometimes he carried a cane. George E. Brenner, who wrote and drew his adventures, had obviously been influenced by such pulp-fiction mystery men as the Phantom Detective, the Spider, and the Shadow, and also the novels about the Saint. After solving a case, the Clock left his calling card behind. It showed the face of a timepiece and bore the line "The Clock has struck."

Brenner's dapper sleuth first struck in the November 1936 issues of both *Funny Pages* and *Funny Picture Stories*. Like so many comic-book masked men to come, the Clock was in reality a wealthy young sportsman and amateur criminologist. His civilian name was Brian O'Brien. Toward the end of 1937, the Clock moved into *Feature Comics* for a long stay. He then switched to *Crack Comics*. Everett "Busy" Arnold was responsible for the Clock showing up in the latter two titles. Arnold had been the printer for the earlier comics, and when he started his Quality line, he hired Brenner.

For the run in *Crack*, O'Brien took on a chauffer named Pug Brady, who was not only tough but his boss's exact double. Pug was eventually dropped, replaced by a tough teenage girl named Butch. The Clock struck for the last time in *Crack Comics* #35 in the summer of 1944.

CLOWES, DANIEL (1961–)

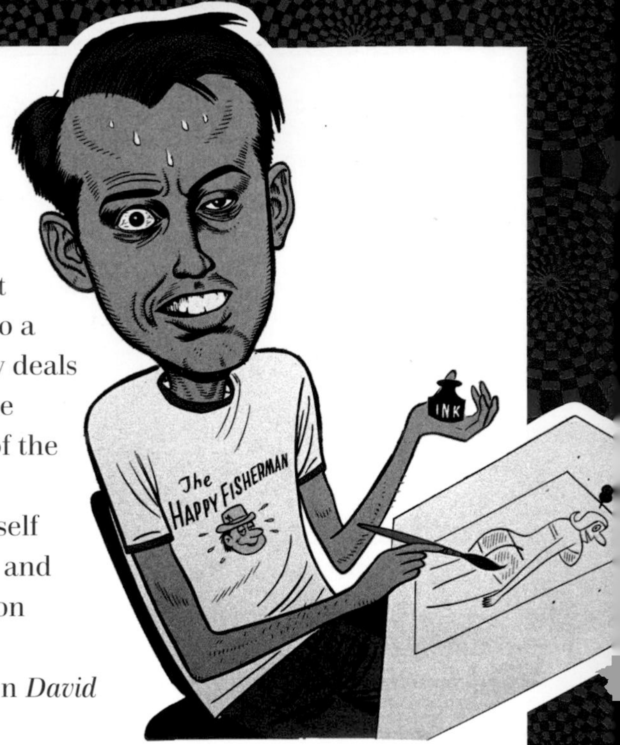
INK
The HAPPY FISHERMAN

■ Another disgruntled and independent cartoonist, Clowes achieved his biggest burst of fame thus far by way of his graphic novel *Ghost World.* It was turned into a moderately successful movie in 2001, with Clowes cowriting the script. The story deals with, among other things, the sorrows of late adolescence and the oddness of the world in general. His style is somewhere between that of Peter Bagge and that of the gentler Seth, two of his successful independent contemporaries.

Although he attended the Pratt Institute in Brooklyn, Clowes considers himself chiefly self-taught. He hooked up with Fantagraphics Books in the middle 1980s and they published his *Lloyd Llewellyn,* which has been described as a satirical take on "such popular genres as science fiction/horror films of the 50s, superheroes and detective novels." He later produced an anthology comic titled *Eightball* and then *David Boring,* which he swears is not autobiographical.

COLE, JACK (1914–1958)

■ His colleagues, his fans, and just about everyone who's seen Jack Cole's comic-book work agree that he was one of the few geniuses in the field. That never gave Cole much satisfaction, since what he really wanted to be was a magazine gag cartoonist. When Cole and his wife moved to New York City in the middle 1930s, his ambition was to become a cartoonist selling to such slick mass circulation periodicals as *The Saturday Evening Post* and *Collier's.*

Born in New Castle, Pennsylvania, "on a frosty December morn in 1914," Cole had wanted to be a cartoonist since childhood. In his teens, by siphoning his school lunch money, he was able to come up with enough to enroll in the then still popular Landon correspondence course in cartooning. Cole's early life sounds like the stuff of local-boy-makes-good stories. Barely out of his teens, he married his longtime sweetheart, Dorothy Mahoney. After two years working at the American Can Company, Cole borrowed $500 from local merchants, and he and his wife embarked for Manhattan. He'd sold his first gag cartoon to *Boy's Life* in 1935, and he had expectations of making it big in the big city. Cole did become a palpable success, though not exactly in his chosen field.

He made a few sales, including one to *Collier's,* but nothing like a comfortable income was coming in. Looking for other markets for his work, Cole discovered comic books. In 1937 he went to work for the enterprising Harry "A" Chesler. Chesler ran a shop at 276 Fifth Avenue, packaging comic-book art for the assorted publishers who were moving into the burgeoning new field, and he also tried publishing comic books of his own. At that early point Cole's style was broadly slapstick, having affinities to that of Dr. Seuss, Bill Holman, and the wackier animated cartoons. He turned out one- and two-page fillers and an occasional page of gag cartons for such pioneering titles as *Funny Pages, Funny Picture Stories* and *Star Ranger Funnies.* By 1940, after the advent of Superman and sundry imitators, Cole branched out on his own and began drawing superheroes and masked men as well as funny filler pages. His style had matured considerably, and his adventure stuff was eccentric, forceful, and attractive, as well as never being completely serious. He'd also developed an ability to draw attractive young women.

Among the characters Cole drew over the next few years were the original Daredevil, the Comet, Silver Streak (Cole also edited *Silver Streak Comics* for a while), Quicksilver, Death Patrol, and Midnight. At the same time he turned out humor pages featuring the likes of Wun Cloo, Slaphappy Pappy, and Burp the Twerp—this latter a parody of superheroes. His major creature, written and drawn for the Quality line's *Police Comics*, was Plastic Man. With Plas, Cole had a feature where he could make use of all the skills he'd been developing since hitting New York. His narratives mixed fantasy, cops and robbers, violence, and humor. His matured drawing style was ideally suited to Plastic Man's bouncy gangbusting adventures. The character soon became the star of *Police*.

When Cole left comics in the early 1950s, he said that he'd been "sidetracked from freelancing" in the gag cartooning field and had put in fourteen years in comic books "on a feature called Plastic Man." He had no way of knowing that the character he dismissed in a single line would survive into the next century and that his Plastic Man stories would be reprinted in expensive and very successful hardcover volumes.

In Cole's second try at becoming a successful gag cartoonist, he sold first to "minor class magazines," such as the humor digests published by Martin Goodman's Humorama line. The same year that Jack Cole returned to the field, Hugh Hefner started *Playboy*. Cole heard about the impending magazine before it hit the stands and sent "a sample wash drawing." A longtime comic-book fan, Hefner remembered and admired Cole's work on Plastic Man and a string of other features. He bought Cole's cartoon and "one OK followed after another." His first cartoon for the magazine appeared in the fifth issue, in the spring of 1954. Soon his wash cartoons, his color drawings, and his *Females by Cole* panels made him the magazine's premier cartoonist.

Late in 1955, Hefner suggested that Cole relocate to the Chicago area so that he'd be nearer the magazine offices. Cole was less than enthusiastic, but the money offered was very good, and so he and Dorothy left Connecticut and eventually settled in the town of Cary, Illinois, about forty miles from Chicago. "That's as near as I want to get to the joint," Cole wrote a friend. "Hef offered me a staff job but I prefer to work at home." In 1958 Cole sold a comic strip titled *Betsy and Me* to the Chicago Sun-Times Syndicate. He had walked in cold, not mentioning his comic-book background or the fact that he was *Playboy*'s star cartoonist. A few months later he bought a gun in his new hometown of Cary and, sitting in his parked car, killed himself. Some of the notes he left survive, but they offer no reason.

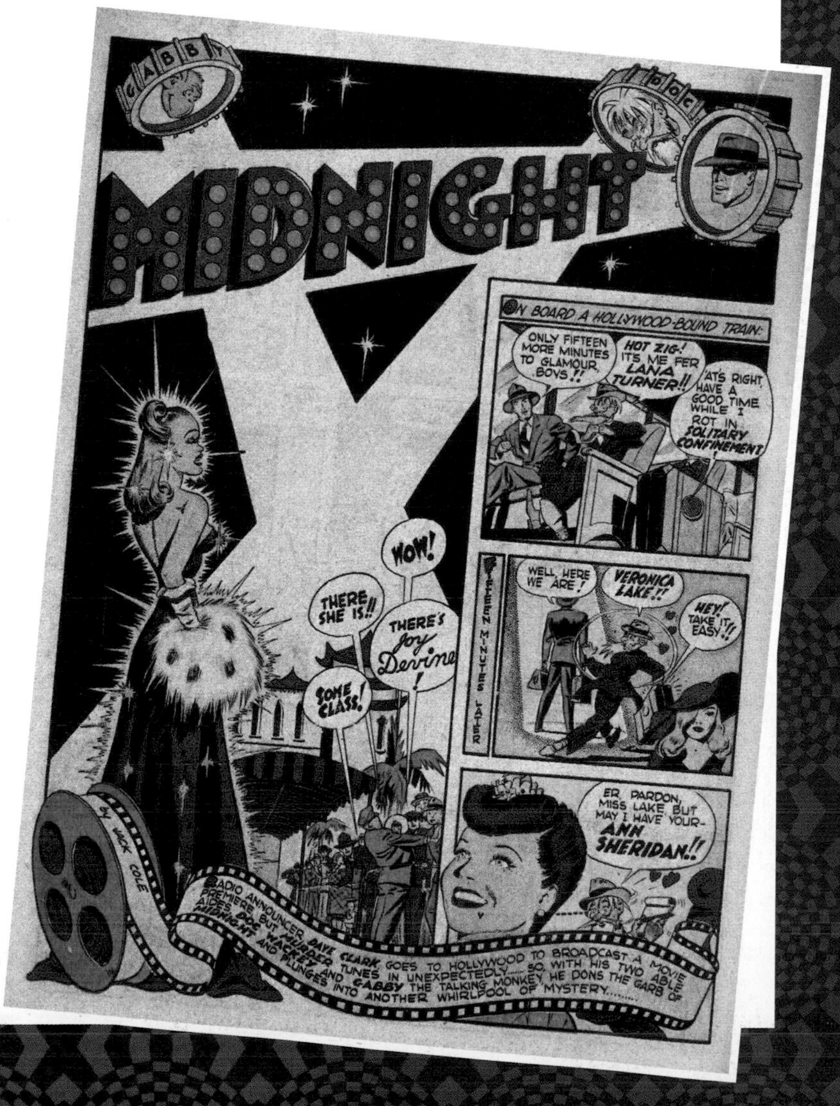
GABBY
DOC
MIDNIGHT
WOW!
THERE SHE IS!!
THERE'S Joy Devine!
SOME CLASS!
BY JACK COLE
RADIO ANNOUNCER DAVE CLARK GOES TO HOLLYWOOD TO BROADCAST A MOVIE PREMIERE BUT MURDER TUNES IN UNEXPECTEDLY..... SO, WITH HIS TWO ABLE AIDES DOC WACKEY AND GABBY THE TALKING MONKEY HE DONS THE GARB OF MIDNIGHT AND PLUNGES INTO ANOTHER WHIRLPOOL OF MYSTERY.........
ON BOARD A HOLLYWOOD-BOUND TRAIN:
ONLY FIFTEEN MORE MINUTES TO GLAMOUR, BOYS!!
HOT ZIG! IT'S ME FER LANA TURNER!!
'AT'S RIGHT, HAVE A GOOD TIME WHILE I ROT IN SOLITARY CONFINEMENT!
FIFTEEN MINUTES LATER
WELL, HERE WE ARE!
VERONICA LAKE!!
HEY! TAKE IT EASY!!
ER, PARDON, MISS LAKE, BUT MAY I HAVE YOUR—ANN SHERIDAN!!

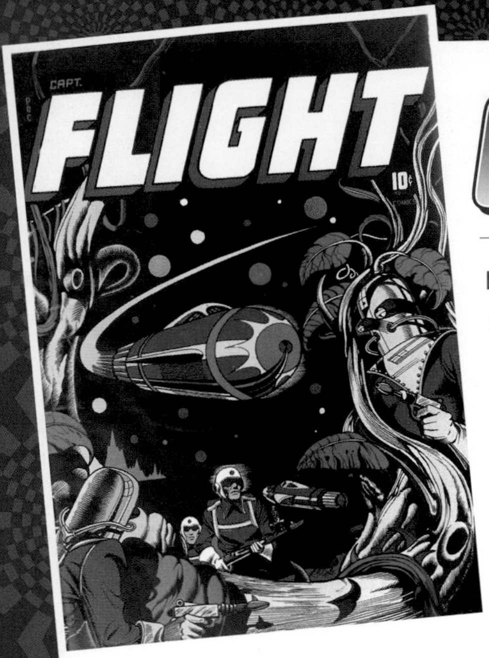
CAPT.
FLIGHT
10¢

COLE, L. B. *(1918–1995)*

■ Many a mediocre comic book of the 1940s is a collector's item today because it bears a cover drawn by L. B. Cole. His bright, bold, and often bizarre covers graced over 1,500 comics of that era. When explaining his philosophy of doing a cover, Cole once said, "There are three colors I found most saleable . . . black, yellow and red. Keep your backgrounds simple, keep your cover subjects simple, even though it looks like a lot is going on."

A former designer of labels, Leonard Cole became active in comics in the early 1940s. He put in time in a small shop run by the incomparable Lou Ferstadt, working alongside Harvey Kurtzman. He also drew for some of the smaller comic-book publishers, doing striking, poster-like covers for such titles as *Captain Aero, Contact Comics, Terrific Comics, Suspense, Mask Comics,* and *Cat-Man Comics.* Late in 1949, he took over the publishing of *Blue Bolt,* turning out some of his most colorful, and sometimes strange, covers for the magazine, particularly after changing its title to *Blue Bolt Weird Tales.*

Cole later edited *Classics Illustrated* for Dell. He published a men's outdoor magazine titled *World Rod & Gun* and painted the covers. The eleventh edition of Bob Overstreet's *Comic Book Price Guide* sported a cover by Cole and contained a long article praising his work. That contributed considerably to making him a favorite of collectors.

COMBAT KELLY

■ Unlike other American wars, past and present, the Korean War (1950–1953) triggered a boom in comic books devoted to combat, past and present. Marvel, then operating under the Atlas banner, was especially gung ho, issuing over two dozen different war titles in the 1950s. Combat Kelly appeared in forty-four issues of his own title from late in 1951 to the spring of 1957.

A tough, unshaven, cigar-smoking infantryman, Kelly began his career in the thick of the fighting in Korea. The blurbs on the covers explained his approach to war—"Rough, tough and sudden death to the Commies!"; "'Death to the Reds!' Is the Battle Cry of Combat Kelly"; and "There Isn't Room Enough in China for COMBAT KELLY and the Commies!"

The dependable Russ Heath was the first artist and David Berg, later to gain fame for his mild suburban satires in *Mad,* served a long hitch illustrating Kelly's tireless combats with the Red Menace. A new version of Combat Kelly had a brief run in the early 1970s.

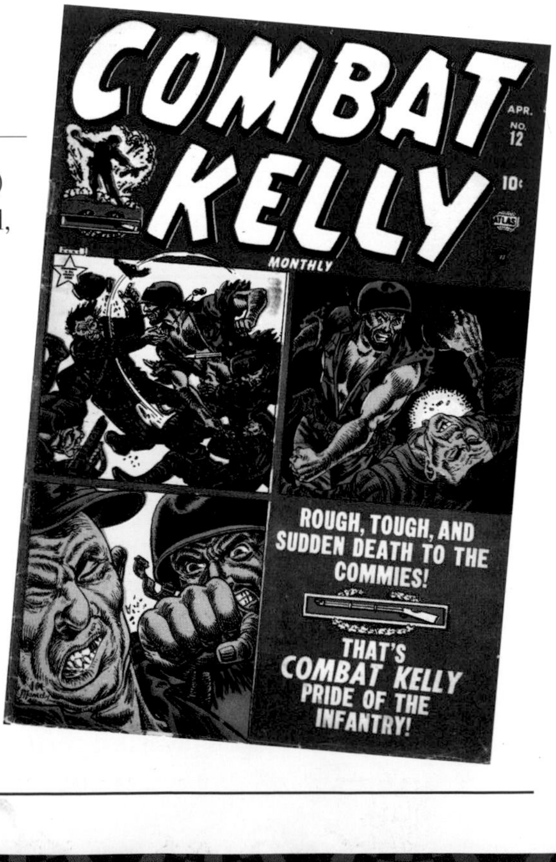
COMBAT KELLY
APR. NO. 12
10¢
MONTHLY
ROUGH, TOUGH, AND SUDDEN DEATH TO THE COMMIES!
THAT'S COMBAT KELLY PRIDE OF THE INFANTRY!

THE COMET

■ Nowadays comic-book heroes frequently drop dead, but during the Golden Age such a thing rarely happened. The very first superhero to die on the job was the Comet, who first expired in 1941. He has been brought back to life several times since his original demise. None of his return trips has lasted very long. John Dickering, alias the Comet, was introduced in MLJ's *Pep Comics* #1 (January 1940) and prematurely retired in #17 (July 1941).

The initial Comet story, written and drawn by Jack Cole, opened exuberantly. The splash panel showed the brightly costumed hero whizzing across the sky, nearly flying off the page. Cole also provided his own blurb—"Smashing adventures of the most astonishing man on the face of the Earth." Readers learned that Dickering, a young scientist, had discovered "a gas that was fifty times lighter than hydrogen." He found that "by injecting small doses of the gas into his bloodstream, his body becomes light enough to make leaps through the air!" Dickering further discovered "that the gas accumulates in the eyes and throws off two powerful beams—these rays, when they cross each other, cause whatever he looks at to disintegrate completely!!!" Glass was the only thing the cross-eyed rays couldn't penetrate, so young Dickering fashioned a glass eyeshield to wear. While he was at it, he designed himself a costume as well, a red, black, and yellow outfit with stars and crescent moons all over the tunic.

The Comet was a merciless crimebuster and thought nothing of melting crooks or dropping them to their deaths from high places. Cole produced three more grim episodes of the saga before moving on. After his departure, the stories toned down some. Bob Wood drew the character for a spell, then Lin Streeter. In the seventeenth issue of *Pep*, the Comet was gunned down by gangsters, and his brother Robert Dickering vowed to hunt down and bring to justice those responsible for his death. To accomplish that, he became the Hangman.

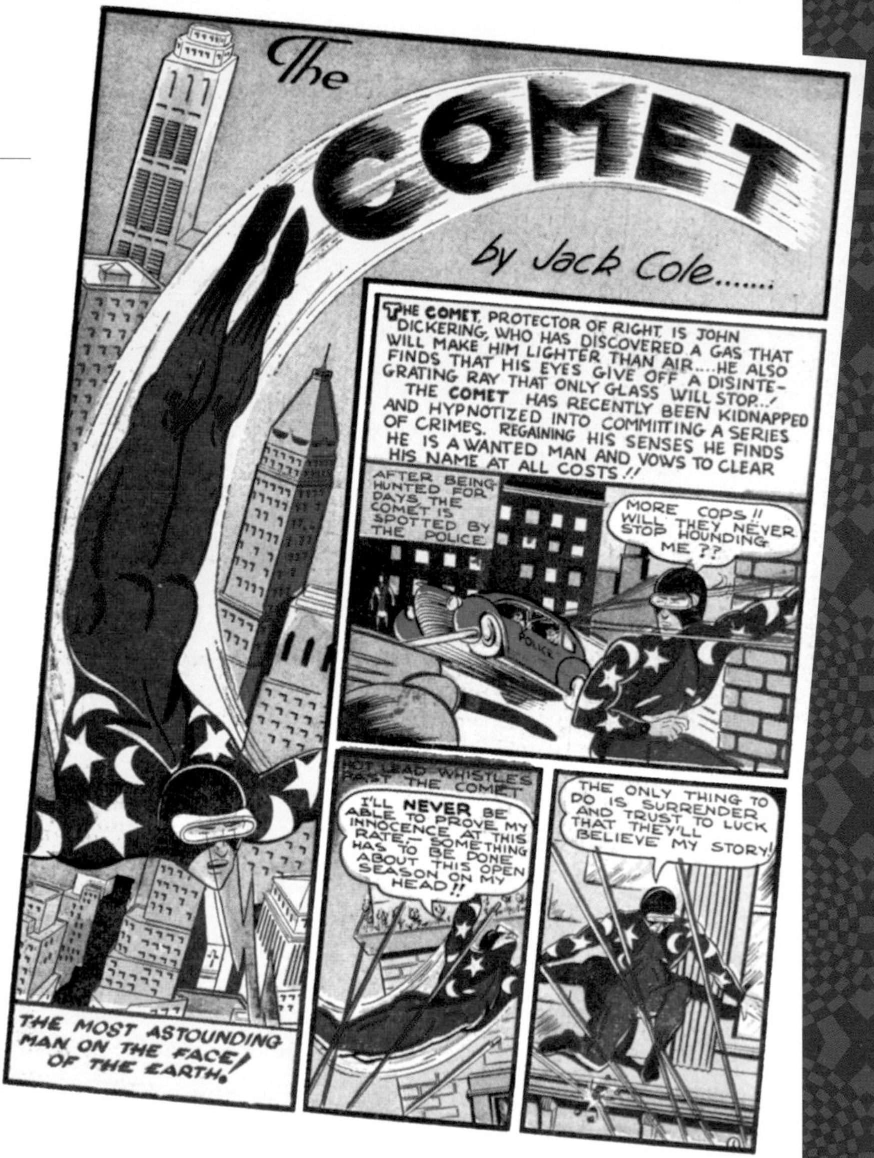
The COMET
by Jack Cole.......
THE COMET, PROTECTOR OF RIGHT, IS JOHN DICKERING, WHO HAS DISCOVERED A GAS THAT WILL MAKE HIM LIGHTER THAN AIR....HE ALSO FINDS THAT HIS EYES GIVE OFF A DISINTEGRATING RAY THAT ONLY GLASS WILL STOP..! THE COMET HAS RECENTLY BEEN KIDNAPPED AND HYPNOTIZED INTO COMMITTING A SERIES OF CRIMES. REGAINING HIS SENSES HE FINDS HE IS A WANTED MAN AND VOWS TO CLEAR HIS NAME AT ALL COSTS!!
THE MOST ASTOUNDING MAN ON THE FACE OF THE EARTH!
AFTER BEING HUNTED FOR DAYS THE COMET IS SPOTTED BY THE POLICE.
MORE COPS!! WILL THEY NEVER STOP HOUNDING ME??
POLICE
HOT LEAD WHISTLES PAST THE COMET
I'LL NEVER BE ABLE TO PROVE MY INNOCENCE AT THIS RATE,— SOMETHING HAS TO BE DONE ABOUT THIS OPEN SEASON ON MY HEAD!!
THE ONLY THING TO DO IS SURRENDER AND TRUST TO LUCK THAT THEY'LL BELIEVE MY STORY!

The first Comet comeback was made in a Fly Girl story in *The Fly* #30 (October 1964). The magazine, after being off the stands for several months, became *Fly Man.* The Comet, along with the Shield and the Black Hood, aided the titular hero in his fight against crime. Jerry Siegel did the writing, Paul Reinman the drawing. It was explained that the Comet hadn't actually died in 1941, but had spent much of the intervening years on the planet Altrox. For his rekindled career, he wore a new costume and grew a moustache. He became part of the Mighty Crusaders and appeared in their comic book as well as a one-shot titled *Super Heroes Versus Super Villains.*

That appearance, in the summer of 1966, was followed by his retirement.

In 1983, Archie included a Comet title in its Red Circle series of revivals. Editor Bill DuBay wrote the scripts and the art was by the team of Carmine Infantino and Alex Niño. The hero looked and sounded considerably better than he had in the 1960s. In the DuBay version, the Comet reverted to his original costume. After being shot in 1941, the Comet had been teleported to Altrox, where friends on that distant planet brought him back to life. During his long stay there, he didn't age. However, he no longer felt the enthusiasm for the superhero profession that he had in his youth. He called himself an anachronism, felt that "I was a butcher. . . . Every bit as ruthless as the savages I hunted!" This angst-ridden Comet, more depressed that the most depressed Stan Lee Marvel hero, made it through only two issues.

In 1991 DC took the name but abandoned most everything else for their Impact series Comet. Now the flying hero was twenty-year old Rob Conners, who, because of a "bizarre accident," became "a hero who can fly and project beams of heat and tremendous energy." This Comet fell to earth after eighteen issues.

COMIC MONTHLY

■ Over a decade ahead of its time, *Comic Monthly* was the first comic book sold on a monthly basis on newsstands. All by itself, it showed up at the end of 1921. Priced at ten cents, the magazine consisted of twenty-four pages that measured 8½" x 10" and offered black-and-white reprints of popular newspaper strips, one title per issue.

Among the comic strips reprinted were *Barney Google*, *Polly & Her Pals*, *Little Jimmy*, and *Tillie the Toiler*. *Comic Monthly* was published by Embee Distributing Company. The *Em* was George McManus, whose *Bringing Up Father* gave Jiggs and Maggie to the world. He was an early though unsung pioneer of the comic book. The *boo* stood for Rudolph Block, Jr., whose father was William Randolph Hearst's comics editor. The Hearst Sunday comic section was subtitled *The Comic Weekly*, which probably suggested the magazine's name. The majority of the reprints were from Hearst syndicates such as King Features.

Comic Monthly maintained its schedule throughout 1922, but inspired no imitator and nobody followed its footsteps. Regularly issued comics and the comic-book industry had to wait another decade to be born.

COMICS ON PARADE

■ See TIP TOP COMICS.

CONAN

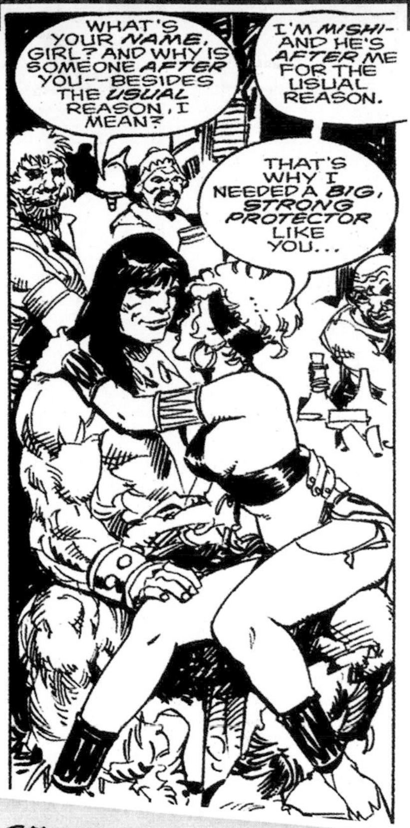
WHAT'S YOUR NAME, GIRL? AND WHY IS SOMEONE AFTER YOU--BESIDES THE USUAL REASON, I MEAN?
I'M MISHI--AND HE'S AFTER ME FOR THE USUAL REASON.
THAT'S WHY I NEEDED A BIG, STRONG PROTECTOR LIKE YOU...

■ With over seventy years in business, he is the most successful barbarian going. He first set up shop in the December 1932 issue of the pulp magazine *Weird Tales*. Conan was the invention of Robert E. Howard, a young Texan who'd begun turning out large quantities of pulp stories while still in his teens. When he wasn't writing for the pulpwoods, he was reading them. The swords-and-sorcery facet of his work was much influenced by such authors as Harold Lamb and Talbot Mundy. Howard borrowed from both of them, though he was never able to imitate their restraint.

"As nearly as such things can be calculated, Conan flourished about 12,000 years ago," explained L. Sprague deCamp, who revised and refurbished the Conan pulp material for book publication. "In this time," according to Howard, "the western parts of the main continent were occupied by Hyborean kingdoms. . . . Conan, a gigantic adventurer from Commeria, arrived as a youth in the kingdom of Zamora. For two or three years he made his living as a thief in Zamora, Corinthia and Nemedia. Growing tired of this starveling existence, he enlisted as a mercenary in the armies of Turan. For the next two years he traveled widely and refined his knowledge of archery and horsemanship." Conan had several odd jobs thereafter. He was a super-muscular, skull-splitting fellow who was fond of spending his days with lovely princesses and slave girls, or in struggling against malignant magic and sorcery. The rest of the time he got into fights.

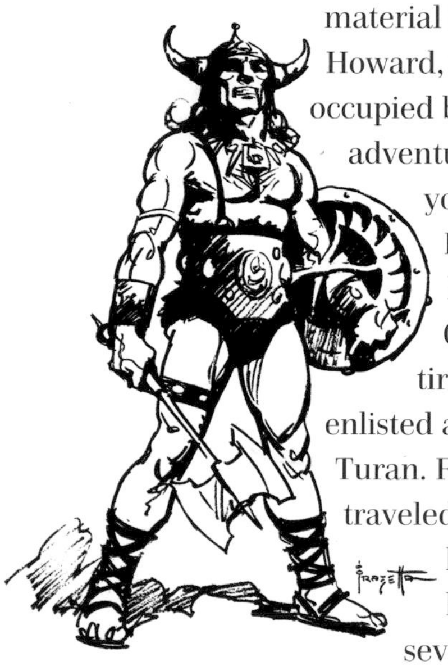

In 1936 Howard, depressed over the death of his mother, killed himself. He was just thirty years old. His stories of Conan, epics of adolescent fantasies and fears, were forgotten for nearly two decades. Then gradually they began coming back into print, first as hardcovers and then, with striking covers by Frank Frazetta, as paperbacks.

Conan found his widest and most enthusiastic audience in the 1970s, thanks to Roy Thomas and Marvel Comics.

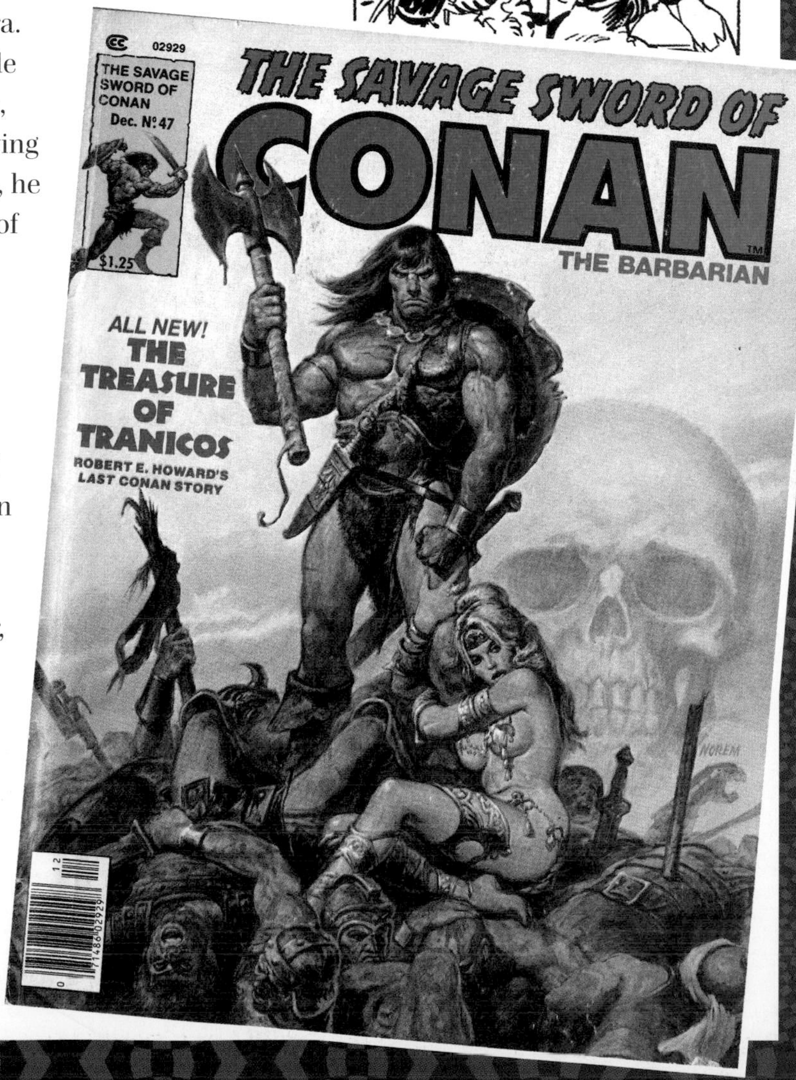
02929
THE SAVAGE SWORD OF CONAN
Dec. No. 47
$1.25
THE SAVAGE SWORD OF
CONAN
THE BARBARIAN
ALL NEW!
THE TREASURE OF TRANICOS
ROBERT E. HOWARD'S LAST CONAN STORY

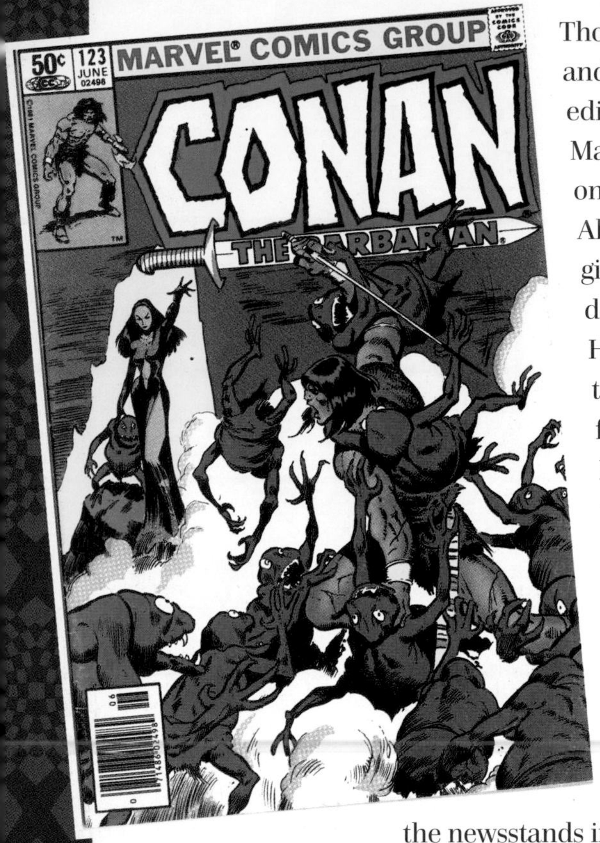

MARVEL COMICS GROUP
50¢
123
JUNE
CONAN
THE BARBARIAN

Thomas began as a fan and by 1970 he was an editor and writer at Marvel, concentrating on superheroes. Although he is often given sole credit for deciding to adapt Howard's barbarian to the comic-book format, artist Gil Kane maintained that he was the one who originally got Thomas and Marvel interested in experimenting with the character. At any rate, *Conan the Barbarian* hit the newsstands in the fall of 1970. Scripts were by Thomas, and the art was by transplanted British artist Barry Windsor-Smith. Although he initially worked in a variation of the Marvel house style, Smith soon developed his own approach. His work became more personal, more intricate, and demonstrated distinct Pre-Raphaelite touches.

Thomas's adaptations drew much praise at the time. Smith, too, attracted attention and was soon winning awards from both his peers and his fans. He left the character in 1973 and was followed by several other artists, among them John Buscema, Ernie Chan, and Gil Kane. The shaggy hero continued for decades. The original *Conan the Barbarian* title ended with the 275th issue (July 1995). The black-and-white *Conan Saga* ended with the 97th issue (April 1995). These were followed through the late nineties by a series of Conan miniseries. While Conan seems to be on leave at the present time, there is little doubt that he shall return.

Conan's early success sparked a small swords-and-sorcery boom. Marvel, for instance, tried Thongor, Kull, and Red Sonja. Justifiably called the "She-Devil with a Sword," Red Sonja first appeared in late 1972 in *Conan* #23. Thomas took the character from another Howard pulp tale and, changing her name slightly, let her loose in the Hyborean Age. She was the guest star in two *Conan* issues and returned in 1974 for a single appearance in a black-and-white magazine, *The Savage Sword of Conan.* Next she fought her way through two issues of *Kull and the Barbarians* in 1975, with Howard Chaykin rendering her sword-wielding escapades. Sonja then became the star of *Marvel Feature,* and Frank Thorne depicted her from the second issue onward. With her bright orange hair and her chain-mail bikini, Thorne's version of the female barbarian attracted considerable interest. Late in 1976, the she-devil got a book of her own that continued, with a lapse or two, until the middle 1980s. Thorne was so affected by the experience of drawing *Red Sonja* that he has drawn little else but barbarian she-devils ever since.

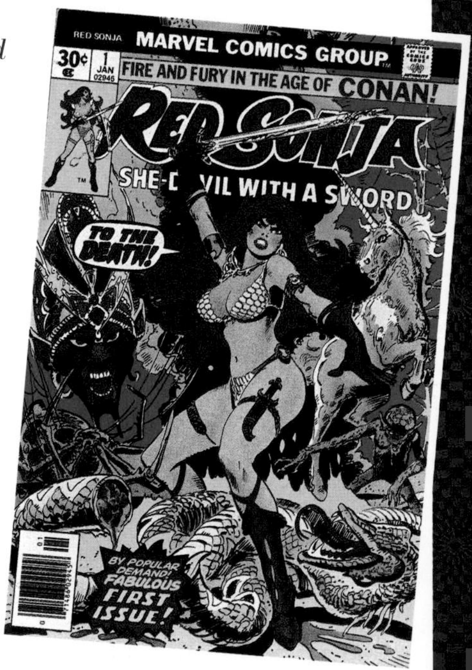

RED SONJA
MARVEL COMICS GROUP
30¢
1
JAN
FIRE AND FURY IN THE AGE OF CONAN!
RED SONJA
SHE-DEVIL WITH A SWORD
TO THE DEATH!
BY POPULAR DEMAND: FABULOUS FIRST ISSUE!

Among the other comic-book barbarians at the gates in the 1970s, many of them from DC, were Beowulf, Claw the Unconquered, and Iron Wolf. Atlas tried Iron Jaw, and Gil Kane produced Blackmark in a paperback format.

CONCRETE

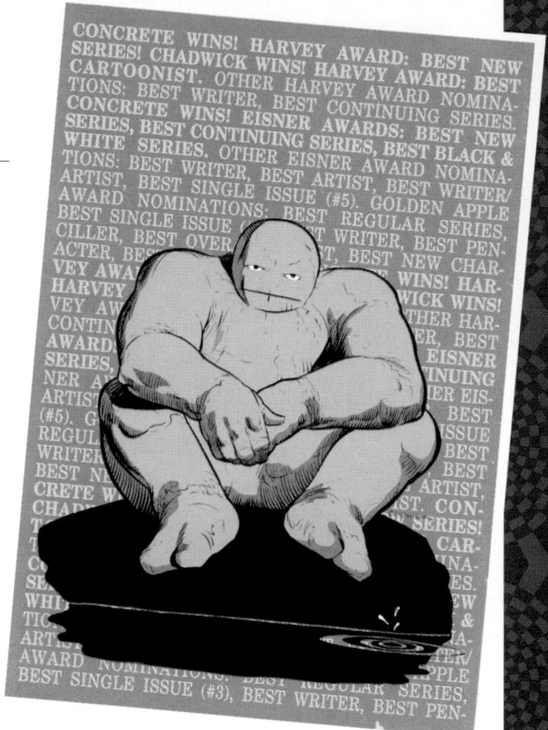
CONCRETE WINS! HARVEY AWARD: BEST NEW
SERIES! CHADWICK WINS! HARVEY AWARD: BEST
CARTOONIST. OTHER HARVEY AWARD NOMINA-
TIONS: BEST WRITER, BEST CONTINUING SERIES.
CONCRETE WINS! EISNER AWARDS: BEST NEW
SERIES, BEST CONTINUING SERIES, BEST BLACK &
WHITE SERIES. OTHER EISNER AWARD NOMINA-
TIONS: BEST WRITER, BEST ARTIST, BEST WRITER/
ARTIST, BEST SINGLE ISSUE (#5). GOLDEN APPLE
AWARD NOMINATIONS: BEST REGULAR SERIES,
BEST SINGLE ISSUE (#3), BEST WRITER, BEST PEN-

■ Though he has some physical resemblance to a couple of bulky and belligerent Marvel characters, Concrete is a mild-mannered and thoughtful fellow. His creator Paul Chadwick once explained, "Concrete is in no way a spin-off or comment on the Thing. Concrete's a gentle, ivory-tower speechwriter grafted into an alien body."

Chadwick, who'd painted paperback covers and storyboarded such films as *The Big Easy* before getting into comics, drew up his first *Concrete* samples in 1983. It wasn't until 1986, after he'd worked on *Dazzler* for Marvel, that Dark Horse tried the character out in the first issue of *Dark Horse Presents.* The next year a *Concrete* bimonthly was started. Chadwick was interested in exploring the idea of what an ordinary fellow would do when trapped in a superpowered body. With pauses now and then, he continued his explorations well into the 1990s.

CONGO BILL

■ Before being upstaged by a gorilla, Congo Bill enjoyed a long, happy life as a guide and jungle adventurer of the Alan Quatermain sort. After residing in *More Fun Comics* for nearly a year, Bill trekked over to *Action Comics* #37 (June 1941) and remained in that magazine for close to two decades. When he moved in, another jungle adventurer, Clip Carson, moved out to settle into Bill's old spot in *More Fun.*

George Papp, who'd been drawing both features, continued with Clip. But over at *Action* a new, young artist named Fred Ray took over *Congo Bill.* Ray obviously enjoyed the feature, and he put considerable effort into it. Gradually its looks changed and its stories moved away from lost cities and evil hunters to take notice of World War II. The 1942 episodes are especially fine, inventively staged and filled with accurately drawn planes, weapons, and uniforms. Ray avoided heroic poses, favoring natural figures. All of this gave *Congo Bill* a sophistication that was missing from the adventures of any of the other jungle heroes.

Congo Bill was drawn by Ed Smalle and John Daly after Ray and the feature hung on in *Action.* Early in 1954, Bill acquired a sidekick in the person of Janu the Jungle Boy. The lad was also on view in seven issues of the *Congo Bill* comic book that appeared from 1954 and 1955. Nick Cardy provided the artwork for that one. Late in 1956, Congo Bill had his fateful first meeting with the Golden Gorilla, and in *Action* #248 (January 1959) a dying native chieftain/witch doctor gave him a magic gorilla ring that enabled him to trade bodies with the Golden Gorilla for one-hour stretches. With this rather dubious ability, Bill began a new career as Congorilla. Under that title the strip went on for another year or so.

DC issued four issues of a *Congorilla* comic book in the early 1990s, and late in 1999 brought out a four-issue miniseries titled *Congo Bill* with artwork by Richard Corben.

COWBOY COMIC BOOKS

■ Heroes on horseback were a staple of comics from the 1930s onward. Major Malcolm Wheeler-Nicholson featured cowboy Jack Woods on the cover of his first original-material comic book, *New Fun*, in 1935. Actually it was an interior page by Lyman Anderson that the canny major used twice and paid for once—if that. Nicholson's second publication, *New Comics*, offered *Captain Jim of the Texas Rangers* among its many features. Many later DC titles made room for a cowboy—Buck Marshall in *Detective Comics*, Chuck Dawson in *Action*, later the Vigilante in *Action*.

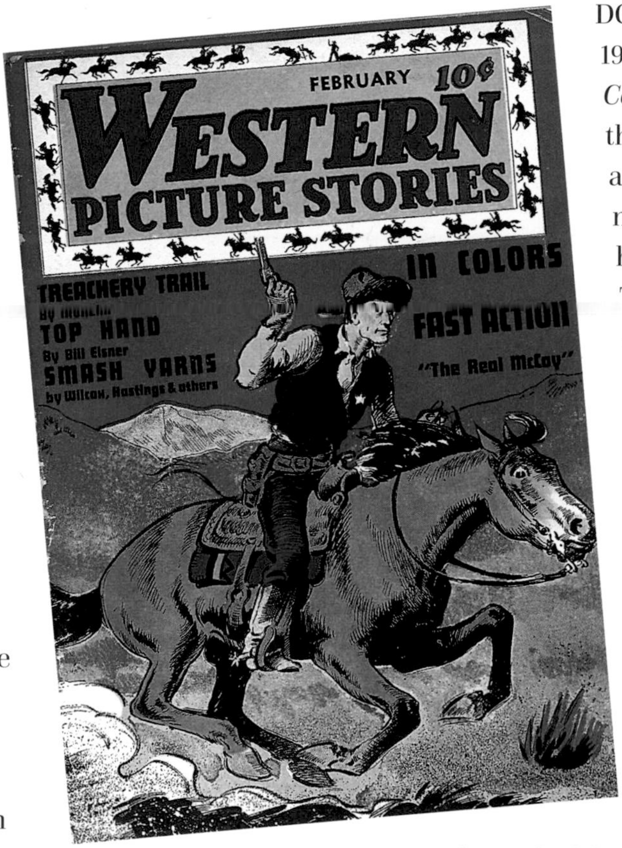
FEBRUARY 10¢
WESTERN
PICTURE STORIES
IN COLORS
TREACHERY TRAIL
TOP HAND
By Bill Eisner
SMASH YARNS
by Wilcox, Hastings & others
FAST ACTION
"The Real McCoy"

Early competitors of the major also paid attention to Western heroes. Early in 1937 two magazines devoted exclusively to cowboy fare came out—*Star Ranger Comics* and *Western Picture Stories*. As the number of titles on the newsstands grew, so did the number of cowboys, especially those who were masked men. The Lone Ranger's newspaper strips were being reprinted and among similar masked cowboys were the Phantom Rider, Tex Maxon—The Phantom Rider, and Nevada Smith—Quick Trigger Man. Publisher Ned Pines featured adaptations of some of his pulp fiction cowpokes in his comic books, including *The Rio Kid*, *Jim Hatfield—Texas Ranger*, and *The Masked Rider*.

Movie cowboys were also popular, and the likes of Buck Jones, Tom Mix, Tex Ritter, and Gene Autry showed up in various funny books. Hopalong Cassidy, looking very much like actor William Boyd, started appearing in comic books in the early 1940s. Both Dell and Fawcett began devoting entire magazines to motion-picture cowboys, resulting in titles like *Roy Rogers*, *Gene Autry*, and *Hopalong Cassidy*. As the public turned away from superheroes in the years after World War II, publishers tried expanding the Western genre. DC introduced *Western Comics* in 1948, then converted *All-American Comics* to *All-American Western* at the end of 1949. Never one to miss a trend, Martin Goodman added numerous cowboy magazines to his line, commencing in 1948. These included *Two-Gun Kid*, *Kid Colt*, *The Outlaw Kid*, *The Apache Kid*, *The Kid from Texas*, *The Ringo Kid*, *The Texas Kid*, and *The Rawhide Kid*. Before he was through Goodman had published fifty different Western titles. Other publishers also went west for a while with such titles as *Western Crime Busters*, *Western Heroes*, *Western Love*, *Western Killers*, *Western Romances*, *Western Tales*, and *Western True Crime*.

By the end of the 1960s almost all of the cowboy comics were long gone. Marvel revived the Rio Kid in the early 1970s and kept the Rawhide Kid going from 1960 to 1979. In 2003 Marvel introduced a gay Rawhide Kid, accompanied by considerable publicity and low sales. DC has had some luck bringing back offbeat Western characters such as the nasty Jonah Hex, first seen in the 1970s. But for the most part the cowboy comic book has ridden off into the sunset for good.

CRACKAJACK FUNNIES

■ Possibly to avoid a conflict with the manufacturers of the then popular Cracker Jack confection, the Whitman Publishing Co. used the variant spelling for the title of their comic book. Launched in the spring of 1938, *Crackajack Funnies* was roughly two-thirds newspaper strip reprints—*Dan Dunn, Wash Tubbs, Boots and Her Buddies, Don Winslow of the Navy*, etc.—and one-third original material. The editor was Oskar Lebeck.

Lebeck also drew many of the early covers as well as writing and drawing a humor feature about Looney Luke, the inventor of a time machine. He used the pen name Ole. Other original features, most of them using characters from Whitman's line of Big Little Books, included cowboys Tom Mix and Buck Jones, both drawn by Ken Ernst, and G-Man X32 by Milt Youngren.

Reprints of funny paper cowboy *Red Ryder* were added in #9 (March 1939). Stephen Slesinger, who specialized in licensing and packaging comic strips, owned Fred Harman's Western comic strip and also put together BLBs for Whitman. Some of the other original material in *Crackajack* was provided by him and drawn by his protégé Jim Gary. Win Smith, an erstwhile Disney artist, took over *Looney Luke* and later introduced his own *Pete and his Pal Pudge*, about a talking penguin and a plump Boy Scout. From #15 to #36 there was a one-page Tarzan text story attributed to Edgar Rice Burroughs.

As the magazine progressed, more and more original material replaced the reprints. *Ellery Queen, Stratosphere Jin and His Flying Fortress, The Crusoes*, and *The Owl* all moved in. The Queen stories weren't based on the mystery novels, though a few were adapted from scripts from the radio show. Bill Ely was the artist for most of the run. Stratosphere Jim's aerial adventures were scripted by Lebeck and drawn by Alden McWilliams, a specialist at drawing airplanes. The Crusoes were a modern-day Swiss Family Robinson and drawn by Al Micale. The Owl, Whitman's answer to Batman, was the work of Frank Thomas.

The ultimate issue, #43 (January 1942) added reprints of *Terry and the Pirates* and used Milton Caniff's newspaper characters on the cover.

CRAIG, JOHNNY *(1926–2001)*

■ Although he drew hundreds of pages and dozens of covers during his twenty-some years in and out of comics, Craig is best remembered for just one cover. That's the cover of EC's *Crime SuspenStories* #22 (May 1954). It shows the decapitated head of a blond young woman being held up by the hair. Displayed during a Senate inquiry in 1954, the cover elicited a response from EC publisher William Gaines that is quoted to this day. Over the years Craig's cover has been reprinted many times, and it was even mentioned in some of his obituaries.

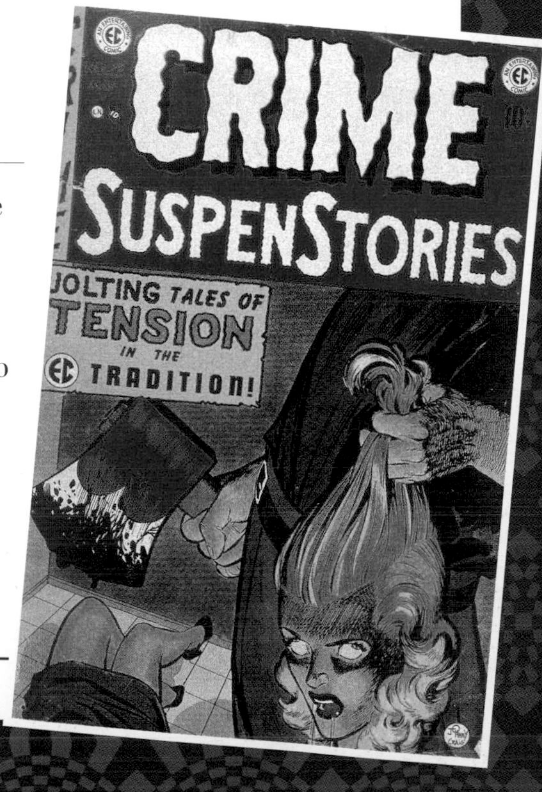
CRIME
SUSPENSTORIES
JOLTING TALES OF TENSION IN THE EC TRADITION!

Craig, like many of his contemporaries, got into the comic-book business while still a schoolboy. He did low-paying art chores for M.C. Gaines's All-American division of DC. After World War II, he got a job with Gaines's new EC line. When William Gaines took over after his father's death in 1947, Craig stayed on to work on the new line of crime and horror titles. In addition to interior artwork, he drew many of the covers for the expanding EC list. His well-designed, poster-like covers appeared on *Crime Patrol* and its successor *The Crypt of Terror* as well as *War Against Crime* and its successor *The Vault of Horror*. Craig, in fact, drew the covers for all twenty-nine issues of *Vault*. He was also responsible for the majority of *Crime SuspenStories*, and in addition to the famous severed head effort he drew a cover showing a close-up of a hanged man, a shot of a man getting his brains blown out, plus one of a man burying his wife alive in a cemetery and a wife burying her dead husband in the woods. Many of the stories Craig illustrated dealt with domestic conflicts of one sort or another, often concluding with one spouse doing the other in.

Craig's work got into the limelight during the U.S. Senate hearings into juvenile delinquency held at the Federal Courtroom in Manhattan. There had by that time in 1954 been considerable complaints about and attacks upon crime and horror comics. William Gaines was called as a witness and during his questioning, Senator Estes Kefauver held up the cover of #22 and said, "Here is your May issue. There seems to be a man with a bloody axe holding a woman's head up, which has been severed from her body. Do you think that's in good taste?" Gaines made the fateful mistake of answering, "Yes, sir, I do—for the cover of a horror comic. A cover in bad taste, for example, might be defined as holding the head a little higher so that blood could be seen dripping from it."

EC, as did many another publisher, had to drop its horror and crime magazines in order to survive. They turned to tamer titles, one of which was *Extra*. Craig did some of his best work for the title, also editing it. The magazine survived for only a few issues.

Craig, after the collapse of EC (except for *Mad*), did some work for DC and in the late 1960s drew *Iron Man* for Marvel. By 1970 he was out of comics and doing advertising art. He also found time to do some painting.

CRANDALL, REED *(1917–1982)*

■ Crandall, like Lou Fine, was an illustrator and not a cartoonist. His early influences were book and magazine illustrators such as Howard Pyle, Henry Pitz, and N. C. Wyeth. When he started in comic books in 1940, he produced pages that stood out from those of many of his contemporaries. He was one of the most proficient artists in the field and a master of drawing the figure in action. Crandall was the best artist to draw Blackhawk in that militant's long career, and he did first-rate work on everything from *Dollman* to horror tales for EC and Warren.

Coming to Manhattan from out of the Midwest, he worked briefly for the Eisner-Iger shop before signing up with Busy Arnold's Quality line. Arnold later referred to Crandall as "the best man I ever had." In addition to *Dollman*, Crandall also illustrated *Uncle Sam*, *Stormy Foster*, *Firebrand*, and *The Ray*. When Quality shut down in the early 1950s, he moved to EC. He excelled at every type of story, including crime, horror, adventure, and science fiction. EC publisher William Gaines loved his work, saying, "He was a fine, fine craftsman and did some of our very best stuff." The 1960s found Crandall working for markets ranging from the Catholic *Treasure Chest* to Warren's *Creepy* and *Eerie*. Teaming with George Evans, he drew *The Hunchback of Notre Dame* and *Julius Caesar* for *Classics Illustrated*. Crandall also illustrated several of the Canaveral Press editions of Edgar Rice Burroughs' novels. By the 1970s he was out of comics. Beset by illness and personal problems, Crandall ended his days doing menial jobs somewhere in the Midwest.

THE CREEPER

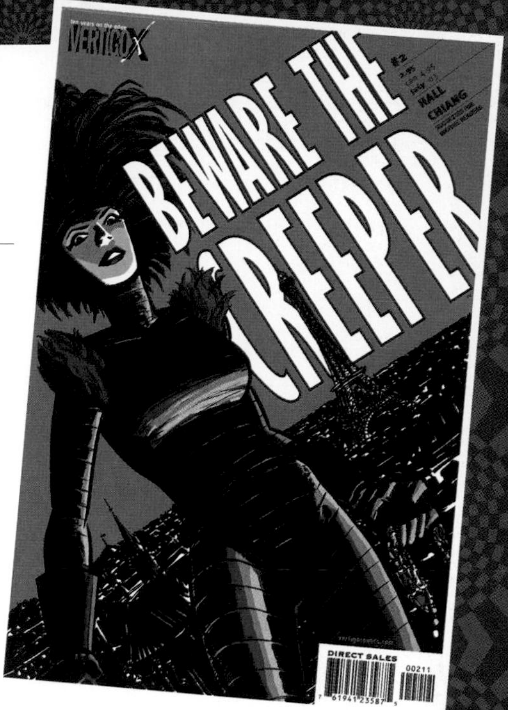
VERTIGO X
HALL
CHIANG
BEWARE THE CREEPER
DIRECT SALES

■ After over three decades of trying to figure what to do with one of the silliest superheroes ever to come down the pike, DC finally arrived at a practical solution. Throw out everything but the name and start all over again. In the spring of 2003 their Vertigo line introduced *Beware the Creeper*, an exemplary title that is both well written and well drawn. Jason Hall provides the scripts, Cliff Chiang the art. This Creeper operates in the Paris of 1925 and is a woman. While her costume is on the flamboyant side, it is not the strange mess that the original Creeper flaunted.

The earlier creeper was thought up and drawn by Steve Ditko and introduced in an issue of *Showcase* in 1968. He soon moved into a short-lived comic book of his own before turning into a perennial guest in other heroes' titles for many a year. After TV newsman Jack Ryder swallowed another of those magic serums that are so popular with a certain class of superheroes and hooking up with a molecule-shuffling gadget, he was transformed into a costumed superman. Don Markstein, Internet comics maven, has described the Creeper's appearance thusly—"He was wearing a green wig and yellow make-up, with a large, hairy red rug glued to his back." And yet, with all that going for him, the character was not a hit.

The new *Beware the Creeper*, aimed at an older audience, is a successful blend of mystery, adventure, romance, and history. Minor characters include Ernest Hemingway, Jean Cocteau, Gertrude Stein, and Pablo Picasso. There are also roving killers and sadistic aristocrats. Chiang's visualization of the 1920s City of Lights is very good and also has a suggestion of early French thriller novels like *Fantomas*. This version was a five-issue series and ended with the apparent death of the new Creeper. But other Creepers await in the wings.

CRIME DOES NOT PAY

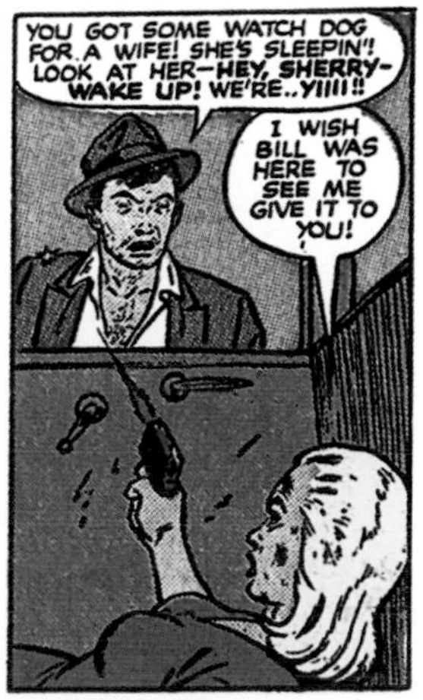
YOU GOT SOME WATCH DOG FOR A WIFE! SHE'S SLEEPIN'! LOOK AT HER—HEY, SHERRY—WAKE UP! WE'RE..YIII!!
I WISH BILL WAS HERE TO SEE ME GIVE IT TO YOU!

■ One of the most influential comic books ever published, it changed the comic-book industry in the late 1940s and early 1950s and contributed to the ruin or near ruin of a good many publishers. The first regularly issued true-crime comic, it was published by Lev Gleason and Arthur Bernhard and edited by cartoonists Charles Biro and Bob Wood. *Crime Does Not Pay* began in the spring of 1942 and remained in business until the spring of 1955. Bernhard withdrew fairly soon, and Gleason continued alone as publisher.

When asked who had come up with the idea for the magazine, Bernhard replied that "Lev conceived the whole thing," turning it over to Biro to edit. The new title was launched in 1942 with typical Biro enthusiasm. Teaser ads in other magazines proclaimed, "IT'S COMING! The most sensational comic magazine ever created!!! The spectacular masterpiece is in production NOW! Get it at your newsstand soon!" Once *Crime Does Not Pay* appeared, full-page ads in the company's other titles announced, "THE MOST SENSATIONAL COMIC IDEA ever is sweeping the country! Crime comics give you the REAL FACTS!! SEE for the first time how real criminals lived, stole, killed and then—" A line of copy below this ad, indicating they had a larger audience in mind, read, "Get 'Crime Does Not Pay'! Show it to Dad, he'll love it."

Major influences on the genesis and evolution of *Crime Does Not Pay* were such hardboiled periodicals as *True Detective*, *Master Detective*, and *Official Detective*. Printed on somewhat better paper than pulp fiction magazines and illustrated with grainy photos of vicious criminals, blowzy gun molls, and bloody corpses, they offered breathless nonfiction accounts of bank robberies, brutal murders, and assorted crimes of passion. *Crime Does Not Pay* came closer than any comic book had before to emulating this particular blend of gritty reality, shoot-'em-up action, and titillation.

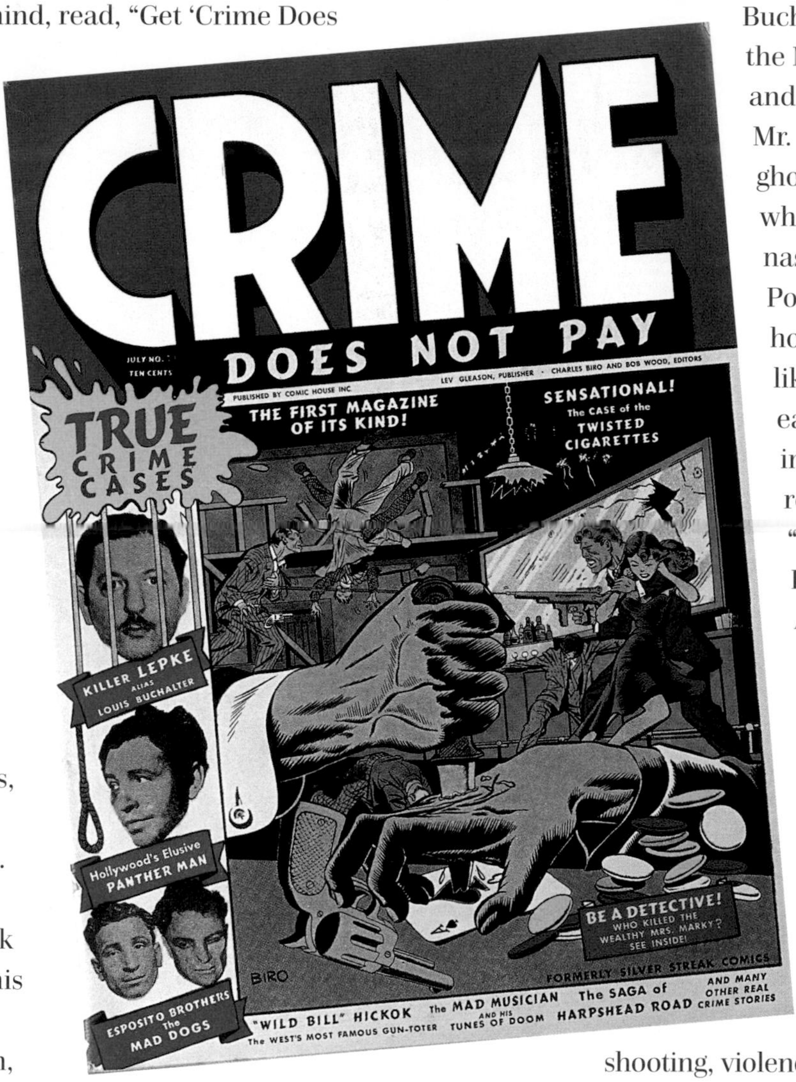
CRIME
DOES NOT PAY
TEN CENTS
PUBLISHED BY COMIC HOUSE INC
LEV GLEASON, PUBLISHER - CHARLES BIRO AND BOB WOOD, EDITORS
TRUE CRIME CASES
THE FIRST MAGAZINE OF ITS KIND!
SENSATIONAL! The CASE of the TWISTED CIGARETTES
KILLER LEPKE ALIAS LOUIS BUCHALTER
Hollywood's Elusive PANTHER MAN
ESPOSITO BROTHERS The MAD DOGS
BE A DETECTIVE! WHO KILLED THE WEALTHY MRS. MARKY? SEE INSIDE!
BIRO
FORMERLY SILVER STREAK COMICS
"WILD BILL" HICKOK The WEST'S MOST FAMOUS GUN-TOTER
The MAD MUSICIAN AND HIS TUNES OF DOOM
The SAGA of HARPSHEAD ROAD
AND MANY OTHER REAL CRIME STORIES

It was the contention of Gleason and his editors that the magazine was "dedicated to the eradication of crime" and for a while the covers carried the slogan "A force for good in the community!" The letters page, which paid $2 for each one published, frequently feature testimonials from both teens and parents stating that the reading of the magazine served as a deterrent to criminal activity and delinquency.

Since *Crime Does Not Pay* replaced the superhero title *Silver Streak*, it assumed that title's numbering and the first issue was #22 (July 1942). The cover assured potential readers that this was "The First Magazine of Its Kind!" Inside were the true crime cases of Louis "Lepke" Buchalter of Murder, Inc., fame, the Mad Dog Esposito Brothers, and Wild Bill Hickock. In #24, Mr. Crime was introduced, a ghostly, all-knowing wiseguy who was a cross between the nasty Mr. Coffee Nerves of the Postum ads and the sardonic hosts of radio mystery shows like *Inner Sanctum*. He hosted each issue's leadoff story and inevitably offered a pithy remark in the final panel—"They got ALL of them! Ralph Fleagle, Royston, and Absher were all hanged in Colorado Sate Penitentiary at Canon City! Good pupils, too, tsk tsk!"

The magazine chronicled the careers of crooks of recent vintage, such as "Legs" Diamond and older heavies like Billy the Kid. Most of the cases were packed with shooting, violence, and action, but little actual bloodshed. Mild sexual activity was typical, usually provided by the lady friends of the various crooks and killers. In later years things got more violent and bloodier.

Artwork in the early issues was by such as Creig Flessel, Harry Lucey, and Bob Montana. As World War II progressed, some lesser artists worked for the magazine. In the middle and late 1940s George Tuska, who has been called "the premier crime comic artist," Bob Fujitani, Dan Barry, and Fred Kida were among those who improved the comic's looks. Biro limited himself to drawing the majority of covers. He usually dealt in anticipation, showing the moment just before the hapless gas station attendants were burned alive or just before the bootlegger was dropped into the lime pit.

By 1945, the combined sales of all the Gleason titles had climbed to 1.5 million, and by 1947 it was over 2 million. Late that year the cover of *Crime Does Not Pay* boasted, "More that 6,000,000 Readers Monthly!" Gleason and Biro were fudging here by assuming that several readers looked at each copy sold.

Crime Does Not Pay had the field pretty much to itself, despite its impressive sales, for several years. But because of the uncertain economics of the postwar period and the decline of interest in superheroes, other publishers turned to crime. Dozens of titles appeared, including Gleason's *Crime and Punishment*. Much of the criticism, censorship, and boycotting that hit the comic-book field in the early 1950s was inspired by the more flamboyant imitators, who went even further than the pioneering *Crime Does Not Pay*.

CRIME SUSPENSTORIES

■ The comic book that got EC publisher William Gaines into the most trouble, *Crime SuspenStories* first reached the stands in the summer of 1950. Although crime comics were already plentiful by this time, a blurb on the cover of the initial issue promised "A New Trend in Magazines." That trend was defined as "Startling Tales of Tension!" For good measure a "Terror-Tale" from EC's *Haunt of Fear* was included from the fourth to the twelfth issue.

The covers, mostly drawn by Johnny Craig, depicted a variety of violent crimes, including a hanging, a strangling, an axe murder, a premature burial, a slashing with a razor, another strangling, and a decapitation. Later issues bore the claim "Jolting Tales of TENSION in the EC Tradition!" Al Feldstein, the editor, also wrote and drew for the magazine. Artists included such EC regulars

as Jack Davis, Bernard Krigstein, Joe Orlando, Wally Wood, George Evans, and Craig.

The tales within dealt with the same topics depicted on the covers, sometimes toned down a bit. Spousal abuse was a frequent theme, and the twist ending, popular at the time on such radio shows as *Suspense* and *The Whistler*, was common. *Crime SuspenStories* lasted from late in 1950 to early in 1955. Its demise was hastened in part by the reaction to Gaines' appearance at a senate inquiry into juvenile delinquency. When Senator Estes Kefauver held up the cover of #22—the one with the severed female head being held up by the hair—and asked Gaines for his ideas on good taste, the hapless publisher did not handle the situation well. (For further details see the entry on Johnny Craig.)

CRIMEBUSTER

■ See BOY COMICS.

THE CRIMSON AVENGER

■ A costumed crimefighter who was appearing in *Detective Comics* over six months before Batman arrived there, the Crimson Avenger lacked the charisma to become the star of the magazine. That might have been because he was too close an imitator of an earlier hero of a different color. The Crimson, who debuted in *Detective* #20 (October 1938), owed a great deal to radio's Green Hornet.

The Hornet, accompanied by his "Flight of the Bumblebee" theme, first took to the airwaves over Detroit's WXYZ and by the spring of 1938 was being heard nationwide on the Mutual network. Whereas the Hornet was in reality Britt Reid, wealthy young publisher of the *Daily Sentinel*, the Crimson was Lee Travis, wealthy young publisher of the *Globe Leader*. The only person who knew the Hornet's true identity was his faithful valet Kato, and the Crimson's secret was shared only by his Chinese servant Wing. Like the Green Hornet, the Crimson Avenger never used a deadly weapon and preferred to put his adversaries to sleep with a blast from his gas gun. He wore a dark blue slouch hat, a domino mask, and an Inverness-style cape of crimson hue.

A SLICK JEWEL SMUGGLER STAGES A FOOLPROOF SCHEME WITH THE AQUARIUM AS A BACKGROUND—BUT FAILS TO PICTURE THE DISASTROUS RESULTS WHEN HE CLASHES WITH THE CRIMSON AVENGER!
THE CRIMSON AVENGER
BY JACK LEHTI

The creation of artist Jim Chambers, in his early adventures the Crimson fought civic corruption and organized crime. Unfortunately for him, Batman showed up in #27, and he was relegated to second-banana status for the rest of his career. In fact, he dropped out of the magazine soon after his more flamboyant rival appeared and didn't return for nearly a year.

He came back in #37 (March 1940). The following month, Jack Lehti, who was very much under the spell of Alex Raymond at the time, took over the drawing. By the fall of 1940, when superheroes in tights were in fashion, the Crimson Avenger switched to crimson tights and tunic, yellow shorts, plus a crimson cowl and cape. The gas gun became much more futuristic-looking. He added a costumed sidekick in #59 (January 1942) in the person of his very own Wing. They remained in *Detective* until #89 (July 1944).

The Crimson Avenger also appeared in *World's Finest Comics* and *Leading Comics*. DC brought him back, in his original outfit, for a short while in 1988.

CRISIS ON INFINITE EARTHS

■ Through the offices of writer Gardner F, who always had one foot in the sci-fi camp, DC introduced the venerable pulp convention of parallel universes to their comic books early in the Silver Age. The initial result was the introduction of Earth-1 and Earth-2 and the coexistence of both versions of the Flash, the Green Lantern, and other characters who now had two separate identities. What with various writers joining in and adding their assorted spins to the concept, by the middle 1980s it was felt that the DC universe had become as overly complex and unwieldy a place as the real world.

So in 1985 writer Marv Wolfman and artist George Perez were assigned the Herculean task of cleaning things up and simplifying everything. That resulted in a twelve-issue series entitled *Crisis on Infinite Earths*, which blended science fiction, fantasy, mythology, theology, and hundreds of DC characters from all eras. By series end many were dead, many changed. It was hoped that the survivors would henceforward exist comfortably in one world.

But in the years that followed, DC has continued to fiddle around, raising the dead and otherwise tweaking things.

THE CROW

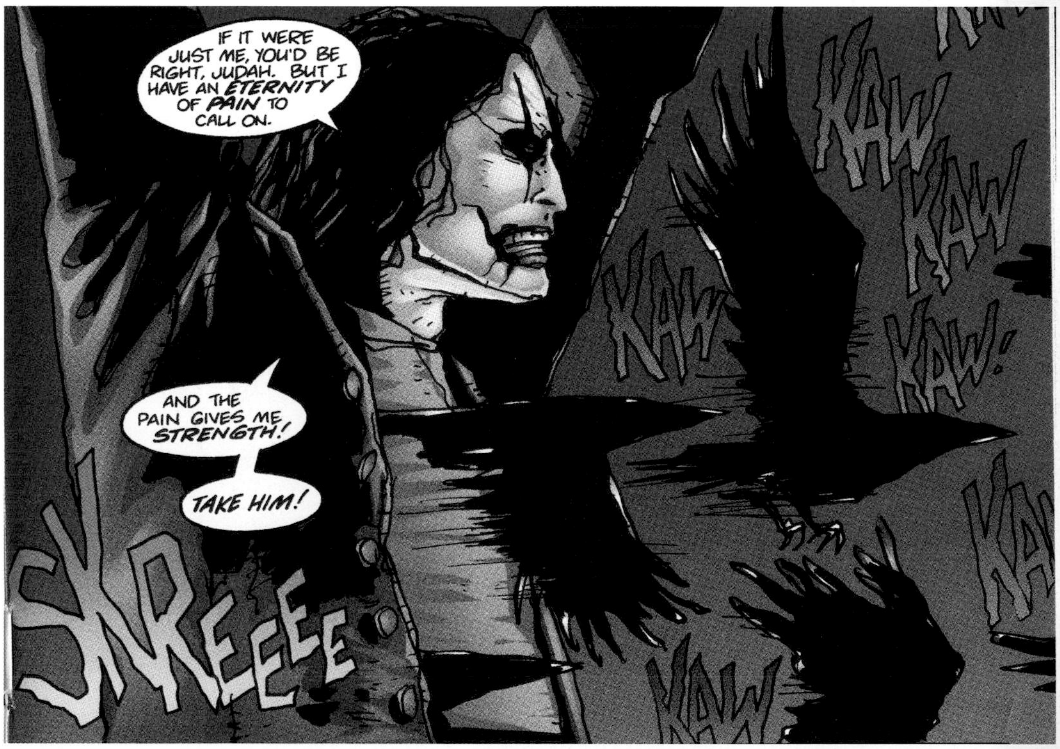
IF IT WERE JUST ME, YOU'D BE RIGHT, JUDAH. BUT I HAVE AN ETERNITY OF PAIN TO CALL ON.
KAW
KAW
KAW
KAW!
AND THE PAIN GIVES ME STRENGTH!
TAKE HIM!
SKREEEE
KAW

■ Yet another dead man who came back to life to seek revenge, he looked somewhat like a leftover member of KISS. Created by James O'Barr, he was introduced late in 1988 in the *Caliber Presents* anthology title. He returned the next year in his own title, a four-part miniseries. The limited series was his métier and there were several through the 1990s. O'Barr both wrote and drew *The Crow*. The second edition of *The Comic Book Heroes* said of his work, "He wove in the storytelling structures and design tricks of superheroes, along with some bloody vigilante fantasies—his protagonist rises from the dead to slaughter the 'inner city' gang responsible for killing him and his fiancée."

The character's popularity was greatly increased by the 1994 movie *The Crow*. It starred Brandon Lee, who was killed during the filming. The film did well at the box office and garnered rave reviews from the likes of *Variety* and Roger Ebert, who called it "the best version of a comic book universe I've seen." A second film in 1996, with a different star, did not fare as well. That second movie was adapted in a three-part comic-book series.

CRUMB, ROBERT

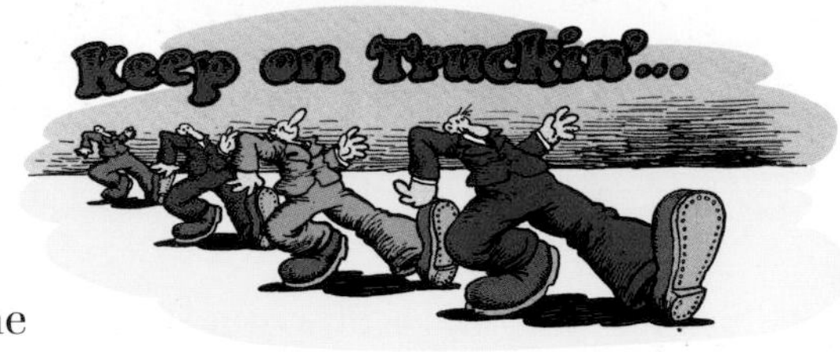
Keep on Truckin'...

■ Like Woody Allen, R. Crumb has parlayed his hang-ups and preoccupations into a long, profitable career. The most popular and widely reprinted of the underground cartoonists, he established himself in the mainstream some years ago and recently his comics have even appeared in *The New Yorker.* Many of his characters and catchphrases—such as Mr. Natural, Fritz the Cat, Devil Girl, and "Keep on truckin'"—are familiar to a great many people who've never been near an underground comic book. And his *Zap Comix,* begun in 1968, is a cornerstone of the independent publishing movement. Crumb's work has always exemplified both the energy and the audacity of the underground approach, and he's a major exponent of the fine art of nasty sex and bad taste.

Born in Philadelphia, Crumb grew up left-handed and Catholic. He was fascinated with comic books, especially the funny animal stuff of Walt Kelly and Carl Barks, and by the time he was three he was already drawing. His two brothers and two sisters also liked to draw, and he and his brother Charles took to drawing their own comic books, chiefly devoted to funny animals, early on. Crumb's teenage years were not happy—"I was such a big jerk, nobody liked me. . . . There was a ten-year period when I felt fiercely alienated from the world. I probably wouldn't have gotten that deeply into cartooning if that hadn't happened."

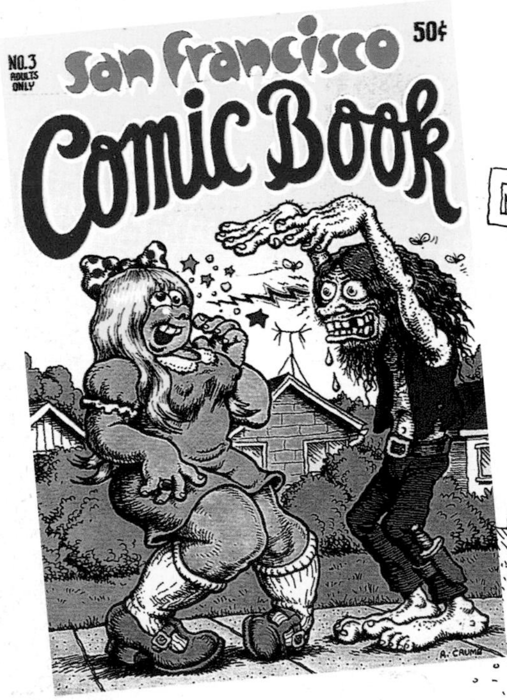
NO.3
ADULTS ONLY
San Francisco
50¢
Comic Book
R. CRUMB

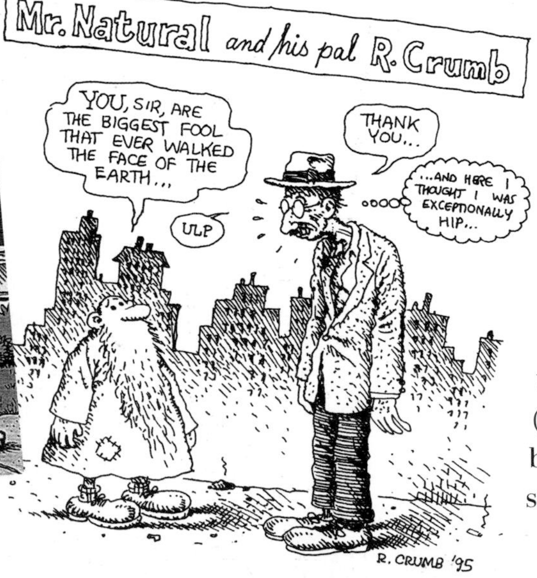
Mr. Natural and his pal R. Crumb
YOU, SIR, ARE THE BIGGEST FOOL THAT EVER WALKED THE FACE OF THE EARTH...
ULP
THANK YOU...
...AND HERE I THOUGHT I WAS EXCEPTIONALLY HIP...
R. CRUMB '95

Crumb went through a conventional phrase in the early 1960s, working in Cleveland for the American Greetings Corporation. After his greeting cards phase, he ventured to New York in 1964, becoming a protégé of Harvey Kurtzman and a contributor to *Help.* By 1967 he was in San Francisco, arriving in the Haight-Ashbury just as the hippie movement was starting to flourish. He became a sort of crotchety Boswell of the movement. An outsider at heart, he was able to write and draw about drugs, love, protest, and violence with a detachment lacking in some of the other chroniclers of the flower children. In addition to starting *Zap,* Crumb drew the lecherous *Fritz the Cat* for the men's magazine *Cavalier.* His highly personal style was an amalgam of various influences, including the funny animals he'd loved as a kid, the cute greeting cards he'd drawn, and the newspaper funnies of the twenties and thirties. He also tossed in references to jazz, current television, and country-blues singers (the phrase "Keep on truckin'" was borrowed from a record by blues singer Blind Boy Fuller).

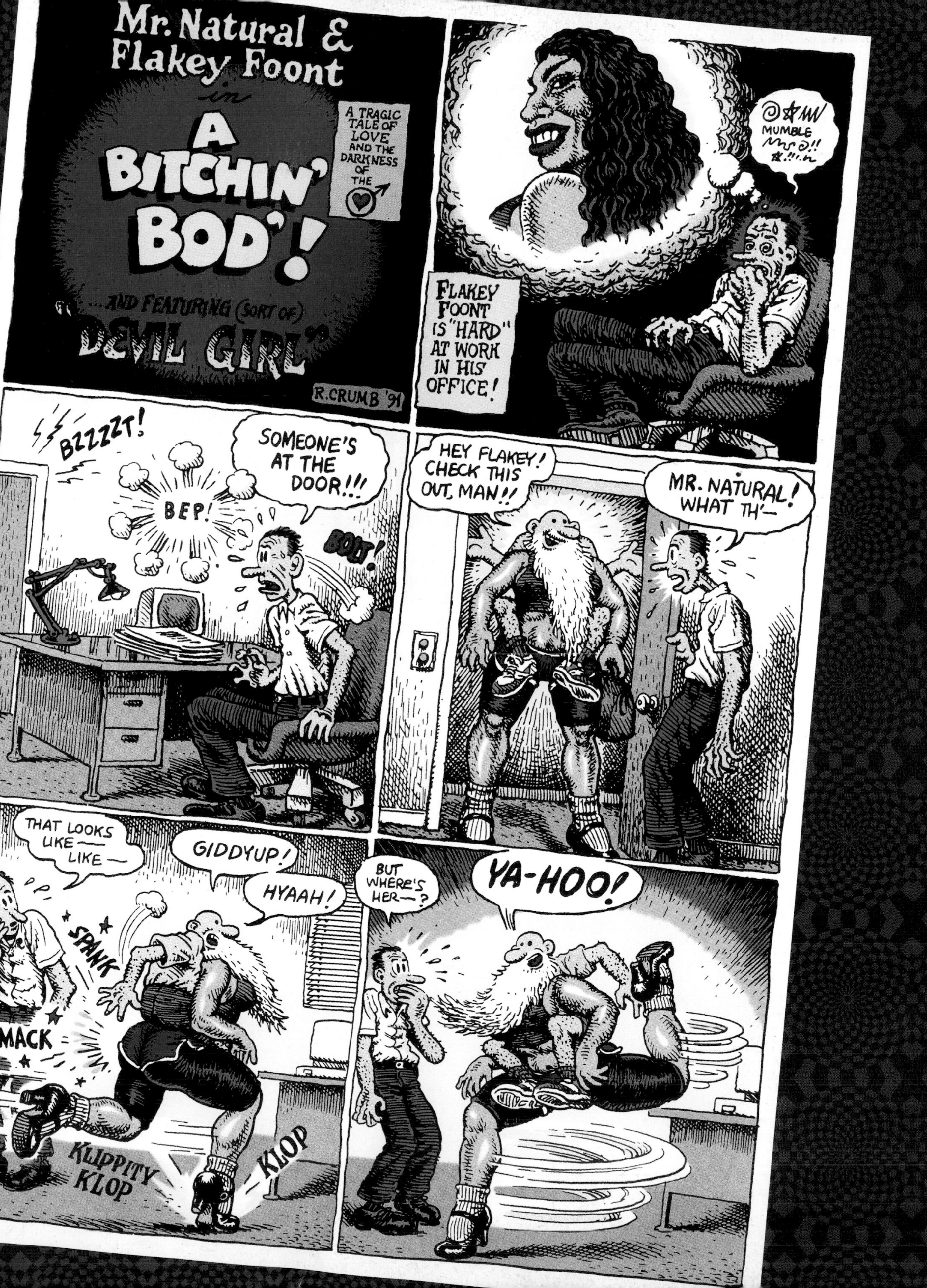
Mr. Natural & Flakey Foont
in
A BITCHIN' BOD'!
A TRAGIC TALE OF LOVE AND THE DARKNESS OF THE ♥ ♂
"...AND FEATURING (SORT OF) "DEVIL GIRL"
R. CRUMB '91
MUMBLE
FLAKEY FOONT IS "HARD" AT WORK IN HIS OFFICE!
BZZZZT!
SOMEONE'S AT THE DOOR!!!
BEP!
BOLT!
HEY FLAKEY! CHECK THIS OUT, MAN!!
MR. NATURAL! WHAT TH'—
THAT LOOKS LIKE— LIKE—
GIDDYUP!
HYAAH!
SPANK
SMACK
KLIPPITY KLOP
KLOP
BUT WHERE'S HER—?
YA-HOO!

During the heyday of undergrounds, his work was also to be found in such publications as *Bijou Funnies*, *Big Ass Comics*, *Bizarre Sex*, *Head Comix*, and *Snatch Funnies*. One of his favorite characters over the years has been himself. He usually appears as a sex-crazed, long-winded bore with bad posture and an obscene moustache. Mean-minded and petty, he's obsessed with women who have large buttocks. Whereas the Ziegfeld Follies glorified the American girl, Crumb has concentrated on glorifying the American girl's backside. The decline and fall of underground comics didn't phase him. He did record covers, gum cards, trading cards, and independent comic books, such as *Weirdo*, subtitled "The Comic Magazine for Low-Life Scum."

Crumb and his wife, cartoonist Alice Kominsky, and his daughter settled in the South of France in the early 1990s. He was supposedly given the house in exchange for six of his art notebooks. In recent years Fantagraphics has undertaken an ambitious program to reprint Crumb's entire output in a series of volumes. He's been compared to George Grosz, Max Beckman, and George Cruickshank, and the *New Yorker* has lauded him.

CRUSE, HOWARD *(1944-)*

■ One of the most gifted cartoonists working mostly outside the mainstream, Cruse has produced an impressive amount of comic-book work in his thirty-plus years of independent output. Although Cruse's most ambitious work to date, the *Stuck Rubber Baby* graphic novel, was published by DC, it was also an independent work as well. Cruse had complete autonomy and was allowed four years to complete it.

...their gay son, Les...
HE USED TO PUSH ME TO GET MARRIED, BUT HE'S LEARNED THAT AIN'T IN THE CARDS.
PAPA'S THE PREACHER IN THE FAMILY AN' I'M THE FAGGOT.
MARTIN LUTHER KING HIMSELF COULD WALK UP AN' SAY TO ME, 'LES, YOU GOTTA QUIT BEIN' GAY!'...
...AN' I'D SAY TO HIM, 'SURE THING, DR. KING—
'—JUST AS SOON AS YOU STOP BEIN' NEGRO!'

A pioneer in drawing and writing comics about everyday gay life, Cruse started a comic strip called *Wendel* for *The Advocate* in the late 1970s. These strips were later collected into trade paperback comic books published by Kitchen Sink. Cruse also created, edited, and contributed to *Gay Comix*. The award-winning *Stuck Rubber Baby* deals with both sexual identity and the civil rights movement in the South in the 1960s. Although the most serious work by Cruse, it still has moments of his more characteristic humor. While Cruse works as an illustrator and commercial artist, his favorite field remains comics.

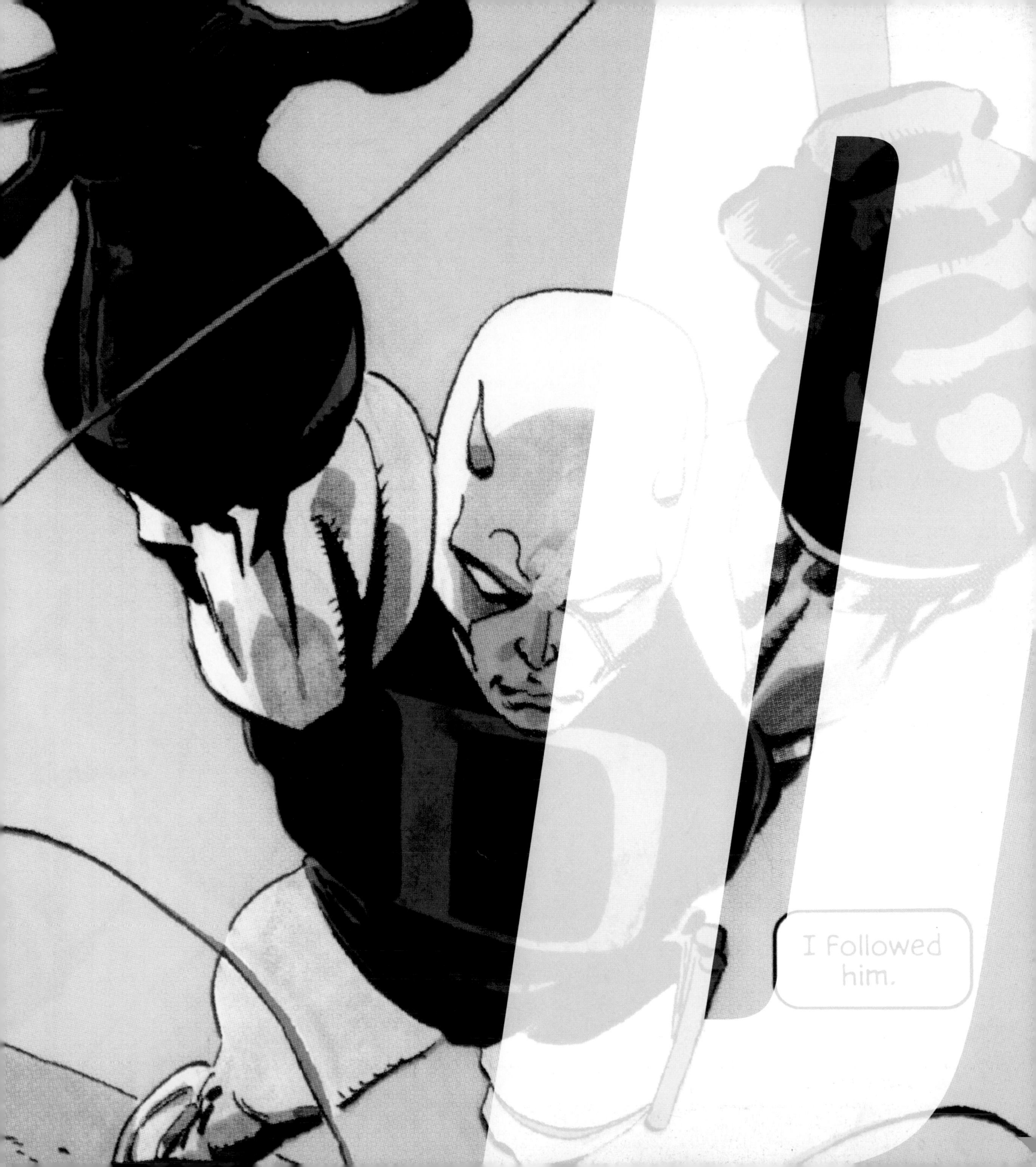
I followed him.

DANGER GIRL

■ Since the name Charlie's Angels was already taken when these three young ladies entered the danger business, they were christened Team Danger Girl. Introduced in Image's *Cliffhanger* #0 in 1997, they moved into a sporadically issued magazine of their own the next year. *Danger Girl* was a joint creation of writer Andy Hartnell and artist J. Scott Campbell, also noted for his work on *Gen 13*. Were the term Good Girl Art still in use, Campbell would certainly be ranked one of its prime practitioners.

The basic team consists of Abbey Chase, Sydney Savage, and Natalia Kassle. Like the Angels, a mysterious gent runs their operation. His name is Deuce, and he operates from a vessel called the Danger Yacht. In his case, Deuce actually appears now and then, looking somewhat like Sean Connery with a ponytail. A redheaded teenager named Valerie assists Deuce about the yacht and sometimes works alongside the other three young women.

Mixing international intrigue, parody, and cheesecake, *Danger Girl* somewhat resembles a merger between a James Bond movie and *Little Annie Fanny*. In addition to Campbell, both Arthur Adams and Phil Nito have drawn the feature. The group appeared most recently in a two-part series called *Danger Girl Kamikaze* published late in 2001.

ABBEY AND JOHNNY MANAGE TO ENTER THE PARTY AS GUESTS.

WHILE SYDNEY AND NATALIA ARRIVED EARLIER AS SERVERS, ALLOWING THEM TO LOOK THE PLACE OVER.

DANGER TRAIL

■ As one postwar alternative to superheroes, DC gave foreign intrigue a try. The first issue of *Danger Trail* appeared in the summer of 1950. The blurb above the title promised "World-wide Adventure in Mystery and Intrigue!" The leading exponent of trench-coat diplomacy was King Faraday, a creation of Robert Kanigher and Carmine Infantino. Alex Toth used the magazine to try out a new and pared-down style, one that produced some striking one-shot stories, including a very effective

Foreign Legion yarn. Faraday was bumped after the fourth issue, replaced by a new improved version of Johnny Peril. An interesting experiment, possibly ahead of its time, *Danger Trail* was canceled after its fifth issue early in 1951.

DC gave it one more try, reviving *Danger Trail* as a four-issue miniseries in 1993. King Faraday returned, again drawn by Infantino, with Len Wein as writer. And there the trail ended.

DAREDEVIL: I

■ The first costumed crimebuster to bear the name of Daredevil was born in 1940 in the pages of *Silver Streak Comics.* He added a magazine of his own the following year and enjoyed a career that lasted throughout the 1940s. He had no superpowers, relying on his wits, his striking bilateral crimson-and-midnight-blue costume, and his boomerang to help him fight werewolves, ladykillers, stranglers, the enormous Asiatic villain known as the Claw, and even Adolf Hitler. He also wore an awe-inspiring belt that resembled a large spiked dog collar. Daredevil had started life as a rather bland fellow, but soon changed into a violent and virile fellow. Among those who worked on his adventures were two of the most influential artist/writers of the period, Jack Cole and Charles Biro.

SILVER STREAK COMICS
DAREDEVIL
BATTLES
THE
CLAW
AN. No. 7
10c

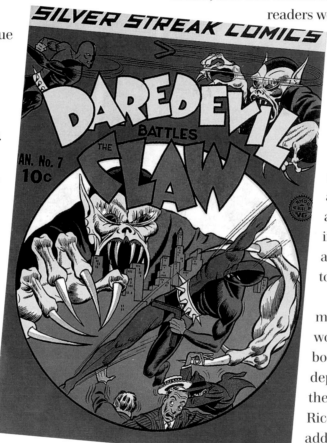

Late in 1939, Arthur Bernhard, who had been involved in publishing magazines of all sorts, ventured into comics with *Silver Streak.* After a few issues he hired Cole to edit. The youthful cartoonist wrote and drew the adventures of the speedy Silver Streak, cramming the pages with action, violence, monsters, pretty women, and humor.

The magazine's only other costumed hero was Daredevil, who was introduced in a bland six-page story in #6 (September 1940). Jack Binder was the artist. The next month Cole took over the character and did something audacious by pretending he was working with a well-established hero. "DAREDEVIL BATTLES THE CLAW," announced his flamboyant cover. This was only a few months after the Human Torch and Sub-Mariner had carried on a monumental battle over in *Marvel Mystery Comics,* and Cole must have assumed that comic-book readers were ready for another full-scale fracas. He devoted sixteen pages of the issue to round one. It started off with an impressive splash page that mixed sex, violence, and the Yellow Peril, and included a teaser disclaimer that cautioned, "WARNING!! You are about to read one of the most astonishing tales ever portrayed in a comic magazine! If you have a weak heart, we advise you NOT to venture further!"

The battle continued for four more issues and by the time it wound up, Lev Gleason had bought into the company. Cole departed, and Daredevil fell into the heavy hands of artist Don Rico. The publishers, however, had additional plans for the hero, and in the summer of 1941 Daredevil graduated to a book of his own.

The first issue was entitled *Daredevil Battles Hitler.* Bernhard has said that the comic was an expression of his own antifascist, anti-Hitler activities. His views were shared by Gleason. The cover was a joint effort of Biro and Bob Wood, signed Woodro. The contents, however, were produced by the Funnies, Inc., shop and included contributions from George Mandel, Harry Sahle, Bill

Everett, and Bob Davis (who wrote and drew a bio of Hitler). The inside back cover carried an ad for the upcoming *Daredevil Comics*—"By Popular DEMAND—What you've all been waiting for—the DAREDEVIL'S OWN COMIC BOOK." Bernhard and Gleason brought in Biro and Wood to edit and produce the new titles. Besides exploiting the combination of violence and titillation that would become a Gleason hallmark, Biro added packaging tricks that eventually became industry standards. From its first issue, *Daredevil* bore an aggressive slogan—"The Greatest Name in Comics." Covers were also littered with boxes of copy that promised all sorts of thrills and delights, including money. "$100 CASH PRIZES You May WIN" was a typical Biro cover come-on.

Among the other characters to be found in the new title were *London* by Jerry Robinson, who was assisting on *Batman* at the time, and *Nightro* by George Roussos, who was assisting on *Batman* at the time. Bob Montana contributed fillers.

In #13, Daredevil met the little Wise Guys. The idea that a gang of feisty, two-fisted boys could be entertaining had become popular in 1937, after the Warner Brothers movie version of the hit play *Dead End* was released. Joe Simon and Jack Kirby had already introduced several kid gangs to comic books, so Biro wasn't covering especially new ground. He did, however, kill off one of the kids after only a couple of issues. Something unheard of until then.

Gradually the Daredevil dropped back into an avuncular role as the Wise Guys got involved with street crime, delinquency, and other pop sociology topics. It's possible that Biro intended these rather preachy tales to counterbalance the blood-and-guts fare he was helping to concoct for Gleason's *Crime Does Not Pay*.

At any rate, the bizarre villains and plots of Daredevil's salad years vanished, and more uplifting and wordier tales took over. After playing a smaller and smaller role, Daredevil dropped out for good in the winter of 1950. The magazine, still bearing his name, continued until 1956 with the Little Wise Guys as stars. Biro had long since farmed out the artwork on his strip to Carl Hubbel, Dan Barry, and Norman Maurer and most of the scriptwriting to Virginia Hubbell.

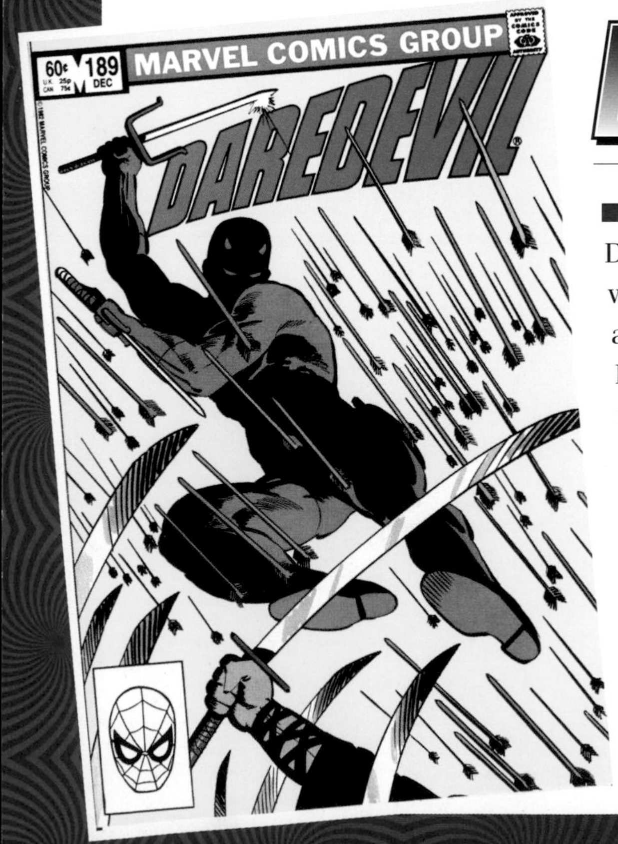
MARVEL COMICS GROUP
60¢ 189 DEC
DAREDEVIL

DAREDEVIL: II

■ Borrowing the name of his favorite Biro character, Stan Lee came up with a Daredevil of his own early in 1964. His Daredevil, known as the Man Without Fear, was introduced in his own magazine. The Silver Age was an era of flawed heroes, and the Daredevil's affliction was blindness. In everyday life he was attorney Matt Murdock. Because he'd lost his sight after being struck by a truck hauling radioactive materials, he acquired "incredible powers" that allowed him to navigate the city's rooftops with an uncanny sixth sense that was somewhat like radar. Daredevil headed out for his first adventures garbed in a red, yellow, and black costume that he sewed up himself. By the seventh issue, his outfit was a deep red. Bill Everett illustrated Daredevil's first adventure, Stan Lee wrote the script. It's possible that Steve Ditko also sat in on the early planning sessions.

Everett was followed by Joe Orlando, Wally Wood, and John Romita. In 1966, Gene Colan became the regular artist on the acrobatic avenger's adventures and remained on the job until the early 1970s. In 1979 Frank Miller took over the drawing. He worked in a highly personal style that showed a variety of influences, including Will Eisner, Steranko, Bernard Krigstein, Japanese prints, martial arts movies, and European comic-book artists such as Moebius and Guido Crepax. Miller was much aware that page breakdowns could be used to control and manipulate time. He chopped them up horizontally and vertically and sometimes sliced each tier into a half dozen or more frames. Readers soon took notice of Miller's new approach and although *Daredevil* didn't shoot straight up to the lead position on the sales charts, it was very soon in the top twenty.

Late in 1980, Miller also assumed the scriptwriting. He soon introduced one of the most formidable women ever seen in comics. She was Elektra, Daredevil's most fascinating foe, and the two of them carried on a complex and engaging love-hate relationship. "Coming in at the end of a decade of wordy, introspective, unimaginative fare, Miller distinguished himself not only as a good plotter but as a dazzlingly effective storyteller," observed Will Jacobs and Gerard Jones in *The Comic Book Heroes.* A notable element of Miller's storytelling was its explicit violence. Censorship standards had relaxed considerably since the days when comic books had been tossed on bonfires by their critics, and Miller's *Daredevil* became increasingly bloody and violent. "Elektra was truly ruthless in her assaults with an arsenal of Oriental death-devices," commented Jacobs and Jones.

After leaving Daredevil in 1983, Miller returned in 1986 for a stint as writer, with Dave Mazzuchelli doing the drawing. Elektra made a notable return in 1986 to 1987, with scripts by Miller and very impressive art by Bill Sienkiewicz. And she is around to this day. The Man Without Fear continued in his grim mode throughout the 1990s. In the twenty-first century Brian Michael Bendis has done most of the *Daredevil* scripting and the drawing of the latest artist, Alex Maleev, perfectly fits the downbeat noir scripts.

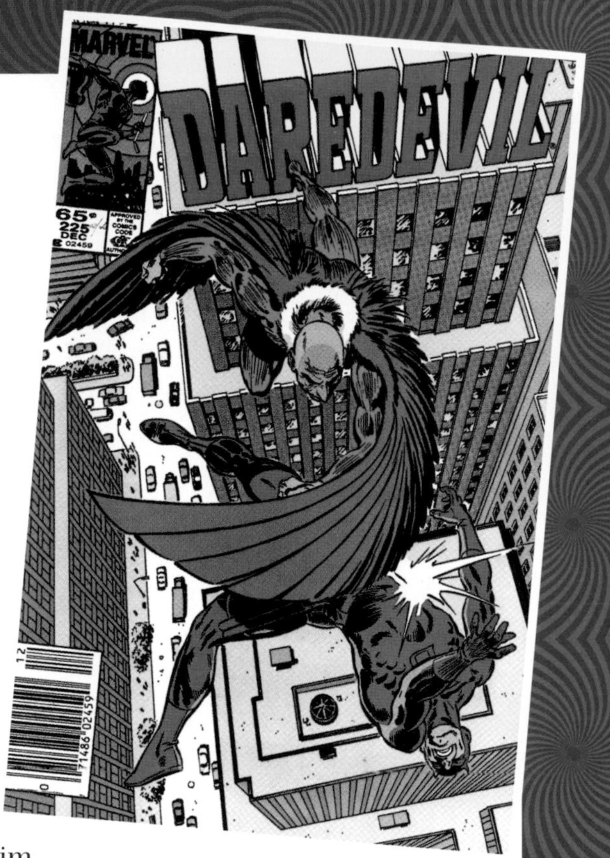
MARVEL
DAREDEVIL
65¢
225
DEC

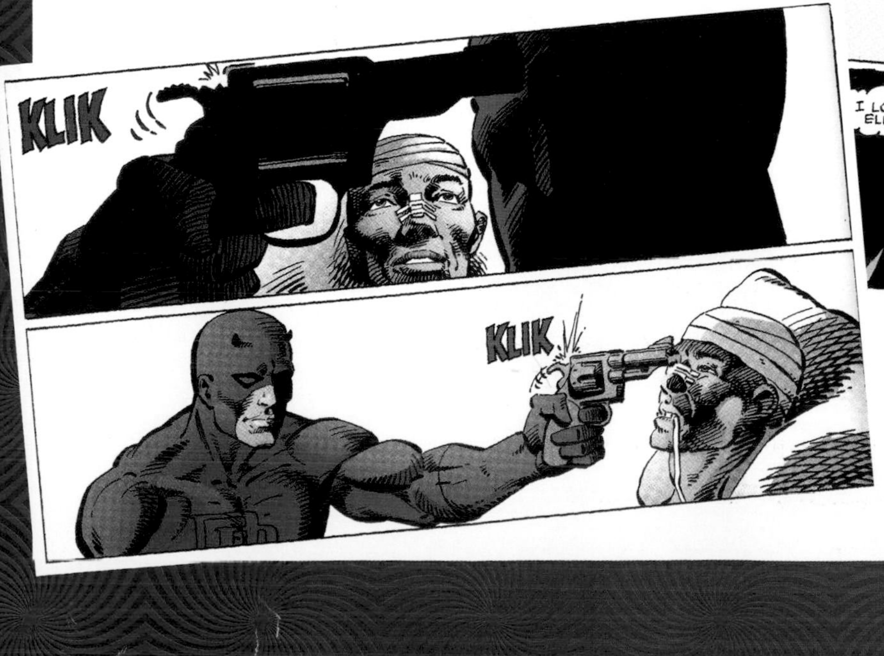
KLIK
KLIK

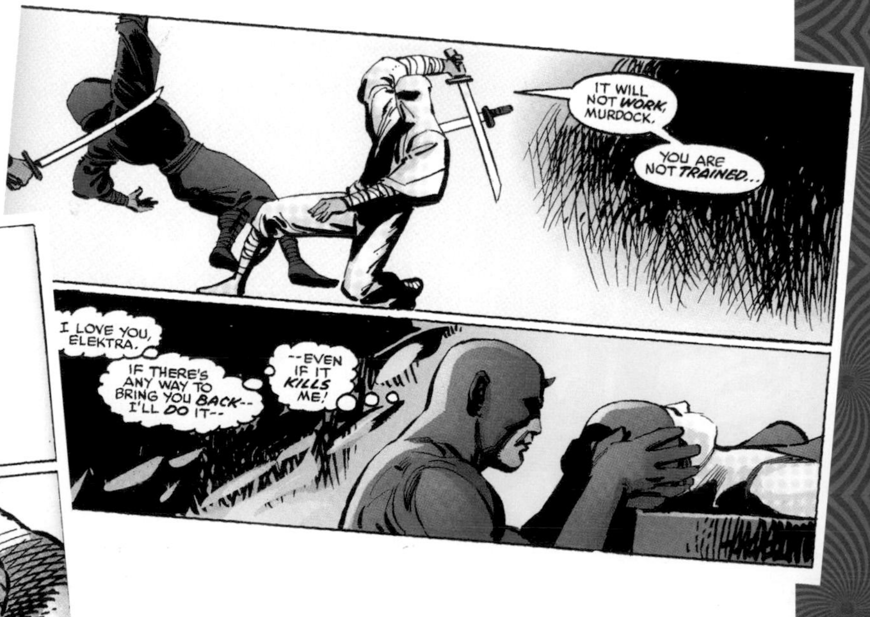
IT WILL NOT WORK, MURDOCK.
YOU ARE NOT TRAINED...
I LOVE YOU, ELEKTRA.
IF THERE'S ANY WAY TO BRING YOU BACK-- I'LL DO IT--
--EVEN IF IT KILLS ME!

DARING MYSTERY COMICS

■ Proving that it's very tough to make lightning strike twice in the same place, *Daring* was basically a flop. That in spite of the fact that, eventually, it was packaged by the same studio that had produced the highly successful *Marvel Mystery Comics.* Intended as a newsstand companion for *Marvel,* it achieved only eight sporadically published issues from late 1939 to 1941. Never sure of itself, Timely's *Daring Mystery* auditioned over three dozen characters during its short life and never settled on a regular lineup. Among the many tryouts were Marvel Boy, the Fin, Captain Daring, Citizen V, the Silver Scorpion, the Phantom Bullet, Zephyr Jones, the Fiery Mask, the Laughing Mask, and the Purple Mask.

The contents of the early numbers were provided by both the Funnies, Inc., and the Harry "A" Chesler shops. The stodgy Chesler studio provided such clinkers as *The Texas Kid, Flash Foster at Midwestern, Trojak the Tiger Man, K-4 and His Sky Devils, The Falcon, Whirlwind Carter of the Interplanetary Secret Service,* and *Breeze Barton* (drawn by a novice Mac Raboy). The Funnies team didn't do much better with the likes of *Monako–Prince of Magic* and *The Fiery Mask.* Things took a turn for the better with the addition of *Marvel Boy* by Joe Simon and Jack Kirby in #6 (September 1941). But that was the young superhero's only appearance, and thereafter *Daring* went on a seven-month hiatus.

The seventh issue arrived in the spring of 1941 with an entirely new cast, this time all produced by Funnies, Inc. Bill Everett produced the Fin, another of his aquatic heroes, and Carl Burgos drew the Thunderer. Ben Thompson, who was drawing *Ka-Zar* over at Marvel, came up with the *Blue Diamond,* Kirby drew *Captain Daring* (a sci-fi chap, not a superman), and Harry Sahle offered a costumed lady crimefighter known as the Silver Scorpion. This seemingly viable lineup was modified with the addition of Citizen V, a costumed guerrilla fighter in #8, which didn't arrive on the stands until after a lapse of nine months. The Fin and the Silver Scorpion remained aboard when *Daring* changed its named to *Comedy Comics* with #9 (April 1942). They were gone by the following number. Then an assortment of comedy characters appeared for an issue or two. Among them were Archie the Gnome, Maymee Hazzit (by George Tuska), the Vagabond, Casey McCann, etc. By #14 (March 1943) *Comedy* was a funny animal book starring Super Rabbit.

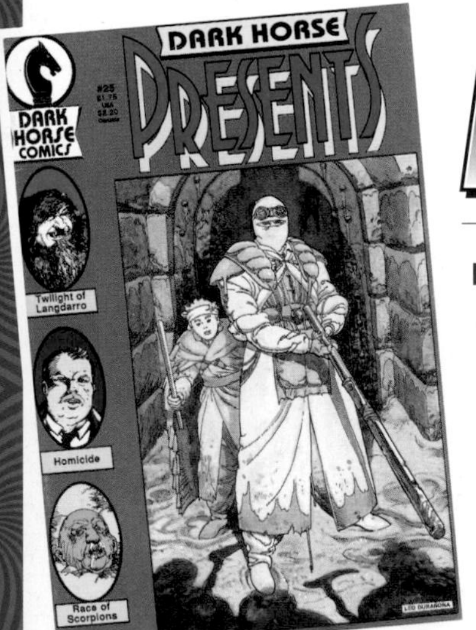
DARK HORSE
PRESENTS
DARK HORSE COMICS
Twilight of Langdarro
Homicide
Race of Scorpions

DARK HORSE PRESENTS

■ A combination sampler and auditioning spot, *Dark Horse Presents,* a black-and-white comic, thrived for 157 issues from the summer of 1986 to the summer of 2000. During that time it introduced such features as Paul Chadwick's *Concrete* and John Byrne's *The Next Men* and also ran episodes of Frank Miller's *Sin City,* Evan Dorkin's *Milk & Cheese,* Mike Mignola's *Hellboy,* and Arthur Adams' *Monkeyman & O'Brien.* In addition, the monthly showcased adaptations of such movie-generated characters as the Predator and Buffy the Vampire Slayer.

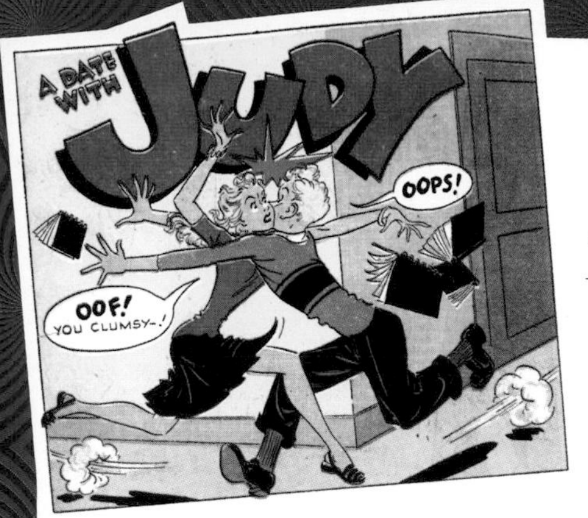
A DATE WITH
JUDY
OOPS!
OOF! YOU CLUMSY--!

A DATE WITH JUDY

■ Judy Foster was a teenager for almost twenty years. Nowhere near as long as Archie Andrews, but still not a bad run. Her first medium was radio, where *A Date with Judy* began, as a weekly half-hour comedy show in June of 1941. The show was created and written by Aleen Leslie. After three years of being heard only as an NBC summer replacement, *Judy* was promoted to a year-round spot in 1944. Judy achieved greater fame in 1948 when MGM brought a musical version of *A Date with Judy* to the screen. Jane Powell was Judy and the supporting cast included Elizabeth Taylor, Wallace Beery, and Carmen Miranda. There was also a *Judy* television show from 1951 to 1953.

DC Comics, during a postwar crusade to woo more teens and preteens, introduced its bimonthly comic-book version in the autumn of 1947. The comic book kept Judy alive until the end of 1960. Each issue offered a quartet of stories about the hyperactive, modestly boy-crazy blonde, her often perplexed parents, her boyfriend Oogie, and her kid brother Randolph. The continuities, which mixed situation comedy with simple slapstick, were drawn for most of the magazine's run by Graham Place, a former animator. Paul S. Newman, destined to become one of the most prolific writers in comics, turned out his first scripts for *Judy*.

DAVIS, BOB

■ See BLUE BOLT.

DAVIS, JACK *(1926-)*

■ The heyday of his comic-book career came in the 1950s, when he was one of the busiest cartoonists working for William Gaines's EC line. Versatile, Davis excelled at both serious and humorous drawing. That meant his work fit into not only *Tales from fhe Crypt* and *Two-Fisted Tales* but also *Mad*.

Davis drew cartoons for the campus newspaper while attending the University of Georgia and also worked for an off-campus humor magazine. He moved to Manhattan in 1950. After various arts jobs, he eventually signed on with EC. Some of the more explicit horror tales he illustrated while there, Davis later regretted—"At the time, I didn't realize how bad it was . . . But now that I look back, I know it was."

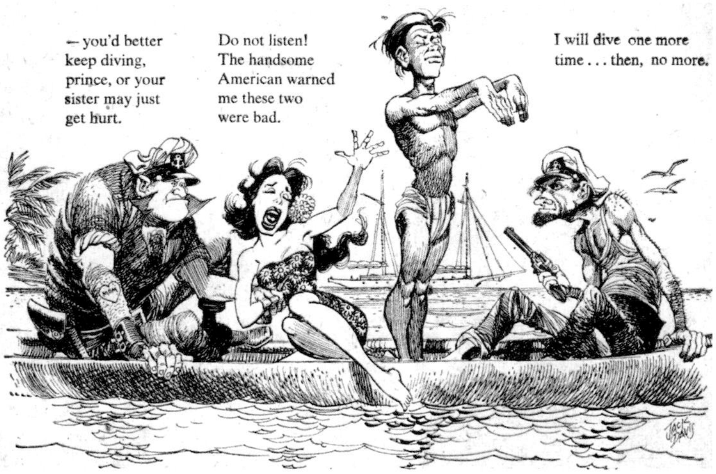
—you'd better keep diving, prince, or your sister may just get hurt.
Do not listen! The handsome American warned me these two were bad.
I will dive one more time . . . then, no more.

He worked several years for *Mad*, the only EC title that lasted beyond the 1950s. Davis was also a contributor to Harvey Kurtzman's ill-fated *Humbug*. Later on he became a highly successful commercial artist, because, as he once explained, quite a few young art directors had been fans of his *Mad* efforts in their youth.

DAZZLER

■ The only disco singer who ever became a superhero, Allison Blaire was given a Marvel comic of her own early in 1981. A mutant and a reluctant law student, she was first on display in *X-Men* #130 (February 1980), an issue drawn by John Byrne and written by Chris Claremont. After a few more appearances with the X-bunch, she graduated to *Dazzler.* Her basic ability involved converting sound, especially music, into bursts of radiant light that were so intense they temporarily blinded her opponents and usually knocked them cold. In other words, she could dazzle people.

According to an article by Richard Gagnon in a 1986 issue of *Amazing Heroes,* "the idea to create a singer who has super-powers came not from Marvel Comics, but from Casablanca Records. . . . The idea was to have a singer tour the country dressed as the Marvel character, thereby both the comic and the singer would gain free publicity." The project, initiated in the late 1970s, eventually produced Dazzler, but by that time the record company had long since withdrawn. Marvel continued alone and after trying the character out in *X-Men* launched their *Dazzler* title with considerable fanfare. They also offered the book for sale only in comic shops, something that could be done in the days when newsstands still handled comics. The first issue sold well.

Allison had a tendency in her early days, when she wasn't acting as a one-woman light show, to speak in a slangy show biz manner—"World savin' ain't my style . . . I prefer singin' my heart out to an audience that really digs me." She eventually modified her speech patterns, particularly in the later issues written by Archie Goodwin.

Dazzler's initial run, mixing singing with combating such villains as Dr. Sax, the Enchantress, and Dr. Doom, ran until #42 early in 1986. Like many another singer, Allison's popularity faded and the cover of that final issue carried the unkind blurb—"Because you demanded it—the LAST issue of Dazzler!"

Dazzler also appeared in a four-part series with the Beast. She has made occasional comebacks since then and even had an affair with Longshot.

DEADMAN

■ Following in the ghostly footsteps of the Spectre, he didn't really get going as a superhero until he'd been killed. Created by writer Arnold Drake and drawn initially by Carmine Infantino, Deadman first died in DC's *Strange Adventures* #205 (October 1967). Boston Brand did a circus trapeze act wearing a red costume and his face painted a ghost-white. That his circus name was Deadman may indicate that Brand had a premonition that he'd be killed one night while in the midst of his aerialist stuff. He didn't die by accident, but from a sniper's bullet.

Normally that would have been that. However, a benevolent entity known as Rama Kushna intervened. He arranged for Brand's sprit to remain earthbound until he found his killer and brought him to justice. Deadman would be invisible, to everybody but the reader, but he would have the power to take over other folks' bodies for a temporary stay if he needed a human form for his quest. You'd think that a mystical entity with Rama Kushna's powers could simply have told Deadman the name of his killer and saved a lot of trouble, but such was not the case. Brand, therefore, spent considerable time in *Strange Adventures* and then in his own title tracking down the killer who was known only as the Hook. For most of this run Neal Adams was the regular artist.

After finding his killer, Deadman had his mission extended to the fighting of evil in general. That he's done, with a few fallow periods, ever since. He returned, for example, in a two-part series in 1989, wherein he met and fell in love with the ghost of a lady aerialist. That was written by Mike Baron and drawn by Kelly Jones, whose

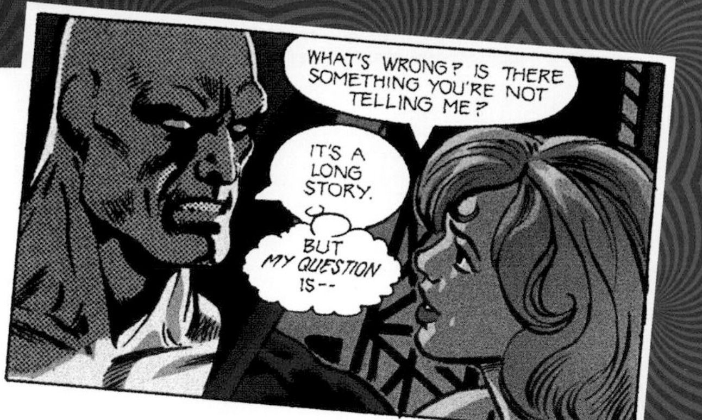
WHAT'S WRONG? IS THERE SOMETHING YOU'RE NOT TELLING ME?
IT'S A LONG STORY.
BUT MY QUESTION IS--

Deadman was an extremely skinny chap. Most recently, in 2002, there was a nine-issue run of *Deadman.* Written by Steve Vance, it was drawn by various artists. Mike Mignola contributed some covers and Jose Luis Garcia-Lopez drew two very impressive issues. Once again Brand fell in love with a ghost, this time an attractive blond young woman who'd just been murdered. Once he catches her killer, her spirit moves on to the hereafter and Deadman is once again alone.

DENNIS THE MENACE

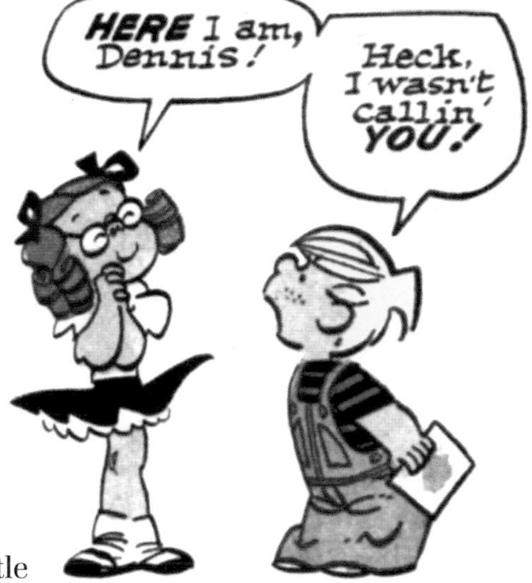
HERE I am, Dennis!
Heck, I wasn't callin' YOU!

■ Hank Ketcham's daily cartoon panel started appearing in newspapers in March of 1951 and a Sunday page was added the following year. At its height of popularity *Dennis the Menace* ran in close to eight hundred papers in the United States. The boisterous five-year-old entered comic books in 1953. These were published first by Ned Pines, then from late 1958 by Fawcett. This was several years after Fawcett had abandoned Captain Marvel and the other members of the Marvel Family.

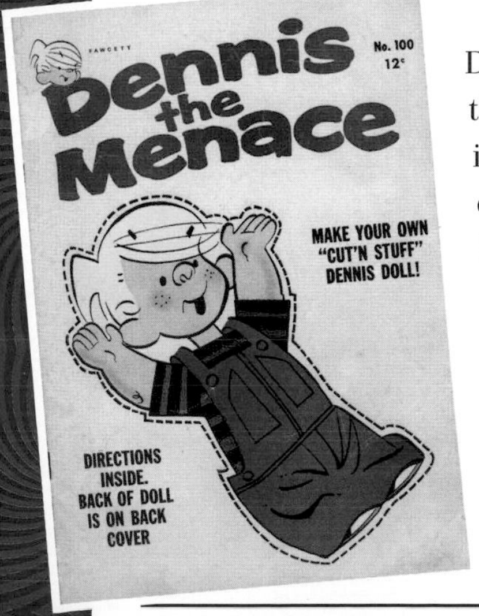
No. 100
12¢
Dennis the Menace
MAKE YOUR OWN "CUT'N STUFF" DENNIS DOLL!
DIRECTIONS INSIDE. BACK OF DOLL IS ON BACK COVER

As comics historian Dennis Wepman has pointed out, little Dennis Mitchell was "neither malicious nor aggressive . . . destructive more to the composure than to the property of his staid family or neighbors." Chief among those neighbors was the irascible Mr. Wilson, a perennial foil for Dennis. Wilson and the Mitchells made up the core cast of the comic books, all of which continued original adventures of the miniature menace. Not limited to the typical town of the panel, the books took Dennis and his family all over the country, including vacations in Hawaii, Hollywood, and Mexico. The comic book was well done, proving popular with younger readers in the days when there were still kid-oriented titles. Longtime Ketcham ghost Al Wiseman, who was a much better artist than his boss, drew the majority of the comics, including the Giant Specials. Fred Toole provided most of the scripts.

The Fawcett series concluded at the very end of 1969. Marvel brought back Dennis for a short run in the early 1980s.

DETECTIVE DAN

A STORY IN CARTOONS
DETECTIVE DAN
SECRET OPERATIVE NO. 48
STICK 'EM UP, TWO FINGER—YOU'RE UNDER ARREST!
THE WHITE CAT MURDER

■ In 1933, Norman Marsh, a pugnacious ex-marine and second-rate cartoonist, decided to become a comic-book publisher—not a crowded field at the time. He formed the Humor Publishing Company, based in Chicago, and his first title was his own *Detective Dan.* Also known as Secret Operative 48, Dan was a shaky imitation of Chester Gould's Dick Tracy, who'd been successfully appearing in a newspaper strip since 1931. Later in 1933 Dan morphed into Dan Dunn for a Marsh comic strip released by the Publishers Syndicate. A thirty-six-page black-and-white magazine printed on pulp paper, *Detective Dan* was not exactly a template for other original-material comic books to come. It was, however, a pioneering precursor of original comic books that followed.

Since Marsh included drug dealers and naked women in his comic book, it's obvious he wasn't aiming at a kid audience. What's also likely is that he intended *Detective Dan* as a showcase to use in selling his *Dick Tracy* knockoff to a syndicate. The only other two Humor titles he published were *Ace King,* with a detective billed as "the American Sherlock Holmes," and *Bob Scully, the Two-Fisted Hick Detective.* Possibly distracted by the sale of his newspaper strip, Norman Marsh closed shop after publishing those three issues.

According to comics historian Robert Beerbohm, Humor Publications had also agreed to publish an early version of Siegel and Shuster's *Superman* but shut down before getting around to it. The artwork for the cover still exists.

DIAL H FOR HERO

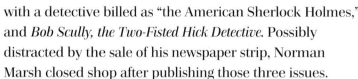

■ Replacing the traditional magic word with a gadget, *Dial H for Hero* offered a young protagonist who could turn into a multiplicity of superheroes. The only problem for Robby Reed was he never knew in advance what sort of hero he'd turn into when he dialed H-E-R-O on the strange dialer he'd stumbled upon. This added an element of Russian roulette to the process. The feature, written by Dave Wood and drawn by Jim Mooney, was introduced in DC's *House of Mystery* #156 (January 1966).

Robby, a blond teenager, found the dial in a hidden cavern. It looked like part of an alien telephone. Once he'd figured out how to translate the interstellar language on the device, Robby realized it was a "transformation tool" and that when he dialed the alien equivalent of *hero* he'd be transformed into one. Somewhat more time consuming than shouting, "Shazam!" but offering a wider range of alternate identities. Robby was only the star of *House of Mystery* for seventeen issues before being dumped early in 1968. During that time he'd fought such villains as the Thunderbolts and Dr. Light in the form of such superhumans as the Cometeer, Sphinx Man, Giant-Boy, and, once, Plastic Man.

The hero dial returned to DC comics in the early 1980s, but without Robby Reed using it. This time, in fact, there were two dials and thus both Vicki Grant and Chris King could be transformed. This version of *Dial H* lasted until 1984. Marv Wolfman wrote the scripts; Carmine Infantino did the drawing. The feature appeared in *Adventure Comics* and *New Adventures of Superboy.*

DICK TRACY

FIRST OF THREE $3.95 US $4.95 CAN
DICK TRACY
BOOK ONE:
BIG CITY BLUES

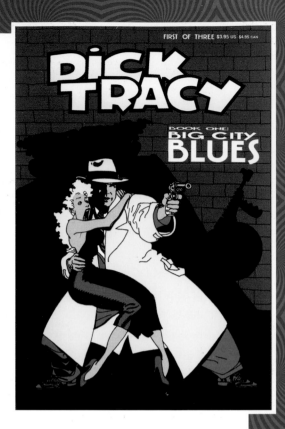

■ A widely reprinted detective, Chester Gould's hawk-nosed Dick Tracy was first seen in a newspaper strip in 1931. The very first Big Little Book reprinted some of the Tracy strips in 1932 and one of the last Cupples & Leon hardcover comic books did the following year. By 1936 the *Dick Tracy* strip was being reprinted in full color as one of the many features in Dell's *Popular Comics*. Dick, his sidekick Pat Patton, his girlfriend Tess Trueheart, and Junior moved over to *Super Comics* two years later, and several issues of McKay's black-and-white Feature Books were devoted to them. There were also, over the years, quite a few thirty-two-page paper-covered *Dick Tracy* comic books that appeared as premiums and giveaways.

Dell launched a *Dick Tracy Monthly* in 1948, which was taken over by Harvey Publications in 1950. Some issues used original stories ghosted by Art Huhta. Various small publishers have reissued Tracy material in the decades since then.

UNUSUAL TALES
PUPILS MATERIALIZED ON WHAT HAD BEEN STONE-BLANK EYES... HER BEAUTIFUL LIPS PARTED IN A WON-DERING SMILE...

DITKO, STEVE (1927-)

■ He was present at the creation of Marvel's most successful superhero. And in addition to being the cocreator of Spider-Man, he created Dr. Strange. Ditko broke into comics in the early 1950s, drawing fantasy and horror tales for *Strange Suspense Stories*, *Fantastic Fears*, and *Black Magic*. By 1956 he'd linked up with Charlton to draw *Tales of the Mysterious Traveler*. Later in the 1950s, Ditko went to work for Marvel, turning out somewhat quirky tales of fantasy and horror for titles like *Journey into Mystery* and *Tales of Suspense*. One of his specialties was alien invaders.

Ditko invented Captain Atom for Charlton in 1960 and in 1962, working with Stan Lee, he began his run with Spider-Man. He designed all the major characters—Peter Parker, Aunt May, J. Jonah Jameson, etc.—as well as such major villains as Dr. Octopus, the Vulture, and the Green Goblin. By this time Ditko had developed a distinctive style of his own, inspired in part by both Jack Kirby and Joe Kubert. He went on to draw Iron Man and upgrade his costume and also to revitalize the Hulk.

Leaving Marvel in 1966, Ditko worked for Dell and then DC, where one of his creations was the strange and flamboyantly costumed Creeper. Later he worked again for Marvel. Highly independent, Ditko left mainstream comics some years ago.

DR. FATE

■ A variety of people, some of them reincarnated, have done business as Dr. Fate since the character was introduced in the spring of 1940. Created by Gardner Fox and artist Howard Sherman, he was a cross between a superhero and an occult detective. He was introduced in *More Fun Comics* #55 a few months after the Spectre, making that DC periodical one of the spookier publications of the day.

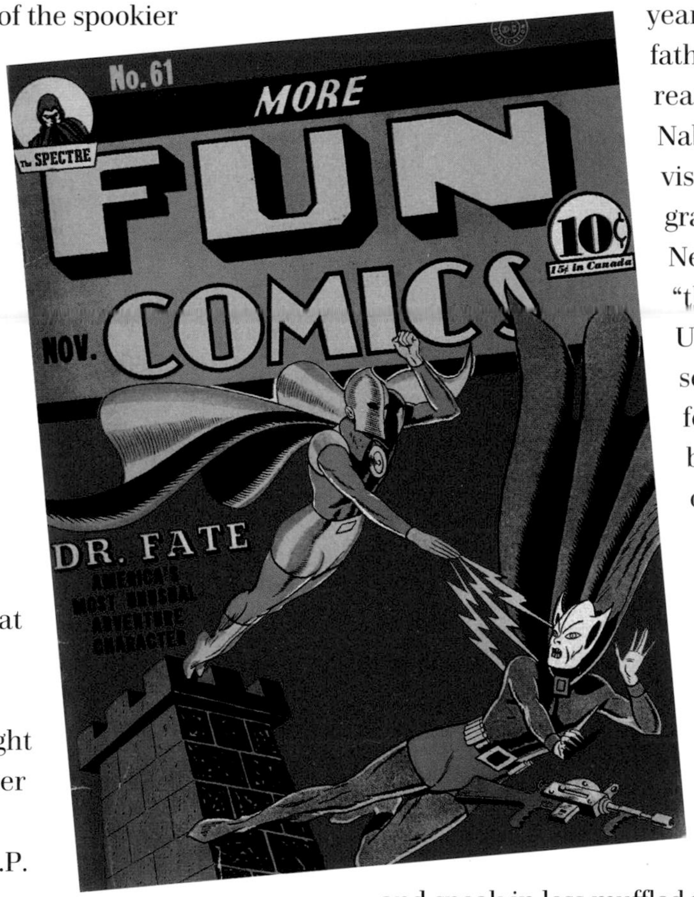
No. 61
MORE
FUN
COMICS
NOV.
10¢
15¢ in Canada
The SPECTRE
DR. FATE
AMERICA'S MOST UNUSUAL ADVENTURE CHARACTER

An early caption spoke of the original Dr. Fate, who wore a blue-and-gold costume and a golden helmet that completely covered his face, as a "man of mystery, possessor of ancient secrets." He resided "apart from mankind in his lonely tower north of ghost-ridden Salem" and called "upon secret and ancient sources for the power with which he fights unusual crimes." He described himself at this time as being "not human. . . . The elder gods created me here on Earth to fight evil sorcery!" A dedicated reader of pulp fiction, Fox turned to *Weird Tales* and especially to H.P. Lovecraft and his circle for his inspiration. Ancient gods, evil entities, and sorcerers who practiced black magic abounded. Dr. Fate could rattle off mystical incantations—"Fyoreth dignaleth!"—that rivaled the best Lovecraftian gibberish. Fox often saw to it that, like the Shadow, his heroes had a trusted female companion that was in on the secret of their dual identity. A young woman named Inza Cramer shared most of Fate's occult adventures with him and knew, eventually, whose face was behind the mask.

In *More Fun* #67 (May 1941), the doctor was given an origin and a civilian name. It turned out he was Kent Nelson, son of a noted archeologist. While Kent and his dad were exploring a pyramid in the Valley of Ur, "in the year 1920 or thereabouts," Kent's father was killed after the youth reanimated the ancient sorcerer Nabu, who was actually a long-ago visitor from another planet. In gratitude, Nabu offered the young Nelson the opportunity to learn "the secrets of the universe." Understandably, this took several years, and when Nabu felt that his pupil was ready, he bestowed upon him the Dr. Fate outfit and bid him go forth.

A few issues later, the character made another step toward becoming a more conventional superhero. He showed up wearing a new helmet, one that allowed the lower part of his face to show. While this allowed him to smile at friend and foe alike and speak in less muffled tones, it also robbed him of a good deal of his mystery. Late in 1942, Dr. Fate experienced yet another change. Inza came upon Nelson surrounded by "a pile of ponderous medical books." He explained, "I'm going to become a doctor . . . a *real* doctor!" After getting through medical school in two panels, he became an intern. A caption then informed readers that "this new Dr. Fate is to have even more understanding of mankind—

more dignity, more humanity!" That Dr. Fate made his final house call late in 1943.

Written again by Gardner Fox and drawn by Murphy Anderson, Dr. Fate was brought back as part of the Silver Age renaissance. Several writers and artists thereafter worked on the doctor's cases, including Roy Thomas, William Messner-Loeb, and Keith Giffen. Along the way, Kent Nelson and Inza Cramer got married. A 1991 *Who's Who in the DC Universe* volume explained some of the later changes thusly—"As time passed, Inza was driven mad by her life of solitude and Nelson's body began to age rapidly due to the stress of his many battles as Fate. Soon Inza died, and Nabu, expecting Nelson to die as well, transformed a young boy named Eric Strauss into an adult. He became the new Dr. Fate. . . . When Eric and Linda Strauss died in battle . . . Nabu summoned the sprits of Kent and Inza back to physical existence, giving them new bodies that were identical to their original ones. . . . Kent and Inza at long last merged to become Dr. Fate . . . The Nelsons soon discovered that Kent could no

longer join in the mystical merger for reasons that remain unknown. As a result, Inza alone now acts as Doctor Fate." This resulted in the brief appearance of a Dr. Fate with a bosom.

In the 1980s yet another Dr. Fate came upon the scene. He was said to be the son of Carter Hall, the original Hawkman, and Shiera Sanders, the original Hawkgirl. Hector Hall, in a process too complex to detail here, who'd been known as the Silver Scorpion, had died, come back to life, and become a member of the All Star Squadron as a new Dr. Fate. For a while after that he resided inside the Amulet of Anubis with Kent Nelson and Inza. Apparently that was a very roomy amulet.

To mystify readers ever further, DC published *JSA: All Star 3* in the spring of 2003. Therein a gray-bearded Hector Hall once again donned the golden headgear to act as Dr. Fate. In the back of the book was a short "macabre tale from a bygone era" that featured the old original Dr. Fate and Inza. This was written and drawn by Darwyn Cooke.

DR. MID-NITE

■ Very much in the tradition of pulp fiction mystery men, the doctor was introduced in *All-American Comics* #25 (April 1941). Like the Black Bat in the *Black Book Detective* pulp, Dr. Mid-Nite was blinded, then regained his sight but kept the fact a secret. In his case he could only see in the dark. So by day he continued as blind Dr. McNider and after darkness fell, putting on special dark glasses of his own design, he combated crime. To guarantee he'd always have sufficient darkness to work in, McNider also invented blackout bombs. For a nocturnal companion he had an owl he'd named Hooty. Dr. Mid-Nite was invented by Charles Reizenstein and

drawn by Stan Josephs (pen name of Stanley Aschmeir). Also invited to join the Justice Society, he was to be found in *All Star Comics* from #8 in 1941 through #58 in 1951.

When the old JSA now and then got together with the new Justice League in the 1960s, Dr. Mid-Nite returned to comics. He was known to team up with Batman in the 1970s and the 1980s every so often. He was brought back again in the ten-issue run of *The Justice Society of America* in 1992 to 1993. In 1994's *Zero Hour* his age caught up with him and he passed away. But in the DC universe death is not always permanent, and a Dr. Mid-Nite was back again in a three-issue series in 1999.

DR. OCCULT

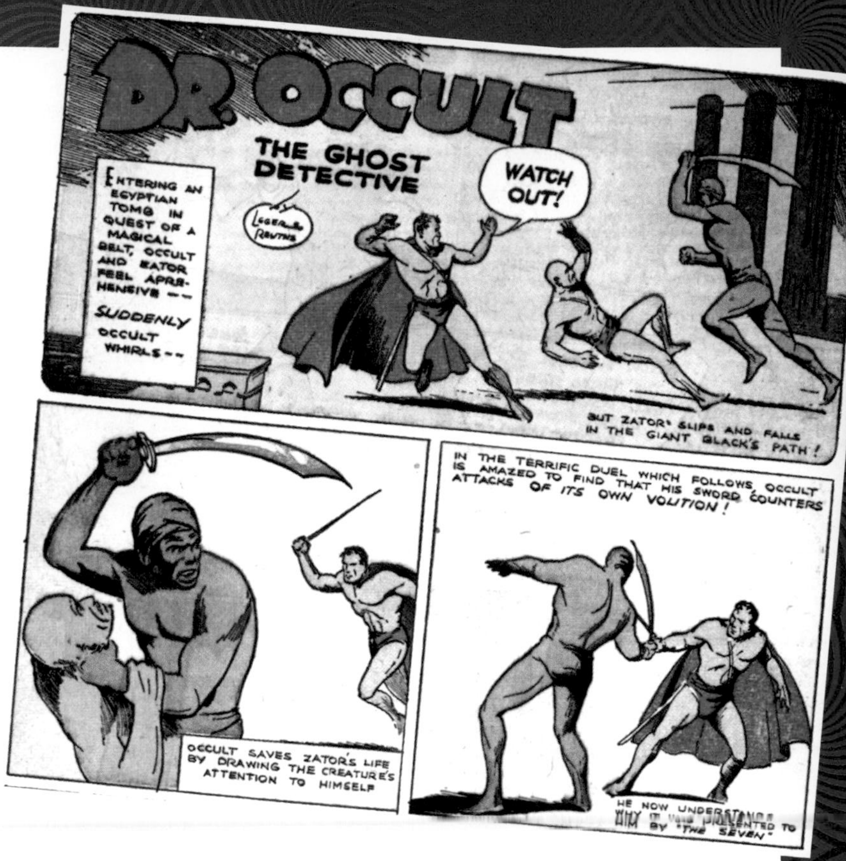
DR. OCCULT
THE GHOST DETECTIVE
ENTERING AN EGYPTIAN TOMB IN QUEST OF A MAGICAL BELT, OCCULT AND ZATOR FEEL APPREHENSIVE -- SUDDENLY OCCULT WHIRLS --
LEGAR & REUTHS
WATCH OUT!
BUT ZATOR' SLIPS AND FALLS IN THE GIANT BLACK'S PATH!
OCCULT SAVES ZATOR'S LIFE BY DRAWING THE CREATURE'S ATTENTION TO HIMSELF
IN THE TERRIFIC DUEL WHICH FOLLOWS, OCCULT IS AMAZED TO FIND THAT HIS SWORD COUNTERS ATTACKS OF ITS OWN VOLITION!

■ The first ghostbuster in comic books, he was created by writer Jerry Siegel and artist Joe Shuster and appeared initially in 1935, almost three years before their major hero Superman. Called Doc Occult in his early appearances—a possible nod to one of Siegel's favorites, Doc Savage—the ghost detective was introduced in *New Fun* #6 (October 1935). The magazine was retitled *More Fun Comics* with the next issue, and Dr. Occult, as he was eventually dubbed, remained there until #32 (June 1938).

Occult wore a fedora and a trench coat, the accepted attire of many movie and funny paper sleuths. Since both Siegel and Shuster, who used the pen names Legar and Reuths, were devoted pulp-fiction fans, Dr. Occult's caseload involved him with the sort of problems to be found in weird and fantasy pulpwoods. He encountered a vampire master, werewolves, zombies, and a variety of evil spirits. His steady girl was named Rose Psychic. Perhaps she never married him because she didn't want to be known as Rose Psychic Occult.

In a later adventure Dr. Occult journeyed to a mystic realm, confronted a supernatural villain in an Egyptian tomb, and dressed up in trunks and cape, somewhat resembling the yet to be published Man of Steel. He returned to his trenchcoat in his final adventures.

Doc remained in limbo for nearly three decades. Then in 1985, DC resurrected him for an appearance in the All-Star Squadron. After a couple more turns there, he was not seen again until Neal Gaiman updated him and his lady friend in the first four issues of *Books of Magic*. Since then the doctor has appeared off and on in such DC titles as *Sandman*, *Trenchcoat Brigade*, and *Day of Judgment*. Somewhere along the way he picked up a first name, which is Richard.

DOC SAVAGE

■ Even though he was one of the primary inspirations for Superman and was known as the Man of Bronze before the Man of Steel was born and Clark Kent borrowed his first name from him, Clark Savage never did especially well in comic books. Several publishers have given him a try, the first in 1940 and the most recent in 1995.

The *Doc Savage* pulp-fiction magazine was launched by Street & Smith early in 1933 and introduced Doc and his five-man crew of gifted and colorful sidekicks. They were Renny Renwick, Long Tom Roberts, William Harper Littlejohn, Ham Brooks, and Monk Mayfair. Ham, the dapper attorney, and Monk, the tough, apelike chemical genius, were continually bickering. They were also the most popular members of Doc's crimefighting crew. Lester Dent, using the house name Kenneth Robeson, created the series and wrote the majority of the monthly novels. He mixed mystery, fantasy, and considerable humor. Doc was called a Superman in early pulp ads. A scientific wizard, incredibly strong and an expert at most forms of combat, he couldn't fly and bullets didn't bounce off him. He gained his superior status by hard work, diligent research, and a good genetic code to start off with. The *Doc Savage* pulp-fiction magazine did very well, becoming a top seller.

Doc Savage made an inauspicious comic-book debut in Street & Smith's *Shadow Comics* #1 (March 1940) in a dull, ill-drawn six-page story drawn by Maurice Gutwirth of the Chesler shop. Doc was "in the heart of Africa," accompanied only by "his trusted assistant Monk," to put an end to the activities of a foreign agent who was selling rifles to the natives. After two more appearances in *Shadow*, the Man of Bronze was given his own magazine. The adventure that began in the former magazine was continued in the first issue of *Doc Savage Comics* (May 1940). It was a greatly condensed version of the early pulp novel *The Land of Terror*. S&S was apparently aware of the competition and ads now referred to Doc as the "greatest of all Supermen." Several other characters, most of them borrowed from the pulps, shared the magazine. In his own stories, Doc Savage worked only with Monk and Ham.

In 1941, a story written by Carl Formes and drawn by Jack Binder abruptly converted Doc into a costumed superhero. He took to wearing a Sacred Hood that had a Sacred Ruby stuck in it, all acquired in Tibet. He continued in that fashion until his magazine folded with the twentieth issue in the summer of 1943. He then returned to backup status in *Shadow Comics*, abandoned the ruby, donned a business suit, and, aided by Ham and Monk, worked as a scientific detective. Among the artists who drew his adventures were William A. Smith, Al Bare, and Bob Powell. Street & Smith folded all its comics in 1949.

In 1966, after Doc had returned to public view by the way of Bantam's very successful paperback reprints of the Dent novels, Dell issued a one-shot comic book, drawn by Jack Sparling. Marvel attempted two short-lived series, one in color and the other in black-and-white, in the middle 1970s. Next came DC with a title that lasted from 1987 to 1990. In 1991 Millennium took over the character, and in 1995 Dark Horse had a turn. All the later Docs looked like the blond stormtrooper type designed originally by artist James Bama for the paperback covers.

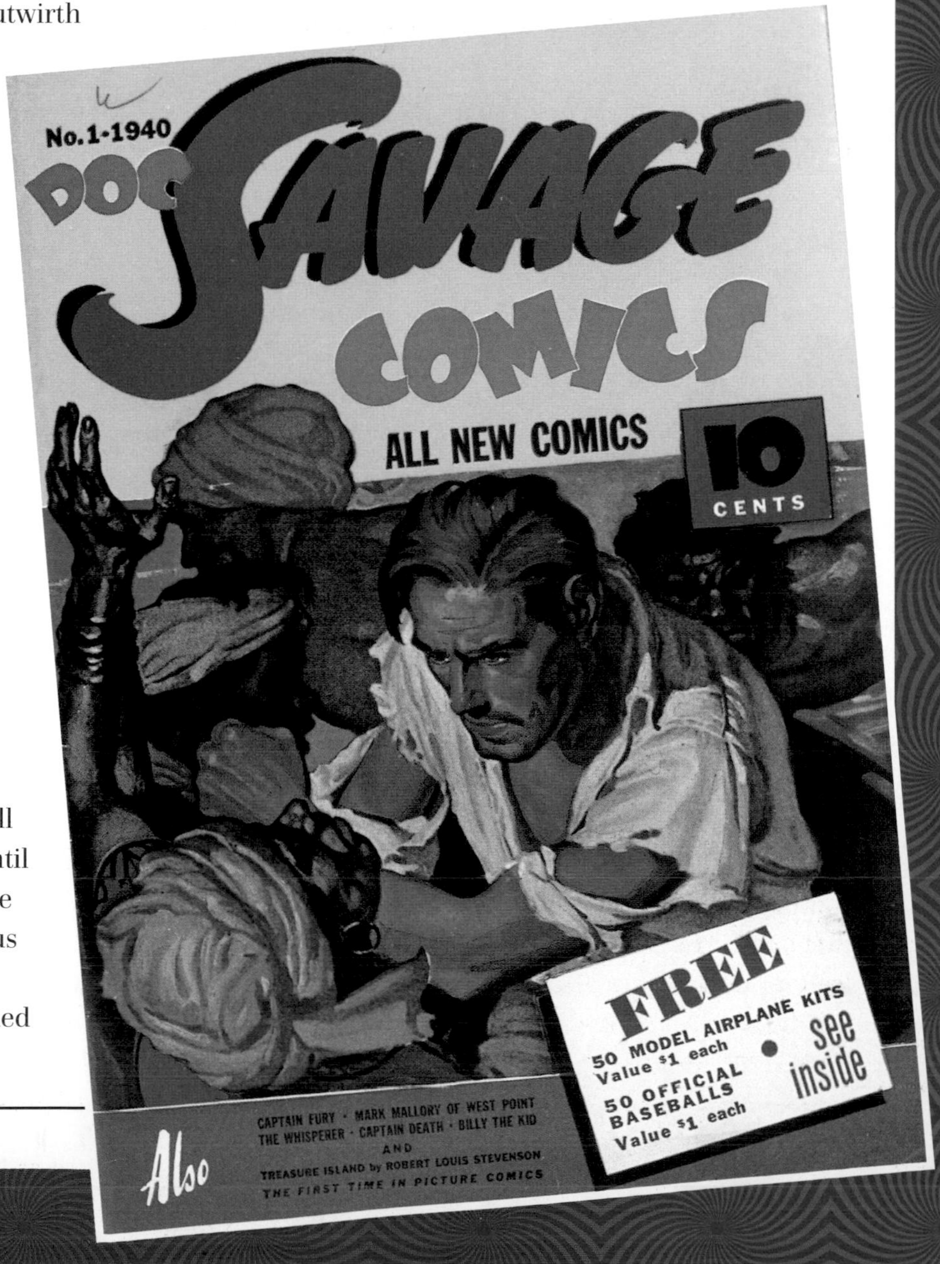
No. 1-1940
DOC SAVAGE COMICS
ALL NEW COMICS
10 CENTS
FREE
50 MODEL AIRPLANE KITS Value $1 each
50 OFFICIAL BASEBALLS Value $1 each
see inside
Also
CAPTAIN FURY • MARK MALLORY OF WEST POINT
THE WHISPERER • CAPTAIN DEATH • BILLY THE KID
AND
TREASURE ISLAND by ROBERT LOUIS STEVENSON
THE FIRST TIME IN PICTURE COMICS

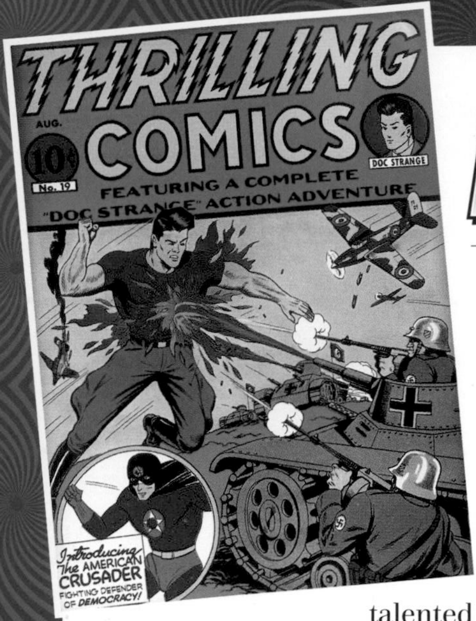
THRILLING COMICS
AUG.
10¢
No. 19
DOC STRANGE
FEATURING A COMPLETE "DOC STRANGE" ACTION ADVENTURE
Introducing The AMERICAN CRUSADER
FIGHTING DEFENDER OF DEMOCRACY!

DOC STRANGE

■ The first superhero to do business as Dr. Strange, he entered the field in *Thrilling Comics* #1 (February 1940). He was created by editor/writer Richard E. Hughes and drawn by the minimally talented Alexander Kostuk. Until the seventh issue he performed his heroics clad in a business suit, but from then on he wore a red T-shirt, blue riding pants, and brown boots. When he showed up for work in #11 (December 1940), he had changed his name to Doc Strange, no doubt inspired by the popular pulp-magazine hero Doc Savage. By that time, George Mandel, a much better artist, had been illustrating Strange's adventures for several months.

Publisher Ned Pines must have had considerable faith in the character, allotting him thirty-seven pages in the first issue of *Thrilling*. In that initial, and unusually lengthy for the time, story, readers learned that the doctor, a dedicated young scientist with an impressive head of slick black hair, had invented something he called Alosun, "a distillate of sun-atoms endowing its possessor with limitless powers." The early version of the brew gave him "super-human strength." In that same #7 where he changed outfits, he cooked up a new, improved Alosun, and it enabled him "to soar through the air as if winged."

Kostuk drew the first few covers, in his usual clunky fashion, and then the nonpareil Alex Schomburg was assigned the job. Doc's looks improved, but even Schomburg couldn't do much with that hair. On the covers Doc Strange started fighting Nazis toward the end of 1940, over a year before the United States and Germany were officially at war.

While covers continued to be well done, the interior artwork took a serious downturn in the early and middle 1940s. Doc suffered at the hands of several cartoonists of diminished capacity, including the prince of bad artists, Ken Battefield. Doc acquired a boy companion in 1942, when that was a fad among superheroes. His name was Mike. After the war, they devoted themselves to homeland security. They left the magazine early in 1948. A jungle girl named Princess Pantha replaced Doc as star of *Thrilling*. During his heyday Doc Strange was also a regular in *America's Best Comics*. And in recent years a Doc Strange lookalike has popped up now and then in Alan Moore's *Tom Strong*.

DR. STRANGE

■ A character who combines the best qualities of Zatara and Dr. Fate, he began humbly as a backup character in somebody else's comic book in the early 1960s. Gradually, though, the popularity of the Master of Mystic Arts increased, and by the late 1960s he had a title of his own. He was able, with a layoff now and then, to keep working for several decades.

Dreamed up and initially drawn by Steve Ditko, with scripts by Stan Lee, the scholarly sorcerer entered comics by way of a five-page story in Marvel's *Strange Tales* #110 (July 1963). Lee cited as one of the sources of inspiration the radio serial *Chandu the Magician*, which first aired in the early 1930s. The show, years earlier, also inspired the funny paper magician Mandrake. In the

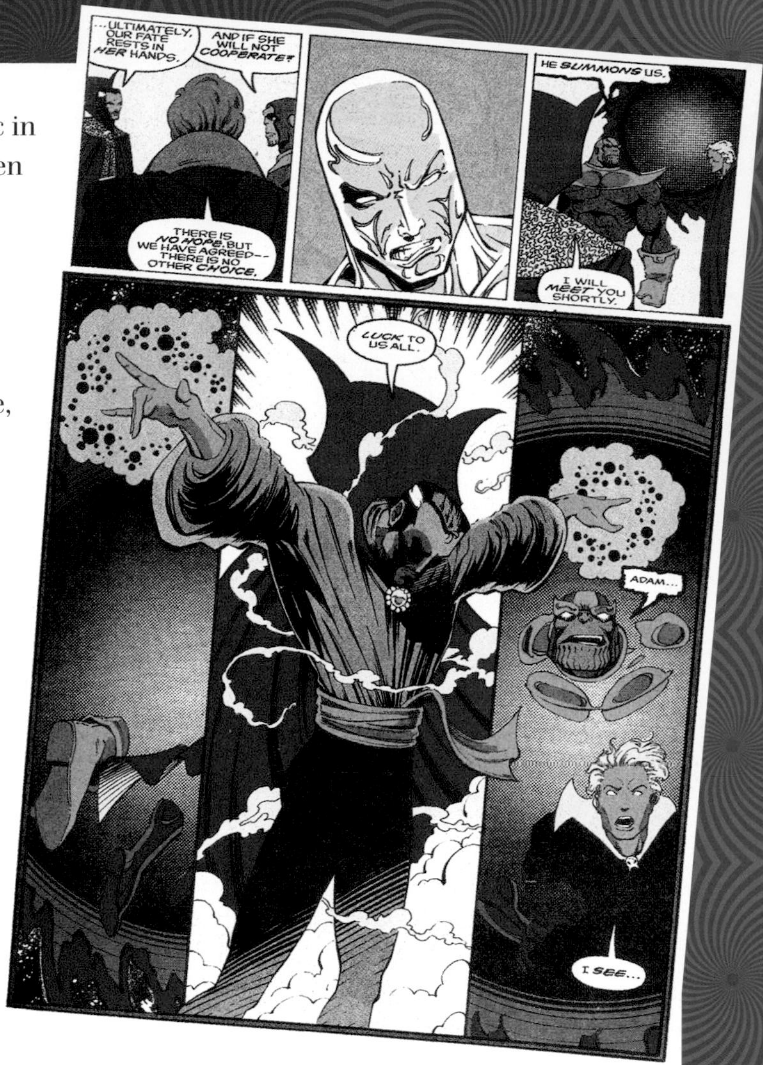
...ULTIMATELY, OUR FATE RESTS IN HER HANDS.
AND IF SHE WILL NOT COOPERATE?
THERE IS NO HOPE, BUT WE HAVE AGREED-- THERE IS NO OTHER CHOICE.
HE SUMMONS US.
I WILL MEET YOU SHORTLY.
LUCK TO US ALL.
ADAM...
I SEE...

radio serial, American Frank Chandler learned the secrets of magic in the mysterious East. Similarly, the eminent and arrogant Dr. Stephen Strange found his way to India after an accident ended his medical career. There he studied with a world-class mystic known as the Ancient One.

Back in America, Dr. Strange set up shop as a sort of freelance ghostbuster. Among his frequent early opponents were Baron Mordo, a turncoat pupil of the doctor's own mentor, and Nightmare, a nasty strangler from the realm of dreams. Ditko rendered the doctor's supernatural adventures in inventive ways, assimilating some of the techniques of the psychedelic posters of the sixties.

Strange's popularity continued to grow. He became the star of *Strange Tales.* Then the magazine title was changed to *Dr. Strange* with #169 (June 1968). Except for one hiatus, that title continued until 1987. From 1988 through 1996, the magus was seen in a new title *Doctor Strange, Sorcerer Supreme,* and in 1999 there was a four-part *Doctor Strange* limited series.

Among the other artists and writers who contributed to the doctor's mystical saga were Frank Brunner, Roy Thomas, Jim Starlin, Gene Colan, J. M. DeMatteis, Dan Jolley, and Tony Harris.

DR. VOODOO

■ His career changed considerably during the two years his shingle was hanging out in *Whiz Comics.* When first seen, in issue #7 (August 1940), young Hal Carey, M.D., was practicing medicine "deep in the trackless jungles of Brazil." He was practicing among the Biancas, "a head-hunting tribe of white Indians." Because of his medical abilities and his besting of the local witch doctor in combat, "the ignorant white Indians" took to calling him Dr. Voodoo. During his very first appearance he also met a blonde jungle girl Maxinya, who palled around with a jaguar.

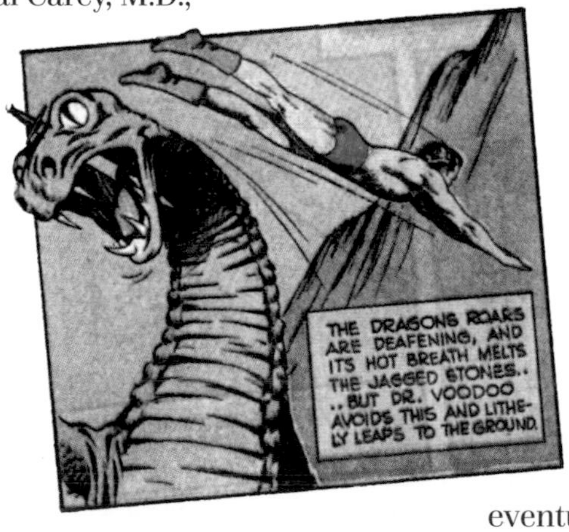
THE DRAGONS ROARS ARE DEAFENING, AND ITS HOT BREATH MELTS THE JAGGED STONES.. ..BUT DR. VOODOO AVOIDS THIS AND LITHE-LY LEAPS TO THE GROUND.

The gifted and meticulous Mac Raboy soon took over the drawing of *Dr. Voodoo.* A short while after that the good doctor began wearing a loincloth and swinging through the trees. In *Whiz* #18 (June 1941), Voodoo was "thrown back in time" and had to remain several centuries in the past "until he recovers . . . the legendary Golden Flask." His quest included fighting pirates on the Spanish Main, falling in love with Anita the Queen of the Giants (not a giant herself), and facing Attila the Hun in combat. Before dropping off the project, Raboy produced quite a few handsome pages. Dr. Voodoo did eventually find the Flask, but he never got home to Brazil before he was dropped from the magazine in the summer of 1942.

DOLL MAN

■ See FEATURE COMICS.

DONALD DUCK

Mickey Mouse
Magazine
10¢
JANUARY
1940

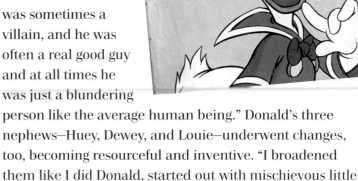

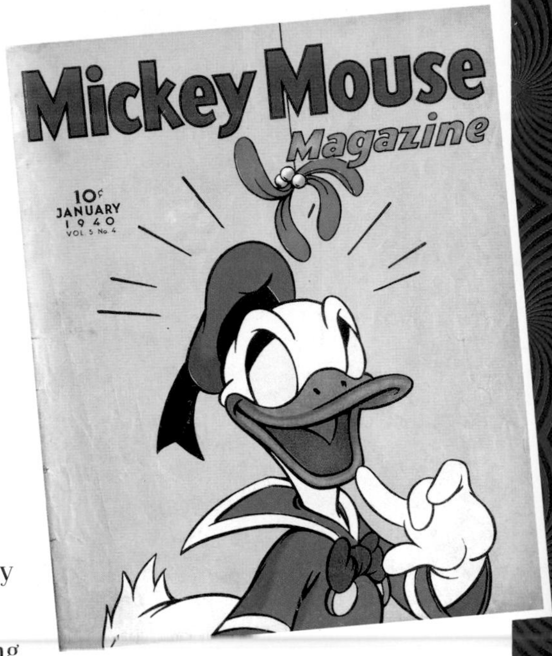

■ The antithesis of Mickey Mouse, Donald Duck was short-tempered, cunning, vindictive, and generally pugnacious. He was, aided by the memorable voice characterization supplied by Clarence Nash, introduced to the world in 1934 in the Walt Disney short *The Wise Little Hen.* Starting out in bit parts, the short-fused fowl fought his way to stardom by 1937. Donald first appeared in newspaper comics in 1934 and was part of the lineup of *Mickey Mouse Magazine* when it got rolling in 1935. His first appearances in *Walt Disney's Comics & Stories*, which began in 1940, were by way of reprints of the newspaper strip by Al Taliefero. Then in 1942 Carl Barks came into Donald's life.

Barks had gone to work for the Disney studios in the 1930s. Though originally hired as an in-betweener, he soon displayed an inventiveness that convinced the studio he was better suited for the story department. He remained there until the early 1940s, when he decided to quit Disney and try his hand at something else. That something turned out to be comic books. Before leaving Disney, Barks (along with fellow artist Jack Hannah) had worked on a one-shot 1942 comic book titled *Donald Duck Finds Pirate Gold*, written by Bob Karp. Based on a never-produced animated cartoon, it was the first original Donald Duck comic book. Late that same year, Barks heard that Dell/Western was looking for someone to do ten-page original Donald Duck stories for *Walt Disney's Comics & Stories.* He got the assignment, and his first duck original appeared in issue #31 (April 1943).

Soon after, Barks was writing as well as drawing. His most notable innovation was to broaden Donald's character. "Instead of making just a quarrelsome little guy out of him, I made him a sympathetic character," Barks once recalled. "He was sometimes a villain, and he was often a real good guy and at all times he was just a blundering person like the average human being." Donald's three nephews—Huey, Dewey, and Louie—underwent changes, too, becoming resourceful and inventive. "I broadened them like I did Donald, started out with mischievous little guys and ended up with little scientists, you might say."

Barks added full-length duck books to his schedule in 1943. It was in the stories produced from this point onward—"The Mummy's Ring," "Frozen Gold," "Volcano Valley," etc.—that he hit his stride. With plenty of space to move around in, he created carefully plotted graphic novels. The stories were full of adventure, action, comedy, and satire. They were set in exotic locales and featured some of the best cartooning and visual storytelling to be found in comic books.

A 1947 adventure titled "Christmas on Bear Mountain" introduced Barks's major creation, Uncle Scrooge. Penurious, paranoid about protecting his vast fortune from the scheming Beagle Boys and other threats, Scrooge was nonetheless likable and fond of Donald and the nephews. Other characters that Barks brought to life included the unconventional inventor Gyro Gearloose and the supremely insincere Gladstone Gander.

Barks retired at the age of sixty-five, never having been allowed to sign his work. Since Walt Disney's death in 1966, his contribution to the duck saga has been publicly acknowledged by comic-book publishers and the Disney organization. Barks's material has been frequently reprinted over the years. In addition, both the Gladstone line of comics and the Disney line introduced new Donald Duck and Uncle Scrooge stories. Most notable among the newer artist/writers, and the closest in spirit to Barks, was William Van Horn. Although absent from the newsstands in recent years, Donald Duck and several of his colleagues returned in 2003.

DOOM PATROL

■ One of the great unsolved mysteries of comics is how both DC and Marvel came up with virtually the same idea at about the same time. DC's Doom Patrol first appeared in 1963, three months before Marvel's X-Men. Like Marvel's considerably more successful group, they were a gang of misfits presided over by a genius in a wheelchair.

The Doom Patrol first set up shop in *My Greatest Adventure* #80 (June 1963). They were recruited by a crippled, red-bearded mastermind known as the Chief. The original bunch consisted of Robotman, a mechanical fellow with a human brain; Elasti-Girl, who suffered from a sort of Plastic Man affliction and could grow to a great height or shrink down to an extremely small size; Negative Man, who could send out a dark, negative-energy duplicate of himself for up to sixty seconds. If his negative self didn't get back together with his positive self under the time limit, he'd die. Arnold Drake wrote the series, and it was drawn by Bruno Premiani, who brought an appealing realism to Drake's entertaining, though somewhat peculiar, narratives. Although clearly inspired by the needling character interplay that turned Marvel's Fantastic Four into a hit team, the Doom Patrol developed a special weirdness of its own by emphasizing story elements such as disembodied brains, superannuated militarists, and a whole parade of villains

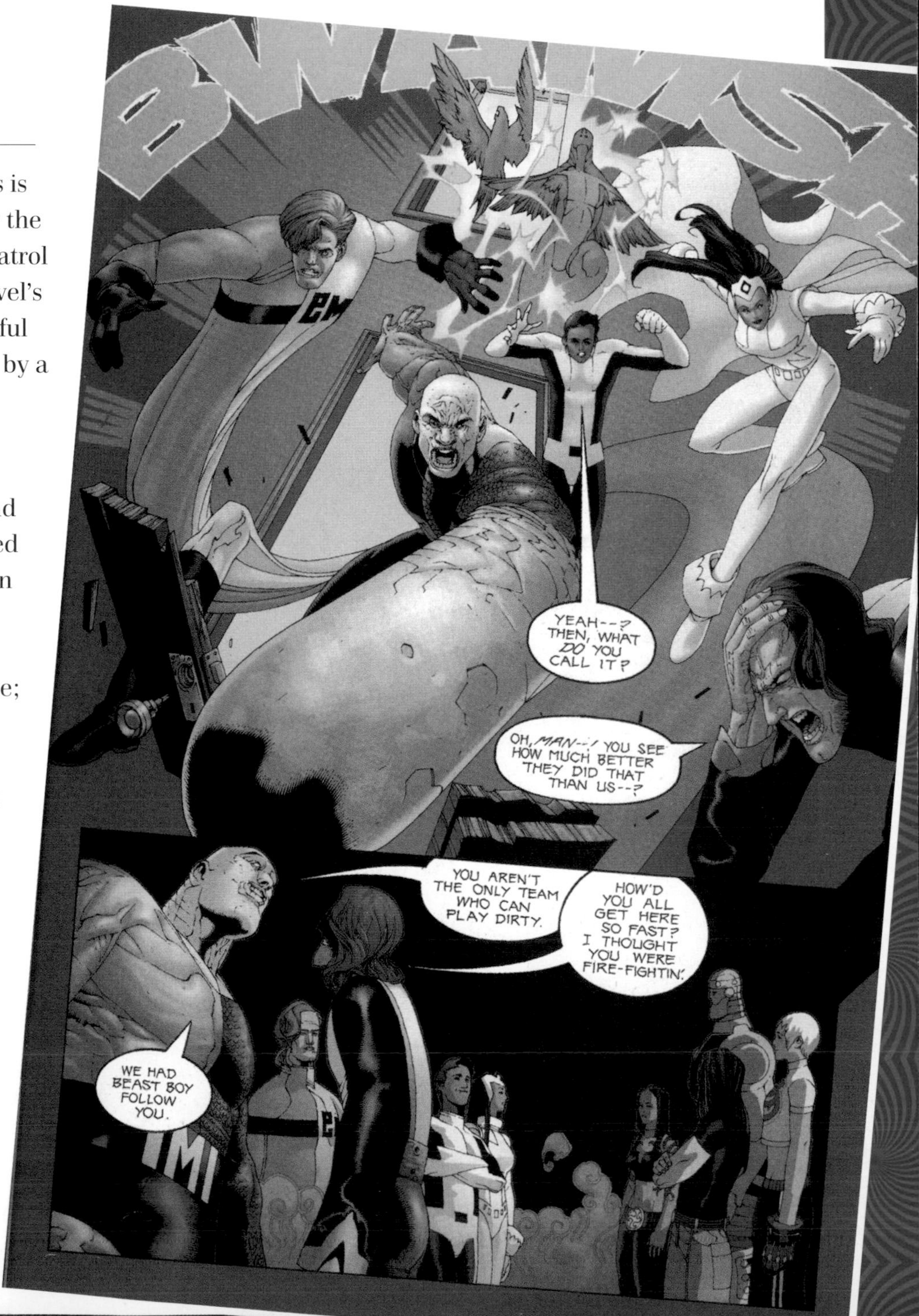
YEAH--? THEN, WHAT DO YOU CALL IT?
OH, MAN--! YOU SEE HOW MUCH BETTER THEY DID THAT THAN US--?
YOU AREN'T THE ONLY TEAM WHO CAN PLAY DIRTY.
HOW'D YOU ALL GET HERE SO FAST? I THOUGHT YOU WERE FIRE-FIGHTIN'.
WE HAD BEAST BOY FOLLOW YOU.

with physical deformities. In a recent interview Drake mentioned that he had never heard of DC's earlier Robotman. He'd originally named the character the Automaton.

Because readers responded positively to the group, *My Greatest Adventure* was officially retitled *The Doom Patrol* with issue #86. Despite similarities to the X-Men, the Doom gang never enjoyed high sales. DC ended their lives with issue #121 in 1968 in a story titled "The End of the Doom Patrol?" The answer proved to be yes, and the team remained moribund until the summer of 1987, when they came back to life for a new series. Grant Morrison wrote the majority of scripts until the Vertigo division took over that title with the sixty-fourth issue early in 1993. The stories grew stranger during the Vertigo period and the Chief went through a phase where he was seen as a severed head resting in a pan of ice cubes. The Vertigo version ended in 1995. In 2000 DC began a series called *Silver Age* and the old original Doom Patrol was revived for a one-shot. Then at the end of 2001 an entirely new Doom Patrol—except for Robotman and a much changed Negative Man—reached the comic shops. The talented Malaysian artist Tan Eng Huat did the drawing. The scripts by John Arcudi placed more emphasis on bickering than on action. In the summer of 2003, the title was canceled once again.

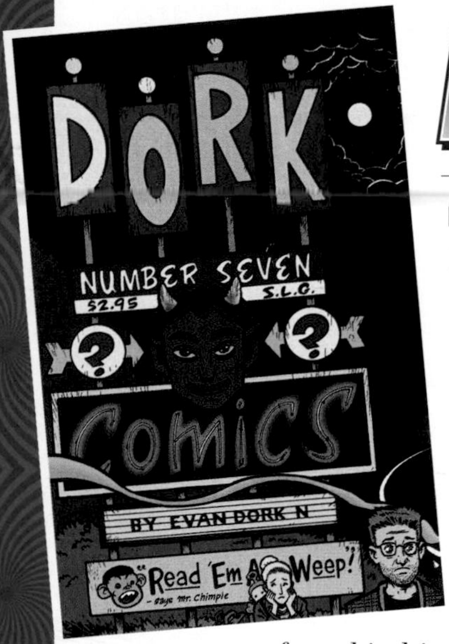
DORK
NUMBER SEVEN
$2.95
S.L.G.
COMICS
Read 'Em & Weep!

DORKIN, EVAN *(1965-)*

■ A dual identity cartoonist, he's been doing both mainstream and independent comics since the early 1990s. Dorkin has written and drawn comic books for both Marvel and Slave Labor Graphics and also worked for the Cartoon Channel. His most personal and iconoclastic work can be found in his own *Milk and Cheese* and *Dork*.

Milk and Cheese, known as "dairy products gone bad," came along in 1991 and have been sporadically appearing since. The seven issues published thus far have all enjoyed multiple printings. The title characters are a carton of milk and a hunk of cheese, both of whom have faces and tiny arms and legs. Foul-mouthed and triggered to violence by the many inanities and stupidities of society and popular culture, they go forth on frequent rampages of mayhem and, now and then, murder. They favor such expletives as "@*#%!" *Dork* is an anthology founded in 1993. All eight of its issues have been frequently reprinted. Dorkin has described the magazine as a "collection of @*#% that doesn't fit into my other comic titles."

He draws in an angry, cluttered cartoon style and has admitted that on occasion he's pressed so hard that he's broken pen nibs. In his gentler manner he's contributed to both DC and Marvel and worked on such TV shows as *Space Ghost Coast to Coast*.

DOUGLAS, STEPHEN A.

■ See FAMOUS FUNNIES.

DRACULA

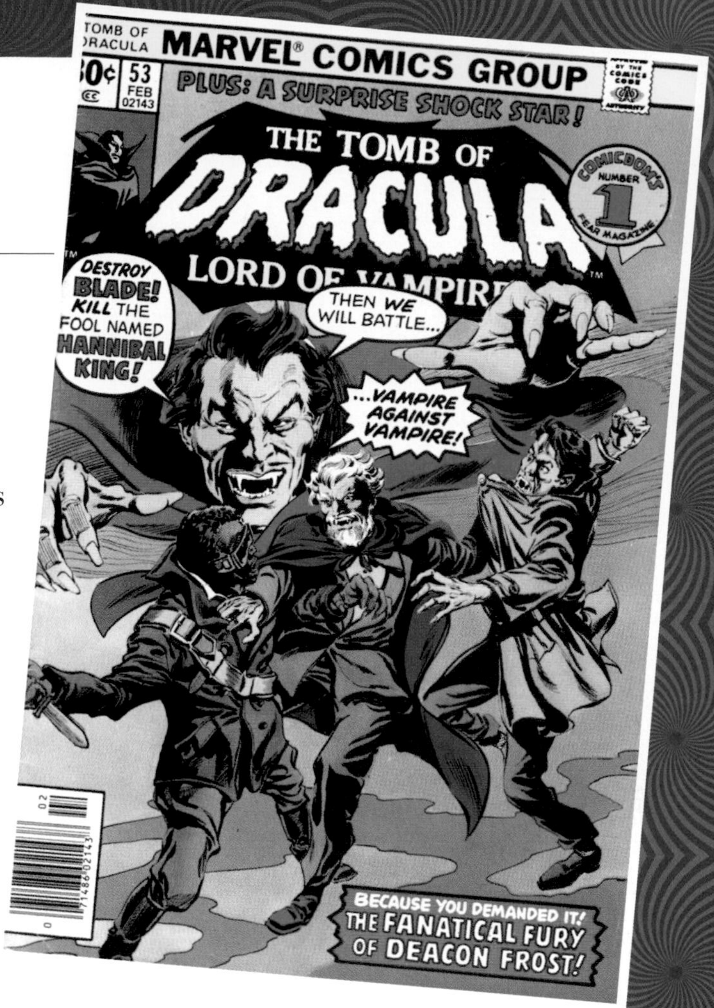
TOMB OF DRACULA
MARVEL® COMICS GROUP
53 FEB 02143
PLUS: A SURPRISE SHOCK STAR!
THE TOMB OF DRACULA
LORD OF VAMPIRES
COMICDOM'S NUMBER 1 FEAR MAGAZINE
DESTROY BLADE! KILL THE FOOL NAMED HANNIBAL KING!
THEN WE WILL BATTLE...
...VAMPIRE AGAINST VAMPIRE!
BECAUSE YOU DEMANDED IT! THE FANATICAL FURY OF DEACON FROST!

■ Dracula, who has a knack for coming back to life, was introduced in Bram Stoker's novel *Dracula* in 1897. He reached the Broadway stage in 1927 and was first seen upon the silver screen, in the definitive performance by Bela Lugosi, early in 1931. The count, however, did not appear in a regularly issued comic book of his own until 1972, when Marvel introduced *The Tomb of Dracula*. The artist for the entire run was Gene Colan and the writer for most of that time was Marv Wolfman.

There had been numerous comic-book vampires before Dracula, especially in the early 1950s. Even the count himself had appeared sporadically in the heyday of horror comics in the early 1950s. As comics historian Lou Mougin has pointed out, "Adaptations of *Dracula*, both the novel and the character, had been around for at least twenty years before Marvel's version." Avon had used the count in *Eerie* in 1953, Dell issued an adaptation in its Movie Classics series in time for Halloween of 1962, and *Creepy* featured a two-part Dracula tale by Archie Goodwin and Reed Crandall in the middle 1960s. The strangest use of the character occurred late in 1966, when Dell issued a Dracula comic book in which he appeared as a costumed superhero who vaguely resembled Batman. Tony Tallarico drew all three issues.

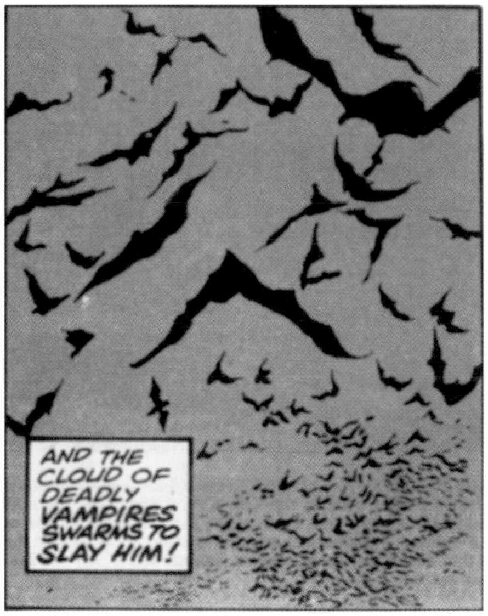
AND THE CLOUD OF DEADLY VAMPIRES SWARMS TO SLAY HIM!

The Marvel version of Dracula was set in the 1970s and dealt with a Lord of Vampires who "spreads his reign of terror across a twentieth century world." The Colan-Wolfman count was a nasty, brutal fellow with a moustache and none of the Continental manners or sly humor of the Lugosi characterization. Among those who pursued him through the continued narrative were Rachel Van Helsing, a blond young woman who was descended from Dracula's original nemesis, and Blade the Vampire Stalker, a costumed ghostbuster. The title was relatively successful and lasted for seventy issues before expiring in 1979.

To tie in with Francis Ford Coppola's 1992 film, *Bram Stoker's Dracula*, Topps Comics produced a four-issue series of the same name, starting late in 1992. Mike Mignola did the artwork. Marvel produced three issues of *Dracula: Lord of the Undead* late in 1998. They also gave Blade several miniseries of his own in the nineties. And, with Lesley Snipes starring, he appeared in three successful motion pictures.

DUBOIS, GAYLORD *(1899–1993)*

■ Nearly anonymous throughout his career, DuBois was a very prolific comic-book scriptwriter for several decades. His most notable achievement was writing most of the scripts for Dell's *Tarzan.* "I wasn't the first scriptwriter for Tarzan comic books," he once explained, "and I haven't been the only one. But it would be fair to say that I have done most of the Tarzan magazine scripts." DuBois chronicled the adventures of the ape-man from the late 1940s to the early 1970s.

A former seminarian, he started writing in the 1930s. DuBois hooked up with Whitman Publishing to turn out both Big Little Books and juvenile novels, including the first *Lone Ranger* novel. He next wrote comic strips, working for packager Stephen Slesinger on *King of the Royal Mounted.* Then he was hired by editor Oskar Lebeck to write for the Whitman/Dell comic books. In 1947, when Dell began publishing original *Tarzan* material, Dubois was given the script assignment. Jesse Marsh was the artist and DuBois' first script was for the second issue. He also wrote the *Brothers of the Spear* backup feature.

DuBois once told an interviewer that he had been reading Edgar Rice Burroughs's books, including all the *Tarzan* novels, since the 1920s. For Dell he also wrote the *Bat Masterson, Lassie, Bonanza,* and many another title. But, he said, "The Tarzan scripts were always the most fun."

THE DURANGO KID

■ Yet another masked cowboy on a white horse, this one imported from the movies. His comic book, published by Magazine Enterprises, started in the fall of 1949 and continued until the fall of 1955. The black-clad Durango, who wore a black bandana to mask the lower part of his face, appeared in a series of sixty some Columbia Pictures B-Westerns from 1940 to 1952. Charles Starrett, a veteran of low-budget action films, portrayed Durango and plump, perennially perspiring Smiley Burnette was his frequent sidekick. Vincent Sullivan, the ME publisher who also put cowboy actor Tim Holt into a comic book, once explained, "If it's in the movies, it's pre-sold."

The early issues of *The Durango Kid* used photo covers of Starrett in costume with an overline proclaiming him "The Movies' Most Colorful Western Star." The stories, most of them written by Gardner Fox, took place in the post–Civil War West. A dual identity hero, Durango was also Steve Brand, a rambling cowboy. Changing clothes and donning the mask was the easy part, but sometimes producing that white stallion could cause problems. His sidekick was a Burnette type named Muley Pike. Joe Certa, inked by John Belfi, drew *The Durango Kid* until the nineteenth issue, then the dependable Fred Guardineer became the artist. Guardineer has said he considered this among his best work.

One of the magazine's backup features was *Dan Brand,* dealing with a "white Indian" and drawn for a time by Frank Frazetta.

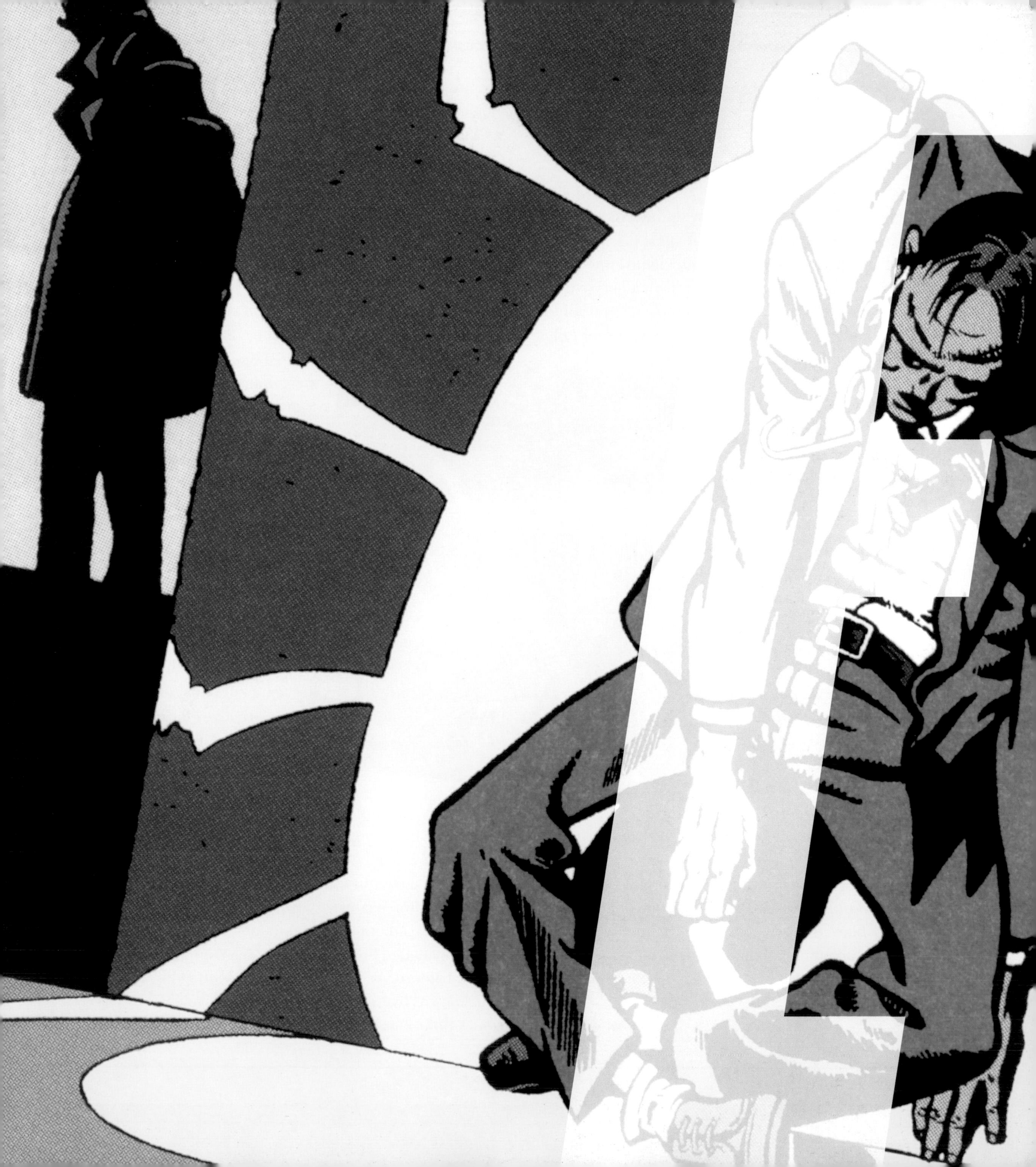

ECLIPSO

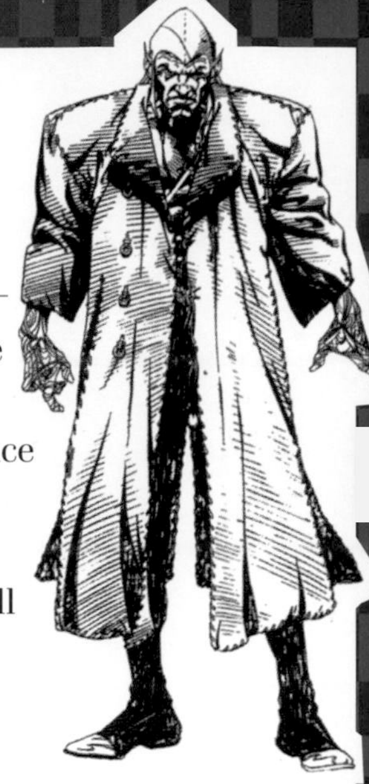

■ For some comic-book characters having a dual identity was no fun at all. Far from elated by his own magical transformation was Bruce Gordon. Against his will, he would change from a clean-cut blond scientist into a nasty and violently destructive villain with a purple-and-black costume and a face that was half blue. His troubles started in *House of Secrets* #61 (August 1963). Writer Bob Haney, with some input from editor Murray Boltinoff, invented Eclipso. Lee Elias was the first artist, followed shortly by Alex Toth and then Jack Sparling.

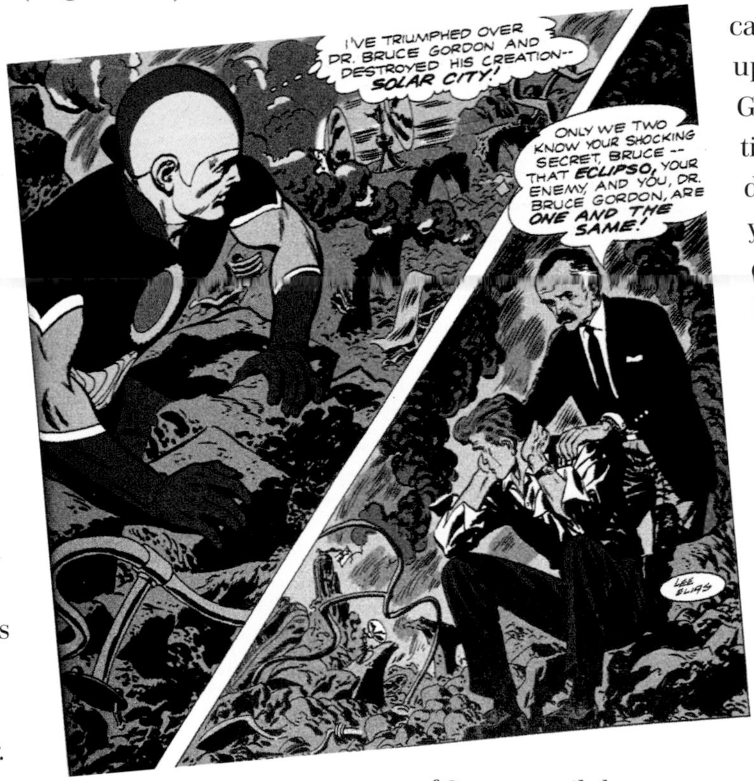

I'VE TRIUMPHED OVER DR. BRUCE GORDON AND DESTROYED HIS CREATION-- SOLAR CITY!
ONLY WE TWO KNOW YOUR SHOCKING SECRET, BRUCE -- THAT ECLIPSO, YOUR ENEMY, AND YOU, DR. BRUCE GORDON, ARE ONE AND THE SAME!
LEE ELIAS

As an early caption explained "the vast unknown powers of the sun and moon combined with a freakish fate to divide Dr. Bruce Gordon into two beings—one dedicated to humanity—the other to ruthless destruction!" That freakish fate befell Dr. Gordon on the aptly named Diablo Island where he'd gone to study a solar eclipse. An unfortunate encounter with a local wizard resulted in his being slashed with a mysterious black diamond as the eclipse unfolded. From then on "every time he is within reach of an eclipse, Dr. Bruce Gordon becomes the demon ECLIPSO!"

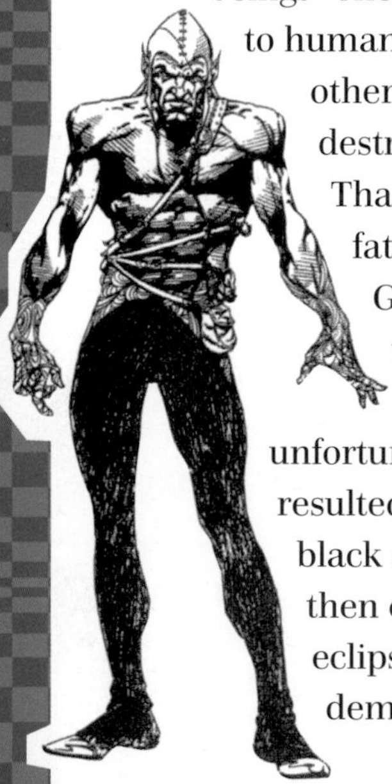

Eclipso was a bestial fellow, one side of his face tinted blue to symbolize the duality of his nature. He wore the purple-and-black costume that had once belonged to that local mystic back on Diablo. He was devoted to crime, violence, mayhem, and destruction. All in all, he caused the upstanding Gordon endless grief. His first time at bat, he single-handedly destroyed Solar City, which young Dr. Gordon had helped develop and was intended to be "the world's first community to be run by the sun's limitless energy." To aid him in his mean-minded missions of destruction, Eclipso was able to use that fateful black diamond to send out powerful rays of destructive black light.

Billed as "hero and villain in one man," Eclipso hung out in *House of Secrets* until the summer of 1966, then temporarily retired. He has returned at intervals since. In 1992 he came back with a bang in a title of his own and in a multi-issue adventure titled *Eclipso: The Darkness Within.* This pitted him against a virtual army of superheroes and was played out in assorted titles, including some of those devoted to Superman, Wonder Woman, and the Green Lantern. Another *Eclipso* title, with plots and breakdowns by Keith Giffen, ran through eighteen issues from 1992 to 1994.

EERIE: I

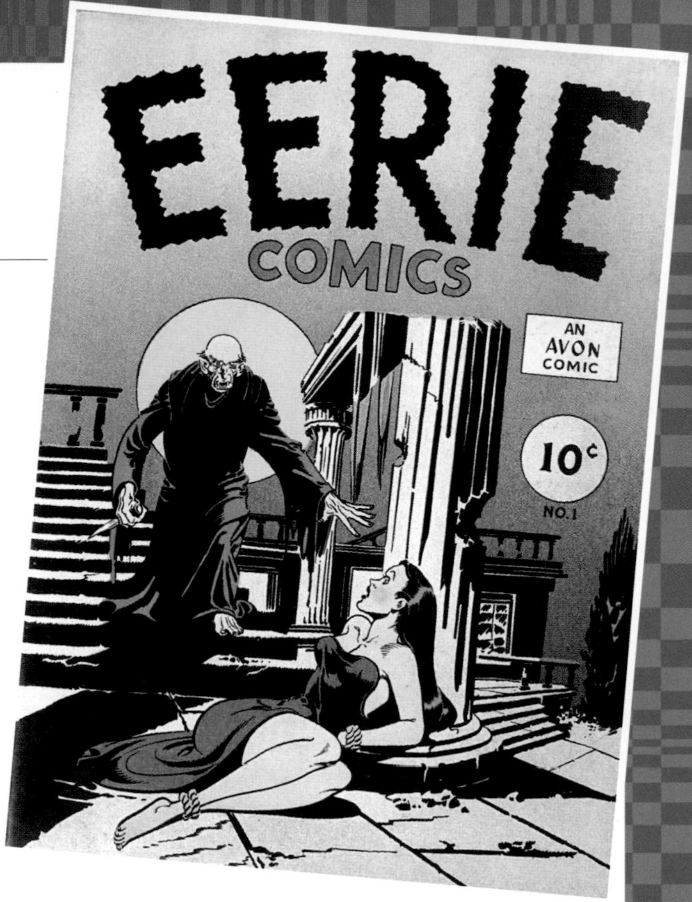
EERIE
COMICS
AN
AVON
COMIC
10¢
NO.1

■ While never an especially innovative or inventive publisher of comic books, Avon Periodicals did issue the very first horror comic book. A single issue of *Eerie Comics* was published in 1947, offering creepy twist-ending yarns of the sort heard on such popular radio shows of the day as *Inner Sanctum* and *Lights Out.* They dealt with demons, walking corpses, and giant man-eating lizards. Art was by such as Joe Kubert, Fred Kida, and Bob Fujitani, already a horror expert from his association with *The Hangman.*

In 1951, Avon began again, shortening the title to just plain *Eerie.* This version made it through seventeen issues before succumbing in the summer of 1954. Kubert was again one of the artists, as were Wally Wood and Joe Orlando.

EERIE: II

■ James Warren, the publisher who would eventually give the world Vampirella, entered the comic field in 1964 with *Creepy* and the following year added *Eerie.* Like *Creepy*, *Eerie* was a black-and-white and sold for a quarter. The admirable Archie Goodwin, who was associate editor from 1965 to 1970, also provided many of the horror scripts. On the list of regular artists were Alex Toth, Al Williamson, Richard Corben, Reed Crandall, Esteban Maroto, and Tom Sutton. Warren's *Eerie* lasted until early 1983 and its 139th issue.

EISNER, WILL *(1917-)*

■ Not only is Eisner an excellent cartoonist and writer, he is also an astute businessman. That's why he has fared much better than many of his Golden Age peers and is still profiting from characters, especially *The Spirit*, that he created well over a half century ago. Among the many other characters Eisner had a hand in inventing are Blackhawk, Sheena, Hawks of the Sea, Blue Beetle, the Flame, and Doll Man.

Born in Brooklyn and reared in tenements (which helped encourage his noir approach to storytelling), Eisner attended DeWitt Clinton High School in the Bronx. One of his fellow students was Bob Kane. While still in his teens, Eisner started drawing for a short-lived comic book called *Wow.* He was also a contributor to such early magazines as *Detective Picture Stories.* Next he and former *Wow* editor Jerry Iger formed one of the earliest shops

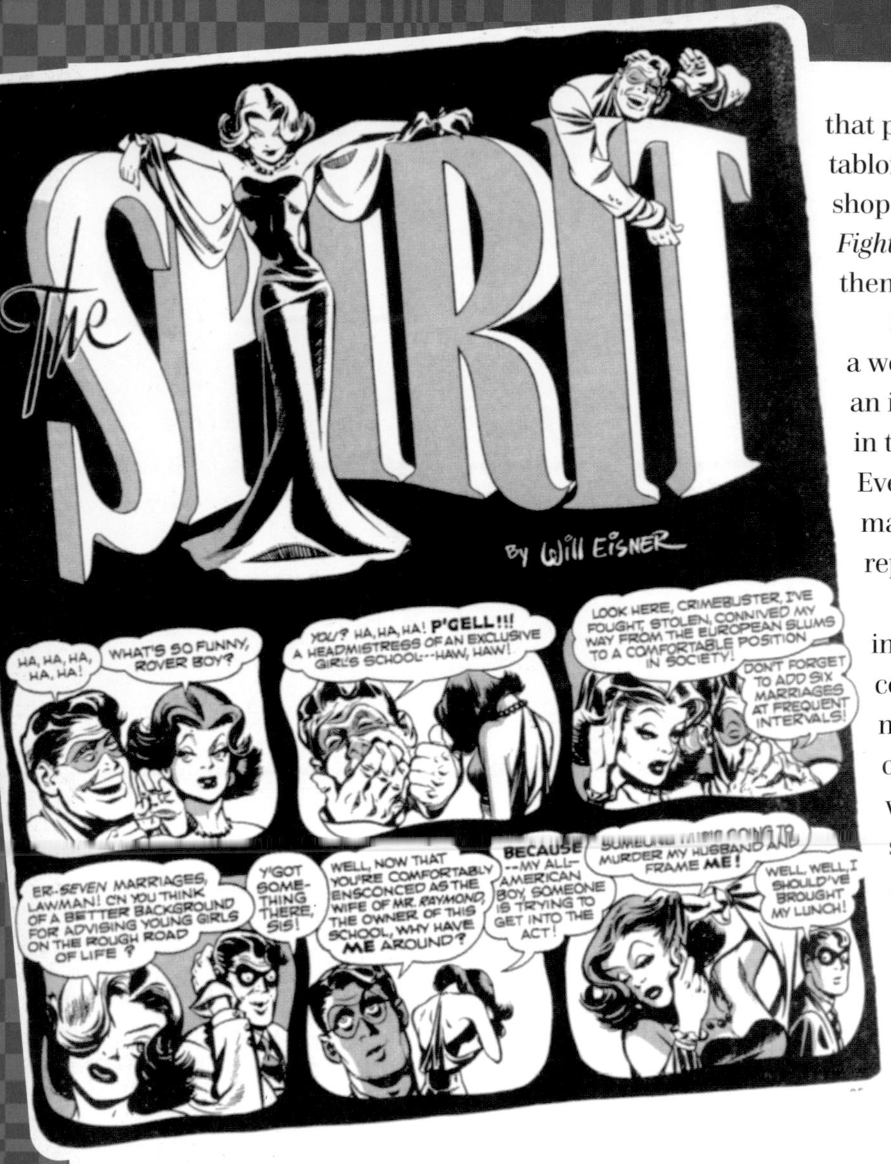
The SPIRIT
By Will Eisner
HA, HA, HA, HA, HA!
WHAT'S SO FUNNY, ROVER BOY?
YOU? HA, HA, HA! P'GELL!!! A HEADMISTRESS OF AN EXCLUSIVE GIRL'S SCHOOL--HAW, HAW!
LOOK HERE, CRIMEBUSTER, I'VE FOUGHT, STOLEN, CONNIVED MY WAY FROM THE EUROPEAN SLUMS TO A COMFORTABLE POSITION IN SOCIETY!
DON'T FORGET TO ADD SIX MARRIAGES AT FREQUENT INTERVALS!
ER-SEVEN MARRIAGES, LAWMAN! C'N YOU THINK OF A BETTER BACKGROUND FOR ADVISING YOUNG GIRLS ON THE ROUGH ROAD OF LIFE ?
Y'GOT SOME-THING THERE, SIS!
WELL, NOW THAT YOU'RE COMFORTABLY ENSCONCED AS THE WIFE OF MR. RAYMOND, THE OWNER OF THIS SCHOOL, WHY HAVE ME AROUND?
BECAUSE --MY ALL-AMERICAN BOY, SOMEONE IS TRYING TO GET INTO THE ACT!
MURDER MY HUSBAND AND FRAME ME!
WELL, WELL, I SHOULD'VE BROUGHT MY LUNCH!

that packaged comic books. After putting together issues of a tabloid-sized overseas magazine called *Wags*, the Eisner-Iger shop moved on to producing work for Fiction House (*Jumbo, Fight, Jingle, Wings*, etc.), Fox (*Wonder, Mystery Men*, etc.) and then Quality (*Crack, Hit, National*, etc.).

In 1940, after parting with Iger, Eisner began producing a weekly sixteen-page *Spirit* booklet that was distributed as an insert in Sunday newspaper funnies sections. His partner in the enterprise was Busy Arnold, the Quality publisher. Eventually Eisner became the sole owner of the unorthodox masked man, and he has benefited from frequent reprintings of the 1940s and 1950s weekly adventures.

An excellent storyteller and artist, and an expert at innovative layout, Eisner has influenced generations of comic-book creators. He began exploring the graphic novel format some years ago and has gone on to turn out many successful titles in that area, including original works such as *A Contract with God* and adaptations of such classic novels as *Don Quixote*. Not surprisingly, the annual awards for excellence in the comic-book field given out at the vast San Diego comics convention are named in Will Eisner's honor.

ELDER, WILL *(1922-)*

■ Inside many a serious illustrator there is a zany satirist waiting to break out. Elder was one such. After inking straight adventure stuff with penciler John Severin for *Prize Comics Western* and then various EC titles, he broke loose when his old high school buddy Harvey Kurtzman started *Mad* in 1952. "I was always a cut up," he once explained, "and I felt if I could expose this zaniness, this bottled up zaniness in me, I would really burst forth. . . . *Mad* gave me a tremendous amount of license."

When Kurtzman and *Mad* parted company in the middle 1950s, Elder left, too. He worked with Kurtzman on his next three unsuccessful magazines—*Trump*, *Humbug*, and *Help*. In 1962 the two of them cooked up *Little Annie Fanny* for *Playboy*. Elder stuck with that project for well over a score of years.

ELIAS, LEE (1920–1998)

■ A violinist as well as a cartoonist, and the most accomplished disciple of Milton Caniff, he got into comic books in 1943, working originally for the Fiction House line. The British-born Elias, who contributed to such tiles as *Wings Comics* and *Planet Comics*, soon discovered that drawing pretty women was his forte. He cocreated the feisty Western lady Firehair for Fiction House's *Rangers Comics*. Moving to Harvey Comics in 1946, he became the artist on *Black Cat*, about another feisty lady who wore a minimum of clothes.

Elias also worked quite a bit in the romance and horror genres for Harvey before going over to DC in the late 1940s. There he illustrated adventures of the Flash, Green Arrow, Tommy Tomorrow, Adam Strange, and Eclipso, as well as more weird tales. Briefly in 1947 he even drew *Sub-Mariner* for Timely. In the early 1950s he drew *Beyond Mars*, a Sunday page written by science-fiction veteran Jack Williamson. Elias's last comic-book work was in 1980, where he drew *The Rook* in the black-and-white Warren magazine of that name.

ELLSWORTH, WHITNEY (1908–1980)

■ Ellsworth, both a cartoonist and a writer, was the editorial director of Detective Comics, Inc., from 1939 to 1953. In addition, he was the producer of the 1950s *Superman* television show starring George Reeves. Before being put in charge of the entire creative end of DC, Ellsworth had earlier worked with Major Nicholson on *More Fun Comics* and *New Comics*, the cornerstones of what became the DC empire. And while in Hollywood in the fifties he also produced the pilot for the unsold *Superpup*, which starred midgets in dog suits.

12 BIG LAUGH FEATURES!
OLD FRIENDS AND NEW IN BRAND-NEW STORIES
10¢
ALL FUNNY COMICS
A BIT EARLY FOR SWIMMING, ISN'T IT?

He was born in Brooklyn and in the later 1920s got a job in the King Features Syndicate bullpen in Manhattan. There he wrote, and sometimes ghosted, such comic strips as *Tillie the Toiler* and *Dumb Dora*. After an art staff job with the *Newark Star*, Ellsworth went to work for Major Malcolm Wheeler-Nicholson in the middle 1930s. He drew gag cartoons, did a kid feature titled *Little Linda*, drew covers, and coedited along with Vincent Sullivan. His drawing was in the basic cartoon style known as bigfoot, influenced by his time spent at King. He left the major after a couple of years to try his hand at writing pulp fiction.

Returning to DC in 1939, after both Nicholson and Sullivan had departed, he was offered the job of editorial director. Ellsworth was on hand when DC expanded to producing dozens of titles. He hired Mort Weisinger, Jack Schiff, and Murray Boltinoff. In addition to producing the *Superman* show, he also was one of the writers on the *Superman* newspaper strip and the *Batman* strip of the 1960s.

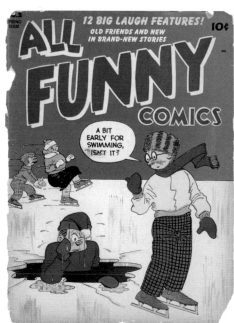

ELONGATED MAN

■ Although his approach to crimefighting was similar to that of both Plastic Man and Reed Richards of the Fantastic Four, he offered an entertaining and well-drawn variation on the theme. The stretchable sleuth was introduced in *The Flash* #112 in the spring of 1960. During his third appearance in #119, he met and married Manhattan debutante Sue Dearborn. Starting with *Detective Comics* #327 (May 1964), the couple moved into a backup spot there.

Red-haired Ralph Dibney came by his malleability after experimenting with gingo (not to be confused with ginkgo). The juice of this Mexican fruit, when distilled to its quintessence, gave him the power to stretch and extend himself in assorted ways useful in catching crooks. Somewhat of a showoff, Dibney fashioned a purple costume for himself and always made sure he got credit for solving each and every mystery that he solved. He and Sue traveled the world, managing to find a challenging crime wherever they stopped.

Elongated Man was able to stretch his arm as far as a mile. But he usually extended it only a block or so in order to punch a fleeing culprit or collar a crook. He could also stretch his neck so that his ability as a Peeping Tom was greatly enhanced. The malleable manhunter and his missus left *Detective* late in 1968. However, he and Sue also put in time as members of the Justice League.

FOUR-ISSUE MINISERIES
DC
1
US $1.00
CAN $1.25
UK 60p
ELONGATED MAN
EUROPE '92
NORTH SEA
Having a wonderful time—
Wish you were here! Love, Sue
PARIS
CHAPTER 1
CONCORDE to DISCORD!
Gerard Jones
Mike Parobeck
Ty Templeton

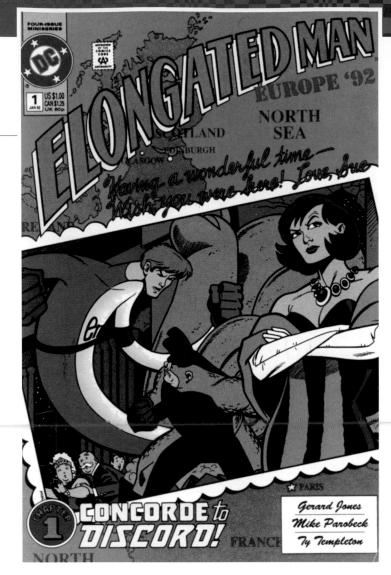

The initial writer was Gardner Fox and Carmine Infantino did the penciling. Early in 1992, DC issued a four-issue *Elongated Man* miniseries. Scripts were by Gerard Jones, art by Mike Parobeck and Ty Templeton. That time around the Dibneys were visiting Paris.

ERNST, KEN *(1918–1985)*

■ Ernst is best remembered as the artist on *Mary Worth* for over forty years. It was the most successful soap-opera strip ever done and the one, during Ernst's early tenure, that established the slick, sophisticated brush style that just about all subsequent soapers imitated. Before moving into the realm of romance, melodrama, and heartbreak, Ernst had been active in comic books. He entered the field in 1936, while still in his teens. Leaving his native Chicago, Ernst went to New York City and lived there for roughly a year. During that period he worked in the shop of Harry "A" Chesler. His earliest comic book stuff appeared in such titles as *Funny Pages*, *Star Comics*, and *Keen Detective Funnies*.

Later in the 1930s, Ernst returned to Chicago. By traveling to nearby Racine, Wisconsin, he was able to sell material to the Whitman line of comic books—*Crackajack*, *The Funnies*, and *Super Comics*. His most successful and longest-running feature was *Magic Morro* for *Super Comics*. Initially, Morro hung out on a desert island and was "versed in magic and sorcery." Ernst himself was an amateur magician. Whitman also published Big Little Books, and Ernst illustrated several of those as well, notably volumes devoted to movie cowboys Tom Mix and Buck Jones. Some of these illustrations were recycled into comic-book stories by the frugal Whitman editors. Working through the mail, Ernst also sold to New York comic books. He drew *Larry Steele*, a tough private-eye feature for *Detective Comics* and for *Big Shot Comics*, there was *Tom Kerry*, about a tough D.A.

MAGIC
MORRO
by Ernst
THE PLANE IN WHICH SAM GOODWIN'S KIDNAPPERS ESCAPED, AFTER GOODWIN'S TIMELY RESCUE BY MORRO, HAS REAPPEARED AND IS DIVING DIRECTLY TOWARD THE CAR IN WHICH MORRO AND HIS FRIENDS, AND ONE OF THE KIDNAPPERS ARE RIDING!

When the Mary Worth strip was searching for a new artist to replace Dale Ulrey, Ernst's Whitman editor recommended him. He took over the strip in 1942.

EVANS, GEORGE (1920–2001)

■ He loved to draw airplanes and during his half century as a cartoonist he got to draw a great many of them. Especially when he was with EC in the early and middle 1950s working for *Two-Fisted Tales*, *Frontline Combat*, and the short-lived *Aces High*. Versatile, Evans also illustrated stories for EC's horror, crime, and science-fiction titles. During his long career, he worked as well for Fawcett, Marvel, DC, and *Classics Illustrated*. He also ghosted the *Terry and the Pirates* newspaper strip for several years in the 1960s and drew *Secret Agent Corrigan* from the early 1980s to the end of its days.

After leaving the air force at the end of World War II, George Evans went to work for Fiction House. He drew airplanes for *Wings Comics*, but also quite a few pretty women for their other titles such as *Fight Comics* and *Planet Comics*. Next he moved to Fawcett and *Captain Video*, based on a then popular kids' TV show. After EC closed up shop, he illustrated such classics as *Lord Jim*, *Oliver Twist*, and *Romeo and Juliet* for *Classics Illustrated*. On some of these jobs he was teamed with the equally gifted Reed Crandall.

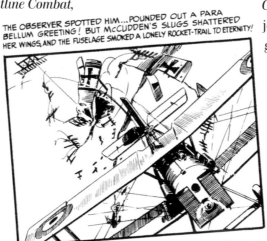

THE OBSERVER SPOTTED HIM...POUNDED OUT A PARA BELLUM GREETING! BUT McCUDDEN'S SLUGS SHATTERED HER WINGS, AND THE FUSELAGE SMOKED A LONELY ROCKET-TRAIL TO ETERNITY!

For Dell and Gold Key he contributed to *The Twilight Zone* and *Believe It or Not*. An excellent artist, though not as flamboyant as those who specialized in superheroes, he produced a considerable amount of first-rate work. At DC his was one of the best versions of *Blackhawk*. He wrote and drew *Secret Agent Corrigan* for King Features Syndicate for many years. What he once said about that strip also sums up his feelings about his comic-book work. "It [doesn't] pay much, but I have been having such fun drawing it."

EVERETT, BILL (1917–1973)

■ Both an artist and a writer, Bill Everett created Sub-Mariner in 1939. In all the years since then no one has done a better job with Prince Namor. In a 1970 interview, he said of his antihero, "He was an angry character and I probably expressed some of my own personality." In talking about the early days of Sub-Mariner, he added, "I was allowed full expression. There were no limitations set by editors, no limitations set by publishers, no limits set by anyone . . . and this was a case where an artist or artist/writer could freely express himself." Whenever Everett returned to Sub-Mariner in later years, he no longer had such autonomy.

Everett's early life was fairly adventurous. He'd spent time on cattle ranches out West, served in the merchant marine, and worked in the art departments of *the Boston Herald-Traveler* and *the New York Herald Tribune*. Everett admitted that his formal education was limited, saying, "I dropped out of high school, I dropped out of art school as well." But he devoted considerable time to teaching himself, both drawing and writing. His favorite artists were Dean Cornwall, Floyd Davis, and Milton Caniff, and his favorite writer Jack London. He got into comics in the later 1930s, hooking up with the Centaur line. He'd been unemployed for a while until that happened. "I came back to New York to take the world by the heels—and wound up on the unemployment breadline." For *Amazing Mystery Funnies* he did his earliest features, *Skyrocket Steele* and *Dirk the Demon*, both in the sci-fi category. Then came Amazing Man for the comic of the same name. With editor Lloyd Jacquet, Everett and a few other Centaur contributors formed Funnies, Inc. Their shop provided art and editorial for comic-book publishers. An early customer was Martin Goodman. Everett's contribution to *Marvel Mystery Comics* was Prince Namor the Sub-Mariner. By now he'd developed a highly individual and attractive drawing style, one that mixed illustration with cartoon elements. His scripts were good, too. Colleague Gil Kane once told Everett, "You were always, in my estimation, one of the best writers that comics every produced."

HYDROMAN
By Bill Everett
HARRY THURSTON, A YOUNG CHEMICAL ENGINEER, ACCIDENTLY COMPOUNDED A FORMULA TO CONVERT HUMAN FLESH AND BLOOD INTO WATER.
A HUGE CONTAINER OF THE REMARK-ABLE SOLUTION WAS SPILLED, AND SPLASHED OVER BOB BLAKE, HARRY'S FRIEND, CAUSING HIM TO DISINTEGRATE AND BECOME A POOL OF WATER ON THE LABORATORY FLOOR! —PROMPTLY AN ANTIDOTE WAS CONCOCTED, AND WITH THE AID OF THIS, BOB REGAINED HIS NATURAL FORM~ HE THEN DISCOVERED THAT HE COULD CONTROL THIS PHENOMENAL CHANGE MERELY BY POWER OF THOUGHT — THUS WAS CREATED HYDROMAN!

Among the other aquatic heroes, what Everett called "water characters," he later came up with were the Fin for Goodman's *Daring Mystery* and Hydroman for *Heroic Comics*. Returning from the service in 1946, he went back to work for both *Marvel* and *Heroic*. He created another water character named Namora, drew Venus, Marvel Boy, and vast quantities of zombies, ghosts, and murderous creatures for Timely's assorted horror titles.

In the 1950s, when comic books fell upon hard times—"The whole bunch of us were thrown out on our respective ears, and that was when I decided I'd better find another outlet for whatever talent I might have." Eventually moving with his family to Massachusetts, Everett worked in the greeting card field. The 1960s flourishing of Marvel brought him back into comics again. He drew a much altered Prince Namor, was the original artist on Daredevil (for one issue only), and drew such characters as the Hulk and Captain America. At the time of his death, he was once again drawing Sub-Mariner.

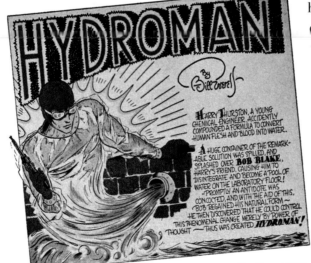

EXCITING COMICS

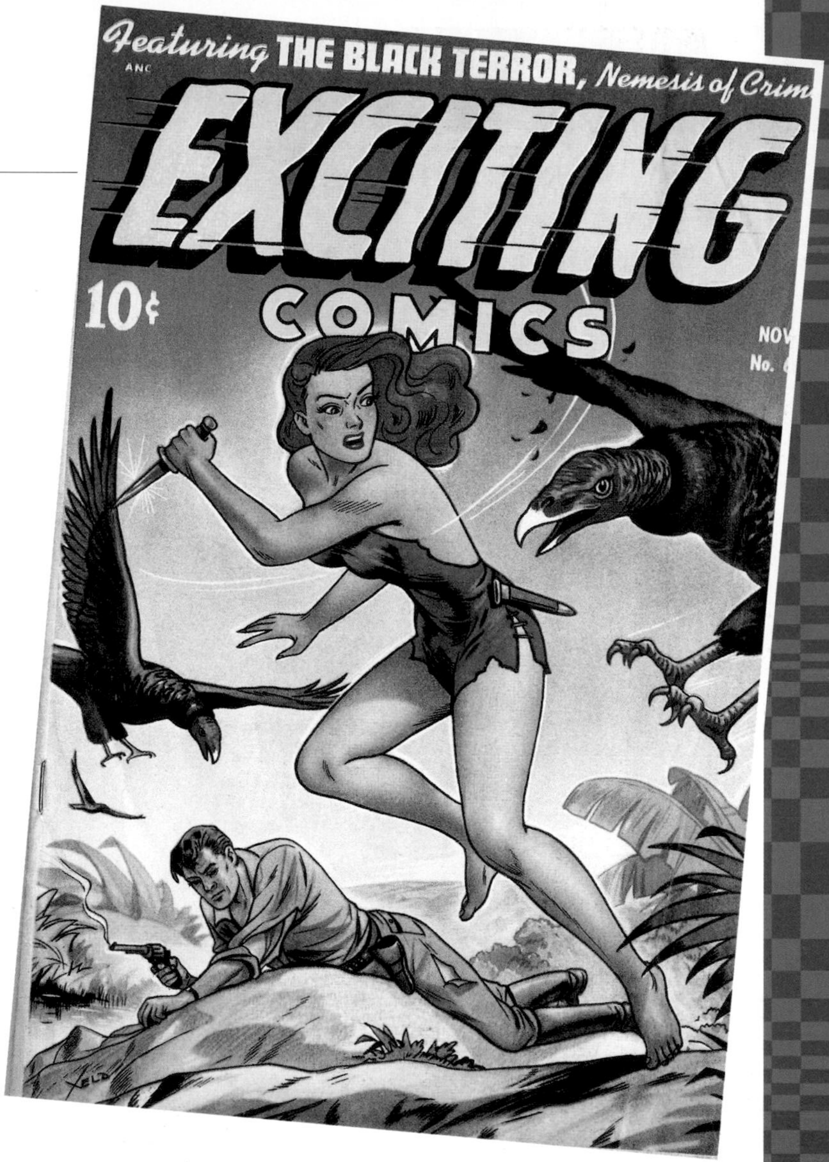
Featuring THE BLACK TERROR, Nemesis of Crim
EXCITING
10¢
COMICS

■ Another comic book from Ned Pines's Better Publications, it was introduced in the spring of 1940. Over a year was to pass before *Exciting Comics* installed a viable hero. Meanwhile the lineup of characters was in the pulp tradition Pines and editor Leo Margulies had established in their fiction magazines. In fact, several were adaptations of existing pulp heroes.

Major Mars, seen only in the first issue, was actually Edmond Hamilton's Captain Future from the pulp magazine of the same name. From the SF magazine came Future's robot Grag ("endowed with a synthetic brain"). Max Plaisted, who also worked for *Spicy Detective*, was the artist. With the second issue Plaisted introduced a new planet story, *The Space Rovers*, and managed to sneak in his *Spicy* specialty, women in their underwear. The designated star of the new comic was the Mask. He was a supposedly blind district attorney who battled crooks wearing a hood. Pulp readers of the day would've recognized him as the successful mystery man the Black Bat under a different name. To confuse things further, *Exciting* had originally intended to call the Mask the Owl. That accounts for the fact that in the early stories the mask has a beak and the hero leaves behind a card that has an owl's head printed on it. Raymond Thayer, formerly an illustrator for mass-circulation magazines like *Collier's* and *Liberty*, was the artist.

Another pulp retread was Jim Hatfield, Texas Ranger, who galloped through a pulp magazine of his own. The Masked Rider, yet another pulp figure, was also in *Exciting*. George Mandel drew *Ted Crane*, about a daring explorer, and *Son of the Gods*, about a fellow who discovers he's the reincarnation of a powerful ancient god.

The Black Terror, with the skull and crossbones on his black tunic, was introduced in #9 (May 1941), written by Richard Hughes and drawn by Elmer Wexler. Other supermen followed, such as the American Eagle and the Liberator. After artists like Wexler, Mandel, and Plaisted left, the artwork took a decided turn for the worse. Not until after World War II did such artists as Frank Frazetta, the team of Jerry Robinson and Mort Meskin, and Ruben Moreira start appearing. The only bright spot during the bland war years was the cover work of the gifted Alex Schomburg.

Miss Masque was added in #51 (September 1946) and *Judy of the Jungle* in #55 (May 1947). Overreacting to the growing trend for cowboy comics, Pines added Billy West to the magazine and featured him on covers. After two more issues the magazine shut down, in the fall of 1949.

THE EYE

■ One of the strangest superheroes ever to appear in comic books was the star of *The Eye Sees.* Not only did he not have a civilian identity, the Eye didn't even have a body. Living up to his name, he was nothing else but an eye. Albeit an enormous, extremely impressive eye with the ability to fly and hover. When the eye looked at you, you paid attention.

He first floated into view in *Keen Detective Funnies* #16 (December 1939), the invention of Frank Thomas. The Eye was a huge disembodied orb that was dedicated to helping the oppressed and punishing evildoers. "I AM THE EYE!" he would exclaim. "The Eye! To whom time and distance are nothing—who bares man's thoughts and pierces his conscience! The Eye's powers are limitless—his vengeance is terrible!"

MAY
Nº 20
THE MASKED MARVEL!
Keen
DETECTIVE
FUNNIES
10¢
IN THIS ISSUE–
MASKED MARVEL
SPARK O'LEARY
DAN DENNIS–F.B.I.
AMATEUR G-MAN
SPY HUNTERS
THE EYE!
DEAN DENTON
Frank Thomas
THE EYE'S POWER RAY REPELS THE ATTACKING ALIENS

He was able to materialize just about anywhere—high in the sky to strike an escaping airship with a bolt of fire out of his pupil or in a cemetery at midnight to discourage grave robbers. The Eye could expand and shrink and, besides shooting bolts of flame and power rays, he was also capable of projecting a searchlight beam. Vindictive and vengeful, his notion of justice included the killing of villains.

The Eye remained in *Keen Detective* until its twenty-fourth and final issue (September 1940). He also starred in both issues of Centaur's *Detective Eye* late in 1940 and then was seen no more.

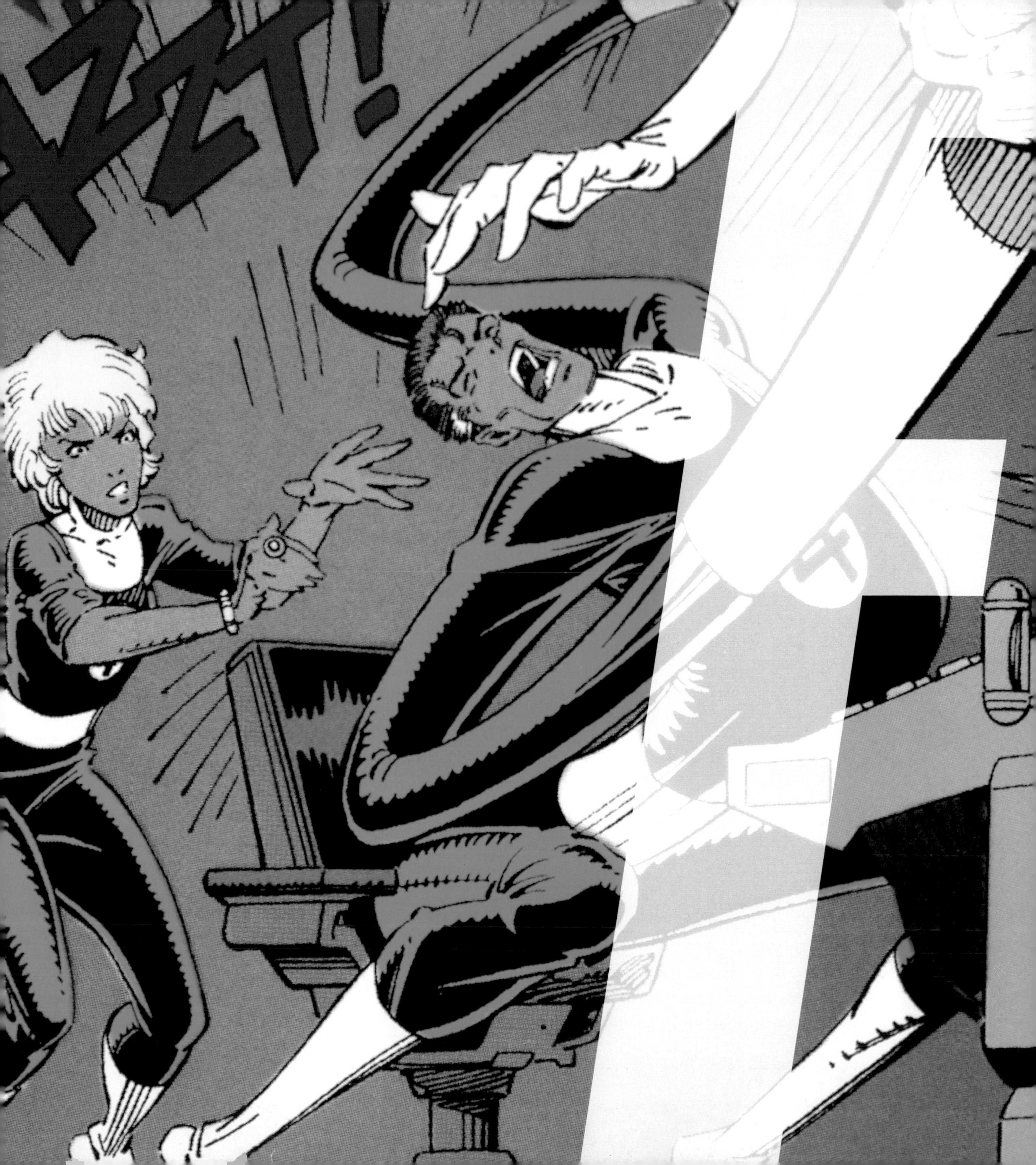
ZZT!

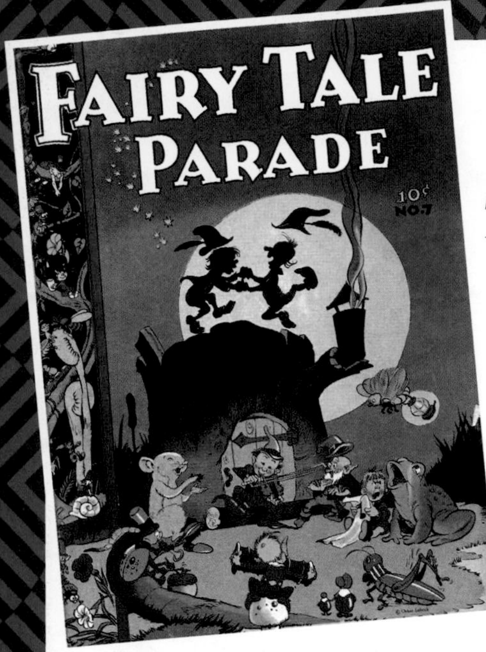
FAIRY TALE
PARADE
10¢
NO.7

FAIRY TALE PARADE

■ Another kid-oriented title put together by editor Oskar Lebeck for Dell, *Fairy Tale Parade* was introduced in the spring of 1942. Each issue offered several comic-book versions of both familiar and little known fairy tales. The undisputed star of the magazine was Walt Kelly, recently back in the East after serving several years in animation at the Walt Disney studios. His many fairy tale adaptations mixed Disney cuteness with Kelly's own slapstick and satirical approach. Another contributing artist was veteran children's book illustrator, and sometime Kelly drinking buddy, George Kerr. After making it through fifteen sporadically released issues, *Fairy Tale Parade* was retied in the autumn of 1946.

FAMOUS FUNNIES

■ Originally it didn't occur to the people who invented the modern-format comic book that you could sell them on newsstands. The first titles that the Eastern Color Printing Company of Connecticut produced were used as advertising giveaways. As soon as they realized that kids might pay ten cents for a comic book, *Famous Funnies* was born. The magazine became the cornerstone for one of the most lucrative branches of magazine publishing. *Famous* reached the stands in the Depression year of 1934. For anyone who could spare a dime, the sixty-four-page, full-color book offered dozens of strips reprinted from newspapers. These included *Joe Palooka*, *Mutt & Jeff*, *Dixie Dugan*, *Hairbreadth Harry*, *Connie*, and, from the third issue on, *Dan Dunn* and *Buck Rogers*.

The chief inventor of the modern comic book was a man named Harry I. Wildenberg. Eastern Color employed him as a sales manager. Among many other printing jobs, Eastern Color turned out the Sunday comic sections for many East Coast newspapers. Wildenberg, who had an advertising background, first thought of using the funnies as advertising premiums. He sold Gulf Oil on the idea of giving away a tabloid-sized book of comics at its gas stations, and that proved a successful gimmick. Wildenberg and some of his associates—including M. C. Gaines and Lev Gleason—noticed that reduced Sunday pages that they'd made as a promotion for the *Philadelphia Ledger* would fit two to a page on the standard tabloid sheet of paper. After further figuring, fiddling, and folding, Wildenberg worked out a way to use Eastern's presses to print sixty-four-page color comic books.

With the help of Gaines, an Eastern Color salesman, Wildenberg interested other advertisers in using comic books as premiums. They produced books for Procter & Gamble, Canada Dry, Kinney Shoes, Wheatena, and other companies

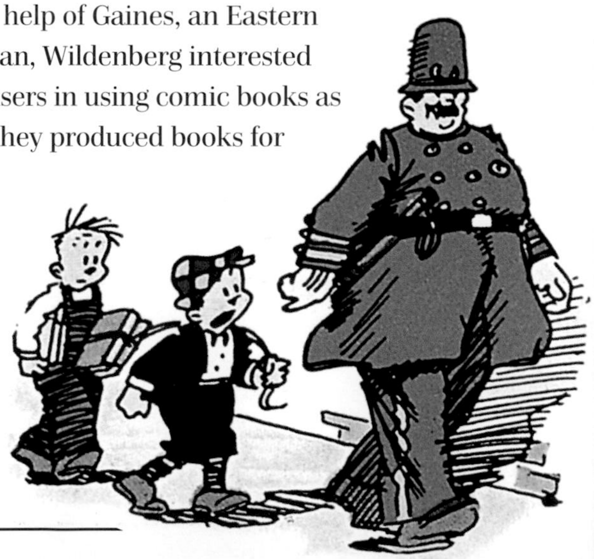

with kid-oriented products. The giveaway editions usually had print runs ranging from 100,000 to 250,000. Wildenberg and Gaines then considered sticking a ten-cent pricetag on the comic books and selling them directly to children. They approached the Woolworth's chain but were told that sixty-four pages of old comics wasn't enough value for a dime. Eventually in 1934, they persuaded the American News Company to distribute a monthly comic book to newsstands across the country. The new magazine was called *Famous Funnies*, a title Wildenberg had originally thought up for a soap company premium. Although the initial issue sold 90 percent of its 200,000 print run, Eastern Color lost over $4,000 on it. But by issue #12, *Famous* was showing a net profit of $30,000 each month.

No. 35
FAMOUS FUNNIES
The Nation's Comic Monthly
10 CENTS
SCRATCH MY BACK, WILL YOU!
June
A world of delightful comics and thrilling adventure for everybody! Don't miss these:
BEAU GESTE
DICKIE DARE
WAR ON CRIME

Editorial offices for the fledgling magazine were set up in Manhattan. Although Harold A. Moore, a longtime Eastern Color employee, was listed as editor, the actual editor of *Famous Funnies* throughout its entire long run was Stephen A. Douglas. Brooklyn-born Douglas was working as a professional cartoonist before he even reached his teens. He was in his late twenties when he when he went to work as an editor and production manager for *Famous*. During its early days, the magazine printed mostly Sunday pages. Besides those listed above, there were *Tailspin Tommy*, *The Bungle Family*, *Jane Arden* (complete with paper dolls), and *The Nebbs*.

Gradually some original filler pages began to show up. The earliest contributor was Victor E. Pazmino, who signed himself VEP. A man with a knack for being in on the ground floor, VEP had contributed to *The Funnies* in 1929. For *Famous* he drew a monthly page of gag cartoons and then a page about Seaweed Sam, a bubble-nosed sailor who was fond of traveling and speaking in rhyme. VEP also drew nearly all the covers during the magazine's first seven years. Jerry Iger also contributed filler pages. Some of his later ones were ghosted by Bob Kane in the days before *Batman*.

As it moved into its third year, *Famous Funnies* made quite a few changes in content. Some of its features, such as *Joe Palooka*, *Dixie Dugan*, and *Dan Dunn*, had moved into the rival reprint comics that were starting up. They added several of the top Associated Press daily strips, including *Scorchy Smith*, *Dickie Dare*, *Adventures of Patsy*, and *Oaky Doaks*. By the end of the 1930s, the magazine had a lineup that included, in addition to the AP strips and *Buck Rogers*, *Roy Powers*, *Eagle Scout* by Frank Godwin, *Skyroads* by Russell Keaton, and *Big Chief Wahoo* by Allen Saunders and Elmer Woggon. By this time, with dozens of superhero comic books elbowing onto the stands, the sales of *Famous Funnies* declined. But they stayed in business.

FAMOUS FUNNIES
Featuring BUCK ROGERS
10¢
DEC. #209
BUCK IS A One Man ARMY OF GREASED LIGHTNING
This is a FAMOUS FUNNIES Publication

After a brief fling in the early 1940s with an original superhero of its own named Fearless Flint, drawn by H. G. Peter, *Famous* stuck pretty much to reprints. Douglas drew a great many covers after VEP departed. Bill Everett did a few, and Frank Frazetta drew a series of memorable Buck Rogers covers in the magazine's declining years. The final issue was #218 (July 1955).

It was a slim thirty-two pages and contained no reprints save those of *Buck Rogers*. Appropriately enough, a television set figured prominently on the final cover.

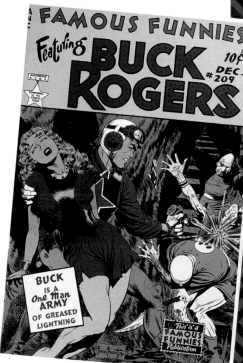

FANTASTIC COMICS

In his continuing efforts to rival Detective Comics, Inc., the ambitious Victor Fox issued his third monthly toward the end of 1939. Included on *Fantastic*'s early roll call were Samson, Space Smith, Yank Wilson—also known as Super Spy Q4, the Golden Knight, and the inimitable Stardust the Super Wizard. The magazine ended with its twenty-third issue late in 1941.

Samson, no relation to the biblical strongman, was the chief superhero and appeared on each and every cover. The long-haired blond muscleman, who wore a pair of lion-skin shorts for his costume, often looked better on those covers than he did inside the magazine, since the chief cover artists were Lou Fine and Edd Ashe. Since *Fantastic Comics* was originally packaged by the Eisner-Iger shop, several of their regular artists were in evidence. Dependable Alex Blum was the first artist on *Samson*, followed by Al Carreño (working very hurriedly) and Louis Cazeneuve. In the tenth issue (September 1940), Samson acquired a boy sidekick named David, no relation to the little fellow who slew Goliath.

10¢ FEB. No. 3

FANTASTIC COMICS

64 PAGES IN FULL COLOR

SAMSON Slays the Iron Monster

YANK WILSON, Super Spy | STARDUST | SUB SAUNDERS

Space Smith was a future space pilot who made "regular inter-lunar trips," usually accompanied by his girlfriend Dianna. The inimitable Henry Fletcher was the initial artist. The Golden Knight practiced "during the Crusades." Yank Wilson, the invention of newspaper old-timer Jack Farr, did his spy work in the near future after the United States had been invaded by "crazed Eskimongolians from North Poleria." Stardust, Henry Fletcher's other contribution, is of sufficient unusualness to require an entry of his own. An early humor filler was *Professor Fiend* by the admirable Fred Schwab, using the pen name Boris Plaster. Artists and writers changed every few issues on all the features.

Later issues added new characters. There was the Black Fury, in reality a gossip columnist, and his boy companion Chuck. A very nasty lady, the Queen of Evil, entered *Fantastic* in its waning days. She was "Nagana, risen from three thousand years of living death, to once more weave her sinister plots against mankind!" Pierce Rice and Louis Cazeneuve drew her unsettling adventures. The Gladiator and the Wraith also made it into the magazine just before closing time.

THE FANTASTIC FOUR

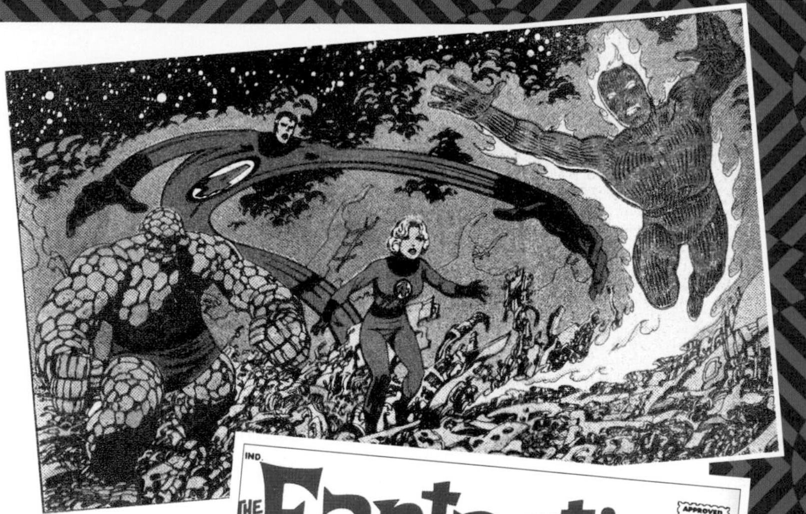

■ Instructed by Marvel publisher Martin Goodman to invent something similar to DC's very successful Justice Society, Stan Lee and Jack Kirby came up with a group that was basically Kirby's earlier Challengers of the Unknown with superpowers added. In their debut issue the Four even wore costumes that were purple, like those of the Challs. Be that as it may, the Fantastic Four proved to be extremely popular, changing the fortunes of Marvel, Lee, and Kirby.

They began their career in the late autumn of 1961 and are still going strong. The quartet consisted of Reed Richards (aka Mr. Fantastic), Sue Storm (the Invisible Girl), Johnny Storm (the Human Torch), and Ben Grimm (the Thing). To come up with the characters abilities, Kirby and Lee had borrowed from here and there. The powers of the new Human Torch came from Marvel's 1940s superhero, the original Human Torch. Mr. Fantastic had similar abilities to those of Plastic Man, and Invisible Girl owed something to both H. G. Wells and the old newspaper strip *Invisible Scarlet O'Neil.* The Thing was the sort of monster that Lee and Kirby had been producing for Marvel's fantasy and horror titles for years. Lee added problems and hang-ups for his characters, a trick that would become a Stan Less specialty, and one that had special appeal for angst-ridden teenage readers. "It would be a team such as comicdom had never known," he once modestly explained. "The characters would be the kind of characters I could personally relate to; they'd be flesh and blood, they'd have faults and foibles, they'd be fallible and feisty, and—most important of all—inside their colorful costumed booties they'd still have feet of clay."

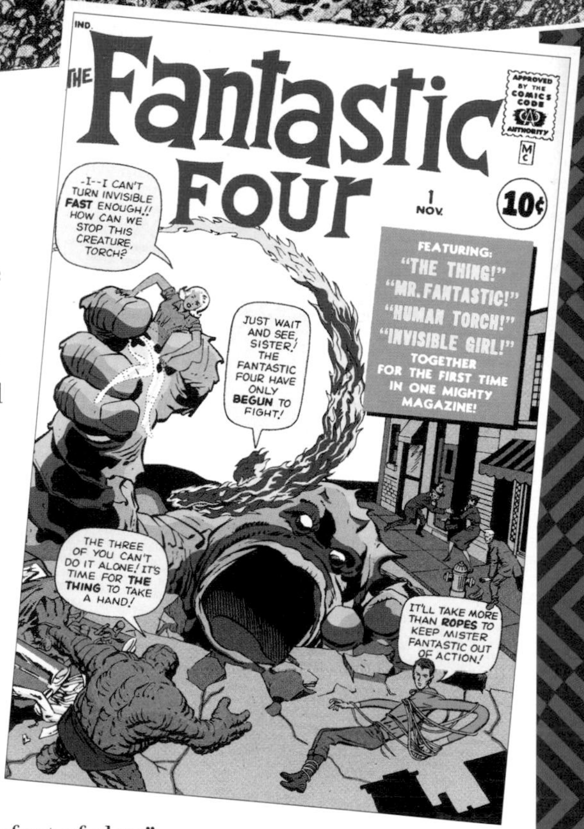
IND.
THE Fantastic Four
APPROVED BY THE COMICS CODE AUTHORITY
MC
1 NOV.
10¢
-I--I CAN'T TURN INVISIBLE FAST ENOUGH!! HOW CAN WE STOP THIS CREATURE, TORCH?
FEATURING: "THE THING!" "MR. FANTASTIC!" "HUMAN TORCH!" "INVISIBLE GIRL!" TOGETHER FOR THE FIRST TIME IN ONE MIGHTY MAGAZINE!
JUST WAIT AND SEE, SISTER! THE FANTASTIC FOUR HAVE ONLY BEGUN TO FIGHT!
THE THREE OF YOU CAN'T DO IT ALONE! IT'S TIME FOR THE THING TO TAKE A HAND!
IT'LL TAKE MORE THAN ROPES TO KEEP MISTER FANTASTIC OUT OF ACTION!

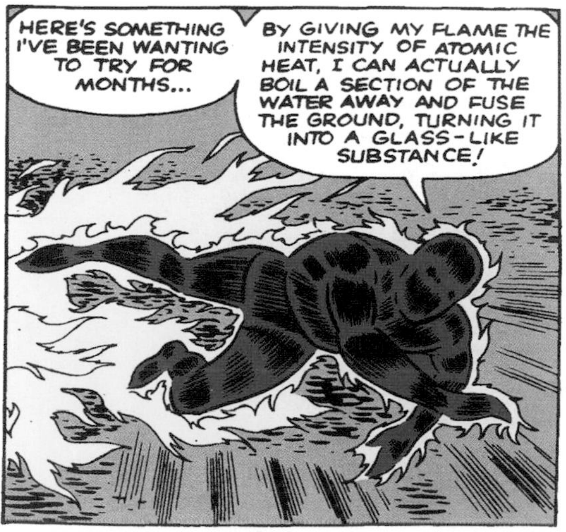
HERE'S SOMETHING I'VE BEEN WANTING TO TRY FOR MONTHS...
BY GIVING MY FLAME THE INTENSITY OF ATOMIC HEAT, I CAN ACTUALLY BOIL A SECTION OF THE WATER AWAY AND FUSE THE GROUND, TURNING IT INTO A GLASS-LIKE SUBSTANCE!

Fantastic Four #1 (November 1961) helped launch Marvel on the successful course that would sustain them for the rest of the century and lead to the addition of Spider-Man, Thor, Daredevil, X-Men, and the Hulk to their lineup. Jack Kirby, with an assortment of inkers, remained with FF for nearly ten years. Other artists and writers who worked on the feature include George Perez, John Byrne, Chris Claremont, Steve Englehart, Arthur Adams, Walt Simonson, and Jim Lee. Eventually the members of FF also showed up in other books, including titles of their own.

THE FANTOM OF THE FAIR

■ See AMAZING MYSTERY FUNNIES.

FAT & SLAT

■ This team had been perpetrating old vaudeville gags since the 1920s, long before the modern comic book was born. Originally they were supporting players in the group of recurring actors Ed Wheelan used in his newspaper strip *Minute Movies*. In the strip, which ran from the early 1920s to the middle 1930s, Fat was a character now and then portrayed by Fuller Phun and Slat was a role handled by Archibald Clubb. In the twelfth issue of *Flash Comics* (December 1940), Wheelan reassembled his company of actors and *Minute Movies* appeared in the magazine for the next four years.

Now and then, Wheelan would add a *Fat & Slat* page, filled with venerable jokes, as a short to accompany that month's feature film. Publisher M. C. Gaines, who was especially fond of *Mutt & Jeff* and had reprinted Bud Fisher's strip in several of his comic books, must have seen a similar team in Wheelan's two clowns. After Fat and Slat left *Flash* and after W. H. Wise had published a full issue of new *Fat & Slat* material, Gaines brought the pair into his new Fables Publications (later EC) fold. There were four issues of his *Fat & Slat* title and they also included Wheelan's superhero spoof *Comics McCormick*.

FEATURE COMICS

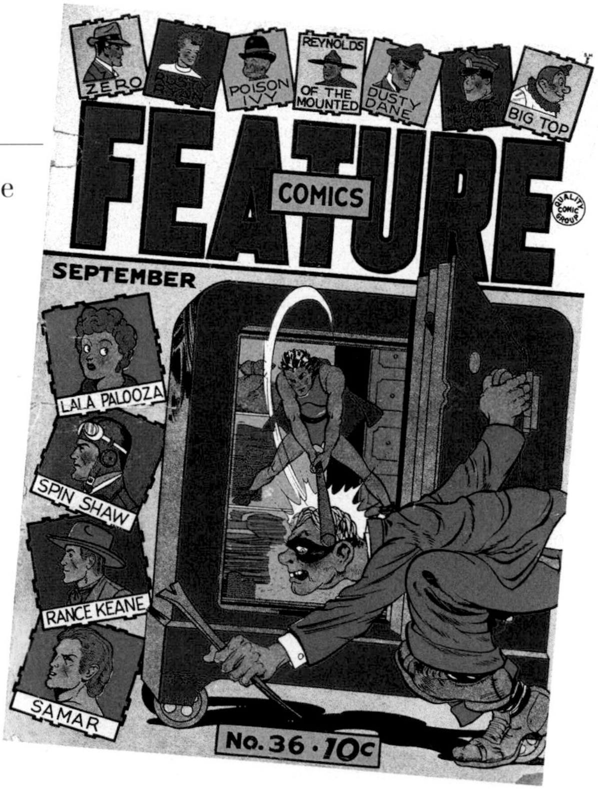
ZERO
POISON IVY
REYNOLDS OF THE MOUNTED
DUSTY DANE
BIG TOP
FEATURE
COMICS
QUALITY COMIC GROUP
SEPTEMBER
LALA PALOOZA
SPIN SHAW
RANCE KEANE
SAMAR
No. 36 · 10c

■ Originally called *Feature Funnies*, this was the first title of what became E. M. "Busy" Arnold's Quality line. Initially it was a reprint magazine of the *Famous Funnies* sort. In fact, such newspaper strips as *Joe Palooka*, *Dixie Dugan*, *Jane Arden*, and *The Bungle Family* had all been appearing in *Famous* before switching allegiance to *Feature*. Arnold's partners in his comic-book venture included Frank Markey and Henry Martin, executives with the syndicates that controlled these particular comic strips. *Feature* contained some original material in its early issues, including Will Eisner's *Espionage* and editor Ed Cronin's *Jack Swift*.

Fairly soon more new features were added—Vernon Henkel's *The Gallant Knight*, Art Pinajian's *Reynolds of the Mounties*, and George Brenner's *The Clock*, who by this time had struck in several earlier comic books. With the twenty-first issue (June 1939) the title was changed to *Feature Comics* and with the twenty-seventh (December 1939) the first superhero was added. Written by Eisner and drawn by

Lou Fine, the Doll Man was a fellow with the ability to shrink to a height of about eight inches to combat crime. Avoiding getting squashed underfoot, he remained in the magazine until the autumn of 1949. Later artists included John Celardo, Reed Crandall, and John Spranger.

Other new additions over the years were *Zero the Ghost Detective*, *Spin Shaw of the Naval Air Corps*, *Rusty Ryan and the Boyville Brigadiers*, *The Spider Widow*, and *Swing Sisson.* Gill Fox and Arthur Beeman both provided one- and two-page humor fillers, and when reprints of Rube Goldberg's *Lala Palooza* and Ed Wheelan's *Big Top* ran out, Goldberg's assistant Johnny Devlin, and then Bernard Dibble, drew new pages. *Feature Comics* concluded in the spring of 1950. For the final five issues the diminutive Doll Man was replaced by a dull Hollywood amateur sleuth named Stunt Man Stetson.

FELIX THE CAT

FELIX THE CAT
I WISH I COULD GET INSIDE OF A WARM HOUSE TONIGHT
by PAT SULLIVAN

■ Until Mickey Mouse unseated him, Felix was the most popular animated cartoon character in the world. Produced by Pat Sullivan, created and animated by the uncredited Otto Messmer, the feisty and tricky little black cat was first seen on the movie screen in 1919. The silent black-and-white one-reel cartoons were well received and Felix's popularity with movie audiences kept growing. In 1923 King Features started syndicating a Sunday *Felix the Cat* page, drawn by Messmer. A daily strip, eventually turned out by Messmer, was added in 1927. Messmer, one of the most talented of cartoonists, had a distinctive humorous style that was all his own. That same year a cardboard-covered Felix comic book appeared, with another issued in 1931.

WHEN IT COMES TO BIDDING FOR TROUBLE, I PASS— I'M AN ACE THAT'S HARD, TO TRUMP!
?
S.O.S!
NOBODY HEARS ME — BUT I'VE GOT AN IDEA!
S.O.S.
?
IF I CAN ONLY LASSO A TREE OR SOMETHING ON SHORE, EVERYTHING WILL BE HUNKY-DORY!
SAVED! I HOOKED ON TO SOMETHING!
?
SO!
THIS IS MY CUE FOR AN EXIT!
TO THINK I SHOULD CATCH YOU FISHING WITH THE MAID — PREPARE FOR A GRAND SLAM!
PAT SULLIVAN
TO BE CONTINUED

Though Messmer favored the sort of inventive visual gags he used for the movies, the strip also made use of continuity. In addition to domestic sequences, with Felix trying to find shelter and a home, there were many adventure yarns involving seagoing treasure hunts, safaris, and journeys to fantasy worlds. The cat started appearing in conventional comic books in 1942, as one of the features in Dell's *New Funnies.* Dell also reprinted Messmer's newspaper strips in a series of occasional *Felix* comics that commenced in 1943.

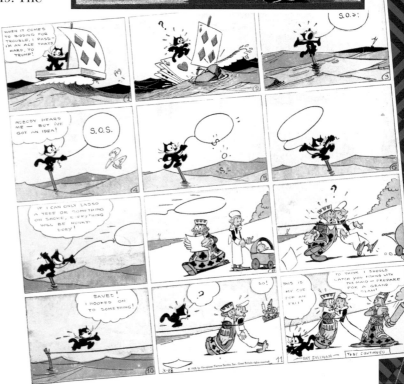

It was also Dell that introduced original Felix material in 1946—"For the first time Felix the Cat comics written and drawn for this book." Messmer drew this brand-new material, going on to turn out several dozen issues before stepping down in 1955. Toby Press and then Harvey published *Felix the Cat* from 1948 onward. Joe Oriolo, an animator who eventually became owner of the Felix property, drew some of the later comic books.

Felix had another brief life in comic books in the 1990s in both original and reprint formats.

FERSTADT, LOUIS *(1900–1954)*

■ The drawing Ferstadt did on *The Flash* in the early 1940s field was unlike anything seen before or since. His characters were chunky and his layouts, particularly his splash pages, often alluded to the cubist approaches of painters like Picasso. Ferstadt was a gallery painter and muralist who turned to comics to boost his income. He drew in a bold, proletarian style and was the only cartoonist ever to draw both *The Flash* and a comic strip for *The Daily Worker.* He worked for DC, Timely, Hillman, Ace Magazines, and several others. The brightest employee Ferstadt had in the small shop he ran out of his apartment was Harvey Kurtzman.

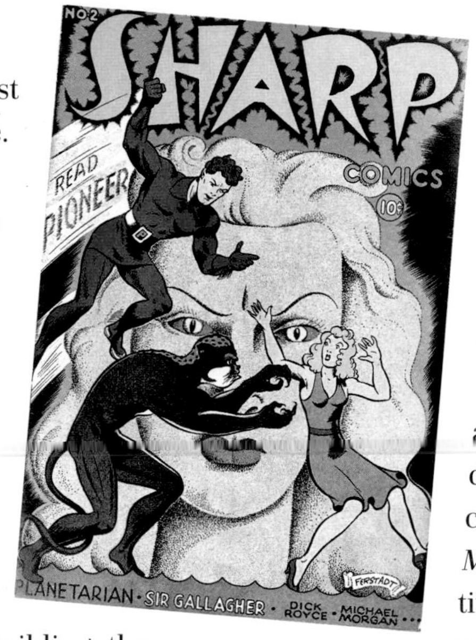
NO.2
SHARP
COMICS
10¢
READ PIONEER
FERSTADT
PLANETARIAN · SIR GALLAGHER · DICK ROYCE · MICHAEL MORGAN ...

Born in the Ukraine, Ferstadt came to the United States in his youth and established himself as a painter and sculptor. His murals decorated the RCA Building, the WNYC radio station, the 1939 New York World's Fair, and a few schools and post offices. Today his paintings hang in museums like the Whitney, but then he wasn't earning enough from his serious work. After a brief bit of comic-book work in the middle 1930s, he seriously entered the field in the early 1940s.

For a couple of years his shop was responsible for the contents of Ace's *Super-Mystery*, *Lightning Comics*, and *Four Favorites.* That meant that he, Kurtzman, and such employees as L. B. Cole were drawing *Magno*, *Mr. Risk*, *"Lash" Lightning*, and a bunch of others. The Ace stories were among the earliest that Harvey Kurtzman ever signed.

Ferstadt also had a humorous side and, usually signing himself Looey, he drew some odd somewhat surrealistic comedy fillers with titles like *Casey McCann* and *Ulysses, Jr.* for Timely's funny titles. After World War II, when younger artists began coming home, Ferstadt's highly individual style, with its heroes who didn't always look especially heroic, was not as much in demand. By the late 1940s he was no longer active in the field.

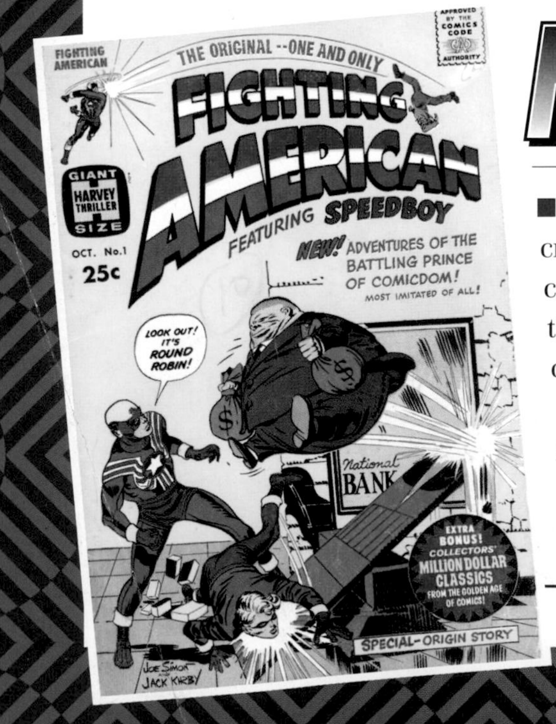
FIGHTING AMERICAN
THE ORIGINAL --ONE AND ONLY
APPROVED BY THE COMICS CODE AUTHORITY
FIGHTING AMERICAN
FEATURING SPEEDBOY
GIANT HARVEY THRILLER SIZE
OCT. No.1
25¢
NEW! ADVENTURES OF THE BATTLING PRINCE OF COMICDOM! MOST IMITATED OF ALL!
LOOK OUT! IT'S ROUND ROBIN!
National BANK
EXTRA BONUS! COLLECTORS' MILLION DOLLAR CLASSICS FROM THE GOLDEN AGE OF COMICS!
SPECIAL-ORIGIN STORY
JOE SIMON
JACK KIRBY

FIGHTING AMERICAN

■ Who better qualified to create an imitation Captain America than the team who'd created Captain America. Thus it was that early in 1954 Joe Simon and Jack Kirby created Fighting American for the Prize Group of comic books. According to Simon, there was a distinct advantage to this star-spangled simulacrum—"This time the copyright belonged to Simon and Kirby."

Since World War II had segued into the Cold War, this new red, white, and blue superhero fought not Nazis and Japanese but Communist spies, saboteurs, and home-grown traitors. In everyday life Fighting American was a television newscaster named Johnny Flagg, who called himself "the voice of freedom" and broadcast over

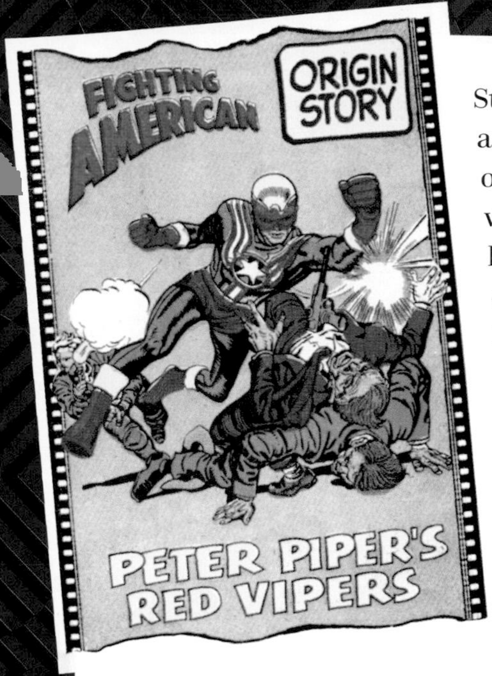
FIGHTING AMERICAN
ORIGIN STORY
PETER PIPER'S RED VIPERS

Station U.S.A. Well, actually, he was Flagg's mild-mannered brother Nelson, who, thanks to a complex and secret U.S. government machine, took over his brother's body after the original Johnny was murdered by Red agents. The transition process also provided him with superhuman powers and a snappy variation of the Captain America costume. Simon has said that, "The first stories were deadly serious. Fighting American was the first commie-basher in comics." But then, as he and Kirby lost faith in Senator Joseph McCarthy and other communist hunters, they decided to lighten up. This resulted in the introduction of such antagonists as Poison Ivan, Hotsky Trotskie, and a formidable lady known as Rhode Island Red (who somewhat resembled Kirby in drag).

Humor didn't help, and the Fighting American and his Bucky-esque sidekick Speedboy made it through only seven issues before folding up. That was early in 1955. In 1966, Harvey Publications brought out one issue of *Fighting American*, which mixed new material with old. DC and others tried, briefly, an updated version in the middle and late 1990s.

FINE, LOU

(1915–1971)

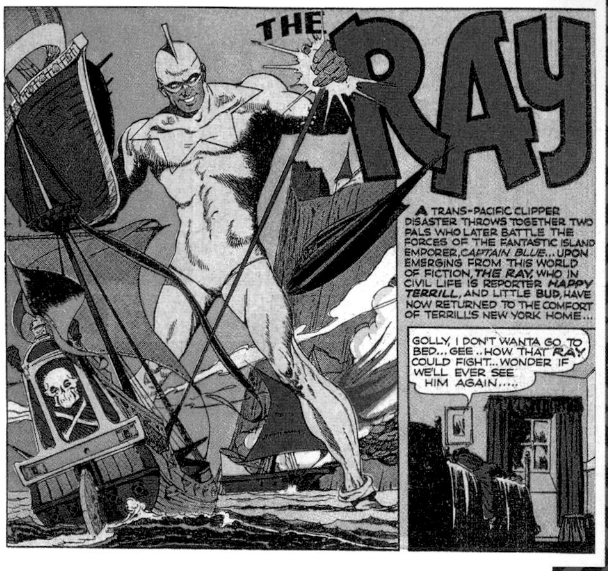
THE RAY
A TRANS-PACIFIC CLIPPER DISASTER THROWS TOGETHER TWO PALS WHO LATER BATTLE THE FORCES OF THE FANTASTIC ISLAND EMPORER, CAPTAIN BLUE... UPON EMERGING FROM THIS WORLD OF FICTION, THE RAY, WHO IN CIVIL LIFE IS REPORTER HAPPY TERRILL, AND LITTLE BUD, HAVE NOW RETURNED TO THE COMFORT OF TERRILL'S NEW YORK HOME...
GOLLY, I DON'T WANTA GO TO BED... GEE .. HOW THAT RAY COULD FIGHT... WONDER IF WE'LL EVER SEE HIM AGAIN.....

■ Fine, a much admired and much collected comic-book artist, spent less that ten years in the field. He joined the Eisner-Iger shop in the late 1930s to draw such features as *Wilton of the West* and *The Count of Monte Cristo* for *Jumbo Comics*. For the Fox line Fine drew *The Flame* as well as a series of striking covers for *Fantastic Comics* and *Mystery Men*. Eventually hired by publisher Busy Arnold, he started working directly for Quality. He drew Doll Man, the Black Condor, Uncle Sam, and the Ray. In addition, he drew a batch of impressive covers for *Hit Comics* and *National Comics*.

Fine's ambition was to be an illustrator, and his early comic-book work was very much influenced by such illustrators as J. C. Leyendecker. His work was unmatched in the early 1940s, and his closest competitor, Reed Crandall, lacked Fine's ease and grace. After a few years, however, he tired of his lyrical, heroic style and began developing a much more realistic approach. This was evident when he took over the weekly *The Spirit* newspaper inserts while Will Eisner was in the army. Next Lou Fine moved into advertising and turned out a large quantity of handsome Sunday comic-section advertising strips. By this time he'd perfected his mature style, drawing such things as a Sam Spade strip for Wildroot Cream Oil hair tonic and Mr. Coffee Nerves for Postum. In the middle 1940s he also drew a weekly black-and-white page titled *The Thropp Family* for the then popular *Liberty Magazine*.

Fine drew comics for *Boy's Life* and was also involved with newspaper strips. He illustrated a soap opera daily called *Adam Ames* and then one about a tough private eye named Peter Scratch. Both these were scripted by Elliot Caplin and neither thrived. At the time of his death, he was working on samples for a new sports-oriented newspaper strip.

FIREHAIR

RANGERS COMICS
Firehair
by JOHN STARR
ALMOST AS OLD AS TIME ITSELF, TREATY TREE HAS STOOD ON THE BANKS OF BLOODY CREEK. FOR GENERATIONS, THE CROWS AND DAKOTAS MET UNDER ITS GNARLED AND TOWERING BRANCHES TO SMOKE THEIR PEACE PIPES... MARK THEIR BOUNDARIES, AND MAKE TRADE TALK. SO ONCE MORE, THE CHIEFS HAVE GATHERED BENEATH ITS BRANCHES...
HERE, WHITE WOLF, THE BEAVERS MADE THEIR DAMS, AND SO CHANGED THE RIVER'S COURSE.
AYE, TEHAMA...AND SO WE GAINED A BIT OF GROUND. BUT AT THIS SPOT A MOUNTAIN LANDSLIDE AGAIN CHANGED THE CHANNEL AND ROBBED US.
QUITE TRUE... BUT THAT LAND WAS JUST A USELESS SWAMP. NOW AT THIS SPOT...

■ The woman who brought Good Girl Art to the Old West, Firehair was first seen in *Rangers Comics* #21 (February 1945). Like many another Western character, she had been raised by Indians after the death of her parents. Adopted by the Dakota tribe that took her in, the redhead remained with them after reaching maturity. Clad in a skimpy buckskin dress that grew skimpier over the years, Firehair acted as the champion of her adoptive people and helped them battle a continuous stream of predatory white men who were out to cheat, rob, murder, and otherwise take advantage of them.

Also known as "The Warrior-Maiden of the Wilderness" and "The Flame Girl of the Wild West," Firehair was soon the leading character in the magazine. From #40 (April 1948), she was featured on every cover until her departure in 1952. The scripts were always attributed to the house name John Starr and in her early years her adventures were illustrated by two of the acknowledged experts at drawing heroic women. The first was Lee Elias, who'd later draw Harvey's Black Cat, and the second was Bob Lubbers.

Firehair remained in *Rangers* through #65 (June 1952). She was also featured in eleven issues of her own magazine from 1948 to 1952. Giving way to a trend of the times, *Rangers* concentrated on war stories in the final four issues after Firehair left. They installed a new leading lady named G.I. Jane.

In the early 1970s, DC borrowed the Firehair name for a young red-haired boy, also raised by Indians, who was a backup character in their *Tomahawk* magazine. Joe Kubert drew the short-lived feature.

STANDARD COMICS
Starlet O'HARA in Hollywood
Her Romantic Adventures in Movieland
No. 3
10¢
SOMEDAY I'LL BE A STAR!

FITZGERALD, OWEN (c. 1918–1994)

■ A moonlighting Hollywood animator, Fitzgerald worked anonymously in comic books in the 1940s and 1950s. His style had a loose, lively look, and his pages resembled fast-moving animation storyboards. A Fitzgerald specialty was pretty girls, often of the scatterbrained sort. He was attached to the West Coast Sangor shop, which was run by fellow animator Jim Davis.

Fitzgerald's longest-running assignment was for DC's *The Adventures of Bob Hope*, a title he worked on from the first issue in 1950 and for several years thereafter. He also drew all four issues of Standard Comics' *Starlet O'Hara in Hollywood.*

In addition to being employed by such cartoon studios as Walt Disney, Hanna-Barbera, and DePatie-Freleng, Fitzgerald found time to ghost the *Dennis the Menace* Sunday page and also draw some of the *Dennis* comic books.

THE FLASH: I

■ He got going in the winter of 1939, debuting in *Flash Comics* #1 (January 1940), a title he shared with such characters as Hawkman, the Whip, and Johnny Thunder. The magazine was edited by Sheldon Mayer. In the original story, scripted by Gardner Fox and drawn by Harry Lampert, readers learned that college student Jay Garrick came by his incredible speed after accidentally inhaling "the deadly fumes of the gas elements of 'heavy water.'" The first thing Jay did with his new swiftness was join the football team to impress his blonde girlfriend, Joan Williams. Unlike less bright comic-book ladies, Joan was fully aware that Garrick was also the Flash. Once he became a practicing superhero, she was not above asking him to do her a superhuman favor now and then. His costume consisted of a red tunic with a lightning bolt on the front, blue tights, winged red boots, and a winged hat in the Mercury fashion.

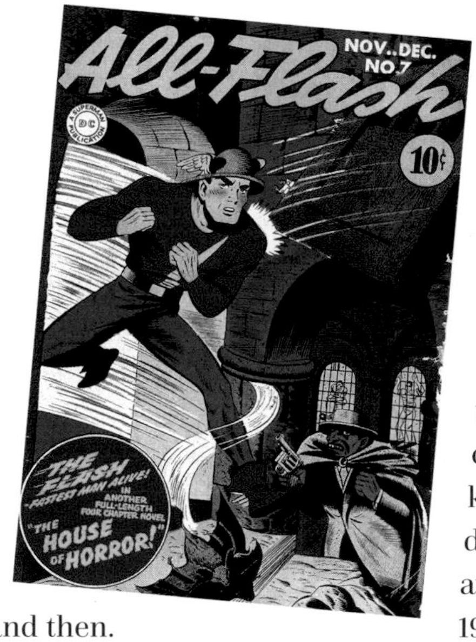
All-Flash
NOV..DEC. NO.7
10¢
THE FLASH
"THE HOUSE OF HORROR!"

Lampert left the feature after the second issue and was replaced by Everett E. Hibbard, an erstwhile commercial artist. He gave the feature a somewhat more realistic look, showing the influence of two of his newspaper comic-strip idols, Milton Caniff and Noel Sickles. Gradually Fox moved away from completely serious continuities and began to indulge in a certain amount of kidding and satire. Speedily becoming a hit with readers, the Flash soon branched out into a spot in *All Star Comics* and in the spring of 1943 an *All-Flash* title hit the stands. He also appeared in *Comic Cavalcade,* the fat fifteen-cent anthology he shared with the likes of Wonder Woman and Green Lantern. Other speedsters followed the trail he'd blazed, notably Johnny Quick in DC's *More Fun Comics.*

A great many of the heroes overseen by Mayer lightened up even further during World War II, possibly in an attempt to boost morale. During this period some heroes picked up clowns rather than boy wonders as sidekicks. The Green Lantern, for example, added Doiby Dickles, and the Flash took on a trio of buffoons, fellows obviously based on the Three Stooges of the screen and known as the Three Dimwits. They debuted in *All-Flash* #5, but were kept away from *Flash Comics* until #46 (October 1943). Named Winky, Blinky, and Noddy, they plagued the Flash's life for several years and ruined his chances of being taken seriously as a superhero.

To meet the demands for the increased number of stories about the Fastest Man Alive, other artists were brought in. Hal Sharp ghosted quite a few stories in the early 1940s, as did the incomparable Louis Ferstadt. In 1947 after Hibbard moved on, such artists as Joe Kubert, Alex Toth, Carmine Infantino, and Lee Elias took turns drawing the Flash. The postwar adventures looked and sounded, now with scripts by Robert Kanigher, much more serious, and the Three Dimwits were gone. The Flash took his first leave of comics in 1949 as the Golden Age waned.

THE FLASH: II

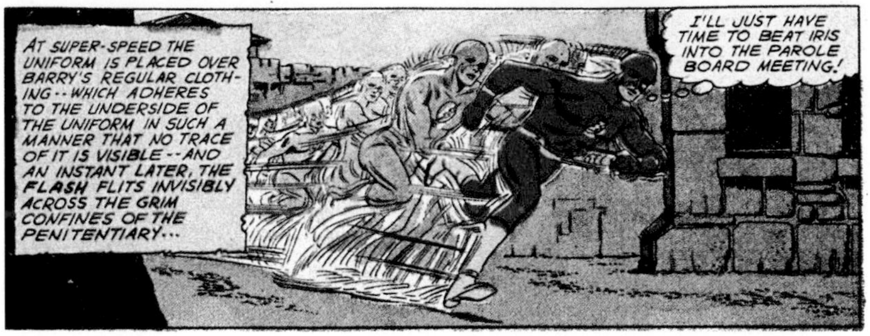
AT SUPER-SPEED THE UNIFORM IS PLACED OVER BARRY'S REGULAR CLOTHING--WHICH ADHERES TO THE UNDERSIDE OF THE UNIFORM IN SUCH A MANNER THAT NO TRACE OF IT IS VISIBLE--AND AN INSTANT LATER, THE FLASH FLITS INVISIBLY ACROSS THE GRIM CONFINES OF THE PENITENTIARY...
I'LL JUST HAVE TIME TO BEAT IRIS INTO THE PAROLE BOARD MEETING!

■ The harbinger of the new wave of superheroes, this Flash zoomed into view in 1956 and launched what was to become the Silver Age of comic books. In the middle fifties, while other editors were contemplating new genres, DC's Julius Schwartz was turning his thoughts again to superheroes. The first hero he took out of mothballs was the Flash.

"Someone, I don't know who, said, 'The Flash was always one of my favorites and maybe we ought to take a crack at putting him out again.' All eyes turned to me," Schwartz once recalled. "So I said, 'OK. I'm stuck.' For some reason, I decided not to revive the original Flash, but to do a *new* Flash with the same power, super-speed. I think I wanted to do an origin, which I always found fascinating, and I didn't like the original. I worked out a story with Bob Kanigher—new costume, new secret identity, new origin. The Flash's name, Barry Allen, came from two show-business personalities, Steve Allen and Barry Gray. The thing I like best about what we did was that the Flash got his inspiration of naming himself from a comic-book character he read as a kid after he got doused with that lightning bolt and realized he had super-speed himself."

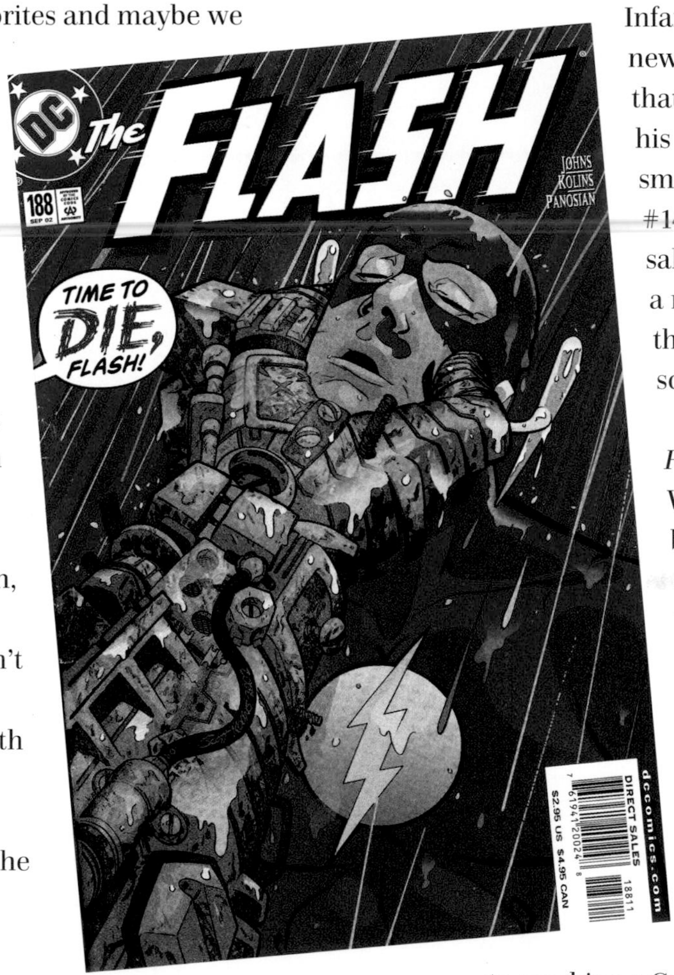
DC
The FLASH
188
SEP 02
JOHNS
KOLINS
PANOSIAN
TIME TO DIE, FLASH!
dccomics.com
DIRECT SALES
$2.95 US $4.95 CAN

The revamped Fastest Man Alive was introduced on *Showcase* #4 (September–October 1956). Carmine Infantino penciled, Joe Kubert inked. The new updated Flash wore a bright red costume that offered less wind resistance than that of his predecessor. It also folded up very, very small. He returned in *Showcase* #8, #13, and #14. Early in 1959, after proving he was a saleable commodity, the Flash was granted a magazine of his own. Infantino remained the artist, John Broome became the scriptwriter.

The speed king got a boy sidekick in *Flash* #110 late in 1959, in the person of Wally West, aka Kid Flash. (Schwartz borrowed this name from a venerable science-fiction pulp writer known as Wallace West.) In *Flash* #123, the Golden Age Flash returned and teamed up with his newer counterpart. "I had a discussion with Gardner Fox," Schwartz explained. "I said, 'Gardner, the easiest way to do it is to say you're communicating with another Earth, a parallel Earth in another dimension. Let the Flashes cross over and meet.' It was a breakthrough, to combine a Golden Age hero with a modern counterpart and have them team up." The parallel universe notion, a familiar gimmick in many a pulp sci-fi yarn, not only enabled the two Flashes to work in tandem, it allowed the elder to have a career of his own again. Over on his separate-but-equal Earth, Jay Garrick was now married to Joan Williams.

By the middle 1980s the parallel earths concept had been used so lavishly in so many DC titles that confusion tended to reign. That's why *Crisis on Infinite Earths* came along in 1985 and attempted to bring order. One of the many changes wrought was the death of Barry Allen.

FLASH COMICS

■ When M.C. Gaines got around to putting together his third title for Detective Comics, Inc., his young editor Sheldon Mayer was able to persuade him that superheroes were more than a passing fad. Thus *Flash Comics* #1 (January 1940) contained two serious superheroes and one silly one.

The three were the Flash, also known as the Fastest Man Alive, the Hawkman, and the nitwit with superpowers provided by his own personal thunderbolt, Johnny Thunder. For good measure, Mayer added a Zorro type called the Whip, a daring secret agent named Cliff Cornwall, and, in the third issue, the King, a master of disguise. Since Mayer was a fan of newspaper comics, he invited out of work comic-strip artist Ed Wheelan to provide a *Flash Picture Novelette* for each early issue. And since Gaines had been associated with such reprint magazines as *Famous Funnies* and *Popular Comics*, there was even a reprint of Paul Jepson's little-known science-fiction Sunday page, *Rod Ryan of the Sky Police*.

Most of the scripts were by nonpracticing attorney Gardner Fox, who was near the beginning of his comic-book career. "I wrote everything except Johnny Thunder and the Whip," Fox once recalled. "Both were by a fellow in Maine, John Wentworth, and Ed Wheelan . . . I did the Flash, Hawkman, even Cliff Cornwall." The early artists included Harry Lampert, then E. E. Hibbard on *The Flash*;

Thereafter Kid Flash grew up, donned the red suit and became the third Flash. As a recent caption explained it, "After the death of his forerunner, and years of training as Kid Flash, Wally has inherited the identity of the scarlet speedster. Today he carries on the legacy of the Fastest Man Alive. Today Wally West is the Flash." Scripter of the twenty-first century adventures has been Geoff Johns with Scott Kolins as penciler.

Dennis Neville and then Sheldon Moldoff in *Hawkman*; George Storm and then Homer Fleming on *The Whip*; Stan Josephs on *Johnny Thunder*. By *Flash* #12 (December 1940) Wheelan had switched to *Minute Movies*, a full-color revival of his popular 1920s to 1930s newspaper strip.

Hawkman acquired a partner, Hawkgirl, in #24 (December 1941). *The Ghost Patrol*, featuring three dead aviators who returned to plague the Nazis, began in #29. It was the product of the small Emanuel Demby shop and drawn by Frank Harry. As the magazine continued, Mayer, a man of strong opinions and an individual outlook, hired men whose work hadn't been seen in other DC titles. He picked the highly individualistic Joe Gallagher to draw *The King* and young and inventive Joe Kubert to draw *Hawkman*.

The years after World War II brought changes to *Flash Comics*. Hibbard was replaced, and both Lee Elias and Carmine Infantino drew *The Flash*. Infantino also applied his Caniff-inspired style to *Johnny Thunder*. The humorless Robert Kanigher had assumed the scripting of this latter feature, and Johnny, along with his thunderbolt, was eased out. The Black Canary, who'd been sharing the feature, became the sole occupant.

In this incarnation *Flash Comics* ended with #104 (February 1949). But many of its characters would return, in various forms, in the coming years.

BUT THE HUNGRY TENDRILS CATCH FLASH-----
--AND DRAW HIM INTO THE AIR!--------
1-24
Copr. 1937 King Features Syndicate, Inc., World rights reserved.

FLASH GORDON

■ In the company of Dale Arden and Dr. Zarkov, Flash Gordon embarked for the planet Mongo in 1934. That was in the Sunday funnies in a page drawn by Alex Raymond and written anonymously by former pulp-fiction editor Don Moore. This space opera became one of King Features Syndicate's most popular features, and Raymond's illustrative art was to have a strong influence on many of the young artists who began drawing for comic books in the late 1930s and the early 1940s—Tom Hickey, Sheldon Moldoff, Jack Lehti, George Papp, Mac Raboy, Dan Barry, etc.

Flash Gordon entered comic books early in 1936 by way of reprints in *King Comics.* His battles with the merciless Ming, a sort of galactic Fu Manchu, unfolded in the magazine from the first issue.

In the early 1940s Dell began issuing now and then *Flash Gordon* reprint titles. Later in the decade came an occasional comic-book offering Flash adventures "especially written and drawn for this magazine." The artist was Paul Norris, who also began drawing the *Jungle Jim* newspaper page in 1948.

Harvey Publications tried reprinting the Raymond material in 1950 and 1951, giving up after a few issues. King Features experimented with publishing comic books in the late 1960s. These used original material, and the *Flash Gordon* book made use of such artists as Al Williamson, a devoted Raymond disciple, Gil Kane, and Reed Crandall. When King quit, Charlton took over and finally Gold Key. The final *Flash Gordon* comic book was printed in 1982. He reappeared briefly in 1987 as part of a team that included Mandrake and the Phantom in the TV-inspired *Defenders of the Earth.*

"FLASH" LIGHTNING

■ See LIGHTNING COMICS.

FLESSEL, CREIG *(1912–)*

■ In the course of a very long career, Flessel has drawn everything from the original *Sandman* in *Adventure Comics* to *Baron von Furstinbed* for *Playboy.* Along the way he worked for Major Malcolm Wheeler-Nicholson on the first original-material comic books in the middle 1930s, drew dozens of attractive covers for *Detective Comics* and *Adventure Comics*, served time in the Harry "A" Chesler shop, cocreated *The Shining Knight*, designed the Mr. Crime character who hosted many a story in *Crime Does Not Pay*, had his true-crime artwork cited by Dr. Fredric Wertham in *Seduction of the Innocent*, drew the *David Crane* newspaper strip for many years, ghosted the *Li'l Abner* strip, worked on many advertising strips, and even drew Joe Simon's ill-fated *Prez* in the 1970s.

THE FLY

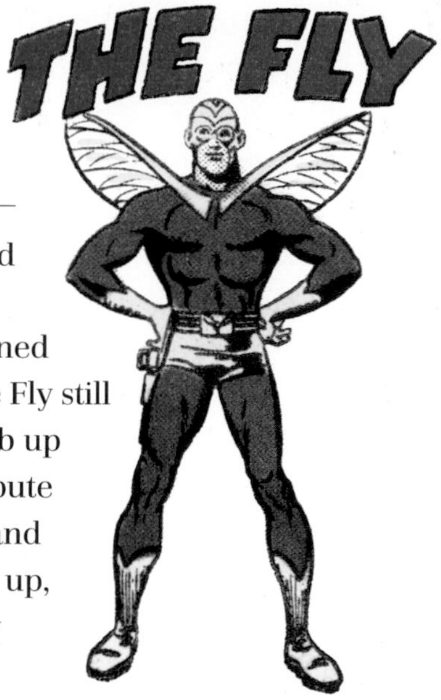
THE FLY

■ A moderately successful Silver Age superhero, the Fly had a rather illustrious creative team behind him. It included Joe Simon, Jack Kirby, and C. C. Beck. Published as part of the Archie Adventure Series, the first issue of *The Fly* appeared in the summer of 1959. The title was soon changed to *The Adventures of the Fly,* and then, toward the end of the run in the middle 1960s, it was switched to *Flyman.* According to Simon, the character was originally to have been christened Spiderman.

In his book *The Comic Book Makers*, Joe Simon says that in the middle 1950s, he and C. C. Beck, cocreator of the original Captain Marvel, and writer Jack Olek put together a pitch for a character they originally called Spiderman. As work progressed the name of the new superhero was changed to the Silver Spider—"A 'tribute' to one of the earlier features I had done—the Silver Streak." Basically this was Billy Batson and Shazam revisited, with the orphan boy now blond and named Tommy Troy. When he rubbed a magic ring, he became the full-grown Silver Spider. Simon submitted the idea to Harvey Publications, but it was rejected.

Then in 1959, John Goldwater of Archie asked Simon for a new superhero. With the moribund Silver Spider in mind, Simon invented a similar character called the Fly. After getting an okay, he called in his erstwhile partner Jack Kirby. Although Kirby redesigned the Silver Spider costume, the Fly still maintained the ability to climb up walls like a spider. After a dispute with the Archie folks, Simon and Kirby quit. Tommy Troy grew up, picked up a partner called Fly Girl, and buzzed around for several more years.

John Rosenberger, who'd been working for ACG in such magazines as *Adventures into the Unknown* and *Romantic Adventures*, signed with Archie in the summer of 1960. He became the official Fly artist with #11 (March 1961), drawing both covers and stories. An illustrator as well as a cartoonist, Rosenberger worked in a somewhat more formal and less flamboyant style than his predecessors. When he switched to *The Jaguar*, John Giunta undertook the drawing.

The Fly returned briefly in the early 1980s and was last seen on the stands as one of DC's ill-fated Impact titles. "Like a lot of flies," Joe Simon once observed, "it took several swats before his legs stopped moving."

THE FOX AND THE CROW

■ A comedy team for more than a quarter of a century, they first got together in a 1941 Columbia animated cartoon. Four years later, Fauntleroy Fox and Crawford Crow became the stars of DC's *Real Screen Comics.* In 1952 came a separate *The Fox and the Crow* title, which survived until 1968.

The cartoon introducing the con man Crow and the gullible fox was titled *The Fox and the Grapes.* Released in December 1941, it was directed by Frank Tashlin. Bob Wickersham took over the direction with the second Fox and Crow and stayed on to direct sixteen more of them between 1942 and 1946. The Fox, a mild-mannered fellow, was the perennial mark of the cunning Crow. Wearing a derby, smoking a stogie, and talking with a Brooklyn accent, Crawford Crow devoted much of his energy to conning Fauntleroy Fox out of his money, his food, and just about anything else he possessed.

When DC sent editor Whit Ellsworth to Hollywood to arrange for licensing animated characters, all the major funny animals, such as Mickey Mouse, Woody Woodpecker, and Bugs Bunny, had long since been signed by Dell. Ellsworth had to settle for the Fox and the Crow plus some of Columbia's even lesser-known characters. *Real Screen Funnies*, which became *Real Screen Comics* with the second issue, first appeared in the spring of 1945. The Fox and the Crow were backed up by Tito and his Burrito, Flippity and Flop, and the Polar Playmates. The magazine, chiefly because of the Fox and the Crow, was relatively successful and remained in business until 1961, having changed its name to *TV Screen Cartoons* in 1959. The team's own title lasted from 1952 to 1968. They were also featured in the revamped *Comic Cavalcade* from 1949 to 1954. The animated movie series had ceased in 1949.

The Fox and the Crow comic books were a product of Hollywood, being produced by the West Coast Sangor shop managed by animator Jim Davis. The first artist was Wickersham, who was also in charge of the animated cartoons. The chief scriptwriter was Hubert Karp, another worker in animation. Wickersham quit in 1948, and Davis himself took over the drawing, little suspecting how long he'd be at it. "I had no way of knowing it was going to be my bread and butter for the next twenty years," he once said. Karp died in 1953, and Cecil Beard took on the writing. Beard, who also had an animation background, enjoyed his job. "We sometimes had a rough time getting the work out," he once admitted. "We would be rolling on the floor in hysterics over some preposterous situation the characters . . . seemed to develop."

While meant for younger readers, the Fox and the Crow also attracted a loyal, albeit smaller, older audience as well.

FOX, GARDNER E. *(1911–1988)*

■ One of the most prolific and most inventive of comic-book writers, Fox had a hand in the creation of several major characters from the 1930s to the 1960s. Trained as a lawyer, he started writing scripts for DC in 1937. He cocreated the original Sandman, Zatara, Dr. Fate, Hawkman, Starman, and the Justice Society. He also wrote for *Batman*. In the 1960s, he was in at the creation of Adam Strange, the new Flash, the new Green Lantern, the new Hawkman, and the Justice League. He later wrote for Marvel. In his spare time, Fox contributed stories to such pulp-fiction magazines as *Planet Stories* and *Amazing Stories* and turned out, sometimes using pen names, well over one hundred paperback novels.

FOX, GILL (1915–2004)

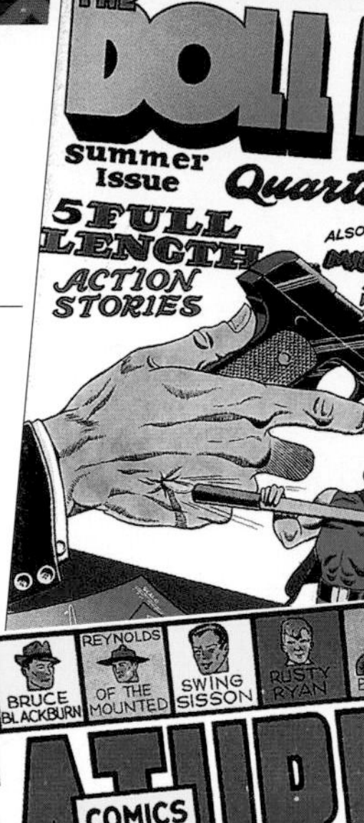
THE DOLL MAN
Summer Issue
Quarterly 10¢
5 FULL LENGTH ACTION STORIES
ALSO The DRAGON
AMERICA... IT'S WORTH DEFENDING!

■ Fox's career as a cartoonist extended over sixty years. He worked regularly in comic books from the late 1930s, with time out for overseas service in the army and staff work on *Stars and Stripes*, to the early 1950s. He was first with the Quality line from 1939 to 1943, drawing humorous fillers, editing such titles as *Police Comics*, and drawing covers showcasing such heroes as the Black Condor, Plastic Man, and Doll Man. After World War II, Fox returned to Quality to do more humor stuff and also to draw *Torchy*.

While still in his teens Fox got himself a job with the Fleischer animation studio, located in New York City at that time. He went from there to the Harry "A" Chesler shop. He soon made a connection with Everett "Busy" Arnold's Quality outfit, where his funny features included *Poison Ivy*, *Slaphappy Pappy*, and *Wun Cloo*. He also did a lighter version of Jack Cole's *Death Patrol*. He put in time at the Johnstone and Cushing agency in the 1950s, drawing advertising strips alongside such colleagues as Creig Flessel, Stan Drake, and Dik Browne. He drew several newspaper features and panels, putting in many years with the NEA *Side Glances* panel. Next Fox became a political cartoonist, once nominating himself for a Pulitzer Prize, and was still at it until quite recently. Versatile, Fox was a master of many styles, but there are those who think the humor pages he drew and wrote back in the 1940s represent his best work.

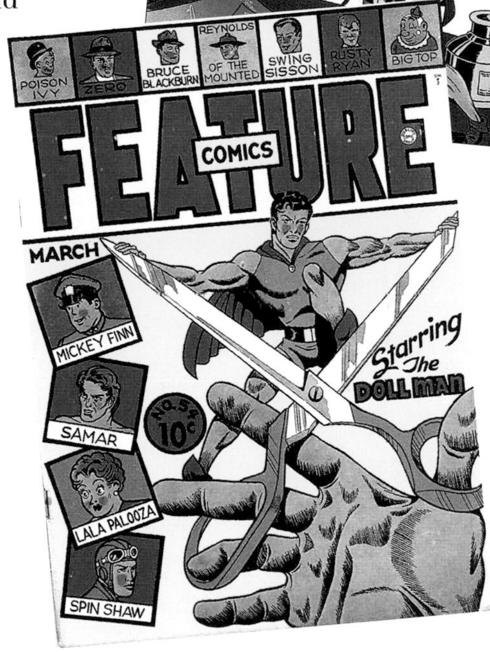
POISON IVY
ZERO
BRUCE BLACKBURN
REYNOLDS OF THE MOUNTED
SWING SISSON
RUSTY RYAN
BIG TOP
FEATURE COMICS
MARCH
MICKEY FINN
SAMAR
LALA PALOOZA
SPIN SHAW
Starring The DOLL MAN
10¢

FRADON, RAMONA (1927–)

■ Ramona Fradon established herself as a first-rate comic-book artist during a period when very few women were to be found working in that capacity. An art school graduate, she started in the field in the early 1950s. She was married to Dana Fradon, who'd not yet become a top *New Yorker* cartoonist. Back then, as she recently explained, "We were poor. We needed money." At the suggestion of a friend she did some sample comic-book pages and took them up to DC. Fradon was hired by Murray Boltinoff and fairly soon became the regular artist on *Aquaman*. Her work was direct and colorful, easy to spot even though she rarely signed it. She stayed with the underwater superhero for several years and also drew *Metamorpho*. In the early 1970s, she worked at Marvel for a while, drawing *The Cat* and *The Fantastic Four*. Returning to DC, she was involved in one of the unsuccessful attempts to revive *Plastic Man*. She left comic books in the early 1980s to take over the drawing of the *Brenda Starr* newspaper strip and remained with it until her retirement in 1995.

FRANKENSTEIN

■ Undoubtedly one of the oldest characters to appear regularly in comic books, the Frankenstein monster was created, in more ways than one, in 1818 in Mary Wollstonecraft Shelley's novel *Frankenstein; or, the Modern Prometheus.* In the book Dr. Victor Frankenstein cobbled the monster together from parts he'd gathered and gave him life. The patchwork man proved indestructible, living throughout the nineteenth century in numerous reprints. He survived into the twentieth century, and in 1931 Universal Pictures adapted him to the screen. In 1940, the Frankenstein monster lurched into comic books to make the first of many appearances.

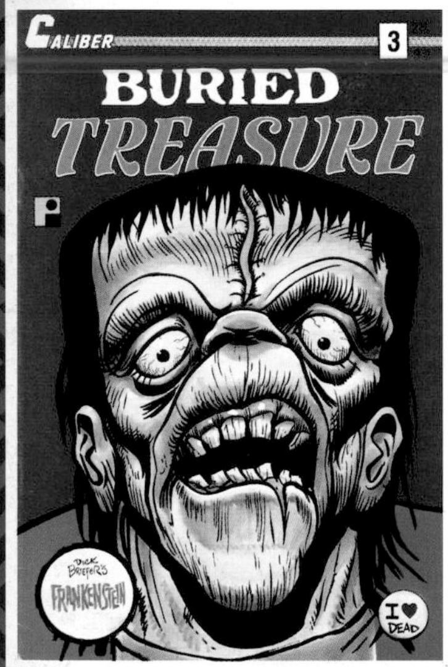
CALIBER
3
BURIED TREASURE
I ♥ DEAD

Artist/writer Dick Briefer introduced him in *Prize Comics* #7 (December 1940), modeling him after actor Boris Karloff, who'd appeared in three Frankenstein movies by then. Since the novel was in public domain and Karloff wasn't, Briefer was careful to state at the start of each comic-book episode that it was "suggested by the classic of Mary Shelley." He updated the story, gave it an American setting, and showed his hulking, dead-white monster rampaging through streamlined urban settings. Within a few months he began calling the monster Frankenstein, explaining "the name is universally accepted to be that of the ghastly creation."

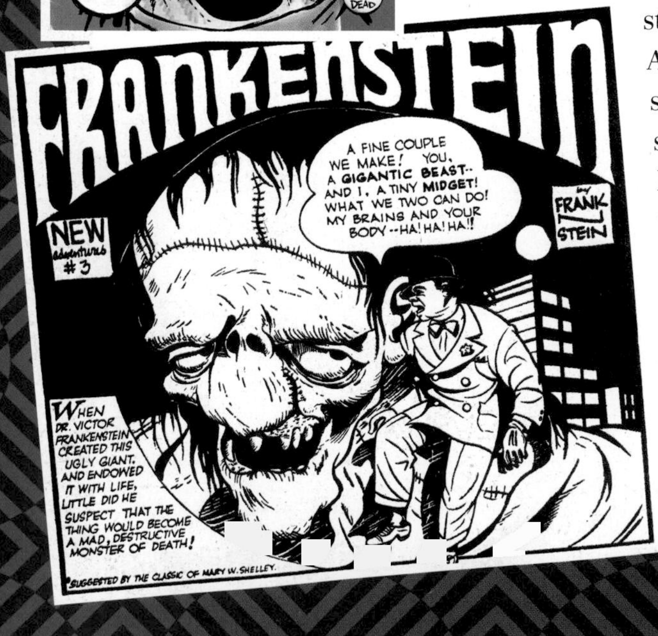
FRANKENSTEIN
A FINE COUPLE WE MAKE! YOU, A GIGANTIC BEAST-- AND I, A TINY MIDGET! WHAT WE TWO CAN DO! MY BRAINS AND YOUR BODY--HA! HA! HA!!
by FRANK STEIN
NEW adventures #3
WHEN DR. VICTOR FRANKENSTEIN CREATED THIS UGLY GIANT, AND ENDOWED IT WITH LIFE, LITTLE DID HE SUSPECT THAT THE THING WOULD BECOME A MAD, DESTRUCTIVE MONSTER OF DEATH!
SUGGESTED BY THE CLASSIC OF MARY W. SHELLEY.

A man with a strong though perverse sense of humor, Briefer gradually tired of doing all the ghastly stuff straight. By the middle 1940s, he had converted *Frankenstein* into a comedy feature. He kidded the whole horror genre, made fun of such current fads and foibles as quiz shows and crooners. The monster became the star of *Prize* and in 1945 also began appearing in a bimonthly magazine of his own. Briefer afterward admitted that the funny Frankenstein was the favorite of all his comic-book work. "I look back into the old comic mags of *Frankenstein*," he said, "and really marvel at most of the art and ideas and scripts that I turned out."

The humorous Frankenstein ended in the late 1940s, but the character came back in the early 1950s in a new, grim version that lasted until late in 1954. Also from the Prize Group, it was written and drawn by Briefer.

Back in 1945, *Classics Illustrated* had offered an adaptation of the novel. Packaged by the Jerry Iger shop, it had artwork by Bob Webb. In 1964, Dell issued a one-shot *Frankenstein* in their Movie Classics series, offering the Universal version with the slogan "The Monster Is Back!!!" Two years later, in an example of flop-oriented thinking, Dell introduced a new Frankenstein who was "the world's newest, greatest, and strangest super hero!" This unlikely combination of horror and heroics managed to struggle through only three quarterly issues. Marvel came up with *The Monster of Frankenstein* in 1973—"The most famous, most fearsome MONSTER of all!" Drawn initially by Mike Ploog and later by John Buscema and others, the magazine ended in 1975 after eighteen issues. The monster rose again in comic-book novel adaptations in the 1980s and 1990s.

FRAZETTA, FRANK

(1928-)

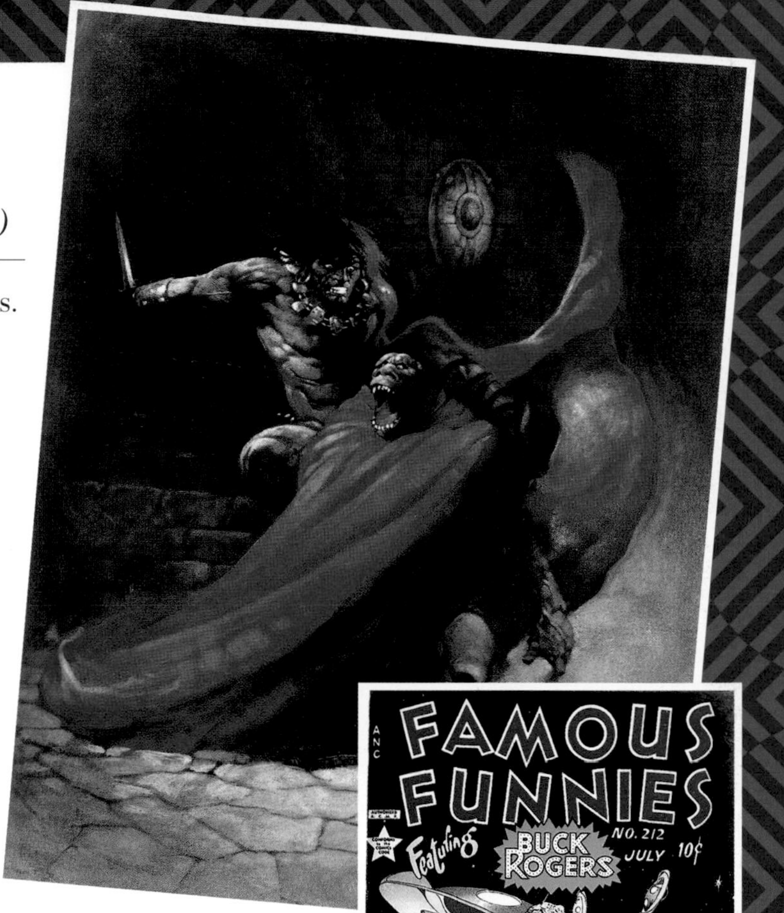

■ Another boy wonder, Frazetta entered comics while in his teens. After working as an assistant to John Giunta, he joined the Bernard Baily shop in 1945. The next year he was appearing in such Ned Pines titles as *Startling Comics* and *Thrilling Comics.* He was doing mostly light stuff at this point, teenage characters, funny animals, and a hillbilly strip called *Looie Lazybones.* By the time he went to work for Vincent Sullivan's Magazine Enterprises in 1949, Frazetta had perfected his straight illustration style, which owed a good deal to his idol Hal Foster. For ME he drew *Dan Brand* in *The Durango Kid* and produced some striking covers for *Ghost Rider.* His most ambitious work for ME was the first issue of *Thun'da.*

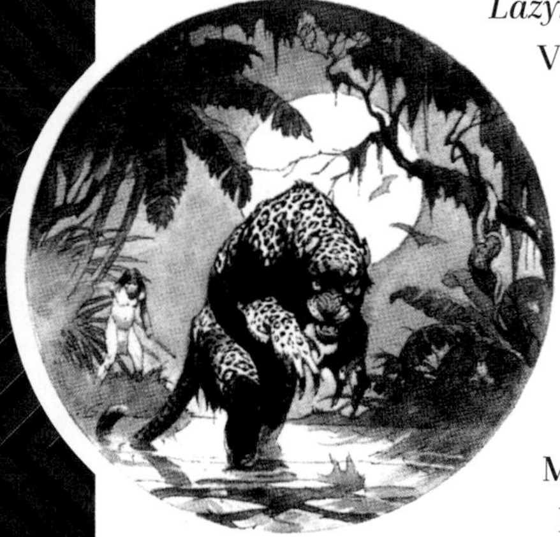

Next at DC Frazetta drew some episodes of *Tomahawk* and *The Shining Knight.* Over at *Famous Funnies,* he did a series of memorable covers featuring Buck Rogers and also drew some true stories for *Heroic Comics.* Frazetta did a few jobs for EC before taking on the newspaper racing-car strip *Johnny Comet* in the early 1950s. He also began a several-year run ghosting *Li'l Abner* for Al Capp, who was later outraged that many fans could tell Frazetta's work from his.

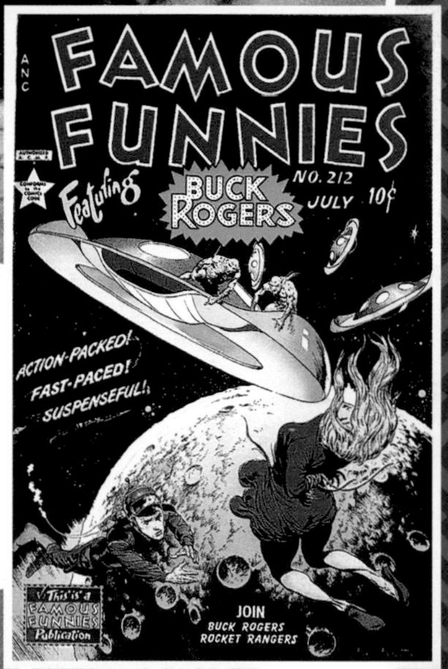
FAMOUS FUNNIES
Featuring BUCK ROGERS
NO. 212
JULY 10¢
ACTION-PACKED! FAST-PACED! SUSPENSEFUL!
This is a FAMOUS FUNNIES Publication
JOIN BUCK ROGERS ROCKET RANGERS

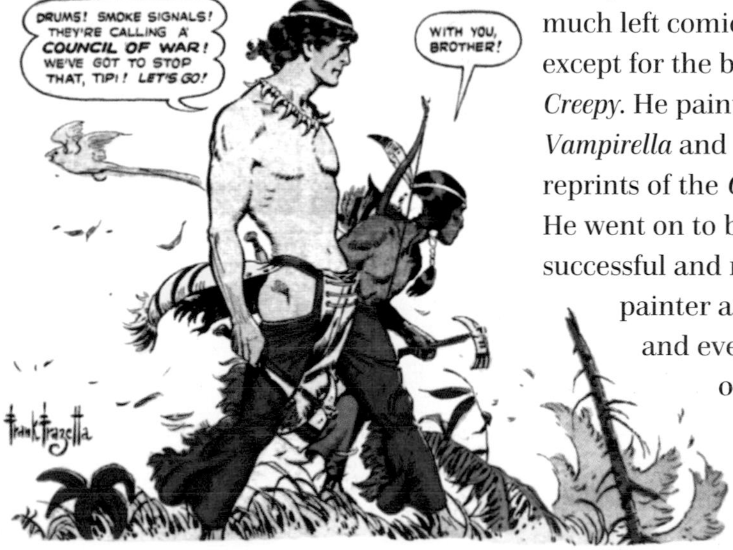
DRUMS! SMOKE SIGNALS! THEY'RE CALLING A COUNCIL OF WAR! WE'VE GOT TO STOP THAT, TIPI! LET'S GO!
WITH YOU, BROTHER!
Frank Frazetta

By the 1960s he had pretty much left comic books, except for the black-and-white *Creepy.* He painted covers for *Vampirella* and for the Ace reprints of the *Conan* novels. He went on to become a highly successful and much collected painter and illustrator and even set up his own museum.

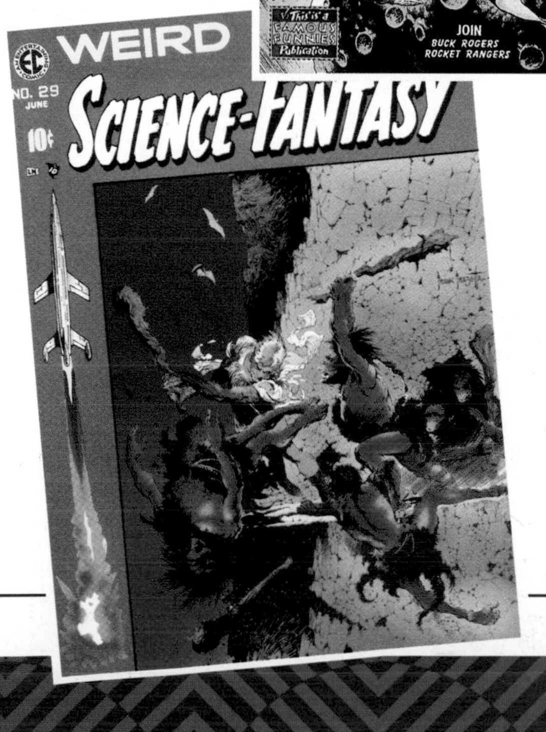
WEIRD
NO. 29
JUNE
10¢
SCIENCE-FANTASY

FRONTLINE COMBAT

■ See TWO-FISTED TALES.

FUJITANI, BOB (1921–)

■ It was while using the pen name Bob Fuje in the 1940s that he did some of his best, as well as some of his most gruesome, drawing in comic books. His art credits for that period include *Shock Gibson*, *Cat-Man*, *The Black Condor*, *Hack O'Hara*, *Sky Wolf*, *The Zebra*, and *Hangman*. He'd first worked on the latter character when assisting the earlier artist Harry Lucey. Appearing in *Pep Comics*, Hangman dealt with some of the nastiest and most bloodthirsty criminals of the era. Fujitani did them all justice, especially the ones who had a tendency to drool while at their work. He was also a regular contributor to Lev Gleason's *Crime Does Not Pay* and contributed to the pioneering but short-lived horror comic *Eerie*.

Later on, using a milder and more subdued style, he drew such things as *Dr. Solar*. He was the first artist on a comic strip titled *Judge Wright* in the middle 1940s and from the middle 1960s to the middle 1980s he ghosted the *Flash Gordon* strip.

FUNG, PAUL (1897–1944)

■ A gifted cartoonist with a direct, lively style, Fung had been a newspaper cartoonist in Seattle before going east in the early 1920s to work for William Randolph Hearst's King Features Syndicate. He assisted Billy DeBeck on *Barney Google*. On his own he drew *Bughouse Fables*, *Gus & Gussie*, and *Dumb Dora*, which he inherited from *Blondie* creator Chic Young. Later in the 1930s, he ghosted the daily *Polly and Her Pals* strip and also worked on advertising comics. Fung drew a great many Sunday advertising strips for such products as Nestlé's, Postum, Ralston cereals, and a tonic with the appealing name of Scott's Emulsion.

His comic-book career at DC, cut short by his early death, lasted only during the early 1940s. He drew several visually inventive episodes of *Penniless Palmer* in *Star Spangled Comics*. Fung was also a regular early contributor to *All Funny Comics*, and he drew one less-than-serious adventure of *Superman*. Like most of his advertising work, his comic-book stuff was done anonymously.

HELP!
SOCK!
DOUG ...... HE KISSED ME
OH, HE DID---- DID HE?
SOCK!
I'LL GET EVEN WITH YOU, ROD, AND I'LL LIKE IT--- I'LL KISS DORA----
!
KISS DORA, EH?
KISS BESSIE, EH?
SLAP!
SLAP!

THE FUNNIES: I

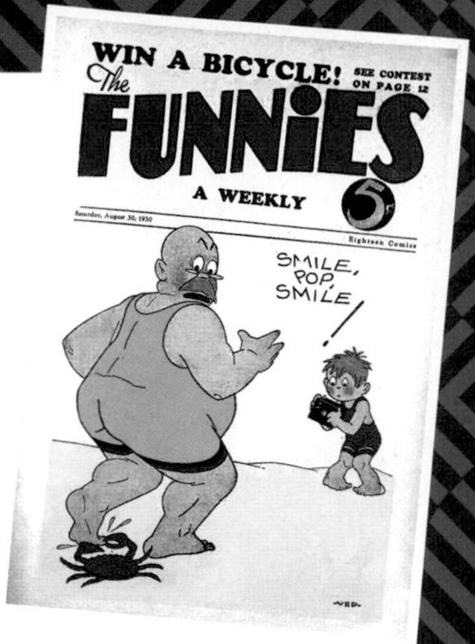
WIN A BICYCLE!
SEE CONTEST ON PAGE 12
The FUNNIES
A WEEKLY
SMILE, POP, SMILE

■ An early and noble experiment, this was more a Sunday comic section without the rest of the newspaper than a true comic book. But it did offer all original material and was sold on newsstands. A sixteen-page four-color tabloid, *The Funnies* was published by Dell and priced at a dime initially. Henry Steeger, who later published such pulp-fiction magazines as *Dime Detective*, *The Spider*, *Black Mask*, and *Adventure*, was the editor. He never went near comics again.

The features, laid out like Sunday funnies, included *Clancy the Cop* by Vic Pazmino, *Deadwood Gulch* by Boody Rogers, *My Big Brudder* by Tack Knight (later by Frank Engli), and *"Frosty" Ayre* by Joe Archibald. The premier issue of *The Funnies* arrived late in 1929, just as the Depression got rolling. By the summer of the next year, the price had been lowered to a nickel. Not helped by the price reduction, the ailing publication halted in October 1930. Dell revived the title for a conventional format comic book in 1936. Some of the material was reused in Dell's *The Comics* in 1937.

THE FUNNIES: II

■ Not one to abandon a perfectly good title, Dell resurrected *The Funnies* in 1936. This time for use on a monthly sixty-four-page comic book to rival the increasingly successful *Famous Funnies*. It was packaged by M. C. Gaines and Sheldon Mayer and was devoted to newspaper strip reprints. The early issues drew heavily on the NEA syndicate stable, *Alley Oop*, *Captain Easy*, *Myra North*, and *Salesman Sam*. Among the other reprints, mostly Sunday pages, were *Dan Dunn*, *Tailspin Tommy*, *Don Dixon*, *Bronc Peeler*, and *Mutt & Jeff*.

In the second issue, editor Mayer, a boy cartoonist himself, introduced *Scribbly*, a strip about a boy cartoonist. The two or three pages devoted to *Scribbly* each issue were laid out to look like Sunday page reprints, each with its own logo.

Gradually other new material began slipping into the magazine. Starting with #20 (May 1938), six-page adaptations of cowboy B-movies were featured. A four-page true-crime continuity called *The Crime Busters*, drawn by Alden McWilliams, started in the twenty-first issue. After Gaines and Mayer departed late in 1938 to put together comic books for DC, *The Funnies* underwent further changes. With the exception of *Alley Oop* and a couple of others, the reprints were dropped. Among the new features were *Mr. District Attorney*, adapted from the popular radio show, and *John Carter of Mars*, adapted from Edgar Rice Burroughs's novels and illustrated after a few issues by his son, John Coleman Burroughs.

Early in 1940, the magazine added *Rex, King of the Deep*, and *Speed Martin*, about a reporter in war-torn Europe. With July 1940 came Phantasmo, *The Funnies*' first honest-to-gosh superhero. A year later saw the advent of another radio hero, Captain Midnight. Drawn by Dan Gormley, the captain and his Secret Squadron supplanted Phantasmo as the leading characters.

Then, after allowing Andy Panda and Felix the Cat into its pages, the magazine made another, more drastic change. With #65 (July 1942), it became *New Funnies*. Added to the revised lineup were Raggedy Ann and Andy, Oswald the Rabbit, the Brownies, and Woody Woodpecker. This proved to be the book's most durable phase, and it reached issue #288 before ending its life in 1962.

FUNNYMAN

■ Eager to come up with another major hit after being dismissed from *Superman*, Jerry Siegel and Joe Shuster pinned their hopes on *Funnyman*. This lighthearted take on costumed crimefighters, however, failed first as a comic book and then as a syndicated newspaper strip.

Their hero was a TV comedian named Larry Davis, who put on a slapstick costume and hopped into his Jet Jalopy to combat assorted clownish crooks and criminals. While Siegel wrote the scripts, Shuster, suffering from failing eyesight, did none of the drawing. A good deal of it was provided by John Sikela, the best of the *Superman* ghosts.

Vincent Sullivan, the editor at *Action Comics* who'd bought *Superman* from the team in 1938, had since become a publisher. His Magazine Enterprises bought *Funnyman*. The first issue was dated January 1948. Asked about the venture several decades later, Sullivan said, "I lost quite a bit of money. It just didn't sell." Even the cover line "The creators of SUPERMAN present their NEW HERO" didn't help. After the sixth issue (August 1948) the *Funnyman* comic book was gone.

Just as the magazine faded away, the Bell Syndicate took a chance with a *Funnyman* comic strip. That only made it to the autumn of 1949 before expiring. Sikela drew most of the strips, daily and Sunday.

FUNNY PAGES
IN THE HIDDEN UNDERGROUND TRAP, MING SHOWED HIS DAUGHTER THE G-MAN IN THE GRASP OF A GIANT OCTOPUS!
INDIAN MAGIC
MAKER
CIRCUS U SUK
MAD MING
MAGIC
PLUTON

FUNNY PAGES

■ The first magazine to imitate Major Malcolm Wheeler-Nicholson (whose company later became DC) and use all original material was founded early in 1936 by two deserters from the major's camp, William Cook and John Mahon. The initial title published by their shoestring Comics Magazine Company, Inc., was called *The Comics Magazine*. With the second issue, the title was changed to *Funny Pages*.

As with the early Nicholson titles, the new magazine offered a couple of dozen characters, mostly in two-page episodes. The first issue contained several familiar features, either pilfered from Major Nicholson or given to Cook and Mahon in lieu of severance pay. These included two by Sheldon Mayer and Siegel and Shuster's *Federal Men* under the title *Federal Agents* and their *Dr. Occult* posing as *Dr. Mystic*.

Cook and Mahon gave up their magazine in the spring of 1937, and it eventually became a Centaur publication. The characters now were fewer, the stories longer, and not all of the pages funny. A red-clad mystery man known as the Arrow, drawn by Paul Gustavson, was added in the summer of 1938, making him the first costumed crimefighter in comics after the advent of Superman. Soon Jack Cole contributed *Mantoka*, about a shape-changing native American magician, and Harold DeLay drew *Mad Ming*, which dealt with yet another Fu Manchu impersonator. *Funny Pages* also made room for two of the few women cartoonists around at the time, Claire Moe and Tarpe Mills. The magazine ended with its forty-second issue in 1940.

Funny Picture Stories, the second Cook-Mahon venture, also turned eventually into a Centaur title. It lasted from 1936 to 1939 and helped launch the Clock, but contained no other major characters.

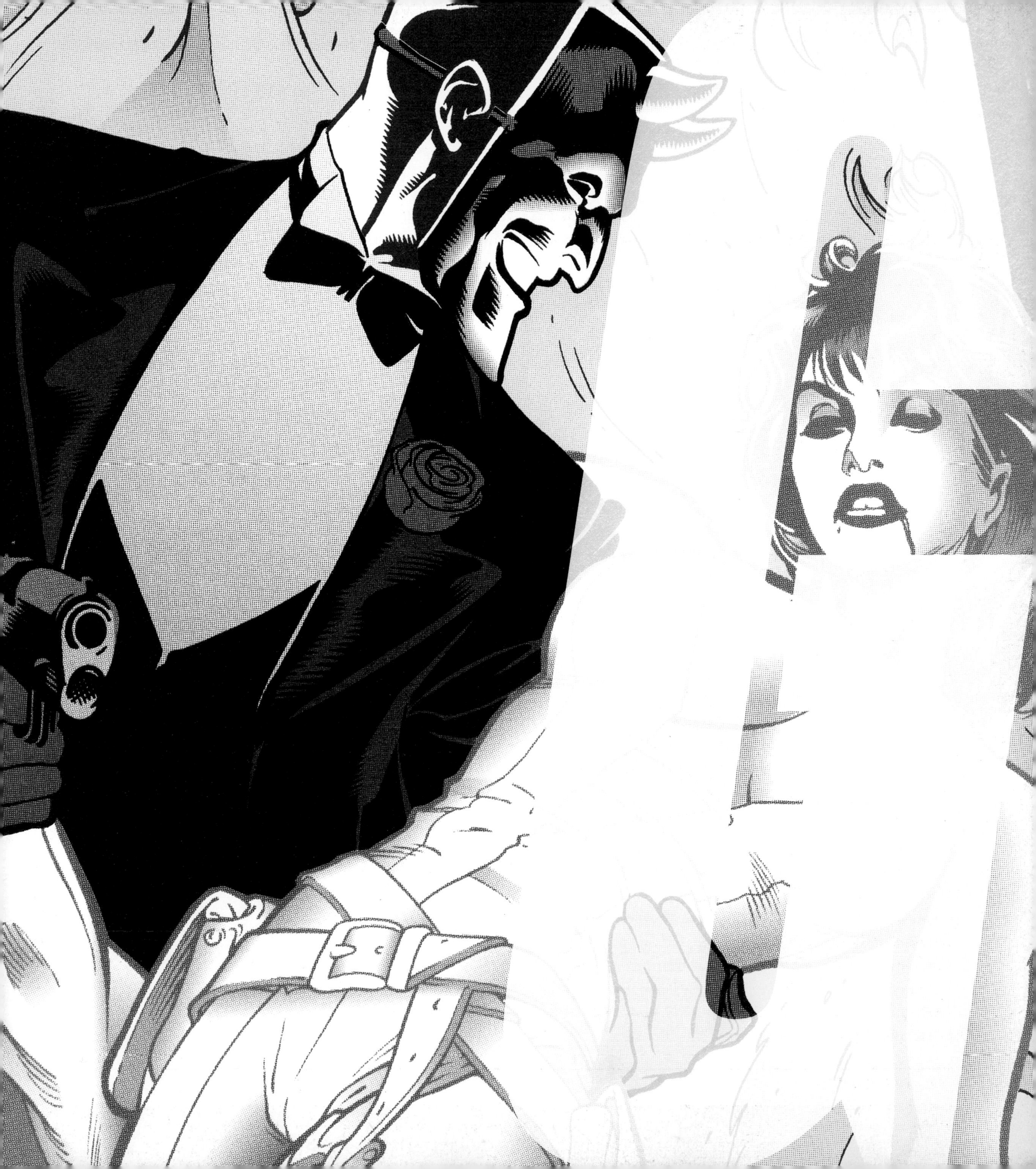

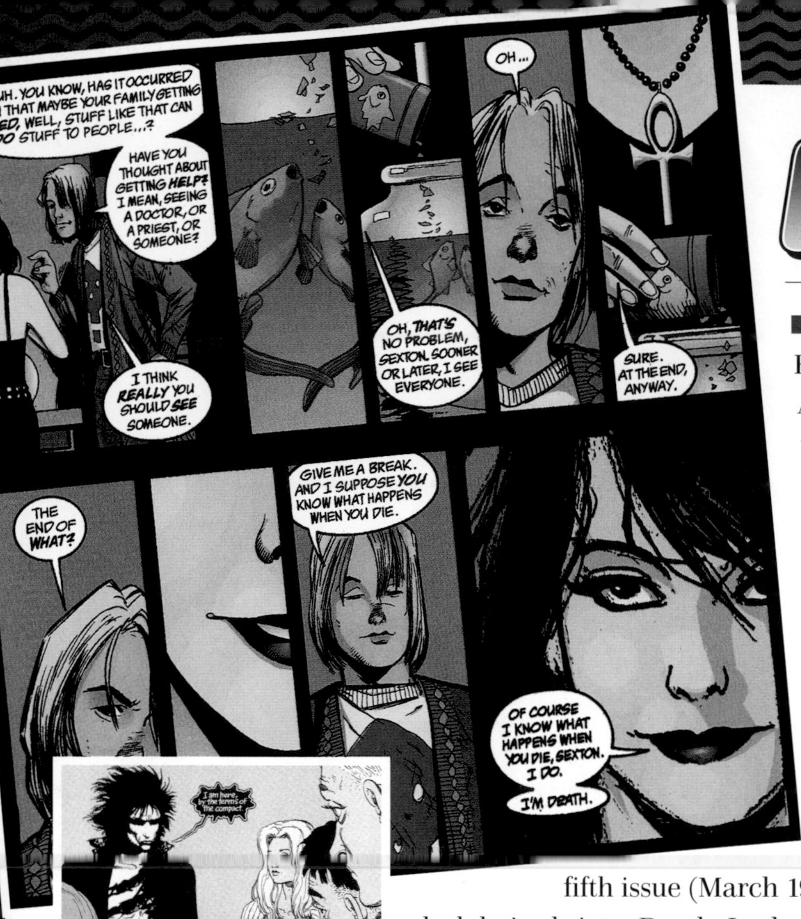
UH-HUH. YOU KNOW, HAS IT OCCURRED TO YOU THAT MAYBE YOUR FAMILY GETTING KILLED, WELL, STUFF LIKE THAT CAN DO STUFF TO PEOPLE...?
HAVE YOU THOUGHT ABOUT GETTING HELP? I MEAN, SEEING A DOCTOR, OR A PRIEST, OR SOMEONE?
I THINK REALLY YOU SHOULD SEE SOMEONE.
OH, THAT'S NO PROBLEM, SEXTON. SOONER OR LATER, I SEE EVERYONE.
OH...
SURE. AT THE END, ANYWAY.
THE END OF WHAT?
GIVE ME A BREAK. AND I SUPPOSE YOU KNOW WHAT HAPPENS WHEN YOU DIE.
OF COURSE I KNOW WHAT HAPPENS WHEN YOU DIE, SEXTON. I DO.
I'M DEATH.

GAIMAN, NEIL

(1960-)

■ A much revered writer and a frequent award winner, British journalist Gaiman first came to the attention of American comic-book readers in the late 1980s when, working with artist Sam Keith, he invented a brand-new Sandman. Unlike the old gas mask–wearing Sandman, Gaiman's protagonist was actually Morpheus, god of sleep and ruler of the land of dreams. The stories mixed fantasy, horror, New Age philosophy, and mysticism, and attracted a fairly sizeable audience for the *Sandman* comic book.

During the next few years, *Sandman* and Neil Gaiman won an impressive array of awards, everything from the Will Eisner to the World Fantasy Award. Gaiman decided to end the series with the seventy-fifth issue (March 1996). He later wrote a limited series about Sandman's dark-haired sister Death. In the middle 1990s, Gaiman also was hired by Tekno Comix to script several books, among them *Neil Gaiman's Mr. Hero—The Newmatic Man* and *Neil Gaiman's Wheel of Worlds.* Even his name in the titles didn't help, and none survived beyond 1996. He has also branched out into writing best-selling novels as well as screenplays. In 1999, he wrote a novel about Sandman titled *The Dream Hunters.*

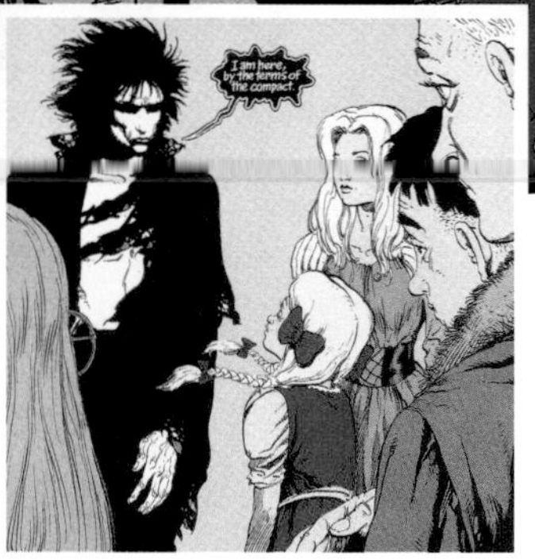
I am here, by the terms of the compact

GARCIA-LOPEZ, JOSE LUIS

(1948-)

■ If there were a list of the ten Most Underrated Artists in Comics, Garcia-Lopez's name would be near the top. Born in Spain, he grew up in Argentina. After becoming a contributor to various Spanish-language comics, he began working for American comic books while still living in Argentina. His earliest work was for such Charlton titles as *Ghostly Tales* and *Hollywood Romances.* In 1975 Garcia-Lopez moved to the United States and also moved up the ladder. He went to work for DC,

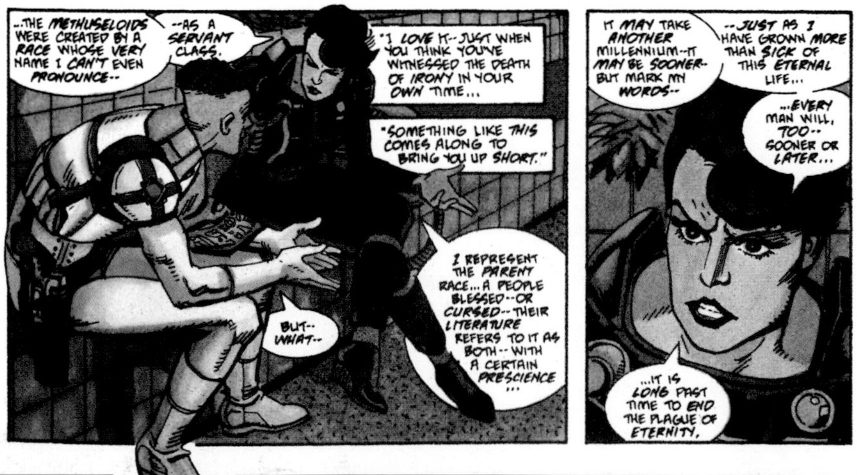
...THE METHUSELOIDS WERE CREATED BY A RACE WHOSE VERY NAME I CAN'T EVEN PRONOUNCE--
--AS A SERVANT CLASS.
"I LOVE IT--JUST WHEN YOU THINK YOU'VE WITNESSED THE DEATH OF IRONY IN YOUR OWN TIME...
"SOMETHING LIKE THIS COMES ALONG TO BRING YOU UP SHORT."
I REPRESENT THE PARENT RACE...A PEOPLE BLESSED--OR CURSED--THEIR LITERATURE REFERS TO IT AS BOTH--WITH A CERTAIN PRESCIENCE ...
BUT-- WHAT--
IT MAY TAKE ANOTHER MILLENNIUM--IT MAY BE SOONER-- BUT MARK MY WORDS--
--JUST AS I HAVE GROWN MORE THAN SICK OF THIS ETERNAL LIFE...
...EVERY MAN WILL, TOO-- SOONER OR LATER...
...IT IS LONG PAST TIME TO END THE PLAGUE OF ETERNITY.

where his first major assignment was drawing *Superman.*

Asked some years ago for his advice to young artists, he said, "Get a solid art education . . . The rest comes with hard work and observation." Garcia-Lopez obviously has followed his own advice, and he is one of the best illustrative artists in contemporary comic books. All the hard work that went into arriving at his current style doesn't show. He conveys an ease and grace, plus an enjoyment of drawing and a mastery of everything from anatomy to design sense.

Over the years he's also worked on *Jonah Hex*, *The Phantom Stranger*, *Teen Titans*, and *Wonder Woman.* He's drawn several impressive graphic novels, including *Star Raiders, Twilight*, scripted by Howard Chaykin, and *Batman—Reign of Terror*, wherein an Elseworlds Batman gets involved in the French Revolution and behaves in the swashbuckling manner of the Scarlet Pimpernel. One of Garcia-Lopez's most recent accomplishments was penciling two issues of the *Deadman* return. Respected and admired by colleagues and readers, he has yet to reach the fan favorite status of many a lesser artist.

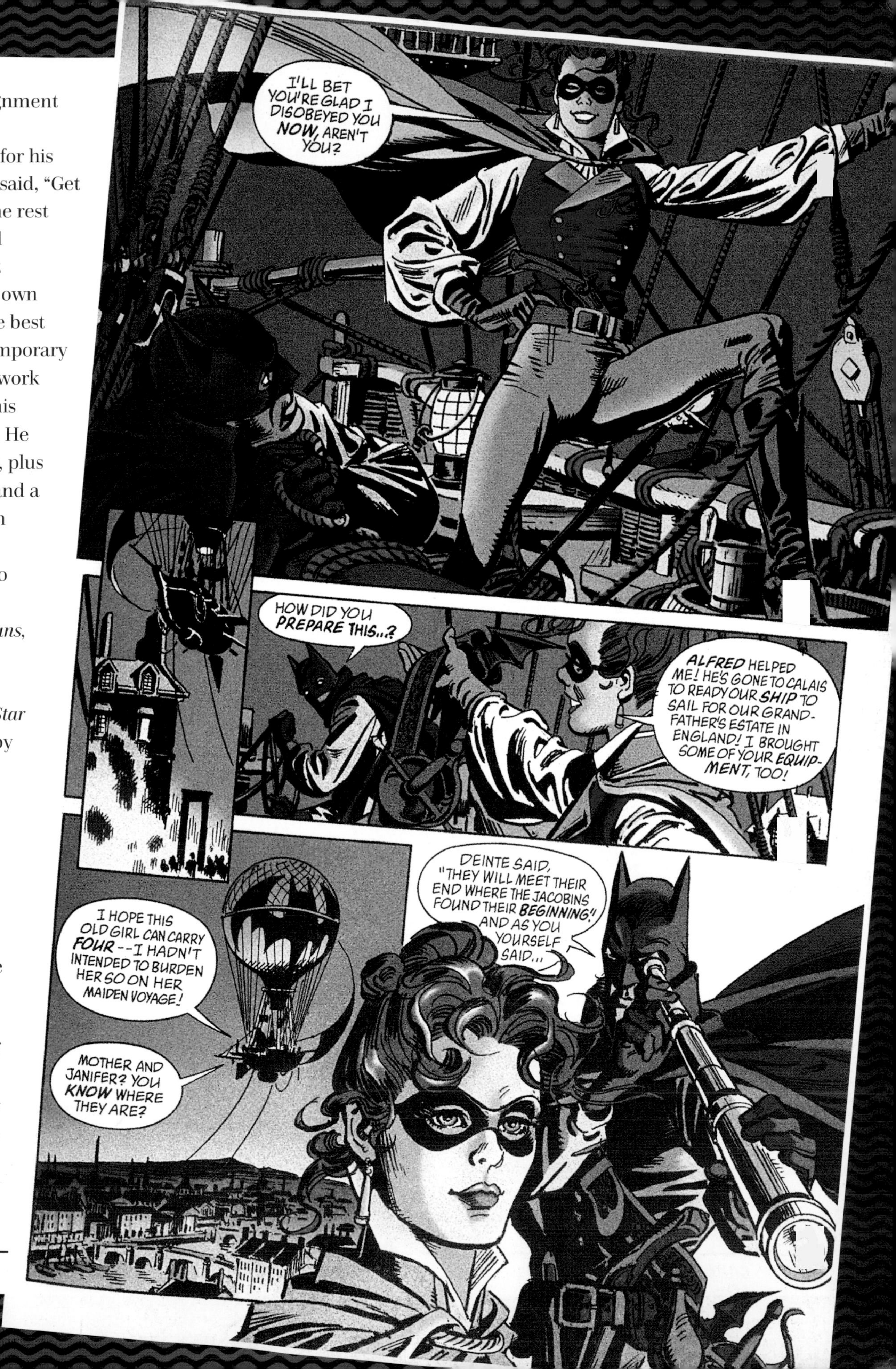
I'LL BET YOU'RE GLAD I DISOBEYED YOU NOW, AREN'T YOU?
HOW DID YOU PREPARE THIS...?
ALFRED HELPED ME! HE'S GONE TO CALAIS TO READY OUR SHIP TO SAIL FOR OUR GRANDFATHER'S ESTATE IN ENGLAND! I BROUGHT SOME OF YOUR EQUIPMENT, TOO!
I HOPE THIS OLD GIRL CAN CARRY FOUR--I HADN'T INTENDED TO BURDEN HER SO ON HER MAIDEN VOYAGE!
MOTHER AND JANIFER? YOU KNOW WHERE THEY ARE?
DEINTE SAID, "THEY WILL MEET THEIR END WHERE THE JACOBINS FOUND THEIR BEGINNING!" AND AS YOU YOURSELF SAID...

GARY CONCORD, ULTRA MAN

■ See ALL-AMERICAN COMICS.

THE GAY GHOST

■ See SENSATION COMICS.

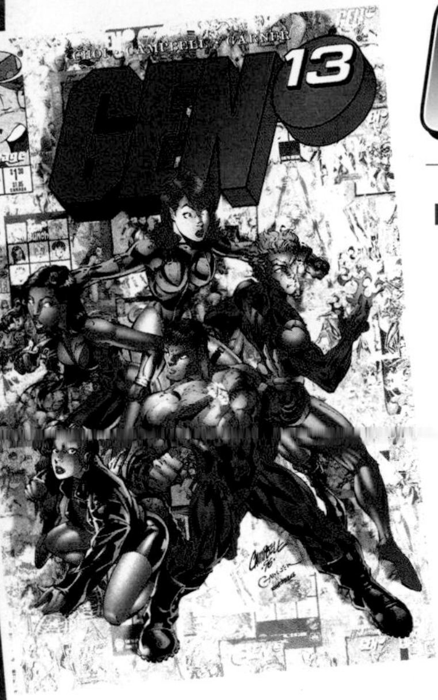
GEN
13
image

GEN 13

■ Another group of teenagers with superpowers, they entered comics in 1995. Jim Lee came up with this variation on the X-Men and Brandon Choi was the chief scriptwriter. Since the team included three young women who wore tight costumes while fighting hulking monsters and exposing complex conspiracies, J. Scott Campbell was a natural choice for regular artist. The ladies wore wristbands that allowed them to disassemble the molecules of their civilian clothes and exchange them for costumes concealed in the wristbands. Among the guys in the band were Grunge, who had the ability to turn to steel, and Burnout, who could operate as a minor Human Torch. The recurrent villain was a huge green chap named Helmut, who wore a massive suit of armor when on his appointed rounds.

The original Gen 13 bunch was replaced in 2003 by a new collection of gifted teenagers. Chris Claremont wrote the scripts.

GENIUS JONES

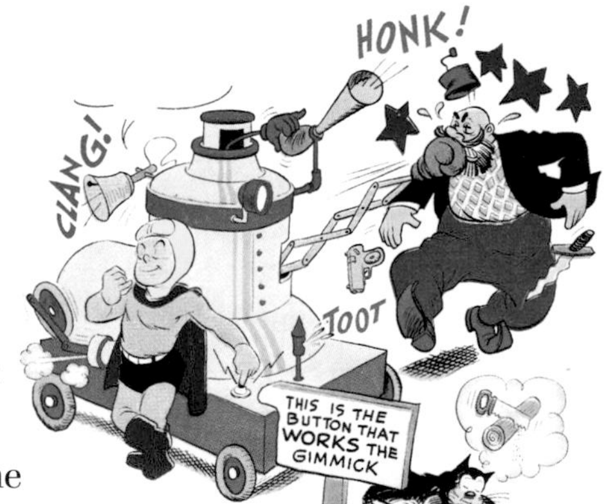
HONK!
CLANG!
TOOT
THIS IS THE BUTTON THAT WORKS THE GIMMICK

■ A few years before he wrote the classic science-fiction novels *The Demolished Man* and *The Stars My Destination*, Alfred Bester (1913–1987) wrote scripts for comic books. It was for DC's *Adventure Comics* in 1942 that he created Genius Jones. The artist was Stan Kaye. Bester wrote scripts for several features—including *The Green Lantern*, for which he created the villain Solomon Grundy—but *Genius Jones* was the only one he ever signed his name to.

The diminutive Johnny Jones was marooned on an uncharted island when a boy and was not rescued until he reached adulthood. Washed ashore with him after the shipwreck were several hundred mostly scholarly books, including a complete set of the *Encyclopedia Britannica*. To while away the time when he wasn't hunting, fishing, or swinging through trees, young Jones memorized the contents of just about all the books that shared his island with him.

Returned to the real world and with no means of support, Jones set up a sidewalk stand—later motorized to add to his mobility—and took to calling himself the Answer Man. Not as altruistic as some heroes, Genius

Jones always charged ten cents to answer a question or solve a mystery. When fighting crime he wore a costume that consisted of a cape, tights, and a crash helmet donated by friends in his theatrical boardinghouse.

Facing killers, criminal masterminds, or foreign spies, Genius used his vast knowledge of everything from physics to world history to get himself out of various traps and sticky situations. He usually made his more serious costumed colleagues appear a bit dense.

During his initial case Genius met, and extricated from a serious mess, a young woman named Mary Brown. She continued as his girlfriend and sidekick throughout Bester's association with the feature. Among the cases Bester chronicled for his pint-sized crimefighter were "The Enigma of the Nonagenarian Natator," "The Case of the Love-Sick Submarine," and "The Enigma of the Absent-Minded Artists." In the introduction to this latter adventure, he described his hero as "the prince of problems, the king of questions, the emperor of enigmas" and as someone who "outmaneuvers the master-spies, expunges and exterminates espionage and incarcerates intriguers." In a footnote Bester suggested that "for the usual fee Genius Jones will answer any question on the meaning of these words."

Bester's name ceased to appear on the strip after #92 (June–July 1944). Genius, with Kaye as the artist, continued in comic books until late 1947. He moved over to *More Fun Comics* in 1946, when the venerable magazine was converted to all humor. He was also a regular in *All Funny*, an eventual bimonthly that began in 1943. Throughout Genius's career, Kaye drew his adventures in an inventive and appealing way.

GERBER, STEVE

■ See HOWARD THE DUCK.

GHOST

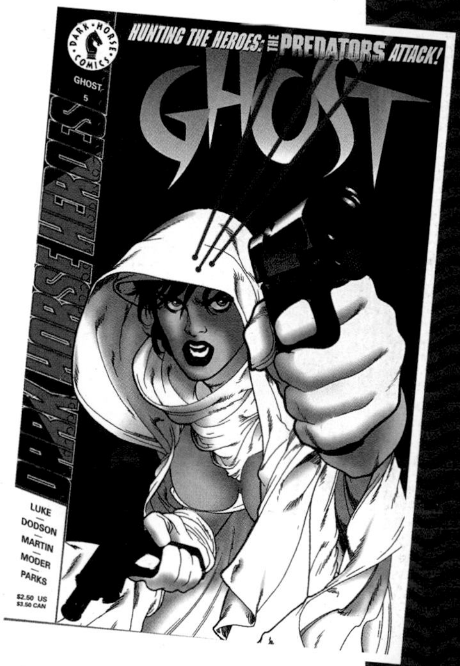
HUNTING THE HEROES: THE PREDATORS ATTACK!
DARK HORSE COMICS
GHOST 5
GHOST
LUKE
DODSON
MARTIN
MODER
PARKS
$2.50 US
$3.50 CAN

■ Like the Spectre and Deadman, reporter Elisa Cameron's adventures didn't begin until after she'd been killed. Then she turned into Ghost, a very perturbed spirit whose white costume was part flowing shroud and part a dominatrix's low-cut, laced outfit. She also acquired two automatics. Written by Eric Luke and drawn at the start by Adam Hughes, Ghost was introduced in Dark Horse's Comics *Greatest World* in 1993. Early in 1995, a *Ghost* title materialized. Hughes also drew the early covers.

The stories were set in Arcadia, "a thriving metropolis of dark waterfronts, art deco canyons and shimmering skyscrapers." The city was run by "organized crime, corrupt politicians, and corporate robber barons." When Eliza's investigative reporting looked to be about to unearth too much about Arcadian corruption, she was murdered. As Ghost she roamed the city trying to find who did her in. She also had to look after her younger sister, who had a tendency to fraternize with porno entrepreneurs and other Arcadian lowlifes. Among the other residents were a group of very strange folks called paranormals. So in addition to seeking revenge, Elisa also had run-ins with monsters, thugs, and assorted other criminals.

Several artists followed Hughes, including Matt Haley, Terry Dodson, and H. M. Baker. The first run of *Ghost* went to thirty-six issues, ending early in 1998. She then returned in a new series that made it through twenty-two issues from 1998 to 2000. And Ghost appeared in one-shots and limited series with the likes of Hellboy and Batgirl.

THE GHOST PATROL

■ See FLASH COMICS.

GHOST RIDER: I

■ Probably the only comic-book hero inspired by the once popular crooner Vaughn Monroe, the original Ghost Rider first galloped onto the scene as a backup feature in ME's *Tim Holt* #11 in 1949. In reality he was Rex Fury, a federal marshal in the Old West who dressed up in a luminous white outfit that included a glowing cape and Stetson. Eventually he added a skull mask to his ensemble, and the sight of him mounted on his glowing white stallion was sufficient to scare even hardened owl-hoots out of their wits.

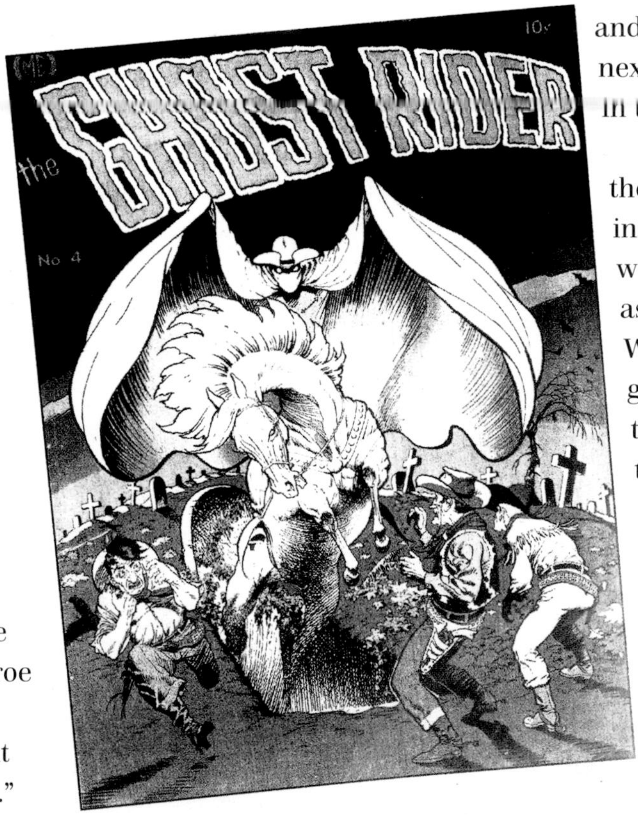
10¢
the GHOST RIDER
No 4

Publisher Vincent Sullivan came up with the original idea for the phantom cowboy. Dick Ayer drew the feature and in a 2001 interview in *Alter Ego* he explained, "Vin would come in and sit down and describe what he wanted in *The Ghost Rider.* He told me to go see Disney's *Sleepy Hollow*–Ichabod Crane, the Headless Horseman–and then he told me to play the Vaughn Monroe record, 'Ghost Riders in the Sky.' And then he started talking about what he wanted the guy wearing."

Many of the tales contained supernatural elements and ghosts, werewolves, and vampires occasionally roamed the range along with rustlers and gunmen. During part of his run, Ghost Rider wore a cloak of darkness given to him by a "strange creature from another dimension," which enabled him "to create mystic illusions to thwart evildoers." He spoke in a flowery style, never using a contraction.

He proved popular and ME introduced a separate *Ghost Rider* title in 1950. Dick Ayers drew all the stories and covers, except for a few covers done by Frank Frazetta. The magazine ended in 1954 and the Western mystery man was next seen in the *Tim Holt* magazine in the summer of the following year.

Early in 1967 Marvel assimilated the character and brought out its initial version of the Ghost Rider, with Ayers again as the artist. Billed as "The World's Most Mysterious Western Hero," he dressed in a glowing costume that was identical to that of his predecessor. This time around he was Carter Slade, who'd been given his phosphorescent costume by a Comanche medicine man. His horse was named Banshee. This series ended after seven issues. The character returned in 1970 and graced the first seven issues of Marvel's revived *Western Gunfighters.* During the course of this short run, Carter Slade was gunned down, and his brother Lincoln Slade, also a marshal, assumed the role. Marvel reprinted earlier tales in the middle 1970s in a six-issue series with the hero using the alias of the Night Rider.

GHOST RIDER: II

■ Marvel proved that bikers were more popular than cowboys with their next version of *Ghost Rider.* In 1973 they introduced a contemporary Ghost Rider who rode a motorcycle. Johnny Blaze was a clean-cut, blond young cyclist who became the unwilling host of a spirit named Zarathos. When Zarathos was in ascendancy, the hapless Johnny turned into a demon biker with a blazing skull instead of a head. When in this mode, much like the Hulk, he didn't take any crap from anybody. More successful than any prior Ghost Rider, he survived for eighty-one issues until the spring of 1983.

The cowboy and the biker also coexisted at times. In *Ghost Rider* #56, Hamilton Slade, a descendant of the Old West Riders, showed up. In order to save Johnny Blaze from danger, he was taken over by the spirit of the old Ghost Rider.

In 1990, writer Howard Mackie, working with artists Javier Saltares and Mark Texeira, came up with yet another Ghost Rider. This time he was a clean-cut young cyclist named Danny Ketch who got possessed by spirits and became the biker with the blazing skull. This Rider has appeared periodically throughout the nineties and was also seen in a six-issue series that commenced in the summer of 2001.

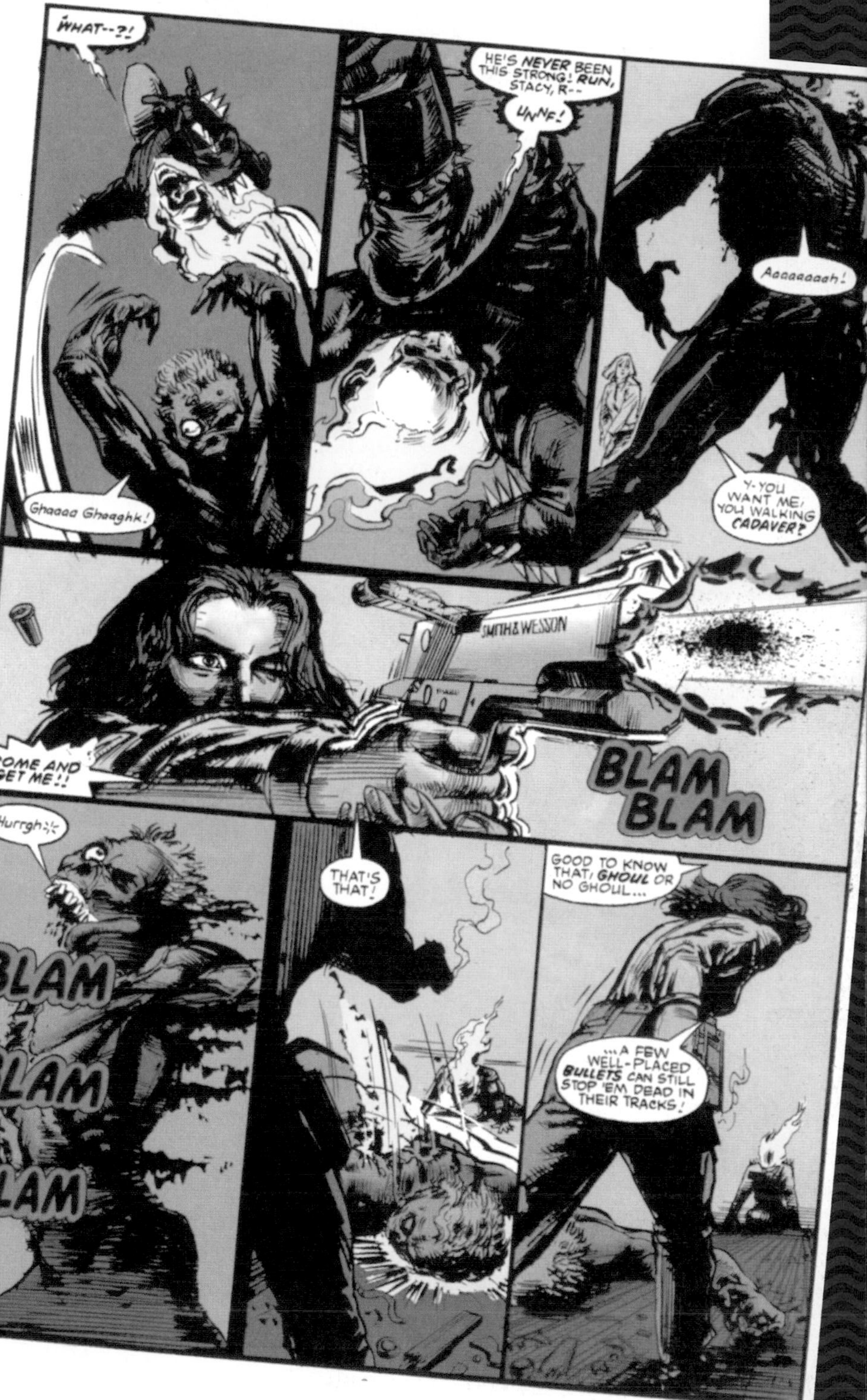
WHAT--?!
Ghaaa Ghaaghk!
HE'S NEVER BEEN THIS STRONG! RUN, STACY, R--
UNNF!
Aaaaaaaah!
Y-YOU WANT ME, YOU WALKING CADAVER?
SMITH & WESSON
COME AND GET ME!!
BLAM BLAM
Hurrgh
BLAM BLAM BLAM
THAT'S THAT!
GOOD TO KNOW THAT, GHOUL OR NO GHOUL...
...A FEW WELL-PLACED BULLETS CAN STILL STOP 'EM DEAD IN THEIR TRACKS!

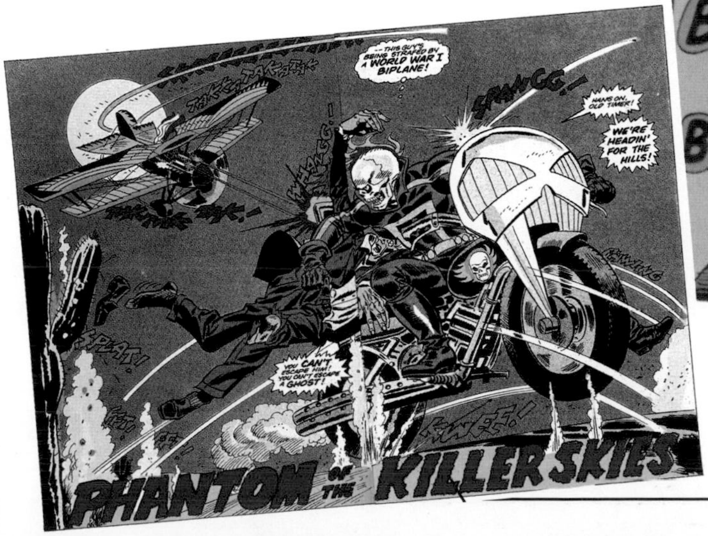
--THIS GUY'S BEING STRAFED BY A WORLD WAR I BIPLANE!
SPANGG!
HANG ON, OLD TIMER!
WE'RE HEADIN' FOR THE HILLS!
YOU CAN'T ESCAPE HIM! YOU CAN'T ESCAPE A GHOST!
PHANTOM OF THE KILLER SKIES

GIBBONS, DAVE

(1949–)

■ Another British artist who made a name for himself in American comics, Gibbons's first major attention-getting work was DC's twelve-part *Watchmen* series, which hit the stands in the summer of 1986. By then, Gibbons had been working, by mail for the most part, for DC for four years and drawing such dependable heroes as Batman, Superman, and the Green Lantern. It was *Watchmen*, however, with scripts by Alan Moore, that won him a much larger audience, considerable attention from his peers, glowing reviews in both fanzines and mainstream publications, and a variety of awards. For English comics Gibbons had done artwork for such titles as *2000 A.D.* and *Dr. Who.*

Working in his assured illustrative style, Gibbons has continued contributing to American comics. One of his more ambitious projects in the early and middle 1990s was drawing the *Give Me Liberty* series of graphic novels published by Dark Horse and scripted by Frank Miller. Set in the near future, they deal with an American turned fascist and have an African-American woman named Martha Washington as the main focal character. Once again Gibbons did an impressive job in depicting an alternate world.

More recently he drew the Green Lantern issue in DC's Just Imagine series, bringing to life Stan Lee's take on the character. Working with such writers as Alan Moore and Frank Miller has apparently had an effect on Gibbons, and he has been doing some writing of late. He's scripted a *World's Finest* Batman and Superman team-up, drawn by Steve Rude, and worked with artist Andy Kubert on *Batman Versus Predator.*

LAURIE? WHAT'S ...?
OH.
OF COURSE.
PLEASE FORGIVE ME...
SOMETIMES THESE THINGS SLIP MY MIND.
HHHUUHHHHR
3

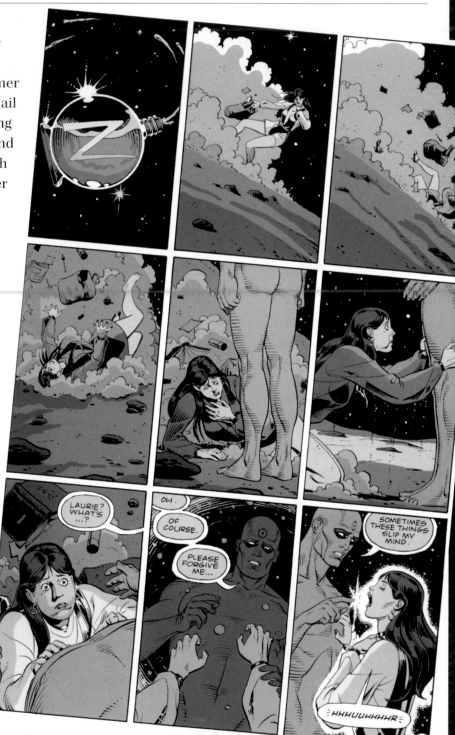

GIGGLE COMICS

GIGGLE
COMICS
10¢
READER, BE MY VALENTINE!
Luv, Superkatt

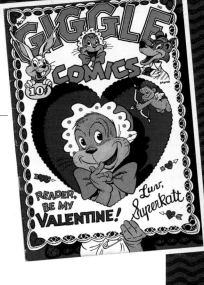

■ This was one of the two initial titles published by the company that would eventually become the American Comics Group. Cover-dated October 1943, *Giggle* was devoted to funny animals, with the material provided by both moonlighting West Coast animators and Manhattan-based cartoonists. Among the Californians who contributed were Ken Hultgren, Jim Davis, Bob Wickersham, and Lynn Karp. Based in the East were the likes of Dan Gordon and Vic Pazmino.

The backup characters fluctuated, sometimes from issue to issue, and included Byron Bunny, Wacky Wolf, Clarence Canary, and Fremont Frog. The first real star of *Giggle Comics* was Superkatt, who signed on in the ninth issue (June 1944). As drawn by Dan Gordon, with scripts by Richard Hughes, the Superkatt stories had the pace and wackiness of animated cartoons. A onetime animator, Gordon's work always looked lively and, more important, funny. Superkatt had one of the more unusual hero costumes of the era. It consisted of a blue baby bonnet, a blue bow tie, and a diaper fastened with a safety pin. He and his dog sidekick, Humphrey, were the featured players in *Giggle* for years and were seen on each and every cover. But then a latecomer, and not an animal but a ghost, usurped the lead spot. That was Spencer Spook. For the last two issues the magazine even changed its named to *Spencer Spook.*

Ha Ha Comics, the sister magazine, was introduced in the same month as *Giggle,* and they both ended early in 1955. It too was devoted to the funny animal genre.

GIORDANO, DICK *(1932-)*

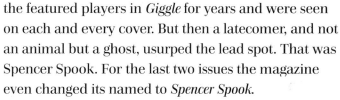

■ Accomplished as an artist, an editor, and an inker, Giordano began working in comics in the early 1950s. He started at the Jerry Iger shop, where his major assignment was drawing the backgrounds for the *Sheena* stories. Moving on from foliage, he went to work for Charlton in 1952 and remained with the Connecticut-based publisher into the late 1960s. There he drew such features as *Rocky Lane* and *Billy the Kid*, as well as covers for *The Fightin' 5* and *The Blue Beetle.*

Giordano also worked for Dell, drawing everything from *Nukla* to movie adaptations like *Beach Blanket Bingo.* For DC in the early 1960s he drew *Batman.* Returning there in the 1970s, he worked on *Elongated Man* and *The Human Target.* Much in demand as an inker, he served in that capacity on such features as *Superman, Green Lantern/Green Arrow*, *John Carter*, *Kid Flash*, and *The Atom.* He was also an editor at DC and he formed an art shop known as Continuity Associates with Neal Adams. He is still active as an inker.

GIRAUD, JEAN

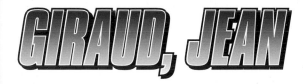

■ See MOEBIUS/JEAN GIRAUD.

THE GOLDEN AGE

■ A term applied to the comic books of the 1930s and the 1940s, it has been used by fans, dealers, and historians for several decades. The highest priced and rarest magazines date from this period.

There has, however, never been universal agreement as to exactly what year the Golden Age began and when it officially ended. Some, such as *Comic Buyer's Guide,* say the term "indicates the first era of comic book production—which occurred in the 30s and 40s." *The*

Overstreet Price Guide, on the other hand, defines it as "the period beginning with *Action* #1 (June 1938) and ending with World War II in 1945."

For the purposes of this encyclopedia, the Golden Age is considered to run from the middle 1930s to the late 1940s, encompassing the launching of *Famous Funnies, New Fun,* and the advent of Superman in 1938, and including the decline of the first generation of superheroes in the late 1940s.

THE GOLDEN ARROW

■ See CAPTAIN MARVEL.

GOODWIN, ARCHIE *(1937–1998)*

■ Undoubtedly the best-liked editor in comics, Archie Goodwin was also a cartoonist and, more important, a clever and prolific writer. He was an editor and scriptwriter at Warren, DC, and Marvel and also wrote such newspaper comic strips as *Secret Agent Corrigan, Captain Kate, Star Hawks, Tarzan,* and *Star Wars.*

A graduate of Manhattan's School of Visual Arts, Goodwin did some cartooning for Harvey Publishing before joining Warren in the early 1960s. In addition to editing such titles as *Creepy* and *Blazing Combat,* he wrote

a great many scripts for *Vampirella* and had considerable to do with developing the character and the supporting cast. Moving to Marvel, Goodwin wrote *Spider-Man, The Hulk,* and *Wolverine.* He also edited Marvel's Epic Comics line and invented *Epic Illustrated.*

During one of his stays at DC, he, with artist Walt Simonson, updated and revived Manhunter. In his last years he was again at DC, editing such titles as *Starman* and *Batman: Legends of the Dark Knight.*

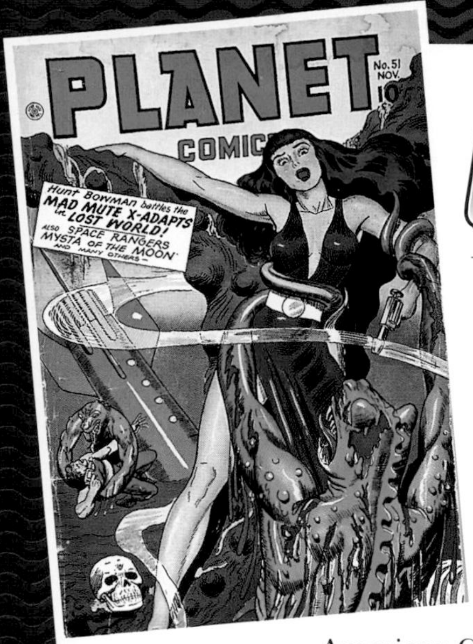
PLANET
No. 51
NOV.
COMICS
Hunt Bowman battles the MAD MUTE X-ADAPTS in LOST WORLD!
ALSO SPACE RANGERS
MYSTA OF THE MOON

GOOD GIRL ART

■ A phrase now used by dealers and collectors to refer to comic books that were once intended for pubescent boys in the 1940s and 1950s, it was first popularized in the mail order catalogs of the American Comic Book Company some years ago. It alludes not to comics that contain drawings of virtuous girls but to those that showcase good drawings of pretty women, usually scantily clothed.

The Comic's Buyer's Guide has defined Good Girl Art as "pinup-type pictures of leggy, busty females in 'cheesecake' poses." They add that "some find the term offensive." Overstreet's *Comic Book Price Guide* includes Good Girl Art as one of the comic-book categories.

The publishers that specialized in the genre include Fiction House, Fox and Farrell, and to a lesser degree MLJ and Lev Gleason. The first heyday of Good Girl Art was the early and middle 1940s, when the young male audience for comics was added to by a large readership among servicemen. Included in the characters who owed a considerable portion of their newsstand success to the sexy way they were depicted were the Phantom Lady, Sheena, and quite a few of her jungle-dwelling sisters. Matt Baker was one of the masters of the craft, as were Nick Cardy, Joe Doolin, Bob Lubbers, and Bill Ward. In the postwar years Good Girl Art spread into true crime and horror comics and eventually drew the ire of an army of critics.

GRAPHIC NOVELS

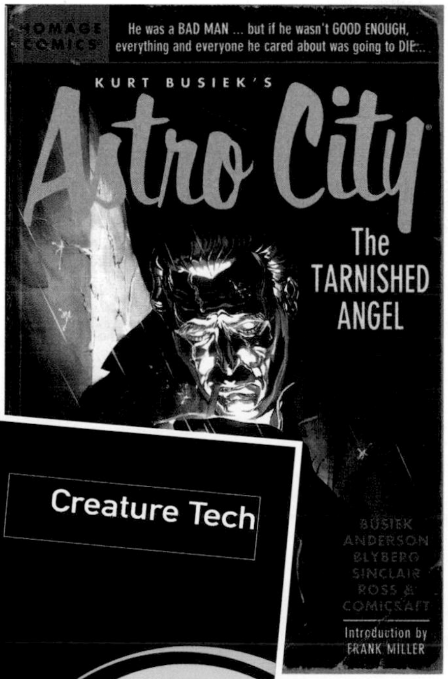
HOMAGE COMICS
He was a BAD MAN ... but if he wasn't GOOD ENOUGH, everything and everyone he cared about was going to DIE...
KURT BUSIEK'S
Astro City
The TARNISHED ANGEL
BUSIEK ANDERSON BLYBERG SINCLAIR ROSS & COMICRAFT
Introduction by FRANK MILLER

■ Graphic novels have become an important part of the American comics industry over the past quarter century. Packaging comic-book material in trade paperback and hardcover formats has broadened the sales base considerably. Not only can graphic novels be purchased in most bookstores, they can also be found, in increasing numbers, on the shelves of libraries across the country. The term has comprehensive applications, embracing everything from *Maus* to *The Death of Superman* to *Creature Tech.*

It was in the middle 1970s that graphic novels started appearing here. Among the pioneer creators were James Steranko, whose "visual novel" *Red Tide* was published in 1976, and Will Eisner, who turned out his *A Contract with God* in 1978. Many of the early efforts in the genre involved material that was considered too different from the standard superhero fare to fit into conventional comic books.

Two basic sorts of graphic novels have developed—those that offer original material and those that collect episodes of a comic-book serial into a single volume. While a fairly recent innovation in the United States, the

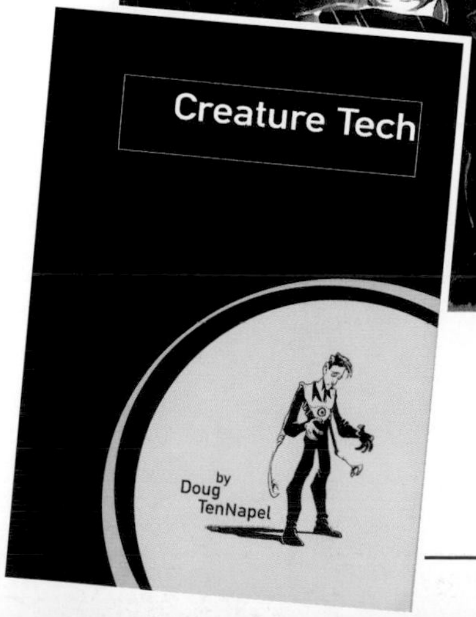
Creature Tech
by Doug TenNapel

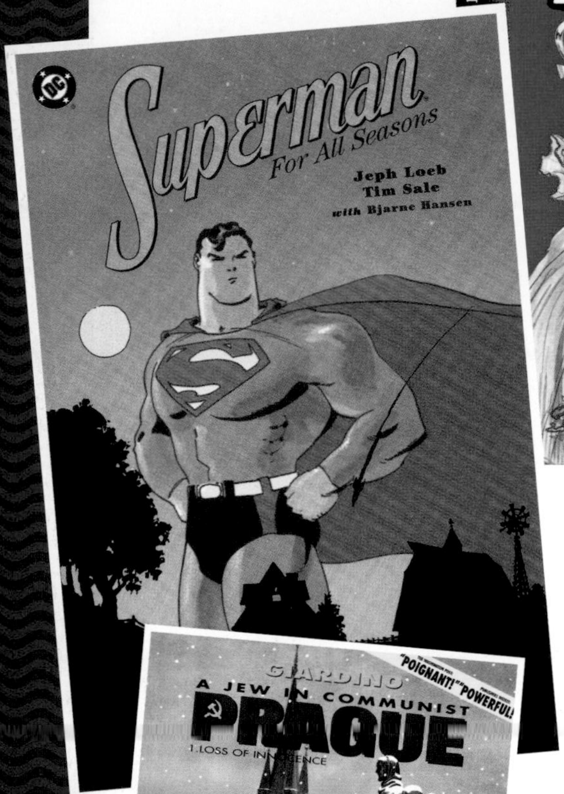
Superman
For All Seasons
Jeph Loeb
Tim Sale
with Bjarne Hansen

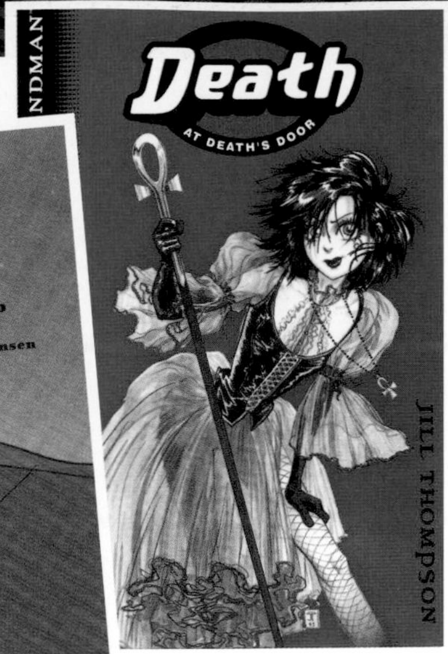
Death
AT DEATH'S DOOR
JILL THOMPSON

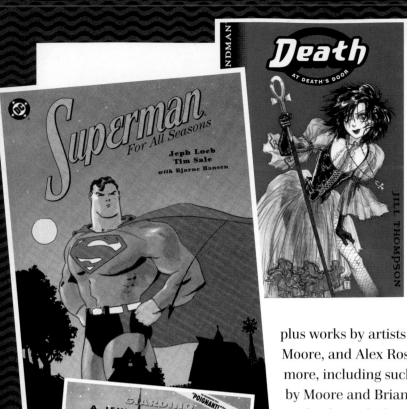

practice of gathering previously issued magazine stories into single volumes has long been popular in Europe. There the *Tintin* albums have been successful for decades, as have Jean Giraud's *Lt. Blueberry* compilations and hundreds of other albums.

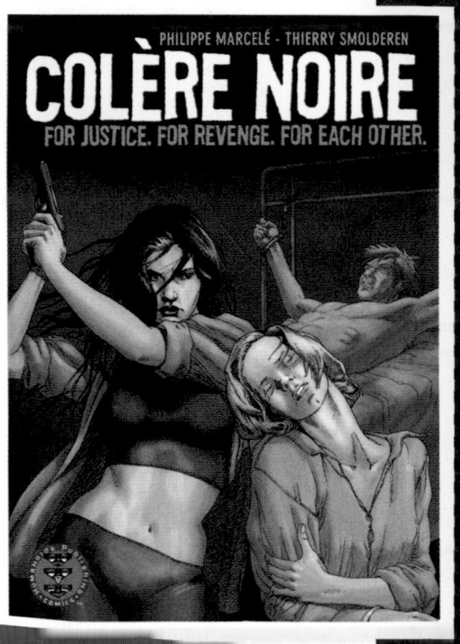
PHILIPPE MARCELÉ - THIERRY SMOLDEREN
COLÈRE NOIRE
FOR JUSTICE. FOR REVENGE. FOR EACH OTHER.

The largest comic-book publishers, notably DC and Marvel, have long since entered enthusiastically into the genre. There have been numerous Superman graphic novels, notably such titles as *Superman for All Seasons* by Tim Sale and Jeph Loeb, plus works by artists and writers such as John Byrne, Alan Moore, and Alex Ross. Batman has appeared in even more, including such innovative books as *The Killing Joke* by Moore and Brian Bolland, *The Long Halloween* by Loeb and Sale, and *The Dark Knight Returns* by Frank Miller. Other notable DC efforts include *Kingdom Come* by Mark Waid and Alex Ross, *Watchmen* by Moore and Dave Gibbons, and *Superman & Batman: Generations* by John Byrne. Marvel has taken fewer risks than DC and the majority of their graphic novels collect and recycle adventures of such popular characters as Spider-Man, the Fantastic Four, X-Men, Wolverine, and Thor.

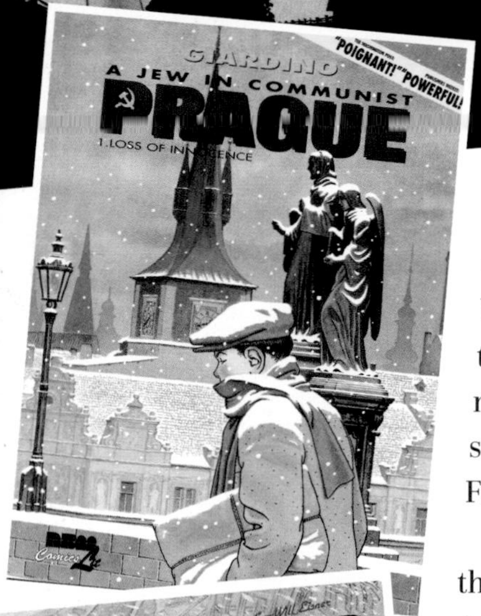
GIARDINO
"POIGNANT!" "POWERFUL!"
A JEW IN COMMUNIST
PRAGUE

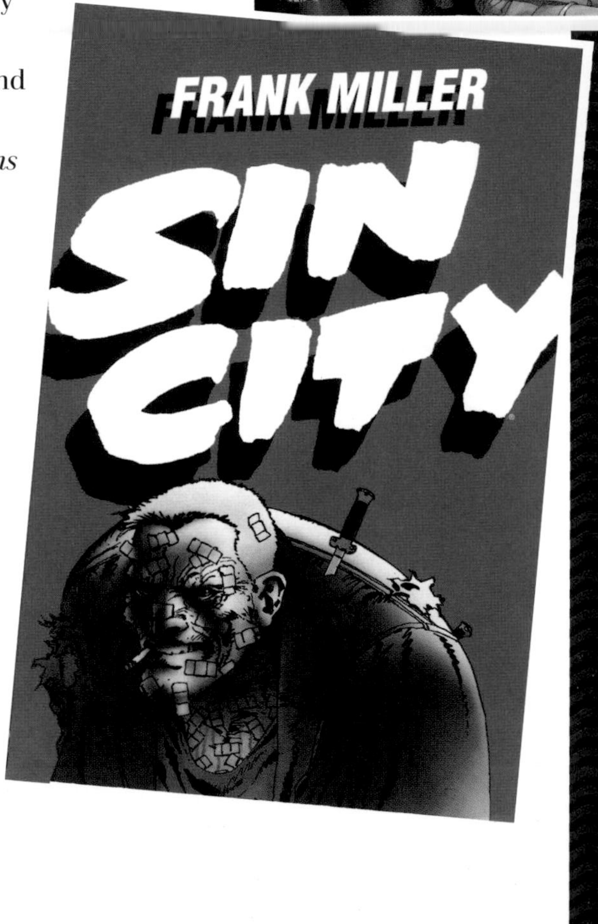
FRANK MILLER
SIN CITY

Interesting and innovative titles from the independents include Kurt Busiek's *Astro City*, *Tom Strong* by Moore and Chris Sprouse, the ever-popular *Elfquest* by Wendy and Richard Pini, and Stan Sakai's rabbit samurai *Usagi Yojimbo*. Howard Cruse's *Stuck Rubber Baby*, Chris Ware's *Jimmy Corrigan, The Smartest Kid in the World*, and Doug TenNapel's *Creature Tech* all demonstrate the quality and variety available in the genre. It might just be that the graphic novel may well outlive the comic book.

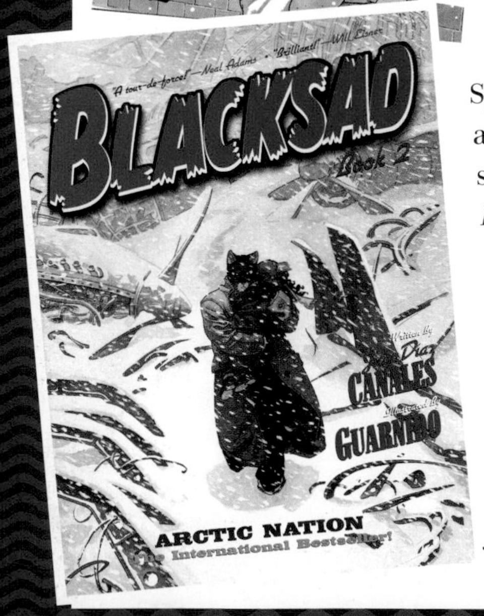
BLACKSAD
Book 2
CANALES
GUARNIDO
ARCTIC NATION

THE GREEN LAMA

■ The creation of writer Kendell Foster Crossen, the Green Lama was pretty much a multimedia failure. He first showed up in the Munsey pulp *Double Detective* early in 1940 and was added to the cast of *Prize Comics* later that year, had a short-lived comic book of his own in the middle 1940s and a summer replacement radio show in 1949.

Initially he was intended to be a pulp-fiction rival for Street & Smith's popular Shadow. Writing as Richard Foster, Crossen invented Jethro Dumont, who turned into the Green Lama to fight crime with tricks and techniques he'd learned in Tibet. All told there were fourteen Lama short novels in *Double Detective*. Crossen's mystery man, with scripts credited to Richard Foster, was added to *Prize* in #7 (December 1940) along with a batch of other new characters that were intended to perk up circulation. The Green Lama, who wore a green robe and hood, always intoned, "Om! Ma-ni Pad-me Hum!" before going into action. This was translated in captions as "the prayer of the Buddhist priest—which means, Hail! The jewel in the lotus-flower."

The first artist was Mac Raboy. Later cartoonists included Jimmy Thompson and Dick Briefer. The Lama remained in *Prize* until #34 (September 1943), then was dropped to make room for another shuffling of characters.

Late the next year, Crossen founded Spark Publications. His maiden title was *Green Lama Comics*. Mac Raboy returned to draw the twelve-page story that led off the issue and in this reincarnation Dumont wore a conventional superhero costume, skin-tight and green. Now when he recited the Buddhist prayer, he was transformed into a flying crimebuster. Though Raboy's work had greatly improved since 1940, he remained notoriously slow. Harry Anderson was the cartoonist who most frequently ghosted pages when Raboy couldn't meet the deadline. Raboy always managed to draw the striking covers. The magazine ended with the eighth issue early in 1946.

Versatile radio actor Paul Frees, later the voice of the Pillsbury Doughboy, played the Green Lama of CBS for eleven weeks in the summer of 1949.

THE GREEN LANTERN: I

—AND I SHALL SHED MY LIGHT OVER DARK EVIL... FOR, THE DARK THINGS CANNOT STAND THE LIGHT... THE LIGHT OF THE GREEN LANTERN!

■ The original holder of the title, he was introduced in *All-American Comics* #16 (July 1940). There he was on the cover, as depicted by Sheldon Moldoff, in his green-and-red costume and flowing cape, charging along a girder at a tommy-gun wielding thug. That was just about the only glimpse readers got of the costume that month, since the eight-page origin story inside didn't get around to showing GL dressed for crimefighting until the final panel. That original story told how blond engineer Alan Scott came to own a mysterious green lantern made of a strange off-planet metal. By making a ring of the metal and then putting it on and touching the lantern with it, he was

converted into a superhero who could fly, be immune to bullets, and walk through walls. He had to recharge himself every twenty-four hours, however. The only thing he was vulnerable to was wood, so that a conk on the head with a chair would render him out cold.

The Green Lantern was the joint invention of artist Mart Nodell and writer Bill Finger, the uncredited cocreator of *Batman*. Editor Sheldon Mayer also had a hand in reshaping Nodell's original notion, which Mayer saw as an updating of the Aladdin legend with the addition of superhero elements. From #26 (May 1941), Irwin Hasen was the ghost artist on the feature. In #27, Finger and Hasen introduced Doiby Dickles, the tough, overweight cabbie who became the Green Lantern's equivalent of Robin. Mayer once mentioned that Doiby was inspired by movie character actor Ed Brophy.

Finger concentrated on stories of urban crime, and the Green Lantern and Doiby tackled civic corruption and racketeering. Along the way Scott became a radio engineer and worked for a large radio station. There was mystery in the stories, fantasy, and usually more comedy than was to be found in the adventures of your average superman. Other scriptwriters included Henry Kuttner and Alfred Bester. In the middle 1940s the nasty Solomon Grundy, a villain who combined the best qualities of the Frankenstein monster and the Heap, rose up to plague GL. Bester later admitted he was probably the one who thought up Grundy. After World War II, when Alex Toth was doing much of the drawing, several more colorful villains came along, most notably the mystery woman who called herself the Harlequin. For a while Doiby was replaced by a wonder dog.

The Lantern was one of the more popular of the DC characters, and he starred in thirty-eight issues of his own magazine between 1941 and 1949. He was also one of the featured characters in the first twenty-nine issues of *Comic Cavalcade* and appeared frequently in *All Star Comics*, being a member in good standing of the Justice Society. He left *All-American* in 1948, after being nudged out by the cowboy Johnny Thunder. He took his final bow in *All Star* #57 early in 1951.

He returned in 1963 in the *Justice League of America*. Since then he has frequently revisited the DC universe, having become a recurrent houseguest in various titles. Sometimes Doiby tags along.

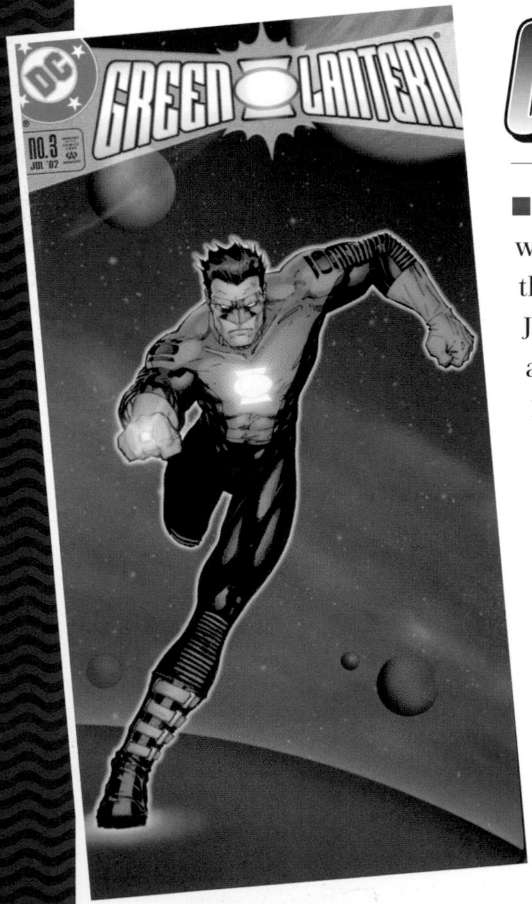
DC
GREEN LANTERN
NO.3
JUL '02

GREEN LANTERN: II

■ Hal Jordan started doing business as the Green Lantern in 1959. Over the years it was revealed that he wasn't the only one, and there were more Green Lanterns in the universe than you could shake a stick at, over three thousand of them actually. Jordan, all by himself, was first seen in DC's *Showcase* #22 (October 1959). After auditioning again in the next two issues, he moved into his own title in the spring of 1960. "When the returns started coming in on the Flash and we saw we had a hit, the natural instinct was to do something similar," editor Julius Schwartz once recalled. "That's how we decided to go ahead with the Green Lantern, and I worked out the same theory of giving him a new personality, a new costume, a new everything."

This time the Green Lantern was test pilot Hal Jordan, who got his ring and lantern from an alien who'd crashed on Earth. The dying, red-skinned spaceman explained that he was a "space-patrolman in the super-galactic system" and that the ring, which had to be recharged at the lantern every twenty-four hours, gave the wearer incredible powers to be used "against forces of evil and injustice." Taking over the ring, the lantern, and the alien's uniform, Jordan assumed the role of the Green Lantern. John Broome was the original scriptwriter, Gil Kane the artist.

Gradually Schwartz and Broome embellished the background of their hero. They invented the Guardians of the Universe, an immortal bunch who had set up the Green Lantern Corps, "a group of living beings chosen from all parts of the universe to fight evil and given rings of power." Over the years, Jordan appeared in assorted contexts. In the early 1970s, when DC was undergoing a relevance phase, he teamed up with the Green Arrow to fight social ills. Later he worked as part of the Green Lantern Corps, along with such alternate GLs as the black John Stewart, the red-headed Guy Gardner, an alien lady named Katma Tui, a dog-faced native of the planet Bolovax Vik named Killowog, and potentially nearly 3,600 other official Green Lanterns. Jordan was pronounced dead in 1994, by way of the *Zero Hour* limited series, and was replaced by yet another Green Lantern. He came back to life briefly, then died again. In 1999, his spirit assumed the role of the Spectre.

THE GREEN TURTLE

■ See BLAZING COMICS.

GROO

MARVEL
SERGIO ARAGONÉS
GROO
THE WANDERER
$2.95 US
100
APR

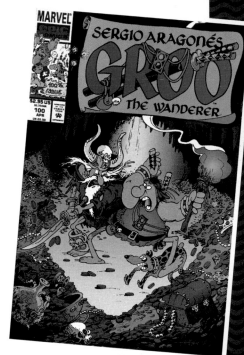

■ A spoof of Conan and all similarly inclined comic-book barbarians, Groo the Wanderer, who looked as though he might have stepped out of the pages of *Mad*, began his sword-wielding career late in 1982 in a twelve-issue run from Pacific Comics. The pudgy barbarian stayed longest with Marvel. From 1985 to 1995 there were 120 Marvel issues of *Groo the Wanderer*. Since then both Image and Dark Horse have published miniseries. Artwork by the highly productive doodler Sergio Aragones, scripts by Mark Evanier.

GROSS, MILT *(1895–1953)*

■ A popular cartoonist and a popular author in the 1920s and the early 1930s, Gross did his last cartoon work for comic books in the middle and late 1940s. In 1947 there were even two issues of *Milt Gross Funnies*.

He drew in a loose, attractive style, and his approach toward humor was a mix of slapstick and screwball. Gross was most successful in the twenties, when the use of slang and vernacular were especially popular in American humor. Working in an approximation of Jewish dialect, Gross did a strip titled *Nize Baby*. His newspaper columns, also written in dialect and illustrated by him, were collected into two successful books, *Nize Baby* and *Dunt Esk*. Gross also wrote and illustrated *Hiawatta Mitt No Odder Poems*, *De Night in De Front from Chreesmus*, and *Famous Fimmels Witt Odder Ewents from Heestry*.

His magnum opus in the book field came in 1930 with *He Done Her Wrong*. This graphic novel was all pictures and no words and, as comics historian Bill Blackbeard has pointed out, it parodied both the serious wordless novels of artist Lynn Ward and the waning silent movies.

In addition to *Nize Baby*, Gross drew such newspaper strips as *Count Screwloose*, *Dave's Delicatessen*, and *That's My Pop*. He turned out a daily panel called *Grossly Xaggerated* and also worked in Hollywood, both as a writer and an artist. After his comic-strip career ended, he turned to comic books. For the short-lived *Picture News* in

1946 and 1947, he drew four pages of comments on current events. He drew as well for such comic books as *The Kilroys* and *Hi-Jinx*, zany material that had no relationship to anything else in either magazine. In his own comic book, he brought back *Count Screwloose* and *That's My Pop*.

He died at the age of fifty-eight in 1953 while returning with his wife from a vacation in Hawaii.

GUARDINEER, FRED *(1913–)*

■ He once confessed that he never much liked drawing magicians, much preferring cowboys. Yet in the late 1930s and early 1940s Guardineer drew several of them. The best known was Zatara, whom he created for *Action Comics* #1 in the spring of 1938. He also drew Marvelo, Tor, and Merlin. In addition, Guardineer drew all sorts of other characters, from junglemen to private eyes, for assorted publishers. He even drew Superman once, though only on a cover of *Action*.

A college graduate with a degree in fine arts, he joined the Harry "A" Chesler shop in 1936. He drew humor filler pages as well as adventure stuff. His earliest continuing feature was a sci-fi epic titled *Dan Hastings*. Even in his earliest days, his style stood out. Guardineer had a strong sense of design, and he had early realized that a comic-book page differs from a newspaper funny page, and he laid them out accordingly. His figures, buildings, props, and landscapes were never burdened with feathering or crosshatching, and he believed in flat basic colors.

After leaving the Chesler shop, Guardineer moved to DC, where he drew *Speed Saunders* for *Detective*, *Anchors Aweigh* for *Adventure*, and *Zatara* and *Pep Morgan* for *Action*. On this latter feature he used the pen name Gene Baxter, which, because of his distinctive style, fooled very few. When DC editor Vincent Sullivan left to start *Big Shot Comics*, Guardineer was one of those who went along. He drew the adventures of a DA named Tom Kerry and a magician named Marvelo, who looked quite a bit like Zatara except that he wore a turban instead of a top hat. For the Quality line, he drew *The Marksman*, *The Blue Tracer*, *Tor*, and *Merlin*, also taking over *Mr. Mystic* in Will Eisner's weekly *Spirit* booklet. In the middle 1940s, Guardineer was also a frequent contributor to *Crime Does Not Pay* and some of the Hillman comics. And he drew the articulate jungle lord Lance Hale in *Silver Streak Comics*.

He finally got to draw a regular cowboy feature when he became the artist on *The Durango Kid* in 1952. This was for his frequent editor, Vincent Sullivan. Guardineer remained on the job until 1955. Then, with the comic-book industry experiencing a serious decline, he decided to make a change—"I just had to get out and set up some kind of security." He found that security by becoming a postman in his hometown on Long Island. Guardineer, an active sportsman, continued to draw fishing and hunting illustrations for specialty publications and local newspapers until he left the post office in 1975. In recent years he's been a guest at a few comics conventions.

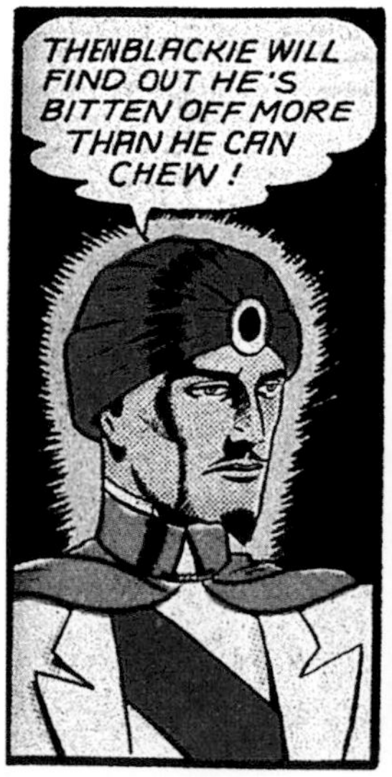
THEN BLACKIE WILL FIND OUT HE'S BITTEN OFF MORE THAN HE CAN CHEW!

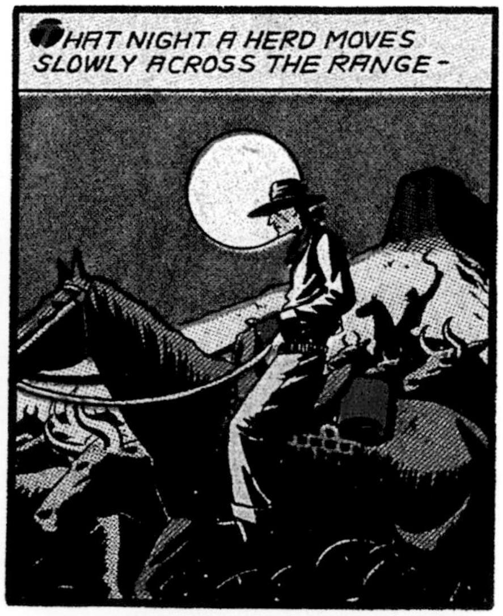
THAT NIGHT A HERD MOVES SLOWLY ACROSS THE RANGE –

GULF FUNNY WEEKLY

■ Possibly because it was free, *Gulf Funny Weekly* soon had a circulation of 3 million copies per week. Originally a four-page tabloid, it was given away at Gulf gas stations from the spring of 1933 to the spring of 1941. The invention of Eastern Color Printing Co. executive Harry Wildenberg, the man who would soon invent *Famous Funnies*, it offered original comics. The front-page feature in the early days was *The Uncovered Wagon* by Stan Schendal. It dealt, logically enough, with travel by automobile. In 1937 *Wings Winfair*, a Flash Gordon surrogate, was added and became the leadoff strip. In 1938 Fred Meagher, who later drew *Straight Arrow*, took over that sci-fi feature. The following year the *Weekly*'s four pages shrank down to comic-book size. It quit publishing in May 1941. Over the years many a parent was persuaded to stop at a Gulf station for gas because the kids wanted that free comic book.

According to research done by Robert Beerbohm and Richard Olsen, and printed in the *Comic Book Price Guide*, Standard Oil and Shell also gave away free funnies at their service stations in the 1930s. The leading feature in *Standard Oil Comics* was a page by venerable King Features artist Frederic Opper that included his famous Happy Hooligan. Cartoonist Sid Hix also contributed. Shell played it safe, sticking to reprints of *Mutt & Jeff* and *Toonerville Folks*.

GUSTAVSON, PAUL *(1917–1977)*

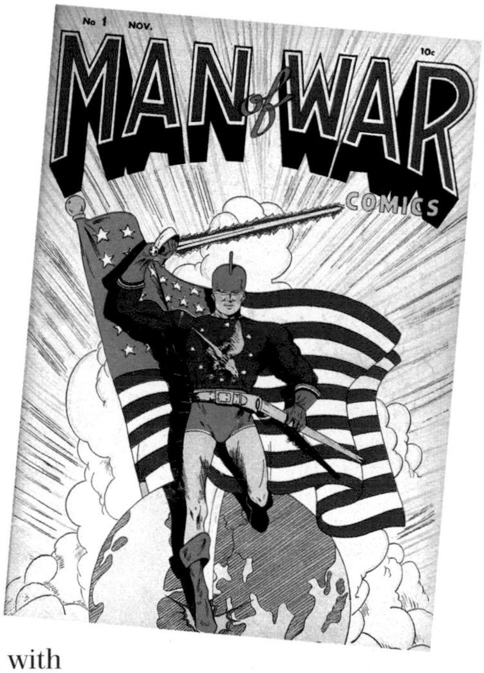
No 1 NOV.
10c
MAN of WAR
COMICS

■ Versatile, Gustavson drew both humor features and serious adventure stuff. In this latter mode, he drew *The Angel* for *Marvel Mystery Comics*, *The Human Bomb* for *Police Comics*, and *Midnight* for *Smash Comics*. Born Karl Paul Gustafson in Finland, he and his family came to America in 1921. His first cartooning job was assisting gag cartoonist Frank Owen, who sold to slick magazines such as *Collier's* and also turned out a wacky syndicated panel called *Jaspar*. Starting in 1938 Gustavson drew funny fillers for DC and Centaur. While with Centaur he branched out into more serious fare, drawing *The Fantom of the Fair* and *The Arrow*, the first costumed hero to appear after Superman.

Gustavson's early adventure style was a mite shaky and crude. But by the time he created *The Angel* he'd developed an attractive and strikingly laid out way of handling action material. Switching to the Quality group, he drew *Alias the Spider*, *Quicksilver*, *The Jester*, and *Rusty Ryan*, as well as taking over *Midnight* after Jack Cole left it. He remained with Quality until 1956, switching from superheroes to romance, true crime, and Western fare. From the late 1950s on, out of comics, he worked as a surveyor for New York State.

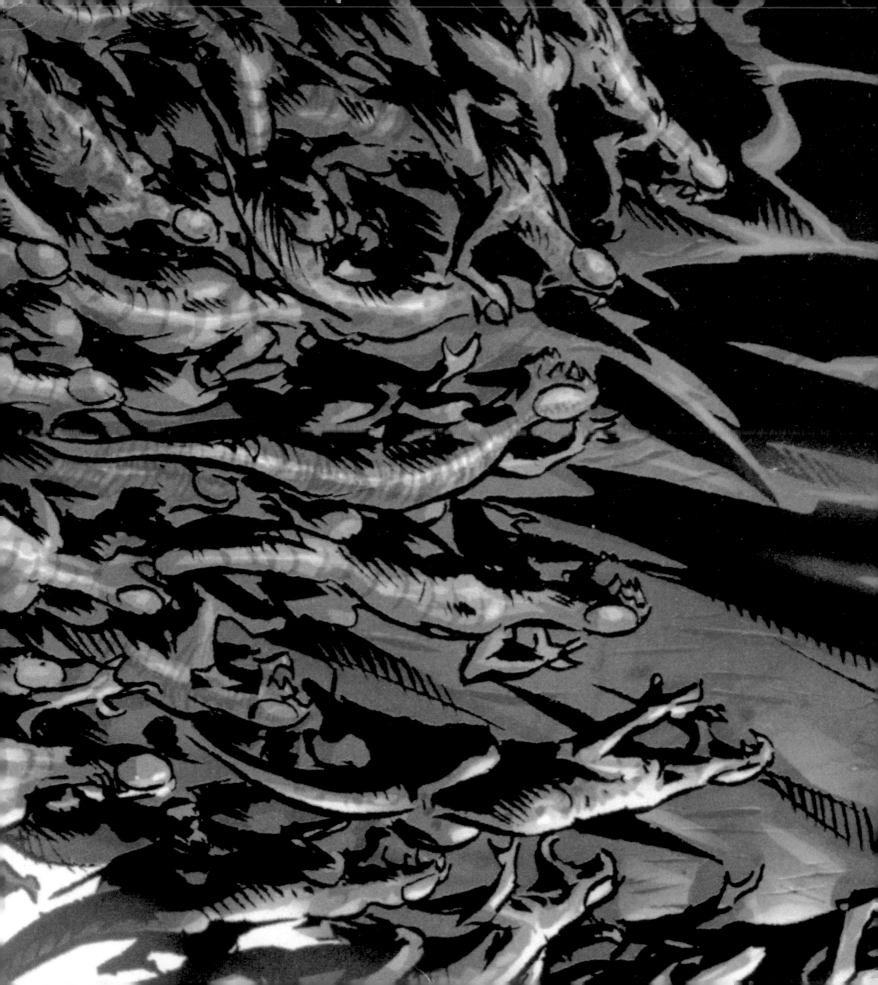

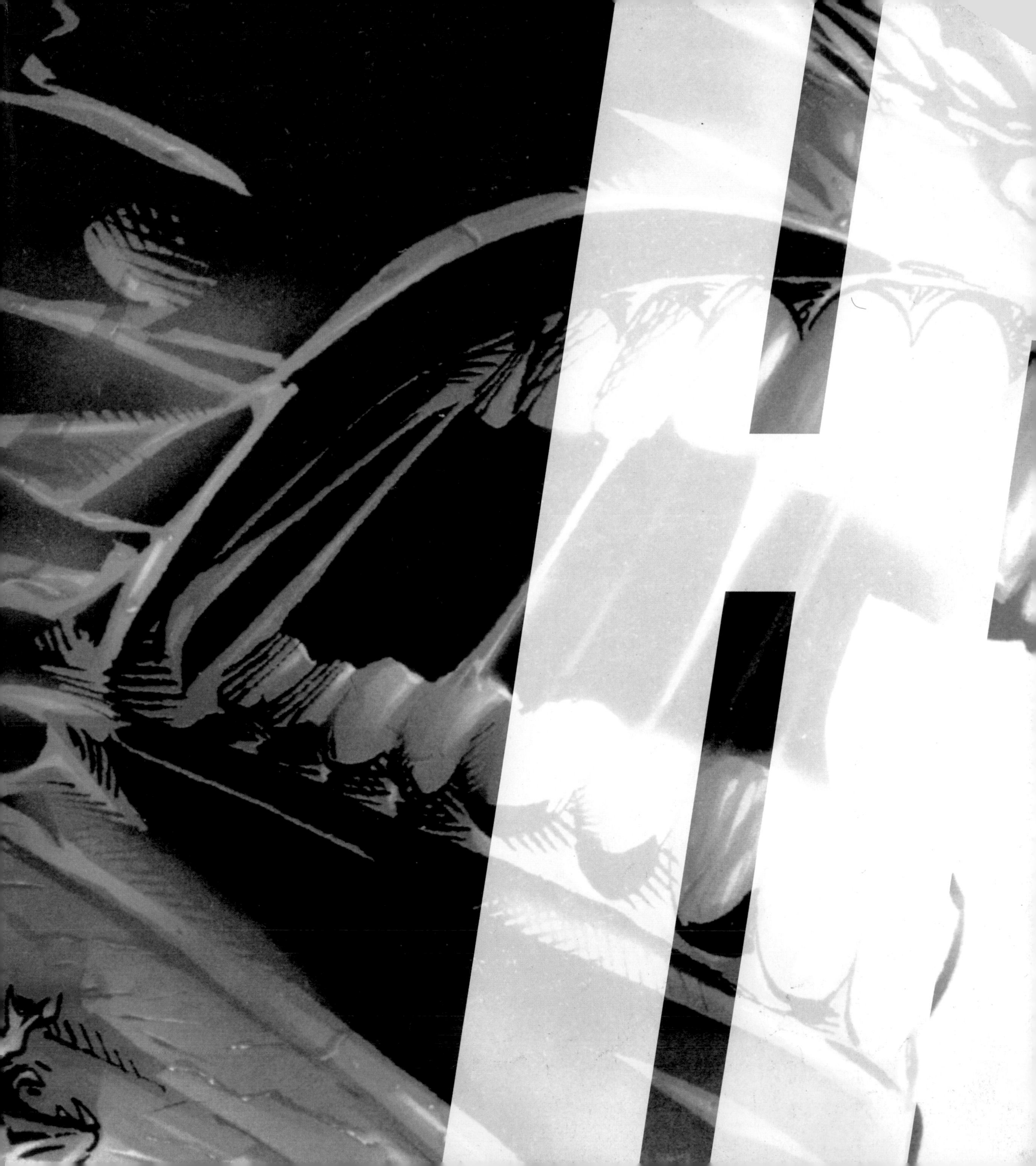

THE HANGMAN

■ Being a costumed crimefighter became a family tradition with the Dickering brothers. When Robert Dickering's brother John, also known as the Comet, was killed by gangsters, he became the Hangman to get revenge. After sending the gang leader to the gallows, he decided to remain a mystery man. At the conclusion of his debut case, he issued a challenge to the underworld—"The Comet has died but his spirit lives on . . . in the Hangman! Beware criminals, you can not outrun your conscience . . . nor escape the gallows!"

The Comet expired and the Hangman replaced him in MLJ's *Pep Comics* #17 (July 1941). Cliff Campbell, probably a house name that was also used in the pulps, was credited with the early scripts, and George Storm drew the first four stories. Then Harry Lucey became the artist, followed by Bob Fujitani.

NAZIS AND JAPS, YOU RATS! BEWARE! THE HANGMAN IS EVERYWHERE!
HANGMAN
NO. 8
FALL
10¢
AN MLJ MAGAZINE

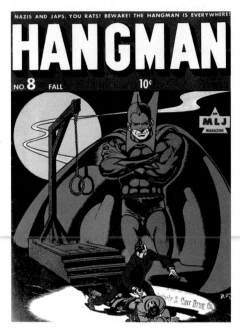

Since the character was introduced while MLJ was going through a Grand Guignol phase, the Hangman escapades were rife with impalings, stranglings, and stabbings, accompanied by much bloodletting, decapitations, and, of course, an occasional hanging. According to a recent Fujitani interview in *Alter Ego*, editor Harry Shorten wrote many of the Hangman scripts. "He'd write stories right on the spot," Fujitani recalled. "He'd just dictate the story right there [in the office]. He'd give me the plot and say, 'We'll fill in the word balloons later.'"

Hangman appeared in eight issues of his own title from late in 1941 to the summer of 1943. Lucey drew the first two issues, followed by Fujitani. He departed from *Pep* after #47 (March 1944). The Hangman was fleetingly revived in the middle 1960s and Fujitani drew him one more time late in 2002 for the cover of *Alter Ego* #23.

HARLEY QUINN

■ A comic-book character who was born on television, Harley Quinn was first seen on the *Batman* animated cartoon show. She was created by writer/producer Paul Dini and animator Bruce Timm and made her debut in an episode titled "Joker's Favor" that first aired on September 11, 1992. "Harley Quinn quickly became a favorite of the audience, the crew, and her creators," Dini has said.

DC introduced *The Batman Adventures* title, based on the animated series, in the autumn of 1992, and early in 1994 came *The Batman Adventures: Mad Love.* Written by Dini and drawn by Timm, it offered Harley in a one-shot of her own. The style that Bruce Timm used on the book, adapting his animated cartoon approach to comics, was infectious, and several other artists have adopted versions of it since. In 1999 there was another one-shot, *Batman: Harley Quinn*, which proved successful enough to go into a second printing. Finally, toward the end of 2000, and drawn in a less cartoony style, she was promoted to a title of her own when the monthly *Harley Quinn* was introduced.

Like many another Batman villain, Harley is a good person gone wrong. Dini has explained that she is a "former psychologist who became personally involved with her patient the Joker." Formerly Dr. Harline Quinzel, she developed an obsessive crush on the vile and prankish Joker, and, abandoning her career, she became the costumed Harley Quinn and joined the purple-suited, white-faced criminal as what Dini has described as "a foil/hench-wench."

Among the creative teams who've worked on her comic books are writer Karl Kessel and the art couple Terry and Rachel Dodson. On her own, Harley has been, at least temporarily, weaned from her attachment to the Joker. She formed a gang of her own known as the Quintet and eventually teamed up with longtime DC female villain Poison Ivy. When asked how the new title differed from other Batman books, Kessel replied, "Um . . . it's funny?" The Harley Quinn adventures are a mixture of action, adventure, crime, and comedy. Careening through such cities as Metropolis and Gotham on her souped-up motorcycle, Harley comes across as a quirky combination of Bonnie Parker, a court jester, and Tinkerbell.

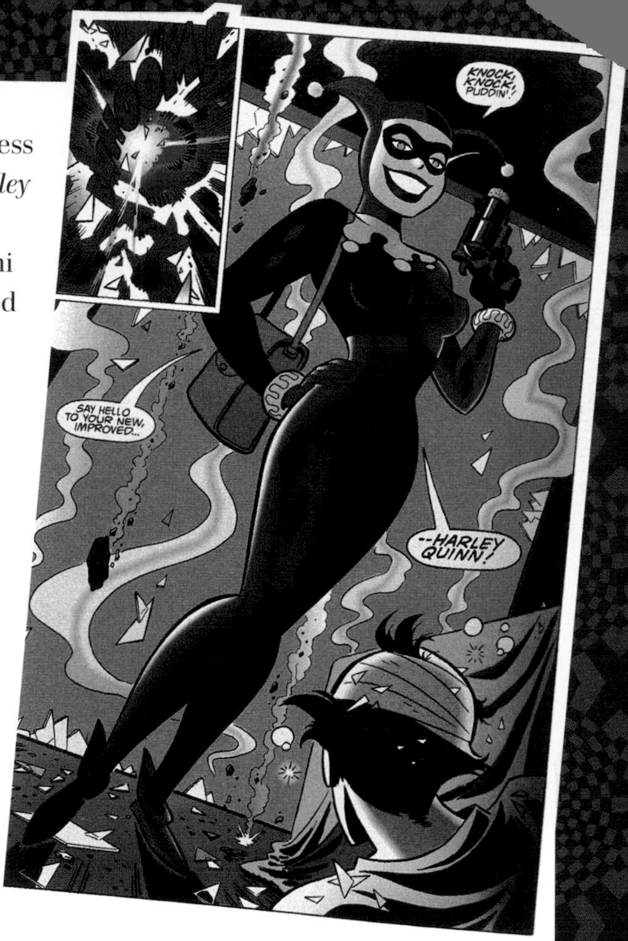
KNOCK, KNOCK, PUDDIN'!
SAY HELLO TO YOUR NEW, IMPROVED...
--HARLEY QUINN!

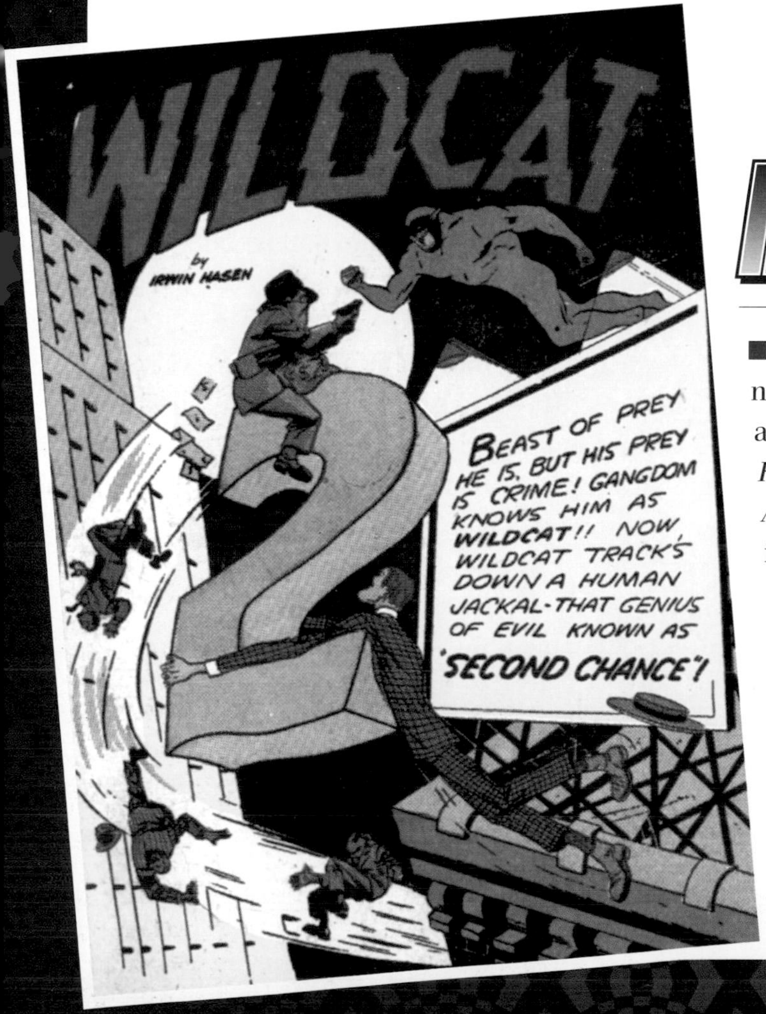
WILDCAT
by IRWIN HASEN
BEAST OF PREY HE IS, BUT HIS PREY IS CRIME! GANGDOM KNOWS HIM AS WILDCAT!! NOW, WILDCAT TRACKS DOWN A HUMAN JACKAL-THAT GENIUS OF EVIL KNOWN AS "SECOND CHANCE"!

HASEN, IRWIN

(1918-)

■ Before he started drawing the wholesome, heartwarming newspaper strip *Dondi* in 1955, Hasen was a crackerjack comic-book artist specializing in costumed heroes. He drew *Cat-Man*, *The Green Hornet*, and *The Fox* before he started ghosting *The Green Lantern* in *All-American Comics* early in 1941. He also turned out some very imaginative covers from #32 (November 1941) through #54 (December 1943). Hasen also provided covers for the *Green Lantern* magazine. For *Sensation Comics*, he teamed with writer Bill Finger to create *The Wildcat*. He got a credit on that one. After World War II, Hasen returned to DC to work again on the Green Lantern. In recent years, he has been frequently found as a guest at major comics conventions.

HEADLINE COMICS

■ *Headline*, which began early in 1943 as a comic book "for the American boy," had by early 1947 turned itself into a hard-boiled crime title. Part of the Prize Group, the magazine was relatively wholesome in its early years. Among the *Headline* characters were the Junior Rangers, Buck Saunders and His Pals, and a fluctuating collection of hyperactive kid protagonists.

Following in the footsteps of such previous funny-book kid gangs as the Boy Commandos and the Newsboy Legion, the Junior Rangers were made up of four disparate youths—Smokey, a tough street kid; Roger Ranger, a former farmboy who still wore his bucolic straw hat; Chin Lee, who spouted Pidgin English; and Jerry Simms, the clean-cut son of an army colonel. In the course of their career, the patriotic lads traveled to war-torn Europe to battle Nazis. They also tussled with villains out of the past, saboteurs, and giant monsters at home. All the material in *Headline Comics* was turned out by the Bernard Baily shop, and several different artists drew the Rangers, including Henry Kiefer, Baily himself, and a youthful Gil Kane.

Abruptly in 1947 Baily and his staff were dismissed, replaced by Joe Simon and Jack Kirby. *Headline* abandoned the American boy in favor of "All TRUE Famous Detective Cases." In addition to Kirby and Simon, John Severin, Will Elder, and Mort Meskin also illustrated the allegedly true crime tales. Later in life the magazine used photographic covers, one of which showed patrolman Simon arresting burglar Kirby. With its slogan "CRIME Never Pays" emblazoned on each cover, *Headline Comics* stayed in business until the fall of 1956.

AND, AS IF BY SHEER INSTINCT, THE TWO GIANTS CLASH IN A STARK DEATH-STRUGGLE THAT SHAKES A VIOLENT CURRENT THROUGH THE STAGNANT WATER!

THE HEAP

■ The inspiration for Swamp Thing and other walking compost piles, the Heap emerged from the muck in the third issue of *Air Fighters Comics* (December 1942) as the antagonist in a yarn about an aviator known as Sky Wolf. After a couple more skirmishes with Sky Wolf, who wore a white wolf's head as a hat while in the air, the Heap was eventually promoted to a feature of his own. That occurred in the thirty-second issue (October 1946). By then the magazine was calling itself *Airboy Comics*. The Heap remained until the final issue in 1952. Sky Wolf, on the other hand, had been grounded in 1947.

Harry Stein was the scriptwriter who first invented the Heap, Mort Leav was the artist who first brought him to life visually. It seems that during World War I a German flying ace named Baron Emmelman had crashed in a lonely swamp and been seriously injured. Instead of dying, his body merged with the vegetation, and he eventually became "a fantastic HEAP that is neither animal nor man." An ambiguous fellow, when the Heap finally left the swamp he tended to be anti-Nazi. And by the time he starred in a feature of his own he'd mellowed a great deal. He wandered from place to place, becoming involved in the lives of assorted people and usually helping them out of their problems and predicaments before shambling on. A sort of vegetarian Fugitive.

HEATH, RUSS (1926-)

■ Heath has been a professional artist for roughly sixty years, and in all that time he has rarely drawn a superhero. A first-rate illustrator, noted for his meticulous realism, he has specialized in war and combat stories, set in various times and climes, and Western tales. Over the years Heath has drawn *Sgt. Rock*, *Robin Hood*, *Kid Colt*, *Two-Gun Kid*, and *The Sea Devils*.

Heath, in his lighter moments, worked with his friend Harvey Kurtzman on *Mad*, *Humbug*, *Trump*, and *Help*. He also was part of the team that helped produce *Little Annie Fanny* for *Playboy*. He did some excellent black-and-white work for magazines like *Eerie* and *Blazing Combat*. In 1981 he was the artist on the revived *Lone Ranger* newspaper strip. The masked man and Tonto never looked better, nor their West more authentic, but the strip didn't succeed. Heath resettled in Southern California some years ago to work in animation. In recent years he's been doing comic-book work again.

HEAVY METAL

■ More or less an American version of the French *Metal Hurlant*, the magazine first appeared in 1977. Initially made up mostly of translated reprints, *Heavy Metal* showcased the work of such European artists as Moebius (Jean Giraud), Philippe Druillet, Jacques Tardi, and Enki Bilal. At that time most readers in this country were not familiar with the work of such artists. *Metal Hurlant* (Screaming Metal) had been launched in France two years earlier by writer Jean-Pierre Dionnet and a group that included Moebius and Druillet. Licensed by Leonard Mogel, publisher of *The National Lampoon*, the American *Metal* started as a monthly comic book in the *Lampoon* format. Among the early U.S. contributors were Richard Corben, Vaughn Bode, and Berni Wrightson.

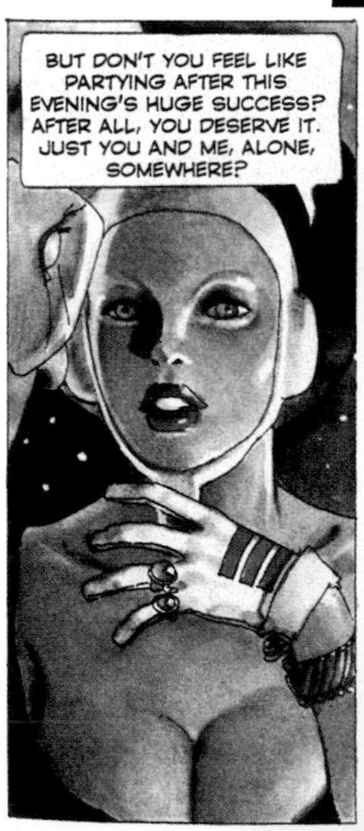
BUT DON'T YOU FEEL LIKE PARTYING AFTER THIS EVENING'S HUGE SUCCESS? AFTER ALL, YOU DESERVE IT. JUST YOU AND ME, ALONE, SOMEWHERE?

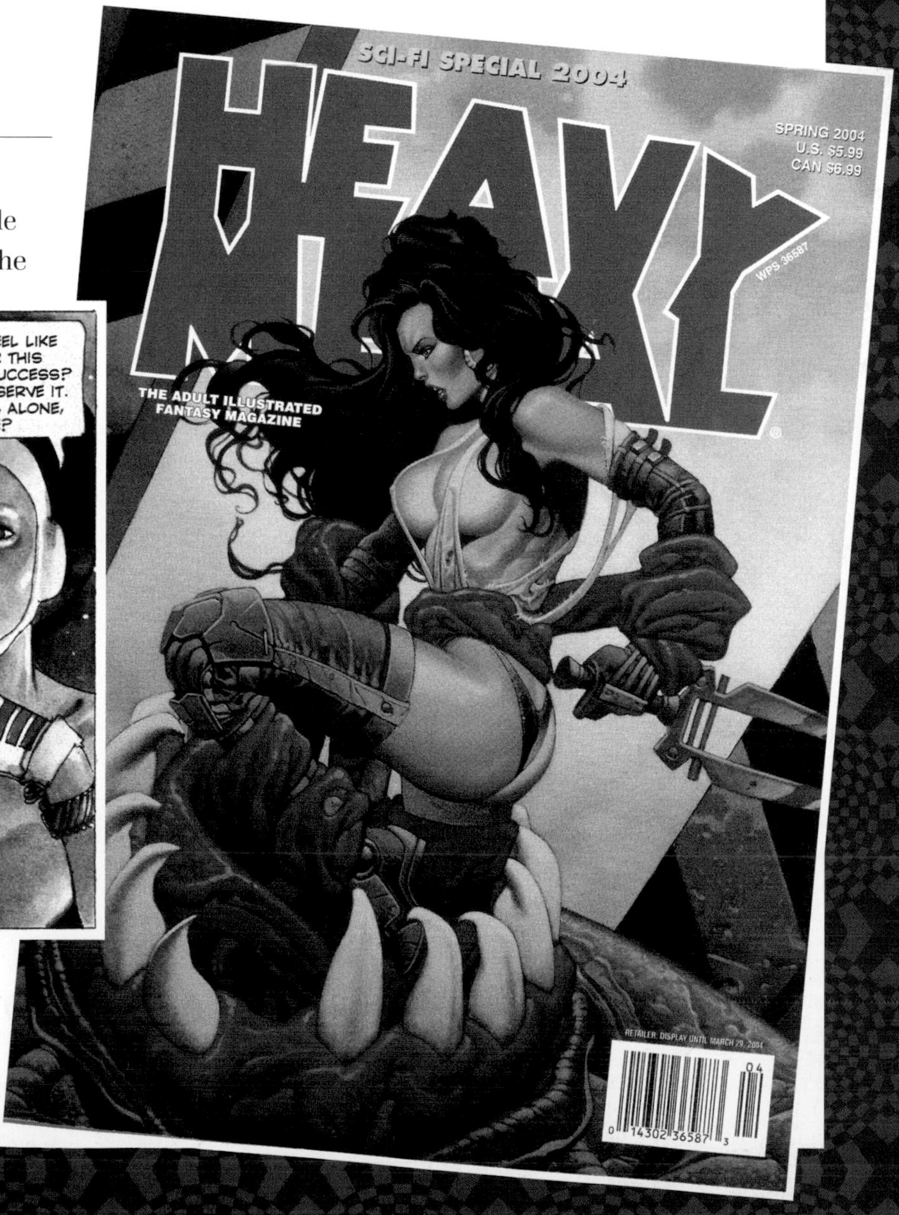
SCI-FI SPECIAL 2004
HEAVY METAL
SPRING 2004
U.S. $5.99
CAN $6.99
THE ADULT ILLUSTRATED FANTASY MAGAZINE

Aimed at an older audience, *Heavy Metal* initially offered continued tales of fantasy and science fiction.

IT'S YOUR TURN NOW, DEAR FRIENDS...

Gradually over the years, there was an increased emphasis on sex. Covers started featuring a sparsely clad and busty female each issue. Artists with experience with erotica were added, including Milo Manara, Paolo Serpieri, and Juan Gimenez. Dionnet recently commented that the American edition "(much to my horror) plummeted to a drooling esthetic . . . truly cheesy . . . with flying horses and sterile images of bimbos with perfect hairdos."

Be that as it may, *Heavy Metal* continues to appear, a monthly once again after a long spell as a bimonthly. Kevin Eastman, one half of the *Ninja Turtles* creative team, became the publisher in 1991. Sci-fi and pinups continue to share the magazine's pages. In 2002 Humanoids Publishing (USA) introduced an English language edition of a revived *Metal Hurlant*. Moebius, as a writer, is once more a contributor and Fred Beltran, who specializes in both science fiction and sexy women, is a regular.

HECK, DON *(1929-1995)*

■ In a better world Don Heck would have spent his forty years in comic books drawing in a wide range of genres—adventure, fantasy, Western, etc. As things turned out, he devoted many years to superheroes, a category of comics that was not his favorite. Heck was the first artist to draw *Iron Man* and served a long stretch with *The Avengers*. He also drew *Spider-Man, Batgirl, The Flash, X-Men, Daredevil,* and *Wonder Woman*.

He broke into comics in 1949, doing paste-up work for Harvey Publications. By the 1950s Heck was working for Marvel, drawing stories for jungle, fantasy, weird, and cowboy titles. He had an easygoing, realistic style, slightly influenced by his favorite cartoonist Milton Caniff. Heck worked at DC in the early 1970s, later for the short-lived Topps line of comic books. He was, unfortunately, one of several underappreciated artists.

HELLBLAZER

■ John Constantine is known as a man of mystery, a master magician, and a total bastard. If Clive Barker hadn't beaten him to the name, he'd be known as Hellraiser. He started off as a now-and-then supporting character in DC's *Swamp Thing* in the spring of 1984. Alan Moore was the first to write of him, Steve Bissette the first to draw him. Constantine was promoted to a book of his own in 1987, and eventually that came under the Vertigo banner.

His early physical appearance was supposedly based on erstwhile Police singer Sting. Constantine also shared qualities with the angry, often amoral, young men found on British movie screens and stages a few decades earlier and personified by the likes of Albert Finney, Richard Harris, and Michael Caine. Constantine divides his time between international pub crawling and getting entangled in horrendous supernatural and occult messes in every part of the world. He's also been involved with a variety of women, ranging from good to evil.

Writers over the years have included Jamie Delano, Garth Ennis, and Warren Ellis. Among the artists were Sean Phillips, Steve Dillon, and Mark Buckingham. Most recently Hellblazer's adventures have been written by both Brian Azzarello and Mike Carey. The artwork underwent an enormous improvement when Argentinean artist Marcello Frusin was given the job.

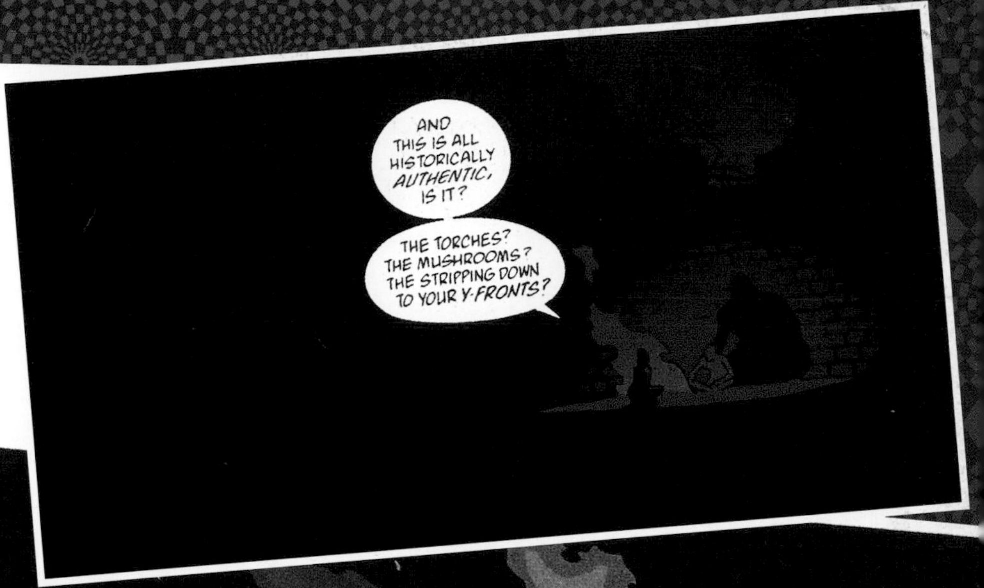
AND THIS IS ALL HISTORICALLY AUTHENTIC, IS IT?
THE TORCHES? THE MUSHROOMS? THE STRIPPING DOWN TO YOUR Y-FRONTS?

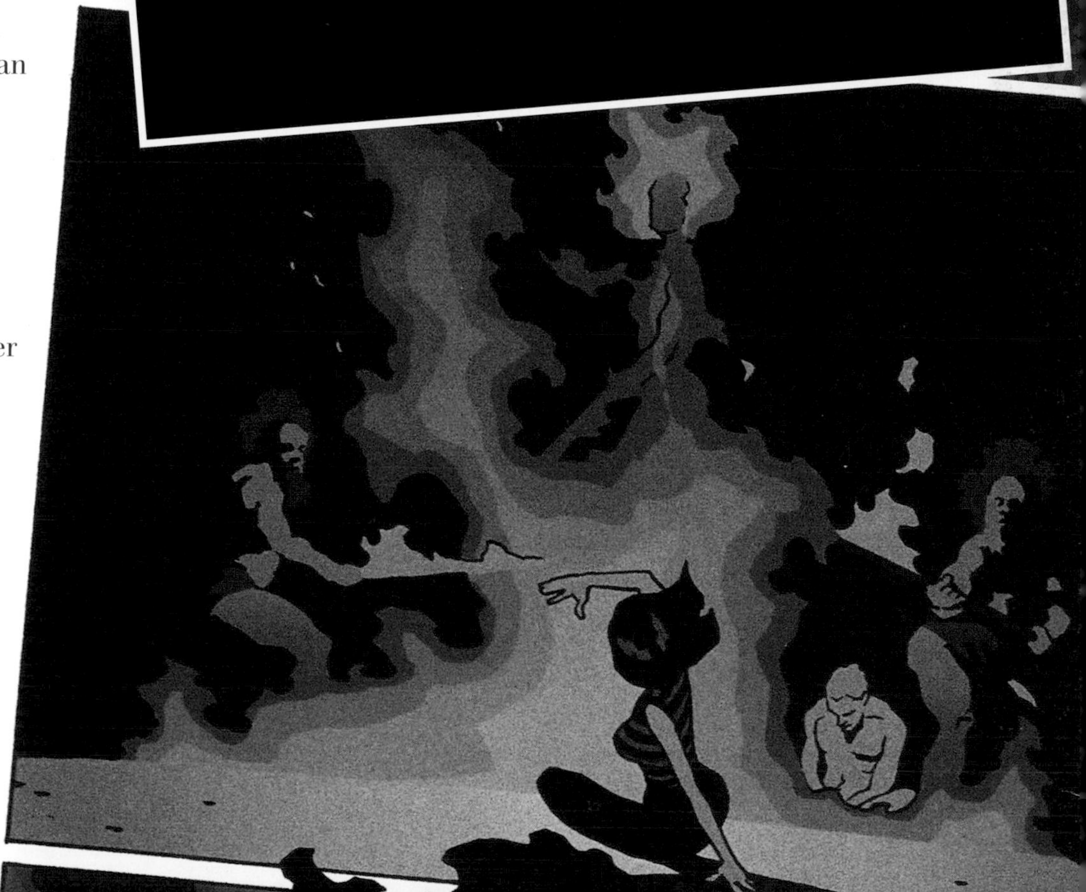

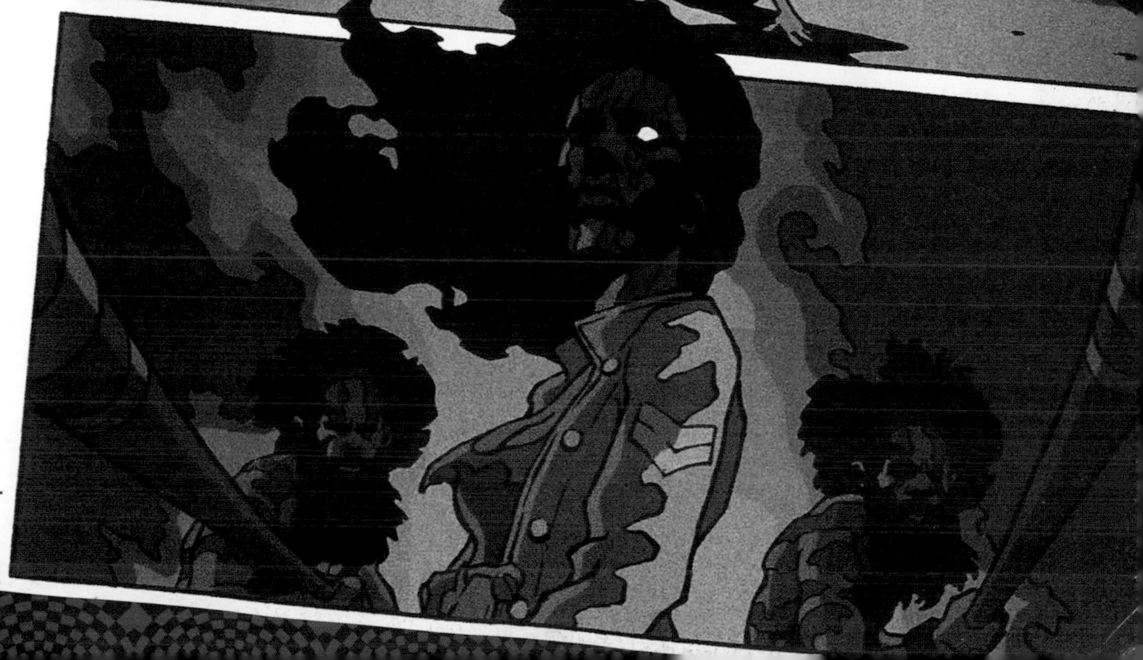

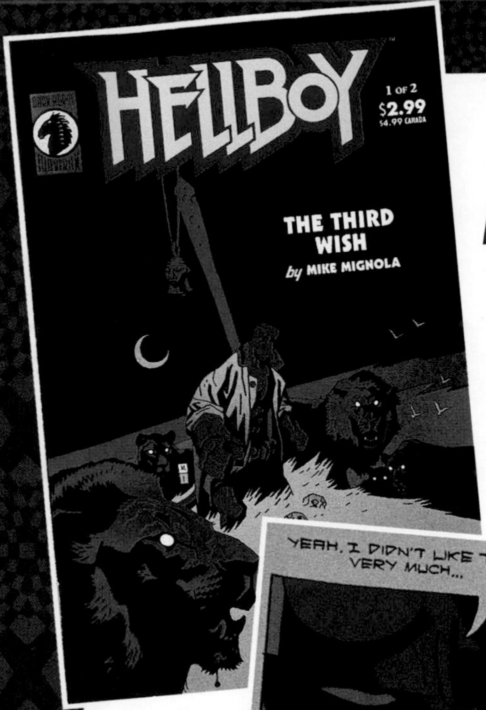
HELLBOY
1 OF 2
$2.99
$4.99 CANADA
THE THIRD WISH
by MIKE MIGNOLA

HELLBOY

His adventures are written and drawn by Mike Mignola, who has described his character as "theoretically the world's greatest occult detective." He further explained that Hellboy "is actually sort of a demon who was brought to Earth at the end of World War II, raised among humans, thinks of himself as a human, but may actually be the Beast of the Apocalypse." Despite that, the red-hued Hellboy is "a good guy and he fights monsters."

Hellboy first appeared as a backup in *John Byrne's Next Men* in 1993. He then graduated to a series of miniseries comics of his own. Hellboy also teamed up with Batman and Starman in a two-issue limited series that was a DC and Dark Horse joint venture in 1999. The most recent *Hellboy* was the four-issue *Conqueror Worm* published in 2001. As usual, Mignola utilized monsters, Nazis, old dark castles, and "as many pulp clichés as I can possibly toss in there." He has developed a highly individual and effective style that rivals those of the best European comic-book artists.

In 2003, Dark Horse introduced *Hellboy Weird Tales*. Hellboy appears, but without Mignola. In the spring of 2004 came a Hellboy movie.

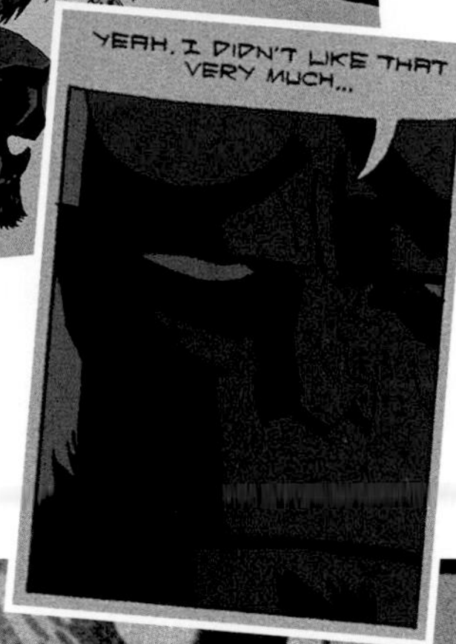
YEAH, I DIDN'T LIKE THAT VERY MUCH...

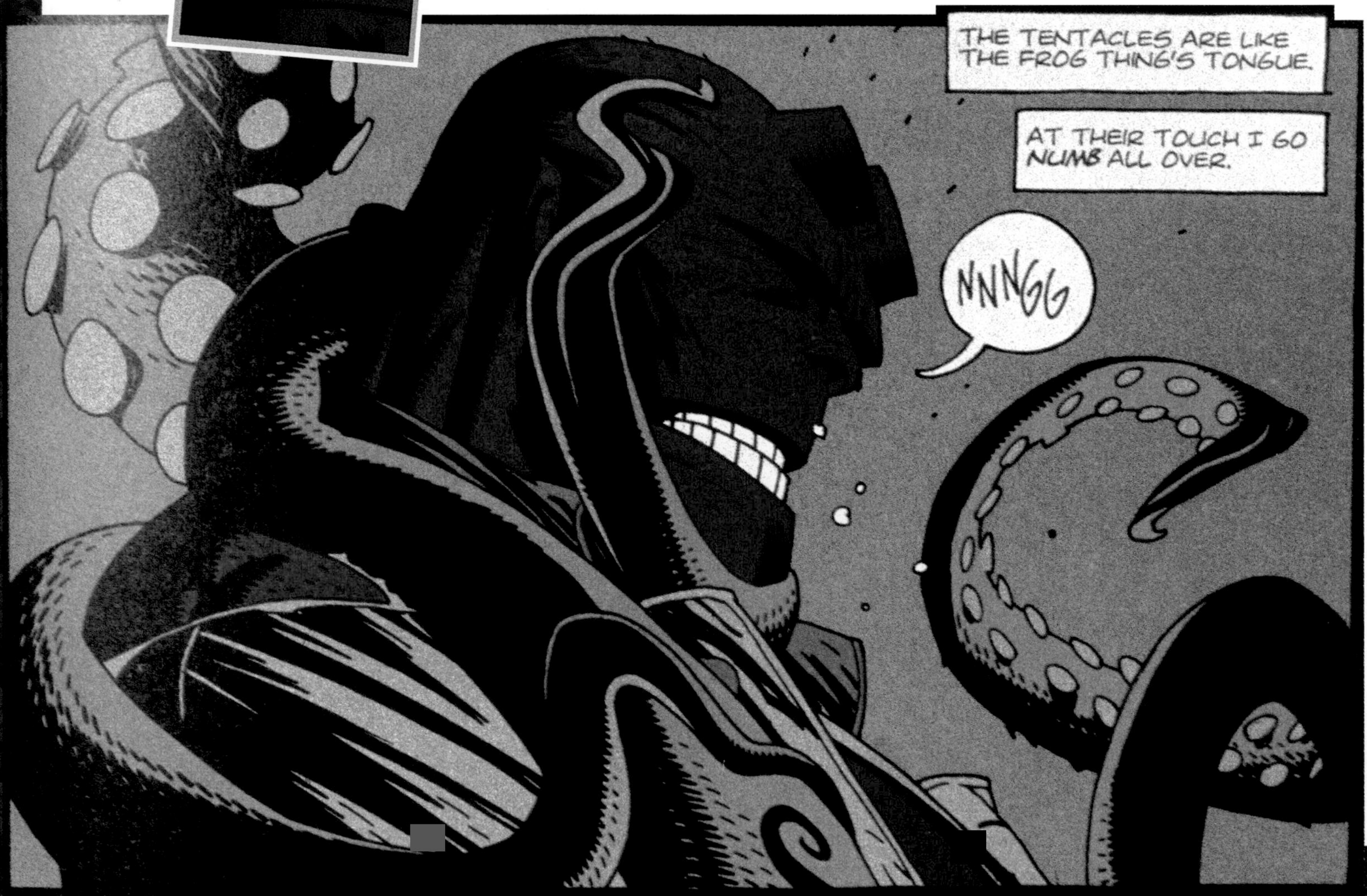
THE TENTACLES ARE LIKE THE FROG THING'S TONGUE.
AT THEIR TOUCH I GO NUMB ALL OVER.
NNNGG

HERBIE

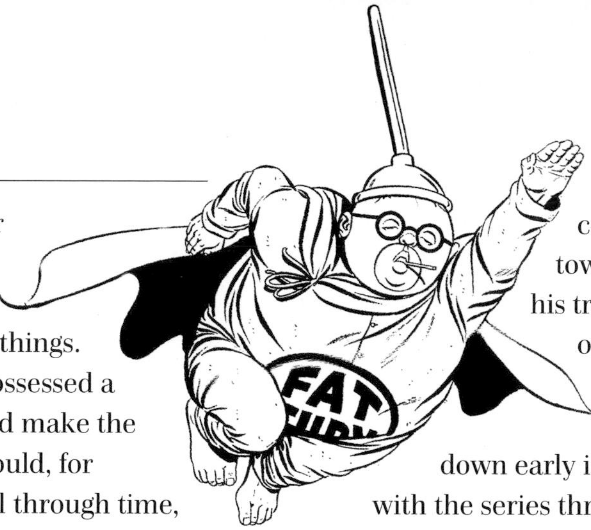
FAT FURY

■ An obese preteen with a father who always alluded to him as "a little fat nothing," Herbie nevertheless accomplished great things. Also known as the Fat Fury, he possessed a range of mystic powers that would make the average superhero envious. He could, for instance, fly, walk on water, travel through time, repel bullets, and foresee the future. Written by editor Richard Hughes under the pen name Shane O'Shea and drawn by Ogden Whitney, Herbie first waddled into view in the American Comics Group's *Forbidden Worlds* #73 (December 1958). In his initial outing, titled "Herbie's Quiet Saturday Afternoon," Herbie Popnecker talks to a tiger in the zoo and convinces him not to escape and kill the zookeeper, floats on the air, turns invisible, rescues a senator lost at sea, thwarts an alien invasion by disintegrating the invaders and their flying saucer with their own Delta Ray, and also consumes several lollipops.

Herbie did not show up again in *Forbidden Worlds* until early in 1961. After a couple more appearances amidst the more serious fare there was, according to ACG historian Michael Vance, "an outpouring of reader demand." *Herbie* #1 was unleashed upon the world in the spring of 1964. Herbie, lollipop in hand, was seen on the cover floating through the air while towing George Washington and some of his troops across the Delaware. The slogan over the title read, "Make Way for the Fat Fury." The magazine lasted for twenty-three issues before closing down early in 1967. Hughes and Whitney stayed with the series throughout, providing stories that were a mix of slapstick, satire, pop psychology, and mysticism.

As the saga progressed it was revealed that Herbie had a large cache of lollipops hidden away. Some were filed under Special Purpose, others under Time Lollipops. Taking out one of these latter, Herbie stepped into the family's grandfather clock, inserted the candy into his mouth, and rode back to whatever period in the past he chose. It might be Pilgrim days, the era of the cavemen, or the Revolutionary War period. Sometimes Herbie wore a costume that consisted of a suit of red flannel underwear with *Fat Fury* scrawled across the chest, a cape, a mask, and a plumber's helper for a hat. In whatever guise, Herbie was always taciturn and unflappable, a stoic compared to other crimefighters.

Herbie stories were reprinted in the early 1990s by A+ Comics and then by Dark Horse. For that final return engagement, John Byrne wrote and drew a new adventure of the fat little nothing.

HEROIC COMICS

■ *Heroic*, another publication of the *Famous Funnies* folks, was a mixture of original material and funny paper reprints. The new stuff came from the Funnies, Inc., shop, and the newspaper reprints included such lesser-known strips as *Flyin' Jenny*, *Don Dixon and the Hidden Empire*, and *Sgt. Stony Craig*. Among the brand-new features were *Hydroman* and *The Purple Zombie*. Other new characters were added over the first two years, including Man O' Metal, the Music Master, and Rainbow Boy. The initial issue bore a cover date of August 1940.

For its first fifteen issues the magazine was titled *Reg'lar Fellers Heroic Comics* and also called itself "the official publication of Reg'lar Fellers." Gene Byrnes, with considerable help from ghost artists such as George Carlson, had been turning out the successful *Reg'lar Fellers* newspaper strip for a score of years. Now, with *Heroic* as a recruiting tool, Byrnes was starting a club to be called Reg'lar Fellers of America. Unlike other comic-book clubs, there were no dues. The early issues devoted a dozen pages to club news and various contests that gave away prizes. Some of the prizes were copies of Byrnes' books on how to cartoon. Kids who didn't win a copy might be tempted to go out and buy one. The club venture was apparently not a success. After the fifteenth issue the words *Reg'lar Fellers* were dropped from the title with no explanation.

The leading hero in *Heroic Comics* was another Bill Everett water-based character. Due to a freak lab accident, Bob Blake achieved the ability to turn into water at will. Calling himself Hydroman, he set about fighting spies and saboteurs of an Asian cast. Because of his unique superpowers, he was able to sneak into criminal strongholds by way of the plumbing, escape from cells through the drains, and hide in the ocean. Among the other new features from Funnies, Inc., were two by Tarpe Mills. *Mann of India* dealt with an international adventurer who was pitted against the followers of Kali. Her *The Purple Zombie* was concerned with an allegedly reanimated corpse who killed only fascists and warmongers.

While still under the *Reg'lar Fellers* banner the magazine added *Man O'Metal* by H. G. Peter (in his pre–*Wonder Woman* phase) and *Music Master*, about a fellow who could turn into music instead of water and was drawn first by Bill Everett and later by Jimmy Thompson. When the Gene Byrnes club notes were dropped, *Heroic* added nonfiction—"True Stories of War Heroes." Painted covers, many of them by Henry Kiefer, depicted war scenes. The thirty-second issue (September 1945) dispensed with the reprints and the superheroes and was completely given over to nonfiction. A few issues later the title became *New Heroic Comics* and all the stories were devoted to the exploits of "truly heroic men and women" in everyday dangerous situations. The new artists included a youthful Alex Toth and a youthful Frank Frazetta. *Heroic Comics* continued until 1955.

HIBBARD, EVERETT E. *(1909–)*

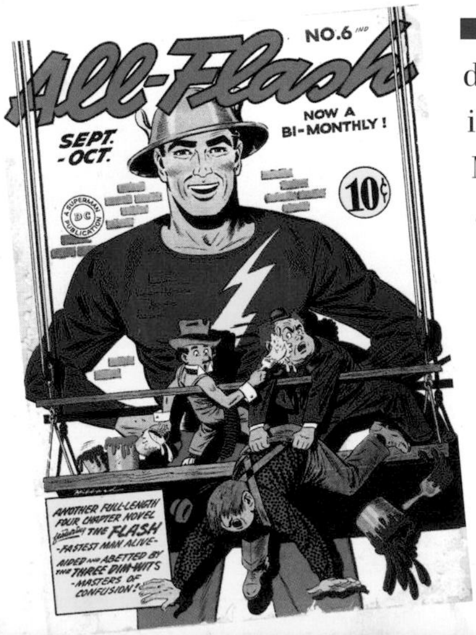
All-Flash
NO.6
NOW A BI-MONTHLY!
SEPT.-OCT.
10¢
ANOTHER FULL-LENGTH FOUR CHAPTER NOVEL
THE FLASH
-FASTEST MAN ALIVE-
AIDED AND ABETTED BY THE THREE DIM-WITS
MASTERS OF CONFUSION!

■ Working in comic books for less than ten years, E. E. Hibbard spent most of that time drawing the original Flash. An advertising artist at heart, his comics style was influenced by Milton Caniff and Noel Sickles. He took over the drawing of the Fastest Man Alive in the third issue of *Flash Comics* (March 1940). An excellent illustrator with a strong sense of design, Hibbard also drew nearly two dozen covers for the magazine. Besides drawing the Flash in *All Star Comics*, he drew the opening chapter of the early issues and several covers. He was the first artist to draw all the members of the Justice Society gathered together. When *All-Flash Quarterly* started in the spring of 1941, Hibbard did the book-length Flash adventures there, too. Leaving comics for good in 1947, he returned to advertising.

HI-JINX

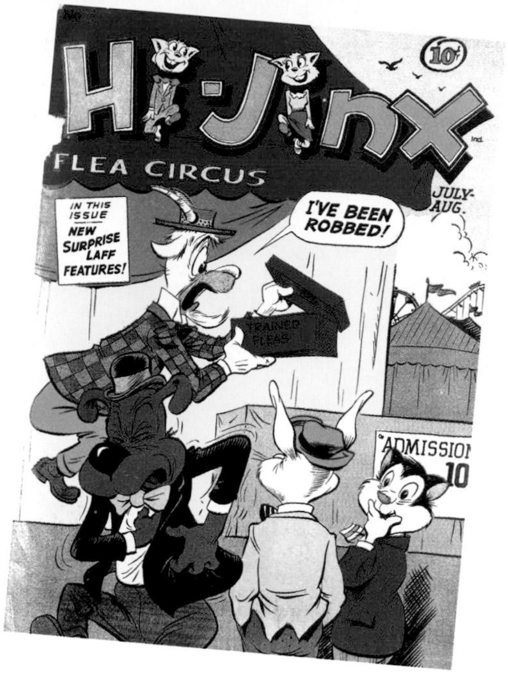
Hi-Jinx
10¢
FLEA CIRCUS
JULY-AUG.
IN THIS ISSUE NEW SURPRISE LAFF FEATURES!
I'VE BEEN ROBBED!
TRAINED FLEAS
ADMISSION
10

■ Mixing two popular genres, funny animal and teen humor, the American Comics Group created a hybrid they christened *Hi-Jinx*. The public was apparently not ready for teenage animals, and the magazine made it through only seven bimonthly issues, from the summer of 1947 to the summer of 1948.

The stars of the book were the Hepcats, led by Tommy Hepcat and his girlfriend Kitty. These two were actually cats in teen attire. There were also a rabbit named Hippity and assorted other teenage animals. Erstwhile animator Jack Bradbury drew the feature, erstwhile animator Cal Howard wrote it, and erstwhile animator Dan Gordon drew the covers. Veteran zany newspaper cartoonist Milt Gross contributed *Pete the Pooch*, which had nothing to do with teens, to the final four issues.

HOP HARRIGAN

■ The media sky was full of boy aviators in the 1930s. You found them in the funny papers, pulp magazines, movies, and on the radio, youths such as Tailspin Tommy, Jimmy Allen, Bill Barnes, and Barney Baxter. Young Hop Harrigan, who was introduced in *All-American Comics* #1 (April 1939), was a notable comic-book representation of the profession. The majority of his aerial adventures were written and drawn by his creator, Jon L. Blummer.

An orphaned farm boy, Hop had run away from his cruel guardian in an old biplane he'd restored. Landing at an airfield run by a test pilot named Prop Wash, he was unofficially adopted by him and a chubby red-haired mechanic named Ikky Tinker. Hop eventually got his pilot's license, acquired a girlfriend named Gerry, and, after America entered World War II, joined the army air force to fly in combat in both Europe and the Pacific. After the war, Hop had adventures as a civilian pilot. Blummer's plotting often relied on tried-and-true air-adventure devices—such as flying the serum to the Eskimos, etc.—but he knew his aircraft and the feature was well illustrated. Ikky changed his name to the more alliterative Tank Tinker in the autumn of 1941.

A *Hop Harrigan* fifteen-minute weekday radio show was introduced in 1942. There was also a short-lived newspaper strip. In 1946, a fifteen-chapter Columbia Pictures movie serial was released. Hop remained in *All-American* until it was changed into a Western in 1948. The last stories were drawn by Howard Purcell.

HOPALONG CASSIDY

■ For a while in the late 1940s and early 1950s, thanks to television, Hoppy was the most popular fictional cowboy in the world. Clarence E. Mulford, who'd never been west at the time, had first written of Hopalong Cassidy back in 1905. The limping cowboy, losing his limp, entered movies in 1935, portrayed by silver-haired actor William Boyd. The black-clad cowboy became a comic-book hero in 1942, a few years before real celebrity struck. Unlike later movie and television cowboys, the fellows who'd gun you down for a fistful of dollars, Hoppy was clean-cut and gentlemanly. He didn't drink or smoke, and he was always on the side of justice. He was, in fact, the sort of ideal father or uncle that most any matinee-going kid would've liked to have. And he struck kids of the fifties the same way.

Fawcett was the first publisher to utilize Hopalong, introducing him as a backup in *Master Comics* #33 (December 1942). The magazine's leading men at the time were Captain Marvel, Jr. and Bulletman. The only similarity between the comic-book Hoppy and the movie Hoppy was that he looked like William Boyd. There was no mention of the cowboy's Bar 20 Ranch, no sign of his usual movie sidekicks. In the Fawcett version Hopalong usually functioned as the sheriff of a generic Old West town named Twin Rivers, and his sole sidekick was a fellow named Mesquite. Ralph Carlson, a former pulp illustrator, was the first artist. Later Harry Parkhurst, another pulp alumnus, drew the feature. It was Parkhurst who illustrated the first issue of Fawcett's *Hopalong Cassidy*, which hit the stands in January of 1943. The second issue didn't arrive until 1946, also drawn by Parkhurst. Thereafter the Hoppy title became a monthly. The stories, usually four to an issue, were standard cowboy fare.

The movies, to which Boyd had purchased the television rights, began airing as early as 1945 in New York and by the late 1940s were being shown on a growing number of stations. A half-hour show, using newly filmed episodes, debuted on NBC in 1949. By that time, Boyd's name was appearing on the covers of the comic, and his photo, usually including his horse Topper, was used on most of the covers as well. Carl Pfeufer drew many of the later issues. When Fawcett left the comic-book business in 1953, DC took over the Hopalong title. The first artist was Gene Colan, followed by Gil Kane. *Hopalong Cassidy* lasted to its 135th issue in the spring of 1959. By that time other idols had replaced Hoppy on television.

HOUSE OF SECRETS

■ This sister magazine to *House of Mystery* reached the stands in the winter of 1956. While offering pretty much the same mixture as before, *House of Secrets* has the distinction of introducing the durable Swamp Thing.

This version of the walking compost heap showed up in #92 in the spring of 1971. Len Wein provided the script, and Berni Wrightson, already specializing in creepy artwork, did the drawing. By the following year, Swamp Thing had a magazine of his own to lurch around in.

The less successful Eclipso had made his debut in *Secrets* back in 1963, with Alex Toth drawing some of his early yarns. Mort Meskin's occult detective Mark Merlin was a regular until he turned into Prince Ra-Man in #73. The magazine added a host, in the person of a sinister chap named Abel, a few issues later.

After retiring in 1978, *House of Secrets* came back to life from 1996 to 1998, under DC's Vertigo banner and offering somewhat more adult fantasy and horror.

MARVEL COMICS GROUP
HOWARD THE DUCK
30¢
8 JAN
TRAPPED IN A WORLD HE NEVER MADE!
HOWARD THE DUCK
DAILY
FINAL
Assassination Attempt Defended By Gunman
Carter Yells Fowl
"Thought He Was In Season," Explains Prisoner

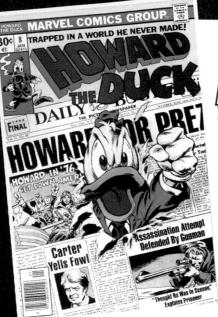

HOWARD THE DUCK

■ The duck who inspired one of Hollywood's biggest turkeys, Howard entered comic books in 1973. He looked like a cigar-smoking funny animal fowl, but he was actually an extraterrestrial. After appearing in Marvel's *Fear* and *Man-Thing*, Howard won his own comic book in 1975. The world in which Howard had to function was a freely rendered version of Cleveland. He was confused and angry at being stranded on Earth and, as cover blurbs reminded readers, "trapped in a world he never made." Howard was as much an antihero as he was a comedy character.

Howard was talkative and cynical. Writer/creator Steve Gerber used him to comment on a wide variety of social issues. Gerber, who'd scripted such superhero titles as *The Defenders*, kidded the fairly rigid formats and formulas of the genre. Frank Brunner, the original artist, was succeeded by Gene Colan commencing with *Howard the Duck* #4. The book lasted for thirty-one issues and was canceled in 1979. Two additional issues that carried on the original numbering appeared in 1986 to coincide with the movie *Howard the Duck*, still considered one of the all-time cinema follies. The sarcastic bird also appeared in a nine-issue run of a black-and-white *Howard* magazine. Gerber and Colan turned out a cryptic and short-lived *Howard* newspaper strip. Howard made another minimal comeback in 2002 in a six-issue series. Gerber once more wrote the scripts, with Phil Winslade the artist. This time around, however, Howard had been reincarnated as a giant rat.

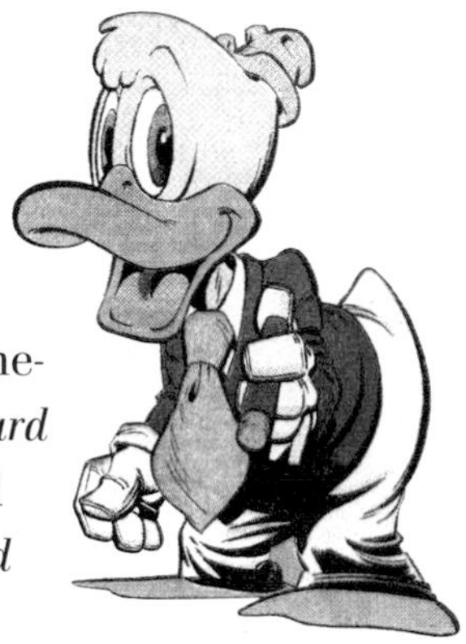

HUGHES, ADAM (1967-)

■ A relative newcomer to comics, getting under way in the 1980s, Hughes has become one of the most popular artists in the field. This is largely because of the imposing covers he's created for such magazines as *Ghost* and, most recently, *Wonder Woman*.

Earlier he penciled features that included *Justice League*, *Nexus*, and *X-Men*. He also drew early issues of *Ghost*. When questioned about his influences in a recent interview, Hughes said, "It changes every couple of years." But he added that he's still influenced by the work of Steve Rude, Mike Mignola, and Kevin Nowlan. Illustrators whom he admires include Norman Rockwell and Robert McGuiness, the prolific producer of paperback covers a few decades ago.

DC
WONDER WOMAN
170
JIMENEZ
KELLY
LANNING
A DAY IN THE LIFE
AH!
dccomics.com
DIRECT SALES
$2.25 US $3.75 CAN

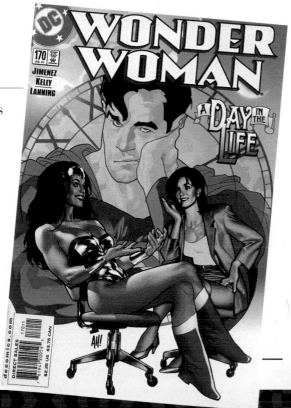

HUGHES, RICHARD E. *(1909–1974)*

■ A longtime editor, a prolific writer, and a man of many pen names, Hughes edited three dozen or so comic books and created such characters as Doc Strange, the Black Terror, Herbie, and Supermouse. Among the many titles he edited was ACG's *Adventures into the Unknown*, the first regularly issued horror comic book. He started as an editor at the Ned Pines's line of comics in 1940 and went on to spend twenty years with the American Comics Group.

He used a great many aliases, most often when writing scripts for the various ACG titles—ranging from *Blazing West* through *Forbidden Worlds* to *Giggle Comics*—that he edited. It's likely that even Richard Hughes was a pen name. In his history of the ACG company, William Vance states that Hughes's real name was probably Leo Rosenbaum.

While at Pines in the early 1940s, he edited such titles as *Thrilling Comics* and *Exciting Comics*. After working for the Sangor shop, Hughes became editor of the ACG line. Able to write in just about any genre, he turned out hundreds of scripts. A large amount of them were for *Adventures into the Unknown* and the companion horror/fantasy titles *Forbidden Worlds*, *Unknown Worlds*, etc. When not dealing in grim and gruesome tales, Hughes wrote scripts for *Supermouse*, *Herbie*, *Cookie*, and assorted funny animals and teenagers.

After ACG suspended nearly all its titles in the late 1960s, Hughes wrote awhile for DC on such characters as Hawkman, Jimmy Olsen, and Lois Lane

THE HULK

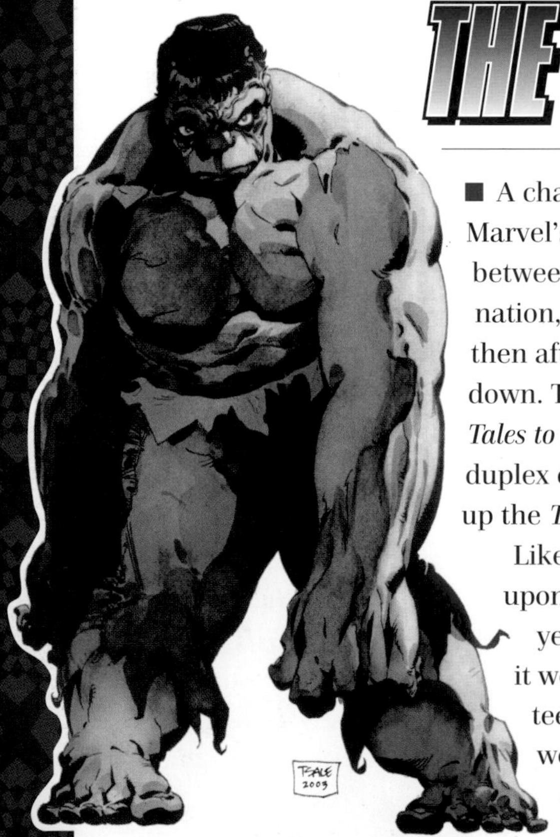

■ A character with a severe anger management problem, he first manifested himself in Marvel's *The Incredible Hulk* #1 (May 1962). This represented another collaboration between Stan Lee and Jack Kirby. Destined to become the best-known green giant in the nation, the Hulk was colored gray for his debut. He turned green in the second issue. And then after the sixth (March 1963), which was penciled by Steve Ditko, the magazine shut down. The Hulk didn't bounce back until the summer of 1964, when he started sharing *Tales to Astonish* with Giant-Man. The summer of the following year found him sharing the duplex comic with Sub-Mariner. *The Incredible Hulk* title reappeared early in 1968, picking up the *Tales to Astonish* numbering and designated #102.

Like many another comic-book character, Dr. Bruce Banner had his alter ego thrust upon him by accident. The Jekyll-Hyde condition that was to afflict him for over forty years was a result of having been too near the test site of the first gamma-bomb when it went off. Mild-mannered Banner, inventor of the bomb, noticed that a foolhardy teenage boy had sneaked onto the proving ground just prior to the detonation. He went rushing out to drag the lad to safety, after warning his sinister associate Igor (actually a Russian spy) to delay the test a few minutes. Banner was able to shove the teen into a protective trench, but the treacherous Igor pushed the button and

"Dr. Bruce Banner is bathed in the full force of mysterious gamma rays!"

Banner screams and is still screaming when he comes to hours later. He's with a project doctor, where the teenager, Rick Jones, has brought him. The medic insists that Banner remain under observation. When night falls, with Rick Jones standing by, Banner turns into a huge, bad-tempered brute. He smashes through a stone wall to go stomping across the desert. Rick tails along.

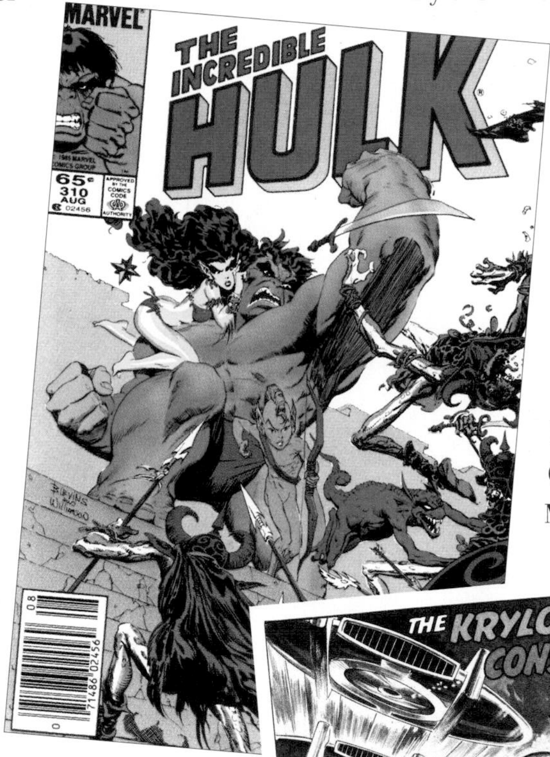
MARVEL
THE INCREDIBLE HULK
65¢
310
AUG

Military guards who try to stop the monster dub him "The Hulk," and the name sticks. The giant gets to Banner's cottage just in time to prevent the Russian spy from stealing the notes to the secret of the bomb. As dawn approaches, the Hulk turns back into soft-spoken Dr. Banner. Rick Jones is the only one who knows Banner's dread secret. When he is the Hulk, besides changing color, he is a violent, destructive fellow who loathes all humanity and speaks in short sentences.

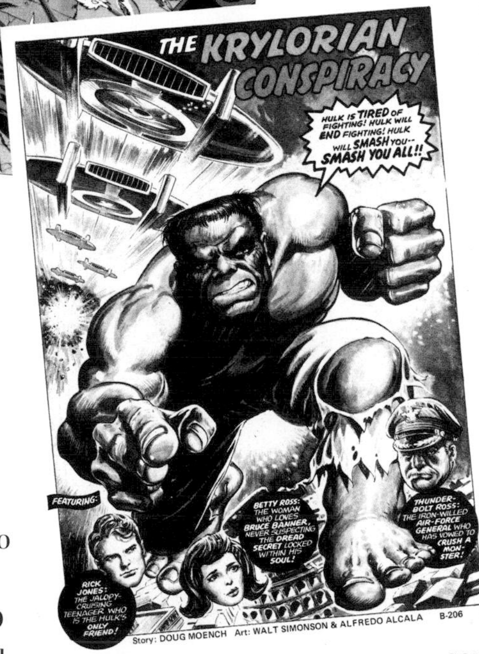
THE KRYLORIAN CONSPIRACY
HULK IS TIRED OF FIGHTING! HULK WILL END FIGHTING! HULK WILL SMASH YOU-- SMASH YOU ALL!!
FEATURING:
RICK JONES: THE JALOPY-CRUISING TEENAGER WHO IS THE HULK'S ONLY FRIEND!
BETTY ROSS: THE WOMAN WHO LOVES BRUCE BANNER, NEVER SUSPECTING THE DREAD SECRET LOCKED WITHIN HIS SOUL!
THUNDER-BOLT ROSS: THE IRON-WILLED AIR-FORCE GENERAL WHO HAS VOWED TO CRUSH A MON-STER!
Story: DOUG MOENCH Art: WALT SIMONSON & ALFREDO ALCALA B-206 3

The other regulars introduced in the first issue were General "Thunderbolt" Ross, who is in charge of the government's gamma-bomb project and considers Banner "a milksop." His daughter Betty Ross, who dresses in Jackie Kennedy fashion (complete with pillbox hat), is fond of Banner. She also feels, even after being assaulted by the Hulk, "in spite of everything there was something . . . something SAD about him!" Rick Jones was to remain the boy sidekick, a confidant to Dr. Banner and a sort of keeper to the Hulk.

In discussing his creation a decade later, Lee admitted that since the Thing was the most popular member of the Fantastic Four, he was aiming for a similar lovable monster with the Hulk. He mentioned as well that he was also trying for a touch of the Frankenstein monster—"Since I was willing to borrow from Frankenstein, I decided I might as well borrow from Dr. Jekyll and Mr. Hyde as well."

By the time the Hulk returned in 1964, he no longer turned from doctor to monster every time the sun went down. His transitions were now triggered by stress, pressure, or anger. Providing, as comics historian Craig Shutt has pointed out, "the unpredictability necessary to add drama to the strip."

Ditko remained the artist only until early in 1965, when Kirby returned. Other artists over the years have included John Buscema, Marie Severin, Herb Trimpe, Gil Kane, Sal Buscema, Al Milgrom, Todd McFarlane, Jeff Purves, Dale Keown, Adam Kubert, and John Romita, Jr. Among the writers were Roy Thomas, Archie Goodwin, Steve Englehart, Len Wein, Roger Stern, Bill Mantlo, and, for eleven years, Peter David.

The original *Incredible Hulk* stopped with its 474th issue (March 1999). The next month came a just plain *Hulk* comic book. With #12 (March 2000) that became *The Incredible Hulk* again. Fans say the Hulk series they'd most like to see collected into a graphic novel would be *The Incredible Hulk Adventures in the Crossroads*, an eighties saga that started with episode #300 and had Bruce Banner banished to a world where he could do no harm.

THE HUMAN TORCH: I

■ He first lit his fire in the autumn of 1939 in publisher Martin Goodman's *Marvel Comics.* Actually, the Human Torch wasn't human, but rather a "synthetic man—an exact replica of a human being." In the comic book he was the creation of Professor Horton, who'd been laboring to come up with a synthetic man. In real life the Torch was cooked up by artist Carl Burgos and writer John Compton.

In the original story, which is not a classic example of coherence, it was revealed that the handsome blond android had an unfortunate and unforeseen tendency to burst into flame when exposed to the oxygen in air. Sure enough, exposed to the stuff, he does burst into flame and rushes out as a flaming hero to capture, appropriately enough, a gang of arsonists. During that initial foray, the Human Torch learned how to melt iron, toss fireballs, and then how to turn his flame off and on at will. He didn't look at all charred or singed after his experiences and yet no one explained what exactly was burning when he was in his Torch phase. Made altruistic by his initial foray, he decided to use his firebug abilities to fight crime. He soon adopted the alter ego of a uniformed policeman.

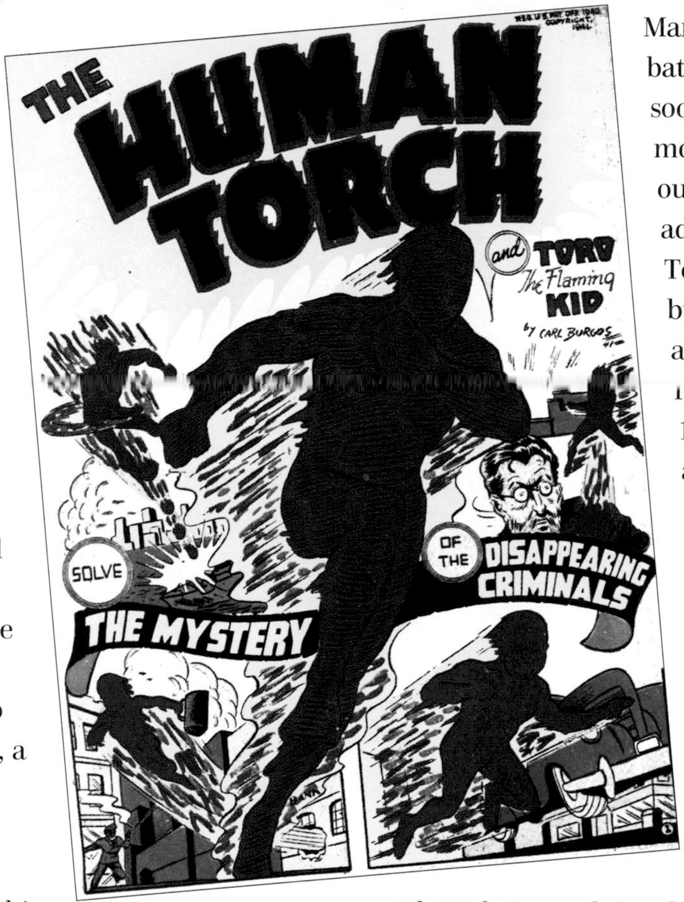
THE HUMAN TORCH
and TORO The Flaming KID
by CARL BURGOS
SOLVE THE MYSTERY
OF THE DISAPPEARING CRIMINALS

Along with Bill Everett's Sub-Mariner, whom he sometimes battled in later issues, the Torch soon became one of *Marvel*'s two most popular heroes. He branched out into his own title in 1940 and added a boy companion named Toro, who also had a knack for bursting into flame. Both the Torch and Toro could also fly. The team remained popular throughout the 1940s. Harry Sahle, Burgos's assistant and sometime ghost, also drew the stories early on. When Burgos went into the service during World War II, Edd Ashe took over the characters, followed by Jimmy Thompson and a host of others.

Marvel made its first attempt to rekindle the Torch in the early 1950s, adding him to the lineup of *Young Men* with Dick Ayers doing the drawing. That was not successful, and in 1961 they loaned his name to Johnny Storm of the Fantastic Four. Since then the old original Human Torch has made occasional comebacks.

THE HUMAN TORCH: II

■ See THE FANTASTIC FOUR.

HYDROMAN

■ See HEROIC COMICS.

HYPER MYSTERY COMICS

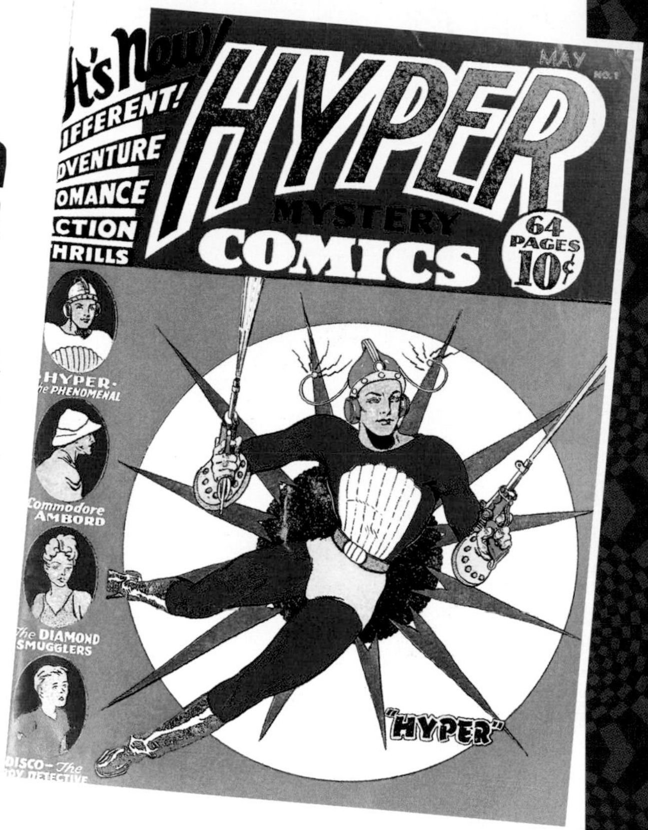
It's Now!
DIFFERENT!
ADVENTURE
ROMANCE
ACTION
THRILLS
MAY
NO. 1
HYPER
MYSTERY
COMICS
64 PAGES
10¢
HYPER-
The PHENOMENAL
Commodore
AMBORD
The DIAMOND
SMUGGLERS
DISCO-The
BOY DETECTIVE
"HYPER"

■ In the heady atmosphere of the early 1940s, when every publisher dreamed of Superman-like success, a great many small companies entered the comic-book field. And quite a few abruptly exited. One such was Hyper Publications, who published two issues of *Hyper Mystery Comics* before vanishing forever.

The magazine is notable for introducing a superhero with the catchy name of Hyper the Phenomenal, whose blue-and-gold helmet seemed to come equipped with earmuffs. Reg Greenwood drew Hyper and H. G. Peter, soon to draw *Wonder Woman,* did his first comic-book work here.

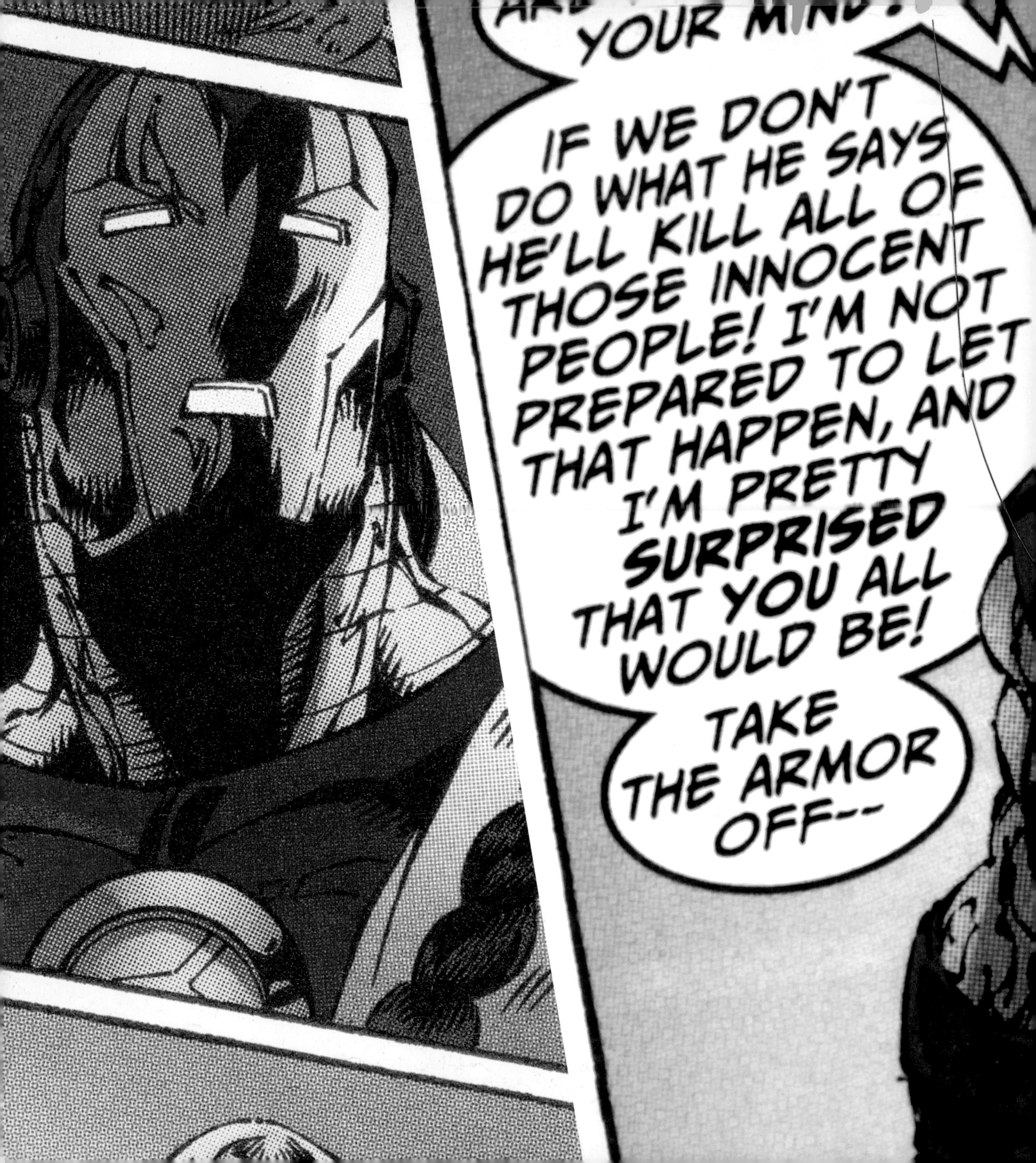
YOUR MIND!
IF WE DON'T DO WHAT HE SAYS HE'LL KILL ALL OF THOSE INNOCENT PEOPLE! I'M NOT PREPARED TO LET THAT HAPPEN, AND I'M PRETTY SURPRISED THAT YOU ALL WOULD BE!
TAKE THE ARMOR OFF--

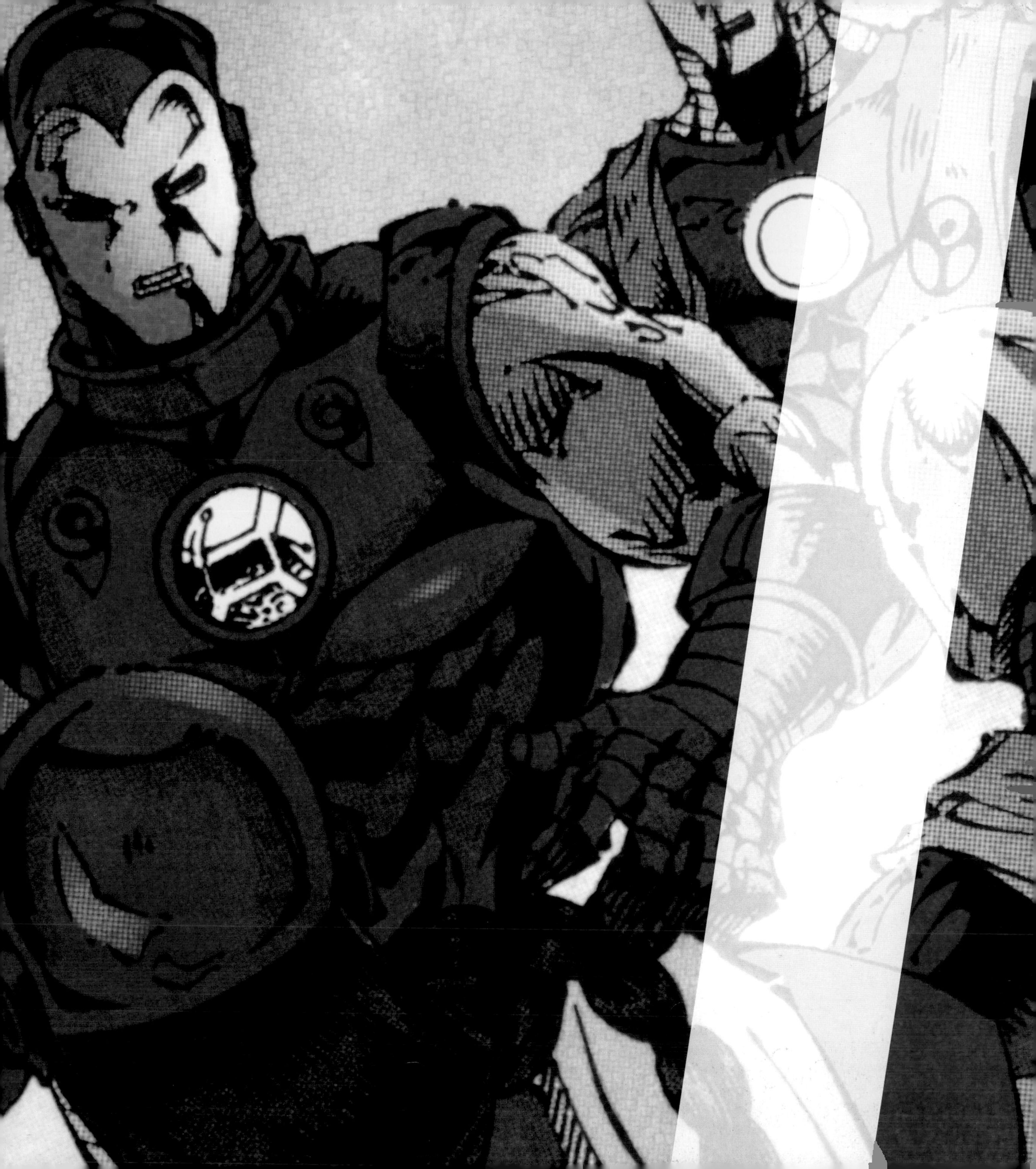

IBIS THE INVINCIBLE

■ See WHIZ COMICS.

IGER, JERRY

■ See JUMBO COMICS.

INFANTINO, CARMINE

(1925-)

■ It was his rendering of the new, improved Flash that ushered DC into the Silver Age. Like many of his contemporaries, such as Gil Kane, Alex Toth, and Joe Kubert, Infantino started drawing for comic books while still in his teens. That was in the early 1940s. By the time he went into semi retirement in the 1990s, he'd also drawn such characters as Batman, Elongated Man, the Phantom Stranger, Rex the Wonder Dog, Adam Strange, Charlie Chan, and the Heap. And Infantino had been both the editorial director and the publisher of DC Comics.

Infantino worked in, and got some of his art training from, first the Jack Binder shop and then the Bernard Baily shop. Branching out on his own, by the middle 1940s he was drawing such features as *Gunmaster* and *The Heap* for Hillman. In 1947 he went to work for DC. At that point he was drawing in a boldly inked style that showed the influence of his idol, Milton Caniff. He drew *The Ghost Patrol*, *King Faraday*, *Pow-Wow Smith*, *Black Canary*, the old, original *Flash*, and even *Rex the Wonder Dog*.

Infantino had developed a new, subtler illustration style by the time editor Julius Schwartz asked him to draw the new Flash. He designed the character and his new costume, introduced in *Showcase* #4. His version of the Fastest Man Alive, with help from Gardner Fox's script, was a success, and in 1959 DC started a regular *Flash* title. Infantino continued as penciler for several years. He also modernized Batman, drawing him in a much more illustrative fashion than had been seen previously. After leaving DC in the middle 1970s, Infantino worked for a while in animation and commercial art. He's occasionally done some comic-book work. In 2002 he produced a profusely illustrated autobiography called *The Amazing World of Carmine Infantino*.

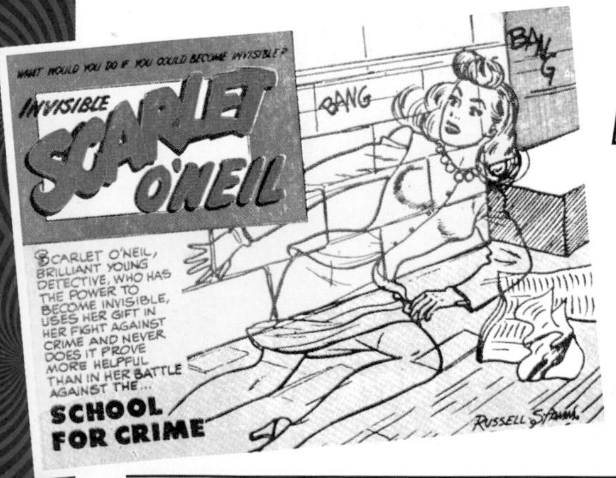
WHAT WOULD YOU DO IF YOU COULD BECOME INVISIBLE?
INVISIBLE SCARLET O'NEIL
BANG
BANG
SCARLET O'NEIL, BRILLIANT YOUNG DETECTIVE, WHO HAS THE POWER TO BECOME INVISIBLE, USES HER GIFT IN HER FIGHT AGAINST CRIME AND NEVER DOES IT PROVE MORE HELPFUL THAN IN HER BATTLE AGAINST THE...
SCHOOL FOR CRIME
RUSSELL STAMM

INVISIBLE SCARLET O'NEIL

■ She began life in a newspaper strip in 1940. In the spring of 1941, *Famous Funnies* started reprinting the strip, which was written and drawn by Russell Stamm. H. G. Peter, soon to be the *Wonder Woman* artist, drew the young woman on the cover of her debut issue.

Invisibility was a popular knack in the thirties and forties. The movies introduced the Invisible Man in 1933 and the Invisible Woman in 1940. The

Shadow was turning invisible on the radio once a week from 1937 onward, branching out into a newspaper strip and comic books in 1940. Scarlet came by her ability due to an accident in the home lab of her scientist father. Thereafter, she could turn invisible and visible at will. Stamm drew her as transparent rather than unseen in the former state. Aware of the growing popularity of comic books, the syndicate advertised Scarlet as "America's new superheroine."

Invisible Scarlet remained in *Famous* until 1948. In 1950 Harvey Publications starred her in a few issues of her own title. Quite obviously she influenced later unseeable folks, particularly Sue Storm, the Invisible Girl of the Fantastic Four.

IRON MAN

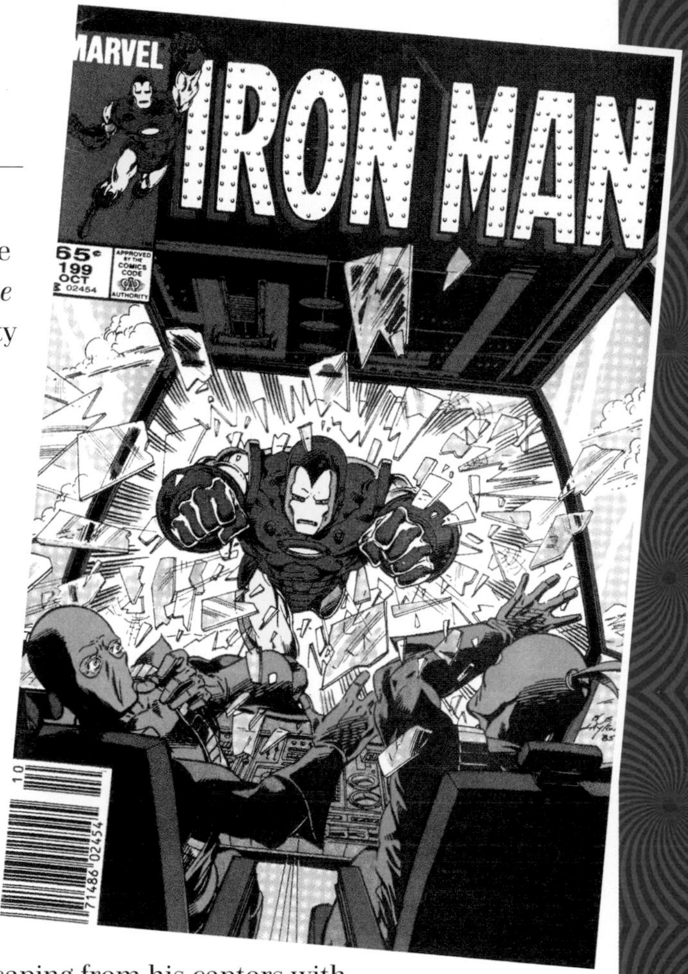
MARVEL
IRON MAN
65¢
199
OCT

■ "When billionaire industrialist Tony Stark dons sophisticated steel-mesh armor of his own design, he becomes a living high-tech weapon—the World's greatest human fighting machine," explained a recent issue of *The Invincible Iron Man.* And thus it's been, with some exceptions, for over forty years. One of the most trouble-ridden heroes of the Silver Age, Iron Man first appeared in Marvel's *Tales of Suspense* #39 (March 1963). Another of Stan Lee's many inventions, his early adventures were written by Larry Lieber, drawn by Don Heck. Tony Stark, then only a multimillionaire, was not a true superhero. But he gained an incredible array of abilities by putting on "an electrically powered, transistorized smart suit of armor equipped with offensive weaponry."

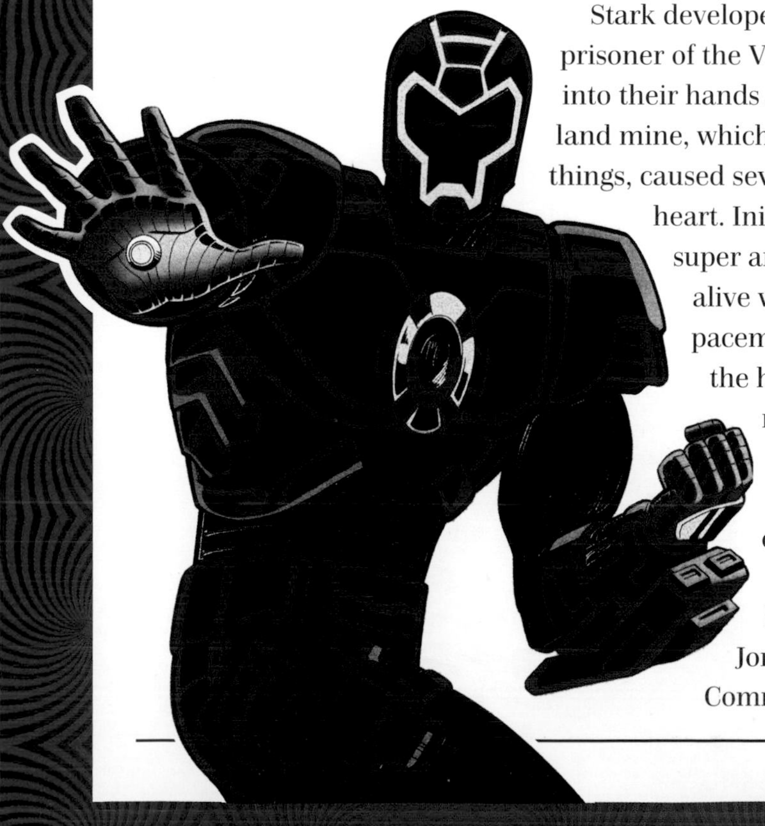

Stark developed the suit while a prisoner of the Viet Cong. He'd fallen into their hands after stepping on a land mine, which, among other things, caused severe damage to his heart. Initially the suit of super armor kept him alive with a built-in pacemaker device. After escaping from his captors with the help of a black chopper pilot named James Rhodes, Stark eventually returned to civilian life. He served as president and CEO of Stark Industries (later Stark International and later still Stark Enterprises), a member in good standing of the military-industrial complex. Rhodes came to work for him, becoming his best friend.

Iron Man's favorite foe over the years was a sinister Oriental known as the Mandarin. In its early years the saga was, as Gerard Jones has pointed out, "an odd mélange of political realism, shrill anti-Communist jingoism and fanciful superheroics." Although he eventually

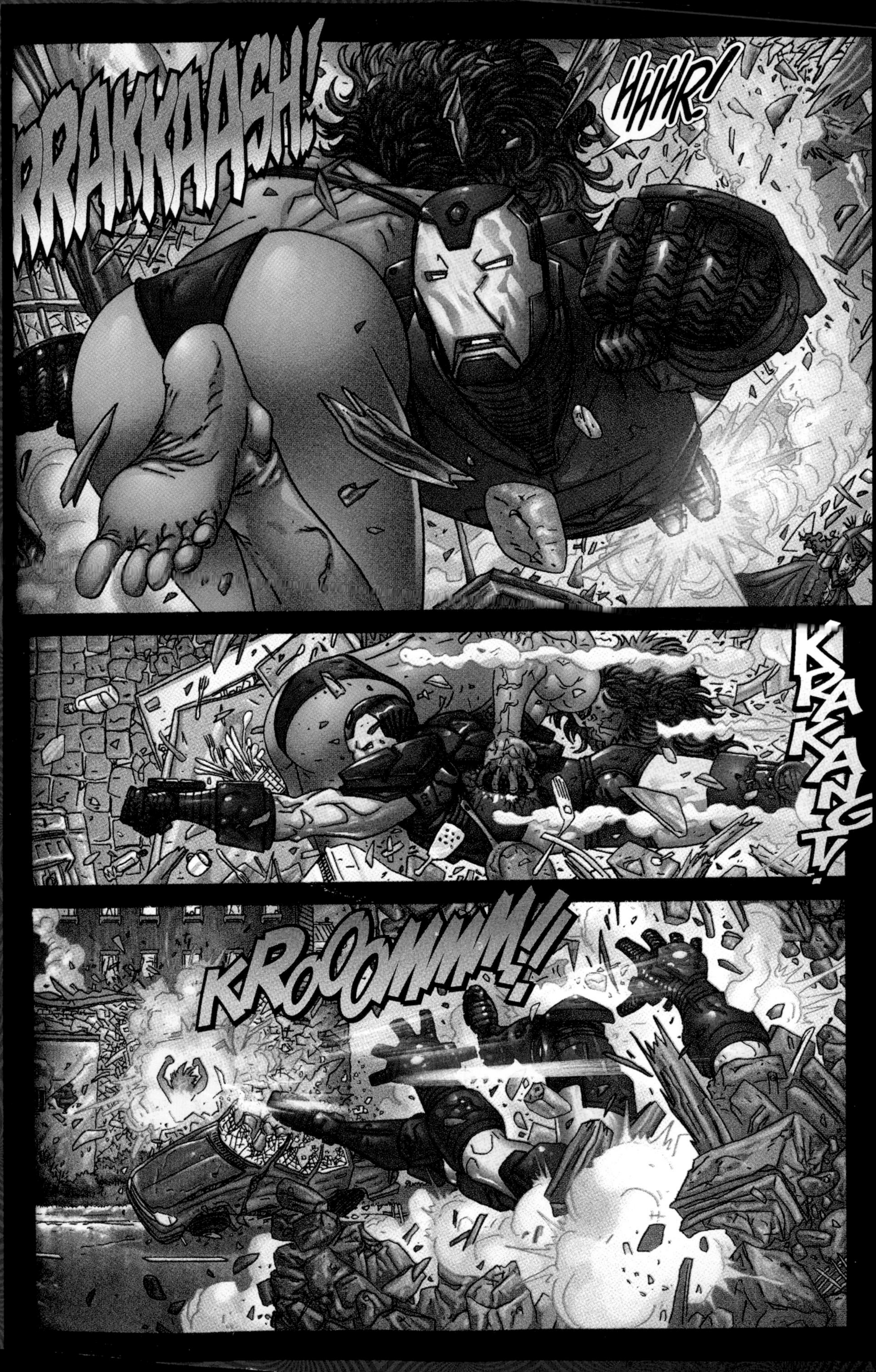
RRAKKAASH!!
HHHR!
KRAKANG!
KROOOMMMM!!

became less of a cold warrior, Stark's life was not especially happy. Unmarried, he suffered a series of romantic setbacks. In addition, a bullet wound to his spine left him crippled for a time and later another injury caused neural damage. For quite a while Stark was also an alcoholic. During the periods when Stark's problems incapacitated him, Rhodes, nicknamed Rhodey, put on the armor and served as Iron Man. That suit of armor has undergone many changes in both design, color scheme, and capabilities.

MARVEL
IRON MAN
$1.00
6
1983
ANNUAL
TO FREE THE ETERNALS!

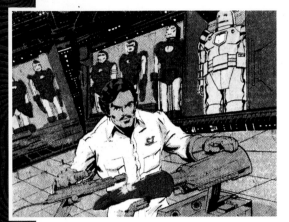

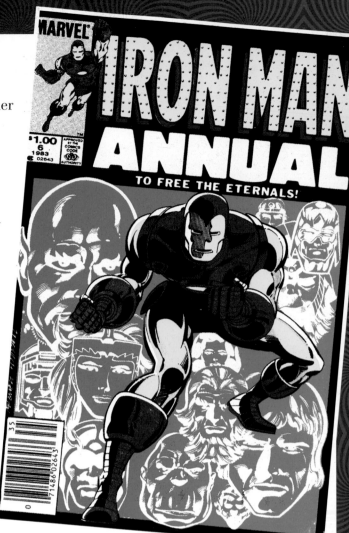

Iron Man has been a member of the Avengers and later of the Avengers West Coast. Numerous other artists and writers have had a hand in producing his adventures, including Gene Colan, Archie Goodwin, George Tuska, John Romita, Jr., Scott Lobdell, While Portacio, Kurt Busiek, Robin Laws, and Robert Teranishi.

Although Tony Stark has died now and then, he appears to have incredible recuperative powers. Currently, in yet another suit of upgraded armor, he can be found in *The Invincible Iron Man* in a comic shop near you.

THE IRON SKULL

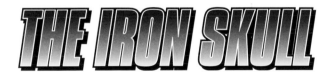

■ See AMAZING-MAN COMICS.

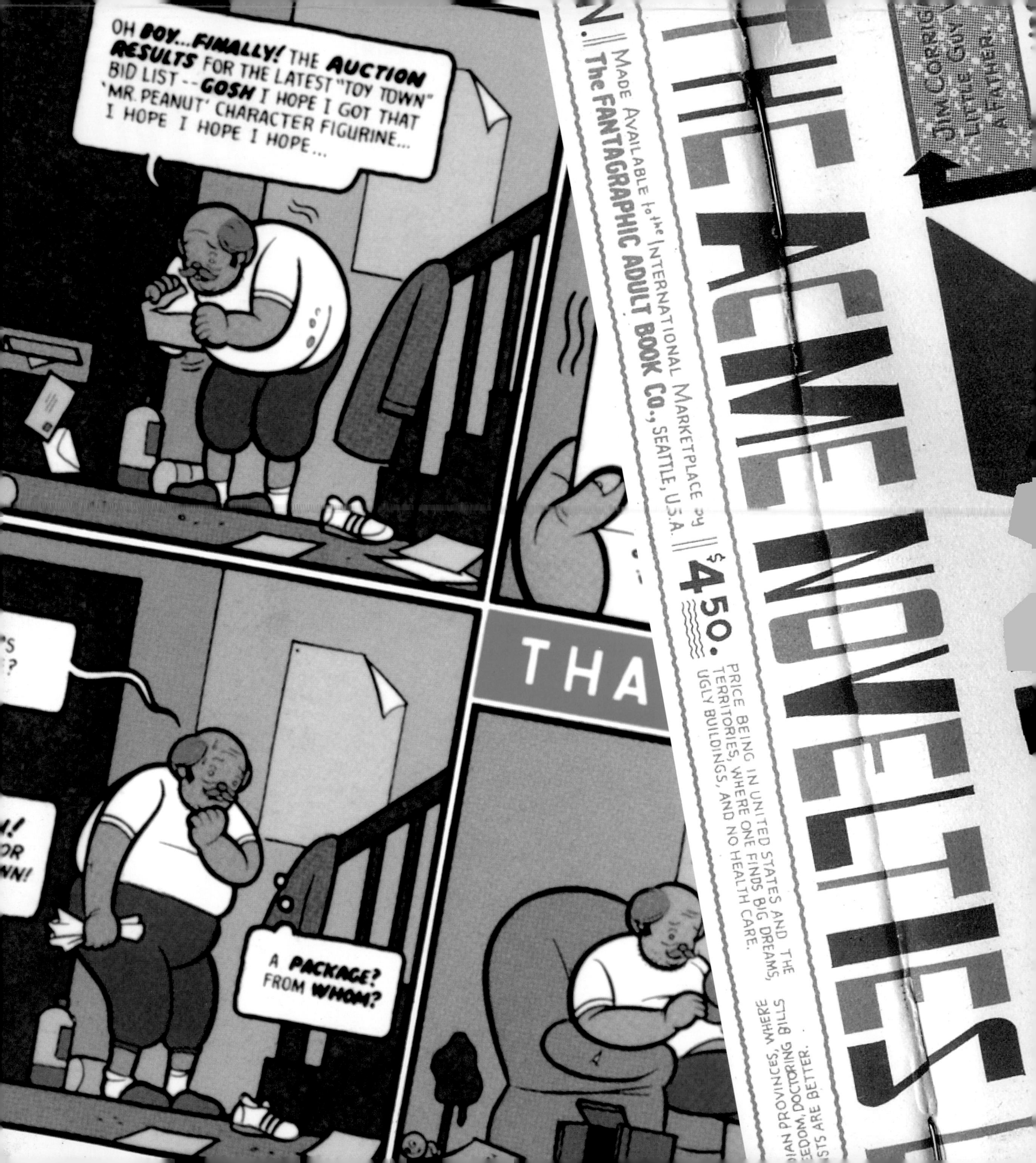
OH BOY...FINALLY! THE AUCTION RESULTS FOR THE LATEST "TOY TOWN" BID LIST--GOSH I HOPE I GOT THAT 'MR. PEANUT' CHARACTER FIGURINE... I HOPE I HOPE I HOPE...
A PACKAGE? FROM WHOM?
MADE AVAILABLE to the INTERNATIONAL MARKETPLACE by The FANTAGRAPHIC ADULT BOOK Co., SEATTLE, U.S.A.
$4.50.
PRICE BEING IN UNITED STATES AND THE TERRITORIES, WHERE ONE FINDS BIG DREAMS, UGLY BUILDINGS, AND NO HEALTH CARE.

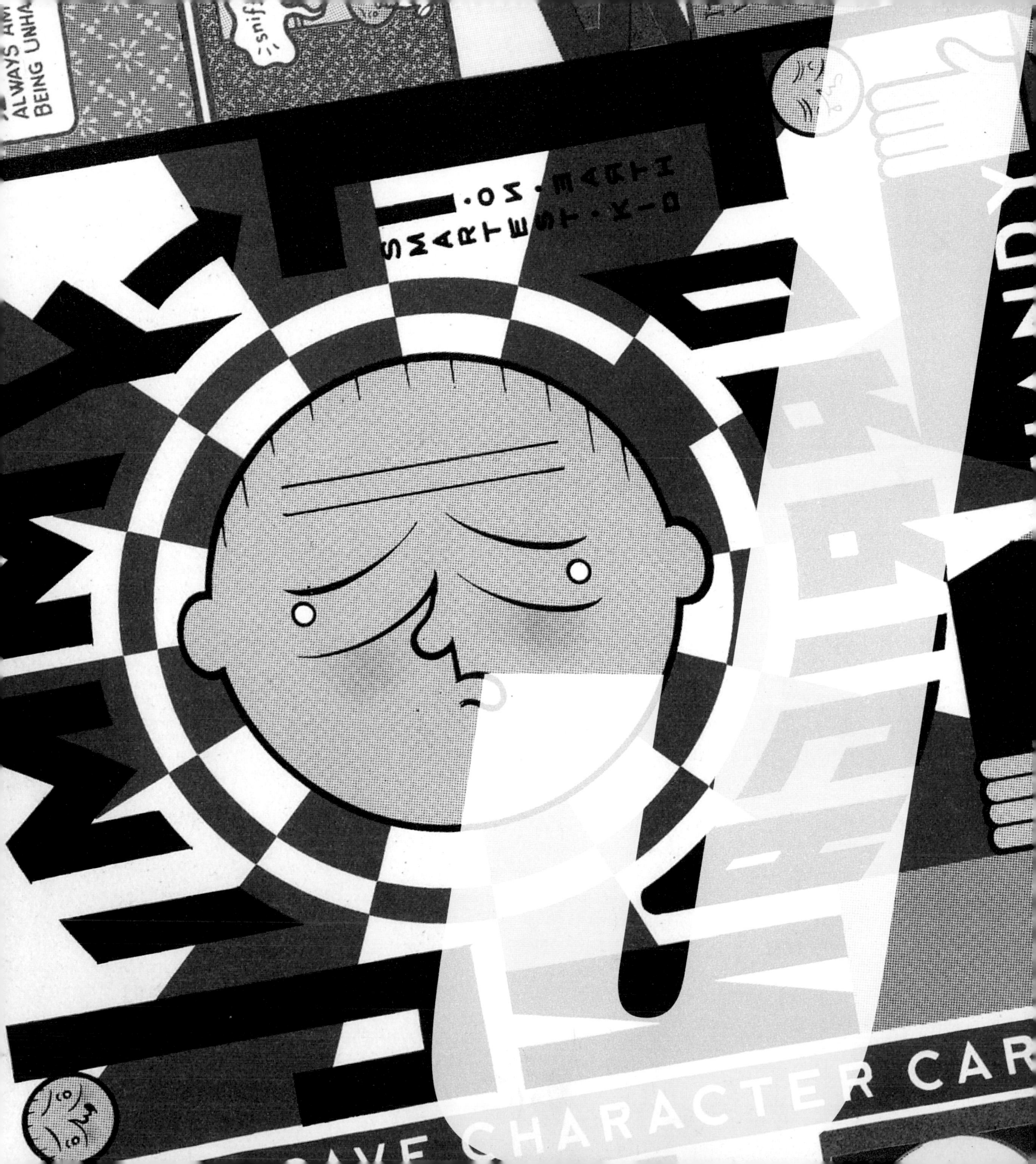
snif
SMARTEST KID ON EARTH
CHARACTER

JAFFEE, AL (1921–)

■ While some cartoonists in the course of long careers in comics have drawn both humorous and serious features, Jaffee has remained staunchly silly for well over a half century. He broke into the field in the early 1940s, drawing a superhero spoof titled *Inferior Man* for *Military Comics*. He also found work at Timely, contributing *Squat Car Squad* to *Joker Comics* and *Ziggy Pig and Silly Seal* to *Krazy Comics*.

After service in the air force during World War II, he returned to Timely to labor on such diverse titles as *Patsy Walker* and *Super Rabbit*. He was an early recruit to *Mad* and is still a contributor. He also drew for *Humbug* and *Trump*.

JIMMY CORRIGAN

■ See WARE, CHRIS.

JOHN CARTER OF MARS

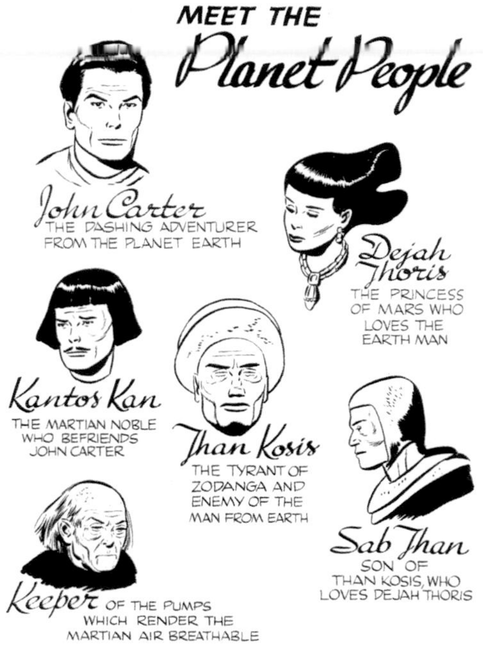
MEET THE
Planet People
John Carter
THE DASHING ADVENTURER FROM THE PLANET EARTH
Dejah Thoris
THE PRINCESS OF MARS WHO LOVES THE EARTH MAN
Kantos Kan
THE MARTIAN NOBLE WHO BEFRIENDS JOHN CARTER
Than Kosis
THE TYRANT OF ZODANGA AND ENEMY OF THE MAN FROM EARTH
Sab Than
SON OF THAN KOSIS, WHO LOVES DEJAH THORIS
Keeper OF THE PUMPS WHICH RENDER THE MARTIAN AIR BREATHABLE

■ John Carter had been swashbuckling on the red planet for nearly three decades before he ever set foot in a comic book. Another creation of Edgar Rice Burroughs, Carter was introduced in the pages of the pulpfiction magazine *All-Story* early in 1912. That first serial was reprinted in book form as *A Princess of Mars* in 1917. Nine other novels appeared over the next twenty-some years, after first being serialized in such pulps as *Blue Book*, *Argosy*, and *Amazing Stories*. Finally in 1939, *John Carter of Mars* appeared as a backup feature in *The Funnies*.

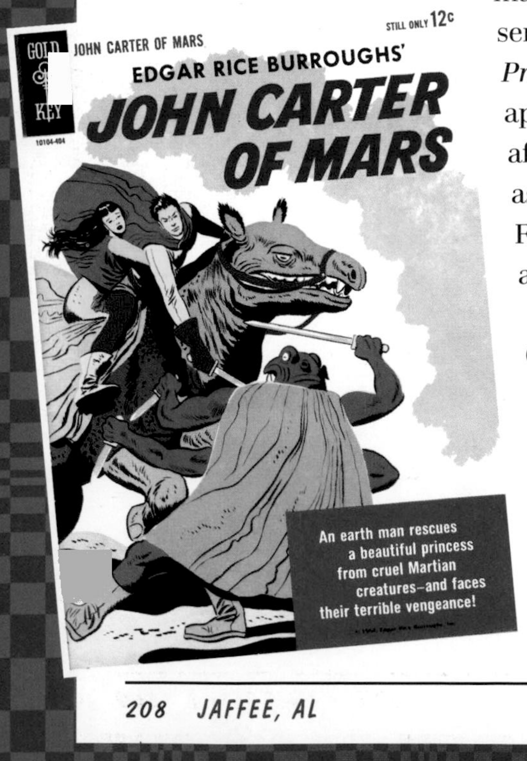
GOLD KEY
JOHN CARTER OF MARS
STILL ONLY 12¢
EDGAR RICE BURROUGHS'
JOHN CARTER OF MARS
An earth man rescues a beautiful princess from cruel Martian creatures—and faces their terrible vengeance!

Three episodes were drawn by Jim Gary before ERB's artist son John Coleman Burroughs took over. Based somewhat loosely on *A Princess of Mars*, the four- and eight-page comic-book chapters retained the senior Burroughs's highly unscientific take on the nature of Mars, a planet the locals in his tales called Barsoom. There was a breathable atmosphere on his Mars as well as canals. There was a race of four-armed giant green warriors and another race who more or less resembled earth folks. There were also such large Martian animals as woolas and calots. Transferred to the red planet in a mystical manner, without benefit of spaceship, Carter fell in love with a beautiful princess with the unromantic name of Dejah Thoris and found himself in the thick of intrigues, violence, and considerable swordplay.

John Carter's adventures ended in #56 (June 1941). At about the same time a Sunday page, also drawn by John Coleman Burroughs, began in a small number of newspapers. Nowhere near as popular as *Tarzan*, it ceased early in 1943. Dell brought the swordsman of Mars back to comic books in 1952, publishing three issues of *John Carter of Mars* with art by regular *Tarzan* comic-book artist Jesse Marsh. These were reprinted under the Gold Key colophon in 1964.

Next came a short-lived DC version in 1972 in *Weird Worlds*. Marvel gave Barsoom a try in 1977 with *John Carter, Warlord of Mars*. This title, with art by Gil Kane initially, lasted a bit over two years. John Carter, Dejah Thoris, and the unique flora and fauna of Barsoom have been absent from comics ever since.

JOHNNY THUNDER: I

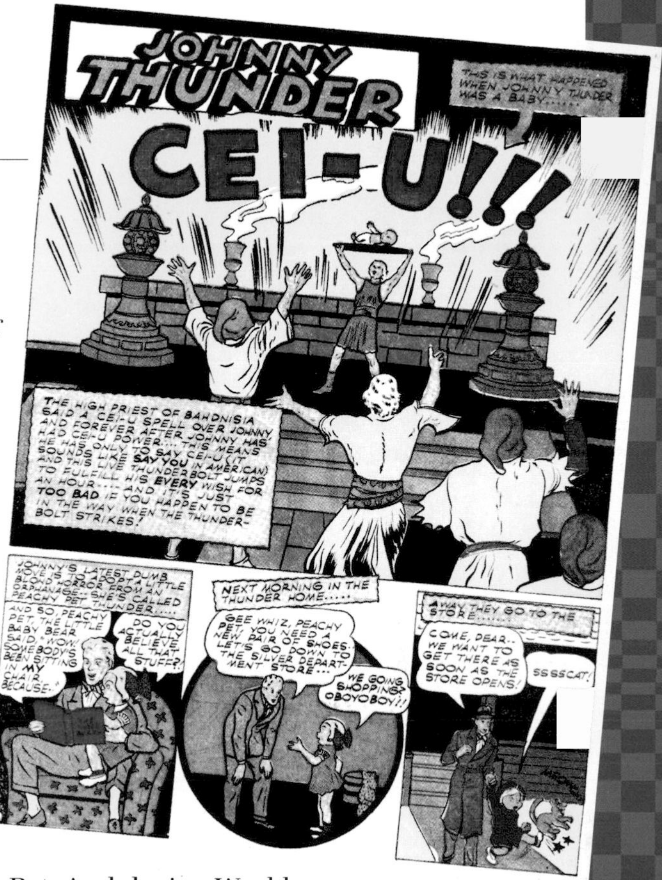
JOHNNY THUNDER
THIS IS WHAT HAPPENED WHEN JOHNNY THUNDER WAS A BABY......
CEI-U!!!
THE HIGH PRIEST OF BAHDNISIA SAID A CEI-U SPELL OVER JOHNNY AND FOREVER AFTER JOHNNY HAS HAD CEI-U POWER.... THIS MEANS HE HAS ONLY TO SAY CEI-U (IT SOUNDS LIKE SAY YOU IN AMERICAN) AND THIS LIVE THUNDERBOLT JUMPS TO FULFILL HIS EVERY WISH FOR AN HOUR.... AND IT'S JUST TOO BAD IF YOU HAPPEN TO BE IN THE WAY WHEN THE THUNDER-BOLT STRIKES!
JOHNNY'S LATEST DUMB MOVE IS TO ADOPT A LITTLE BLOND HORROR FROM AN ORPHANAGE.. SHE'S CALLED PEACHY PET THUNDER.....
AND SO, PEACHY PET, THE LITTLE BABY BEAR SAID, "WOW! SOMEBODY'S BEEN SITTING IN MY CHAIR BECAUSE-"
DO YOU ACTUALLY BELIEVE ALL THAT STUFF?
NEXT MORNING IN THE THUNDER HOME.....
GEE WHIZ, PEACHY PET, YOU NEED A NEW PAIR OF SHOES.. LET'S GO DOWN TO THE SILVER DEPARTMENT STORE...
WE GOING SHOPPING? OBOYOBOY!!
AWAY THEY GO TO THE STORE........
COME, DEAR.. WE WANT TO GET THERE AS SOON AS THE STORE OPENS!
SSSSCAT!

■ Destined to provide comic relief for decades to come, Johnny Thunder was introduced in *Flash Comics* #1 (January 1940). The magazine was also the home of such serious heroes as the Flash, Hawkman, and the Whip.

As presented by writer John Wentworth and artist Stan Aschmeier (under his pen name Stan Josephs), Johnny Thunder—called Johnny Thunderbolt in early issues—was an inept but likeable blond young man who just happened to have a pet thunderbolt that could perform all sorts of magic. This was due to a series of mystical happenings in Johnny's youth. Whenever he uttered "Say you," a phonetic approximation of the word of power "Cei-u," the humanoid thunderbolt would appear, genie-like, make a few snide remarks, and then do Johnny's bidding for one hour. Being dense, it took Johnny quite awhile to realize that "Say you" was a magic phrase and could be used to summon his private electrical genie whenever he needed him.

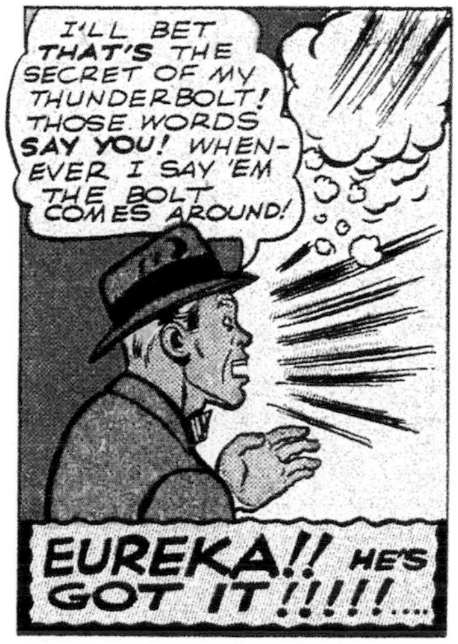
I'LL BET THAT'S THE SECRET OF MY THUNDERBOLT! THOSE WORDS SAY YOU! WHEN-EVER I SAY 'EM THE BOLT COMES AROUND!
EUREKA!! HE'S GOT IT!!!!!...

Wentworth had a good deal of fun with his concept, making fun of superheroes, G-Men, urban life, and assorted other targets. He eventually also burdened Johnny with a mischievous ward, a little girl known as Peachy Pet. And during World War II Johnny served as a very inept sailor. A hanger-on at the early meetings of the Justice Society over in *All Star Comics*, Johnny was begrudgingly initiated in #6. His thunderbolt proved more helpful to the organization than he ever was.

After Wentworth was replaced by the humorless Robert Kanigher, Johnny became much less amusing. He had a fateful meeting with a mysterious lady known as the Black Canary, and before he knew it she took over his strip and he was gone from *Flash Comics*. Not to worry. DC has brought Johnny back at various times over the years, whenever they have need for an affable bumbler.

JOHNNY THUNDER: II

■ A herd of cowboys began invading comic books in the late 1940s. Publishers and editors, seeking replacements for their fading supermen, looked to the West. DC, getting ready to unload the entire cast of *All-American Comics*, introduced a new and different Johnny Thunder to the magazine in #100 (August 1948). "The roar of thunder and the flash of lightning signal the entrance of the sensational new WESTERN fighting team JOHNNY THUNDER and BLACK LIGHTNING!" proclaimed a cover blurb. The dark-haired Johnny, guns ablaze, was seen riding his great white stallion. The horse got his name from a black zigzag mark on his forehead. Alex Toth was the artist, and the writer was Robert Kanigher, who'd seen the original Johnny Thunder to his final rest.

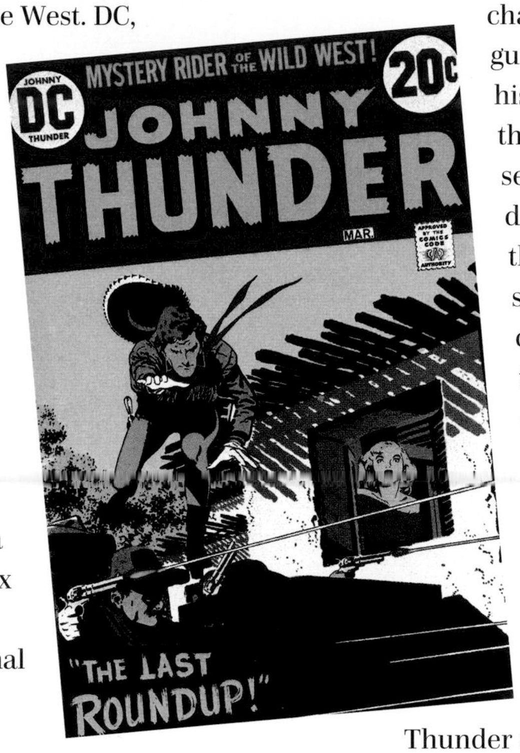
MYSTERY RIDER OF THE WILD WEST!
20¢
JOHNNY
DC
THUNDER
JOHNNY
THUNDER
MAR.
APPROVED BY THE COMICS CODE AUTHORITY
"THE LAST ROUNDUP!"

Like many of his superhuman predecessors, Johnny had a dual identity. By day he was mild-mannered blond schoolteacher John Tane, and a disappointment to his tough sheriff father. When trouble arose, he took off his glasses, quickly dyed his hair black, changed his clothes, strapped on his six-guns, went to the place where he kept his horse hidden, and rushed forth as the avenging Johnny Thunder. On several occasions he aided his aging dad. Comics readers accepted the fact that if Clark Kent could fool Lois Lane simply by taking off his glasses, Johnny could certainly fox his own father by taking off his glasses *and* changing the color of his hair.

With issue #103 (November 1948) the magazine became *All-American Western* with the new Westernized Johnny Thunder as its star. Then in 1952 there came another drastic change and the new title was *All-American Men of War*. Johnny Thunder and Black Lightning moseyed over to *All-Star Western*, remaining there until 1961. Gil Kane drew many of their later exploits.

JOKER COMICS

■ *Joker Comics* was one of the several humor titles Timely added to its list in 1942, along with *Comedy Comics* and *Krazy Komics*. The more illustrious contributors included Basil Wolverton, Harvey Kurtzman, and Al Jaffee. The first issue had a cover date of April 1942.

The magazine introduced Wolverton's peerless Powerhouse Pepper, the bald superhero, to the world. In addition there was Jaffee's screwball police procedural, *Squat Car Squad*. The feature offered not only burlesque accounts of crime and detection but appearances by the artist himself, publisher Martin Goodman, and others of the convivial staff. *Snoopy and Dr. Nutzy* was a detective spoof, and *Rolly & Solly* kidded the army. Both changed artists regularly. Among the other features were *Eustis Hayseed, E. Radicate De Bugs, Tommy Gunz*, and *Dippy Diplomat. Tessie the Typist* commenced in the second issue, initially offering a series of one-page office gags. Tessie was a pretty blonde and soon was being featured on most of the covers. Harvey Kurtzman, who's thus far in his comic-book career drawn mostly superheroes, started doing a strange, funny, and somewhat surrealistic filler page called *Hey Look* in the spring of 1946.

In the years after World War II, pretty girl characters began to dominate the lineup. In addition to Tessie, there were Millie the Model, Nellie the Nurse, Hedy of Hollywood, Patty Pinup, and Daisy. The humor to be found in the stories about these young women wasn't screwball or slapstick but closer to what would now be labeled sitcom. A true loon like Powerhouse Pepper was increasingly out of place in such surroundings and after issue #31, in the spring of 1948, he was seen there no more.

Joker, with the funny ladies in charge, continued until the summer of 1950. As an omen of what was going to happen to comic books in the early years of the upcoming decade, *Joker Comics* became *Adventures in*

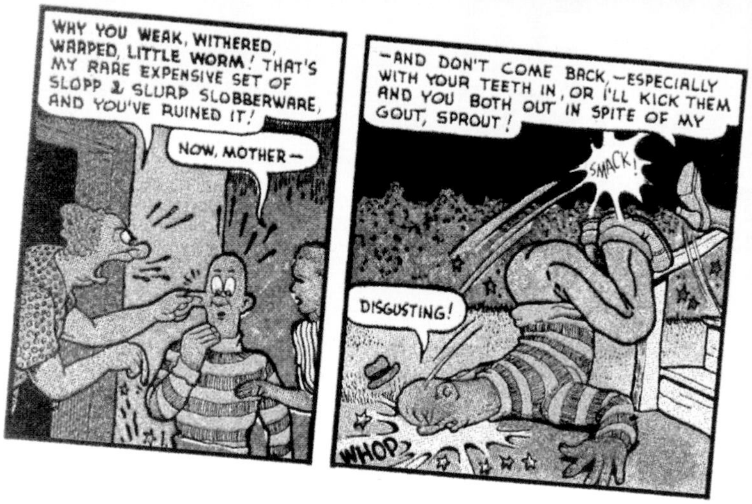
WHY YOU WEAK, WITHERED, WRAPPED, LITTLE WORM! THAT'S MY RARE EXPENSIVE SET OF SLOPP & SLURP SLOBBERWARE, AND YOU'VE RUINED IT!
NOW, MOTHER—
—AND DON'T COME BACK,—ESPECIALLY WITH YOUR TEETH IN, OR I'LL KICK THEM AND YOU BOTH OUT IN SPITE OF MY GOUT, SPROUT!
SMACK!
DISGUSTING!
WHOP

Terror with its forty-third issue. Among the early "tales of strange suspense" that it offered were "The Thing in the Cave," "The Torture Room," and "Spawn of the Vampire."

Joker Comics is not to be confused with the assorted latter-day comic books devoted to Batman's favorite foe, the Joker.

JOURNEY INTO MYSTERY

■ Eventually the birthplace of one of Marvel's enduring superheroes, *Journey into Mystery* was initially one of the many horror comics crowding the newsstands in the early 1950s. Each issue was an anthology of weird tales and the early covers, many of them by Bill Everett, were rich with walking skeletons, walking corpses, and brutal monsters. In 1955, after the Comics Code Authority was set up, the covers and contents became much tamer. Among the artists contributing to *Journey* were, besides Everett, Joe Maneely, Russ Heath, Steve Ditko, Jerry Robinson, George Tuska, and Bernard Krigstein.

Things changed with issue #83 (August 1961), when Stan Lee and Jack Kirby introduced Thor. The helmeted hero was seen on the cover using his hammer against green monsters while a blurb proclaimed, "The Most Exciting Super-Hero of All Time!" From that moment on the Mighty Thor was the leading man in *Journey into Mystery.* With #126 (March 1966) the comic book changed its name to *Thor,* continuing as such until #502 (September 1996). The *Journey into Mystery* title returned until the magazine closed down with #521 (June 1998). A new Thor title began the following month. He'd been absent from the closing issue of *Journey*, replaced by the likes of the Black Widow and Shang-Chi.

NEW YORK WORLD'S FAIR Special EDITION
JUMBO COMICS
FRANK BUCK'S JUNGLELAND
THE CHILDREN'S VILLAGE
FUN AT THE FAIR, etc.
10¢ Bigger & Better Funnies 10¢
WORLD OF TOMORROW
WILTON OF THE WEST
BIG PAGES–BIG PICTURES–BIG TYPE–EASY TO READ

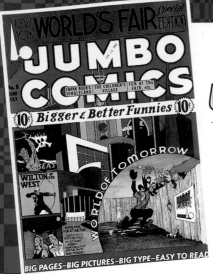

JUMBO COMICS

■ *Jumbo* introduced Sheena the Queen of the Jungle to American comics in the summer of 1938. The magazine was named after an elephant because it was larger than any of the other comic books that had begun showing up on the newsstands. It was 10½" wide and 14½" high. The pages had to be that big in order to reuse the printing plates from *Wags*, an overseas weekly tabloid packaged by the fledgling Will Eisner and Jerry Iger shop. The salesman of the team, Iger had convinced pulp publisher Fiction House to give comics a try. Since the plates printed in black-and-white, Iger suggested various shades of pastel paper to give *Jumbo Comics* some color.

Sheena was written by Eisner, drawn by Mort Meskin. In later years, Iger was fond of taking sole credit for inventing the jungle girl, handing out some preposterous explanations for how he arrived at her name. Eisner has explained, much more logically, that he was inspired by the name of H. Rider Haggard's *She*. Other recycled *Wags* features included Eisner's pirate strip, *Hawks of the Seas, The Count of Monte Cristo* by Jack Kirby under the alias Jack Curtis, *The Hunchback of Notre Dame* by Dick Briefer, *The Diary of Dr. Hayward* also by Kirby, and *Peter Pupp*, a Disneyesque strip by Bob Kane, still some months away from *Batman*. In later issues Lou Fine took over all the Kirby features.

The ninth issue was smaller and in full color and the tenth was standard comic-book size. Bob Powell took over *Sheena*, a red-suited superhero named Lightning was added, and Lou Fine moved on. Sheena's costume was modified over the months, becoming ever skimpier and turning to leopard skin. From the seventeenth issue (July 1940) onward, the jungle queen was featured on every cover—drawn by Dan Zolnerowich, Nick Cardy, Artie Saaf, Joe Doolin, and others. When Eisner and Iger ended their partnership in 1940, Iger's shop held on to the *Jumbo* account. Iger's staff contained many practitioners of Good Girl Art.

Among the new features were *The Ghost Gallery*, drawn by Alex Blum and then Bob Hebberd, with the scripts credited to the ghost hunter star of the strip, Drew Murdoch. A later addition was *Skygirl*, a prime example of the Good Girl school and drawn by one of its masters, Matt Baker. Robert Webb drew *Sheena* after Powell's departure. The jungle girl reigned in *Jumbo* until #167 (March 1953), the final issue.

ACTION ADVENTURE MYSTERY
JUMBO COMICS
NOV No. 57
SHEENA JUNGLE QUEEN
"ARENA OF THE BEASTS"
10¢

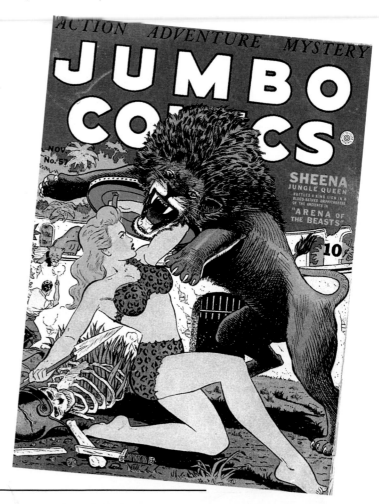

JUNGLE JIM

DELL
ALL BRAND-NEW STORIES
JUNGLE JIM
10¢

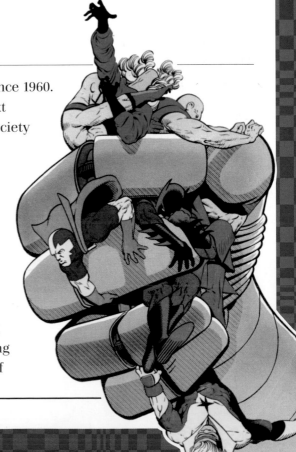

■ Jungle Jim Bradley, who influenced a great many comic-book soldiers of fortune and big-game hunters, began life in the Sunday funnies in January of 1934. He appeared as the topper above the *Flash Gordon* page. Alex Raymond, another influential fellow, drew both features, and they were scripted, without credit, by former pulp-fiction editor Don Moore. Unlike most of his comic-book imitators—Congo Bill, Clip Carson et al—Jim worked not in Africa but in places like Malaya, Borneo, and Sumatra. He helped, along with the movies, to perpetuate the notion that jungle hunters wore pith helmets and riding breeches. He had a faithful turbaned sidekick named Kolu and a recurring lady friend named Lil. *Jungle Jim* became one of the many King Features strips reprinted in *Ace Comics* from 1937 onward.

Early in 1949, Standard introduced a *Jungle Jim* title that used original material. The artist was Paul Norris, who'd assumed the drawing of the Sunday page the previous year. An excellent artist, he had worked on both newspaper strips and comic books and was the cocreator of Aquaman. After ten issues, Standard dropped Jim from their roster. Then in 1954 Dell tried a Jungle Jim title, using such artists as Creig Flessel and Frank Thorne. That version made it through seventeen issues before ending in 1959. A decade later Charlton began a seven-issue run. Wally Wood was one of the artists.

The newspaper Jungle Jim ended his wanderings in the mid-fifties, but thanks to Charlton, Jim survived in comic books until the early seventies.

THE JUSTICE LEAGUE

■ The organization that succeeded the Justice Society, it's been functioning since 1960. After resurrecting the Flash and Green Lantern, DC editor Julius Schwartz next recaptured an entire team of superheroes from the past. Taking the Justice Society from the defunct *All Star Comics*, he rechristened it the Justice League. The membership roster now had the names Flash, Green Lantern, Aquaman, Wonder Woman, and Martian Manhunter on it. Gardner Fox, official scribe for the first gang, was brought back to write the book-length adventures of the new one. The team was introduced in *The Brave and the Bold* #28 (March 1960). Mike Sekowsky was the initial artist.

The Justice League apparently appealed not only to young readers but to older ones who were still nostalgic about *All Star*. After three tryout issues, the JLA was given its own magazine, titled *The Justice League of America*, in the autumn of 1960. It continued through #261 before shutting down in the spring of 1987. A new comic book, called simply *Justice League*, started up the following month. For a time it was called *Justice League International*, and in the spring of

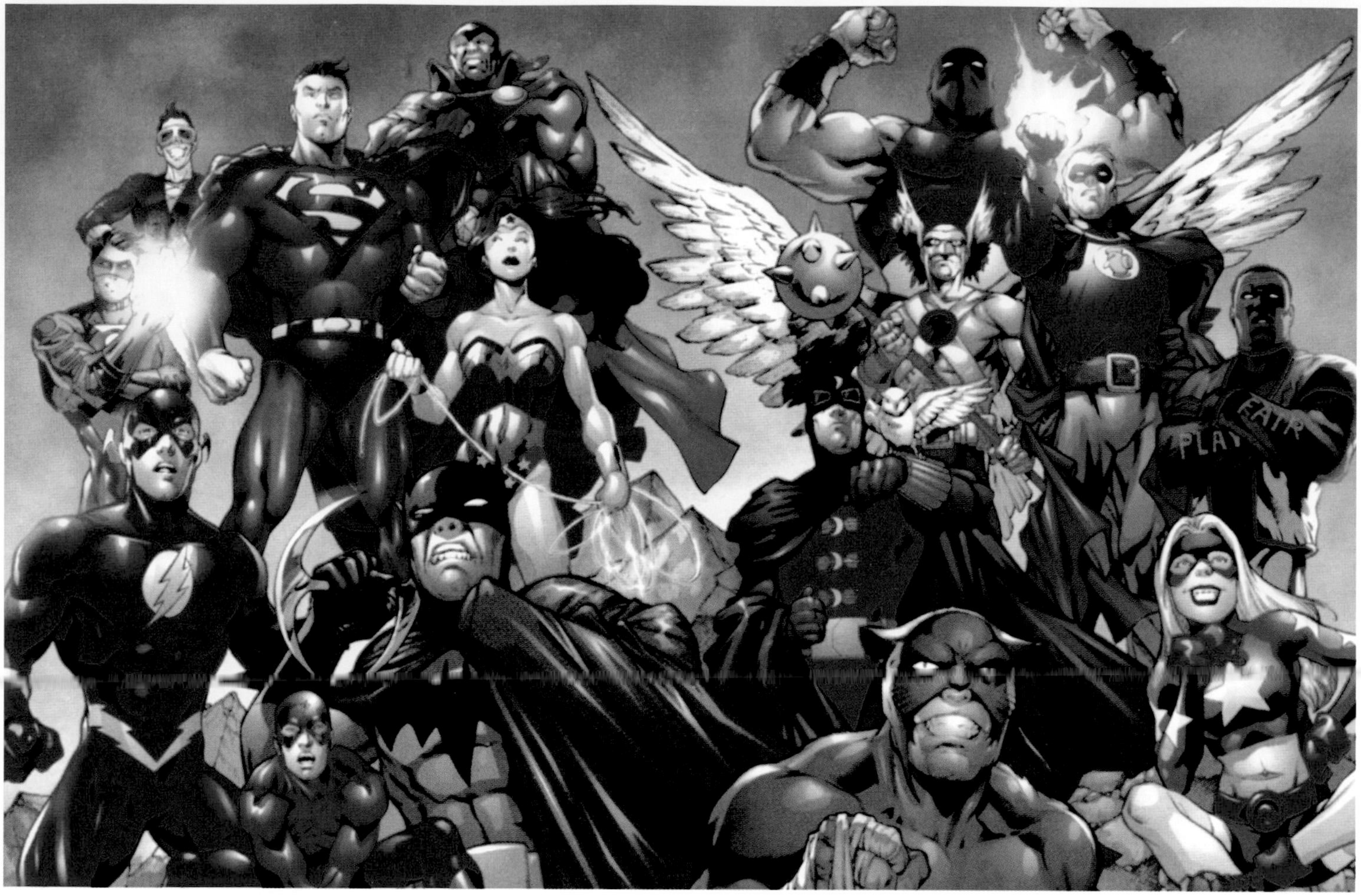
PLAY FAIR

1989 a separate magazine, *Justice League Europe*, was launched. The JLA has waxed and waned in the years since then. Like any organization it has experienced changes in personnel. Such characters as Batman, Green Arrow, Mr. Miracle, Blue Beetle, Black Canary, Firestorm, Captain Marvel, Elongated Man, Booster Gold, and Guy Gardner have all been card-carrying members.

With a fluctuating membership, the League appeared in assorted short-run series in the late 1990s. In 2003 came *Formerly Known as the Justice League* for a six-issue trial run. Included in the new group were Mary Marvel, Booster Gold, and the Blue Beetle.

JUSTICE SOCIETY OF AMERICA

■ See ALL STAR COMICS.

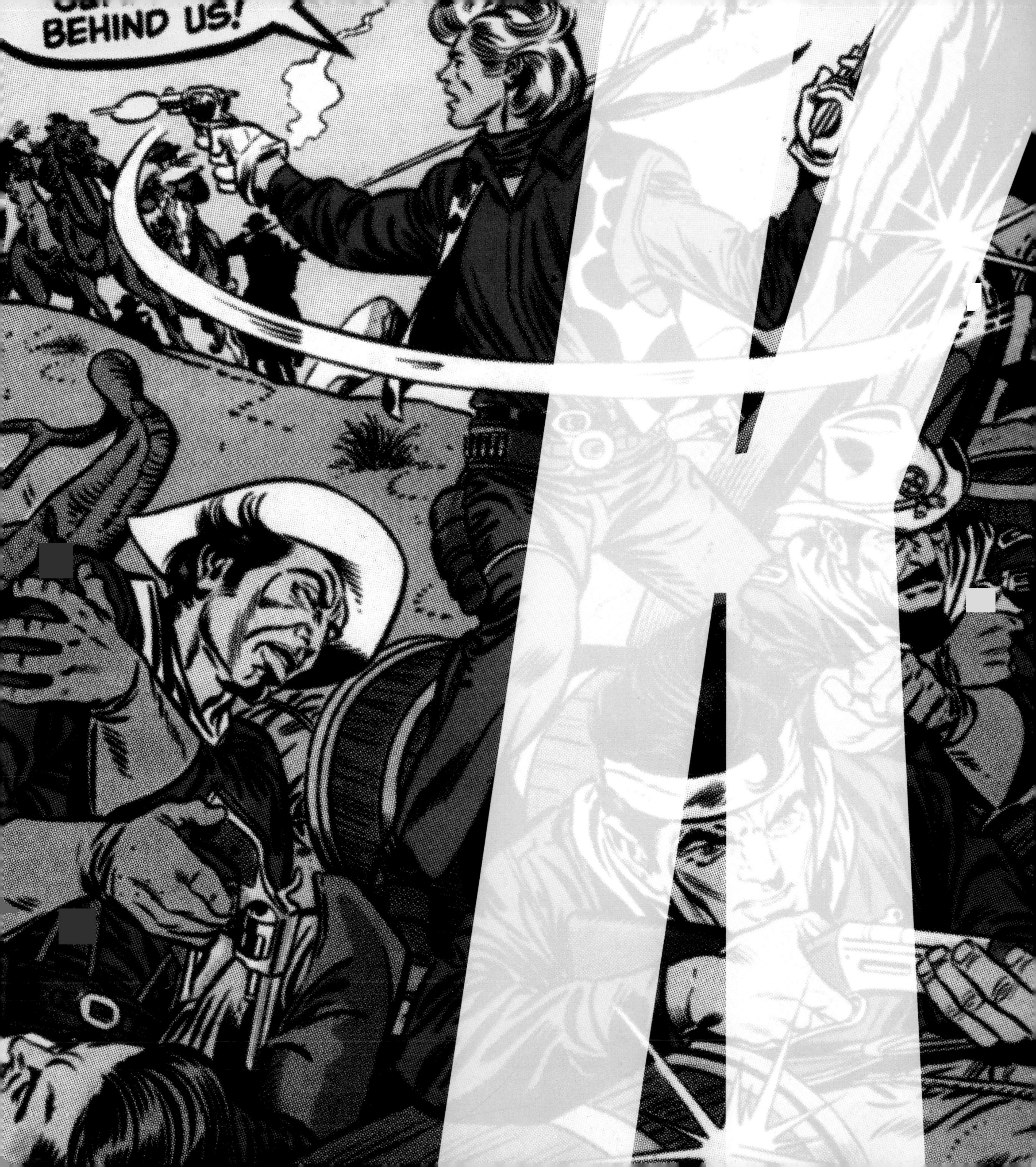
BEHIND US!

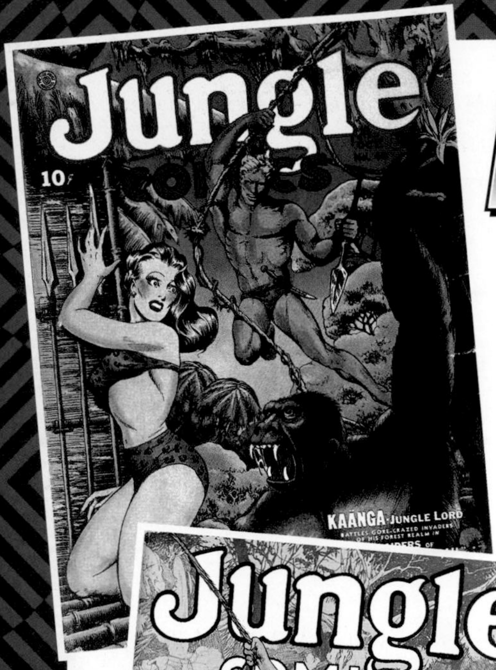
Jungle Comics
10¢
KAANGA-JUNGLE LORD

KAANGA

■ A highly successful Tarzan imitator, the blond lord of the jungle held forth in *Jungle Comics* from 1940 to 1954. Kaanga also appeared in twenty issues of his own magazine from 1949 to 1954. He was the product of the Eisner-Iger shop, the same outfit who'd invented Sheena a few years earlier.

Like many another jungleman, Kaanga was left an orphan when his explorer parents were killed. Whereas the orphaned Tarzan was raised by apes, Kaanga was raised by a strange jungle tribe of ape-men. In his first adventure he met Ann Mason, who'd just been orphaned when a notorious slave trader murdered her explorer father. Kaanga saved her, and Ann taught him English—"Tree, sky, you Kaanga, I Ann." By the fifth issue of *Jungle*, Ann was being referred to as the jungle lord's mate.

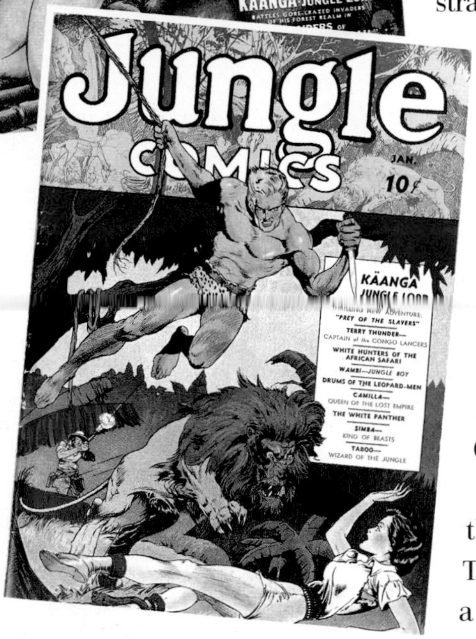
Jungle Comics
JAN.
10¢
KÄANGA JUNGLE LORD
"PREY OF THE SLAVERS"
TERRY THUNDER— CAPTAIN of the CONGO LANCERS
WHITE HUNTERS OF THE AFRICAN SAFARI
WAMBI—JUNGLE BOY
DRUMS OF THE LEOPARD-MEN
CAMILLA— QUEEN OF THE LOST EMPIRE
THE WHITE PANTHER
SIMBA— KING OF BEASTS
TABOO— WIZARD OF THE JUNGLE

While their adventures were standard jungle movie stuff, several first-rate artists drew them. Journeyman Alex Blum drew the initial story, followed by a fellow named Ken Jackson. But then George Tuska took over, and the look of the feature improved greatly. Others who drew Kaanga's adventures were Ruben Moreira, John Celardo, Reed Crandall, and Maurice Whitman. Kaanga appeared on every cover, usually seen in the act of saving Ann from lions, leopards, gorillas, rampaging natives, Nazis, ivory hunters, etc. Lou Fine, Will Eisner, Tuska, Celardo, Crandall, and others provided the cover art.

The jungle lord shared *Jungle Comics* with such wilderness denizens as Wambi the Jungle Boy, Capt. Terry Thunder of the Congo Lancers, Roy Lance—Explorer, Tabu—Wizard of the Jungle, Camilla (who wore a zebra-skin bikini), and Fantomah, a true mystery woman. There was also a strip starring a lion named Simba.

KALUTA, MICHAEL *(1947–)*

■ An artist who admits to being influenced by a range of people that includes Frank Frazetta, Moebius, Maxfield Parrish, Orson Welles, and Aubrey Beardsley is obviously going to produce some interesting stuff. Which is exactly what Kaluta has been doing since he turned professional in the late 1960s. In the decades since he's drawn, among many other features, *The Shadow, Starstruck, Carson of Venus, Conan, Vampirella,* and *Batman.*

More recently Kaluta has drawn a series of handsome art-deco covers for Vertigo's *The Books of Magic.* In addition he's done an impressive series of both color and black-and-white illustrations for a new edition of the science-fiction novel *Metropolis.* Also

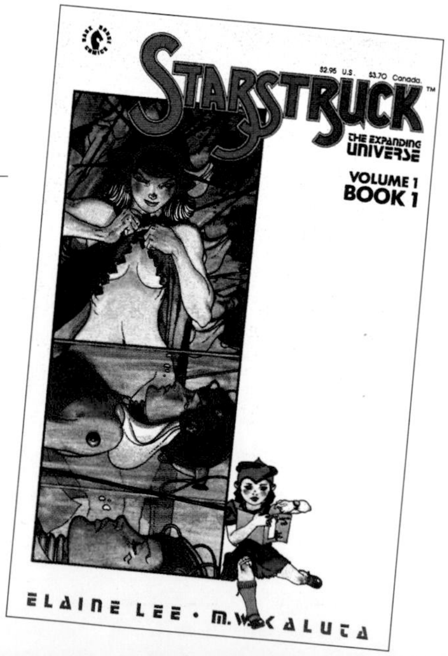
STARSTRUCK
$2.95 U.S. $3.70 Canada
THE EXPANDING UNIVERSE
VOLUME 1
BOOK 1
ELAINE LEE • M.W. KALUTA

active in providing art for the gaming field, he's illustrated a Dungeons and Dragons *Monster Manual* and designed cards for *Magic*. Vanguard Publications has issued *Echoes: The Drawings of Michael William Kaluta*, which provides a fine overview of his career.

Also an admirer of British film director Carol Reed, Kaluta's advice to aspiring artists includes the admonition, "You can't be a comic-book artist without seeing *The Third Man*. You've just got to see it . . . something that's going to change your perspective."

KAMANDI

■ His name being a possible nod to the Boy Commandos, the boy Kamandi had his origin in *Kamandi, the Last Boy on Earth* #1 (October–November 1972). Edited, written, and drawn by Jack Kirby, Kamandi's adventures took place in a future "after a natural disaster of CYCLOPEAN proportions had swept the world with deadly effect. . . . Man is no longer master of all he surveys! The once lowly beast has RISEN to power!"

The muscular blond teen Kamandi, clad in a pair of ragged shorts, teamed up with the surviving adult humans to battle the now upright and articulate gorilla-men, tiger-men, gopher-men, etc., who treat humans as humans once treated animals. When readers of the early issues pointed out a rather close resemblance between *Kamandi* and *The Planet of the Apes*, editor Steve Sherman replied that Kirby had used the "talking animals" notion before and, as a matter of fact, "has only seen about forty-five minutes of the first *Apes* movie and has yet to see the others."

Kirby remained with Kamandi, who like most of the Kirby heroes of the period looked like he was on steroids, until the fortieth issue. Dick Ayers replaced him and stayed until the final issue in the summer of 1978. Kamandi also showed up in *The Brave and the Bold* and in a 1993 miniseries.

KANE, BOB *(1916–1998)*

■ A cartoonist of average attainments, Bob Kane (formerly Robert Kahn) had the good fortune early in his career to become the cocreator of *Batman*. A protégé of Jerry Iger and a schoolmate of Will Eisner, Kane joined the Eisner-Iger shop in 1937. In those early days he limited himself to humorous drawing, turning out gag cartoons and filler pages.

He drew *Peter Pupp*, about a Mickey Mouse sort of dog, that ran first in the overseas weekly *Wags* and was later reprinted in *Jumbo Comics*. Kane also ghosted some of Iger's *Pee Wee* filler pages for *Famous Funnies*. Commencing in 1938 he turned out *Oscar the Gumshoe* for

"CLIP" CARSON
SOLDIER-OF-FORTUNE
BY BOB KANE

Detective Comics, *Professor Doolittle* for *Adventure Comics*, and *Ginger Snap* for *More Fun Comics*. Early that same year he attempted his first adventure strip. It began on *Adventure* #25, was called *Rusty and his Pals*, and was done in a cartoony style. Early the next year, at the suggestion of DC editor Vincent Sullivan, Kane tried a costumed hero. He and his writer friend Bill Finger came up with *Batman*.

BRING WHAT'S LEFT OF THE MOB DOWN TO-MORROW NIGHT. WE'VE GOT A JOB TO DO!
OKAY, BOSS!
LOCKING THE DOOR BEHIND THE DEPARTING HOODLUM, THE OLD MAN SHUFFLES TO THE REAR OF THE STORE, AND LIFTING A STRIP OF CARPET, EXPOSES A TRAP DOOR
DESCENDING TO A ROOM THAT SEEMS TO OVERFLOW WITH ART TREASURES, THE OLD MAN PROCEEDS TO PEEL OFF CLOTHING AND REMOVE MAKEUP...
...TO REVEAL A DEAD-WHITE, MASK-LIKE FACE ..WITH COLD, BLACK EYES... WHILE THE MOUTH IS DRAWN INTO A REPELLENTLY TERRIBLE SMILE ...THE SMILE OF....THE JOKER!
EVEN MY HOODLUMS DON'T SUSPECT THAT OLD WICKED REKOJ-MUSIC DEALER, IS - THE JOKER!
NOW, TO COMPLETE MY REVENGE UPON MY ENEMIES. TO DISTRICT ATTORNEY CARTER, I SEND THE RECORD OF MUSIC.... AND DEATH!!
WHILE THE BATMAN...
THAT FELLOW DIDN'T DISAPPEAR INTO THE THIN AIR.. WHICH MEANS, A SLIDING DOOR-- HIDDEN SOMEWHERE-- WHICH ALSO MEANS I'M GOING TO KEEP AN EYE ON THIS PLACE!
THE NEXT DAY, THE DISTRICT ATTORNEY PUZZLES OVER A RECORD SENT TO HIM ANONYMOUSLY...
PECULIAR! NO TITLE....OH WELL, I'LL PLAY IT ANYWAY
AS THE RECORD REVOLVES, A VIOLIN IS HEARD PLAYING STRANGE, UNEARTHLY MUSIC...
WHAT EERIE, FORBIDDING MUSIC THAT IS!

Kane had the good sense to realize his limitations as an artist, and before Batman, who debuted in *Detective Comics* #27 (May 1939), was a year old, he hired assistants. He was lucky enough to hire Jerry Robinson, a gifted young man, and the nearly as talented George Roussos. The three of them, aided with scripts by Finger and, for a few months, Gardner Fox, made *Batman* one of the most popular heroes of the day. The Dark Knight was soon also appearing in his own magazine as well as *World's Finest* and that created a demand for even more artists. Jack Burnley was one of them and Dick Sprang another, both of them working directly for DC. All of the ghosted material—Robinson had moved up to drawing entire stories as well—was signed Bob Kane. Later ghosts included Lew Schwartz, Sheldon Moldoff, and Win Mortimer. Fred Ray helped out on several covers in the early 1940s.

Bill Finger never did get a credit. Kane stopped being involved in the production of *Batman* material in 1968. Subsequently he worked in animation, inventing such characters as Courageous Cat and Cool McCool. Kane was involved in the *Batman* movies, particularly the one made during the heyday of the Adam West TV version. He also got a screen credit on the movies of the 1990s.

KANE, GIL *(1926–2000)*

■ Although his mature style made him one of the field's top professionals and has influenced many younger artists, Kane was never satisfied with it. Just about every day before starting on a job, he would devote an hour or two to sketching, practicing to improve. No matter how well a story or a cover turned out, he always had the suspicion that it could have been better.

In his long career Gil Kane drew a vast amount of material. In addition to designing and drawing the Silver Age Green Lantern, he drew *Hopalong Cassidy*, *Spider-Man*, *Johnny Thunder*, *Brain Boy*, *Batman*, *Undersea Agent*, *Daredevil*, *Teen Titans*, *Tomahawk*, *Conan*, *Superman*, *Ka-Zar*, *Blue Beetle*, and one issue of *Blue Devil*. He also illustrated DC's four-issue adaptation of Wagner's *Ring of the Nibelung*. In the 1970s and early 1980s, Kane drew two syndicated newspaper strips—*Star Hawks*, written by Ron Goulart, and *Tarzan*, with scripts by Archie Goodwin. In addition, Kane produced over seven hundred covers for Marvel and a considerable number for DC.

Born in Latvia, Kane grew up in Manhattan and entered the comics field while still in his teens. He freelanced for MLJ, assisted Joe Simon and Jack Kirby, and worked in Bernard Baily's shop. Very early in his career he signed his real name, Eli Katz, to a few of his stories, but then began trying out pen names. For a time he was Gil Stack until he finally settled on Gil Kane. Much of his early work wasn't that good. "I think that my triumph was that I was lousy early on," he once explained, "and it wasn't until I really started to work out systems, to really question the work" that it improved.

He first worked for DC in 1947, drawing *Wildcat* in *Sensation Comics* for editor Sheldon Mayer. Long a fan of the Western genre, Kane was pleased when DC assigned him such heroes as Hoppy and Johnny Thunder. He prided himself on his ability to draw animals, especially horses in action. In 1960, DC editor Julius Schwartz selected him to bring the Green Lantern back to life. Kane was also entrusted with the updated Atom a couple of years later. In the middle 1960s, he worked on *Thunder Agents* for the Tower comics line headed up by Harry Shorten. Kane's style changed drastically on this assignment, moving closer to its mature form. "I began to become interested in structure, placement," he said of that period. "Everything that had to do with understanding how things worked and what they looked like underneath." Kane also inked the Tower material, something he hadn't always been able to do at DC.

He shifted to Marvel in the 1970s, turning out stories and a great many of the covers. Back with DC in the 1980s, he worked again on the Atom and drew some of the Superman annuals. Moving to the Los Angeles area, Kane was hired by an animation outfit, Ruby-Spears Productions, to draw character designs and presentation pieces. Slowed down by illness in his final years, he was still able to turn out work. His last drawings, covers for *Legends of the DC Universe*, appeared the year of his death.

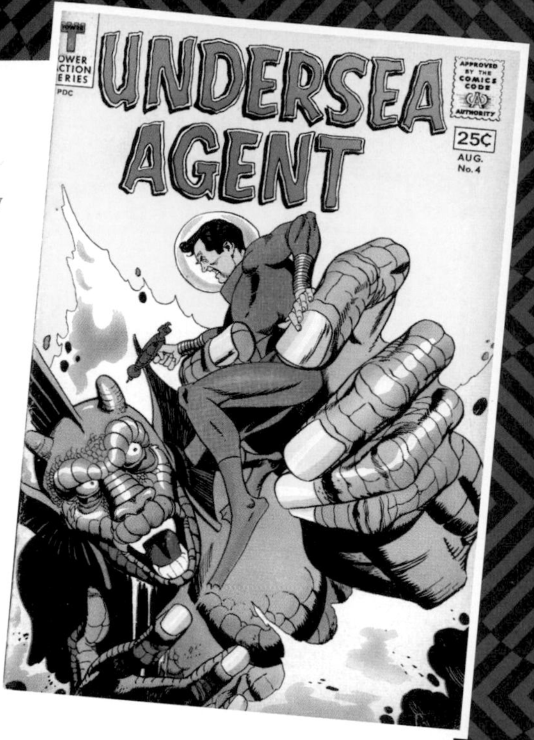
UNDERSEA AGENT
25¢
AUG. No. 4

KATY KEENE

■ Also known as the pinup queen, she was introduced in *Wilbur* #5 (Summer 1945), a publication of the Archie folks. Bill Woggon wrote and drew *Katy Keene* and, more importantly, invited his readership to submit dress designs for Katy's sizeable wardrobe. This gradually built up a following among the virtually untapped girl audience, and by the middle 1950s Katy was appearing in three separate titles of her own. She retired in 1961, but returned in 1983 and remained around for several years.

After her initial appearance in 1945, Katy was added to the lineups of *Laugh*, *Pep*, and *Suzie*. In 1949 she graduated to a magazine of her own. The book appeared just once that year, once in 1950, and twice in 1951. *Katy Keene* became a quarterly in 1952 and a bimonthly a year later. In 1955 two more titles appeared: *Katy Keene Fashion Book Magazine* and a twenty-five-cent comic called *Katy Keen Pin-Up Parade.*

Although the largest part of her audience was composed of teens and preteens, Katy wasn't a teenager. She was a full-grown young woman who worked first as a model and later as a Hollywood starlet. Apparently just about every girl in America goes through a phase where she wants to be a model or a fashion designer. Katy, whose life was taken up mostly with modeling, posing, and dating, appealed to an audience that had been unmoved by supermen or funny animals. Added reader involvement was ensured by Katy's mischievous little sister, Sis, a pigtailed troublemaker who acted as Katy's accomplice, conscience, and cheerleader. Katy's boyfriends included boxer K.O. Kelly, millionaire playboy Rudy Van Ronson, and movie idol Errol Swoon.

THE KATZENJAMMER KIDS

■ Created by cartoonist Rudolph Dirks, Hans and Fritz Katzenjammer began their mischievous, iconoclastic ways at the end of the nineteenth century in a newspaper Sunday page syndicated by William Randolph Hearst. Their endless assaults on the Captain, the Inspector, and society in general were reprinted in various types of comic books from early in the twentieth century onward. In the 1930s, when the modern type of comic book came into being, Hans and Fritz continued their explosive antics in *Tip Top Comics*, *Ace Comics*, *Comics on Parade*, and titles of their own. By that time, due to an earlier legal hassle, there had long been two different versions of the Kids' Sunday page. Dirks had left Hearst in the second decade of the century to draw *The Captain and the Kids* for Joseph Pulitzer, and Hearst hired Harold Knerr, another excellent cartoonist, to carry on *The Katzenjammer Kids*.

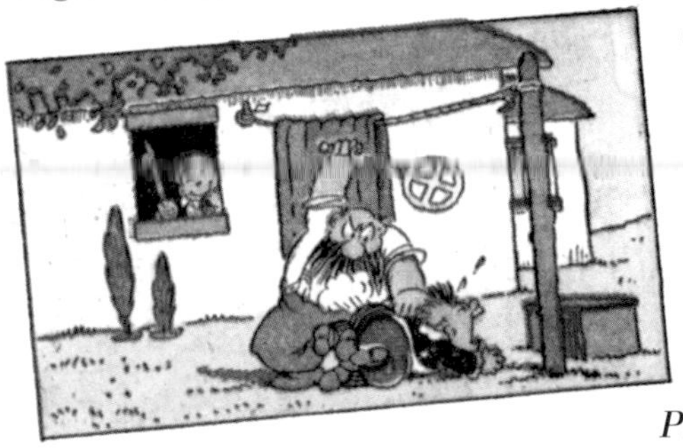

Hans was the dark-haired one, his brother Fritz the blond. Dirks worked with a limited group of performers. There was the plump, forgiving Mama, the two hyperactive boys, and then the Captain, a bewhiskered seadog who became not only a perennial houseguest but the brothers' favorite and most frequent target. The next favored target was the short, white-bearded Inspector, once a sort of truant officer. He also became a permanent part of the household and a perfect foil for Hans and Fritz. The brothers were not above, particularly in their early days, playing violent pranks on each other. As the Captain once explained, while spanking the pair, "One iss just as bad as both der other ones!" Although a spanking or a thrashing was their ultimate fate in a majority of the Katzie pages, corporal punishment never deterred the boys. They remained inventive and unflagging anarchists, intent on bedeviling and deflating established authority as personified by the Captain, the Inspector, and assorted pompous and self-important figures who chanced to cross their path. In the H. H. Knerr version, the kids' names got switched and Fritz was the one with dark hair and Hans the blond. This didn't seem to bother anybody.

Samplings of the Dirks Sunday pages began to be reprinted, usually in cardboard-covered books measuring 10" by 15" in 1902. Usually in full color, over a half dozen different compilations were issued by 1908. After a hiatus came a Katzenjammer one-shot in 1921. United Feature Syndicate, who'd taken over the distribution of *The Captain and the Kids* in the early 1930s, launched *Tip Top Comics* in 1936 and included several pages of reprints in the contents. Two years later they introduced *Comics on Parade*, wherein were included reprints of *The Captain and the Kids* daily strip (ghosted by Bernard Dibble).

Hearst's King Features, in collaboration with the David McKay publishing outfit, also ventured into comic books at about the same time. Knerr's *The Katzenjammer Kids* was one of the reprints in *Ace Comics*, which debuted in 1937. Brand-new Hans and Fritz material, drawn especially for comic books, began appearing in 1947 in McKay's *Katzenjammer* title. When Dell took over *Tip Top* in the late 1950s, original *Captain and the Kids* stories were used. Cartoonist Pete Wells worked on both versions.

By the early sixties Hans and Fritz, in all forms, were gone from American comic books. United killed their newspaper version, then drawn by Dirks's son John, in the late seventies. But King has kept the dynamic duo going as a Sunday page, seen mostly in Europe and drawn by Hy Eisman.

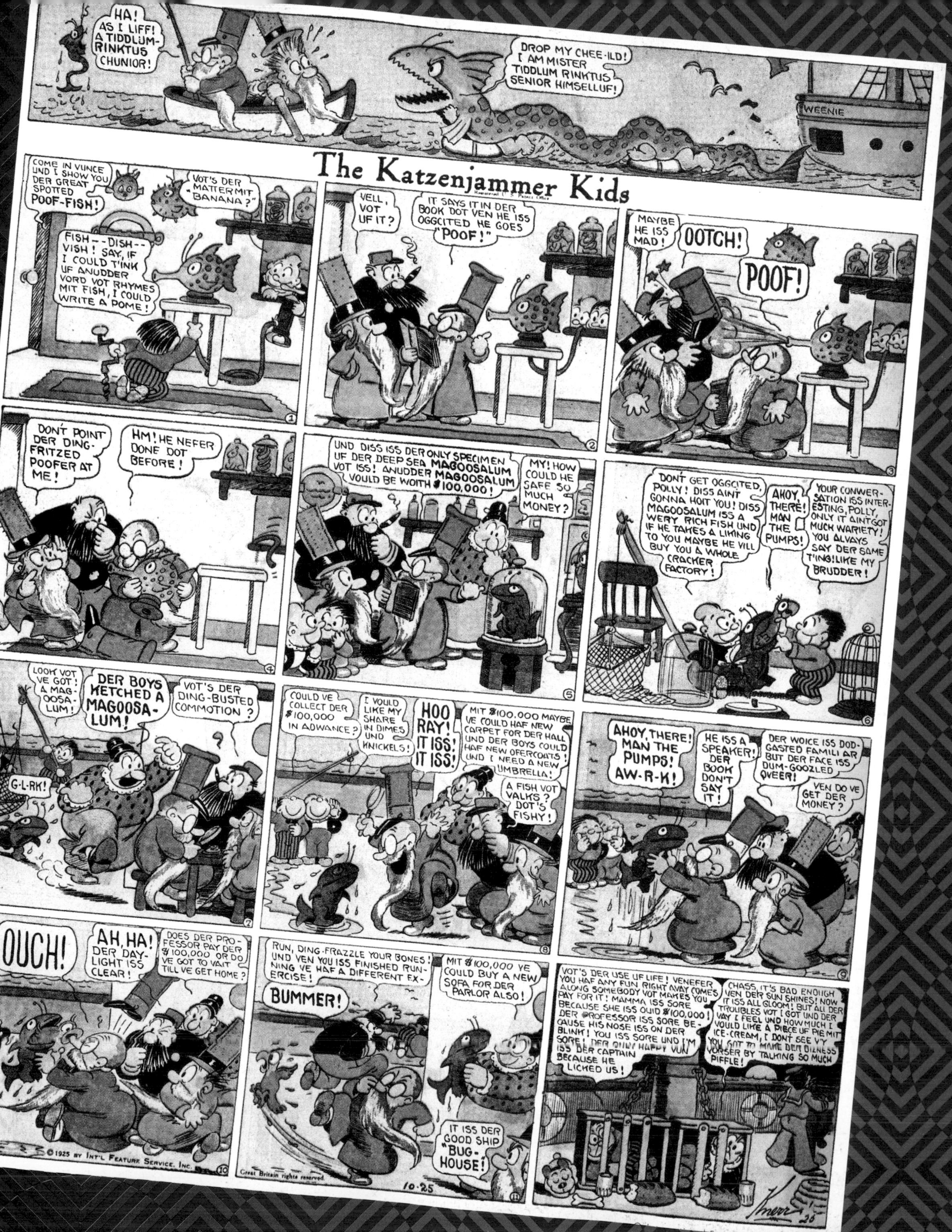
HA! AS I LIFF! A TIDDLUM-RINKTUS CHUNIOR!
DROP MY CHEE-ILD! I AM MISTER TIDDLUM RINKTUS SENIOR HIMSELLUF!
WEENIE
The Katzenjammer Kids
COME IN VUNCE UND I SHOW YOU DER GREAT SPOTTED POOF-FISH!
VOT'S DER MATTER MIT BANANA?
FISH--DISH--VISH! SAY, IF I COULD T'INK UF ANUDDER VORD VOT RHYMES MIT FISH, I COULD WRITE A POME!
VELL, VOT UF IT?
IT SAYS IT IN DER BOOK DOT VEN HE ISS OGGCITED HE GOES "POOF!"
MAYBE HE ISS MAD!
OOTCH!
POOF!
DON'T POINT DER DING-FRITZED POOFER AT ME!
HM! HE NEFER DONE DOT BEFORE!
UND DISS ISS DER ONLY SPECIMEN UF DER DEEP SEA MAGOOSALUM VOT ISS! ANUDDER MAGOOSALUM VOULD BE WOITH $100,000!
MY! HOW COULD HE SAFE SO MUCH MONEY?
DON'T GET OGGCITED, POLLY! DISS AINT GONNA HOIT YOU! DISS MAGOOSALUM ISS A WERY RICH FISH UND IF HE TAKES A LIKING TO YOU MAYBE HE VILL BUY YOU A WHOLE CRACKER FACTORY!
AHOY, THERE! MAN THE PUMPS!
YOUR CONWERSATION ISS INTERESTING, POLLY, ONLY IT AINT GOT MUCH WARIETY! YOU ALVAYS SAY DER SAME T'ING! LIKE MY BRUDDER!
LOOK VOT VE GOT! A MAGOOSALUM!
DER BOYS KETCHED A MAGOOSALUM!
VOT'S DER DING-BUSTED COMMOTION?
G-L-RK!
COULD VE COLLECT DER $100,000 IN ADWANCE?
I VOULD LIKE MY SHARE IN DIMES UND KNICKELS!
HOO RAY! IT ISS! IT ISS!
MIT $100,000 MAYBE VE COULD HAF NEW CARPET FOR DER HALL UND DER BOYS COULD HAF NEW OFERCOATS! UND I NEED A NEW UMBRELLA!
A FISH VOT VALKS? DOT'S FISHY!
AHOY, THERE! MAN THE PUMPS! AW-R-K!
HE ISS A SPEAKER! DER BOOK DON'T SAY IT!
DER WOICE ISS DODGASTED FAMILIAR BUT DER FACE ISS DUM-GOOZLED QVEER!
VEN DO VE GET DER MONEY?
OUCH!
AH, HA! DER DAYLIGHT ISS CLEAR!
DOES DER PROFESSOR PAY DER $100,000 OR DO VE GOT TO VAIT TILL VE GET HOME?
© 1925 BY INT'L FEATURE SERVICE, INC.
RUN, DING-FRAZZLE YOUR BONES! UND VEN YOU ISS FINISHED RUNNING VE HAF A DIFFERENT EXERCISE!
BUMMER!
MIT $100,000 VE COULD BUY A NEW SOFA FOR DER PARLOR ALSO!
IT ISS DER GOOD SHIP "BUG-HOUSE!"
Great Britain rights reserved.
10-25
VOT'S DER USE UF LIFE! VENEFER YOU HAF ANY FUN RIGHT AVAY COMES ALONG SOMEBODY VOT MAKES YOU PAY FOR IT! MAMMA ISS SORE BECAUSE SHE ISS OUID $100,000! DER PROFESSOR ISS SORE BECAUSE HIS NOSE ISS ON DER BLINK! YOU ISS SORE UND I'M SORE! DER ONLY HAPPY VUN ISS DER CAPTAIN BECAUSE HE LICKED US!
CHASS, IT'S BAD ENOUGH VEN DER SUN SHINES! NOW IT ISS ALL GLOOM! BUT ALL DER TROUBLES VOT I GOT UND DER VAY I FEEL UND HOW MUCH I VOULD LIKE A PIECE UF PIE MIT ICE-CREAM, I DON'T SEE V'Y YOU GOT TO MAKE DER BIZNESS VORSER BY TALKING SO MUCH PIFFLE!
Knerr 25

KAYE, STAN (1916–1967)

■ A talented humorous cartoonist, Kaye devoted the majority of his twenty years in comics to inking other artists' work. He was a regular inker on both *Superman* and *Batman*. For a few years in the 1940s, Kaye produced a considerable amount of first-rate comedy features for DC, most notably *Genius Jones*.

Born in Brooklyn and known as Stanley Kalinowski in his early years, he put in time as an assistant to magazine illustrator Dean Cornwall and later studied with illustrator Harvey Dunn. Kaye went to work in the offices of Detective Comics, Inc., in 1941. Before being picked to draw *Genius Jones*, which was scripted by Alfred Bester, Kaye did spot drawings for the two-page text stories. An admirer of Roy Crane's *Wash Tubbs* newspaper strip, Kaye developed a humor style with some affinities to that of Crane. His work had a distinctive look all its own and was obviously done by someone who was enjoying himself.

Genius, who first appeared in *Adventure Comics* in 1942, moved into *More Fun* in 1945 and was also a regular in *All Funny* from 1944 onward. Kaye drew all the covers featuring Genius Jones and quite a few others as well. He also drew *Drafty* in *World's Finest Comics* and *Hayfoot Henry* in *Action Comics*. An unusual strip, *Hayfoot Henry* dealt with a plump policeman, and everybody in it spoke in rhymed couplets.

By the late 1940s, Kaye was no longer drawing funny stuff but was working full-time as an inker. He collaborated a good deal with Wayne Boring on his *Superman* comic-book pages and the newspaper strip. Fired from DC in 1961, during the reign of Mort Weisinger, Kaye left the comics field and spent his last years in an office job in Racine, Wisconsin.

KA-ZAR

■ Ka-Zar was a jungle lord before Martin Goodman ever published a comic book. Borrowing all but one letter of his name from Tarzan, Ka-Zar appeared in a short-lived Goodman pulp magazine containing short novels that chronicled his African adventures. The stories were credited to Bob Byrd. When the Funnies, Inc., shop added Ka-Zar to the group of characters they put together for *Marvel Mystery Comics*, Ben Thompson, borrowing as best he could from *Tarzan* newspaper artist Burne Hogarth, drew the feature.

The first adventure repeated the origin story first told in the pulp. Little David Rand's parents crashed with him in the fierce African jungle. His mother died, and David and his somewhat crazed dad lived on in the wild to become a sort of father-and-son Tarzan team. They made friends with the animals and David—after learning lion lingo—became especially close to a mighty lion named Zar. After his father was murdered by an evil renegade emerald hunter, David more or less moved in with his lion chum and took to calling himself Ka-Zar, which means "brother of the lion." Billed as the "guardian of the wild Belgian Congo animals," he spent a good deal of his time shooing unscrupulous white hunters out of the jungle. Eventually he became more involved with current events and was "successful in destroying Nazi and Fascist fortresses in the jungle." Ka-Zar's jungle was a somewhat spartan place, and few if any women found their way into his domain. He took his leave after *Marvel* #27 (January 1942).

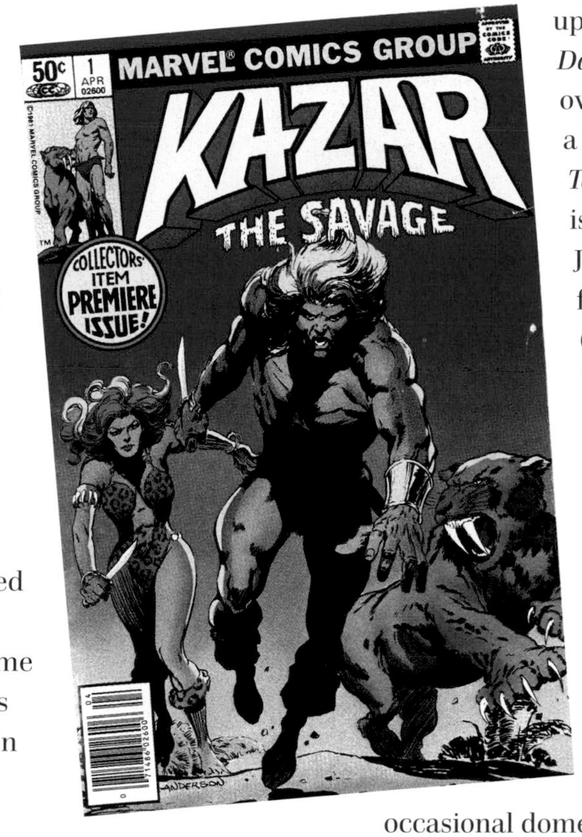
MARVEL COMICS GROUP
50¢
1 APR
KAZAR
THE SAVAGE
COLLECTORS' ITEM PREMIERE ISSUE!

A brand-new Ka-Zar, reinvented by Stan Less, first popped up as a guest in *X-Men* #10 in 1965. This time around, the Lord of the Jungle was actually a British lord named Kevin Plunder. He had grown up in a tropical kingdom known as the Savage Land that was said to lie "buried far beneath the frozen wastes of Antarctica." Like the earlier holder of the title, this Ka-Zar had blond shaggy hair and wore nothing more than an animal-skin loincloth. Unlike his predecessor, he spoke like the Johnny Weissmuller movie Tarzan.

After many guest shots and team-ups, including appearances in *Daredevil, Spider-Man*, and *The Hulk*, over the next few years Ka-Zar earned a permanent berth in *Astonishing Tales.* He appeared in the first twenty issues, beginning in 1970. Lee and Jack Kirby did the original stories, followed by Gerry Conway and Conan artist Barry Windsor-Smith. The jungle man moved into a comic titled *Ka-Zar* in 1974, where he first met up with the feisty Shanna O'Hara, a Sheena lookalike who operated as Shanna the She-Devil. Their initially antagonistic relationship blossomed into a romance and eventually they were married. Ka-Zar was benched in 1977, but returned along with his mate in 1984. In addition to an occasional domestic spat, his life was further complicated by his evil brother Parsival, who sullied the family name by doing vile deeds as a villain known as the Plunderer. He returned once more to the jungle in the late 1990s, with Andy Kubert doing the illustrating.

KEEN DETECTIVE FUNNIES

■ With surely one of the catchiest titles ever bestowed on a comic book, *Keen Detective Funnies* reached the stands in the summer of 1938. A Centaur Publication, the new magazine carried on the tradition of the earlier *Detective Picture Stories.* Both George Brenner's ubiquitous Clock and Bert Christman's Spinner were in the first issue and had also been in the earlier magazine. Drawing in his best imitation of Roy Crane, future *Superman* ghost Paul Lauretta also brought his soldier of fortune Rocky Baird from one title to the next. The rest of the material consisted of one-shot stories.

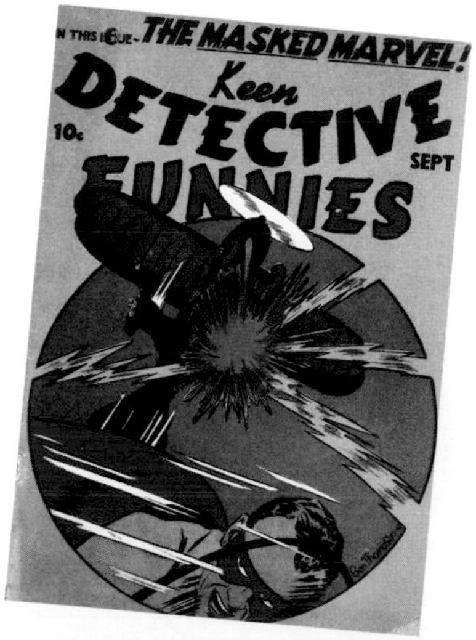
THE MASKED MARVEL!
Keen
DETECTIVE
FUNNIES
10¢
SEPT

As *Keen* continued, regular characters were added, including the Eye, Dan Dennis of the FBI, Dean Denton—Scientific Detective, and TNT Todd. In the eleventh issue (July 1939) the Masked Marvel joined the lineup. Drawn by Ben Thompson, he was a mysterious crimebuster who, with the aid of three former G-Men known as 2R, 2Y, and 2L, was dedicated to breaking up "large and powerful criminal gangs." The Marvel wore a red shirt, red riding breeches, and a red domino mask. His

associates wore business suits and green masks. A relatively successful character, he was featured on several covers and remained in *Keen* until its final issue in the summer of 1940.

Ken Ernst, who would eventually desert comic books for the *Mary Worth* newspaper strip, contributed *Gabby Flynn*, about a tough newspaper reporter. In the final two issues Air Man, a Hawkman impersonator, was given the starring position.

KEITH, SAM

■ See SANDMAN: II.

KELLY, WALT

■ See ANIMAL COMICS.

KIDA, FRED *(1920–)*

■ An excellent illustrative cartoonist, Kida's most memorable work was done in the middle 1940s when he drew Airboy and his feisty lady-pilot colleague Valkyrie. He also did considerable work for *Crime Does Not Pay*. Fellow artists, such as James Steranko and Alex Toth, are admirers of his. Toth has said of him, "Kida demonstrated a rich sense of drama in his underlying black-and-white art."

In the early 1940s, Kida began his professional career with a job in Will Eisner's shop. While there he drew *The Phantom Clipper* for *Military Comics*. Next came Hillman, where he did *Airboy* and later *Gunmaster*. Kida also drew a short-lived newspaper strip titled *Judge Wright*. He was an assistant on both *Flash Gordon* and *Steve Canyon*. In the early 1980s, he penciled the *Spider-Man* newspaper strip.

KING COMICS

■ By 1936 the idea of reprinting comic strips in a format similar to that of *Famous Funnies* was spreading. Early that year, Dell introduced their version, titled *Popular Comics*. Two months later both United Feature Syndicate and King Features entered the comic-book business. United published *Tip Top Comics* and King, in

partnership with Philadelphia publisher David McKay, introduced *King Comics*. The magazine would go through 159 issues before closing down late in 1950.

Relying chiefly on Sunday page reprints for their maiden comic book, the syndicate included *Flash Gordon, Popeye, Mandrake the Magician, Brick Bradford, Little Annie*

Rooney, and *The Little King*. Otto Soglow's pantomime monarch also appeared to the left and right of the cover logo as a sort of mascot. The editor in Philly was Ruth Plumly Thompson, best remembered for carrying on the Oz books after the death of L. Frank Baum. The strips were pasted up in King Features' Manhattan offices, with artist Joe Musial in charge and Bud Sagendorf helping out, and then shipped to McKay. Thompson was responsible for some of the original material. This included a handsome two-page feature about Indian legends drawn by Philadelphia newspaper artist Jimmy Thompson and titled *Redmen*. Thompson herself wrote a series of connected text fairy tales in the humorous manner of her Oz novels. They were usually illustrated by Marge Henderson Buell, creator of *Little Lulu*. Another original feature was a sports panel by Jack Burnley, later to draw DC's Starman. Musial drew most of the covers, the majority of them featuring Popeye and his associates.

As *King Comics* progressed, such syndicate features as *The Lone Ranger*, *Barney Baxter*, *The Phantom*, and *Blondie* were added. The final five issues were published by Ned Pines's Standard outfit.

KIRBY, JACK *(1917-1994)*

■ A key contributor to the rejuvenation of the comics industry in the early 1960s, Kirby'd been in the field for over two decades by that time. He and his partner Joe Simon had created such characters as Captain America and the Boy Commandos and converted the original Sandman into a star long before Kirby got together with Stan Lee to produce a line of Marvel superheroes that included the Fantastic Four, X-Men, the Hulk, and Thor. Jack Kirby wasn't crowned the King of Comics until he helped revive Marvel's fortunes and became one of the most imitated cartoonists of the sixties.

DECEMBER NO. 10
GREEN HORNET
ON THE AIR in the MOVIES
10¢

A street kid named Jacob Kurtzberg who grew up on New York's Lower East Side, he early on decided that he wanted to get out of there and that art was his way. By 1935 he was working for the Manhattan-based Fleischer animation studio, where he worked as an in-betweener on the *Popeye* cartoons. Ambitious, Kirby next drew for a small syndicate run by a second-rate cartoonist named H. T. Elmo. There Kirby drew political cartoons, comic strips, sports cartoons, and imitation *Believe It or Not* panels that were supplied to small-town weekly newspapers.

Moving on to the Eisner-Iger shop, he coined the name Jack Curtiss to sign such features as *Wilson of the West* and *The Count of Monte Cristo*, which appeared first in the overseas weekly *Wags* and later in *Jumbo Comics*. He next drew a fleeting newspaper strip titled *Lightnin' and the Lone Rider*, a Lone Ranger knockoff that he signed Lance Kirby. In 1940, putting two of his earlier aliases together, he became Jack Kirby.

After doing work for the Bert Whitman shop, he met Joe Simon, then an editor at Fox. They joined forces to become the most creative team of the 1940s. With Kirby penciling and Simon inking, they put out *Blue Bolt* then created such characters as Captain America, the Vision, and for DC the Newsboy Legion and the Boy Commandos, as well

"COMMIT A CRIME AND THE WORLD IS MADE OF GLASS"
"GET ME THE GOLDEN GUN"
GUNMASTER PISTOL STAMP
NAMBU PISTOL M'14 JAPAN
THIS PISTOL IS AS FAMOUS AS THE WELL KNOWN GERMAN LUGER.....
With GUNMASTER
YES...EVERY BIG-SHOT IN TOWN BID FOR THE FABULOUS WEAPON---WHICH WAS TAINTED BY AN ANCIENT CURSE AND BROUGHT DEATH TO THE EVIL MEN WHO WANTED IT MOST! ONLY GUNMASTER AND VELVET SILVER SURVIVED THIS EXPLOSIVE LITTLE DEAL! HOW DID THEY DO IT? WELL, YOU SEE.........

as overhauling Sandman and Manhunter. Kirby's style in the 1940s was both forceful and graceful, his layouts innovative. Simon's strong inking added to the dynamic effect. Kirby also became a master of creating impressive splash pages.

Eventually splitting with Simon, after they'd launched such diverse efforts as *Young Romance*, *Black Magic*, and *Boys' Ranch*, Kirby, using a variety of inkers, drew for DC, Marvel, and DC again. The number of characters he created, in addition to those mentioned above, included Challengers of the Unknown. Back briefly with Simon, they invented a brand-new Sandman. An extremely fast penciler, Kirby's later works began to rely on set pieces and Kirby clichés, almost as if he were a younger artist imitating the King. On such later titles as *The Forever People* and *The New Gods*, he let himself go. Writing now as well as drawing, he tossed in his own special brand of cosmology and rendered everybody—men, women, children, and even trees—as spectacularly muscled. He was now and then hired to create characters for other publishers, such as the ill-fated Topps line. His inventions were more variations on a theme, and none succeeded.

But all things considered, few artists gave as much to comics as Jack Kirby.

KORAK

■ See TARZAN.

KRAZY KOMICS

KRAZY
No 8
KOMICS
10¢
JUNE

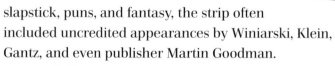

■ Timely's earliest funny animal comic book, *Krazy* was introduced in the late spring of 1942 with a roster of characters that included Toughy Tomcat, Posty and Lolly (a pelican postman and his elephant pal), Ziggy Pig and Silly Seal, the Creeper and Homer Rabbit, and Skinny Bones, a human boy who dwelled in a world populated by humanized animals. Stan Lee was the first editor, followed by Vince Fago in the spring of 1943. The cartooning staff included Al Jaffee, George Winiarski, Dave Gantz, George Klein, Kin Platt, and Mike Sekowsky.

Jaffee wrote and drew the early adventures of Ziggy and Silly, a somewhat pudgy pig and his lisping seal sidekick. Later artists on the feature were Joe Calcagno, a former Milt Gross assistant, and Harvey Eisenberg, a one-time animator. Various bullpen artists worked on the Creeper feature, which pitted Homer Rabbit and his nephew Junior against the mysterious Creeper and his mysterious little son Crawler. A mixture of slapstick, puns, and fantasy, the strip often included uncredited appearances by Winiarski, Klein, Gantz, and even publisher Martin Goodman.

No challenge to Disney or Warner cartoon-derived comic books, *Krazy Komics* had a baggy pants zaniness all its own. The twenty-sixth and final issue (Spring 1947) included a guest appearance by Super Rabbit. Two issues of a new and different *Krazy Komics*, containing no animal products, appeared in 1948 with work by Harvey Kurtzman and Basil Wolverton.

KREMER, WARREN

■ See RICHIE RICH.

KRIGSTEIN, BERNARD

(1919–1990)

■ A stubborn, thoughtful, and innovative artist, Krigstein never quite fit into the comic-book business. Yet the work he produced in the 1950s, especially the forty-some stories he drew for the EC titles, were and continue to be influential. His innovative page breakdowns, staging, and pacing have, along with the work of some European artists, influenced the likes of Frank Miller, Steranko, and John Byrne. One of those EC stories, *The Master Race*, has been frequently reprinted in the half century since he drew it for *Impact* early in 1955.

Krigstein entered comics in 1946 after service during World War II. He put in time at the Bernard Baily shop before venturing out on his own. He drew *Nyoka* and *The Golden Arrow* for Fawcett, illustrated both cowboy and detective stories for Hillman and *Space Patrol* for Ziff Davis. This early work is distinctive, but Krigstein hadn't yet perfected his individual approach to storytelling. The layout was an important factor in the process. "I really felt as if I stumbled upon an important way to tell stories," he once explained, "to break down stories."

When Krigstein reached EC in 1953, he had everything worked out, and he finally was given the freedom to do as he wanted. Editor Al Feldstein encouraged him, although Harvey Kurtzman rarely used Krigstein in the titles he edited. Kurtzman had rigid ideas about layout and wanted his artists to work from rough breakdowns that he produced. One of Krigstein's innovations was to break up a page in unconventional ways. He might use dozens of panels on a single page to slow time or emphasize an action, or he might use a couple of large panels with several events going on at once. In addition to being a thoughtful constructor of pages, Krigstein was an exceptional artist, and the pages he created over fifty years ago still look fresh and appealing today.

He remained in comics for a few years after EC folded its line in the middle 1950s. Krigstein did quite a few fantasy and crime stories for Marvel. Still experimenting, he once used seventy-five panels in a four-page yarn in *Uncanny Tales*. His last comic book was a Dell one-shot in 1961, based on the TV show *The 87th Precinct*. A very strange looking piece of work, Krigstein later confessed that he'd intended it as a joke.

In the early 1960s he worked as an illustrator and commercial artist, later teaching painting at the High School of Art and Design in Manhattan. In his final years he concentrated on painting.

THE NEXT MORNING, EARLY, MOLLY ROSE, DRESSED QUICKLY, AND TIPTOED OUT OF THE HOUSE . . .

BUT SHE NEEDN'T HAVE BOTHERED TIPTOEING. STANLEY HAD ALREADY LEFT...

KUBERT, JOE (1926–)

■ Kubert grew up in the comic-book business, having entered it before he turned thirteen. In the course of his lengthy career, he's worked for just about every major publisher and quite a few minor ones. Among the many characters he's drawn are Hawkman, the Black Cat, Zatara, Tarzan, Sgt. Rock, Tor, and Enemy Ace. In the early 1950s he worked on the development of the short-lived 3D comic-book format, was an editor at DC in the 1960s and 1970s, and later founded the still-thriving Joe Kubert School of Cartoon and Graphic Art.

After working as a sort of apprentice at the Chesler shop, Kubert moved on to freelance for several different publishers, and he had work in such titles as *Police Comics* and *Speed Comics.* He also served as an inker, having the good fortune to be employed by such exemplary artists as Jack Kirby and Mort Meskin. Sheldon Mayer, who was editing the titles for the All-American division of DC, had an affinity for unorthodox artists, and he hired Kubert in 1944 to take over *Hawkman.* Although his work at the time showed the influence of Kirby and Meskin, the young artist's work was already highly individual and especially suited to fantasy.

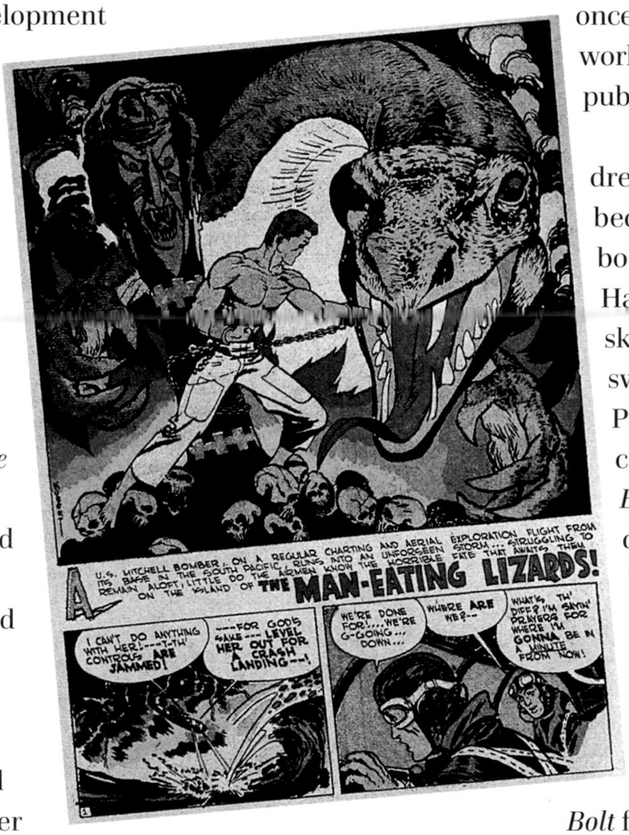
A U.S. MITCHELL BOMBER, ON A REGULAR CHARTING AND AERIAL EXPLORATION FLIGHT FROM ITS BASE IN THE SOUTH PACIFIC, RUNS INTO AN UNFORSEEN STORM... STRUGGLING TO REMAIN ALOFT! LITTLE DO THE AIRMEN KNOW THE HORRIBLE FATE THAT AWAITS THEM ON THE ISLAND OF THE MAN-EATING LIZARDS!
I CAN'T DO ANYTHING WITH HER!---T-TH' CONTROLS ARE JAMMED!
---FOR GOD'S SAKE--- LEVEL HER OUT FOR A CRASH LANDING--!
WE'RE DONE FOR!...WE'RE G-GOING... DOWN...
WHERE ARE WE?--
WHAT'S TH' DIFF? I'M SAYIN' PRAYERS FOR WHERE I'M GONNA BE IN A MINUTE FROM NOW!

Kubert's work continued to improve and change. By the 1950s, after serving in the army, he was closer to the approach he'd use for most of his career. The figure work was stronger, the layouts more assured, and the rendering bolder. Kubert invented his favorite character, the caveman Tor, during that period, drew a few jobs for EC, and drew fantasy stories for St. John titles. Teaming with his longtime friend, Norman Maurer, the two developed one of the systems used to produce 3D comic books. St. John was the publisher, and when 3D proved a fad rather than a staple, the publisher lost considerable money. He once said, "At one time or other, I've worked for possibly every comic-book publishing house in the business."

Returning to DC in the 1960s, he drew a wide range of things and also became an editor of some of the war books. He illustrated the revived Hawkman, drew the World War II skirmishes of Sgt. Rock and the swashbuckling sagas of the Viking Prince, contributed a number of covers to assorted titles including *Batman*, and in 1972 was the artist chosen to handle DC's version of *Tarzan. Tor* has returned now and then, both in new stories and reprints. Kubert had also drawn the unsuccessful newspaper strip *Tales of the Green Berets* in the middle 1960s, ghosted *Big Ben Bolt* for a spell, and, with the help of students from his school, put in a stretch drawing the *Winnie Winkle* strip.

He has continued to work in the medium, but in recent years he has become more ambitious. He produced a handsome graphic novel titled *Fax from Sarajevo* in 1998 and *April 19, 1943: A Story of the Warsaw Ghetto Uprising* in 2003. Two of Kubert's sons, Adam and Andy, have followed in his footsteps to become successful comic-book artists.

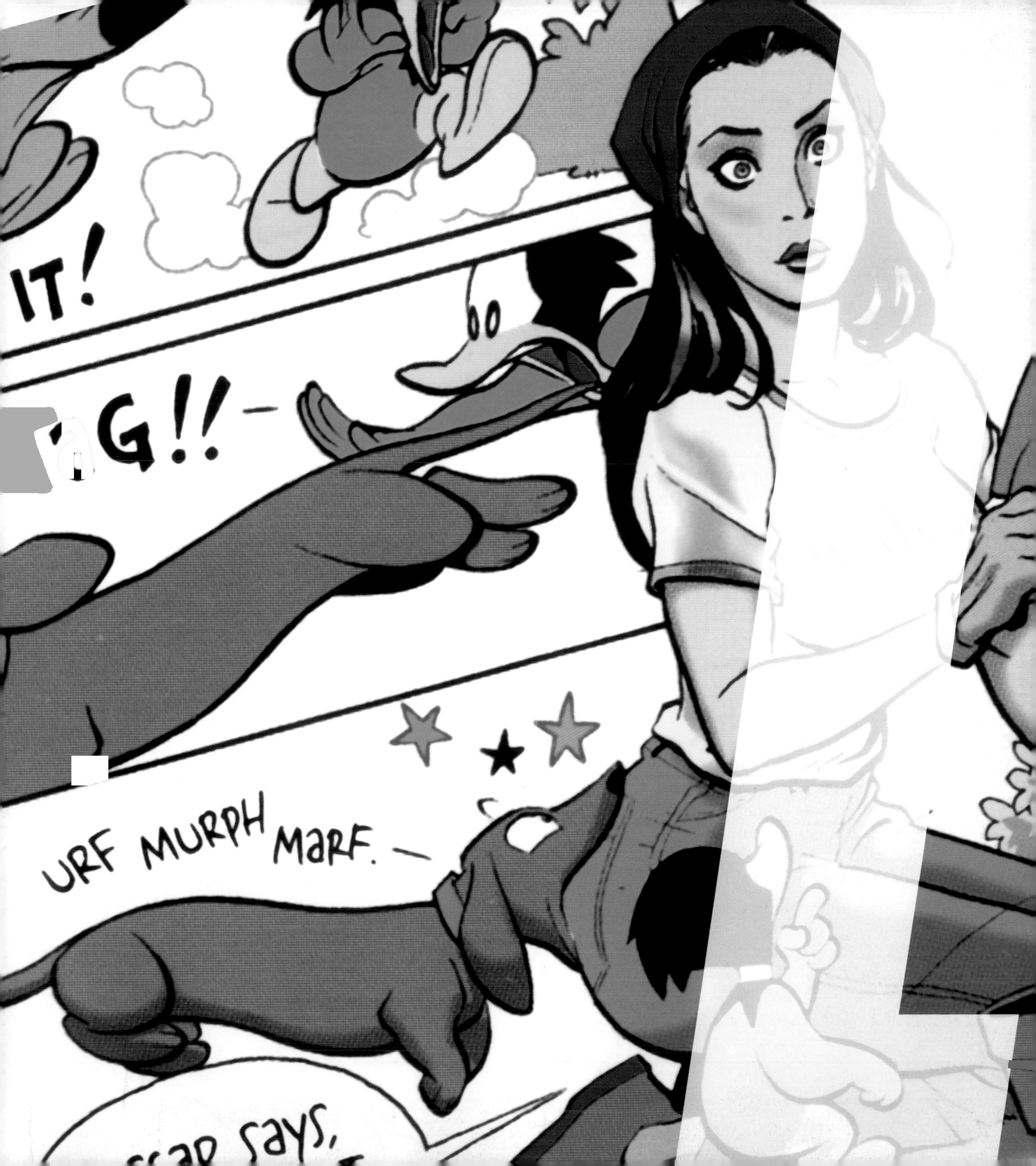
IT!
G!!—
URF MURPH MARF.—
says,

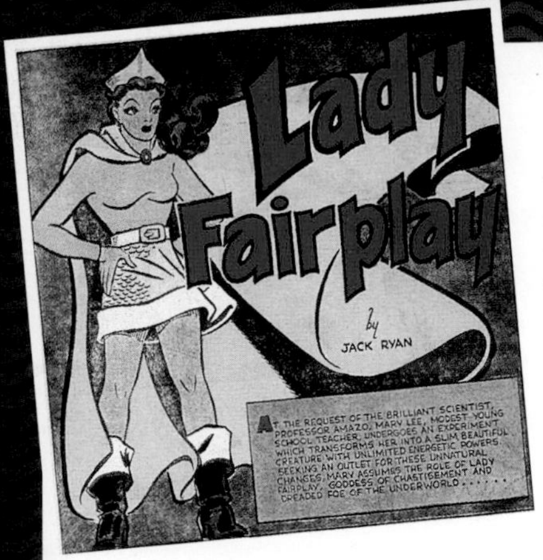
Lady Fairplay
by JACK RYAN
AT THE REQUEST OF THE BRILLIANT SCIENTIST, PROFESSOR AMAZO, MARY LEE, MODEST YOUNG SCHOOL TEACHER, UNDERGOES AN EXPERIMENT WHICH TRANSFORMS HER INTO A SLIM BEAUTIFUL CREATURE WITH UNLIMITED ENERGETIC POWERS. SEEKING AN OUTLET FOR THESE UNNATURAL CHANGES, MARY ASSUMES THE ROLE OF LADY FAIRPLAY, GODDESS OF CHASTISEMENT AND DREADED FOE OF THE UNDERWORLD.....

LADY FAIR PLAY

■ This superhero entered comic books at just about the same time as Wonder Woman. Yet despite having "unlimited energetic powers" and being "gorgeous," she didn't fare anywhere near as well. Her first appearance was in *Bang-Up Comics* #1 (December 1941), and her last was in the magazine's third and final issue six months later. Lady Fairplay never had a full-fledged origin, but readers were informed that a brilliant scientist named Professor Amazo had transformed her into a "slim beautiful creature with amazing superpowers." By day she was bespectacled schoolteacher Mary Lee, but when trouble reared its head, she swiftly converted to a "goddess of chastisement and dreaded foe of the underworld."

Since she didn't posses the ability to fly, Lady Fairplay traveled to and from crime scenes in a red convertible. This sleek vehicle had been built by the helpful professor and was "equipped with everything but the kitchen sink!" The three cases she tackled were fairly mundane. The first involved bank robbers, the second a crooked home for the aged, and the last a hot-car ring.

The Chicago-based *Bang-Up* relied on newspaper artists and writers in the area. *Lady Fairplay* was the work of Jack Ryan. He'd assisted on *Dan Dunn* and *Dick Tracy* and had a Sunday page of his own titled *Streamer Kelly* running in the *Chicago Tribune* at the time.

LADY LUCK

■ A product of the Will Eisner shop, she appeared as a backup for several years in *The Spirit* Sunday newspaper insert that was launched in June of 1940. A masked crimefighter who dressed in green, she was society girl Brenda Banks, who led two lives—"One as an idle heiress . . . the other as the elusive enemy of crime known as Lady Luck." The initial artist was Chuck Mazuojian.

To convert to her alter ego, the blonde Brenda slipped into a simple green frock with a shamrock at the throat, a short green cape, and a wide-brim, flat-crown green hat. For a mask she wore a transparent green veil over the lower portion of her face. Not a very effective disguise, it managed to fool the assorted spies, saboteurs, crooks, and criminal masterminds she rounded up in her weekly four-page capers.

The second artist was Nick Cardy, and during his hitch *Lady Luck* grew lighter in tone. He gave Brenda a large Latino chauffeur named Peecolo, who knew the secret of her dual identity and often helped on her cases. When Cardy was drafted in 1942, Klaus Nordling took over the drawing and the writing. He converted the feature into a mystery comedy. His added character was Count DiChange, a small dithery, trouble-prone fellow.

Nordling stayed on the job for several years, providing over two hundred four-page stories. He was eventually replaced by Fred Schwab. When in 1943 *Smash Comics* began reprinting *Lady Luck*, they used the Nordling material. *Smash* changed its name to *Lady Luck* for the last five issues, and Klaus Nordling returned to write and draw Brenda Banks's new adventures.

LEE, JIM *(1964–)*

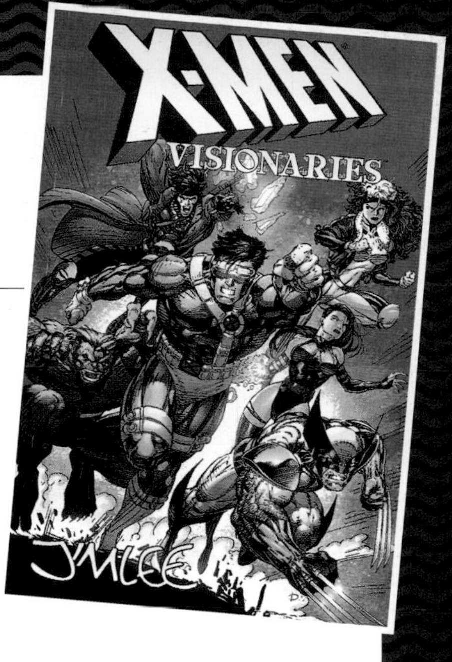
X-MEN
VISIONARIES

■ The cartoonist who drew the best-selling comic book of all time, he began his climb to fame and fortune in 1987 when he took over the penciling of Marvel's *Alpha Flight.* Born in South Korea, Lee moved to the United States with his family in the late 1960s. He attended Princeton and is one of the few comic-book professionals with a medical degree. His first love, however, was drawing, and after submitting samples to Marvel in 1986, he was invited to come to work.

His style was well-suited to the new age of comics that was blossoming in the late 1980s. Lee was a prime exponent of the post-Kirby approach, and his work had affinities to such other young Turks as Todd McFarlane, Arthur Adams, and Rob Liefeld. His layouts were inventive, his characters hyperactive, his pages cluttered with action, and his women tough and endowed with the attributes of centerfolds. Readers took to Lee's work almost immediately, and he was soon moved to *Punisher War Journal.* "My career seemed like it was on the upswing," he's said of that period. By the summer of 1990 he was the official penciler on *Uncanny X-Men,* and he was already coming in first in reader polls. Since Lee entered the fields when artists were paid royalties on sales, he fared considerably better than cartoonists of earlier decades.

In the autumn of 2001, Marvel started up a new improved *X-Men* with Lee as the artist. The first issue, which appeared in five separate versions all with covers by Lee, sold 8 million copies, a feat not matched before nor since. The following year, in partnership with McFarlane, Liefeld, Erik Larson, and others, he cofounded Image Comics and later its Wildstorm subsidiary. For them he invented *Wildcats* and *StormWatch,* as well as plotting and penciling *Fantastic Four* for Marvel. More recently Lee has penciled *Batman* for DC. In 1999 he sold his Wildstorm imprint to them.

LEE, STAN *(1922–)*

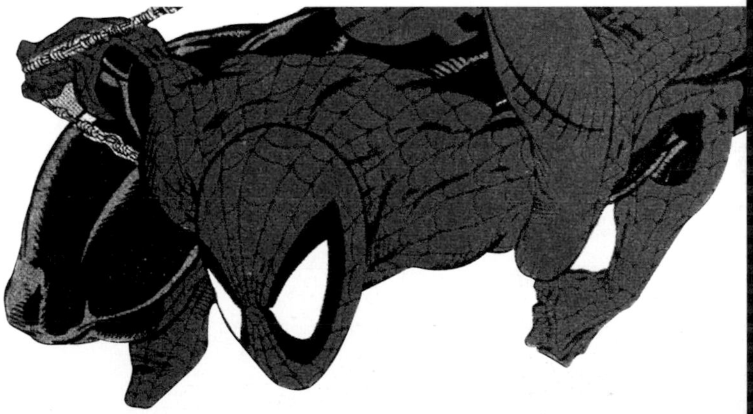

■ In the early 1940s, mild-mannered Stanley Lieber became Stan Lee. Although not a superhero, he eventually had almost as profound an effect on the comic-book industry as the advent of Superman. A relative of publisher Martin Goodman, he started as a writer with what was then Timely Comics. He created *The Destroyer,* wrote scripts for everything from *Captain America* and *The Young Allies* to *Krazy Komics,* plus the two-page text fillers that the postal laws then required. Within a few years he was editor in chief, first at Goodman's Atlas and then at his Marvel Comics. After editing and writing great quantities of cowboy, combat, and monster comic books, Lee helped found the Silver Age. Along with people like Jack Kirby and Steve Ditko, he cocreated *Spider-Man, Dr. Strange, Thor, The Hulk, X-Men, the Fantastic Four, Silver Surfer,* and even *Ant-Man.*

An admirer of Charles Biro, one of the consummate hucksters of the comic field, Lee adapted and expanded on Biro's approach to attracting readers. Lee dubbed every new character who came along as the greatest ever, and he saw to it that the line "Stan Lee Presents" appeared on every Marvel story. He used every cover as a billboard, with bright-colored drawings and numerous boxes of copy promising that the material within was like nothing you'd ever seen. He introduced *Stan's Soapbox*, where he spoke directly to readers and fans, and ran it in all of every month's many titles. Lee had also realized that by crediting everybody who had a hand in each story, including the letterer and the colorist, he could build up a loyal fan following. Of course, the quality of much of the material also helped the enormous sales that Marvel started enjoying.

Involved in recent years with both television and movies, Lee still writes for comic books on occasion. Recently he did a series for DC in which he demonstrated how he would have created such sturdy heroes as Superman.

'Nuff said.

THE LEGION OF SUPER-HEROES

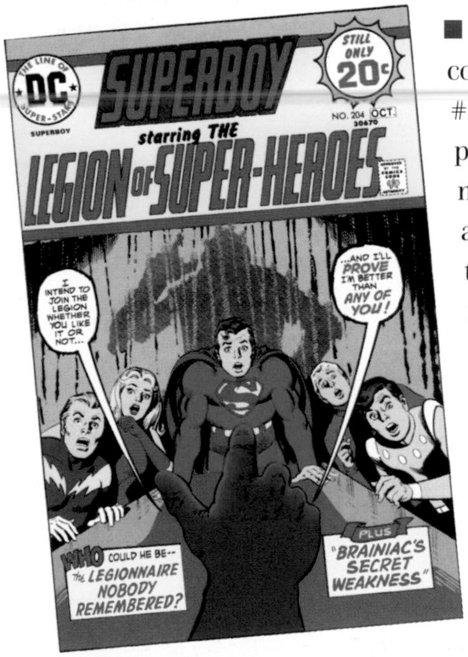
SUPERBOY
STILL ONLY 20¢
NO. 204 OCT.
starring THE
LEGION OF SUPER-HEROES
I INTEND TO JOIN THE LEGION WHETHER YOU LIKE IT OR NOT...
...AND I'LL PROVE I'M BETTER THAN ANY OF YOU!
WHO COULD HE BE-- THE LEGIONNAIRE NOBODY REMEMBERED?
PLUS "BRAINIAC'S SECRET WEAKNESS"

■ A future-based organization that seemed to have more members than a family of cockroaches, the Legion was introduced in the Superboy story in *Adventure Comics* #247 in the spring of 1958. Young Clark Kent met them when, as an official DC history put it, "three time-travelers appeared in Smallville, introduced themselves as members of a far future Legion of Super-Heroes, and invited him to visit their century and join their club. Superboy did so and continued to make periodic journeys to get together with this mass of super-powered young people. The membership list included Ultra Boy, Shrinking Violet, Mon-El, Saturn Girl, Cosmic Boy, Star Boy, Colossal Boy, Element Lad, Invisible Kid, Brainiac 5, Chameleon Boy, Light Lass, Sun Boy, Elastic Lad, Phantom Girl, and Bouncing Boy. To name but a few.

Eventually the Legion eased Superboy out of the top spot in *Adventure*. In the late 1970s, they went further and moved into the *Superboy* magazine and took that over. In their own title the artists who drew their adventures included George Perez, Keith Giffen, and Joe Staton. The bunch was last seen in 2000.

LIBERTY MEADOWS

■ See CHO, FRANK.

LIGHTNING COMICS

■ Thriving pulp fiction publisher A. A. Wynn added comic books to his Ace Magazines line in the spring of 1940. His inaugural title, *Sure Fire Comics*, was changed to *Lightning Comics* with the fifth issue (December 1940). The featured superhero was a fellow known as "Flash" Lightning. His name was changed to "Lash" Lightning with the ninth issue (August 1941). Others on the character docket were the Raven, Whiz Wilson and his Futuroscope, Marvo the Magician, and X the Phantom Fed.

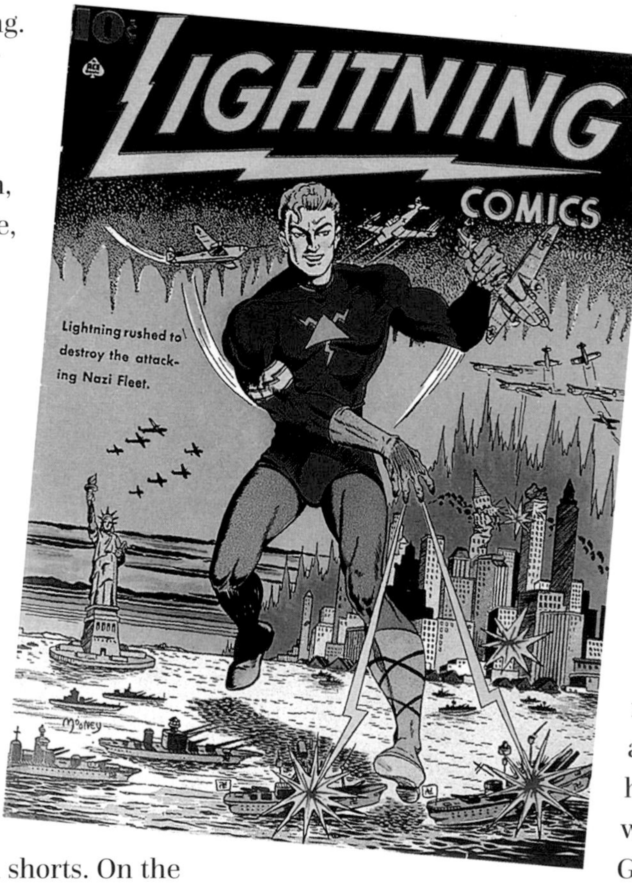
10¢
LIGHTNING
COMICS
Lightning rushed to destroy the attacking Nazi Fleet.
Mooney

"Flash" Lightning was actually a young American schooled in Egypt by "the Ageless Old Man of the Pyramids." Once he'd learned "all the ancient and modern sciences," plus the ability to generate and toss lightning bolts and the knack of flying, he was sent to New York by his mentor to help save the world from crime and doom. Lightning's costume consisted of green tights and red tunic and shorts. On the chest of the tunic was an insignia consisting of a pyramid and three lightning bolts. The first artist was Harry Lucey, followed by Jim Mooney. Lightning did battle against such villains as the Mummy and a slick-haired scoundrel called the Mastermind, both of whom returned to plague him. In the final issue of *Lightning Comics* (June 1942), he was joined by a partner known as Lightning Girl. The team continued for a few more years in *Ace's Four Favorites.*

The Raven was a pulp-style mystery man who wore a purple hood, a purple cloak, and a purple business suit. He was in reality police sergeant Danny Dartin, who donned purple to cut corners in the pursuit of criminals. The first artist was Mart Nodell, before he came up with the Green Lantern. Whiz Wilson, a young scientist, invented the Futuroscope, "with which he can harness gravity, space and time." He used that to travel to the future—the distant year of 1980 in his initial adventure.

Marvo was a moustached and tail-coated stage magician who, like many another comic-book magician, possessed real magic powers and used them to fight crime. His sidekick was a pet monkey named Tito. X the Phantom Fed was an FBI man and also a "man of a thousand faces." Although the comic book never mentioned it, he was an adaptation of Ace's successful pulp-hero Secret Agent X. Harry Lucey was also the first artist on this one. Given the leading place in the first issue, X soon moved aside to give "Flash" Lightning the star spot. The earliest X adventure, which ran to fifteen pages, was based on an earlier X pulp novel.

Among the later characters added were Dr. Nemesis, who wore a surgical mask while fighting crooks, Congo Jack, Ace's answer to DC's Congo Bill, and the Sword, who was a distant relative of King Arthur. Robert Turner acted as editor for at least some of the issues and wrote many of the scripts.

LITTLE LULU

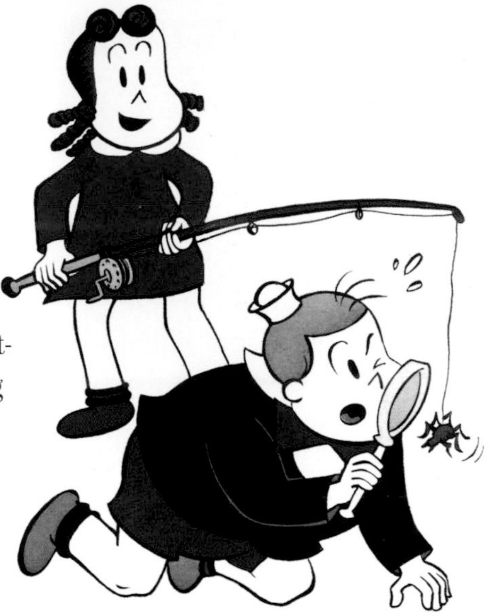

■ One of the few comic-book characters who began her graphic life in the pages of *The Saturday Evening Post*, Little Lulu made her funny-book debut in 1947. She was created by cartoonist Marge Henderson Buell for a series of gag panels that began in the slick-paper weekly in 1935. The smart little girl with the corkscrew curls, bright-red dress, and tiny red hat first showed up in Dell's Four Color #74. The long-running comic, although titled *Marge's Little Lulu*, was actually masterminded by artist/writer John Stanley.

What Stanley provided, after having written and drawn the first couple issues, were rough storyboards for artist Irving Tripp to follow. "To say that Stanley 'wrote' *Little Lulu* is actually deceptive," comics historian Mike Barrier has stated, "since he was responsible for more than plots and dialogue. He sketched each story in rough form, so that he controlled the staging within each panel and the appearances and attitudes of the characters." Stanley's thumbnails would be enlarged, inked by Tripp (with occasional help from Gordon Rose and others), and lettered.

Stanley inherited Lulu's boyfriend/antagonist Tubby from the original cartoons—wherein the fat boy was named Joe—but he invented most of the other characters, including the truant officer Mr. McNabbem, Wilbur Van Snobbe, Witch Hazel and Little Itch, and the bullying West Side Boys. As Barrier has pointed out, Stanley's conception of Lulu is quite different from the bratty kid of the *Post* era. Eventually, Lulu "became a 'good little girl' who outsmarted the boys instead of triumphing through sheer brass, as she had in the past."

Little Lulu's adventures were clever, funny, and low-key. These attributes, coupled with Stanley's simple storytelling style, entertained a generation of kids and inspired many of them to remain fans into adult life. John Stanley worked on *Little Lulu* until 1961. In all, he was responsible for about 150 issues. The comic book continued without him until 1984. Many post-Stanley issues, however, were merely reprints of his earlier work.

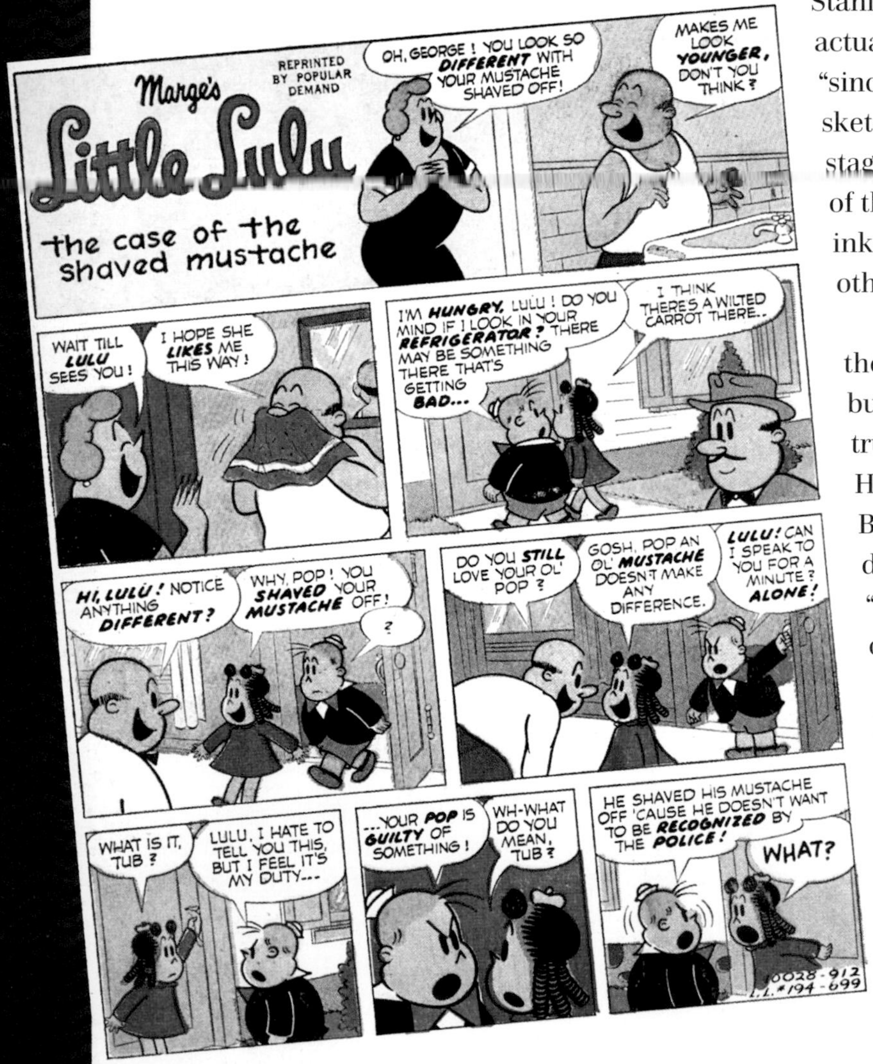
REPRINTED BY POPULAR DEMAND
Marge's Little Lulu
the case of the shaved mustache
OH, GEORGE! YOU LOOK SO DIFFERENT WITH YOUR MUSTACHE SHAVED OFF!
MAKES ME LOOK YOUNGER, DON'T YOU THINK?
WAIT TILL LULU SEES YOU!
I HOPE SHE LIKES ME THIS WAY!
I'M HUNGRY, LULU! DO YOU MIND IF I LOOK IN YOUR REFRIGERATOR? THERE MAY BE SOMETHING THERE THAT'S GETTING BAD...
I THINK THERE'S A WILTED CARROT THERE..
HI, LULU! NOTICE ANYTHING DIFFERENT?
WHY, POP! YOU SHAVED YOUR MUSTACHE OFF!
?
DO YOU STILL LOVE YOUR OL' POP?
GOSH, POP AN OL' MUSTACHE DOESN'T MAKE ANY DIFFERENCE.
LULU! CAN I SPEAK TO YOU FOR A MINUTE? ALONE!
WHAT IS IT, TUB?
LULU, I HATE TO TELL YOU THIS, BUT I FEEL IT'S MY DUTY...
...YOUR POP IS GUILTY OF SOMETHING!
WH-WHAT DO YOU MEAN, TUB?
HE SHAVED HIS MUSTACHE OFF 'CAUSE HE DOESN'T WANT TO BE RECOGNIZED BY THE POLICE!
WHAT?

THE LONE RANGER

The LONE RANGER
and the BLACK SHIRT HIGHWAYMAN
THE BETTER LITTLE BOOK

■ The most popular masked cowboy of the twentieth century was first heard and not seen. The Lone Ranger initially brought law and order to the Old West by way of the radio. He, his great horse Silver, and his faithful Indian companion Tonto came to the air in 1933, originating at Station WXYZ in Detroit. A variation of many earlier masked avengers from dime novels, pulp-fiction magazines, and movies, the character was cobbled together by a team that included station owner George W. Trendle, station dramatic director James Jewell, and freelance writer Fran Striker. The popularity of the thrice-weekly nighttime show was such that considerable merchandising followed. By 1935 the first Big Little Book about the masked man appeared, followed in 1938 by a syndicated newspaper strip and in 1939 by comic books.

THE LONE RANGER
by
FRAN STRIKER
I'LL PROVE TO YOU THAT YOU'VE GOT BLANKS IN YOUR GUN!
LOOK HERE!
SEE? A WAD OF PAPER INSTEAD OF LEAD!
DRILL'EM ALL!

The very first comic book was a giveaway for an ice cream cone company. It adapted Henry Vallely BLB artwork, adding badly lettered dialogue balloons. The David McKay Company issued a black-and-white comic book in 1939 as well, using strips by original artist Ed Kressy, his ghost Jon Blummer, and his replacement from the King Features bullpen, Charles Flanders. McKay also added the Lone Ranger to the roster of strips reprinted in its four-color *King Comics* and *Magic Comics*. For some reason the masked rider was also in their short-lived 1940 *Future Comics*.

In the middle 1940s, Dell began using an occasional *Lone Ranger* reprint issue as part of their Four Color series. That became a regular bimonthly title in 1948, and in 1951, with the thirty-seventh issue, the magazine switched to original material. Artwork was by Tom Gill and his staff, most of the scripts were by the prolific Paul S. Newman. Newman was writing the newspaper strip by this time, and Gill was now and then ghosting it for the ailing Flanders.

During the 1950s, when there was a popular *Lone Ranger* show on television, Dell also published a comic book devoted to Silver and another devoted to Tonto. All the Dell titles ended in 1962. Western Publishing's Gold Key line took over the *Long Ranger* and kept the comic book going until 1969. The Topps Comics line issued four issues of *The Lone Ranger and Tonto* in 1994.

THE LONE RIDER

■ Although he didn't ride a white horse, he was otherwise a pretty good surrogate Lone Ranger. He originated in a very short-lived and sparsely syndicated newspaper strip titled *Lightnin' and the Lone Rider* that began in January of 1939. The masked man and his trusty pinto reached a much wider audience when the strips were reprinted in *Famous Funnies*, beginning in #62 (September 1939). Robert Farrell wrote and distributed the strip by way of his small Associated Features Syndicate. Jacob Kurtzberg moved one step closer to his lifelong pen name when he drew the strip as Lance Kirby.

The Lone Rider had a guitar-playing Mexican sidekick named Diego and initially went after owl-hoots in the Old West. Kirby stayed with the strip for only a few weeks, then Frank Robbins took over. By that time the Rider had shed his mask, revealing himself as a good-looking blond fellow, was living in the present, and was fighting against a female criminal mastermind known as the Panther. When the few existing weeks of *Lightnin' and the Lone Rider* ran out, *Famous* continued with original material. Jack Kirby came back to draw the two pages the hooded hero was allotted each issue. This time around the horse was white. After #80 (May 1941) the Lone Rider rode off into the sunset. The artist in the final days was Dan Gormley.

Never one to give up, Farrell revived his character in 1951 for a *Lone Rider* comic book.

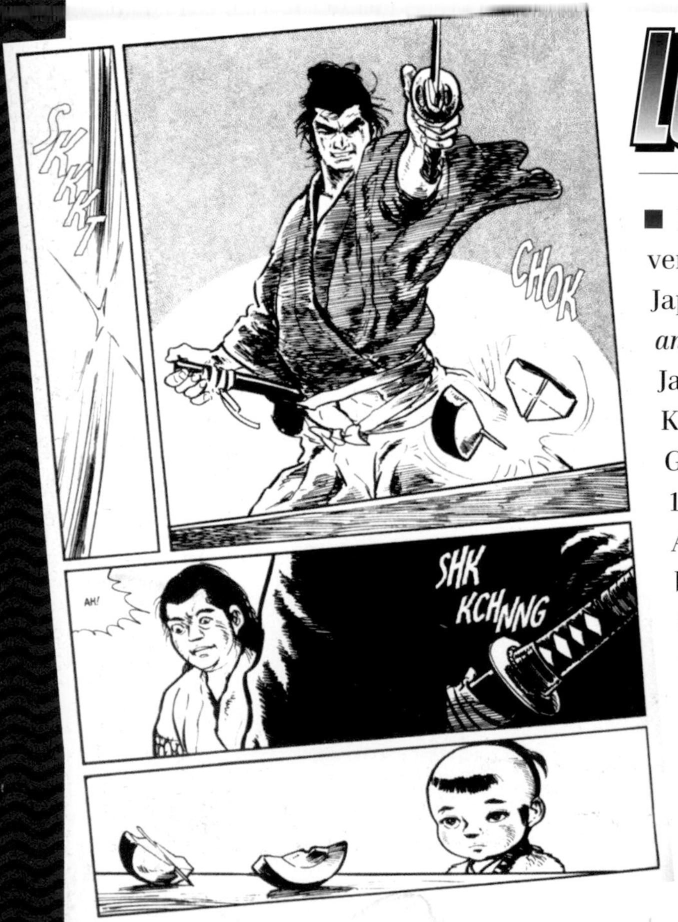
SKKKT
CHOK
AH!
SHK
KCHNNG

LONE WOLF AND CUB

■ In America it has been a very successful and influential Japanese import. *Lone Wolf and Cub* was first seen in Japan in 1970, written by Kazuo Koike and drawn by Goseki Kojima. It was in 1987 that a series of American translations began, published by First Comics. After First went under a few years later, the title didn't appear again in the United States until 2000. At that point Dark Horse began an ambitious series of 296-page black-

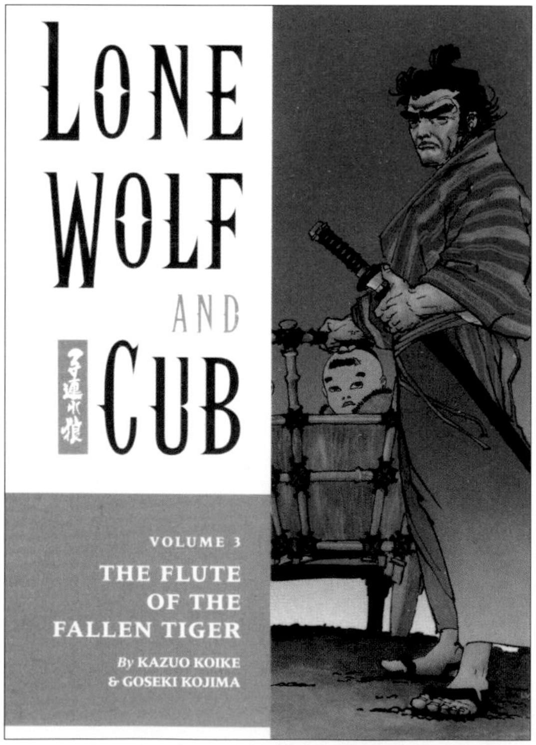
LONE
WOLF
AND
CUB
VOLUME 3
THE FLUTE OF THE FALLEN TIGER
By KAZUO KOIKE & GOSEKI KOJIMA

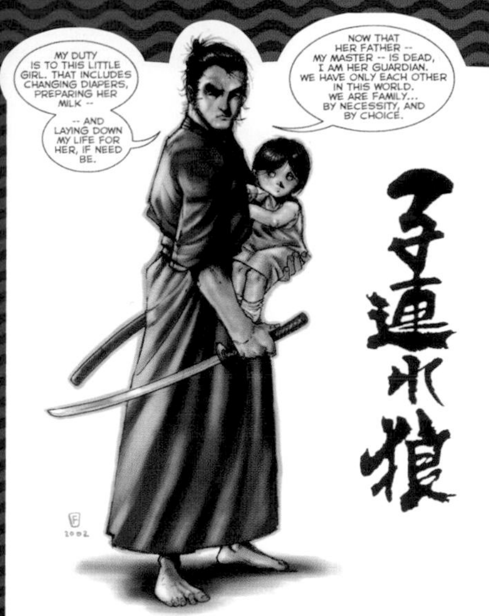
MY DUTY IS TO THIS LITTLE GIRL. THAT INCLUDES CHANGING DIAPERS, PREPARING HER MILK --
-- AND LAYING DOWN MY LIFE FOR HER, IF NEED BE.
NOW THAT HER FATHER -- MY MASTER -- IS DEAD, I AM HER GUARDIAN. WE HAVE ONLY EACH OTHER IN THIS WORLD. WE ARE FAMILY... BY NECESSITY, AND BY CHOICE.
子連れ狼

and-white trade paperbacks aimed at reprinting the entire nine-thousand-some pages of the saga.

A sweeping and complex picaresque set several hundred years in the past, the comic deals with the wanderings of Ogami Itto, a warrior known as the Shogun's assassin, and his three-year-old son, Daigoro. The series is rich with combat, intrigues, bloodshed, ritual, and somewhat fantasized history. It has fascinated not only many American readers but also such artists as Frank Miller.

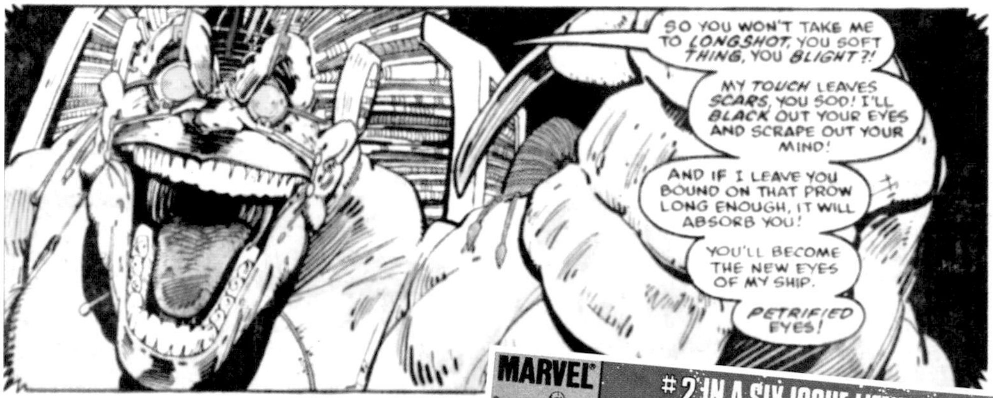
SO YOU WON'T TAKE ME TO LONGSHOT, YOU SOFT THING, YOU BLIGHT?!
MY TOUCH LEAVES SCARS, YOU SOD! I'LL BLACK OUT YOUR EYES AND SCRAPE OUT YOUR MIND!
AND IF I LEAVE YOU BOUND ON THAT PROW LONG ENOUGH, IT WILL ABSORB YOU!
YOU'LL BECOME THE NEW EYES OF MY SHIP.
PETRIFIED EYES!

LONGSHOT

■ An alien visitor from another dimension, he first hit earth in 1985 by way of Marvel's six-part limited series, *Longshot.* Writer Ann Nocenti and artist Arthur Adams, then close to beginning his career, were the joint creators of his complex science-fiction/fantasy adventures. There were also considerable mystical goings-on. Longshot, thus nicknamed because of his tendency to take long chances against heavy odds, moved back and forth between earth and his home dimension.

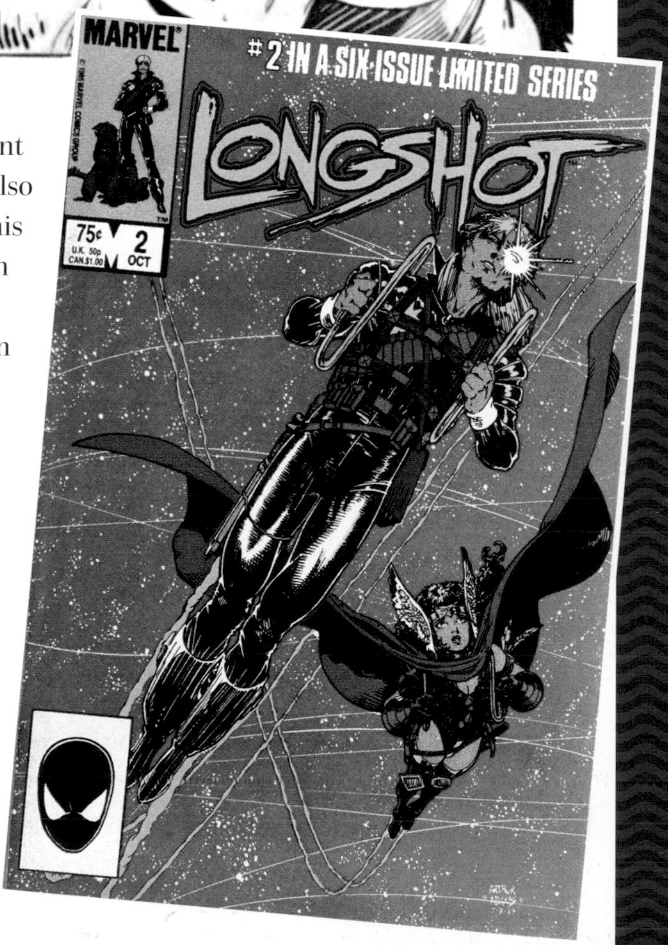
MARVEL
#2 IN A SIX-ISSUE LIMITED SERIES
LONGSHOT
75¢ 2 OCT
U.K. 50p CAN.$1.00

Back there he'd been a slave and a movie stuntman. After sojourns on earth, he made return trips to his other dimension and became a rebel leader of humans who were enslaved by the ruling Spineless Ones. This bunch, led by a chap known as Mojo, also entertained notions of enslaving the population of earth. Later on, while recovering from a bout of enemy-induced amnesia, he was taken under the wing of the X-Men and worked with them. He was helped out by Dr. Strange and later on had an affair with Dazzler.

Among Longshot's powers were the ability to read minds and control future events. Whenever he was exercising one of his wild talents, his left eye would flash green. On a less supernatural level, he was an expert blade-tosser. In addition to a 1989 trade reprint, he has been seen again in a 1998 one-shot.

Some of those who remember *Longshot*'s mixture of sci-fi, mysticism, rebellion, and the questioning of reality feel that his comic books were a source of inspiration for the recent trio of *Matrix* movies.

LOONEY TUNES AND MERRIE MELODIES

■ Following in the footsteps of Walt Disney, Warner Bros. licensed its animated cartoon characters to Dell Publishing in 1941. This resulted in *Looney Tunes and Merrie Melodies*, a title that lasted in its initial run until 1962. Warner had released the first Looney Tunes cartoon in 1930 and the first Merrie Melodies in 1931, the titles of both theatrical series no doubt inspired by Disney's earlier Silly Symphonies. The major characters came along a few years later. Porky Pig in 1935, Daffy Duck in 1937, and Bugs Bunny in 1938. The original lineup of the comic book included Porky and his girlfriend Petunia, Bugs and his nemesis Elmer Fudd, and the mouse Sniffles, who'd also made his screen debut in 1938.

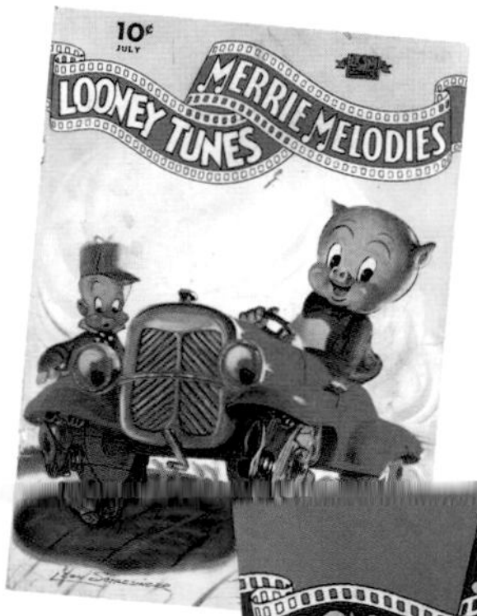

10¢
LOONEY TUNES
MERRIE MELODIES

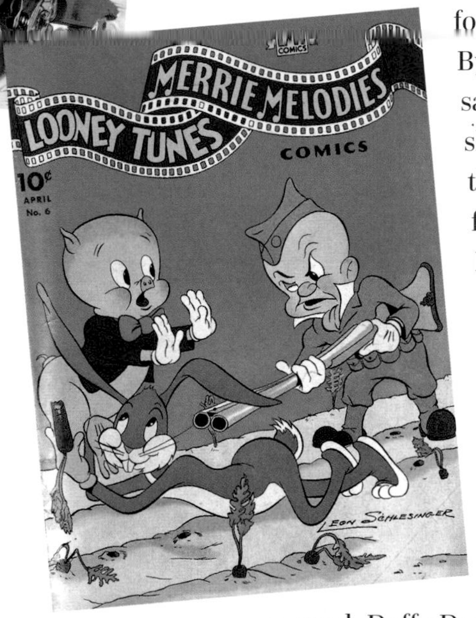

MERRIE MELODIES
LOONEY TUNES
COMICS
10¢
APRIL
No. 6
LEON SCHLESINGER

Early on the artwork was supplied by artists in both the East and in Southern California. The Bugs Bunny story in #1 was drawn by Win Smith, who worked briefly on the *Mickey Mouse* newspaper strip during its beginning months. He was followed by newspaper alumnus George Storm. Other artists who drew Bugs Bunny, Porky Pig, and Elmer Fudd were Chase Craig (also West Coast editor), Carl Buettner, Harvey Eisenberg, and Roger Armstrong.

Smith also drew *Pat, Patsy and Pete*, a creation of his own that recycled his Pete the Penguin character from *Crackajack Funnies* and *Popular Comics.* When he left after just two issues, Storm took over and turned the feature into a fantasy involving the two kids and the talking bird with King Neptune, mermaids, and ghost pirates. Dan Gormley next rendered the penguin strip, transferring the cast to a desert island. Then Walt Kelly took a turn, adding a pot-bellied, peg-legged pirate to the mix. Apparently Kelly was much influenced by the Katzenjammer Kids at this time, and his continuities were built around Pat and Patsy, abetted by Pete, playing horrendous pranks on the grumpy Percy—usually involving such props as dynamite, cannonballs, live crabs, quick-drying cement, and false whiskers.

Earlier Kelly drew *Kandi the Cave Kid.* This, as well as most of the other features, was credited to Leon Schlesinger, the nonwriting, nondrawing producer of the Warner animated cartoons. His name was also signed to the cover art. The mouse Sniffles was teamed up with a blonde little girl named Mary Jane for his comic-book appearances. By the sprinkling about of magic sand provided by Sniffles, she shrank down to mouse size, and the two of them entered into fairy-tale and fantasy settings. Roger Armstrong drew the feature and was the only artist who managed to sign his own name to his work. A onetime newspaper cartoonist and sometime animator named Vevo Risto drew such backup features as *Henery Hawk* and *Beaky Buzzard.* As the years passed, Daffy Duck moved into the magazine, as did Tweety and Sylvester.

In its original incarnation *Looney Tunes and Merrie Melodies* lasted until #262 in the summer of 1962. Gold Key revived it from 1975 to 1984 under the modified title of just plain *Looney Tunes.* In 1994 DC, which shared a parent company with the Warner menagerie, started a new *Looney Tunes* that has continued to thrive.

LUKE CAGE

60¢
90
FEB
02149
MARVEL® COMICS GROUP
POWER MAN AND IRON FIST
ENTER UNUS...
...UNLESS LUKE AND THE FIST FIGURE OUT A WAY TO TOUCH HIM, THEY'RE DEAD!

■ A blend of the best qualities of a tough private eye and a tough superhero, the far from charitable Luke Cage was introduced by Marvel in the aptly named *Hero for Hire* in the spring of 1972. That was a time when blaxploitation movies were doing well at the box office. *Shaft,* about a tough African-American private eye, had been a hit the year before. Marvel being Marvel, they made their latest African-American hero not only a private eye but a superhero as well. Archie Goodwin was the writer, George Tuska the penciler, and Billy Graham, one of the relatively few black artists in comics, the inker.

Like many another superman, Cage became one by accident. Sent to a maximum security prison for a crime he didn't commit, Carl Lucas volunteered for a scientific experiment in order to gain parole and then seek revenge. The experiment went wrong, but it turned him into a powerful superhero. Literally busting out of prison, he returned to Manhattan. After getting revenge out of the way, he changed his name to Luke Cage and set himself up in a tacky office on West Forty-second Street. Not an altruist, he charged any client who was in need of superhuman assistance.

THE FIST'D TELL YOU NICE, BUT HE AIN'T HERE, SO LISSEN, AN' LISSEN GOOD.
EITHER YOU COME LOOKIN' FOR ME AN' THE FIST* OR I'LL COME LOOKIN' FOR YOU!
AN' THAT COULD GET REAL UGLY.
*EVERY MONTH AT NEWSSTANDS AND SPECIALTY SHOPS EVERYWHERE. ASK FOR...
POWER MAN AND IRON FIST
AND BRING 60¢.

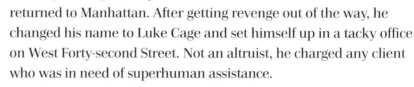

After a couple of so-so years, Marvel, to beef up sales, renamed Cage's comic book *Powerman,* and for some years he and a character known as Iron Fist shared the title. That folded in the middle 1980s, and then in the 1990s a book simply called *Cage* had a short run. Luke Cage was last seen in a five-part series in 2002, with scripts by Brian Azzarello and art by Richard Corben.

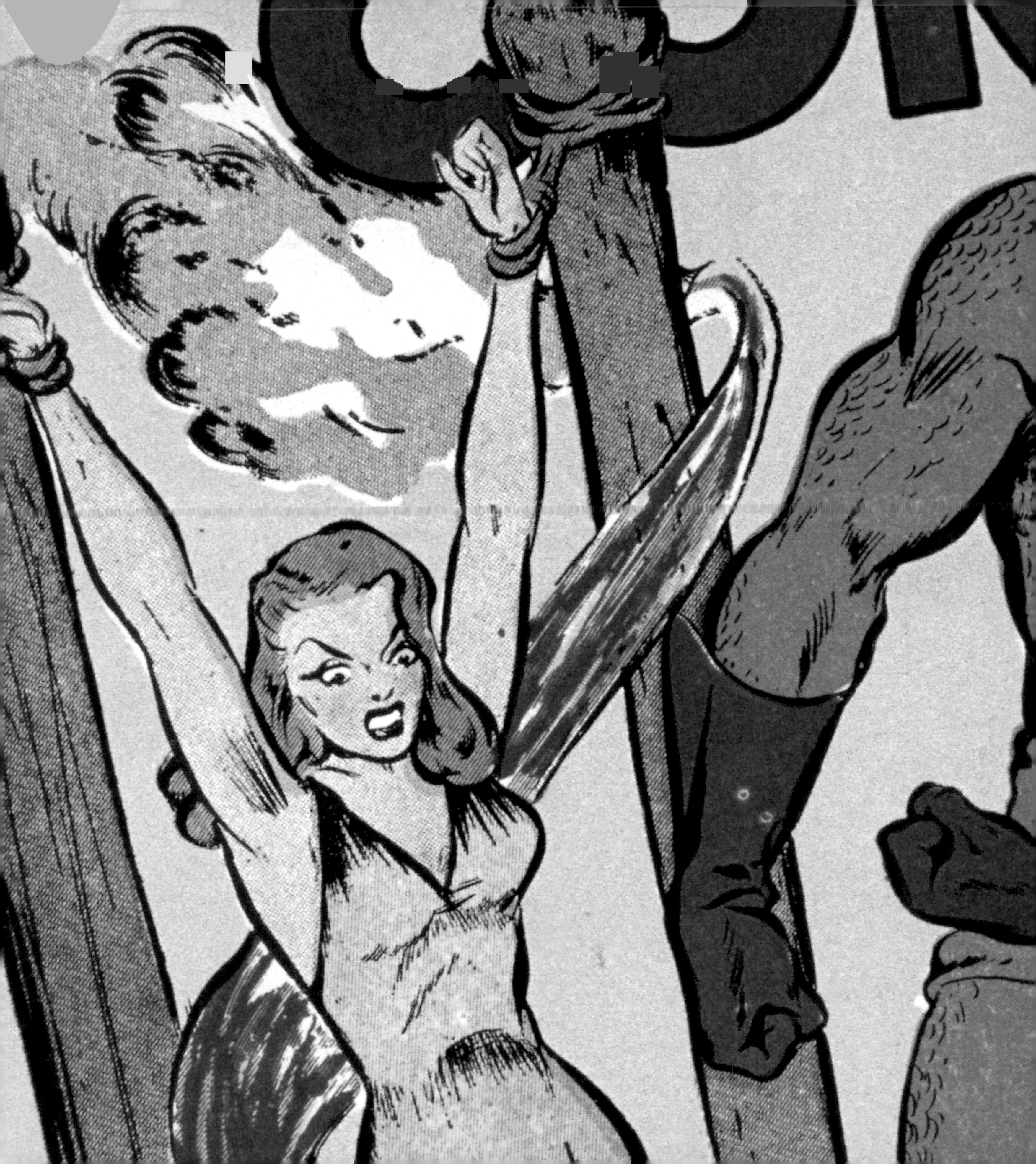

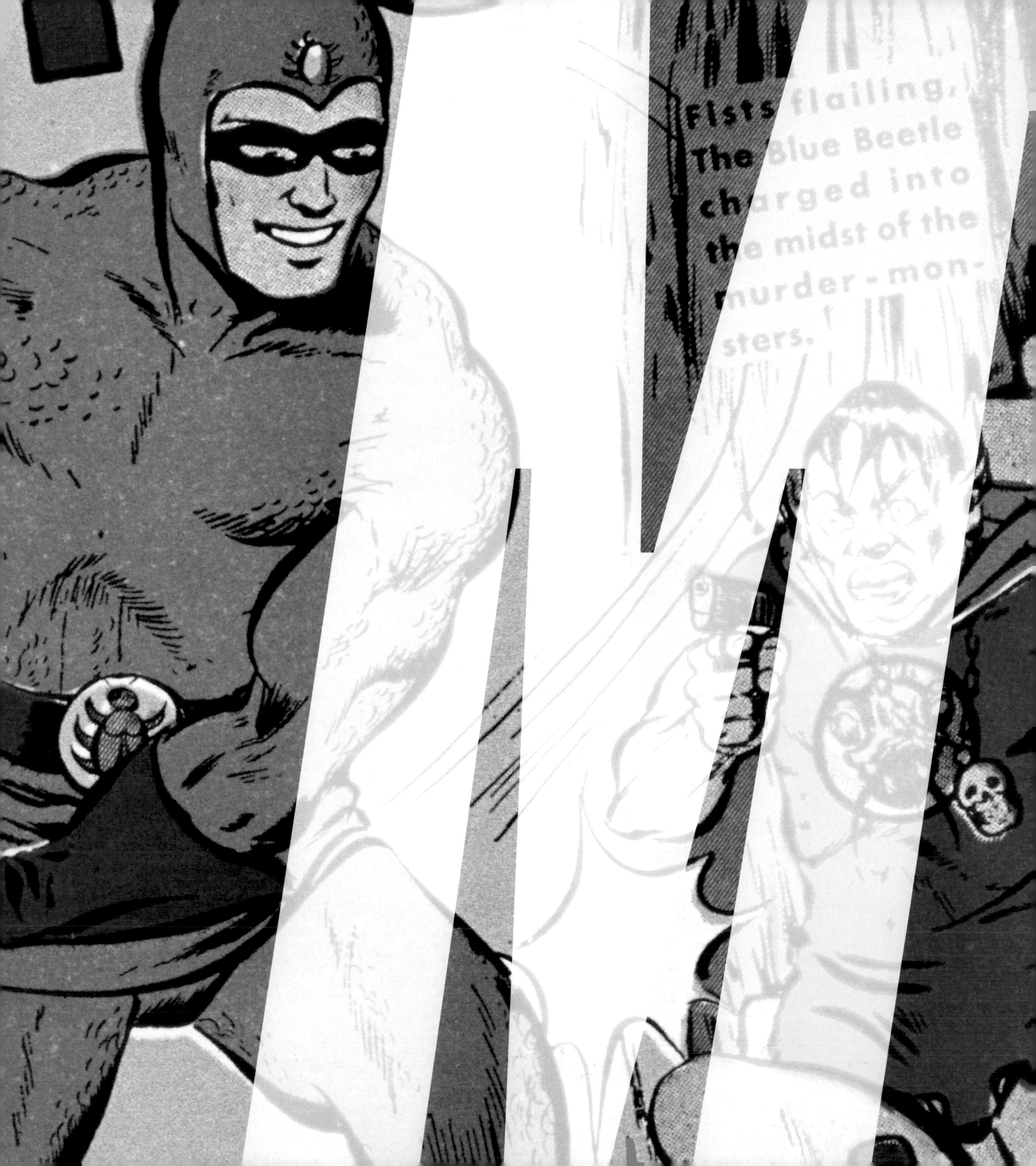
Fists flailing, The Blue Beetle charged into the midst of the murder-monsters.

MACHINE MAN

■ A latter-day Robotman, he first appeared in a magazine of his own in 1978. Published by Marvel, *Machine Man* was written and drawn by Jack Kirby, who'd returned to the Stan Lee fold in 1976 after a sojourn over at DC. Under the name Mr. Machine, the 'bot had debuted the previous summer in the eighth issue of *2001, A Space Odyssey*. He was an addition to the movie adaptation that Kirby invented.

Machine Man, like many a mechanism before him—and not a few superheroes—was originally intended to be a super soldier. Initially he was one of a batch of fifty-one experimental robot warriors produced by a California research facility. He turned out to be the only one without defects. Looked after as a houseguest by a scientist named Dr. Able Stark, Machine Man developed into a well-rounded and non-goofy robot. After Dr. Stark fashioned a believable flesh-like face and convincing hairpiece for him, Machine Man could pass for a human being. That is, if he didn't use his extendable arms or call upon his anti-gravity units to fly.

#2 IN A FOUR-ISSUE LIMITED SERIES
MARVEL
MACHINE MAN
1984 MARVEL COMICS GROUP
75¢
2
NOV
APPROVED BY THE COMICS CODE AUTHORITY

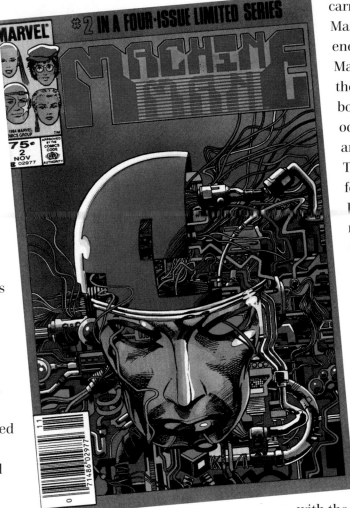

When the doctor died in saving him, Machine Man took to calling himself Aaron Stark, went to work as an insurance agent, and also began carrying on in the manner of a Marvel superhero. His major enemy was a lady known as Madam Menace, and he now and then sat in with the Avengers of both coasts. His enemies would occasionally disassemble him and make off with his head. The same thing was done to his female robot acquaintance Jocasta (why this lady was named after the mother of Oedipus is a matter for psychiatrists to ponder).

Kirby abandoned his android creation with the ninth issue. When the tenth issue finally came along in the summer of 1979, after a hiatus of eight months, Marv Wolfman was the writer and Steve Ditko the artist. They continued as a creative team until the end of the first run of *Machine Man*, which came with the nineteenth issue early in 1981. Aaron Stark returned in 1984 for a four-issue run, with scripts by Tom DeFalco and art by Herb Trimpe and Barry Windsor-Smith. Machine Man was most recently seen in a twelve-issue run that commenced in 1999.

MAD

■ The magazine that brought college humor to the junior high school set, *Mad* began as a ten-cent comic book in the summer of 1952. The brainchild of Harvey Kurtzman, it was published by EC Comics. Making fun of popular comic strips, television shows, and advertising had long been a staple of campus humor such as *The Harvard Lampoon*, *The California Pelican*, and *The Stanford Chaparral*, and in the late 1940s Dell's revived *Ballyhoo* had offered a similar blend on the newsstand. What Kurtzman did was to use such material in comic-book form, making it quicker and easier to assimilate.

Mad was converted to a black-and-white magazine in 1955 and continues as such to this day. Kurtzman departed soon after the changeover and was replaced by Al Feldstein as editor. Nick Meglin succeeded Feldstein. The magazine has remained steadfastly adolescent and irreverent for generations, never tiring of taking satirical potshots at such sitting ducks as movies, television, and advertising. In recent years, due to plummeting sales, the content has become somewhat raunchier. In addition to Kurtzman, the magazine brought fame to such artists as Jack Davis, Don Martin, Al Jaffee, Mort Drucker, and Sergio Aragones. Its mascot, Alfred E. Neuman, became a national celebrity and still appears on every cover. Over the years *Mad* inspired a host of imitations, including *Panic*, *Sick*, *Crazy*, *Cracked*, *Madhouse*, *Plop!*, *Not Brand Ecch*, and *Humbug*.

THE NOSTALGIC
NO. 4
MAD
FREE
AHA, DR. WHATSIT! THE CASE TAKES AN INTERESTING TURN! HERE'S A MUCH MORE SUSPICIOUS CHARACTER TO FOLLOW!

GET ON!
TRUM TRUM TRUM
GRRUMM
SPOK
KSPOK KPAF
SIGH
GOSH-DARN IT!
...OUT OF GAS!
...JUST AT MY BIG MOMENT... OUT OF GAS!
...JUST AS I'M ABOUT TO SAVE THE GIRL FROM THE VILLIANS LIKE A KNIGHT IN SHINING ARMOR...
...OUT OF GAS!
...SAVE THE GIRL FROM THE VILLIANS? WHATAYA MEAN, SAVE THE GIRL FROM THE VILLIANS? WE AIN'T VILLIANS! WE WERE JUST ABOUT TO GIVE HER THE TROPHY FOR THE MOTORCYCLE SPEED RECORD! SHE JUST WON IT... HANDS DOWN!

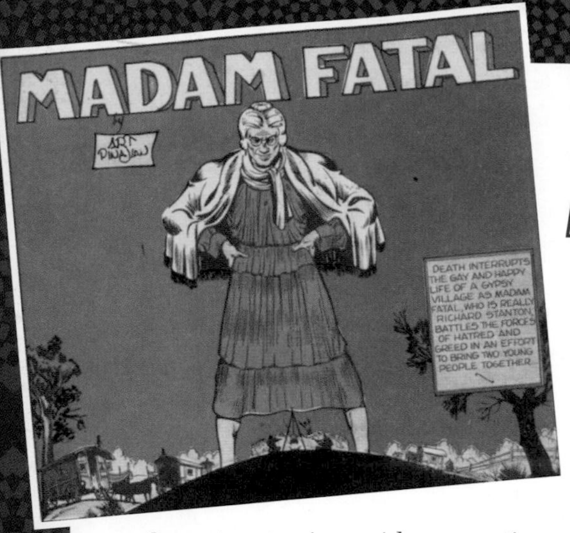
MADAM FATAL
DEATH INTERRUPTS THE GAY AND HAPPY LIFE OF A GYPSY VILLAGE AS MADAM FATAL, WHO IS REALLY RICHARD STANTON, BATTLES THE FORCES OF HATRED AND GREED IN AN EFFORT TO BRING TWO YOUNG PEOPLE TOGETHER.

MADAM FATAL

■ Although a minor early 1940s character, Madam Fatal has retained a certain celebrity because, as the Overstreet price guide never tires of pointing out, "this character is a man dressed as a woman." The man in question was Richard Stanton, "famous character actor and master of makeup." Quitting the stage and assuming the guise of a white-haired little old lady, he devoted years of his life to hunting down the kidnapper of his baby daughter. In the first issue of *Crack Comics* (May 1940), Stanton caught up with the gangster responsible for the kidnapping. The kidnapper, unfortunately, was accidentally killed before revealing what had become of the missing girl. Stanton decided to "go after crime and law breakers as Madam Fatal" and also, possibly, to find his daughter.

Art Pinajian drew the feature. While Stanton was certainly a cross-dresser, he was actually in the tradition of Lon Chaney, who'd disguised himself as a little old lady in the movie *The Unholy Three* and Lionel Barrymore, who'd played a similar role in *The Devil Doll.* He was more an eccentrically costumed crimefighter than a drag queen. Madam Fatal hung up his dress after *Crack* #22 (March 1941), leaving readers to wonder if he ever found his missing daughter.

MADAM SATAN

■ A femme fatale if there ever was one, Madam Satan went her evil way in six issues of *Pep Comics* in 1941. She first materialized in #16 (November 1941). She was a dark-haired, sultry lady, an updated version of the heartless vamp who'd haunted the movies in the years between the two world wars and a forerunner of the destructive duplicitous women of 1940s film noir. An early caption explained her origin—"The Devil searched far and long for an ally to wreak havoc amongst mortals. . . . Then the black, corrupt soul of a beautiful woman, a victim of her own fiendish plan on Earth, left its bodily habitation to stand before the king of Purgatory . . . and his search was at an end . . . the Devil had found himself a fitting mate."

Using the name Iola, occupying her body again and donning a slinky satin evening gown, Madam Satan insinuated herself into various lives and set out to corrupt as many men as possible. On occasion, she also turned into a vampire bat. Although Iola never quite succeeded in shipping an innocent soul off to hell, she did manage to cause an awful lot of death and destruction. She exited *Pep* after #21 to make room for the more amiable Archie. The feature was drawn by Harry Lucey.

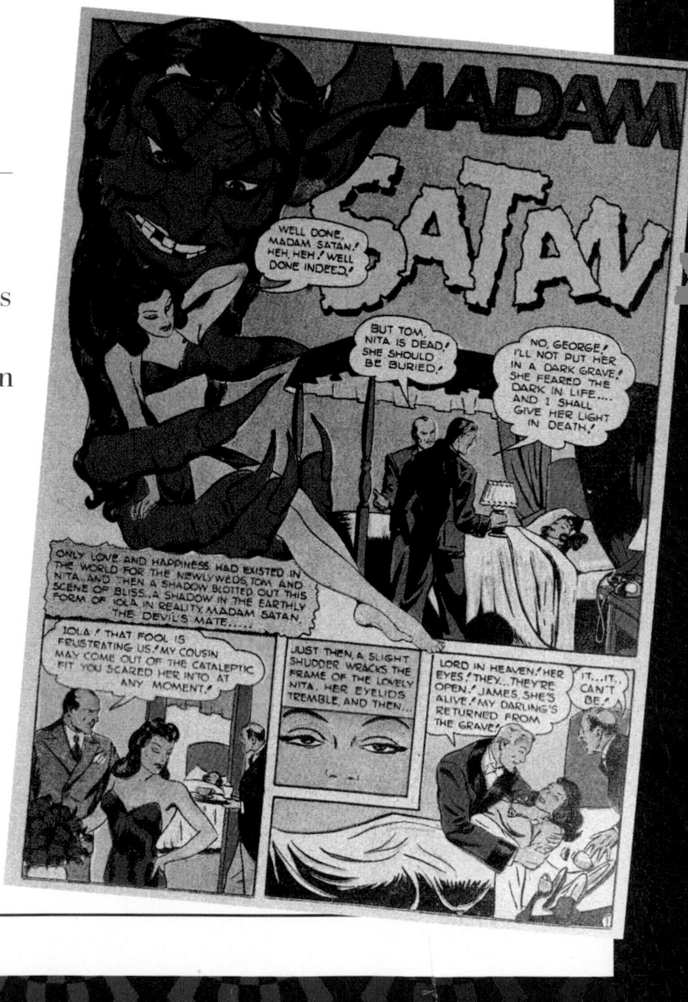
MADAM SATAN
WELL DONE, MADAM SATAN! HEH, HEH! WELL DONE INDEED!
BUT TOM, NITA IS DEAD! SHE SHOULD BE BURIED!
NO, GEORGE! I'LL NOT PUT HER IN A DARK GRAVE! SHE FEARED THE DARK IN LIFE.... AND I SHALL GIVE HER LIGHT IN DEATH!
ONLY LOVE AND HAPPINESS HAD EXISTED IN THE WORLD FOR THE NEWLYWEDS, TOM AND NITA...AND THEN A SHADOW BLOTTED OUT THIS SCENE OF BLISS...A SHADOW IN THE EARTHLY FORM OF IOLA, IN REALITY MADAM SATAN, THE DEVIL'S MATE....
IOLA! THAT FOOL IS FRUSTRATING US! MY COUSIN MAY COME OUT OF THE CATALEPTIC FIT YOU SCARED HER INTO AT ANY MOMENT!
JUST THEN, A SLIGHT SHUDDER WRACKS THE FRAME OF THE LOVELY NITA. HER EYELIDS TREMBLE, AND THEN...
LORD IN HEAVEN! HER EYES! THEY...THEY'RE OPEN! JAMES, SHE'S ALIVE! MY DARLING'S RETURNED FROM THE GRAVE!
IT...IT... CAN'T BE!

MAGNO

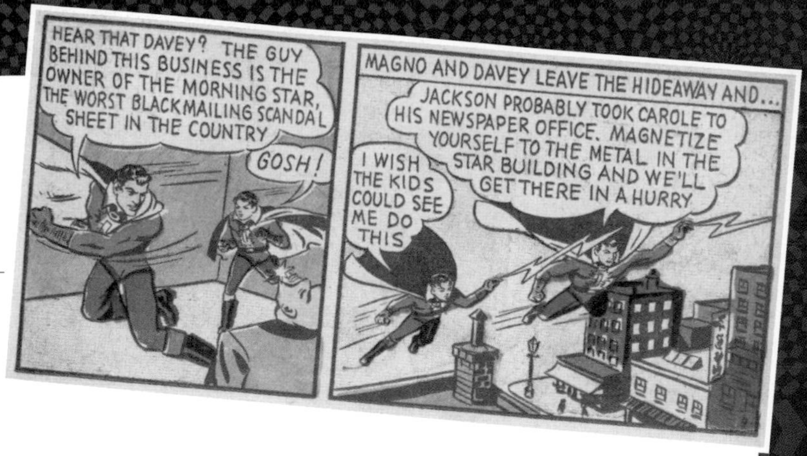
HEAR THAT DAVEY? THE GUY BEHIND THIS BUSINESS IS THE OWNER OF THE MORNING STAR, THE WORST BLACKMAILING SCANDAL SHEET IN THE COUNTRY
GOSH!
MAGNO AND DAVEY LEAVE THE HIDEAWAY AND...
JACKSON PROBABLY TOOK CAROLE TO HIS NEWSPAPER OFFICE. MAGNETIZE YOURSELF TO THE METAL IN THE STAR BUILDING AND WE'LL GET THERE IN A HURRY
I WISH THE KIDS COULD SEE ME DO THIS

■ Also known as the Magnetic Man, Magno had "strange powers which enable him to draw to himself any metal object or project his image upon it. He can also streak through space, drawn by anything metallic. With such forces at his command, Magno goes forth to fight evil."

Magno was the star of Ace's *Super-Mystery Comics* from 1940 to 1946. The probable author of the early scripts was editor Robert Turner. Among those who illustrated Magno's magnetic adventures were Harry Lucey, Jim Mooney, Joe Gallagher, the incomparable Louis Ferstadt, and Harvey Kurtzman. In the fourth issue Magno acquired a magnetic boy companion named Davey. Their chief recurring villain was a white-faced fellow known as the Clown, who behaved in a manner similar to that of the Joker. The team also appeared in twenty-six issues of *Four Favorites.*

MAGNUS

■ Magnus, a rebellious resident of the year 4000 A.D. was dedicated to clobbering robots. He was introduced in Gold Key's *Magnus, Robot Fighter* early in 1963 and stuck to his 'bot-bashing for the next fourteen years. Russ Manning was the original artist and writer. Magnus returned in the early 1990s by way of two Valiant Comics titles and yet again at the end of the decade.

The stories were set in North Am, "the incredible city that covers every habitable area of the North American continent." Robots, originally built to serve humans, had gradually become the "masters of men." Magnus was a sort of futuristic Tarzan, raised in isolation by a benevolent robot and "trained to rely on my brain, rather than on tools." For good measure, his mentor, the gold-plated 1A, also taught him super-karate that enabled him to smash metal with just a chop of his bare hand. Returned to North Am, he set out at once to disable as many tyrannical robots as he could. Teamed with the lovely blond Leeja Clane, Magnus found a wide assortment of mechanical men to disable over the years. Manning, who also drew *Tarzan,* was an excellent fantasy artist, and he quite obviously enjoyed building the future megalopolis and coming up with all sorts of mean-minded 'bots.

Early in the nineties, Jim Shooter's Valiant line licensed the character and featured him in a series of new adventures, drawn by Boy Layton, and a second title that reprinted Manning's earlier work. Magnus was up to his old tricks again in 1997 and 1998 in an eighteen-issue run of *Magnus, Robot Fighter.*

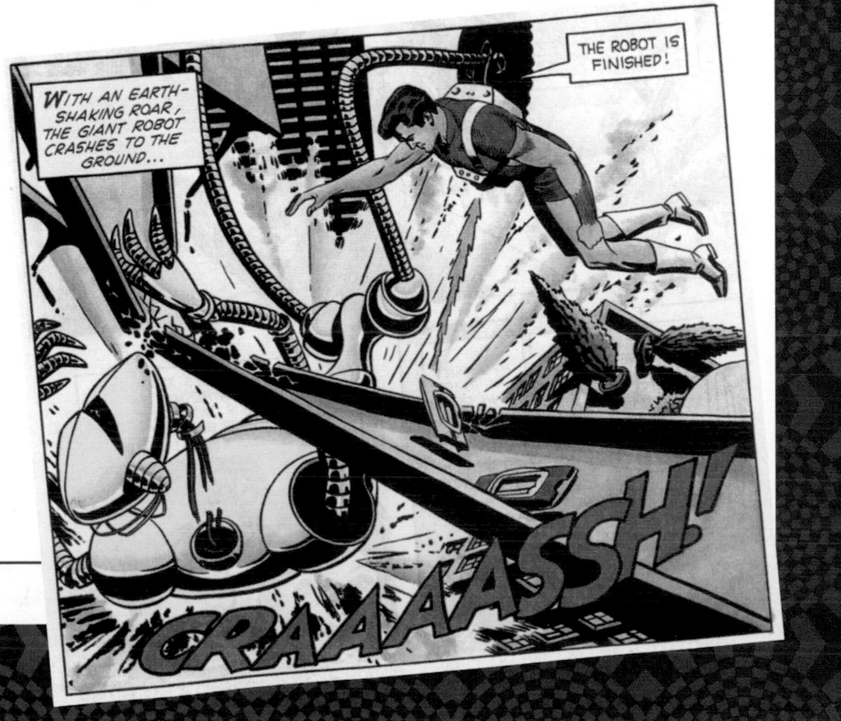
WITH AN EARTH-SHAKING ROAR, THE GIANT ROBOT CRASHES TO THE GROUND...
THE ROBOT IS FINISHED!
CRAAAAASSH!

MANEELY, JOE

(1926–1958)

■ In the decade before Marvel leaped forward into the Second Superhero Age, Maneely was their premier cover artist. In addition to doing considerable interior work, he was responsible for over five hundred covers for every type of Atlas/Marvel comic book from jungle to cowboy. Unlike some of his bullpen contemporaries, Maneely was both fast and good.

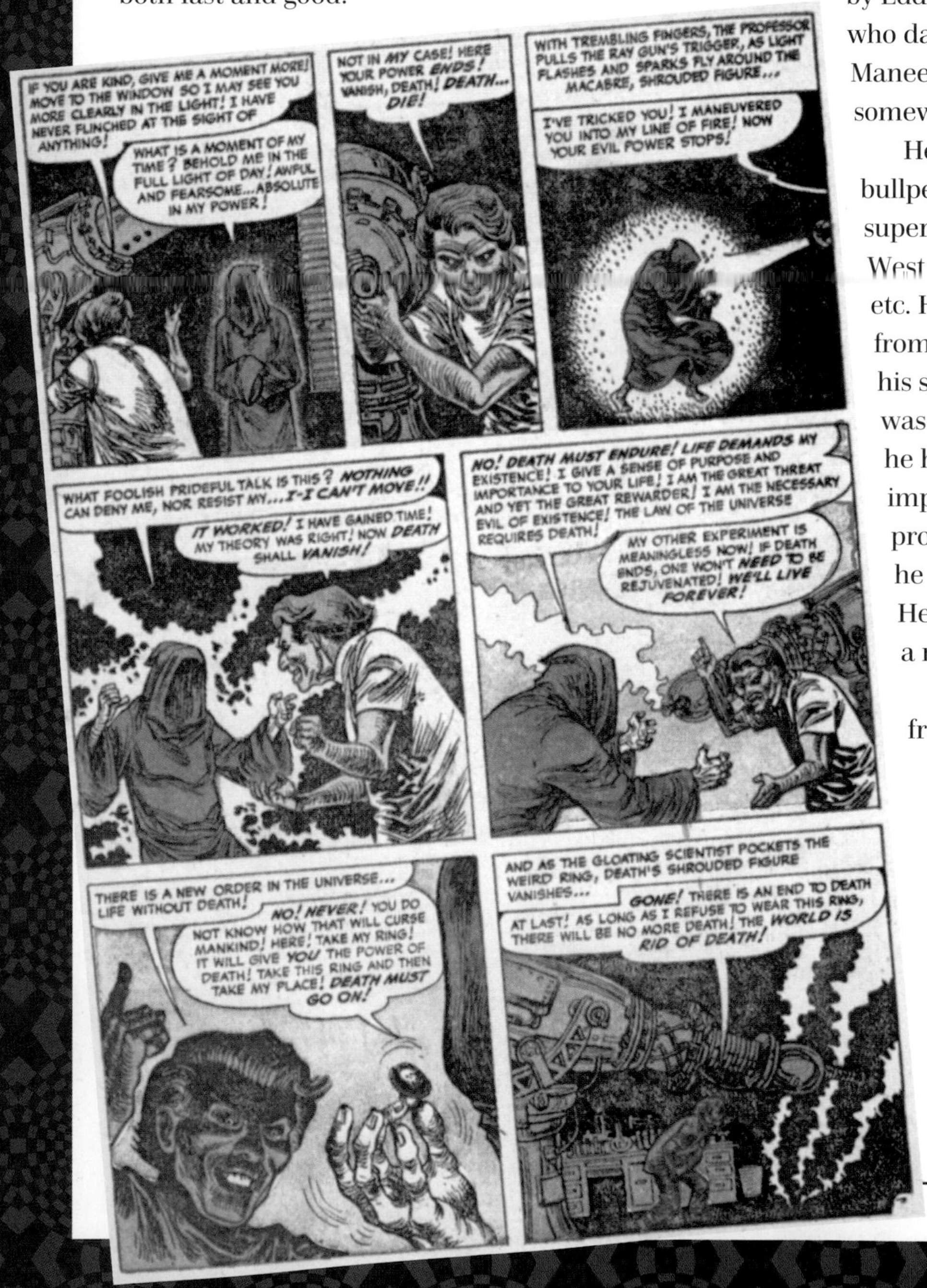

IF YOU ARE KIND, GIVE ME A MOMENT MORE! MOVE TO THE WINDOW SO I MAY SEE YOU MORE CLEARLY IN THE LIGHT! I HAVE NEVER FLINCHED AT THE SIGHT OF ANYTHING!
WHAT IS A MOMENT OF MY TIME? BEHOLD ME IN THE FULL LIGHT OF DAY! AWFUL AND FEARSOME...ABSOLUTE IN MY POWER!
NOT IN MY CASE! HERE YOUR POWER ENDS! VANISH, DEATH! DEATH... DIE!
WITH TREMBLING FINGERS, THE PROFESSOR PULLS THE RAY GUN'S TRIGGER, AS LIGHT FLASHES AND SPARKS FLY AROUND THE MACABRE, SHROUDED FIGURE...
I'VE TRICKED YOU! I MANEUVERED YOU INTO MY LINE OF FIRE! NOW YOUR EVIL POWER STOPS!
WHAT FOOLISH PRIDEFUL TALK IS THIS? NOTHING CAN DENY ME, NOR RESIST MY...I-I CAN'T MOVE!!
IT WORKED! I HAVE GAINED TIME! MY THEORY WAS RIGHT! NOW DEATH SHALL VANISH!
NO! DEATH MUST ENDURE! LIFE DEMANDS MY EXISTENCE! I GIVE A SENSE OF PURPOSE AND IMPORTANCE TO YOUR LIFE! I AM THE GREAT THREAT AND YET THE GREAT REWARDER! I AM THE NECESSARY EVIL OF EXISTENCE! THE LAW OF THE UNIVERSE REQUIRES DEATH!
MY OTHER EXPERIMENT IS MEANINGLESS NOW! IF DEATH ENDS, ONE WON'T NEED TO BE REJUVENATED! WE'LL LIVE FOREVER!
THERE IS A NEW ORDER IN THE UNIVERSE... LIFE WITHOUT DEATH!
NO! NEVER! YOU DO NOT KNOW HOW THAT WILL CURSE MANKIND! HERE! TAKE MY RING! IT WILL GIVE YOU THE POWER OF DEATH! TAKE THIS RING AND THEN TAKE MY PLACE! DEATH MUST GO ON!
AND AS THE GLOATING SCIENTIST POCKETS THE WEIRD RING, DEATH'S SHROUDED FIGURE VANISHES...
GONE! THERE IS AN END TO DEATH AT LAST! AS LONG AS I REFUSE TO WEAR THIS RING, THERE WILL BE NO MORE DEATH! THE WORLD IS RID OF DEATH!

Born in Pennsylvania, he worked in the art department of the *Philadelphia Daily News* and then broke into comic books in 1948. He started with Street & Smith, where he drew *Nick Carter* for *Shadow Comics*, *Tao Anwar*, a boy magician, and *Red Dragon* for both *Super Magician Comics* and *Red Dragon*. He looks to have been influenced by Edd Cartier, a gifted illustrator of S&S pulp magazines, who dabbled in comic books briefly in the late 1940s. Maneely's early approach to drawing and inking and his somewhat humorous approach are similar to Cartier's.

He joined Marvel late in the 1940s, assigned to the bullpen. He worked on every genre in those mainly superhero-free years. One of his specialties was the Old West and he drew *The Ringo Kid*, *Wyatt Earp*, *Kid Colt*, etc. He also did jungle stuff and illustrated everything from *Speed Carter, Spaceman* to *The Black Knight*. Despite his speed, Maneely's work never looked hurried and was always thoughtfully constructed. By this time he had developed his mature style, and it was impressively distinct from a great deal of the Marvel product of the time. The Alex Schomburg of his day, he found time to draw most of Marvel's covers as well. He did a few jobs for DC and, with scripts by Stan Lee, a newspaper Sunday called *Mrs. Lyon's Cubs*.

In 1958 Maneely was killed in an accidental fall from a car on the Long Island Railroad.

MANGA

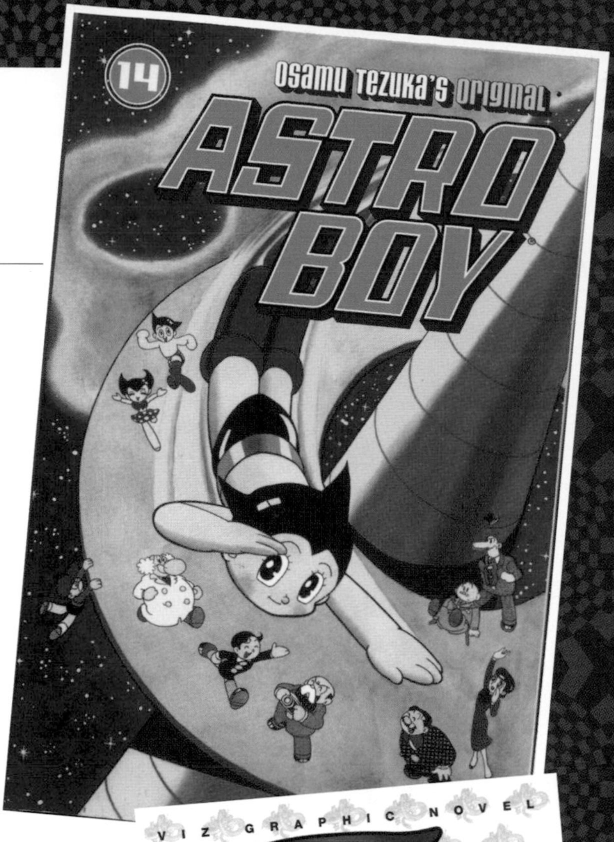
14
OSAMU TEZUKA'S ORIGINAL
ASTRO BOY

■ Manga is the Japanese word for comic book, and in Japan, men, women, and children love comics. Manga sell in the billions there. In this country, mostly in English translations, Manga has a much smaller, but no less enthusiastic, following. The books are printed in black-and-white, with considerable reliance on a wide range of tone patterns. Since Japanese read from right to left, stories start at the back and end at what would be for American readers the front cover. In many of the translated Manga, the page images are flopped and laid out to simulate U.S. comic books, although in recent years some follow the Japanese pattern. In addition to magazine format, Manga are reprinted as trade paperbacks and as fat three hundred- and four hundred-page graphic novels. A typical continuity often stretches across 2,000 or more pages.

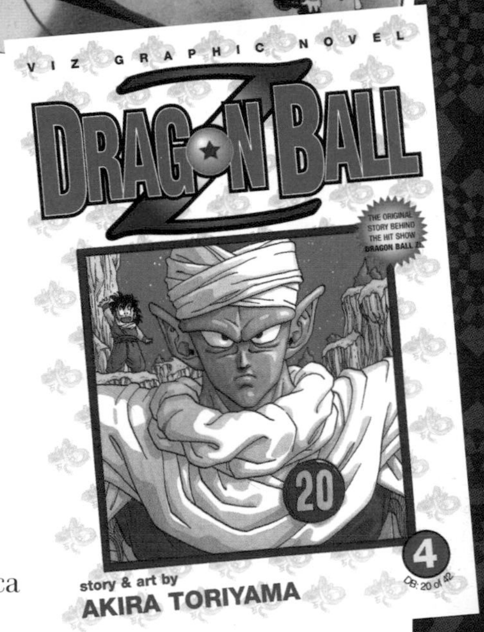
VIZ GRAPHIC NOVEL
DRAGON BALL Z
THE ORIGINAL STORY BEHIND THE HIT SHOW DRAGON BALL Z
20
4
story & art by
AKIRA TORIYAMA

Although the Japanese have been involved with graphic storytelling for centuries, it wasn't until the late 1940s and early 1950s, in the years immediately after the end of World War II, that the modern Manga emerged. The most influential pioneer was Osamu Tezuka, known in Japan as "the Godfather of Manga" and "the God of Comics." In 1951, much influenced by American animated cartoons of the 1930s and 1940s, Tezuka introduced his *Tetsuwan Atom* Manga. The cute robot-child with big eyes became an animated cartoon character in 1963, with Tezuka doing the animation. Renamed *Astro Boy*, the dubbed series became a television hit in the United States. The American *Astro Boy* comic books of the sixties were originals produced in this country.

Tezuka continued in both Manga and Anime. Among his other comic books was a cartoony adaptation of *Crime and Punishment,* also drawn in the cute wide-eyed style. Later on, adopting a more realistic style, he turned out several ambitious and multipart serials. These included *Adolph,* which is a grim thriller that numbers Adolph Hitler and two boys named Adolph in its large cast and takes place in Japan and Germany during World War II. This work, created in the early 1980s, was translated and printed in America in trade paperback format in the middle 1990s. Among Tezuka's other major works are *Black Jack, Phoenix*, and a lengthy biography of Buddha.

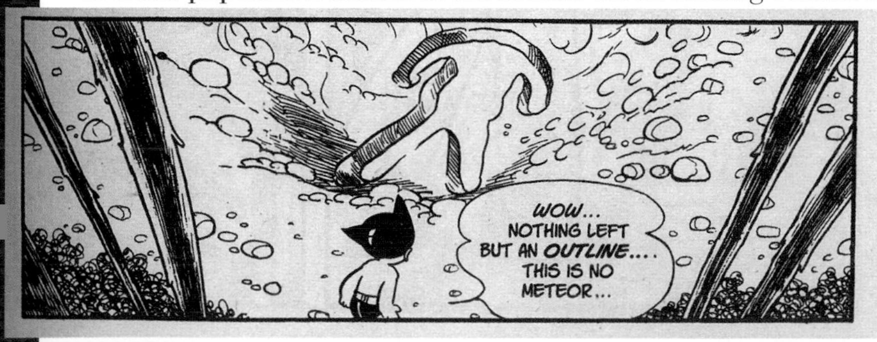
WOW... NOTHING LEFT BUT AN OUTLINE.... THIS IS NO METEOR...

From the late 1980s onward, fueled by the interest in Japanese animation, an increasing number of Japanese Manga have been translated and published in America. The two largest publishers are Viz Comics and Dark Horse. Among the other popular titles available in English are *Sailor Moon* by Naoko

Takeuchi, dealing with a young, saucer-eyed teenage girl who becomes a "sailor-suited soldier of love and justice. . . . Along with her allies, she fights to protect the Earth from evil"; *Crying Freeman*, about a humble artisan who becomes a professional hitman who cries every time he knocks off somebody; *Ranma ½* by Rumiko Takahashi, featuring a young martial arts practitioner who turns into a girl whenever doused with cold water; *Nausicaa of the Valley of the Wind*, a future fantasy that mixes intrigue with ecological concerns and was written and drawn by Japan's premier animator Hayao Miyazaki, creator of such animated features as *Spirited Away* and *Princess Mononoke*.

STAN SAKAI'S
USAGI
YOJIMBO
SAKAI ©1988
FANTAGRAPHICS BOOKS

Another popular Manga stateside is Katsuhiro Otomo's *Akira*, a vast, handsomely drawn and somewhat ponderous adventure set in a bleak, devastated future Tokyo and dealing with weapons of mass destruction, violently gifted mutants, and a cast of thousands. Marvel reprinted some of *Akira* in the middle 1980s, but it is now available in beautiful black-and-white and in its entirety in six massive graphic novels. *Lupin III* is a bawdy adventure series that features the grandson of the early-twentieth-century French gentleman burglar Arsene Lupin. It was written and drawn by Kazuhiko Kato under his pen name Monkey Punch. The 1979 animated film *The Castle of Cagliostro*, directed by Miyazaki, was based on Monkey Punch's Lupin III yarns. *Lone Wolf and Cub* has been a popular favorite in the United States for several years.

One of the most successful current Manga, in America and worldwide, is *Dragon Ball* and its spin-off *Dragon Ball Z*. Begun in a Japanese comic book written and drawn by Akira Toriyama, the quest for the seven magic dragon balls has branched out into animated shows, games, and sundry other merchandise. While in Japan Manga deal with everything from cooking and real estate to erotic romance, the imports deal chiefly with male adventure and adventure featuring empowered young women.

The styles and layouts of Manga have influenced quite a few American comic books. Frank Miller was strongly influenced, as his *Ronin* shows. Some American imitations include *Ninja High School* and *The Dirty Pair*. Stan Sakai's humorous *Usagi Yojimbo*, begun in 1984 and still going, deals with a rabbit warrior in medieval Japan. Americanized Manga continue to grow in popularity and are available not only in comic shops but in the major book chains.

MANNING, RUSS

■ See MAGNUS.

MARSH, JESSE

■ See TARZAN.

MARTIAN MANHUNTER

■ Avoiding the rush, he set up shop as a superhero some months before the Silver Age revival really got rolling. J'Onn J'Onzz, better known as the Martian Manhunter, was introduced in *Detective Comics* #225 (November 1955).

J'Onzz was introduced in a six-page story that explained that he'd been transported from Mars as the result of an experiment conducted by Professor Mark Erdel. Unfortunately for the big, green-skinned alien, the professor's contraption couldn't send him home, and Erdel complicated the situation by dying of a heart attack. J'Onzz, realizing he was stranded, assumed human shape and coloration and changed his name to John Jones. He then—rather easily for someone who'd only been on Earth for a day—got a job as a plainclothes police detective. As a cop, the Manhunter made use of an assortment of abilities not available to the average law officer. The initial writer was Joseph Samachson, who also wrote pulp science fiction under the name of William Morrison. Joe Certa, who was also working on the *Joe Palooka* newspaper strip at the time, was the artist.

John Jones departed *Detective* in the summer of 1963 and seemed to have died, but the Martian Manhunter went on without his alter ego. He took to appearing in various DC titles, including *House of Mystery*, *Adventure*, and *World's Finest*. He was also present in *The Brave and the Bold* #50 (October–November 1963), in a teamup with the Green Arrow. That was the issue that launched the team concept to the title. The Manhunter has also been a now and again member of the Justice League. With the help of an occasional limited series, he's survived into the twenty-first century. Most recently he appeared in a thirty-six-issue run that started in 1998 and ended in 2001.

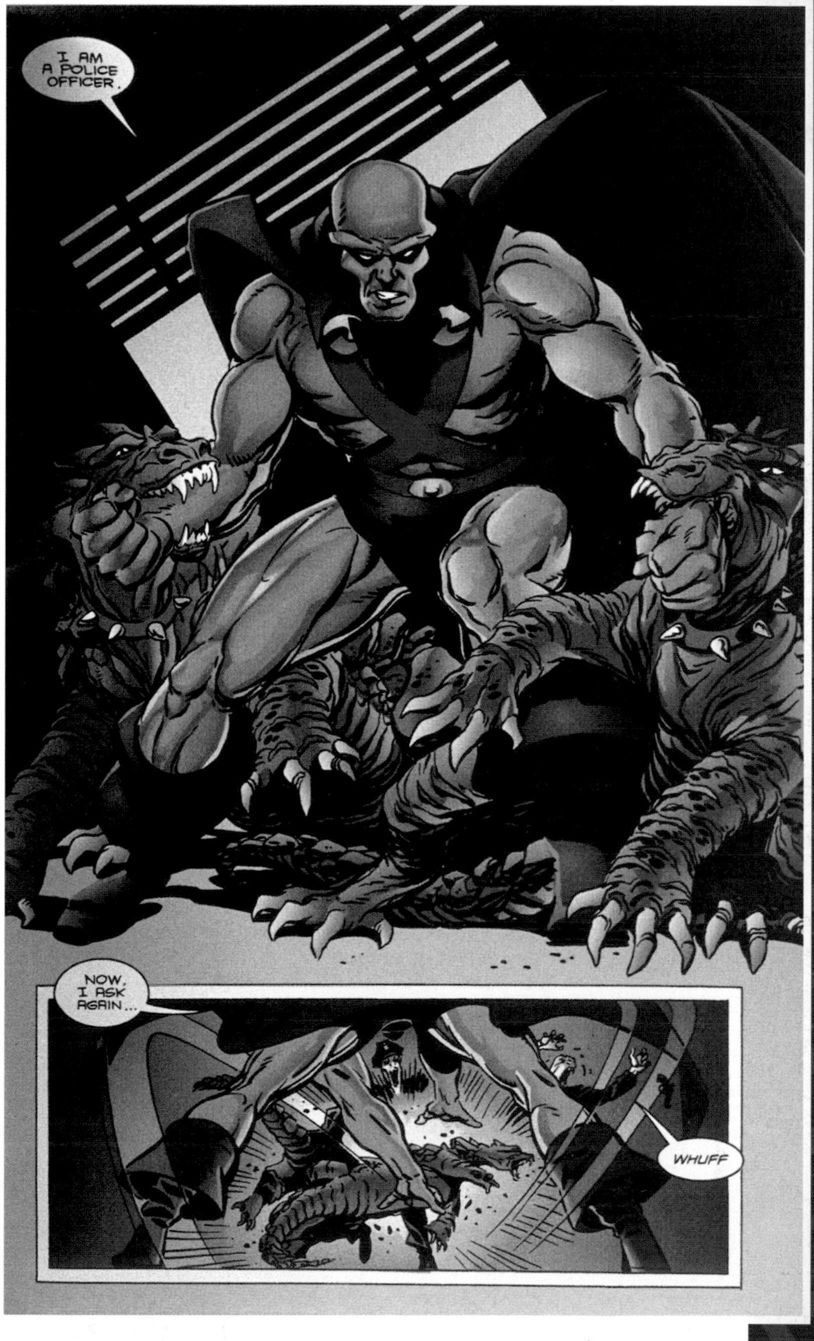
I AM A POLICE OFFICER.
NOW, I ASK AGAIN...
WHUFF

MARY MARVEL

■ Though overshadowed by her big brother, she still managed to do very well in comic books. Mary Marvel was introduced in *Captain Marvel Adventures* #18 (December 1942) and then became the star of *Wow Comics* from #9 (January 1943) onward. She was the first teenage girl superhero, and her initial stay in comics lasted until late 1953.

When Mary Batson first appeared, it was explained that she and her brother Billy Batson had been separated as babies. After being reunited, Mary discovered that Billy's magic word "Shazam!" worked for her as well. Though still a teen when converted to Mary Marvel, she had all the powers of Captain Marvel and wore a skirted version of his red-and-gold costume with the lightning bolt on the chest. Her version of the magic word, though, was an acronym not for Solomon, Hercules, Atlas, Zeus, Achilles, and Mercury but rather for Selena, Hipolyta, Ariadne, Zephyrus, Aurora, and Minerva.

She appeared in *Wow* until the autumn of 1947, in twenty-five issues of her own magazine from 1945 to 1948, and in *The Marvel Family* until late in 1953. Most of the adventures of Mary Marvel were written by the prolific Otto Binder. Marc Swayze was the original illustrator, then Jack Binder became the regular artist. Mary Marvel returned to comics as an occasional backup in the middle 1970s, when DC brought back her brother in *Shazam!* She also made cameo appearances in the 1987 *Shazam!* miniseries and still turns up occasionally for a reunion of what now is known as the Shazam Family. She also figured in a recent revival of the Justice League.

MARVEL BOY

■ Another convert to the wonders of atomic energy, Marvel Boy maintained his superpowers by taking a uranium pill once a day. Introduced late in 1950, when interest in superheros were high, the *Marvel Boy* comic book did not thrive. Marvel's earlier Marvel Boy had appeared once in *Daring Comics* in the summer of 1940.

That earlier version was the creation of Joe Simon, Jack Kirby, and scriptwriter Martin Burstein. Their Marvel Boy was fourteen-year-old Martin Burns, who also happened to be the reincarnation of Hercules. Sent a costume by way of a mysterious messenger and then visited by a shadowy ghost, he became a superhero and went forth to fight Nazi spies. He appeared once again in *U.S.A. Comics* early in 1943 before retiring.

The new Marvel Boy was introduced in his own comic book, with a December 1950 cover date. A cover blurb, an early example of Stan Lee hyperbole, touted him as "The Newest, the Most Amazing Character in Comics!!" This time he was Bob Grayson, living with his scientist father on the planet Uranus. Deciding that earth has more problems than peaceful Uranus, Professor Grayson sends his son there to combat evil. Marvel Boy specialized in combating Soviet spies, zombies, fish-people, and invaders from Saturn.

Each issue featured several adventures of the young hero. Russ Heath illustrated #1 and then Bill Everett took over, staying on until Marvel Boy retired in the autumn of 1951. Marvel brought the character back briefly in the late 1970s and again in 2000.

MARVEL MYSTERY COMICS

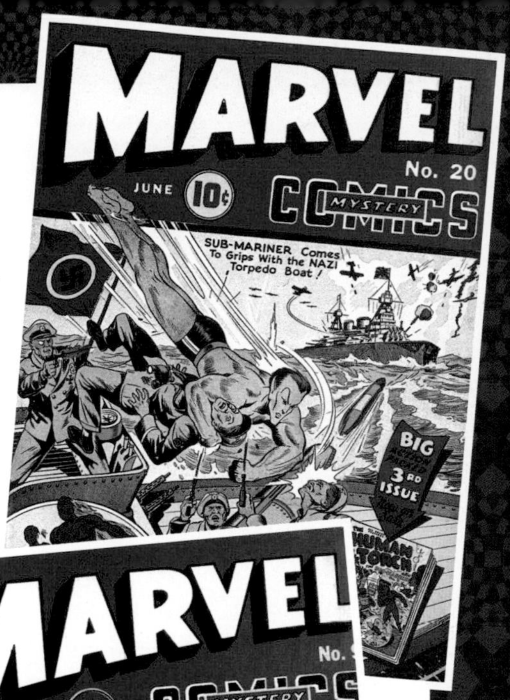
MARVEL
No. 20
JUNE
10¢
MYSTERY
COMICS
SUB-MARINER Comes To Grips With the NAZI Torpedo Boat!
BIG
3RD ISSUE

■ The cornerstone of the mighty Marvel empire, it took its place on the newsstands late in 1939. This was the magazine that introduced such characters as the Human Torch, the Angel, and Sub-Mariner to newsstand audiences. In its original form it lasted until the spring of 1949.

Publisher Martin Goodman went into the comic-book business in the summer of 1939. Until then, he'd been publishing a string of pulp-fiction magazines under various company names. He did cowboy pulps as well as such titles as *Dynamic Science Stories*, *Uncanny Tales*, and *Marvel Science Stories.* When he was approached by the Funnies, Inc., shop, Goodman was persuaded that the time was right to branch out into comic books. The result was *Marvel Mystery Comics* (called simply *Marvel Comics* for its first issue). Goodman called his company Timely Publications for this go-round.

The Torch, the Angel, and Sub-Mariner proved a durable trio. During the magazine's early years other characters came and went, including the Masked Raider, a Lone Ranger look-alike; Electro, a giant red robot; Terry Vance, a schoolboy sleuth and the first character Bob Oksner ever drew; and Ka-Zar, a blond Tarzan borrowed from an earlier Goodman pulp. Later there were the Vision, a mystical green fellow dreamed up by Joe Simon and Jack Kirby, and the Patriot, one more star-spangled hero.

Eventually most of the backup characters were let go. The Human Torch and Sub-Mariner remained, joined in 1946 by Captain America. *Marvel* introduced Miss America in 1943, and she stayed on until the end of 1947. In the postwar years several new women characters were added, including the Blonde Phantom, Sun Girl, and Namora. The magazine sputtered out with its ninety-second issue (June 1949). From #93 (August 1949) it was called *Marvel Tales* and offered horror stories with such titles as "The Ghost Strikes," "A Witch Is Among Us," and "The Thing in the Sewer."

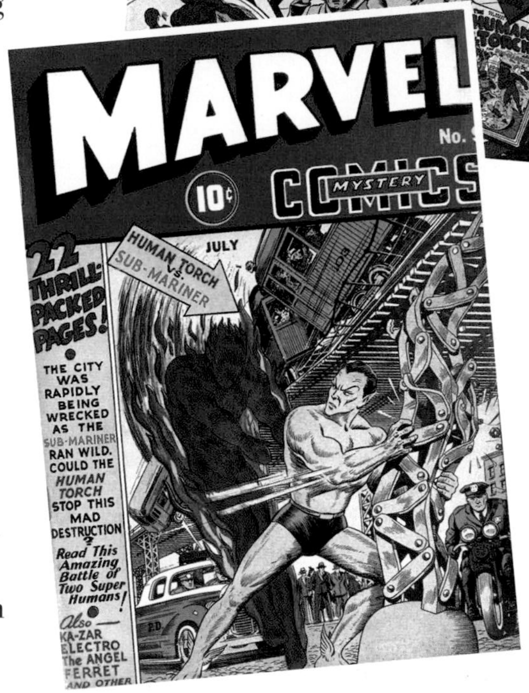
MARVEL
10¢
MYSTERY
COMICS
JULY
HUMAN TORCH VS SUB-MARINER
22 THRILL-PACKED PAGES!
THE CITY WAS RAPIDLY BEING WRECKED AS THE SUB-MARINER RAN WILD. COULD THE HUMAN TORCH STOP THIS MAD DESTRUCTION?
Read This Amazing Battle of Two Super Humans!
Also — KA-ZAR ELECTRO The ANGEL FERRET

Marvel reprinted the first issue in a hardcover format a few years ago, and in 1999 came a one-shot titled *Marvel Mystery Comics* containing an assortment of reprints from early issues. The cover was a reprint of one of Alex Schomburg's many impressive efforts.

THE MASKED MARVEL

■ See KEEN DETECTIVE FUNNIES.

MASTER COMICS

■ At the outset *Master* was a giant among comic books. Its first half dozen issues were jumbos, measuring 10½" by 14". Fawcett Publications introduced the magazine early in 1940, a month after *Whiz Comics*, pointing out to distributors that because of its size, *Master Comics* "makes its own displays!" Furthermore, the eleven new characters were "sure-hit comics" and "MASTER MAN is your pace maker!" Unlike their predictions for *Whiz* and Captain Marvel, none of these came true.

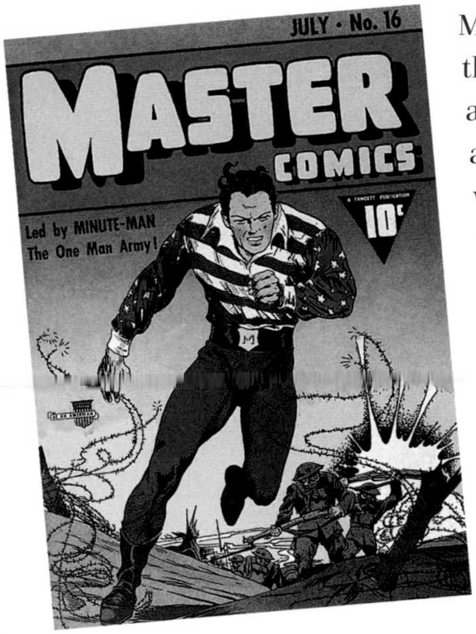
JULY • No. 16
MASTER
COMICS
10¢
Led by MINUTE-MAN
The One Man Army!

By the seventh issue (October 1940), Master Man was gone, along with six of the other sure hits. *Master* was also now the size of ordinary, everyday comic books. For good measure, Fawcett brought Bulletman over from its defunct *Nickel Comics* and Zoro the Mystery Man from its defunct *Slam-Bang Comics*. Much of the material from the unsuccessful oversize issues had been supplied by the Harry "A" Chesler shop, which never seemed to have a firm grasp on what constituted a viable comic-book character.

Bulletman, now drawn by Jon Small, was the new star hero of *Master* for the time being, along with his companion Bulletgirl. Minute Man, also know as the One Man Army, joined up in #11 (February 1941). Drawn by Charles Sultan initially, he was a superpatriot in a star-spangled costume. He arrived on the stands at just about the same time as Captain America, and like Cap he was a soldier in real life. Later artists of the feature included Phil Bard, sometime Simon and Kirby ghost. Minute Man appeared on a few covers as well, but then in *Master* #22 (January 1942) Captain Marvel, Jr. took up residence and also commanded the cover from then on. Mac Raboy, a very impressive artist, drew the junior Marvel on over two dozen covers and handled, with some help from his assistants, the interior stories as well. He was succeeded by Bud Thompson and then Kurt Schaffenberger.

The resident magician from the start was El Carim—"his name spelled backwards is Miracle." George Tuska was one of the artists. Balbo the Boy Magician, created by Bert Whitman, replaced the miracle man. Hopalong Cassidy was a regular from late in 1942 until early in 1944. Nyoka, adapted from the adventures of the Republic Pictures serial queen, started in May of 1944. So did Radar the International Policeman. A trenchcoated hero, he was drawn by Al Carreño and suggested to Fawcett by the Office of War Information as a way to promote understanding among nations, especially in the postwar world that was coming up. He left the magazine in 1948. Bulletman and Bulletgirl dropped out in 1949. In its final years *Master*, slimmed down to thirty-two pages, got by with Captain Marvel, Jr., Nyoka, Tom Mix, and a couple of teens named Ozzie and Babs. The final issue of *Master Comics* was #133 with a cover date of April 1953.

MAURER, NORMAN

■ See BOY COMICS.

MAXON, REX (1892–1973)

■ Although Edgar Rice Burroughs hated his artwork and frequently tried to get him fired, Maxon drew the daily *Tarzan* strip from 1929 to 1947. While he was no match for Hal Foster, Maxon had a passable and distinctive style. In the early 1950s, he went to work for Dell, and his major assignment there was drawing *Turok, Son of Stone.*

A former newspaper artist, Maxon took over the *Tarzan* strip after Hal Foster returned, only briefly, to advertising. Since the job apparently didn't pay that much, Maxon added to his income by doing illustrations for the pulp magazines. He worked for the line published by Frank Armer, whose titles included *Spicy Detective, Speed Western,* and *Hollywood Detective.* For Armer's *Six-Gun Western* he drew a black-and-white filler comic titled *K-Bar Kate.* And he applied what he'd learned about jungles and strange animals while illustrating *Tarzan* to his work on the Turok saga.

MAYER, SHELDON (1917–1991)

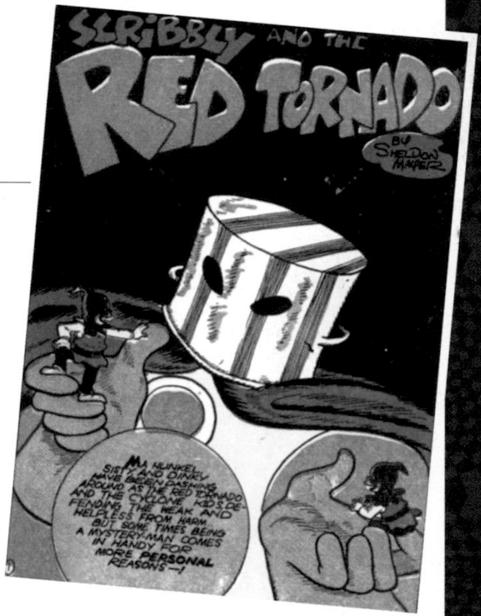
SCRIBBLY AND THE
RED TORNADO
BY SHELDON MAYER
MA HUNKEL, SISTY AND DINKY HAVE BEEN DASHING AROUND AS THE RED TORNADO AND THE CYCLONE KIDS DEFENDING THE WEAK AND HELPLESS FROM HARM... BUT SOME TIMES BEING A MYSTERY-MAN COMES IN HANDY FOR MORE PERSONAL REASONS—!

■ Mayer was one of the chief architects of the Golden Age, as an artist, writer, and editor. While still in his teens he contributed—until he realized he was never going to get paid—to Major Nicholson's pioneering original-material comic books in the middle 1930s and worked with M. C. Gaines in packaging for Dell the early imitations of *Famous Funnies—Popular Comics, The Funnies,* and *The Comics.* He created *Scribbly,* about a boy cartoonist who very much resembled him, for *The Funnies.* It was Mayer who urged DC to buy *Superman* for *Action Comics* and later as Gaines's editor on *All-American Comics* and *Flash Comics,* he was in at the creation of the Flash, Hawkman, Green Lantern, the Atom, Dr. Mid-Nite, and a batch of others. He and writer Gardner Fox cooked up the Justice Society of America for DC's *All Star Comics* (and Mayer even lettered the logo and laid out the first cover). After he'd transplanted *Scribbly* to *All-American,* he introduced the mock superhero the Red Tornado (whose alter ego was that of Ma Hunkel).

Mayer was a great discoverer of talent and hired such young cartoonists as Joe Kubert, Alex Toth, Carmine Infantino, Gil Kane, Joe Gallagher, and Irwin Hasen. He also gave Julius Schwartz his first editorial job. Mayer revived *Scribbly* in 1948 in a book of his own, drew a batch of funny animal characters that included *The Three Mousketeers* and *Doodles Duck,* edited the funny animal title *Funny Stuff* and wrote and drew the entire fifth issue himself, and cocreated *Leave It to Binky* with Bob Oksner (before anyone had so much as thought of leaving it to Beaver). In 1956, no longer editing, he started writing and drawing *Sugar & Spike,* based on looking back at the childhoods of his daughter and son.

He kept drawing even after eye trouble slowed him down in the 1970s. Mayer wrote scripts for DC as well, creating *Black Orchid* in 1974 and writing fantasy tales as well. He did his final cartooning in the middle 1980s, providing covers for some of the digest reprints of the *Sugar & Spike* material.

Vigilante

MESKIN, MORT

(1916–1995)

■ Much admired by such contemporaries as Alex Toth, Joe Kubert, and Gil Kane, he was an artist's artist and seriously underappreciated by the average reader during his years in comic books. Destined never to draw a major superhero, Meskin entered the field in the late 1930s. He was the cocreator of Sheena and the Vigilante and drew such characters as Johnny Quick, Golden Lad, Starman, Wildcat, and the Black Terror. He was also a frequent contributor to such Simon and Kirby ventures as *Young Romance*, *Boys Ranch*, and *Black Magic*. Over the years Meskin worked as well for MLJ, Lev Gleason, and the Prize Group, drawing everything from *The Wizard* to *Tom Corbett*.

Born in Brooklyn, Meskin attended both the Pratt Institute and the Art Students League. He was influenced by newspaper comics, particularly the work of Milton Caniff and Alex Raymond. He was also an admirer of pulp illustrators Edd Cartier and Herbert Morton Stoops. Although Cartier did considerable fantasy and science-fiction art for *Astounding* and *Unknown*, Meskin was most impressed by the graceful, impressionistic drawings Cartier did for *The Shadow*. Stoops was a illustrator for *Blue Book*, and his black-and-white interior drawings with exemplary figure work, layouts, and lighting made a strong impression on Meskin.

After working for the Eisner-Iger shop on *Sheena*, Meskin moved to MLJ and turned out some very effective pages for such titles as *Zip Comics*, *Pep Comics*, and *Blue Ribbon*. An excellent draftsman by this time, Meskin was also a thoughtful artist, and his stories, even those illustrating less than first-rate scripts, are always impressively laid out. He was also a movie buff (*Citizen Kane* was one of his favorites), and Meskin applied cinematic techniques to his work. In 1941 he moved to DC. Collaborating with editor/writer Mort Weisinger, he created the urban cowboy, the Vigilante. The pen name used by the two Morts was Mort Morton, Jr. Meskin did an inventive job on *Johnny Quick*, devising new ways to depict the speed king's rapid movements.

After World War II, he and Jerry Robinson teamed to draw some excellent adventures of both *The Black Terror* and *The Fighting Yank*. In the 1950s and 1960s Meskin concentrated on crime, science fiction, romance, and horror. This later work has a hurried look and doesn't match what he was capable of in the 1940s. A shy, sometimes uneasy man, he left comics in the middle 1960s and became an anonymous storyboard artist at the BBD&O ad agency in Manhattan.

McFARLANE, TODD

(1961–)

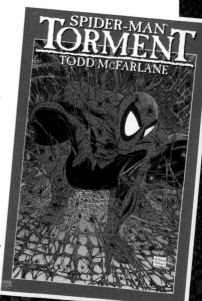

■ Internationally known as the man who paid $3 million for a baseball, he broke into comics in the middle 1980s. He was hired by Marvel and, assimilating the approaches of both Jack Kirby and Steranko and adding a flamboyance of his own, he soon became one of their most popular artists. Assigned *The Amazing Spiderman* title, McFarlane boosted its sales. According to the official McFarlane website, he enhanced the book "with his trademark style, popularizing a new way of rendering webs, transposing the character's human body

SPIDER-MAN
TORMENT
TODD McFARLANE

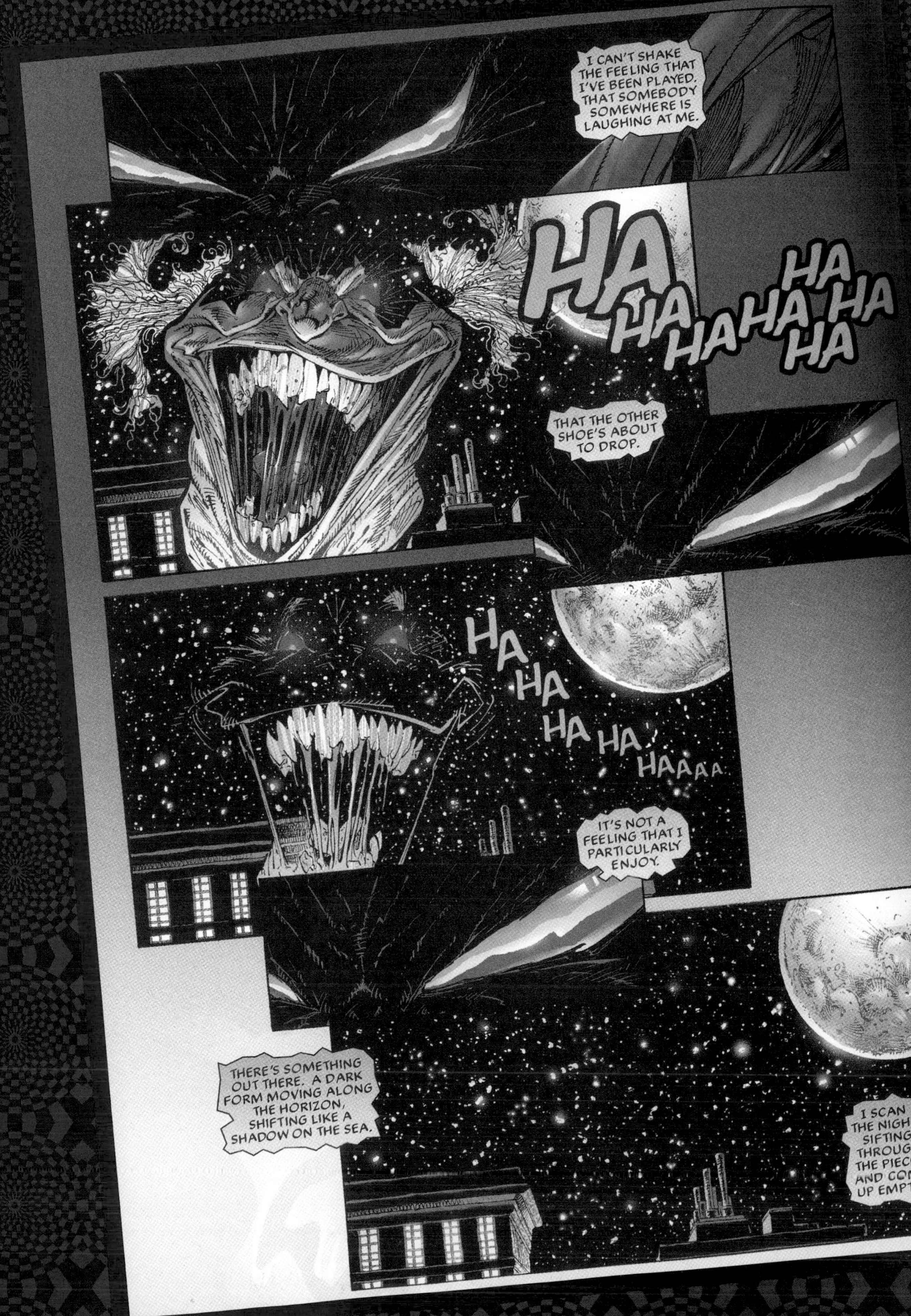
I CAN'T SHAKE THE FEELING THAT I'VE BEEN PLAYED, THAT SOMEBODY SOMEWHERE IS LAUGHING AT ME.
HA HA HA HAHA HA HA
THAT THE OTHER SHOE'S ABOUT TO DROP.
HA HA HA HA HA HAAAA
IT'S NOT A FEELING THAT I PARTICULARLY ENJOY.
THERE'S SOMETHING OUT THERE. A DARK FORM MOVING ALONG THE HORIZON, SHIFTING LIKE A SHADOW ON THE SEA.
I SCAN THE NIGHT, SIFTING THROUGH THE PIECES AND COME UP EMPTY.

to spidery positions and adding spider-looking eyes." Given a brand-new title in 1990 to both write and draw called simply *Spider-Man*, he turned that into a best-seller.

Born in Canada and reared in Southern California, McFarlane's two early ambitions were to be a professional baseball player or a comic-book artist. Never rising further than semi-pro status with baseball, he concentrated on comics. After leaving Marvel, he joined with some of his colleagues—Jim Lee, Rob Liefeld, Jim Valentino, etc.—to form Image Comics. Early in 1992 the company introduced McFarlane's new title, *Spawn*. "Spawn is in this seedy, David Lynch kind of world that isn't quite right," he's explained. "I made it dark to make the guy who he is. If the shadows are removed then the essence of the character is removed." When it came to action, violence, and grotesqueries, *Spawn* out-Marveled Marvel. It became a very successful independent title and has been spun off into toys, movies, animated cartoons, etc. McFarlane formed his own toy company to produce the Spawn action figures.

A wealthy man from all this merchandising, he was in a position to bid on Mark McGwire's seventieth home-run ball from the 1998 season and win. Because of his executive duties, he does little drawing anymore. But *Spawn* continues to be a popular comic book.

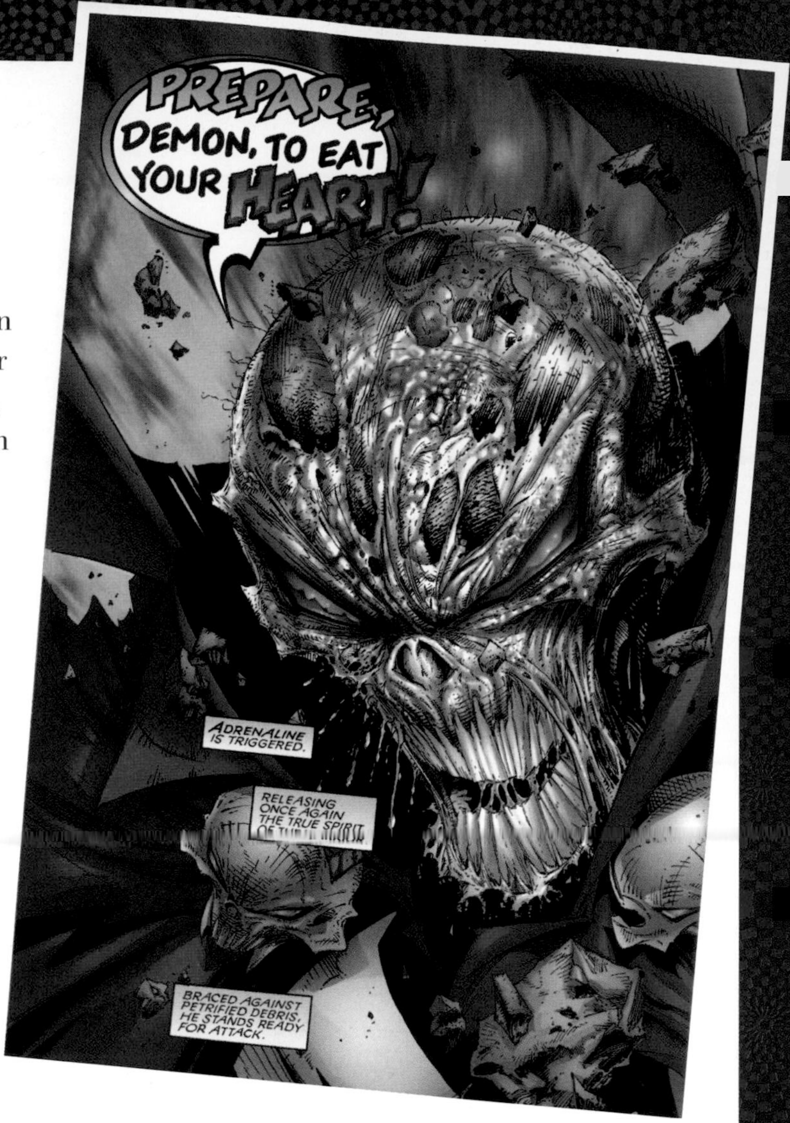
PREPARE, DEMON, TO EAT YOUR HEART!
ADRENALINE IS TRIGGERED.
RELEASING ONCE AGAIN THE TRUE SPIRIT
BRACED AGAINST PETRIFIED DEBRIS, HE STANDS READY FOR ATTACK.

METAL MEN

■ A most unusual team of do-gooders, it consisted of six robots. Each was constructed, by their inventor Doc Magnus, from a different metal. Thought up and written by Robert Kanigher and illustrated by the team of Ross Andru and Mike Esposito, *Metal Men* was introduced in the thirty-seventh issue of DC's *Showcase* early in 1962. Actually there were only five Metal Men plus one Metal Woman. The guys were Gold, Iron, Lead, Mercury, and Tin. The female was Platinum, but was known to the group as Tina.

Proving popular, the six were awarded their own book early in 1963. The *Metal Men* title lasted for fifty-six issues before retiring in 1978. Other artists included Walt Simonson and Joe Staton. DC revived the metallic team for a four-issue run in 1994.

MICKEY MOUSE MAGAZINE

■ The forerunner of *Walt Disney's Comics and Stories*, it reprinted some of the Disney newspaper strips and represents the first monthly newsstand appearances of such characters as Mickey Mouse and Donald Duck. The first issue of the newsstand version went on sale in the spring of 1935. In 1933 Walt Disney merchandising director Kay Kamen had produced a series of digest-sized issues of a *Mickey Mouse Magazine* to be used as promotional giveaways by various dairies around the country. Revising the title and entering into an agreement with Whitman Division of Western Publishing, Kamen became the publisher of the new version. This one was 8½" by 11½", consisted of thirty-two pages and sold for a dime.

Aimed at a very young audience, the magazine was a mix of illustrated stories about Disney animated characters, illustrated fairy tales, contests, puzzles, strip reprints, and ads for Disney merchandise. Donald Duck himself edited a joke page titled *Wise Quacks*. The *Mickey Mouse* newspaper strip was reprinted in two- and four-page sections, using the uncredited work of artist Floyd Gottfredson. Al Taliafero's *Donald Duck* showed up occasionally, as did *Silly Symphonies*. Oskar Lebeck, the probable editor, drew an ongoing original page about Peter the Farm Detective.

The magazine lasted for sixty issues, ending its run in the summer of 1940. *Walt Disney's Comics and Stories*, in a regular sixty-four-page comic-book format, started a month later. Aimed at a slightly older audience, the early issues were made up chiefly of reprints. In 1943 Carl Barks anonymously started drawing original stories of *Donald Duck* and a while after that Paul Murry did the same for *Mickey Mouse*. Walt Kelly put in a few years drawing unsigned covers.

WDC&S proved a best-selling magazine. With some changes in publisher, format, and price, and a few hiatuses, it has survived. In 2003 it returned once again.

ALL NIGHT LONG, MICKEY DREAMS OF THE NEW HOUSE HORACE IS GOING TO BUILD FROM HIS OLD ONE—AND EARLY NEXT MORNING---
THUMP! THUMP! THUMP!
Z-Z-Z- Z-Z-Z- ZUMPP-
HEY! WHAT TH' HECK ARE YOU DOIN'?
I WAS JUST SEEIN' IF YA GOT ENOUGH STRENGTH UP HERE T' BUILD A SECOND STORY, BUT---
!
YA AIN'T!
BUT HERE'S TH' BLUEPRINTS, MICKEY! DON'T YA EVEN WANT T' SEE 'EM?
NOT A CHANCE! I DON'T WANT T' BOTHER WITH 'EM! I'M RICH-- AN' I'M GONNA HAVE FUN WITH MY MONEY!
H. HORSECOLLA
CONTRACTOR
HORACE HORSECOLLAR
CONTRACTOR
!

BATMAN
THE DARK KNIGHT RETURNS
BY FRANK MILLER
WITH KLAUS JANSON
AND LYNN VARLEY
INTRODUCTION BY ALAN MOORE
DC COMICS INC.

MILLER, FRANK (1957-)

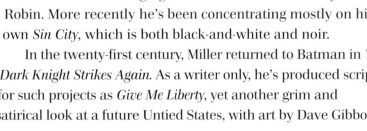

■ Influenced by both European and Japanese comics, Miller started drawing superheroes in a fresh and individual way that had little to do with the approach of far too many artists who relied on muscles and Jack Kirby swipes. Scripting as well as drawing, he rejuvenated Daredevil, invented Elektra, dealt with Batman as no one had before, and went on to do impressive work on such projects as *Ronin* and the more recent and gritty *Sin City*.

Born in Maryland and raised in Vermont, Miller became fascinated with comic books early in life. "I grew up a comic book junkie," Miller once admitted. "I think that came from being miserable in Vermont, from being a maladjusted child." He had little in the way of formal art training—"I've probably learned most of what I know about drawing from reading and working in the field." His first professional work was seen in the *Twilight Zone* comic book in 1977. By 1979 he was drawing *Daredevil* for Marvel. His bravura style and his highly individual approach to layout and staging, plus generous helpings of sex and violence, won him a large audience. Not everyone was awed, and some critics called his work nothing more than "pop culture *kitsch*." But they were in a minority.

FROM THE AUTHOR OF BATMAN: THE DARK KNIGHT RETURNS
FRANK MILLER'S
RONIN

Miller moved on from Daredevil and the attractive assassin Elektra to draw *Wolverine*. Next came *Ronin* for DC, showing a distinct Japanese influence. After that he invented an aging Batman for DC and a feisty female Robin. More recently he's been concentrating mostly on his own *Sin City*, which is both black-and-white and noir.

In the twenty-first century, Miller returned to Batman in *The Dark Knight Strikes Again*. As a writer only, he's produced scripts for such projects as *Give Me Liberty*, yet another grim and satirical look at a future Untied States, with art by Dave Gibbons.

MINUTE-MAN

■ See MASTER COMICS.

MISS AMERICA

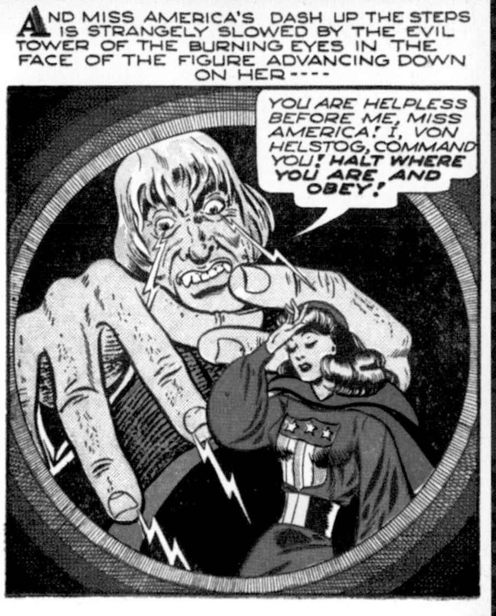
AND MISS AMERICA'S DASH UP THE STEPS IS STRANGELY SLOWED BY THE EVIL TOWER OF THE BURNING EYES IN THE FACE OF THE FIGURE ADVANCING DOWN ON HER----
YOU ARE HELPLESS BEFORE ME, MISS AMERICA! I, VON HELSTOG, COMMAND YOU! HALT WHERE YOU ARE AND OBEY!

■ Not to be confused with any of the young women who paraded in bathing suits at Atlantic City, this Miss America was a superhero introduced in *Marvel Mystery Comics* #49 (November 1943). A superpatriot in the Captain America mode, she was in everyday life Madeline Joyce, "teenage winsome ward of James Bennet, the radio tycoon." She wore a sedate crimson costume with a star-spangled shield emblazoned on the chest, a crimson beanie, and a blue cape. She specialized in combating crooks, spies, and saboteurs on the homefront. Among her powers were the ability to fly and a sixth sense that warned her of impending trouble. The prolific Otto Binder, who'd already created the similar Mary Marvel for Fawcett, was the writer on *Miss America* and Pauline Loth, a former animator, was the chief artist.

Miss America got a title of her own in 1944, but it was soon converted into a combination comic book and slick magazine that was similar to Parents' earlier *Calling All Girls*. She was dropped from the lineup after a few issues, but *Miss America Magazine* continued without her until 1958. The second issue (November 1944) introduced the popular teenage character Patsy Walker, drawn initially by Pauline Loth.

Although ousted from her own magazine, Miss America maintained her residence in *Marvel* until #85 (February 1948). After World War II, Madeline Joyce went to work for a counterspy organization in Washington, where she devoted most of her time to rounding up former Nazis who were attempting comebacks. The stories also emphasized Madeline's regular wardrobe, an indication that Timely was aiming at a female audience. Miss America was also a member of the short-lived All Winners Squad.

MISS FURY

■ A costumed heroine with a touch of the dominatrix in her makeup, Miss Fury brought a comic-book approach to funny-paper crimefighting when her Sunday page began on April 6, 1941. Tarpe Mills (real first name, plain Jane) had been working in comic books since the late 1930s. Like many comic-book heroes, Miss Fury had a dual identity. By day she was bored socialite Marla Drake, and by night, after donning a black leopard skin once "worn by a witch-doctor in Africa," she was the tough Miss Fury.

In addition to slugging both male and female opponents and tossing them around, Miss Fury frequently ran into villains wielding whips and branding irons and chains. In her Marla guise she frequently appeared in frilly lingerie and now and then she got into a clothes-ripping brawl with a female antagonist. All in all, *Miss Fury* was a heady mixture of comic-book action, mystery elements, and some under-the-counter sort of sex.

In spite of its unconventional approach, *Miss Fury* remained in newspapers—though not a large number—until 1952. Marvel, when it was still known as Timely, reprinted the Sunday pages in eight issues of the *Miss Fury* comic book from 1942 to 1946. On the majority of covers she was shown swinging into a room on a rope to kick one or two villains in the face.

MIX, TOM *(1880–1940)*

■ An enormously popular movie cowboy in the silents and early talkies, Tom Mix also had an impressive posthumous career in comic books. Fawcett introduced its *Tom Mix Western* late in 1947, seven years after Mix's death in an auto accident, and continued with the title until 1953.

"According to studio publicity," said Ephraim Katz in *The Film Encyclopedia*, Mix "was the son of a cavalry officer and educated at the Virginia Military Institute, and saw action in the Spanish-American War, the Philippine Insurrection, the Boxer Rebellion, and the Boer War and was later a deputy marshal in Oklahoma and a Texas Ranger." Actually none of this except the Texas Ranger part was true, and Mix was in reality an army deserter. Be that as it may, Mix, an erstwhile rodeo rider, became the most popular motion-picture cowboy by the middle 1920s. And his horse Tony became the first really famous movie horse.

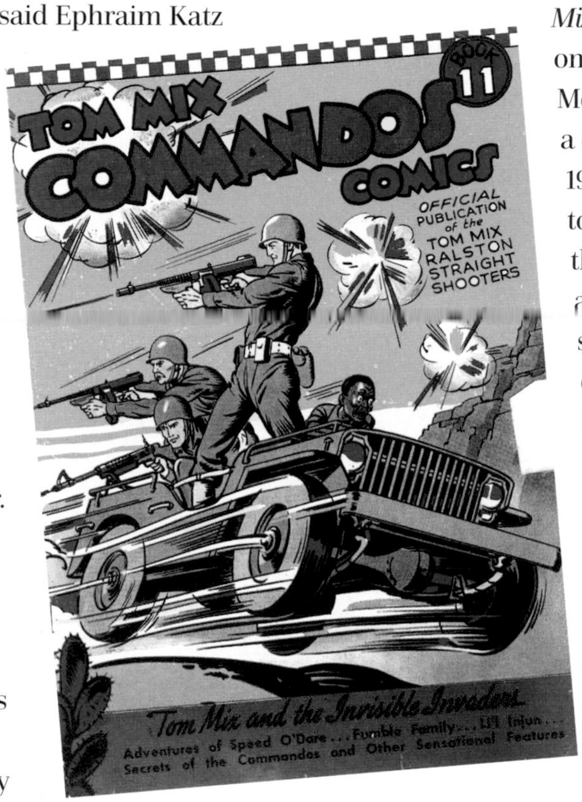
TOM MIX
COMMANDOS
COMICS
BOOK 11
OFFICIAL PUBLICATION of the TOM MIX RALSTON STRAIGHT SHOOTERS
Tom Mix and the Invisible Invaders
Adventures of Speed O'Dare ... Fumble Family ... Li'l Injun ... Secrets of the Commandos and Other Sensational Features

The media Tom Mix was largely a fictional creation. Ralston Cereal put *Tom Mix and His Ralston Straight Shooters* on the air in 1933, keeping it as a kids' hour show until 1950. Since Mix never had anything to do with the radio project, his death didn't affect the show. Radio Tom ran the TM Bar Ranch in Texas, had a black cook named Wash, and was good friends with local sheriff Mike Shaw. When Curley Bradley took over the role in 1944, Tom Mix became a singing cowboy.

Tom Mix first showed up as a comic-book character during his lifetime, appearing in short episodes in *The Comics* and then *Crackajack Funnies*. In 1940, the year Tom Mix was killed, Ralston introduced the first issue of *Tom Mix*, a thirty-two-page giveaway. Based on the radio show, drawn by Fred Meagher, the magazine made it through a dozen issues before shutting down in 1942. In 1947 Fawcett brought Mix back to life in *Tom Mix Western*, with much of the artwork by the team of Carl Pfeufer and John Jordan. This Tom was a strong-jawed, clean-living model citizen, who with the help of Tony tackled the usual Wild West problems. He was nothing like the hard-drinking, much-married, flamboyant real-life Tom Mix who drove a Cord. Like the Tom of radio, Fawcett's ran the TM-Bar Ranch in Dobie, Texas, and often helped out his pal, Sheriff Shaw. There were several clues that he was not based on the authentic Tom Mix. In one story, for example, after Tom is ambushed, pistol-whipped, and shot, the doctor who patches him up tells Mike Shaw, "Only all those years of clean-living saved Tom!"

Ralston issued a final Tom Mix giveaway, a miniature comic written by Jim Harmon and drawn by Alex Toth, in 1983. Bill Black's AC Comics has reprinted some of the Fawcett material in recent years.

MOEBIUS/JEAN GIRAUD

(1938-)

■ Not one major artist but two, Giraud is well known worldwide under a pair of names. As Gir he draws such realistic fare as *Blueberry* and as Moebius he produces fantasy and science fiction. Born in Paris, he became a professional comics artist while still in his teens. In 1961 he became an assistant to Joseph Gillian, who used the pen name Jije, and worked with him on a Western adventure strip titled *Jerry Spring* that ran in the magazine *Spirou.* Two years later, in collaboration with writer Jean-Michel Charlier, he produced a Western strip of his own. The adventures of Lt. Blueberry, set in post–Civil War America and starring a hero who looked and sometimes acted like the then-popular French movie star Jean Paul Belmondo, became a regular feature in the magazine *Pilote.* When the French publisher Dargaud started collecting the *Blueberry* material in a series of hardcover albums, Giraud's audience increased considerably, and his work even started getting a limited amount of attention from American fans.

His early drawing on the Blueberry saga was very much in the Jije style. Gradually, however, Giraud developed a distinctive style of his own. His pages were looking like storyboards for an ambitious John Ford epic or possibly a big-budget spaghetti Western. Moebius was also born in 1963, when Giraud used the pen name for the satirical stuff he began to draw for *Pilote.* He also used the name for his science-fiction illustration efforts. While Giraud relied on a lush, brush-dominated inking approach, Moebius' work was leaner, much given to pen techniques such as crosshatching. Under both aliases his work grew increasingly impressive.

In 1975 Giraud was one of the founders of *Metal Hurlant*, and he drew many science-fiction and fantasy works for the new magazine such as *Arzach* and *Le Bandard Fou.* Two years later *Heavy Metal* started up in

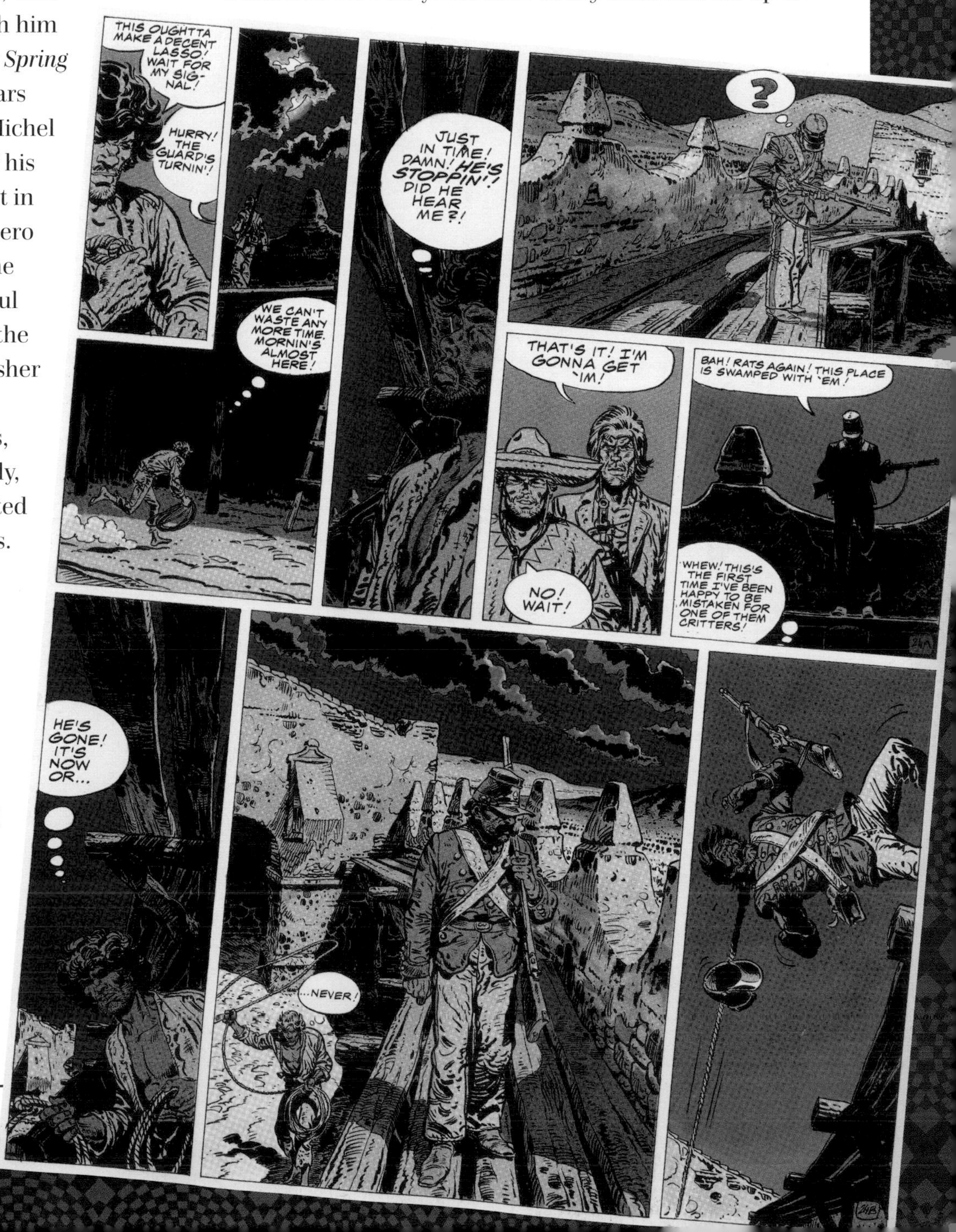

THIS OUGHTTA MAKE A DECENT LASSO! WAIT FOR MY SIG-NAL!
HURRY! THE GUARD'S TURNIN'!
WE CAN'T WASTE ANY MORE TIME. MORNIN'S ALMOST HERE!
JUST IN TIME! DAMN! HE'S STOPPIN'! DID HE HEAR ME?!
?
THAT'S IT! I'M GONNA GET 'IM!
NO! WAIT!
BAH! RATS AGAIN! THIS PLACE IS SWAMPED WITH 'EM!
WHEW! THIS'S THE FIRST TIME I'VE BEEN HAPPY TO BE MISTAKEN FOR ONE OF THEM CRITTERS!
HE'S GONE! IT'S NOW OR...
...NEVER!

the United States, reprinting the Moebius work. Some years after that, Marvel's Epic line began reprinting albums of Moebius material. And the various *Blueberry* albums became available in English. As his international reputation as a gifted and inventive artist continued to grow, Giraud was hired to work on costume design and storyboards for such films as *Alien, Tron,* and *Dune.*

He's also worked for Marvel on such projects as a *Silver Surfer* graphic novel and has continued to produce both sci-fi and Lt. Blueberry comics. In the late 1980s Giraud was telling interviewers that he had turned his back on sex and violence in his work. In the early twenty-first century, however, he's been turning out such erotic works as *Angel Claw.*

MONKEYMAN & O'BRIEN

■ See ADAMS, ARTHUR.

MONTANA, BOB

■ See ARCHIE.

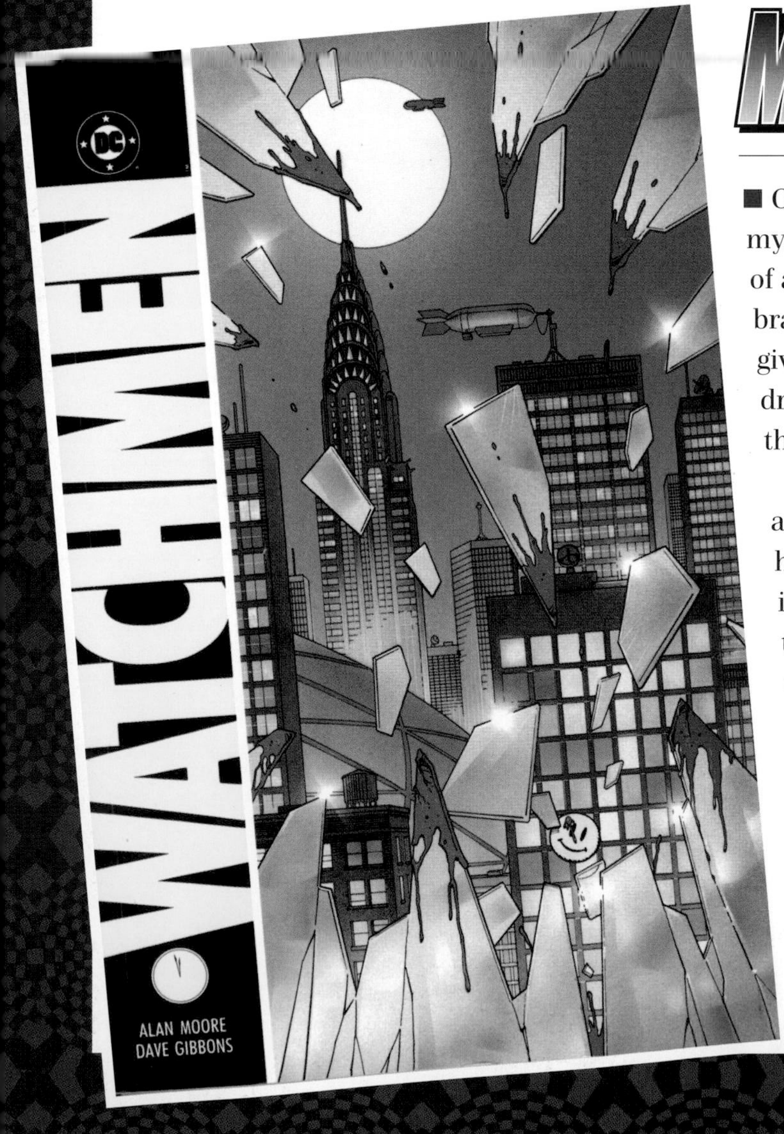
DC
WATCHMEN
ALAN MOORE
DAVE GIBBONS

MOORE, ALAN

(1954–)

■ One of the most inventive of scriptwriters and certainly the most mystical, Moore has been working in comics for close to a quarter of a century. After breaking into the field in his native England, he branched out into American comic books and at the end of 1983 was given *Swamp Thing* to write. His rejuvenation of the muck monster drew considerable attention to Moore's work, and his reputation in the field has continued to grow ever since.

In 1986 DC began publishing his limited series, *Watchmen,* with art by Dave Gibbons. Dealing with a once-famed group of costumed heroes known as the Minute Men, *Watchmen* moved back and forth in time and paid attention to the human side of its heroes. Most of them suffered with enough personal problems to supply a horde of troubled Marvel superheroes. Their ability to function as saviors was frequently hampered by their screwed-up personalities, and they didn't even treat each other very well. In their old age they didn't improve any. The book was a hit, reprinted as a graphic novel almost immediately after the last issue appeared.

Fascinated with the more traditional superheroes, especially those of the 1960s, Moore has returned to them frequently in his

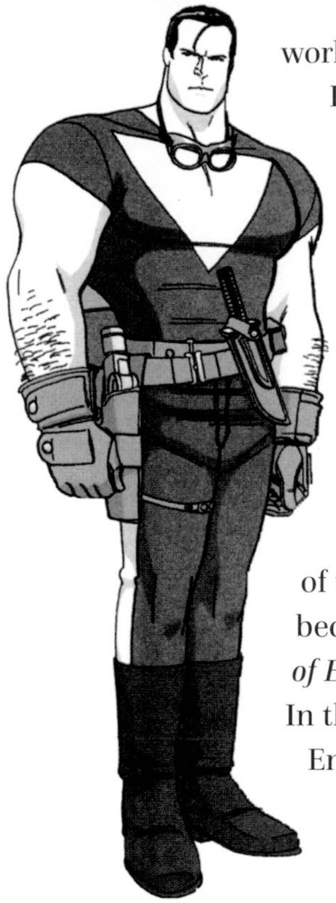

work. In the early 1990s came the 1963 series. Working with artists Rick Veitch, Steve Bissette, and Gibbons, Moore invented a limited series of mock sixties heroes such as the Fury, Horus, and Ultimate Special Agent. The series was limited to six issues, all of them looking as though they'd been slumbering in a Marvel warehouse for thirty years. From 1991 to 1998, Moore and artist Eddie Campbell turned out *From Hell.* This was a detailed well-researched look at the career of the Victorian serial killer, Jack the Ripper.

A few years back, Moore came up with America's Best Comics, a publishing firm that has since become part of DC. For ABC he created and wrote a wide range of titles, including *Tom Strong, Promethea* (his favorite because of its strong magical elements), and *The League of Extraordinary Gentleman* (now a major motion picture). In this latter title, Moore returned again to Victorian England, this time using such fictional characters as Alan Quatermain of *King Solomon's Mines* fame, Captain Nemo, and the Invisible Man.

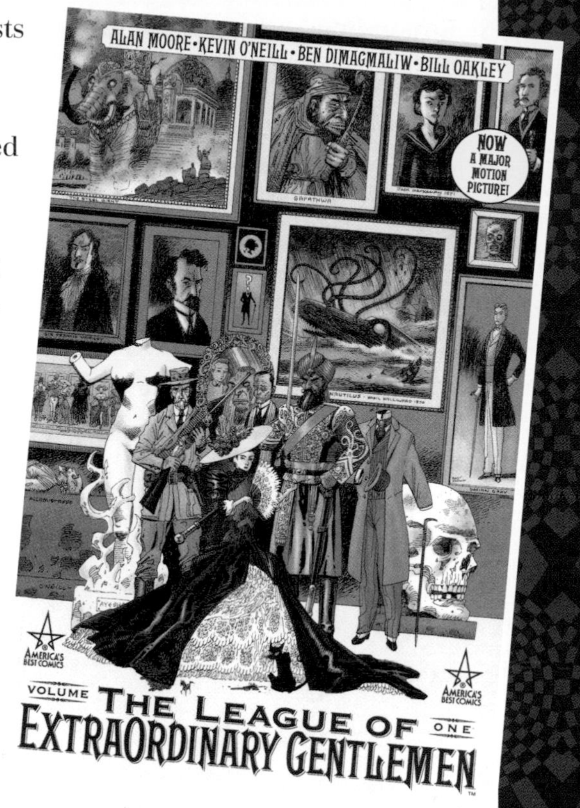
ALAN MOORE • KEVIN O'NEILL • BEN DIMAGMALIW • BILL OAKLEY
NOW A MAJOR MOTION PICTURE!
AMERICA'S BEST COMICS
VOLUME ONE
THE LEAGUE OF EXTRAORDINARY GENTLEMEN

MORE FUN COMICS

■ The first regularly issued original-material comic book, it began at the end of 1934 under the title *New Fun.* Originally a shoestring operation founded by the impecunious Major Malcolm Wheeler-Nicholson, the magazine was the cornerstone of what became the DC empire. It eventually introduced such enduring characters as the Spectre, Dr. Fate, Aquaman, the Green Arrow, Johnny Quick, and Superboy.

Originally Nicholson, a fairly successful pulp author, was more interested in getting some of his features syndicated in newspapers than he was in pioneering original-material comics. Late in 1935, he said he considered "our magazines primarily catalogues of features." When he realized that none of his material was getting a tumble from papers, he apparently decided to concentrate on turning out comic books.

The first issue of *New Fun* bore the cover date of February 1935. Billed as the Big Comic Book and "the New Magazine You've Been Waiting For," it was tabloid-sized. It had a full-color cover, but the thirty-five interior pages were black-and-white. All the features were laid out like Sunday funnies and none, with a single exception, got more than one page. In addition to humor and adventure comics, there was a two-page Western yarn, a sports page, radio news, movie news, instructions for building a model airplane, a popular-science page, and several ads for razor blades.

Among the too-be-continued features were *Sandra of the Secret Service, Buckskin Jim, Barry O'Neill,* and *Jack Andrews, All-American Boy.* Henry Kiefer, a European-trained artist, drew *Wing Brady,* about a Foreign Legionnaire who was also an aviator. Tom McNamara, a veteran newspaper artist, contributed a kid page. Artist Clemens Gretter, collaborating with writer Ken Fitch, drew *Don Drake on the Planet Saro* and *2003/Super Police*, the earliest science-fiction features created for comic books.

Because of the shaky state of the major's finances, he often didn't get around to paying his artists the modest fees—usually $5 per page—he'd promised. This resulted in both ill will and staff changes. Nicholson managed to persuade cartoonists Vincent Sullivan and Whitney Ellsworth to come into the fold and act as editors. The sixth issue of the magazine was dated October 1935 and the next one January 1936. That tardy seventh issue bore the name *More Fun.* Under its new title, the magazine format began shrinking, and by the ninth issue it was the same size as *Famous Funnies.* Color was being added, and as it entered its second year the magazine was looking much more presentable.

Early in 1938, Major Nicholson ceased to be publisher, and *More Fun Comics* was taken over by Harry Donefeld and Jack Liebowitz. Late in 1939, *More Fun* added *The Spectre* to its lineup, written by Jerry Siegel and drawn by Bernard Baily. A few months later in #55 (May 1940) Dr. Fate, another supernatural hero, joined on. Johnny Quick, a Flash surrogate, zipped onto the scene in the summer of 1941, and a couple of months later both Aquaman and the Green Arrow, accompanied by his sidekick Speedy, arrived.

In #101, early in 1945, Superboy was introduced. Aware of the declining interest in superheroes, DC began to convert *More Fun* to a humor book. Superboy moved over to *Adventure Comics* and such characters as Dover and Clover, Genius Jones, and, later, Jimminy and His Magic Book showed up. The final issue was #127 (November–December 1947).

MOREIRA, RUBEN *(1922-1984)*

■ A dependable illustrative cartoonist, Moreira began working in comic books in 1942. In the course of his career he drew such characters as the Shining Knight, Rip Hunter, Alan Ladd, the Golden Arrow, Kaanga, the Black Terror, and Dynamic Man. And in the middle 1940s, using the pen name Rubimor, he drew the Sunday *Tarzan* newspaper page.

Born in Puerto Rico, Moreira came to America with his mother when he was a small child. He later studied art at both Cooper Union and the Pratt Institute. Working first in the Harry "A" Chesler shop, he went on to draw for the Quality line and for Fiction House, for whom he also drew pulp-magazine illustrations. After his fourteen-month stint with the king of the jungle, he returned to comic books. He did considerable work for DC and some for both Fawcett and Marvel. Returning to Puerto Rico in 1958, Moreira continued to draw for DC for a few more years. He then turned to painting.

MR. SCARLET

■ See WOW COMICS.

MYSTERY IN SPACE

■ Launched early in 1951 when a modest science-fiction boom was getting under way in magazines, comics, and movies, DC's *Mystery in Space* offered the kind of sci-fi that had been popular in such pulp-fiction magazines as *Thrilling Wonder Stories* and *Startling Stories* since the 1930s. It was space opera fare, rich with planet-hopping, beautiful women threatened by bug-eyed monsters, ray guns, spaceships, and generous helpings of pseudoscience. *Mystery in Space*'s editor Julius Schwartz had been an agent selling his clients' yarns to those very pulp magazines, and his editorial colleague at DC, Mort Weisinger, had actually edited *Thrilling Wonder* and *Startling* before moving to DC. According to Schwartz, the magazine had *Mystery* in its title at the suggestion of Whit Ellsworth. *House of Mystery* had been a hit, and using the word in another title couldn't hurt.

Several of the scriptwriters for the new magazine had been frequent contributors to the SF pulps. Otto Binder started in the early 1930s; Edmond Hamilton started in the late 1920s, as had Manly Wade Wellman. They were all well versed in turning out science fiction aimed at a juvenile audience. Gardner Fox, a frequent contributor of scripts, was writing for the *Planet Stories* during this same period. Artists included Carmine Infantino, Gil Kane, Lee Elias, and Steve Ditko. Among the regular characters were Space Cabbie, Adam Strange, and Space Rovers. *Mystery in Space* lasted for 110 issues, shutting down in the summer of 1966. The title was briefly revived in 1980.

Strange Adventures, also edited by Schwartz, was DC's first SF title and had appeared in the summer of 1950. It offered the same mixture of stories by many of the same artists and writers as *Mystery*. By the ninth issue, it had installed a regular hero in the person of Captain Comet. Murphy Anderson drew the feature, John Broome scripted. *Strange Adventures* continued until 1973.

MYSTERY MEN

NO. 31
FEB. 10¢
MYSTERY MEN COMICS
Featuring THE BLUE BEETLE in "VENGEANCE OF THE JOSS-HOUSE DEMONS!"
Plus— MORE PAGES OF THE GREEN MASK AND DOMINO in COFFINS FOR COPPERS
In This Issue— MORTIMER THE WRAITH PRIVATE O'HARA and others

■ As its name implies, the magazine was chock full of mystery men—both masked crimefighters and superheroes. Published by the enterprising Victor Fox, *Mystery Men Comics* debuted in the summer of 1939 and introduced Fox's most successful character, the Blue Beetle.

For good measure there were also the Green Mask, the fez-wearing Zanzibar the Magician, Rex Dexter of Mars (a creation of Dick Briefer), and the insidious Fu Manchu clone Chen Chang. Fred Schwab provided comic relief with *Hemlock Shomes and Dr. Potsam*. All the early material was produced by the Eisner-Iger shop. Later on the magazine added a bumbling teenage character, several months before *Pep Comics* unveiled Archie. *Mortimer*, drawn by Edd Ashe, was introduced in #25 (August 1941). The hapless youth didn't enjoy a long life, since *Mystery Men* collapsed after its thirty-first issue a few months later.

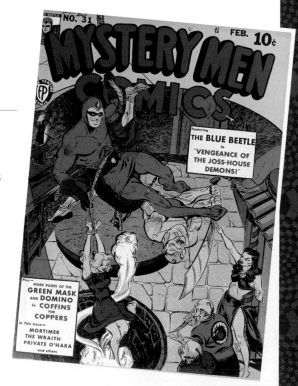

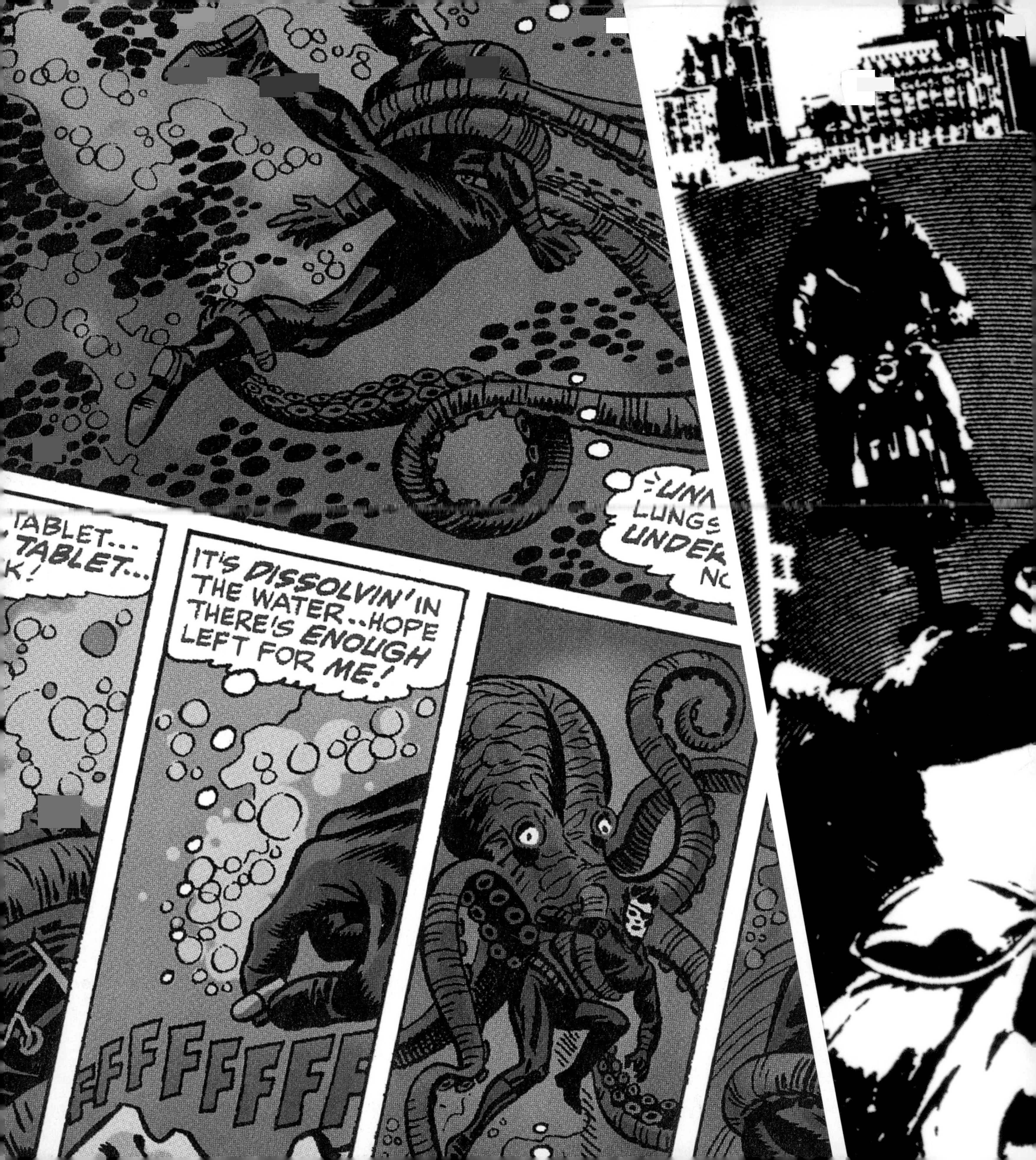

UNN
LUNGS
UNDER
NO
TABLET...
TABLET...
K!
IT'S DISSOLVIN' IN THE WATER--HOPE THERE'S ENOUGH LEFT FOR ME!
FFFFFFFFF

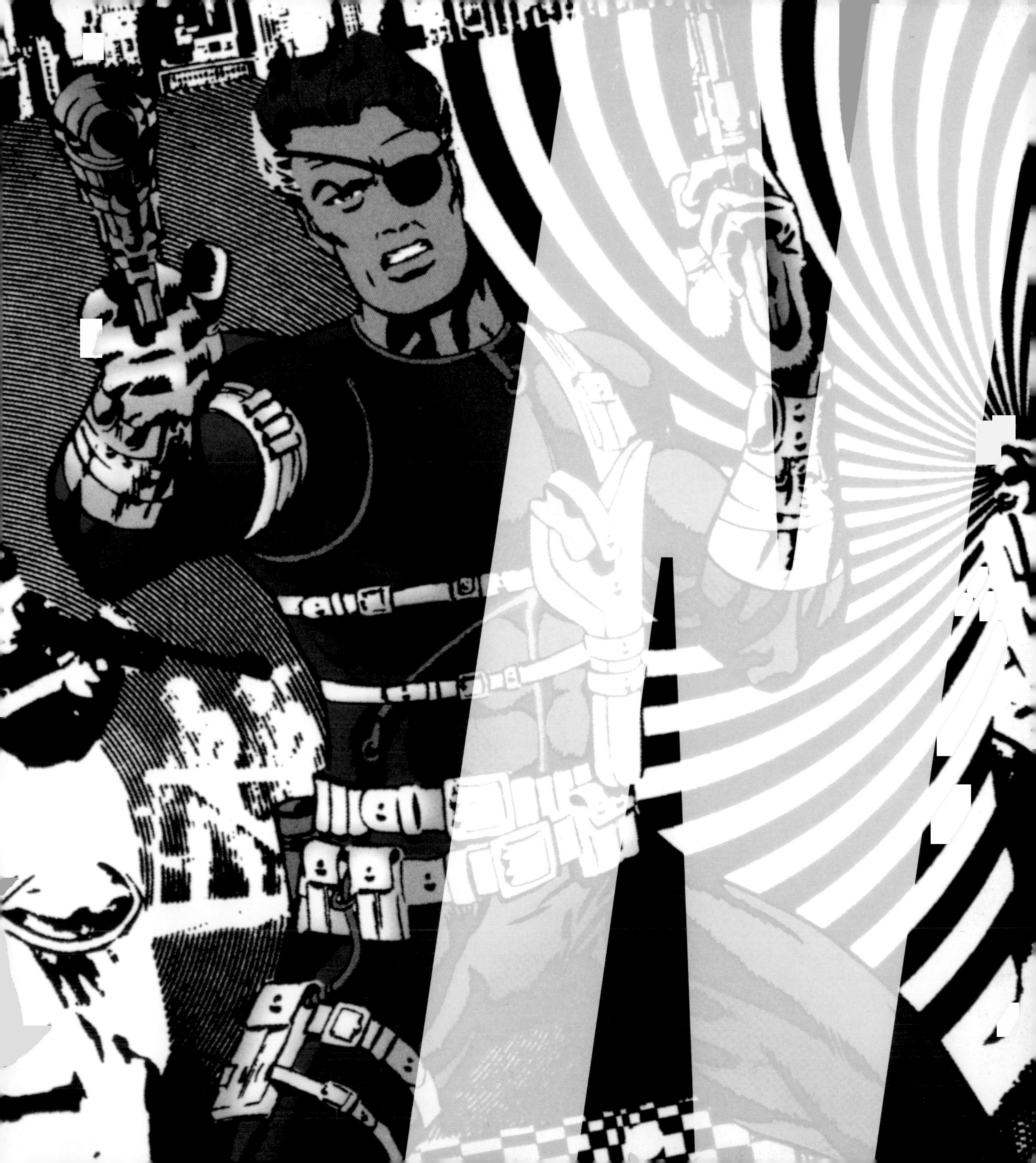

NEW FUNNIES
10¢
OCTOBER
NO. 68
RAGGEDY ANN
RAGGEDY ANDY
FELIX THE CAT
OSWALD
SCHOOL
GO SLOW
DELL

NEW FUNNIES

■ After three years of purveying adventure and superheroes, the format of *The Funnies* was again changed. The sixty-fourth issue added Oswald the Rabbit, Li'l Eightball, and Andy Panda. Actually, Andy had slipped into the magazine a few issues earlier, standing out among the likes of Captain Midnight, Phantasmo, and Rex-King of the Deep. With the sixty-fifth issue (July 1942) the book's title was changed to *New Funnies* and Raggedy Ann and Andy and Peter Rabbit were welcomed aboard.

Andy Panda, Oswald, and that walking racial slur Li'l Eightball were characters who appeared in animated cartoons from the Walter Lantz studios. The early adventures of Andy Panda set him in a world with humans. The artist was veteran illustrator George Kerr, who also drew the Raggedy Ann stories. Frank Thomas, who drew the masked crimebuster the Owl, contributed *Billy and Bonny Bee,* and Walt Kelly drew *The Brownies* for a spell. John Stanley, writer and sometimes artist for the *Little Lulu* comic books, wrote scripts for *New Funnies* in its beginning years.

By the middle 1940s the title had been further modified to *Walter Lantz New Funnies,* and nothing but adaptations of Lantz properties were allowed. Woody Woodpecker was now a regular. The final issue was #288, dated March–April 1962.

NEW MUTANTS

MARVEL
THE NEW
MUTANTS

■ Operating on the theory that you can never have enough mutants, Marvel launched another bunch of them in 1983. Trained by Professor Xavier, the New Mutants were introduced in *X-Men* #167 (March 1983) and *New Mutants* #1 (March 1983). Essentially junior X-Men, the group behaved in a manner similar to that of their now aging predecessors. Chris Claremont, Marvel's mutant maven, wrote the scripts, and Bob McLeod was the initial artist.

Marvel's reader base of the period, containing a large portion of disgruntled and misunderstood teenagers, took this latest bunch of disgruntled and misunderstood mutants to its collective heart. *New Mutants* was a success and continued until 1991. A high point in their appearance occurred in 1984, when Bill Sienkiewicz began drawing them and stuck with the job for a year. The popular Rob Liefeld later drew the feature, as did Al Williamson.

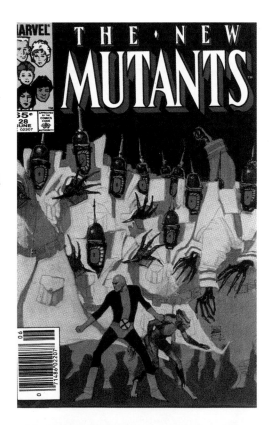

The first recruit was a young woman named Rahne Sinclaire, also known as Wolfbane, who had the ability to "transform from human form to wolf—with a transitional incarnation roughly half way between the two." Then came Xi'an Coy Mahn, also known as Karma, Danielle Moonstar, who was Psyche, Roberto Dacosta, AKA Sunspot, and Samuel Guthrie, better known as Cannonball. A bit later there were Warlock (not to be confused with the earlier hero of that name), described as a "techno-organic being," and Magma, Bird-Boy, Boom-Boom (not to be confused with Pebbles' buddy Bam Bam), Warpath, and Cable. Their major enemies were the members of the notorious Hellfire Club, a group of mean-minded malcontents dedicated to dominating the world by fair means and foul. The leader of the group was industrial billionaire Sebastian Shaw, also known as the Black Bishop. Most of the other variously superpowered members also derived their aliases from chessmen—Black Queen, Black Bishop, Red Rook, White Bishop, etc. One of the most popular members was the sinister White Queen. This bunch also plagued the X-Men from time to time.

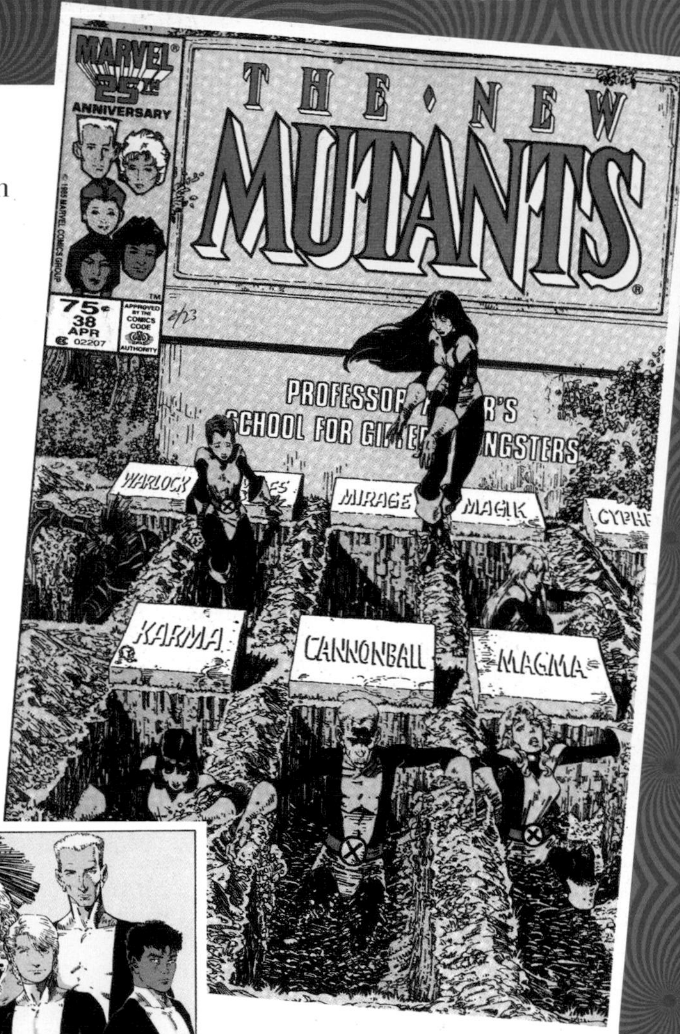
MARVEL
25th ANNIVERSARY
THE NEW MUTANTS
75¢
38
APR
WARLOCK
MIRAGE
MAGIK
KARMA
CANNONBALL
MAGMA

Maturing some, the group changed their name to *X-Force* and stuck with that until 2002. At the moment they are doing business as *X-Static*. In the summer of 2003, Marvel introduced a new bunch of New Mutants.

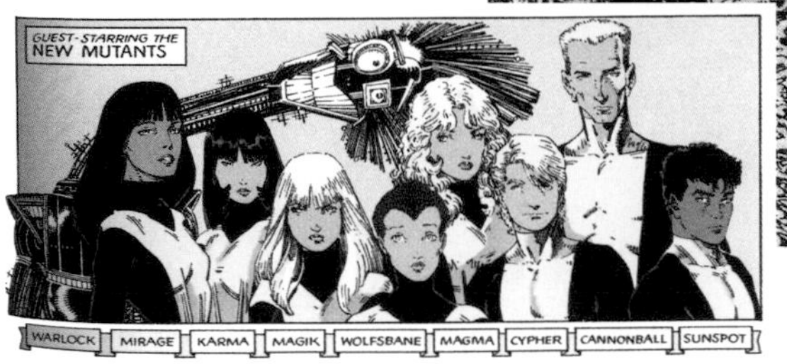
GUEST-STARRING THE NEW MUTANTS
WARLOCK
MIRAGE
KARMA
MAGIK
WOLFSBANE
MAGMA
CYPHER
CANNONBALL
SUNSPOT

NEXUS

■ Dreamed up by writer Mike Baron and artist Steve Rude, Nexus was introduced in a black-and-white comic book published by Capital Comics in the spring of 1981. After the third issue, color was added, and from the seventh, which didn't arrive until early in 1985, First Comics published *Nexus*.

Nexus had no choice about becoming a costumed superhero. As was frequently explained in his magazine, "Nexus dreams of mass murderers. And when he wakes, he is compelled to search them out and assassinate them. His powers, derived from the stars, are almost limitless." He lived several hundred years in the future on an asteroid named Ylum, and his civilian name was Horatio Hellpop. It's possible that a hero with such a name was not meant to be taken completely seriously. *Nexus* ended with #80 in 1991. Since then he carried on his assassinations in one-shots and limited series published by Dark Horse. He was last seen in 1997.

NICK FURY

■ A character who led one of the more unusual double lives in comics, Nick Fury appeared in two separate and distinct Marvel titles. In one he was crusty Sgt. Fury, who went rampaging through World War II with his Howling Commandos, and in the other he was crusty secret agent Nick Fury, blustering his way through James Bond territory.

It was in 1965 that Fury commenced his double life. According to Stan Lee, he was inspired by numerous fan letters asking what the sergeant had done after the war. "I was intrigued by the idea of having two magazines featuring Nick Fury," he once explained, "one dealing with his exploits during World War II and the other bringing him up to the present—but doing what?"

The answer came from television, where *The Man from UNCLE* had begun the previous autumn. Lee invented the secret U.S. intelligence agency known as SHIELD—Supreme Headquarters International Espionage Law-Enforcement Division. "We were going to out-Bond Bond," he said, "and out-UNCLE UNCLE." The new Nick Fury feature was introduced in *Strange Tales* #135 and blurbed as "The Greatest Action-Thriller of All Time!" Middle-aged now and wearing a black patch over his left eye, Fury was initiated into SHIELD. That initiation included having four android replicas made of him and then witnessing them being destroyed by SHIELD's enemies. Thereafter began Fury's seemingly endless battle against the evil organization known as Hydra, which was bent on encircling the earth. As Lee pointed out in the first episode, this wouldn't be an easy task—"But Hydra is immortal! 'Cut off a limb and two more shall take its place!'"

AND, AT THAT VERY MOMENT, APPROXIMATELY THIRTY FEET BELOW THE TWO CONSPIRATORS, THE DEATH-RATTLE SOUNDS FOR COLONEL NICK FURY...
CRIPES! THAT THING..A GIANT OCTOPUS..WRAPPIN' HIS TENTACLES AROUND ME...SQUEEZIN' THE LIFE OUTTA ME...PULLIN' ME CLOSER...
IF ONLY I COULD GET MY ARMS FREE... GOTTA TRY... GOTTA...
UNNNG! NO USE... LUNGS BURSTIN'... UNDER TOO LONG.. NO AIR...
WAIT!
OXYGEN TABLET... OXYGEN TABLET... QUICK!
IT'S DISSOLVIN' IN THE WATER..HOPE THERE'S ENOUGH LEFT FOR ME!
FFFFFFF
COUPL'A MORE SECONDS BOUGHT..! GOTTA REACH FOLDIN' BAYONET --IN MY BOOT--!
GOT IT... BUT..BUT CAN IT WORK? ...CAN IT?

As with many Marvel heroes of the day, Jack Kirby was the first artist, inked initially by dependable Dick Ayers. Jim Steranko also played an important part in the rise of Nick Fury. Late in 1966 he joined Marvel to work as an inker on Kirby's feature. A few issues later, he took over writing and drawing the feisty superspy's escapades. Fans and readers were impressed, and by the spring of 1968 Nick had a magazine of his own. An artist with wide-ranging and eclectic interests, Steranko created a personal and compelling collage for Nick Fury. He mixed the Marvel style, as then personified by Kirby, with the techniques of Will Eisner and Bernard Krigstein, and added the flash of op-art posters. Steranko didn't stay with Nick Fury long, but he left his mark on him.

The first series ended in 1971, but Fury proved to be relatively unsinkable and has returned many times since. Leaner, and possibly meaner, as time went by, he continued to chomp on a cigar and drop his g's. SHIELD was later said to stand for Strategic Hazard Intervention, Espionage, and Logistics Directorate. Fury appeared in a forty-seven-issue run from 1989 to 1993. In the late nineties, most recently in 1998, he came back in three limited series with such titles as *Fury of SHIELD* and *Fury: Agent 13.*

NICKEL COMICS

■ Another attempt by Fawcett Publications to experiment with what had already become the accepted comic-book format. Two months earlier they'd introduced the outsized *Master Comics* and now, with a cover date of May 17, 1940, they launched *Nickel Comics.* Of standard dimensions, the new title contained only thirty-two pages instead of the standard sixty-four and was priced at five cents. Originally planned as a weekly, *Nickel* finally materialized as a biweekly—"New Issue Every Other Friday." The main attraction was Bulletman.

5¢
NICKEL COMICS
NO. 1, MAY 17
NEW ISSUE EVERY OTHER FRIDAY
A FAWCETT PUBLICATION
HERE COMES BULLETMAN!

An anonymous creation, Bulletman was in reality mild-mannered scientist Jim Barr, whose policeman father had been gunned down by gangsters while Jim was a kid. Although Sergeant Barr's dying wish was that his son grow up to become a cop, after devoting years to forensic studies at school, Jim was found too frail to pass the police exam. However, while trying out a "crime-cure" serum he'd invented on himself, he was transformed into "the most powerful man on Earth!" Jim also devised a Gravity-Regulator Helmet. Donning that and an impressive crimson-and-gold costume, he became Bulletman. Only Susan Kent, daughter of the police chief, knows the secret of his dual identity.

Another character in the thin comic book was Warlock the Wizard, "last of the white magicians." He could accomplish impressive feats by shouting the word "Abraxas." Warlock came equipped with a magic staff and a raven named Hugin. The Jungle Twins were two brothers who were separated at birth, one thereafter raised in civilization and the other in the jungle. They got together again in later life in the African jungles. Later additions were *The Red Gaucho* and *Captain Venture*, a space opera drawn by Jack Binder and written by his brother Otto.

After *Nickel* shut down with its eighth issue (August 23, 1940), Bulletman zoomed over to the now normal-sized *Master Comics* with the seventh issue (October 1940). The Red Gaucho and Captain Venture also made the trip, but didn't remain very long.

Fawcett could not foresee that every comic book would someday be only thirty-two pages and sell for quite a bit more than a nickel.

NIGHTWING

■ See BATMAN.

NYOKA the JUNGLE GIRL

WHEN NYOKA GOES LOOKING FOR THE **LOST TRIBE** IN A SOUTH AMERICAN WILDERNESS SHE FINDS, AMONGST MANY OTHER THINGS, TROUBLE!

ADVENTURE OF THE LOST TRIBE!

■ The only jungle girl who worked fully clothed, she was based on a character in a Republic Pictures serial, which was based, sort of, on a novel by Tarzan creator Edgar Rice Burroughs. The 1942 fifteen-chapter movie serial was titled *Perils of Nyoka,* and Fawcett issued a one-shot comic book based on it that same year. *Nyoka,* whose name means snake in Swahili, became a regular backup feature in *Master Comics* in 1944, and the following year a separate *Nyoka* comic book began appearing. The intrepid heroine remained in comics until 1957.

The genesis of the character is somewhat confusing. Republic's 1941 serial *Jungle Girl* starred Frances Gifford as a woman named Nyoka Meredith. The title cards and the publicity credited *Jungle Girl* to a novel by Edgar Rice Burroughs. He had indeed once written a book of that title and the studio had paid him for the serial rights, but his story took place in an entirely different jungle and there was nobody named Nyoka in it. She was entirely the invention of the scriptwriters.

When it came time for a sequel serial, Republic decided not to pay Burroughs any further money, according to Jack Mathis in his *Valley of the Cliffhangers.* So the heroine of the second serial, portrayed this time by Kay Aldridge, was named Nyoka Gordon. She's the one Fawcett used in their comic book. Unfortunately, they titled the magazine *Jungle Girl,* thereby adding to the confusion. Artist Harry Anderson did the drawing.

The Nyoka of the serial was not a jungle girl in the Sheena sense. She didn't dress in a leopard-skin bikini, nor did she swing from tree limbs. She was simply a courageous young woman who, along with her father and boyfriend, encountered numerous perils and pitfalls while exploring a very Hollywood wilderness. She even wore shoes.

The Nyoka who started appearing in *Master* led a similar life and usually wore a blouse, shorts, moccasins, and a gun belt. The title of the feature offered a combination of both serial titles—*Nyoka the Jungle Girl.* Drawn by Jack Sparling, the first story extended over nine issues. As in the movies, each installment ended with a cliffhanger and a teaser. The stories continued in *Master Comics* until the penultimate issue in 1953.

Fawcett's *Nyoka the Jungle Girl* magazine ran from 1945 to 1953, when the company abandoned comics. Charlton took up the jungle girl in 1955 and hung on until 1957. Harry Anderson was also the artist on the early Fawcett issues.

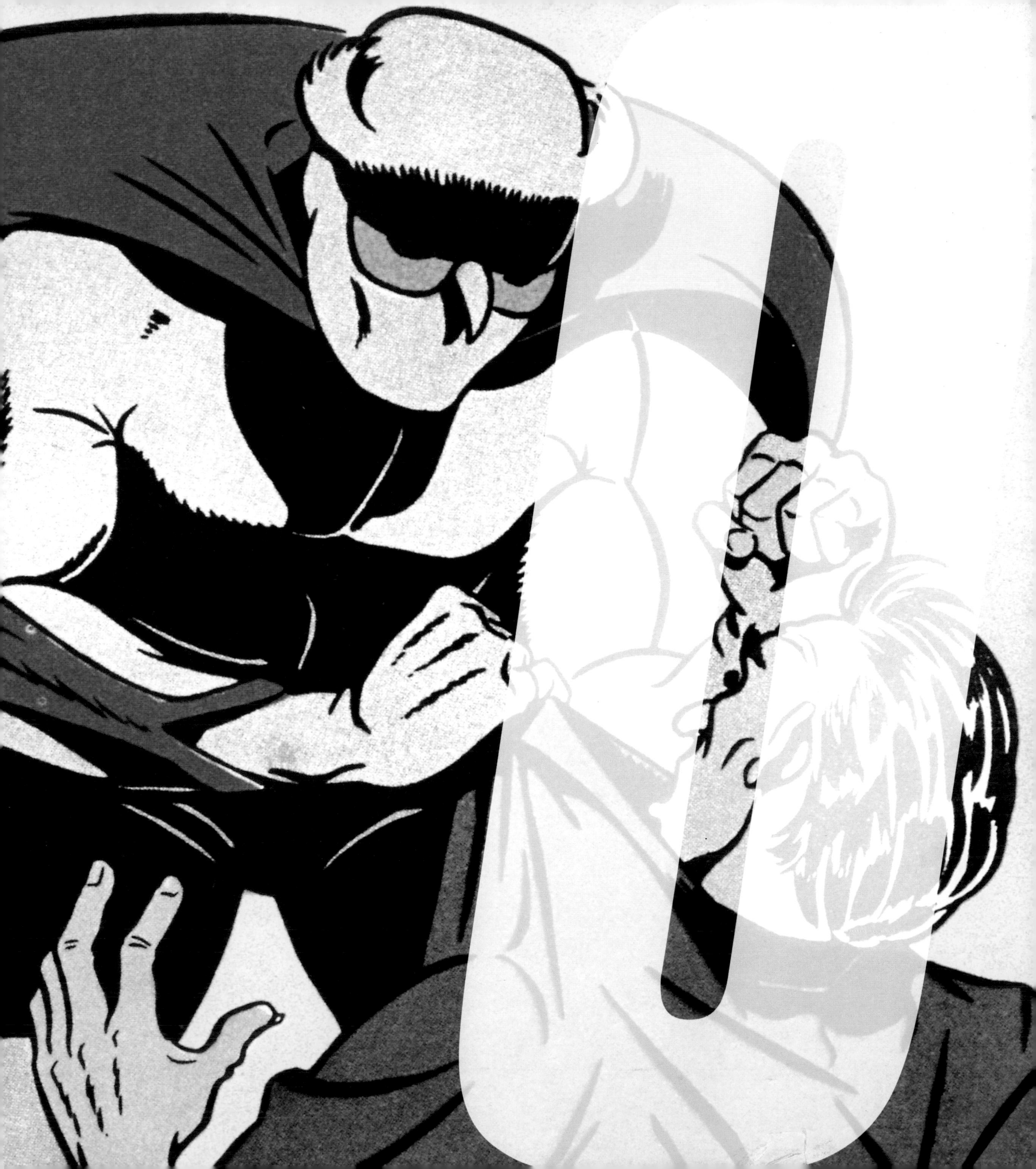

Our Gang
10¢ JULY-AUGUST, No. 18 COMICS
DELL
QUEEN LULU

OUR GANG COMICS

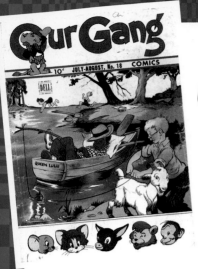

■ A comic book that eventually offered the work of two of the fields shining lights—Walt Kelly and Carl Barks—*Our Gang* arrived on the stands in the summer of 1942. Published by Dell and edited by Oskar Lebeck, most of its features were licensed from Metro Goldwyn Mayer. In addition to the *Our Gang* gang, there were animated cartoon stars Tom & Jerry, Barney Bear, Benny Burro, Droopy (under the more upbeat name of Happy Hound), and text adaptations of Pete Smith's live-action specials.

The movie kid gang had been around since the 1920s, invented by Tom McNamara and Hal Roach and eventually distributed by MGM. The Walt Kelly version was made up of Froggy, Buckwheat, Spanky, Mickey, a blonde girl named Jane, and a pet goat. Kelly's continuities varied from adventure tales involving black marketeers to farces tangling the kids with medicine show con men. He also drew most of the first several years' covers.

Barks signed on with #8 at the end of 1943, drawing stories about MGM animals Barney Bear and Benny Burro. Later the two were teamed in a single story, and Barks drew that until the summer of 1947. He also drew two Happy Hound yarns. With the exception of a single issue of *Porky Pig*, this was the only non-Disney comic-book work Barks ever did.

As interest in funny animals increased, Tom & Jerry assumed a dominant position in *Our Gang* and pushed the kids to the back of the book. After #59 (June 1949), the magazine became *Tom & Jerry* and the animals took over.

THE OWL

■ A nocturnal nemesis of crime in the Batman mode, he was introduced in *Crackajack Funnies* #25 during the spring of 1940 and became the magazine's first costumed hero. In his initial appearance the Owl came off like a surrogate Shadow. With the next issue the Owl got a new costume and a new cartoonist. He went from baggy cloak and floppy-eared sack over the head to purple tights, tunic and cape and owl-like face mask.

Frank Thomas, the new artist, had previously done both humorous and straight stuff. He brought an enthusiasm and a sense of fun to the feature. Nobody was quite sure what the Owl did in everyday life. His civilian name was Nick Terry and sometimes he was referred to as a police detective and at others as a private eye. But when Terry was in his Owl phase it was perfectly clear what he did. He went after a series of bizarre master criminals—including a hooded saboteur named Thor, a beast-masked emperor of crime known as the Panther and a family of crazed killers who palled around with a rather gentle gorilla who wore slacks, a sport coat, and a polka dot bow tie.

One of the things that made this dark knight stand out from many of his contemporaries was his choice of companion. Nixing boy wonders, he teamed up with a pretty blonde lady named Belle. She was Nick Terry's fiancée and a newspaper reporter by day and it only took her a few issues to figure out that Terry was also the Owl. From then on she donned a costume and traveled with him in the Owlplane. When *Crackajack* breathed its last with issue #43 (January 1942), the Owl moved over to *Popular Comics*. He held on there for fourteen issues.

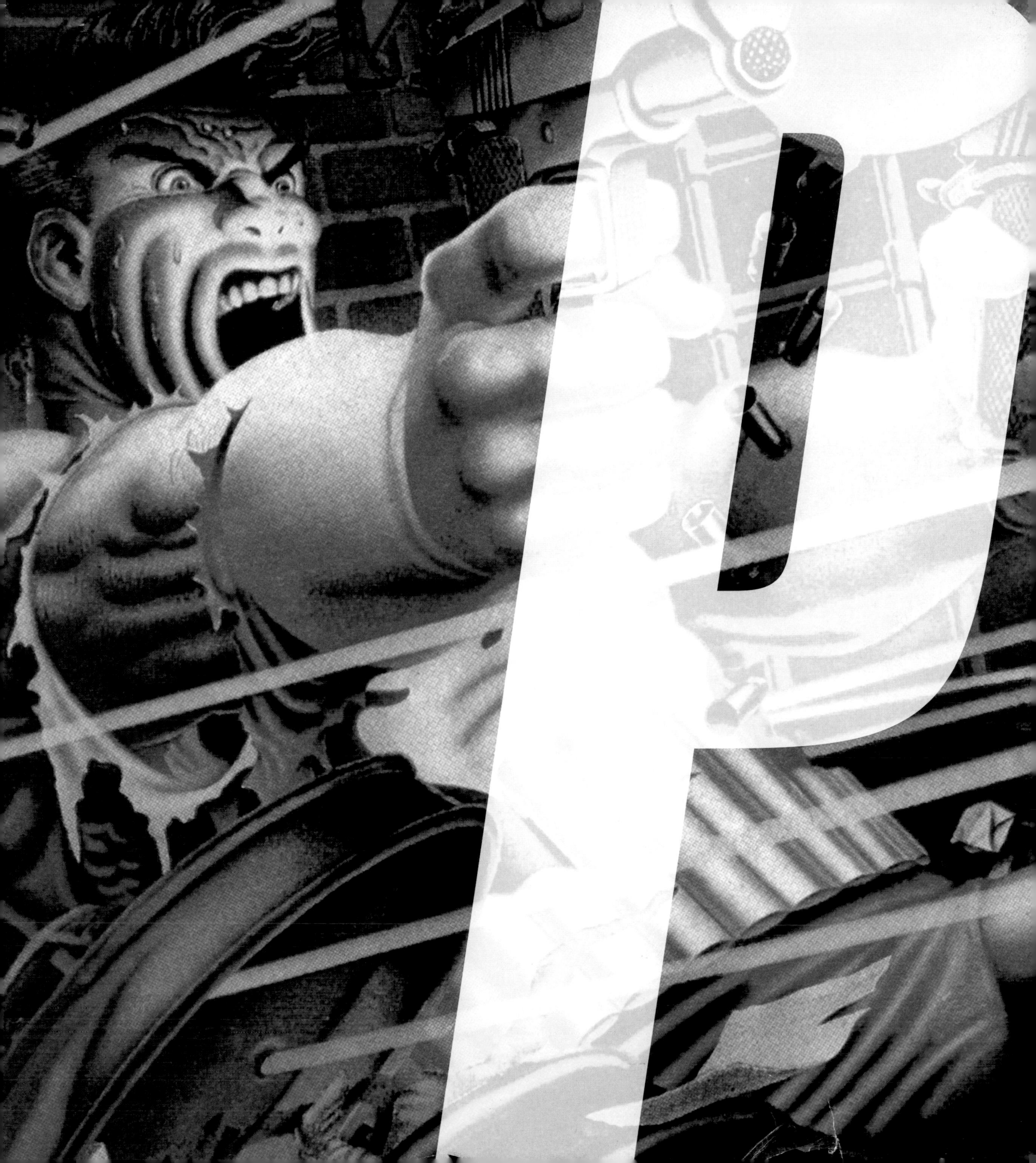

PAZMINO, VICTOR ESTENIO *(1899–1970)*

■ An artist with a knack for getting in on the ground floor, Pazmino was a contributor to both the original *The Funnies* in 1929 and the pioneering *Famous Funnies* in 1934. Signing himself VEP, he also contributed humor features to dozens of other comic books in the 1930s and 1940s. He had a simple, direct individual style, somewhat like that of a very gifted twelve-year-old, and he changed little during the fifteen or so years he was in the comic-book field.

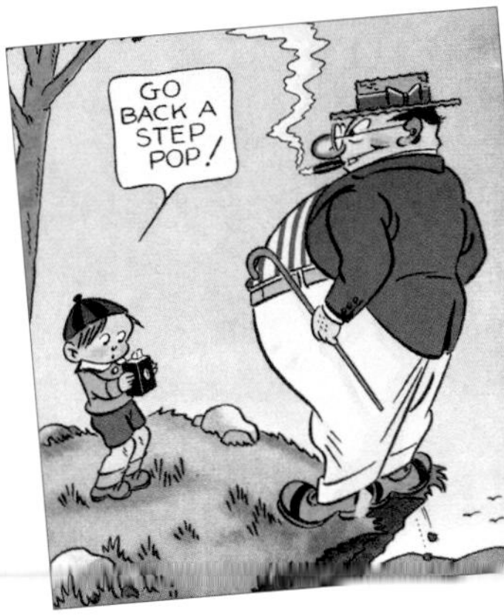
GO BACK A STEP POP!

Born in Ecuador, Pazmino was brought to the United States by his parents when he was less than a year old. They settled in Brooklyn. His father eventually became a magazine editor and one of his younger brothers a newspaper reporter. By the middle 1920s, VEP, who'd earlier worked in a factory, was a professional cartoonist. He drew a syndicated newspaper strip called *The Figgers Family* and then in 1929 drew such features as *Clancey the Cop* and *Jimmy Jams* for *The Funnies.* Pazmino did all but two of the *Famous Funnies* covers from #3 in 1934 through #80 in 1941. Inside the magazine he contributed a monthly page of gag cartoons and a filler about Seaweed Sam, a roving sailor who spoke in rhyme. He also drew covers for such lighthearted magazines as *Coo Coo Comics, Comic Comics,* and *Barnyard Comics.* VEP's filler and four-page comedy features graced a range of magazines that included *Jingle Jangle Tales, Don Winslow of the Navy,* and *Great Comics.*

He left comic books in the middle 1940s, eventually moving into political cartooning for a while. Pazmino underwent a posthumous sex change some years ago, when Denis Gifford, an often reliable comics historian, mistakenly referred to him as Victoria Pazmino. As such Pazmino ended up in more than one database. Recently his relatives have set out to rectify that error. VEP was still residing in Brooklyn when he died.

PEP COMICS

■ The magazine that introduced both comics' first superpatriot and comics' first successful teenager, MLJ's *Pep Comics* #1 arrived late in 1939.

The initial lineup included the Shield, also known as the G-Man Extraordinary, a star-spangled superman who'd devoted his life to "truth, justice, patriotism and courage." In real life he was red-haired Joe Higgins, and the only person who was aware of his dual identity was J. Edgar Hoover. Harry Shorten was the writer, Irv Novick the artist. In *Pep* #11 (January 1941) the Shield was joined by a boy sidekick called Dusty the Boy Detective, also a redhead.

The first issue also included the Comet, written and drawn by Jack Cole, Sergeant Boyle by Charles Biro, plus Bentley of Scotland Yard, and Kayo Ward. In #17 the Comet was killed by gangsters, and his brother set out to avenge him as a brand-new hero named the Hangman. Then in #22 (December 1941) Archie Andrews, a character cocreated by Bob Montana, was added. Gradually *Pep* was converted to comedy, with Archie as the star. The Shield and Dusty were the last to be ousted, departing after #65 (January 1948).

PEREZ, GEORGE (1945-)

■ An artist whose work has been called both powerful and subtle, Perez became a professional in the early 1970s. Born in the South Bronx and self-taught, he was hired as Rich Buckler's assistant in 1973. Soon outshining his boss, he started working directly for Marvel on such features as *Man-Wolf* and *Deathlok*. From there Perez moved up to *Fantastic Four* and *The Avengers*. He became a fan favorite early on, placing high in favorite-artist polls. Of his early work he once said, "The subtleties I developed later were absent, but the power was definitely there."

Perez continued to develop and by the early 1980s, when he was teamed with writer Marvel Wolfman on DC's *New Teen Titans*, he'd arrived at a mature style. In addition to strong characterization and nicely staged action, he excelled at both detailed backgrounds and complex crowd scenes. Perez next worked with Wolfman on the influential *Crisis on Infinite Earths*. More recently he put in time on *Wonder Woman*, and in the past few years he's worked just about exclusively for the new Florida-based Crossgen line of comics.

PETER, HARRY G.

■ See WONDER WOMAN.

PHANTOM LADY

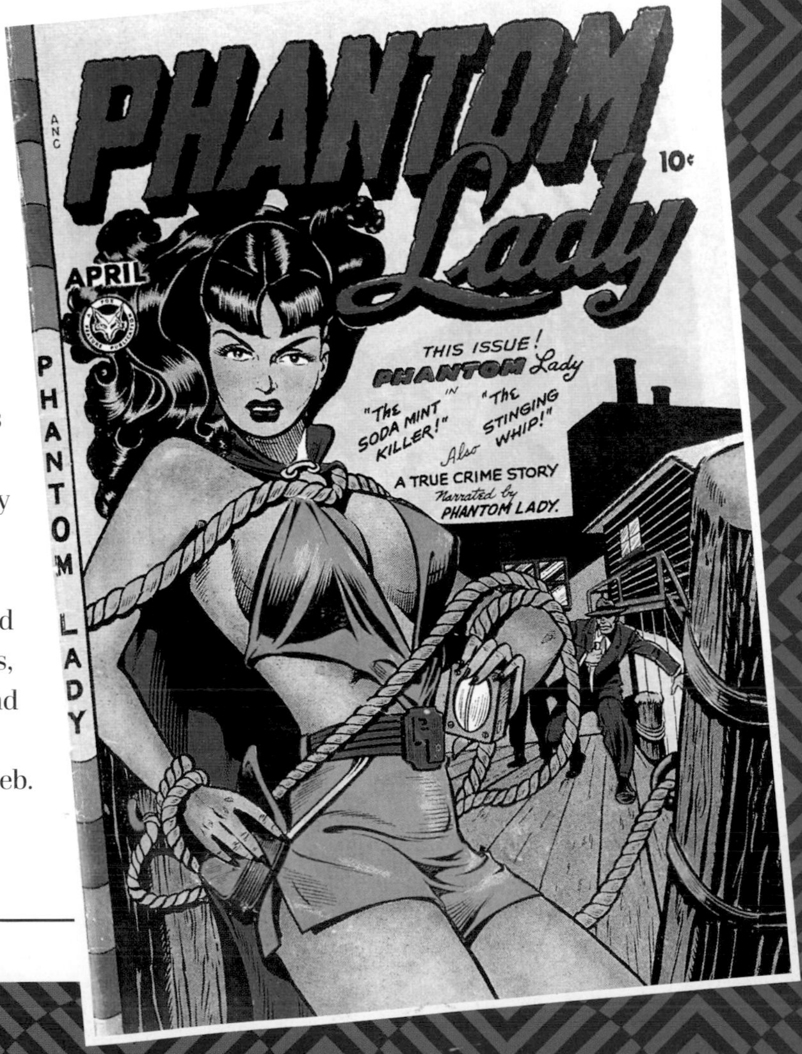
PHANTOM Lady
10¢
APRIL
PHANTOM LADY
THIS ISSUE!
PHANTOM Lady
IN
"THE SODA MINT KILLER!"
"THE STINGING WHIP!"
Also
A TRUE CRIME STORY
Narrated by PHANTOM LADY.

■ A character who became a major icon of Good Girl Art and a target of anti-comics crusaders such as Dr. Fredric Wertham, the Phantom Lady, in a relatively demure incarnation, first appeared in 1941. It wasn't until the opportunistic Victor Fox got hold of her in 1947 that she began combining crime-fighting with cheesecake. She's returned to comics in various stages of undress several times since.

Originally a product of the Eisner-Iger shop, the Phantom Lady was introduced in *Police Comics* #1 (August 1941) and originally drawn by Arthur Peddy. In everyday life she was Sandra Knight, the debutante daughter of a United States senator. The dark-haired Sandra's first costume consisted of a yellow swimsuit, yellow boots, and a green cape. Although she battled crime and espionage in and around Washington, D.C., without benefit of a mask or even a change in hairdo, no one ever recognized her as the well-known deb. She had no special powers, and her only weapon was a blackout flashlight that surrounded her opponents in darkness. When artist/writer Frank Borth took over in 1943, he gave Phantom Lady a fuller figure, a costume with cleavage, and a domino mask. She left *Police* after #23.

Fox began publishing a *Phantom Lady* comic book in the summer of 1947 and also used her in *All Top Comics*. The material was provided by Jerry Iger, who'd been operating a shop of his own since parting with Eisner several years earlier. Matt Baker, one of the leading exponents of Good Girl Art was the artist. This new Phantom Lady wore an even skimpier costume and possessed a distinctly larger bosom. She was also fond of being tied up and chained. The title ended early in 1949 and was replaced on the Fox roster by a romance comic.

Though gone, she was not forgotten. In his *Seduction of the Innocent* in 1954, Wertham reprinted Baker's cover for #17 and captioned it, "Sexual stimulation by combining 'headlights' with the sadist's dream of tying up a woman." Late that same year, Robert Farrell, another satisfied Iger customer, published a *Phantom Lady* title. This time the lady crimefighter appeared in a less-revealing costume and battled communists. Baker also worked on this version. DC brought back Phantom Lady to serve as part of the Freedom Fighters group in the middle 1970s and let her solo, again in a skimpy costume, in the short-lived *Action Comics Weekly*. She has appeared in some of Bill Black's reprint magazines now and again in recent years.

PICTURE NEWS

■ See PICTURE STORIES FROM THE BIBLE.

PICTURE STORIES FROM THE BIBLE

■ The EC comic-book line began its life not with titles offering gritty, realistic war stories; dark, sardonic mystery; grisly, ironic horror; or irreverent satirical humor. The cornerstone of the company was a wholesome, inspirational publication entitled *Picture Stories from the Bible*. And the initial batch of biblical stories was seen first not on newsstands but in the weekly editions of a single Connecticut-based newspaper.

Maxwell C. Gaines, toward the end of 1938, had entered into an agreement with DC to produce a series of comic books that would be published under the DC imprint. His editor was the youthful Sheldon Mayer. Among the titles the team turned out were *All-American Comics, Flash Comics, Wonder Woman*, and *All Star Comics*. Despite his involvement with superheroes, Gaines felt that the comics medium could be used for better things. Sometime late in 1941 he began working on *Picture Stories from the Bible*. Note that he didn't christen his project *Bible*

Comics. Instead he sought a more polite phrase to describe the funny-book format, finally settling on picture stories.

In a 1942 article for *Print* (yet another euphemism for comics was used in the title—*Narrative Illustration*), Gaines touted his newest venture, without identifying himself with it. "Within the last several months," he wrote, "an experiment has been made in the use of stories from the Bible, using the comic-book colored continuity technique. A series of ten ran in a New England paper, and responses indicated such wide acceptance that a ten-cent, sixty-four-page book, *Picture Stories from the Bible*, has lately gone on sale." The newspaper in question was the Bridgeport-based *Connecticut Herald*. A Sunday-only paper, which has been described as the *National Enquirer* of its day, it was owned and operated by the conservative Leigh Danenberg. An entrepreneur, Danenberg also used his plant to print comic books, and his tabloid newspaper had not only a Connecticut edition but editions in Rhode Island and Massachusetts.

The Bible stories appeared in the form of eight-page booklets, emulating the format established by Will Eisner with his Sunday *The Spirit* inserts. The first one appeared on Sunday, April 5, 1942. In order to turn the insert into a viable comic book, the reader had to do a bit of work. The pages were printed on a single sheet of newsprint and "to make your own eight page booklet . . . (1) Cut along this solid line. (2) Fold along dotted line 'A'. (3) Insert pins on inside fold." In concluding his *Print* essay, Gaines had stated that perhaps the next chapter in the history of comic books "will record how beauty, in layout and design, was heightened without estranging people who loved them as they were."

Don Cameron, who drew in a cartoony style, was the artist, and the writer was Montgomery Mulford. An author capable of giving the serpent in the Garden of Eden an aside like, "Ha! Ha! She's tempted!" may not have been the best man for the job. Sheldon Mayer thought the whole enterprise was a mistake and had little to do with it.

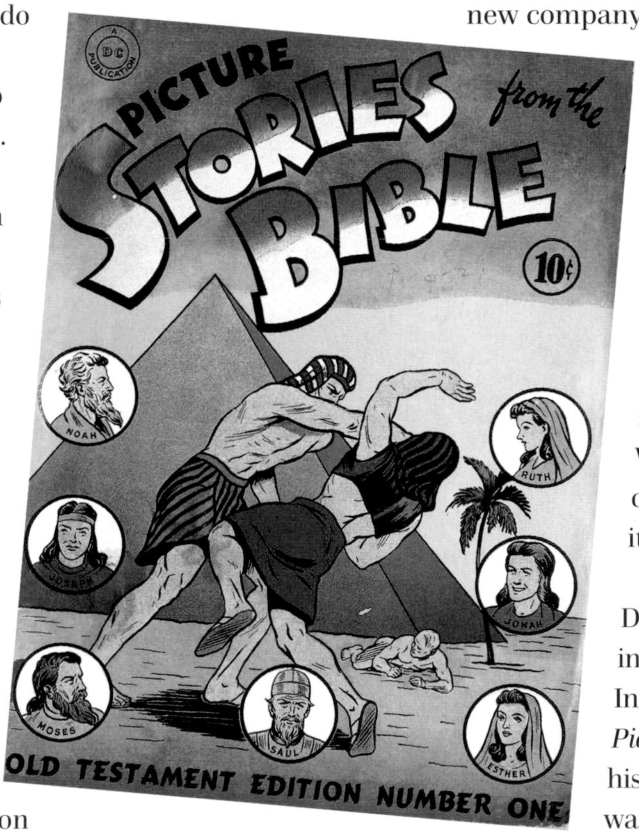
A DC PUBLICATION
PICTURE STORIES from the BIBLE
10¢
NOAH
JOSEPH
MOSES
SAUL
RUTH
JONAH
ESTHER
OLD TESTAMENT EDITION NUMBER ONE

The first issue of *Picture Stories from the Bible*, with the DC logo on the cover, appeared in the summer of 1942. Eventually there were seven issues of the magazine, four devoted to the Old Testament, three to the New Testament. Cameron remained the artist throughout, although E. E. Hibbard drew the covers for the New Testament issues. The series ended up selling several million copies.

In 1945, while Gaines was preparing *Picture Stories from American History*, he ended his association with DC. But he retained the *Picture Stories* series and formed a new company, eventually called Education Comics, Inc. The first two issues of the American history series sold 600,000 copies. He also produced a world history and a science picture story series. He was planning more educational material when he was killed in a boating accident in the summer of 1947. His son, William, took over the EC company and decided to take it in new directions.

The enterprising Leigh Danenberg had apparently been influenced by printing for Gaines. In early 1946 he introduced *Picture News*, borrowing part of his title from the Gaines books. It was intended to be a comic-book version of news magazines like *Life*, and it devoted its space to coverage of Joe Louis's latest fight, a review of the movie version of *Caesar and Cleopatra*, a profile of Cardinal Spellman, a report on atomic bomb tests at Bikini Atoll, etc. It lasted just ten issues. Among the artists were Jack Lehti, Emil Gershwin, Nat Edson, and, of all people, Milt Gross.

THE PIE-FACE PRINCE

■ See CARLSON, GEORGE.

10¢
A VITAL BOOK
PLASTIC MAN IN THE Game of Death!
4 Full Length PLASTIC MAN Picture Stories!
HE STRETCHES, SHRINKS AND BENDS!!

PLASTIC MAN

■ Although several pretenders have claimed to be Plastic Man over the years, the one and only Plastic Man existed only in the 1940s and then was gone forever. What guaranteed his authenticity was the writing and drawing of his creator Jack Cole. Plas made his modest debut in *Police Comics* #1 (August 1941). Cole's narratives mixed fantasy, cops and robbers, violence, and humor. His drawing style, a blend of the illustrational approach with the exaggerations of animated cartoons, was ideally suited to depicting Plastic Man's bouncy gangster adventures.

Part of the fun of the feature were the disguises the shape-changing Plastic Man undertook in his pursuit of crooks and scoundrels. During his first few months, he transformed himself into, among other things, a giant flying squirrel, a quivering junkie, a rather plump matron, a firehose, and a glamour girl. He also stretched, shrank, bounced, rolled like a hoop, and squeezed through keyholes. *Police Comics* hadn't intended Cole's character to be the star. A rather lackluster costumed fellow known as Firebrand had been picked for that chore. But even Reed Crandall's admirable artwork couldn't overcome the fact that Firebrand was a dud. The magazines backup characters, including a fairly tame Phantom Lady and a masked man known as the Mouthpiece, proved no competition either, and within a few issues Plas was the leading man. In #13 (November 1942) Woozy Winks, who looked something like the then popular movie comedian Lou Costello, became the hero's sidekick. From that point on the stories took on more humor, and Plastic Man became an FBI agent.

In 1943 the first complete *Plastic Man* comic book appeared. It was followed by a second a year later, and finally in 1946 the title began a regular schedule. Because of the increasing demands for material, other artists began drawing the bouncy hero. Bart Tumey was the first, followed by Alex Kotzky and John Spranger. Plastic Man was bounced from *Police Comics* after #102 (October 1950). The magazine itself continued for three more years, presenting crime and private-eye material. The *Plastic Man* comic book limped along until 1956, although Cole had long since given up his character.

DC licensed the character and has made several attempts over the years to revive Plas. Artists such as Gil Kane, Ramona Fradon, Phil Foglio, and most recently Kyle Baker have all given it a try, but none have been successful. That's because Cole was really the only one who knew how to do it just right.

COME AND GET IT, BOYS!
TSK-TSK!... AND YOU GUYS ARE SUPPOSED TO BE TOUGH!

PLATINUM AGE

■ In the past few years a new category has grown up among comic-book collectors, as well as researchers and academics. Dubbed the Platinum Age by its earliest and most zealous proponents, it refers to magazines published before what's known as the Golden Age of comic books. Though the Platinum Age has no agreed upon commencement date, as applied to American comic books it is said to include anything published from the middle of the nineteenth century to the middle of the 1930s.

The indispensable *Overstreet Comic Book Price Guide* has been running a special Platinum Age section for several years, and in the latest edition an expanded list covers several hundred titles. Most of them are various-sized comic books that reprint newspaper strips ranging from *Buster Brown and His Resolutions* and *Barney Google and Spark Plug* through *Little Orphan Annie in the Circus* and *The Outbursts of Everett True* to *Winnie Winkle* and *The Yellow Kid*. Thus far no Platinum Age titles have come anywhere near to commanding the sort of prices that the most sought after Golden Age books go for.

POCKET COMICS

100 PAGE POCKET COMICS
POCKET COMICS
No. 2
SEPT.
10¢
CONTINUE THE ADVENTURES OF THE GREAT NEW STARS!
★ SPIRIT OF '76 BATTLES SATAN
★ THE BLACK CAT ★ RED BLAZER
★ THE ZEBRA .... and many others

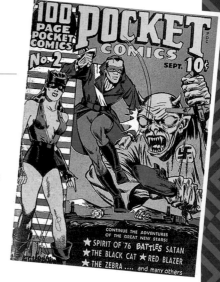

■ The first digest-sized comic book, *Pocket* was the invention of Alfred Harvey and made its debut in the summer of 1941. The cover promised one hundred pages—that's counting the covers—for just ten cents and proclaimed this was "the biggest comic value in the world." The lineup included the Zebra, the Red Blazer, Satan, the Spirit of '76, and the Black Cat. Joe Simon, who'd worked with Harvey at the Fox comics outfit, has said that he drew the covers.

Harvey, who supposedly launched the magazine with a total investment of $400, also started a cartoon digest called *Fun Parade* at the same time. He had acquired the faltering *Speed Comics* and his first issue of that, #14 (September 1941), was in the digest format as well.

Since the public was apparently not ready for digest-sized comics, *Pocket* ceased after its fourth issue (January 1942). And after two more compact issues, *Speed* returned to normal. According to Simon, in his *The Comic Book Makers*, there was a problem with the news dealers as well. Too many kid customers took to heart the suggestion that *Pocket Comics* could easily be slipped into a pocket, neglecting to fork over their dimes.

Before the fall, Alfred Harvey had planned other small comic books, including *Patriotic Comics*, *Historic Comics*, and *Digest Comics*. Harvey went on to do much better with regular-sized comic books, especially with one featuring the Black Cat.

PORKY PIG

■ See LOONEY TUNES AND MERRIE MELODIES.

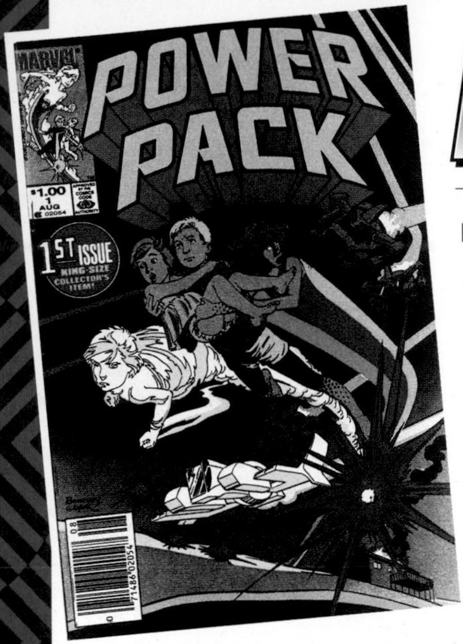
MARVEL
POWER PACK
$1.00
1
AUG
1ST ISSUE
KING-SIZE
COLLECTOR'S ITEM!

POWER PACK

■ This kinder, gentler, and younger version of the usual gang of super-youths was launched by Marvel in the summer of 1984. *Power Pack*, concerning four super-empowered kids, was created by writer Louise Simonson and artist June Brigman. Blending elements of traditional children's fantasy novels, as seen for example in the works of E. Nesbit and C. S. Lewis, with contemporary notions of what sort of fantasy appeals to children, Simonson and Brigman came up with an appealing series about the Power siblings, two brother and sister sets. The kids ranged in age from five to twelve and obtained their assorted superpowers from an alien who appeared in the form of a white horse.

Aimed at a younger and less bloodthirsty audience, *Power Pack* survived until 1991. The four kids did a four-issue encore in 2000.

POWERHOUSE PEPPER

■ See WOLVERTON, BASIL.

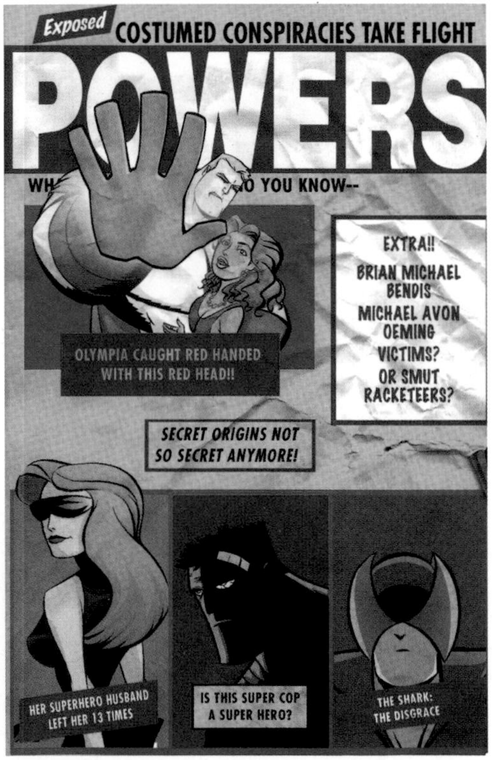
Exposed
COSTUMED CONSPIRACIES TAKE FLIGHT
POWERS
EXTRA!!
BRIAN MICHAEL BENDIS
MICHAEL AVON OEMING
VICTIMS?
OR SMUT RACKETEERS?
OLYMPIA CAUGHT RED HANDED WITH THIS RED HEAD!!
SECRET ORIGINS NOT SO SECRET ANYMORE!
HER SUPERHERO HUSBAND LEFT HER 13 TIMES
IS THIS SUPER COP A SUPER HERO?
THE SHARK: THE DISGRACE

POWERS

■ An interesting variation on the earlier *Watchmen* concept, this is a police procedural series that takes place in a world where superheroes exist. *Powers* began in 2000 and is published by Image. Brian Michael Bendis writes it; Michael Avon Oeming draws it. The superheroes have such names as Olympia (a guy), Retro Girl, Zora, Triphammer, and the Shark. They have feet of clay, at the very least. Some of them consort with hookers, most are as self-centered as movie stars, behave in similar ways, and are media celebrities themselves. All of them have serious personal problems, some have even sued each other.

And now and then one of them, despite his or her powers, gets killed. Then the police get involved, in the persons of Walker, a former power guy himself, and his blond partner Deena Pilgrim. Dialogue and staging are effective, and there isn't another comic quite like *Powers*. Thus far it's been nominated for many of the honors that the comics field offers, such as the Harvey and the Will Eisner awards.

PREACHER

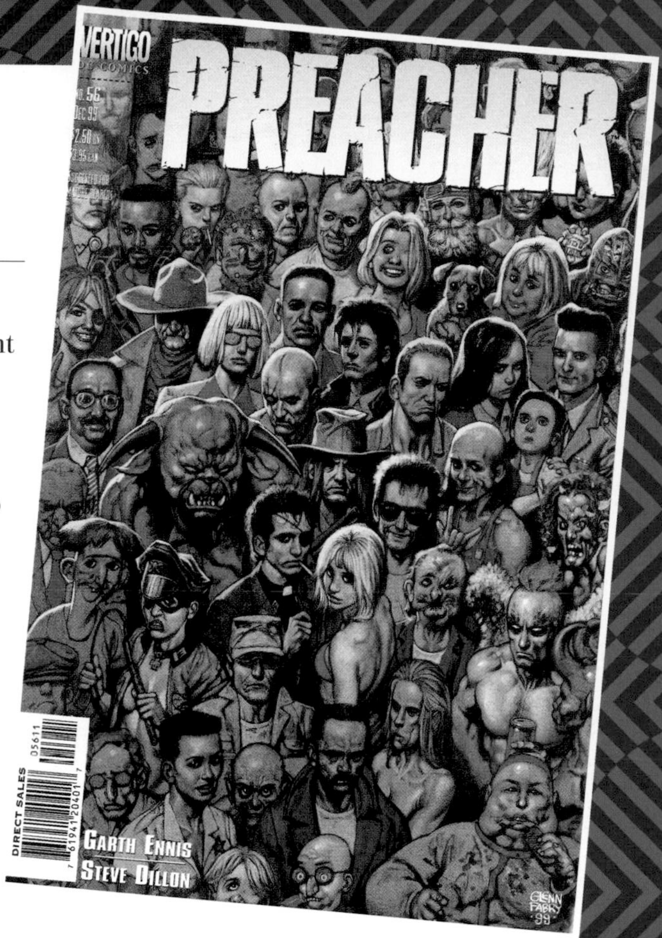
VERTIGO
PREACHER
DIRECT SALES
GARTH ENNIS
STEVE DILLON

■ A frenzied mix of religion, mysticism, Clint Eastwood riffs, family values, and exploding-head violence, *Preacher* was introduced by DC's Vertigo imprint in 1995. The series ended with its sixty-sixth issue in 2000. Throughout its run it was written by Garth Ennis and drawn by Steve Dillon, chaps who'd also worked together on *Hellblazer* for a bit.

The Preacher is the Reverend Jesse Custer, a semi-defrocked priest who decided to leave his small-town Texas parish after a runaway spiritual entity (which is half angel–half devil) seemingly fused itself with him and also caused all two hundred of his parishioners and his church to explode. Thereafter, wearing the top half of his clerical garb with mismatched trousers, Jesse roamed the world fighting evil, helping folks, and getting involved in assorted scenes of slaughter. He traveled with his blond girlfriend Tulip O'Hare and a hard-drinking Irish vampire named Casey. There were also several spooky encounters with a supernatural bloke known as the Saint of Killers, whose assignment is to destroy him and whose fancy it is to dress like a Old West gunfighter. At times *Preacher* somewhat resembled a punk-rock version of *The Fugitive.*

PRIZE COMICS

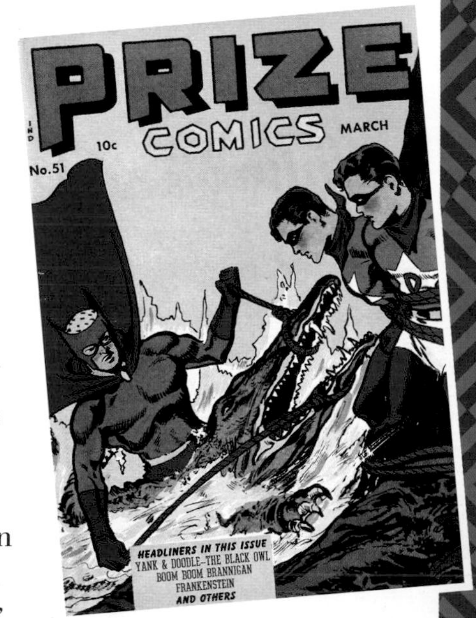
PRIZE
COMICS
10c
MARCH
No.51
HEADLINERS IN THIS ISSUE
YANK & DOODLE—THE BLACK OWL
BOOM BOOM BRANNIGAN
FRANKENSTEIN
AND OTHERS

■ By changing with the times, *Prize* managed to remain on the stands for nearly sixteen years, first as an adventure anthology and then as a Western. Arriving early in 1940, the first issue offered a rather bland blend of features, led off by the blond superhero Power Nelson, aka Futureman. Although Futureman sounds somewhat like Superman, Power was no competition for the Man of Steel and was soon relegated to the back of the book. He and a masked man known as the Black Owl were among the few characters to survive beyond the sixth issue.

One of the ways that *Prize Comics* tried to upgrade was by adding new artists as well as new characters with the seventh issue (December 1940). The recently formed team of Joe Simon and Jack Kirby was brought in to take over *The Black Owl.* An updated version of *Frankenstein*, written and drawn by Dick Briefer, was added as well as a comic-book version of the pulp-fiction mystery man the Green Lama, written by his creator Ken Crossen and drawn by Mac Raboy. *Prize* also installed *"Twist" Turner*, *Dr. Frost*, and *The Great Voodini.*

Yank and Doodle, twin boy wonders of a patriotic bent, joined the magazine in #13 (August 1941). Drawn originally by Paul Norris, Yank and Doodle were billed as "America's Fighting Twins." They wore red, white, and blue uniforms, identical except for a "Y" on the chest of one and a "D" on the chest of the other, and had no special powers. The boys' most persistent antagonist was the Limping Man, "a master of disguise, who cannot be recognized except for his limp! The forces of law and order are helpless in the face of a villain who never looks the same way twice."

In *Prize* #34 (September 1943) the Black Owl got himself drafted. He explained his problem to his old school chum, the twins' father—"While I'm helping take care of international gangsters abroad, who will keep crime in check here?" Dad Walter agreed to take over the role and then teamed up with Yank and Doodle. He knew they were really his sons, but they didn't realize he was the Black Owl. That made for a complicated but stimulating home life. Eventually the lads found out about their pop's alter ego and things ran more smoothly for the "terrific trio." Among the artists who illustrated this unusual *ménage à trois* were Jack Alderman, John Giunta, Fred Guardineer, and a youthful Gil Kane. The father-and-sons act took its final bow in *Prize* #68 early in 1948.

Prize underwent further changes back in that summer of 1943. The Green Lama was dumped, Dick Briefer started changing *Frankenstein* into a horror spoof, and the Bernard Baily shop began producing a batch of new features. One of them was *Buck Saunders and His Pals,* about yet another gang of kid adventurers. Most of the others were strange superhero attempts such as *Airmale and Stampy* and *Flying Fist and Bingo.* Defying description was something entitled *Worldbeater and Unggh.* The following year a boxer named Boom-Boom Brannigan was given the star spot. Baily himself drew that before turning it over to newspaper vet Charles Voight. Voight also contributed a knighthood spoof called *Sir Prize.*

Early in 1948 the magazine decided to become *Prize Western Comics* and junked its former contents. The leading cowpoke was Dusty Bellew, rendered by Al Carreño. Other Western heroes included a Cisco Kid wannabe named the Lazo Kid and a cowboy mystery man who donned a hood with horns and called himself the Black Bull. Harvey Kurtzman, John Severin, and Will Elder all became contributors. Early in 1951, Severin and Elder introduced *American Eagle,* and their Indian hero became the magazine's star character. *Prize* ended with its 119th issue late in 1956.

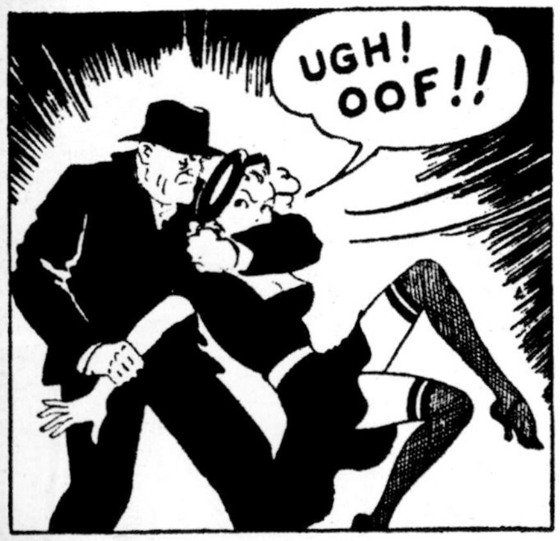
UGH! OOF!!

PULP COMICS

■ Pulp-fiction magazines had begun using original comic book material, albeit in small doses, even before Major Nicholson launched *New Fun,* the first regularly issued comic book using original material. A pioneer in the production of the two- and three-page black-and-white inserts that appeared in several pulps was artist Adolphe Barreaux. He himself drew *Sally the Sleuth,* which started in the November 1934 issue of *Spicy Detective.* In addition, Max Plaisted, who worked in the Barreaux studio, contributed *Diana Daw* to *Spicy Adventure* that year. In 1935 Plaisted began drawing an SF feature called *Ace Jordan* for *Thrilling Adventure* and *Zarnak* for *Thrilling Wonder Stories* the following year.

The pulps also introduced the first true crime comics. Ned Pines's *G-Men* carried a feature titled *Public Enemies* from its first issue (October 1935). In three- and four-page stories, the careers of notorious FBI targets were told. Plaisted, who did more of this stuff than anybody, was once again the artist. The subject of the first episode was bank robber John Dillinger, who'd been gunned down by the G-Men the previous year.

The Spicy line was run by Frank Armer and Harry Donenfeld, soon to be the publisher of Detective Comics, Inc. In their *Spicy Mystery*, a black-and-white strip about a woman with X-ray eyes named Olga Mesmer started in the summer of 1937, almost a year before Superman showed up. The women in all the Spicy comics inevitably lost most, if not all, of their clothes in each episode. The material in the Pines pulp magazines, though turned out by the Barreaux shop, was much more sedate. Barreaux was a contributor to the major's comic books and Plaisted moved into regular comics in the late 1930s.

THE PUNISHER

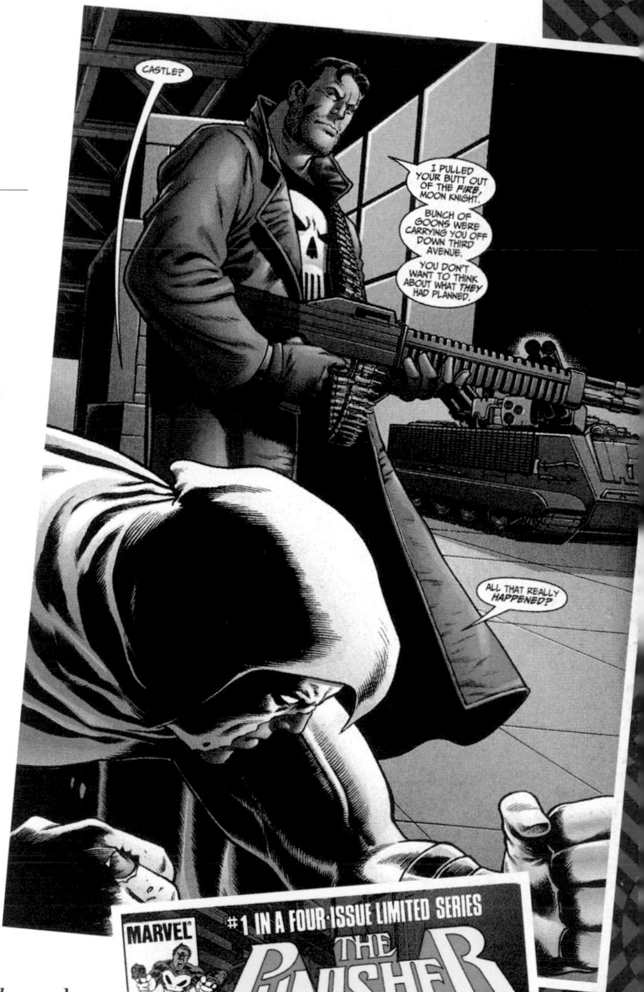
CASTLE?
I PULLED YOUR BUTT OUT OF THE FIRE, MOON KNIGHT.
BUNCH OF GOONS WERE CARRYING YOU OFF DOWN THIRD AVENUE.
YOU DON'T WANT TO THINK ABOUT WHAT THEY HAD PLANNED.
ALL THAT REALLY HAPPENED?

■ Inspired by such popular paperback vigilantes as Don Pendleton's the Executioner, the Punisher started mowing down bad guys in *The Amazing Spider-Man* #129 (February 1974). Dressed all in black, with a huge white skull emblazoned across the chest of his uniform, he mistakenly tried to assassinate Spidey. Disabused of that notion, the Punisher went back to ignoring due process and executing the scum of the criminal underworld. "Right now I'm just a warrior," he told Spider-Man as they parted, "fighting a lonely war." Gerry Conway wrote the script that introduced the character; Ross Andru illustrated it.

Wiping out crime single-handedly is a major undertaking, and it's not surprising that the Punisher is still at it a quarter of a century later. Given his own title in 1986, he soon branched out into a series of magazines, including *The Punisher War Journal*, *The Punisher War Zone*, and *The Punisher Armory*. This last title, issued now and again, was devoted entirely to the weapons of one-on-one destruction in Punisher's arsenal, plus assorted gadgets. A typical issue displayed over two dozen guns and a nice selection of knives.

The Punisher was eventually given the name of Frank Castle and his reason for being was summed up as, "When mobsters slew his family, Frank Castle vowed to spend the rest of his life avenging them! Trained as a Marine, and equipped with a state-of-the-art arsenal, he now wages a one-man war on crime!" Combining all of the favorite aspects of *Rambo*, *Death Wish*, and most Steven Segal movies, the various Punisher titles have been chock full of blazing guns, explosions, and all other known forms of annihilation.

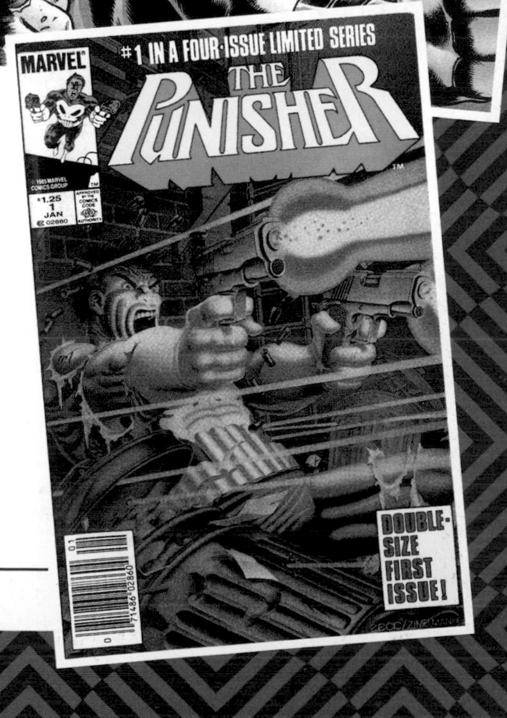
#1 IN A FOUR-ISSUE LIMITED SERIES
MARVEL
THE PUNISHER
DOUBLE-SIZE FIRST ISSUE!

The character has teamed up with a choice selection of Marvel characters over the years, and also with Batman and, in a very strange interlude, with Archie. Among the other artists and writers contributing to the saga of his journey along the road to revenge had been Klaus Janson, Berni Wrightson, and Chuck Dixon. Currently Garth Ennis and Steve Dillon, the erstwhile *Hellblazer* team, are producing the newest Punisher series, which began in the summer of 2001. Frank isn't quite as muscle-bound as in earlier incarnations, and he doesn't grimace or growl much. He has more thoughtful moments, but his collection of guns is about the same.

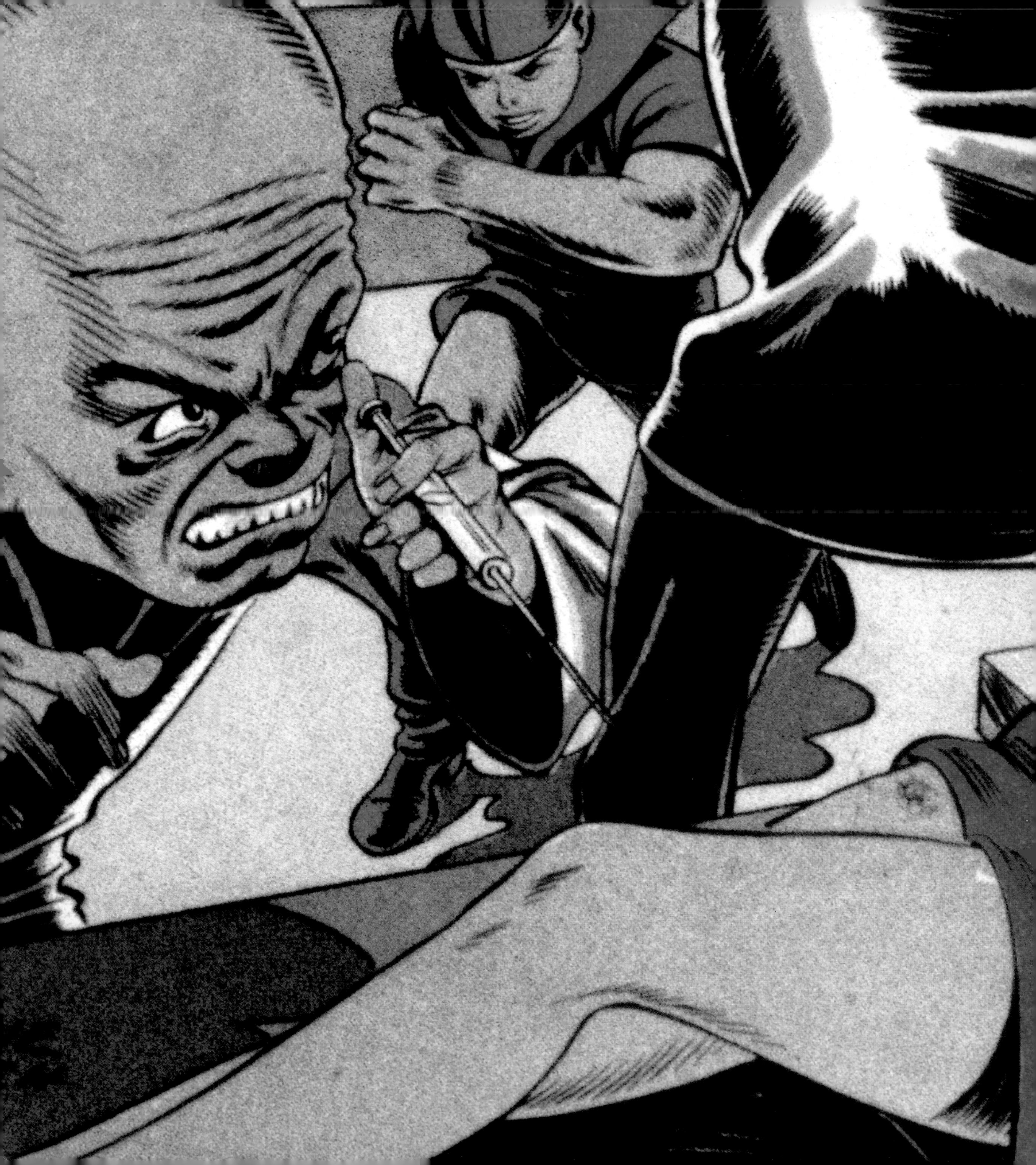

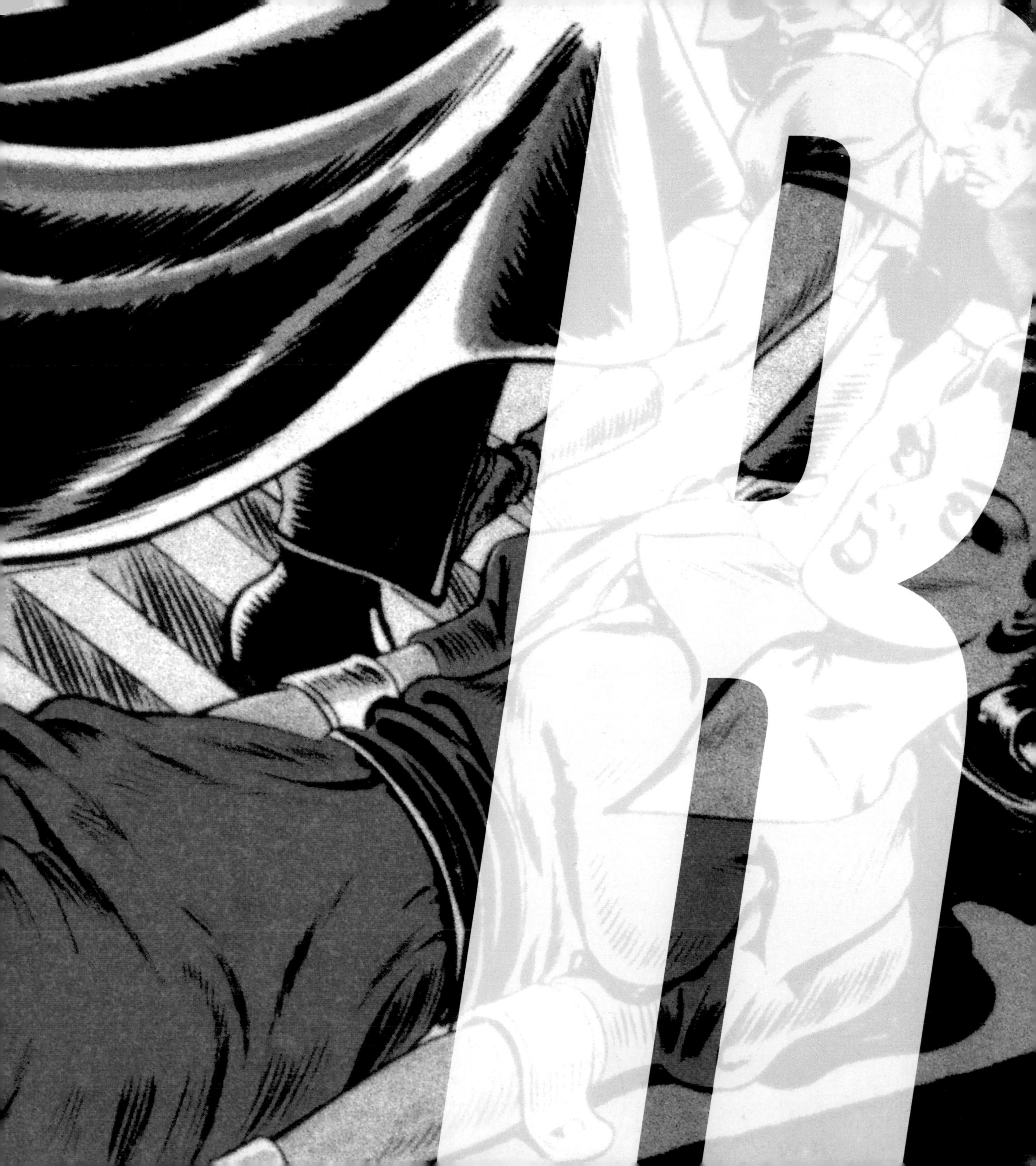
R

RED, WHITE AND BLUE

■ The earliest patriotic team in comic books, this trio of service men began defending their country against spies and saboteurs in *All-American Comics* #1 (April 1939). They were marine Red Dugan, soldier Whitey Smith, and sailor Blooey Blue. John Wentworth was the writer; William A. Smith was the first regular artist.

In that first issue of *All-American*, the three friends met pretty brunette secret agent Doris West while in Panama. After helping her round up a spy ring, they were assigned by the local head of G-2 to be on "special duty to work as a unit to ferret out spy activities!" Their special duties pitted them against saboteurs, fascist groups, Nazi scientists, and other prewar threats to American security. Wentworth used an occasional sci-fi touch, including telepathy and invisibility. As the saga progressed, Red, the good-looking one, and Doris became sweethearts.

When the United States entered World War II in December of 1941, the Red, White and Blue team remained on the homefront for a while, continuing to smash spies. Eventually they split up, each heading to overseas assignments. They were last seen in *All-American* early in 1946.

After Smith, several other artists followed. The most gifted was a young man named Joe Gallagher, who drew in a forceful, gritty style. He shepherded the team through the war and into retirement.

REX THE WONDER DOG

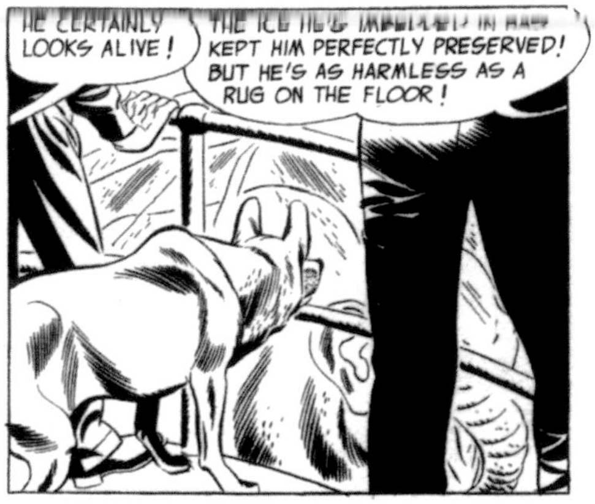
HE CERTAINLY LOOKS ALIVE!
KEPT HIM PERFECTLY PRESERVED! BUT HE'S AS HARMLESS AS A RUG ON THE FLOOR!

■ The movies were fond of wonder dogs, from the highly popular Rin Tin Tin of the silent era and the equally popular Lassie of the 1940s. Television, too, thought highly of heroic hounds. *The Adventures of Rin Tin Tin* was a successful show on ABC from 1954 to 1959, and *Lassie*, in various incarnations, remained on CBS from 1954 to 1971. The most successful wonder dog in comic books was DC's Rex, who had a magazine of his own for most of the 1950s.

The writer was Robert Kanigher; the first artist was Alex Toth. This was not the first German shepherd out of the Toth-Kanigher kennel. They'd introduced Streak the Wonder Dog in *Green Lantern* #30 in 1948. That clever canine soon upstaged his master, even appearing solo on a couple of covers. He also hung out with GL in the final issues of *All-American Comics*. Although Rex was a dog of a different color, he was closely akin to Streak.

The cover of the first issue of *The Adventures of Rex the Wonder Dog*, which reached the stands at the end of 1951, showed the white canine rescuing an unconscious blond young woman from a forest fire. Inside the wonder dog solved a murder in one yarn, worked with forest rangers in another. Owned by a youth named Danny Dennis, Rex adopted a variety of surrogate masters throughout his career. Since Kanigher had a fondness for war stories, by the fourth issue Rex was being referred to as "the Fighting K-9" and showing up on assorted battlefields. Eventually returning to civilian life, the intelligent dog, who thought in English, even found time to tangle with dinosaurs.

Gil Kane followed Toth as artist. The final issue of *Rex* was published late in 1959.

RICHIE RICH

■ The Richest Kid in the World made his modest debut as a backup in Harvey's *Little Dot* #1 (September 1953). After becoming a regular in that comic book, Richie soloed in two issues of *Harvey Hits* in 1957. Then in 1960 the first issue of *Richie Rich* appeared. The little blond lad proved enormously popular with younger readers, and eventually Harvey published nearly fifty different *Richie Rich* titles.

The creative team behind Richie Rich, and never credited in any of the many magazines, initially consisted of editor Sid Jacobson and artist Warren Kremer. In a 2002 interview in *Comic Artist*, Jacobson said, "Warren Kremer and I created the character. More than another mischievous character. And he got richer and richer by the story." Kremer added in an interview in that same issue that it was while watching the TV show *The Millionaire* that he was struck by the thought, "Gee, what about a kid who's the son of a millionaire." He took his notion to Jacobson, and with some help from another staff artist, Richie Rich (named after Kremer's son Richard) was born.

Richie Rich
VAULTS OF MYSTERY
RICHIE RICH
VAULT$ OF
MYSTERY
HARVEY COMICS
MAY No. 10
25¢
D-DAD! WHAT'S WRONG?
THE ANSWER IS IN "THE VOODOO MENACE!"

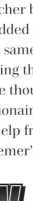

Also known as the Poor Little Rich Boy, Richie usually appeared in five-page humorous adventures. The stories ranged from simple sitcom to mystery, science fiction, and mild horror. They involved a crew of regulars that included Cadbury the Perfect Butler, Irona the robot maid, Richie's pudgy parents, his girlfriend Gloria, Reggie Van Dough, his nasty little cousin, and Dollar, his dog. As Richie's popularity grew, new titles began to proliferate. For many years they were issued at the rate of two or three a week. Among the many were *Richie Rich Millions*, *Richie Rich Vault of Mystery*, *Richie Rich Success*, *Richie Rich Diamonds*, and *Richie Rich Bank Book*. Richie left comics in 1982, returned on a limited basis in 1986, and at present is on hiatus.

Kremer, who died in the summer of 2003, was an enormously productive cartoonist. In addition to drawing *Casper the Friendly Ghost*, he penciled and inked the majority of covers for all the *Richie Rich* titles and penciled a great many of the stories. Another longtime artist was Ernie Colon, who spent twenty-five years drawing Richie. Lennie Herman was one of the most frequent script writers.

ROBIN

■ See BATMAN.

ROBOTMAN

■ An influential mechanical man, he was introduced in DC's *Star Spangled Comics* #7 (June 1942). Jerry Siegel, who'd read many a science-fiction yarn about robots, created the character. Paul Cassidy, Ed Dobrodka, and other artists from the Superman shop took turns drawing the early adventures. Nobody got a credit.

According to the origin story, Robotman had been a regular human being, "rich, young Professor Robert Crane." While working on a new robot with his assistant in his "palatial laboratory-residence," he was fatally shot by burglars. His quick-thinking associate removed his brain and plopped it into the skull of the robot. Thus was born Robotman, who at first looked quite a bit like the Tin Woodman of Oz. In order to function in a world that believed him dead, Crane adopted the alias Paul Dennis and fashioned synthetic skin to wear over his metallic face and hands. He then commenced a dual identity life, passing as human until it was time to fight crime as Robotman.

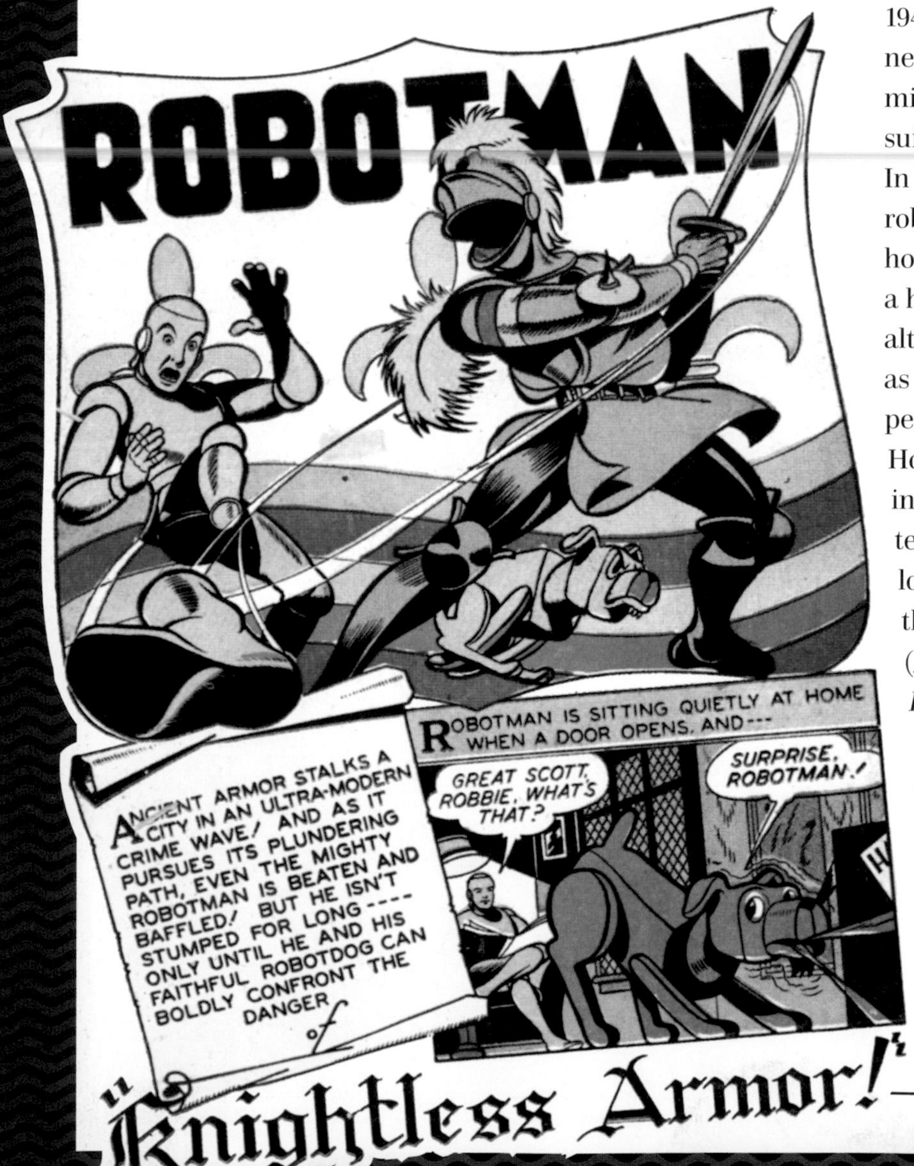
ROBOTMAN
ANCIENT ARMOR STALKS A CITY IN AN ULTRA-MODERN CRIME WAVE! AND AS IT PURSUES ITS PLUNDERING PATH, EVEN THE MIGHTY ROBOTMAN IS BEATEN AND BAFFLED! BUT HE ISN'T STUMPED FOR LONG--- ONLY UNTIL HE AND HIS FAITHFUL ROBOTDOG CAN BOLDLY CONFRONT THE DANGER of
ROBOTMAN IS SITTING QUIETLY AT HOME WHEN A DOOR OPENS, AND---
GREAT SCOTT, ROBBIE, WHAT'S THAT?
SURPRISE, ROBOTMAN!
"Knightless Armor!"

The character's finest hour came in the autumn of 1943, when Jimmy Thompson took over the feature. A newspaper veteran, Thompson achieved just the right mix of humor and straight in his drawing, a blend that suited the not-quite-serious exploits of the metallic sleuth. In *Star Spangled* #29, Thompson introduced Robbie the robotdog. Built by Robotman, the mechanical sleuth hound was initially a polite and sedate creature. But after a hiatus of a few issues, Robbie came back in a slightly altered form. Besides acquiring a shaggy-dog suit to wear as a disguise over his metal body, he had a new personality. Feisty and vain, he now read Sherlock Holmes and assured his master that he was a crackerjack investigator himself. Once Thompson had this basic team, he went on to produce a long string of attractive-looking, entertaining yarns. He drew the character throughout its run in *Star Spangled*, which ended in #82 (July 1948) and stuck with Robotman when he moved to *Detective Comics* as of #138 (August 1948).

Thompson left the job in 1949. Among the later artists were Joe Certa. Otto Binder, who'd written about a robot named Adam Link in the *Amazing Stories* pulp in the late 1930s, contributed scripts in the late 1940s. Robotman ended that phase of his career in 1953. In 1963 an entirely different Robotman became a member in good standing of the Doom Patrol.

ROGERS, BOODY

(1904–1990)

■ He first drew for comic books in 1929, was a contributor to Major Nicholson's original-material comic books in the middle 1930s, ghosted the *Smilin' Jack* newspaper strip from 1936 to the early 1940s, and created the mock superhero Sparky Watts in 1940.

Gordon Rogers was born in the Oklahoma Territory in 1904. "I first thought of being a cartoonist as soon as I was big enough to hold a pencil," he once recalled. He drew for both his high school paper and the humor magazine of the University of Arizona. By the late 1920s, Rogers was studying at the Chicago Academy of Art, which is where he first met fellow Oklahoman Zack Mosley. In 1928 he headed for Manhattan. "My first artwork was tracing my feet on cardboard and cutting them out and placing them in my shoes to plug the holes. I started selling a few cartoons to *Life, Judge, Collier's, Film Fun,* and anyone who would buy. Then came *The Funnies.*"

Rogers worked for George Delacorte's pioneering *The Funnies,* drawing *Deadwood Gulch, Rock Age Roy, Sancho and the Don,* and *Campus Clowns.* After *The Funnies* folded, he turned out a complete black-and-white book of *Deadwood Gulch* for Dell. He was a contributor to *New Comics,* ghosted Frank Beck's *Gas Buggies,* lettered *Dumb Dora,* and did the coloring for the Sunday *Winnie Winkle.* In 1936, when the Chicago Tribune–New York News Syndicate decided to add a *Smilin' Jack* daily strip, Mosley asked his old buddy to lend a hand. During his stay with Mosley, Rogers started his own comic strip. *Sparky Watts* made its debut in 1940 in roughly forty papers around the country. When readers first met Sparky he was working his way through college by selling magazine subscriptions. Exposure to a cosmic ray machine turns him into the strongest man on Earth. Roger's take on superheroes was a humorous one, and he kidded most of the concepts of the burgeoning superhero genre. When Rogers was drafted in 1942, the strip ended.

Big Shot Comics had begun reprinting the strip in 1941 in four- and six-page snippets. After the war, Rogers started drawing original Sparky episodes for *Big Shot* and for a separate *Sparky Watts* magazine. These new adventures involved his hero with Amazons, giant bugs, reanimated mummies, crazed inventors, and a nuclear holocaust. Far from serious about any of these serious topics, Rogers approached them in his usual spirit of burlesque and slapstick, an approach to which his appealing cartoon style was ideally suited.

Big Shot and *Sparky Watts* came to an end in 1949. By that time Rogers was also drawing *Babe* for the Prize Comics group. Babe, also known as the Darling of the Hills, was a beautiful blonde who excelled at sports, especially baseball. The stories mixed fantasy and hillbilly humor. Before he quit comics, Rogers also drew three issues of a teen feature titled *Dudley.* After acting as proprietor of an art-supply house in Arizona, he retired to a small town in Texas.

ROGERS, ROY (1912–1998)

■ The King of the Cowboys and also a king of merchandising, Roy Rogers moved into comic books in 1944. By that time he already had a couple of Big Little Book titles under his belt. Dell published its first *Roy Rogers Comics* in the spring of 1944, the second early in 1945. At the end of 1947, after eleven more issues under the Four Color umbrella, Roy was promoted to a monthly of his own.

. . . . INNOCENT! I'VE COMMITTED NO CRIME AND YOU CAN PROVE IT BY TRIGGER'S TRAIL. . . . I FOUND SOME OF THE LOOT A MILE BACK.

Born in Cincinnati and christened Leonard Slye, by 1935 he and his singing group, the Sons of the Pioneers, were appearing in some of Republic's Gene Autry films. By the late 1930s, he was Roy Rogers and starring in his own series of singing cowboy movies for Republic Pictures.

During World War II, while Autry was away in the service, Republic crowned Roy Rogers the King of the Cowboys and referred to him as such in advertising and promotion articles. An astute businessman, he soon began to branch out into other enterprises, including real estate, cattle, and toys aimed at his many kid fans. And for Dell he became a comic-book cowboy.

Roy Rogers in comic books was the same clean-living, impeccably honest hombre he was in the movies. He even sang an occasional song while riding across the plains on his horse, Trigger. The early artists were Albert Micale and Irwin Hess, the fellow who'd illustrated the first Roy Rogers BLB. Later artists included Jesse Marsh, John Buscema—before he commenced his long run with Marvel—Dan Spiegle, Russ Manning, and Alex Toth. There was a comic book devoted to Trigger from 1951 to 1955. Roy's wife and movie leading lady, Dale Evans, appeared in both Dell and DC comic books of her own.

RUDE, STEVE

■ See NEXUS.

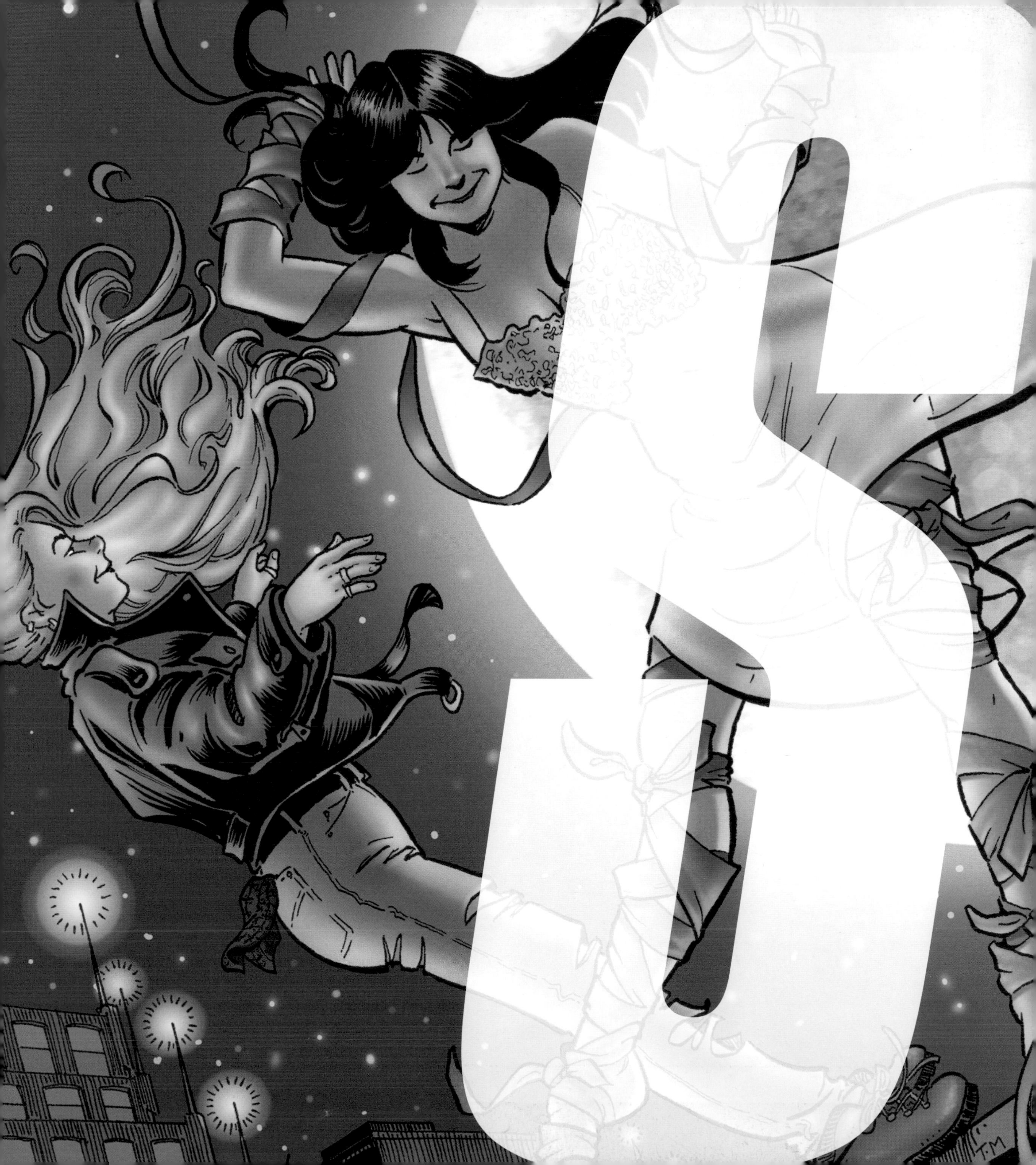

SALLY THE SLEUTH

■ See PULP COMICS.

SAMSON

■ See FANTASTIC COMICS.

THE SANDMAN: I

The SANDMAN
SOUGHT BY POLICE AND UNDERWORLD ALIKE, THE SANDMAN CONTINUES TO THWART BOTH—AND AT THE SAME TIME BRING JUSTICE TO THOSE WHO REALLY NEED IT—BY USING HIS GASGUN AND HELMETED FORM IN A SILENT MYSTERIOUS MANNER....
H'MM-LOOKS LIKE TROUBLE HEADING THIS WAY!
WHY SO?
THE NEWCOMERS HALT IN THE MIDDLE OF THE FLOOR AND DRAW GUNS.
WE'RE PAYING A BUSINESS VISIT! EVERYBODY SIT DOWN AN' NOBODY'LL GET HURT!
WELL, WELL! WES DODDS AND HIS MOLL! HELLO, DEAR! SORRY, LADY, BUT I GOTTA TAKE YER BRACELET!
YOU CAN'T GET AWAY WITH THIS!

■ The first Sandman in a long line of Sandmen, he was introduced in the 1939 edition of DC's *New York World's Fair Comics*. He then moved into *Adventure Comics*, first taking up residence in #40 (July 1939). *The Sandman* was the joint effort of writer Gardner Fox and artist Bert Christman. In everyday life, this modern Robin Hood was Wesley Dodds, a millionaire playboy who was also a brilliant inventor and CEO of the Dodds-Bessing Steel Corporation. When night fell, he put on a green business suit, fedora, gas mask, and purple cape to become the Sandman. Like his namesake, he brought sleep—chiefly to crooks, gangsters, and evildoers—using a special gas gun of his own invention. Although he was dedicated to bringing "justice to a world of injustice," he was often misunderstood and was "wanted by police forces on two continents." Fox got his ideas from such pulp-fiction heroes as the Shadow and the Spider. He was also greatly influenced by the Green Hornet, the popular radio avenger who used a gas gun to subdue his foes and was also considered a criminal by the law. Dodd's constant companion was Dian Belmont, the only person who knew his secret identity. She was not only an expert safecracker but the daughter of the district attorney.

For the next two years, the Sandman operated in a pulp-hero manner, dealing in cases that mixed mystery and fantasy. In addition to his duties in *Adventure*, he found time to serve as a member of the Justice Society over in *All Star Comics*. After Christman, Ogden Whitney,

Creig Flessel, and Chad Grothkopf drew his adventures. In the fall of 1941, Chad and editor Whit Ellsworth, after a convivial evening, decided to update the character. Thus, in *Adventure Comics* #69 Sandman appeared in yellow tunic and tights and purple trunks, cowl, and cape. He traded in his gas gun for a wirepoon gun, which was handy for everything from felling giant bees to scaling skyscrapers. Sandman also gained a boy companion known as Sandy the Golden Lad. Paul Norris carried on with the artwork for two issues before Joe Simon and Jack Kirby took over the feature.

Using the storytelling techniques they'd developed on *Captain America*, the team revitalized Sandman. They began to build some of the stories around dreams, nightmares, and other aspects of the realm of sleep. The old Sandman had been pushed out of the star spot by such latter-day heroes as Hour-Man and Starman, but with the advent of Simon and Kirby the new Sandman moved into the leading spot. From #74 (May 1942) onward, Sandman and Sandy appeared, with one exception, on the next two dozen or so covers. Other artists on the feature were Cliff Young and Phil Bard. Sandman and Sandy called it a night after #102 early in 1946.

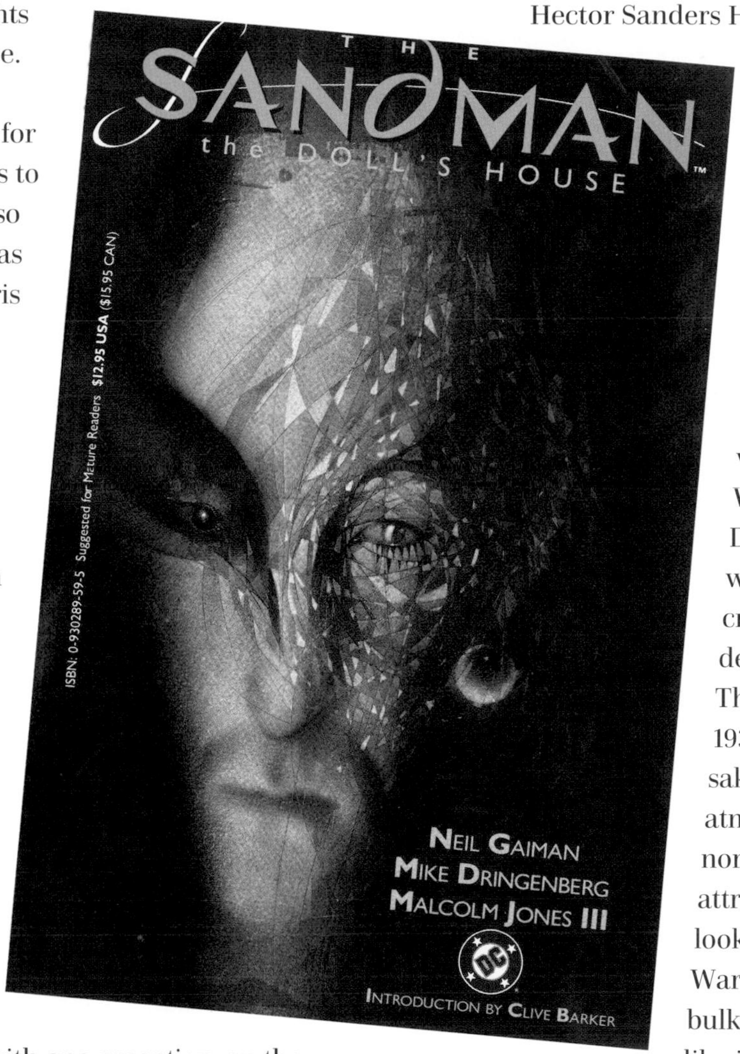
THE
SANDMAN
the DOLL'S HOUSE
ISBN: 0-930289-59-5 Suggested for Mature Readers $12.95 USA ($15.95 CAN)
NEIL GAIMAN
MIKE DRINGENBERG
MALCOLM JONES III
DC
INTRODUCTION BY CLIVE BARKER

The old original Sandman, complete with gas mask, returned now and again during the Silver Age, showing up in *The Justice League of America*. The original Sandy popped up on occasion, sometimes as a member of the All-Star Squadron. Late in 1974 Simon and Kirby, long parted, joined forces again to invent a brand-new Sandman. This one was Dr. Garrett Sanford, who operated as a costumed superhero over in the Dream Dimension, "a plane of existence on which what people see in dreams actually exists." This Sandman made it through six issues of his own magazine. In the late 1980s, Hector Sanders Hall, who'd been the Silver Scarab, assumed the Sandman role and filled in for Dr. Sanford.

A vastly changed version of the old original gas-mask character came along in the spring of 1993. Part of DC's Vertigo line, *Sandman Mystery Theater* was written by Matt Wagner and drawn by Guy Davis. The stories dealt with much seamier big-city crimes than Wes Dodds had dealt with in his heyday. They were set in a grim 1930s urban world. For the sake of the gritty downbeat atmosphere, neither Dodds nor Dian were particularly attractive. Sandman's mask looked like a relic of World War I and his gas gun was a bulky instrument that looked like it would be better suited to decorating wedding cakes. Although striving for a retro sound and feel, the scripts kept putting a 1990s spin on things. For instance, Dodds practices yoga, making him probably the only American businessman so doing in 1939. And Dian criticizes her father for referring to some of her friends as girls, pointing out that at twenty-five they are women not girls. A nice plea for gender equality, but something nobody would have said back then. Full of violence, torture, and partial nudity, the series started sleeping the big sleep in 1999.

SANDMAN: II

■ The most popular Sandman of them all, he was introduced by DC late in 1988. A completely different character, he was created by former British journalist Neil Gaiman and artist Sam Keith. This Sandman was initially Morpheus, the god of sleep and the ruler of Dreamworld. Gaiman's scripts mingled fantasy, horror, and New Age philosophy in a way that attracted an audience of mostly late teen and twenty-something readers. The new version was soon selling near to 100,000 copies each issue, very good for a book that wasn't devoted to a superhero.

John Constantine, better known as Hellblazer, was introduced in the third issue and Morpheus's sister, Death, came along in the eighth. A dark-haired and seemingly anorexic young lady in appearance, she rapidly attracted an audience of her own and branched out into a number of limited series, such as *Death: The High Cost of Living* in 1993.

The continuing popularity of the new *Sandman*, along with the reader interest in such titles as *Swamp Thing*, inspired DC to start its Vertigo line. Aimed at older readers who favored mystics over musclemen, the Vertigo titles were edited by Karen Berger. From the forty-seventh issue onward, *Sandman* bore the Vertigo colophon. The character proved equally popular in graphic novels. The trade paperback compilations of previous issues sold well in both comic shops and bookstores, and eventually Gaiman's entire run was recycled in that format. The series ended with its seventy-fifth issue early in 1996. Since then there have been several *Sandman* limited series, and Gaiman has become a popular mainstream author.

SCHOMBURG, ALEX *(1905–1998)*

■ His specialty was drawing covers, and from the late 1930s to the late 1940s he turned out more than five hundred of them. And with few exceptions, every one was a gem. A former commercial artist and pulp illustrator, Schomburg's first major client was publisher Martin Goodman. His covers were bold, colorful, inventive, and complex. His work graced the covers of such titles as *Marvel Mystery Comics*, *The Human Torch*, *Sub-Mariner*, *Daring*, *All Winners*, *Young Allies*, and a great many of Timely's short-lived and one-shot titles. Schomburg was a master at working the Torch, Captain America, and Sub-Mariner into combat situations that involved planes, submarines, tanks, Nazis, Japanese, monsters, damsels in distress, hooded terrorists, and enough props to stock an armory.

In addition to Timely, he drew a great many covers for such varied titles as *Speed Comics*, *Green Hornet*, and *All New*. There was also a series of covers for the Pines line, everything from *Thrilling Comics* to *Real Fact*. In the late 1940s, Schomburg signed the simpler airbrushed covers he did for Pines with the alias Xela.

By the early 1950s, he was out of comics and working as an illustrator. He had made between $40 and $60 per cover, and during his heyday could draw one a week.

SECRET WARS

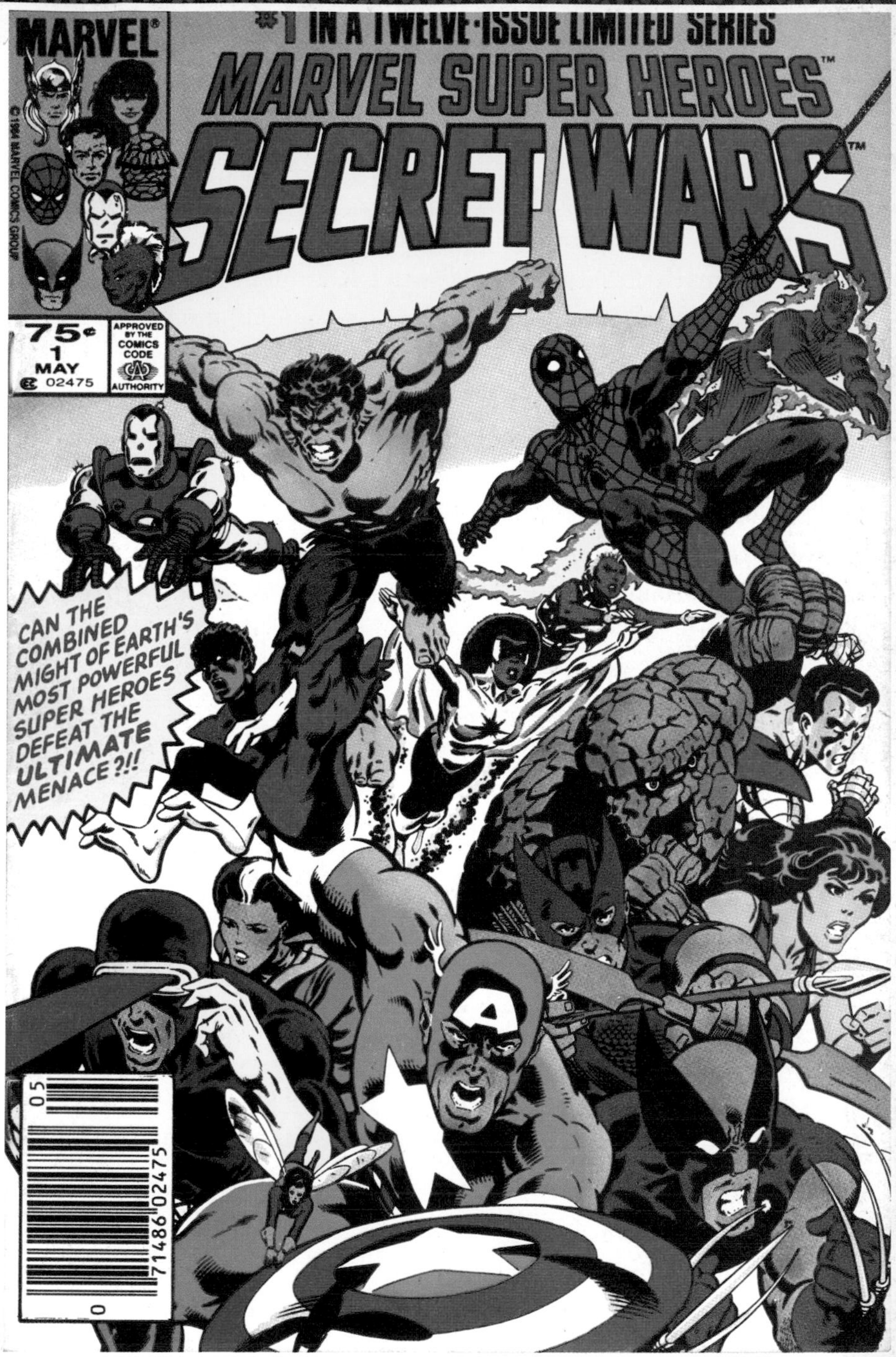
MARVEL
#1 IN A TWELVE-ISSUE LIMITED SERIES
MARVEL SUPER HEROES
SECRET WARS
75¢ 1 MAY
APPROVED BY THE COMICS CODE AUTHORITY
CAN THE COMBINED MIGHT OF EARTH'S MOST POWERFUL SUPER HEROES DEFEAT THE ULTIMATE MENACE?!!

■ A landmark on the road to bigger and better massive groupings of comic-book characters (such as DC's later *Crisis on Infinite Earths*), this twelve-issue series was begun by Marvel in the spring of 1984. The full title was *Marvel Super-Heroes Secret Wars.* Conceived and scripted by then editor-in-chief Jim Shooter and drawn by Mike Zeck, the sequence recruited over two dozen Marvel superheroes and an equal number of notable villains to stage the most complex brouhaha ever seen in comics up to that time.

The participants included Spider-Man, Thor, the Hulk, Iron Man, Wolverine and assorted X-Men, She-Hulk, three out of the Fantastic Four (Invisible Girl sat this one out), and Captain America, who acted as chairman of what was, taking into consideration their various flaws and foibles, the good-guy side. The opposing team, captained by Dr. Doom, included such dependable evildoers as Galactus, Absorbing Man, and Magneto. All the participants were transported to a strange elsewhere by supernatural means by an entity known as the Beyonder. According to Shooter, the Beyonder was a god but not *the* God. As a learning experience for himself, this god wanted to see what sort of free-for-all would ensue. The confrontations that followed, in addition to being packed with traditional Marvel violence, were also rife with mystical and metaphysical overtones. And Marvel heroes being the angst-ridden individuals they were, there was considerable internecine squabbling and bickering. Some characters changed, some were modified, a few expired. All of that, however, seemed to have little permanent effect on the basic structure of the Marvel Universe.

The first series sold so well—"We blew the X-Men out of the water by a large margin," Shooter boasted at the time—that a second was launched in the summer of 1985. This one, consisting of only nine issues, was titled simply *Secret Wars II.* Set this time on earth, it pretty much offered the mixture as before, with the Beyonder once again calling the tune. The battles spilled over into other titles, such as *New Mutants, X-Men,* and *Iron Man.*

SEDUCTION OF THE INNOCENT

■ The early 1950s were thick with government investigations—into communists in the entertainment industry, organized crime, subversives in academia, and too much sex, violence, and gore in comic books. Dr. Fredric Wertham's book *Seduction of the Innocent*, published in 1954, became a sort of bible for all sorts of groups, official and otherwise, intent on purging comic books of both real and imagined faults.

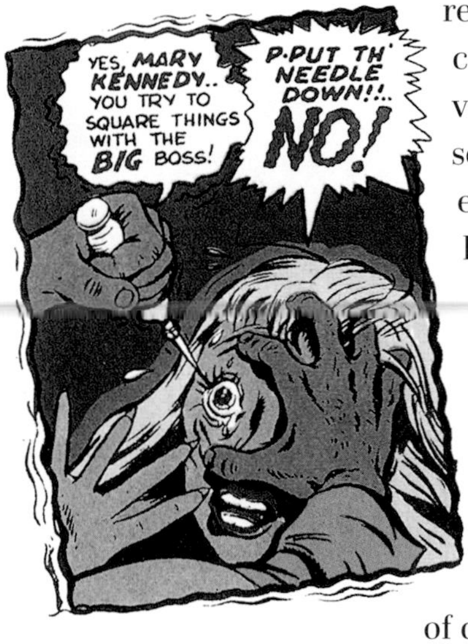
YES, MARY KENNEDY.. YOU TRY TO SQUARE THINGS WITH THE BIG BOSS!
P-PUT TH' NEEDLE DOWN!.. NO!

A psychiatrist in good standing, the German-born Dr. Wertham had come to America in 1920. He served on the staff of Bellevue and in the middle 1940s helped set up the first psychiatric clinic in Harlem. He was, by the late 1940s, senior psychiatrist with the New York Department of Hospitals. He was especially concerned with violence and delinquency among the young.

Wertham (1895–1981) had been a vocal and frequent critic of comic books, citing them as a major cause of juvenile delinquency for several years prior to the publication of his book. Early in 1948, for instance, the Association for the Advancement of Psychotherapy had held a symposium in Manhattan. The doctor, who was the president of the organization, served as moderator, and the topic was "The Psycho-Pathology of Comic Books." Representing the industry were Charles Biro and Harvey Kurtzman. Wertham, however, got most of the media attention by quoting a two-year study of comic books that he'd headed. It was his conclusion that not only were comics "sexually aggressive in an abnormal way," but that they glorified violence and undermined morals. He added that "comic book reading was a distinct influencing factor in the case of every single delinquent or disturbed child."

Despite the fact that Wertham hadn't really established a cause-and-effect relationship between comic-book reading and delinquency and mental illness, his charges fit in with the mood of the times. They were written up in the mass-circulation slick magazine *Collier's* and the middle-brow *Saturday Review of Literature*. Quite a few comic books in the late 1940s and early 1950s, when publishers were looking for something to replace the waning superheroes, turned to crime and horror. Many of these were far too violent and gory, with a strong emphasis on sex. But nobody, including Fredric Wertham, ever proved that consuming trash led to a life of crime.

The same year that the doctor's expanded and illustrated indictment of comic books came out—including his famous suggestion that Batman and Robin were gay—the Senate Subcommittee on the Judiciary staged hearings on the excesses and influence of comics. Although publishers set up a self-regulating Comics Code Authority to tone down the excesses, a great deal of negative publicity had already been created. Many distributors refused to handle comic books; in more than one community aroused officials and parents staged bonfires for comic burning. Quite a few publishers went broke and quit. Wertham was by no means the only cause of this. Television was spreading during this same period, and many comics would have fallen by the wayside without any moral crusade.

Though well-intentioned and concerned with children, Dr. Wertham had produced a book that was long on charges and short on substantial proof. Years later he said, "I never spoke of books. I only spoke of crime comic books." But that was not the impression he gave at the time.

SENSATION COMICS

■ Wonder Woman, after being introduced in *All Star Comics* #8, was given a regular home in *Sensation*. Sharing the book with her were such freshly invented characters as Wildcat, Mr. Terrific, Little Boy Blue, and the Gay Ghost, whose name was to make DC uneasy in years to come. The first issue of *Sensation Comics* was dated January 1942 and had a cover combining H. G. Peter's drawing of Wonder Woman, with additional art by Jon L. Blummer. Sheldon Mayer was the editor.

M. C. Gaines, Mayer's boss, had encouraged psychologist William Moulton Marston to develop *Wonder Woman* and Marston himself had picked the veteran magazine cartoonist H. G. Peter to draw the adventures of the Amazon princess. Mayer was never that fond of the character or Peter's art. During his years as editor of *Sensation*, he had frequent conflicts with Marston over the amount of bondage, domination, and sexual symbolism that was being slipped into the stories. In interviews years later, Mayer maintained that *Wonder Woman* would've been much more excessive if he hadn't kept Marston under control. After about a year and a half, when Peter and his staff were busy with the added burden of the new *Wonder Woman* quarterly, Mayer was able to hire the gifted illustrator and newspaper artist Frank Godwin to draw a half a dozen or so episodes of *Wonder Woman*.

Batman cocreator Bill Finger came up with two of the backup characters. Wildcat was boxing champ Ted Grant, who donned a wildcat costume to fight crime. Irwin Hasen, who'd been ghosting *The Green Lantern*, was the artist. Finger also invented *Little Boy Blue and the Blue Boys*, about a trio of kids who had no superpowers but a lot of chutzpah. Jon Blummer drew that one.

The Gay Ghost was created by Gardner Fox before the underground meaning of gay was as widely known as it later became. At the time using gay to mean lighthearted and possibly dashing was often done in movie titles and so on—*The Gay Divorcee, The Gay Desperado*, etc. Drawn by Howard Purcell, the strip involved the ghost of an Irish nobleman from the eighteenth century who came to share the body of a young American who had died. He took over the body, reanimated it, and deserted it whenever the time came to fight crime and criminals. Basically this was a variation on the premise of *The Spectre*, with some borrowing from the popular 1930s movie comedy *The Ghost Goes West*. The Gay Ghost last materialized in *Sensation* in 1945. When DC later reprinted some of the old material, they renamed the character the Grim Ghost.

While a more glamorous and up-to-date Wonder Woman started to appear on the covers in 1949, the H. G. Peter style was maintained on the stories inside. During its declining years, the magazine added some new women heroes, including Dr. Pat and Astra, the Girl of the Future. Streak the Wonder Dog, who'd been the Green Lantern's sidekick, outlasted him by several months and soloed in three issues of *Sensation* in the summer of 1949. Wonder Woman departed late in 1951. Johnny Peril, now a globetrotting adventurer, became the only recurring character. The rest of the stories were of the mystery and mild horror sort. Alex Toth drew the first three *Johnny Peril* yarns. With its 110th issue (July–August 1952) the magazine turned into *Sensation Mystery*, continuing as such until the 116th and final issue in the summer of 1953.

SGT. FURY AND HIS HOWLING COMMANDOS

■ For comic readers who'd been wondering what the Boy Commandos might be like when they grew up, Jack Kirby and Stan Lee provided something of an answer in 1963. The first issue of Marvel's *Sgt. Fury and His Howling Commandos* had a cover date of May 1963 and introduced Nick Fury, who was, as Lee described him, "a hard-as-nails, two-fisted, tough-talking, fast-moving, cigar-chomping, lusty, gutsy, brawling leader of men, albeit with a soft, easy-touch heart—which hardly ever showed." On the cover of #1, the sergeant was urging his men, "Keep movin', you knuckleheads! Nobody lives forever! So get the lead out and follow me! We got us a WAR to win!" With his crew of misfits, Fury fought World War II until the early 1980s. Kirby penciled the early issues; Dick Ayers inked. Lee took care of the scripts. The concept of the comic book had originally been invented by Kirby for a comic strip he had unsuccessfully tried to sell in the 1950s.

The Howlers included Reb Ralston, Izzy Cohen, Dino Manelli, Dum Dum Dugan (who wore a derby similar to that of the Boy Commando's Brooklyn), and Gabriel Jones, a black jazz musician. Since the army in World War II was not integrated, this was a fantasy. The earlier Sgt. Rock's Easy Co. over at DC was also an anachronistically integrated group.

In 1965 Fury began leading a double life when he also became Nick Fury, Agent of SHIELD. World War II lasted close to twenty years for the Howlers, ending in the 187th issue of the magazine late in 1981. Artists after Kirby included Ayers and John Severin.

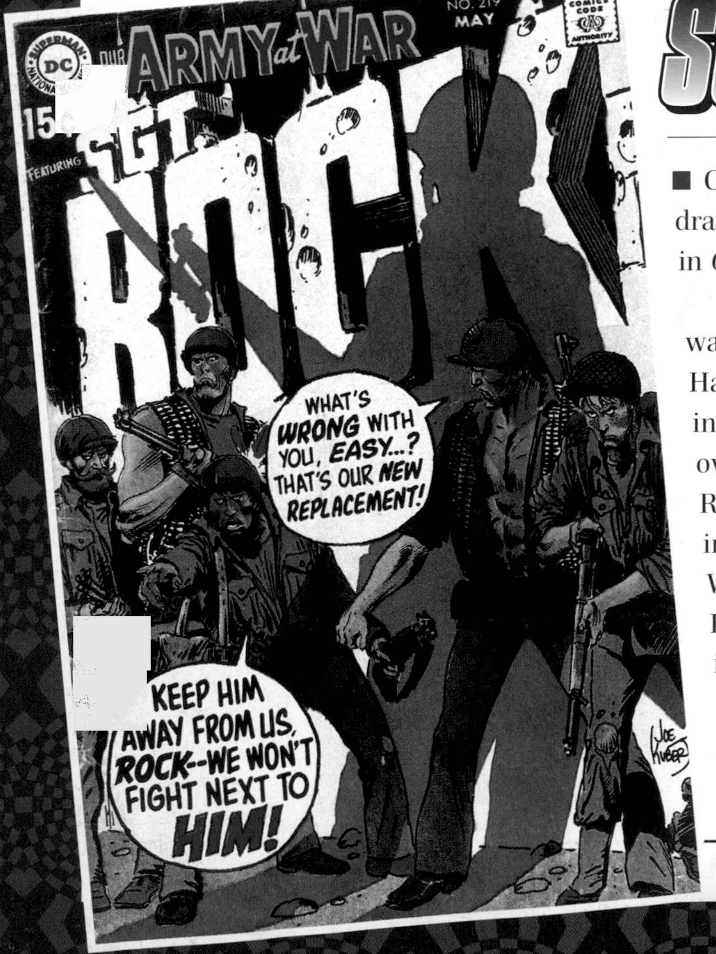
OUR ARMY at WAR
NO. 219
MAY
15¢
FEATURING
SGT. ROCK
WHAT'S WRONG WITH YOU, EASY...? THAT'S OUR NEW REPLACEMENT!
KEEP HIM AWAY FROM US, ROCK--WE WON'T FIGHT NEXT TO HIM!

SGT. ROCK

■ Created by DC's resident war correspondent, Robert Kanigher, and drawn by Joe Kubert, Sgt. Rock as we know him first went into battle in *Our Army at War* #81 (April 1959).

The stories were set during World War II and Sgt. Frank Rock was topkick of a platoon called Easy Co., also known as "the Combat Happy Joes of Easy." He and his men did the majority of their fighting in the European Theater of Operations. Kanigher's idea of combat owed as much to movies and John Wayne as it did to research, and Rock's gang had the same colorful mix of men as might've been found in an MGM epic of a decade or so earlier. Among the personnel were Wildman, Bulldozer, Ice Cream Soldier, and Jackie Johnson, a black. Kanigher fudged on Johnson, giving Rock the only integrated platoon in World War II.

The adventures were gritty, grim, sentimental, and full of Technicolor heroics. The sergeant narrated most of his battle reports himself—"Here's a war story that'll tear at your heart . . . or my name ain't Sgt. Rock." Kubert did a commendable job of illustrating the Easy tales. Russ Heath also drew the feature. The sergeant's name eventually began appearing on the covers in larger and larger letters. Finally, with issue #302 (March 1977), the magazine was retitled simply *Sgt. Rock*. It held on longer than any other war comic, surrendering at last in the summer of 1998. The sergeant re-upped for the *Sgt. Rock Special* that reprinted his earlier combat adventures for a twenty-one-issue run from 1988 to 1992.

SETH *(1962-)*

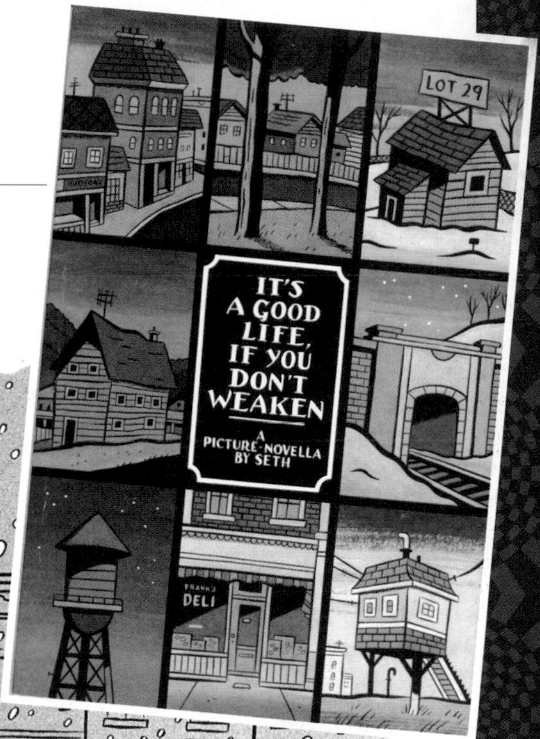
LOT 29
IT'S A GOOD LIFE, IF YOU DON'T WEAKEN
A PICTURE-NOVELLA BY SETH
DELI

■ Next to Chris Ware, the most melancholy cartoonist in comics. An exceptional artist and writer, he's been slowly but surely producing issues of *Palookaville* for the Canadian Drawn & Quarterly outfit since 1991. Born in Canada, "for the first twenty years (or so) he lived under the name his parents had given him: Gregory Gallant," he has said. "In the 1960s he changed it to his nom de plume. Looking back, that may have been a youthful error . . . However, nothing can be done about it now."

Working in black-and-white with a pale blue overlay, Seth has devoted most of the issues of *Palookaville* to chronicling the life of a bespectled, cigarette-smoking cartoonist named Seth. The stories are quiet, blending autobiography with fiction, nostalgia, and an intense love of cartooning, both as a profession and a way of life. Some issues are taken up with *Clyde Fans*, the ongoing saga of a forlorn, bespectacled, cigarette-smoking middle-aged Canadian traveling salesman for the fan company. It too is sad and makes *Death of a Salesman* look like a sitcom.

Seth's work has been collected into several successful and award-winning graphic novels. His work is adult in the best sense of the word, being intelligent, truthful, and drawn in a way that avoids tricks or clichés. His fans include such noted graphic artists as R. O. Blechman and Raymond Briggs.

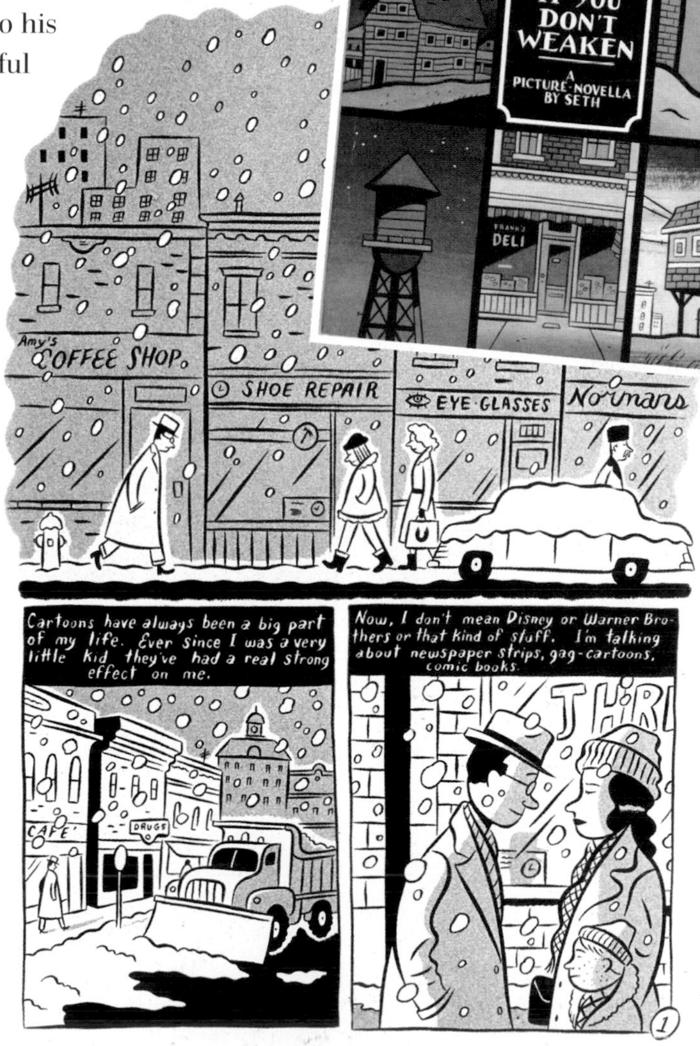
Amy's COFFEE SHOP
SHOE REPAIR
EYE GLASSES
Normans
Cartoons have always been a big part of my life. Ever since I was a very little kid they've had a real strong effect on me.
CAFE
DRUGS
Now, I don't mean Disney or Warner Brothers or that kind of stuff. I'm talking about newspaper strips, gag-cartoons, comic books.
1

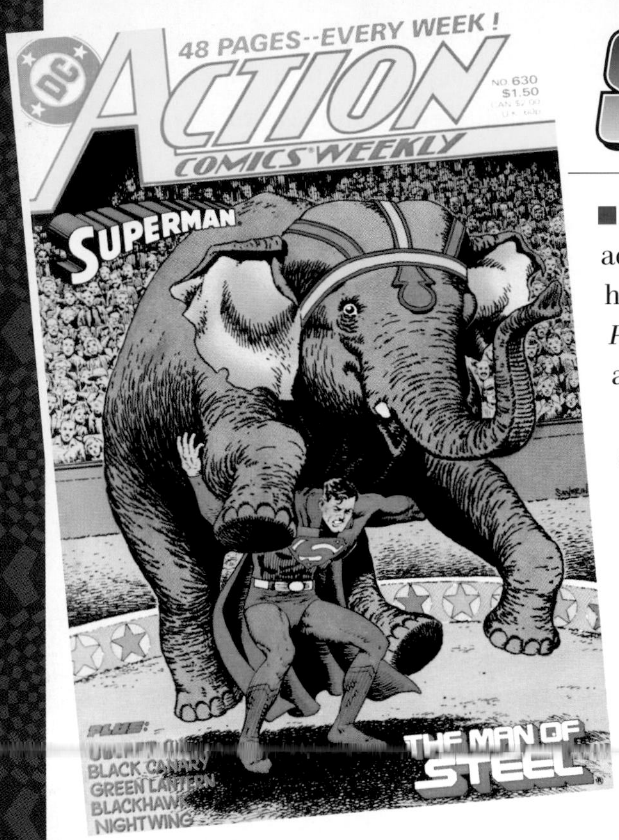
48 PAGES--EVERY WEEK!
DC
ACTION
COMICS WEEKLY
NO 630
$1.50
SUPERMAN
BLACK CANARY
GREEN LANTERN
NIGHTWING
THE MAN OF STEEL

SEVERIN, JOHN

(1921–)

■ An armchair combat artist, Severin has been turning out realistic adventure tales for over a half century. Especially at home in the Old West, he broke into comics in the late 1940s contributing *The American Eagle* to *Prize Comics Western*. He penciled and Will Elder inked that one because, according to Severin, "He couldn't draw and I couldn't ink."

Next the team went to work for EC, contributing to *Mad* as well as fantasy and war titles. Severin started doing solo work, inking in a bolder, more detailed manner than Elder. He expertly handled everything from tales of the Foreign Legion to gritty cowboy yarns. After EC, he worked for Marvel and DC, penciling and/or inking such titles as *The Ringo Kid*, *Sgt. Fury*, *Sgt. Rock*, *The Hulk*, *Combat Casey*, and *Billy the Kid*. In the early 1970s he inked, with his sister Marie penciling, the Conan clone, King Kull. In his spare time he was also a frequent contributor to the poor man's *Mad*, the magazine *Cracked*.

Severin has continued to be one of the top illustrators of two-fisted tales.

SEVERIN, MARIE

(c. 1929–)

■ In addition to being an important colorist, she is an accomplished cartoonist who is capable of drawing adventure stuff as well as wacky comedy. At the urging of her brother John, she ventured into coloring and gave EC titles their distinctive look from 1951 to 1955. Thereafter Marie Severin moved to Marvel, where she eventually became the coloring director.

She also penciled such titles as *King Kull*, *Sub-Mariner*, *The Cat*, *Dr. Strange*, and assorted spoofs for Marvel's *Not Brand Echh*. She especially enjoyed the opportunity to parody such serious super fellows as the Hulk, Spider-Man, and Thor.

THE SHADOW

■ The prince of mystery men, the elusive Shadow first appeared as a pulp hero in 1931 in Street & Smith's *The Shadow* pulp. Written by Walter Gibson under the pen name Maxwell Grant, he was a grim avenger, determined to destroy crooks and evildoers and live up to his reputation as gangdom's foe. He didn't exhibit the slightest tendency to become invisible.

The invisibility came from the radio version, which got going in 1937. There, he was Lamont Cranston in real life and the foe of not only gangsters but mad scientists, ghouls, vampires, and assorted other creepy foes. Years ago he'd picked up in (where else?) Tibet the ability to cloud men's minds so they could not see him. His lovely companion Margo Lane, invented for the radio show, was the only person who knew his secret.

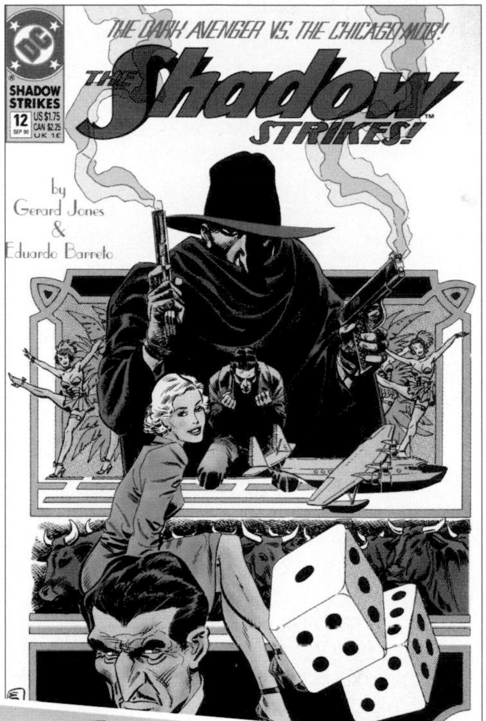
THE DARK AVENGER VS. THE CHICAGO MOB!
DC
SHADOW STRIKES
12
THE Shadow STRIKES!
by
Gerard Jones
&
Eduardo Barreto

The earliest comic-book Shadow, who appeared on stands in 1940, also published by Street & Smith, was based on the pulp version and had absolutely no talent for invisibility. By 1941, however, he was turning invisible with ease. Gibson wrote all the comic-book scripts from 1940 to 1946, and the artists included Vernon Greene, Jon L. Blummer, Charles Coll, and finally Bob Powell. *Shadow Comics* ended in 1949 with its 101st issue. The character was next seen in the summer of 1964 in Archie Comics' *The Shadow*. This ill-advised outing, with scripts by Jerry Siegel and artwork by Paul Reinman, cast him as a costumed superhero. The magazine folded after eight issues.

DC took up the Shadow in 1973, bringing back the hawk-nosed, cloaked avenger of the Gibson pulps. Gangdom's foe for this version, he blazed away with his automatic and hadn't the slightest notion of how to cloud men's minds. Denny O'Neil was the writer and the artists included Mike Kaluta and Frank Robbins. DC's try ended in 1975 after just a dozen issues. They brought him back in a miniseries in 1986 and in a regular series the next year that lasted until 1989. In the 1990s came *The Shadow Strikes*, a monthly written by Gerard Jones and drawn by such as Dan Spiegle and Eduardo Barreto. This was yet again the pulpwood Shadow, with Margo along and the stories set several decades in the past. It folded in 1992. Dark Horse returned him fleetingly in 1994.

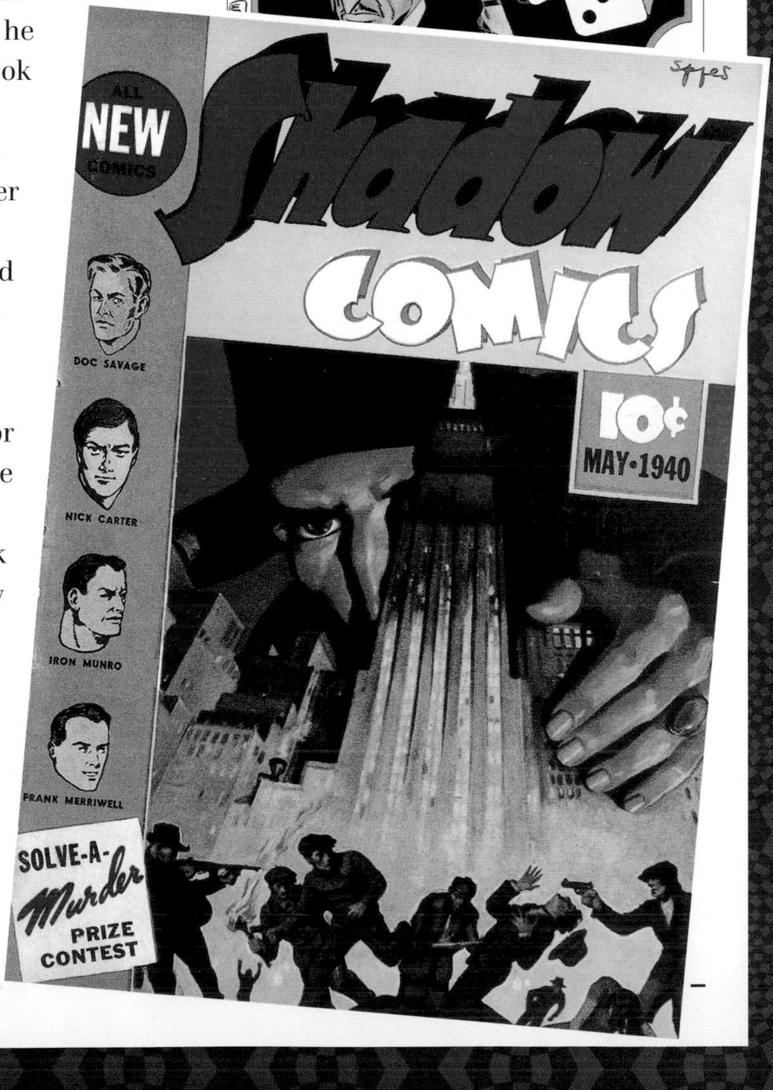
ALL NEW COMICS
Shadow COMICS
10¢
MAY•1940
DOC SAVAGE
NICK CARTER
IRON MUNRO
FRANK MERRIWELL
SOLVE-A-Murder PRIZE CONTEST

SHAZAM

■ A powerful magic word, the name of an extremely old wizard, and a comic-book title. As a magic word it converted teenage radio newscaster Billy Batson into the World's Mightiest Mortal, Captain Marvel.

The word was an acronym that stood for Solomon, Hercules, Atlas, Zeus, Achilles, and Mercury. By saying it aloud, Billy took on the abilities of this group of gods and heroes—wisdom, strength, stamina, power, courage, and speed. The transition from youth to superhero was always accompanied by an impressive boom of thunder and a flash of lightning. To remind readers of his origins, the captain also wore a zigzag of yellow lightning emblazoned on the chest of his crimson tunic.

Shazam was also the name of the ancient wizard who had bestowed superpowers on Billy. And in 1973, when Captain Marvel returned to comics after a layoff of nearly two decades, DC entitled his magazine *Shazam!* This was because during that hiatus Marvel Comics had introduced a completely different Captain Marvel and trademarked the name.

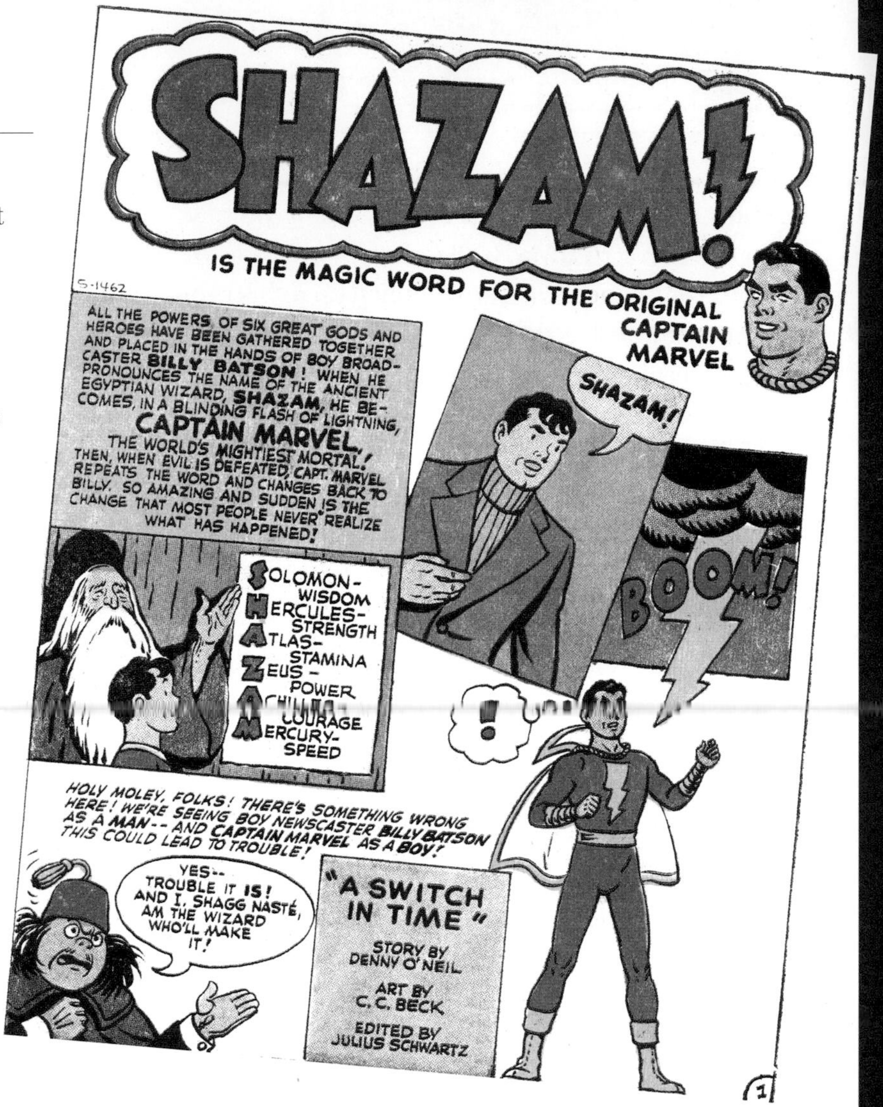
SHAZAM!
IS THE MAGIC WORD FOR THE ORIGINAL CAPTAIN MARVEL
S-1462
ALL THE POWERS OF SIX GREAT GODS AND HEROES HAVE BEEN GATHERED TOGETHER AND PLACED IN THE HANDS OF BOY BROAD-CASTER BILLY BATSON! WHEN HE PRONOUNCES THE NAME OF THE ANCIENT EGYPTIAN WIZARD, SHAZAM, HE BE-COMES, IN A BLINDING FLASH OF LIGHTNING, CAPTAIN MARVEL, THE WORLD'S MIGHTIEST MORTAL! THEN, WHEN EVIL IS DEFEATED, CAPT. MARVEL REPEATS THE WORD AND CHANGES BACK TO BILLY. SO AMAZING AND SUDDEN IS THE CHANGE THAT MOST PEOPLE NEVER REALIZE WHAT HAS HAPPENED!
SHAZAM!
BOOM!
SOLOMON-WISDOM
HERCULES-STRENGTH
ATLAS-STAMINA
ZEUS-POWER
COURAGE
MERCURY-SPEED
!
HOLY MOLEY, FOLKS! THERE'S SOMETHING WRONG HERE! WE'RE SEEING BOY NEWSCASTER BILLY BATSON AS A MAN-- AND CAPTAIN MARVEL AS A BOY! THIS COULD LEAD TO TROUBLE!
YES-- TROUBLE IT IS! AND I, SHAGG NASTÉ, AM THE WIZARD WHO'LL MAKE IT!
"A SWITCH IN TIME"
STORY BY DENNY O'NEIL
ART BY C. C. BECK
EDITED BY JULIUS SCHWARTZ
1

SHEENA

■ See JUMBO COMICS.

THE SHINING KNIGHT

■ See ADVENTURE COMICS.

SIEGEL, JERRY

■ See SUPERMAN.

SHOWCASE

■ A stage devised by DC editor Julius Schwartz on which to audition potential new stars, *Showcase* was first published in 1956. The fourth issue of the bimonthly (October 1956) introduced the Silver Age Flash, the sixth, Challengers of the Unknown, and the twenty-second, the new, improved Green Lantern. *Showcase* also resuscitated Aquaman and launched the diminutive Atom. Adam Strange made his maiden voyage to the planet Rann in the magazine, the Sea Devils (formerly the Frogmen) debuted there as did the time-traveling Rip Hunter.

Later contestants for a permanent job at DC included Metal Men, the updated Spectre, the Inferior Five, the Creeper, Bat Lash, and a new version of the Doom Patrol. Among the characters who didn't quite click were the Human Eel, Fireman Farrell, and B'wana Beast. *Showcase* shut its doors with the 104th issue in 1978. DC revived the title as *Showcase '93*, etc., from 1993 to 1996.

SHUSTER, JOE

■ See SUPERMAN.

SILVER AGE

■ This term denotes the period commencing in the middle 1950s when superheroes made their successful comeback in comic books.

It's generally agreed that the Silver Age started with the publication of DC's *Showcase* #4 (October 1956), which introduced the new improved Flash. Other early milestones, also masterminded by editor Julius Schwartz, included the advent of DC's new Green Lantern and the introduction of the Justice League of America in 1960. Marvel and editor Stan Lee got into the act in 1961 with the *Fantastic Four*.

The Silver Age ended with the decade of the 1960s.

THE SILVER SURFER

■ Unlike many surfers, he was not a suntanned Southern California beach boy but a visitor from the far reaches of space. The most mystical and philosophical of Marvel superheroes, he was a silver-colored, bald-headed alien who looked somewhat like a giant hood ornament and zoomed through the galaxies on his atomic surfboard. Also known as the Sentinel of the Spaceways, he was another creation of editor/wrier Stan Lee and artist Jack Kirby and was first seen in *Fantastic Four* #48 (March 1956). He moved into a magazine of his own in the summer of 1968.

In the original story, which took up thirty-eight pages, readers learned that the Surfer had once been a bald headed but pink fleshed resident of the planet

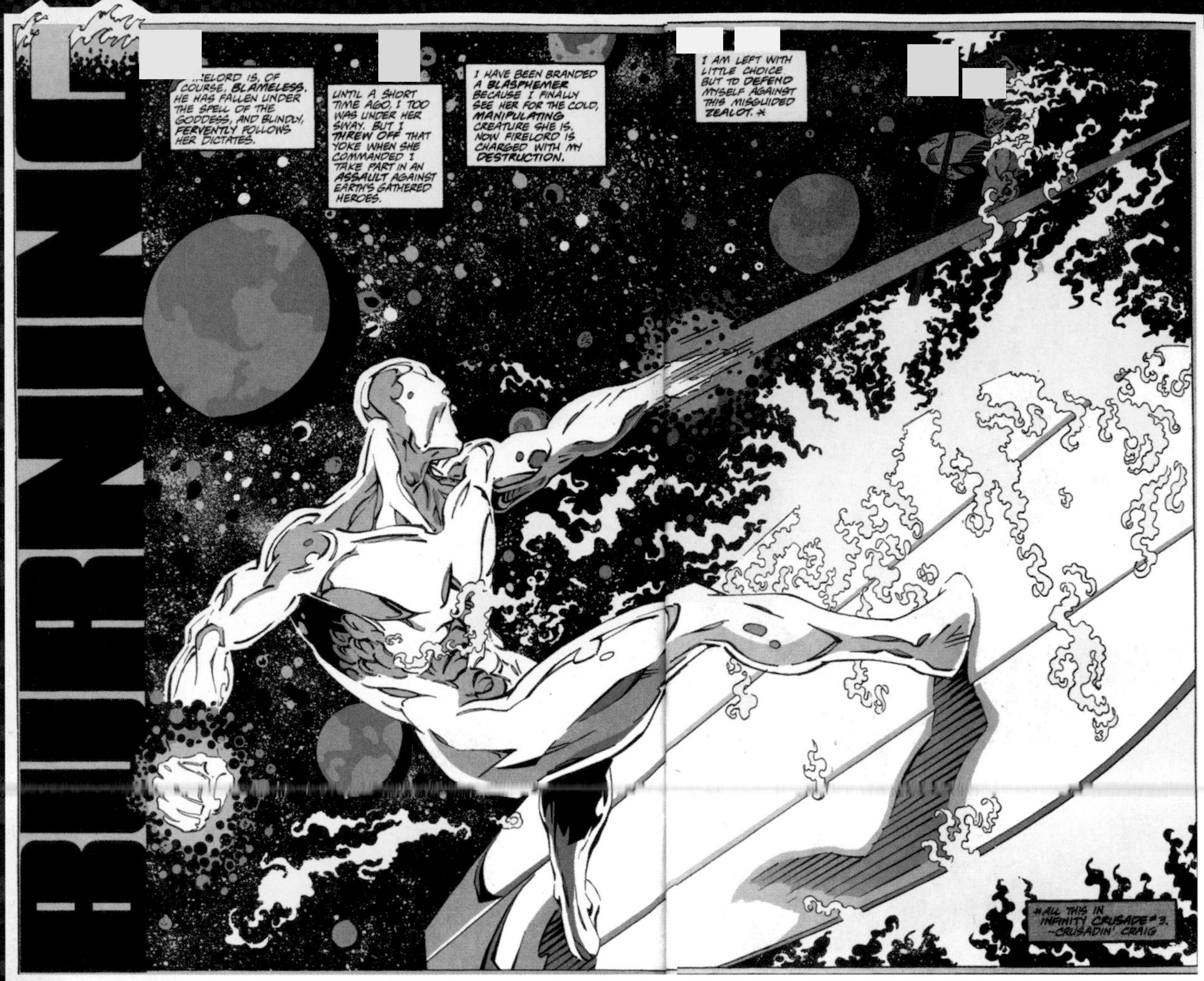
ELORD IS, OF COURSE, BLAMELESS. HE HAS FALLEN UNDER THE SPELL OF THE GODDESS, AND BLINDLY, FERVENTLY FOLLOWS HER DICTATES.
UNTIL A SHORT TIME AGO, I TOO WAS UNDER HER SWAY. BUT I THREW OFF THAT YOKE WHEN SHE COMMANDED I TAKE PART IN AN ASSAULT AGAINST EARTH'S GATHERED HEROES.
I HAVE BEEN BRANDED A BLASPHEMER BECAUSE I FINALLY SEE HER FOR THE COLD, MANIPULATING CREATURE SHE IS. NOW FIRELORD IS CHARGED WITH MY DESTRUCTION.
I AM LEFT WITH LITTLE CHOICE BUT TO DEFEND MYSELF AGAINST THIS MISGUIDED ZEALOT. *
*ALL THIS IN INFINITY CRUSADE #3. --CRUSADIN' CRAIG

Zenn-La. Through a complex chain of events, Norrin Radd came face-to-face with the villainous Galactus, also known as the Eater of Worlds, who decided to make him his herald. Part of the initiation process involved encasing Radd's body "in a life-preserving silvery substance of my own creation." Galactus also provided the newly minted Surfer with "an indestructible flying board . . . yours to command . . . with but a single thought!" Due to a policy conflict that arose during Galactus's initial confrontation with the Fantastic Four, the Surfer was dismissed and dumped on earth. Being chrome-plated seemed to add to Radd's introspective bent, and he was frequently given to zooming around on his board, hands locked behind his back, pondering such imponderables as, "How much longer am I destined to endure a fate I cannot even comprehend?" and "Time is long and fate is fickle." Like many of Lee's more serious characters, the Silver Surfer never used a contraction in speech or thought.

His first magazine ended in 1970, but he continued as a guest star in other titles such as *Fantastic Four.* In 1987 he got his own title once more, with Marshall Rogers as the first artist. In 1998 Lee and Moebius collaborated on a miniseries/graphic novel. He continues to breeze in now and again, and he resurfaced once more in the summer of 2003.

SIM, DAVE

■ See CEREBUS.

SIMON, JOE *(1915-)*

■ Unlike his longtime partner Jack Kirby, Simon was never crowned King of the Comics. He was, however, a major creative force in the field. He created, often in collaboration with Kirby, *Captain America*, *The Blue Bolt*, *The Vision*, *The Young Allies*, *The Boy Commandos*, *Stuntman*, and *Brother Power the Geek* (well, nobody's perfect). Simon also thought up the romance comic book.

In the early 1940s, Simon was an editor at both Fox and then Marvel. On his own he wrote and drew features such as *The Silver Streak*. After they formed a team, Kirby penciled and Simon provided the bold inking. After leaving *Captain America*, they went to DC, creating *The Newsboy Legion* and *The Boy Commandos* and upgrading and revitalizing *Manhunter* and *Sandman*.

After World War II, during which Simon served in the Coast Guard, he and Kirby tried *Stuntman*, *Boy Explorers*, and other features akin to their earlier creations, without much success. In 1947 Simon thought up *Young Romance*, which he and Kirby illustrated. The comic, which was soon selling 1 million copies an issue, inspired the hundreds of romance comics that followed. Simon had seen to it that he and Kirby shared in the profits of *Young Romance*. He was associated again with DC in the 1960s and 1970s, which gave birth to such flops as *Prez* and *Brother Power*. In the 1980s he and Kirby teamed again for a new version of *Sandman*. Simon also devoted several years to editing and drawing for *Sick*.

SLAM BRADLEY

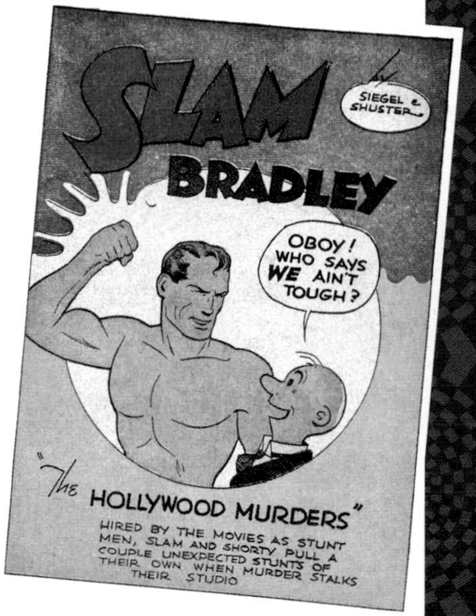
SLAM
BRADLEY
by
SIEGEL & SHUSTER
OBOY! WHO SAYS WE AIN'T TOUGH?
"The HOLLYWOOD MURDERS"
HIRED BY THE MOVIES AS STUNT MEN, SLAM AND SHORTY PULL A COUPLE UNEXPECTED STUNTS OF THEIR OWN WHEN MURDER STALKS THEIR STUDIO

■ Slam Bradley has been around longer than Batman or Superman. Created by Jerry Siegel and Joe Shuster, he entered comics by way of *Detective Comics* #1 (March 1937). He was billed as an "ace freelance sleuth, fighter and adventurer." By going on some very long hiatuses, Slam has managed to survive to the present and can currently be found in DC's *Catwoman*. As it might be expected of a character who's been around for such a long time, Slam is considerably weather-beaten in looks, and somewhere along the way his nose got broken.

As his name hints, Slam was a rough-and-tumble operative who used his fists more than he used his magnifying glass. He owed as much to Roy Crane's freewheeling Captain Easy as he did to the private eyes of pulps and the movies. And just as Easy had the diminutive Wash Tubbs as his comic-strip sidekick, Slam had Shorty Morgan. The two investigated crimes and misdemeanors in Hollywood, on Broadway, in the frozen North, and even in the future. After *Superman* became a hit, Shuster turned over the drawing to assistants. Then came Mart Bailey, Howard Sherman, and John Daly, among others. Slam and Shorty occupied eight pages at the back of the book, handling murders, kidnappings, and assorted rackets with ease and humor. Shorty, who'd grown a bit taller by this time, was feisty and cynical and not always anxious to rush into danger. Slam remained as belligerent as ever.

By the middle 1940s, Slam's caseload was made up mostly of whimsical and slapstick crimes. Sherman returned in the postwar years and remained with the duo until they solved their final case in *Detective* #152 (October 1949). DC has revived Slam on several occasions, and he is now a private eye in Gotham City. A DC *Who's Who* that was issued some years ago announced that Shorty was dead. Eventually, like many a tough PI before him, Slam became involved with a lady with a shady past. For the past few years he carried on a romance with Selina Kyle, also known as Catwoman. Although not romantically involved as of today, they remain good friends.

SKYROCKET STEELE

■ See AMAZING MYSTERY FUNNIES.

SMASH COMICS

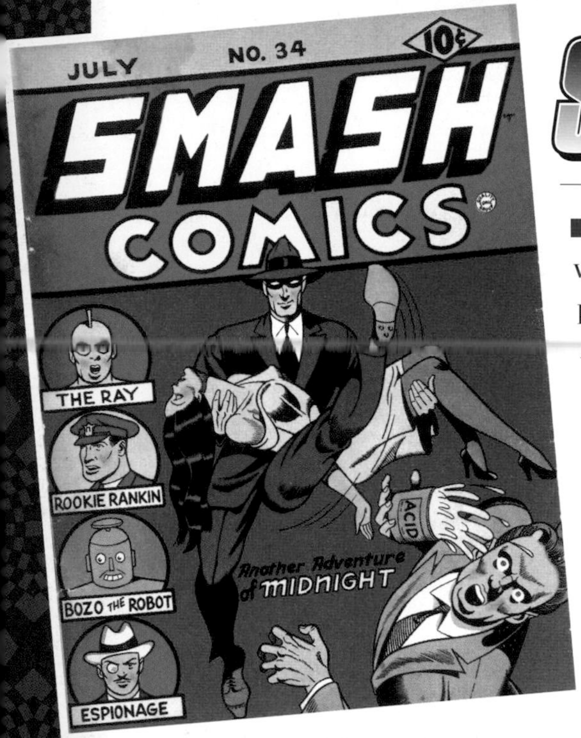
JULY
NO. 34
10¢
SMASH
COMICS
THE RAY
ROOKIE RANKIN
BOZO THE ROBOT
ESPIONAGE
ACID
Another Adventure of MIDNIGHT

■ The second title in what would become publisher Everett Arnold's Quality Comic Group, *Smash*, edited by Ed Cronin, opened for business with nary a superhero to be seen. Issue #1 (August 1939) did offer an invisible man and a robot, but nothing in the way of a Superman surrogate. It was over a year before a single one was added.

The leading feature at the offset was Will Eisner's *Espionage*, transferred from Arnold's *Feature Comics*. The dapper, monocle-wearing spy changed his name from Black Ace to Black X early on. Among the other early characters were Wings Wendall, Captain Cook of Scotland Yard, Abdul the Arab, Invisible Justice, and Bozo the Robot.

Finally, in the summer of 1940, superheroes were added. First came Magno, a blond fellow who came by his powers because his body had been "electrically charged." Next was the Ray, who came by his powers because he'd been struck by lightning while up in a balloon. A reporter named Happy Terrill in everyday life, the yellow-clad Ray was basically a dull hero. What made his electrified adventures noteworthy was the fact that they were drawn by Lou Fine and then Reed Crandall. Both used the pen name E. Lectron.

Issue #18 (January 1941) saw the addition of Midnight, a masked man who somewhat resembled Eisner's Spirit. As written and drawn by Jack Cole, Midnight had a quirky individuality that set him off from the competition. The Cole stories managed to be both grim and slapstick at the same time, as well as inventively staged. Before long Midnight acquired a talking monkey and a reformed mad scientist as partners. After Magno departed, his artist Paul Gustavson introduced the Jester, yet another policeman impatient with the law's delays who became a costumed vigilante.

Reprints of *Lady Luck*, from the weekly *Spirit* Sunday insert, began in *Smash* #42 (April 1943). After its eighty-fifth issue in 1949, *Smash Comics* became *Lady Luck* for five issues before retiring. Klaus Nordling drew new Lady Luck stories for the occasion.

THE SPECTRE

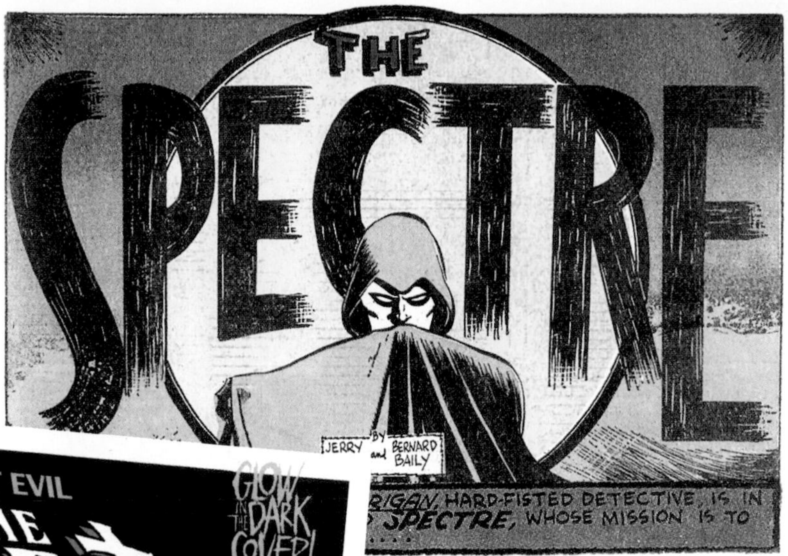
THE SPECTRE
BY JERRY and BERNARD BAILY
RIGAN, HARD-FISTED DETECTIVE, IS IN
SPECTRE, WHOSE MISSION IS TO

■ For someone who died back in 1940, he's done pretty well for himself and can still be found in comic books. The Spectre was given a two-part send-off in DC's *More Fun Comics* #52 and #53 early in 1940. Jerry Siegel, who was already doing very well with *Superman*, wrote the scripts, and Bernard Baily provided the drawing. Baily also designed the costume and gave the Spectre his ghostly look and blank eyeballs.

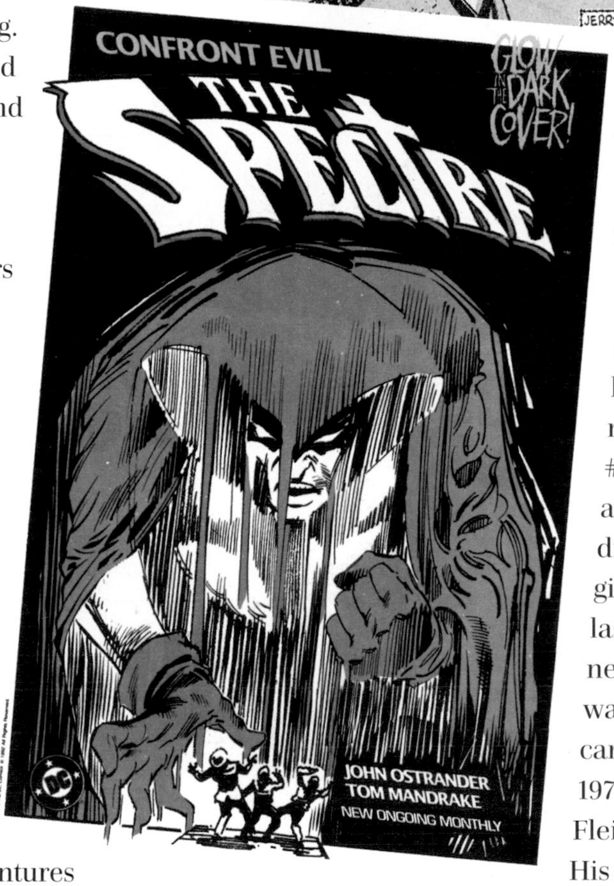
CONFRONT EVIL
THE Spectre
GLOW IN THE DARK COVER!
JOHN OSTRANDER
TOM MANDRAKE
NEW ONGOING MONTHLY

According to the original story, a tough, redheaded cop named Jim Corrigan was murdered by gangsters by being dumped in the river in the traditional barrel of cement. He returned as a spirit, cloaked in green and sporting a pasty white complexion. Corrigan could cause his spirit to look like his former body. Early on, he would turn himself into the Spectre, but later the Spectre was a projection that left the defunct policeman's body to sail off and fight crime. Originally he operated in the city of Cliffland, obviously a surrogate for Siegel's native Cleveland. The Spectre's early adventures were decidedly odd. He had frequent conversations with the Almighty, made occasional trips to the hereafter to get clues from departed souls. He could walk through walls, turn crooks into skeletons, and grow as tall as a downtown office building. A grim, uniquely talented fellow, he didn't simply catch criminals, he enjoyed himself by destroying them. After one instance of spectral vigilantism, he observed, "One less vermin to peril decency."

Not an especially likeable fellow, the Spectre never achieved great popularity. He was dumped from *More Fun* late in 1944. He remained in limbo for two decades and finally made a comeback in *Showcase* #60. Gardner Fox wrote the scripts and Murphy Anderson did the drawing. In 1967 the Spectre was given a book of his own, but that lasted for only ten issues. When he next returned the Ghostly Guardian was much nastier and meaner. He came back in *Adventure* #431 late in 1973 in a story written by Michael Fleisher and drawn by Jim Aparo. His goal was to destroy "the vermin of the underworld." His career has waxed and waned ever since and he's returned as a guest and in titles of his own. In 1999 Jim Corrigan's spirit went on to glory and the ghost of Hal Jordan, the hero formerly known as Green Lantern, assumed the role. The Spectre still has blank eyeballs. The new Spectre recently explained that he was no longer "the vessel of the Lord's wrath. Now I serve as the spirit of redemption."

SPIDER-MAN

■ Not a mutant, he's been Marvel's most successful and popular character. After auditioning in *Amazing Fantasy* #15, he moved into his own title, *The Amazing Spider-Man*, early in 1963. He was he creation of Stan Lee and Steve Ditko, with possible input from Jack Kirby.

The original story introduced mild-mannered high school student Peter Parker, who lived with his Uncle Ben and Aunt May. Clean-cut, hardworking, and bespectacled, Peter was a brilliant science student but was shunned by his fellows and labeled a "bookworm." After being bitten by a radioactive spider at a science exhibit, he gained "spider powers" that included superhuman strength and agility and the ability to cling to any surface and spin webs. Peter first donned a costume so that he could pursue a career in show business doing stunts of the sort then popular on *The Ed Sullivan Show*. But when his Uncle Ben was murdered he went after and caught the killer. He became convinced that "in this world, with great power there must also come—great responsibility." Following in the footsteps of Clark Kent, Peter got a job on a newspaper. He worked as a freelance photographer, serving under the irascible editor J. Jonah Jameson.

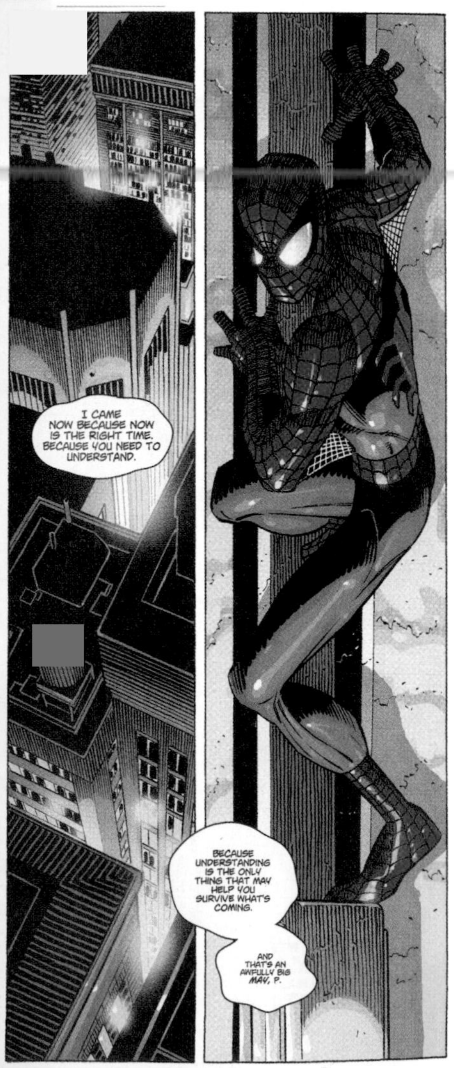
I CAME NOW BECAUSE NOW IS THE RIGHT TIME. BECAUSE YOU NEED TO UNDERSTAND.
BECAUSE UNDERSTANDING IS THE ONLY THING THAT MAY HELP YOU SURVIVE WHAT'S COMING.
AND THAT'S AN AWFULLY BIG MAY, P.

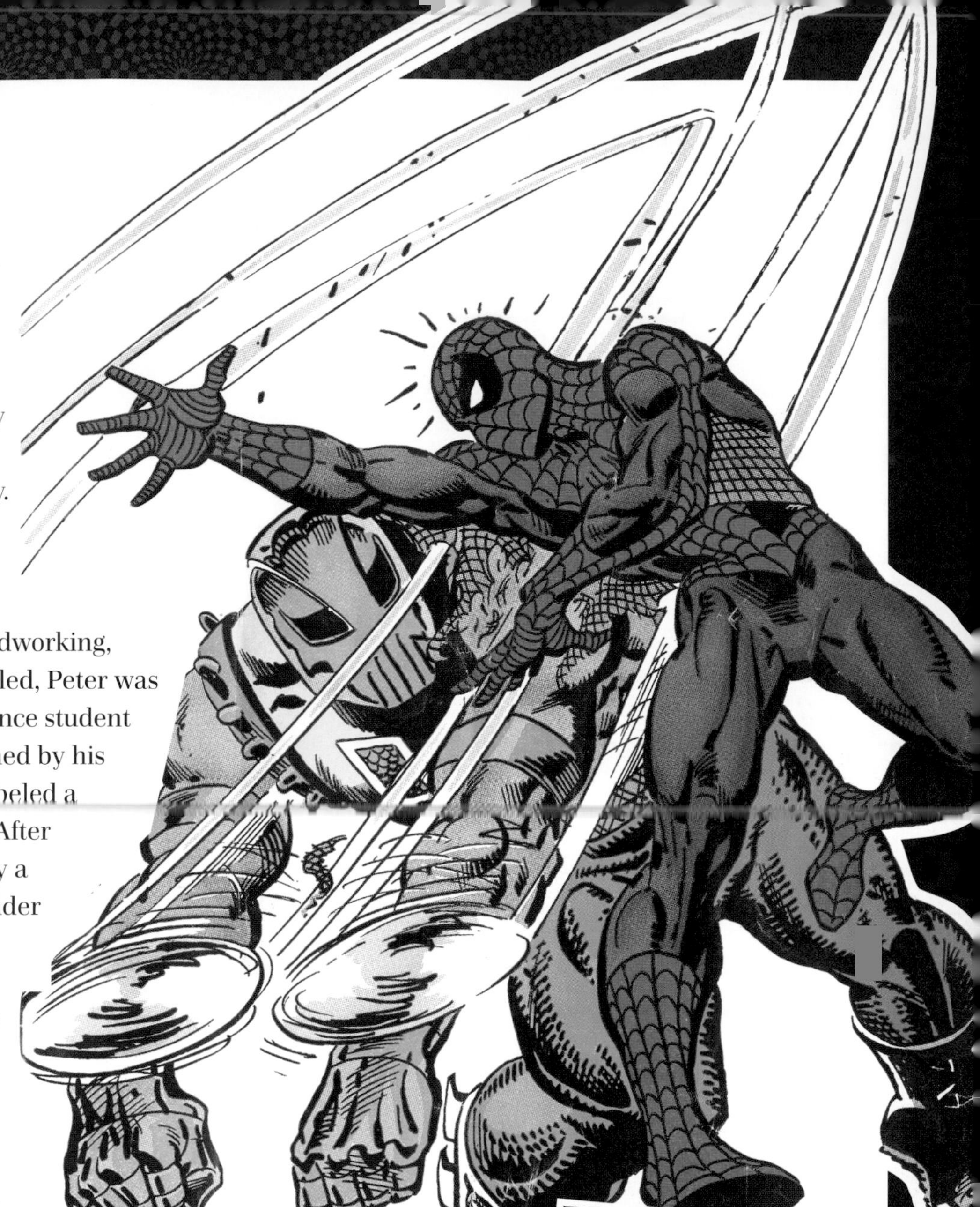

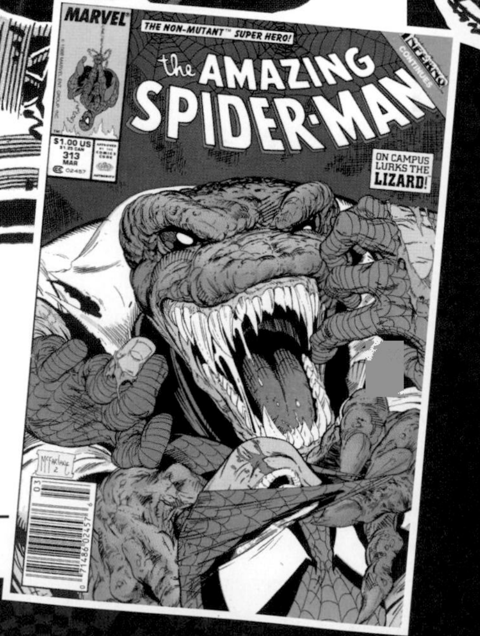
MARVEL
THE NON-MUTANT SUPER HERO!
the AMAZING SPIDER-MAN
$1.00 US
313 MAR
ON CAMPUS LURKS THE LIZARD!

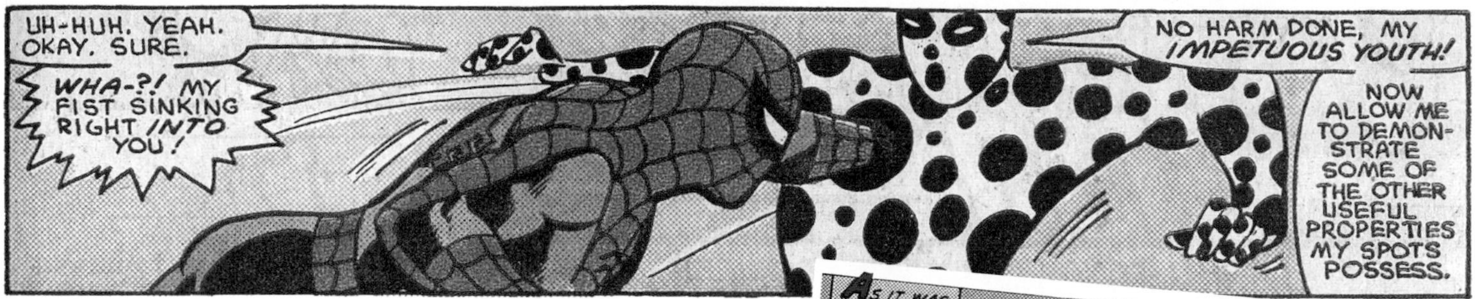
UH-HUH. YEAH. OKAY. SURE.
WHA-?! MY FIST SINKING RIGHT INTO YOU!
NO HARM DONE, MY IMPETUOUS YOUTH!
NOW ALLOW ME TO DEMON-STRATE SOME OF THE OTHER USEFUL PROPERTIES MY SPOTS POSSESS.

Readers enjoyed the Spider-Man's flippant heroics and Peter Parker's adolescent angst, and he quickly became Marvel's best-selling character.

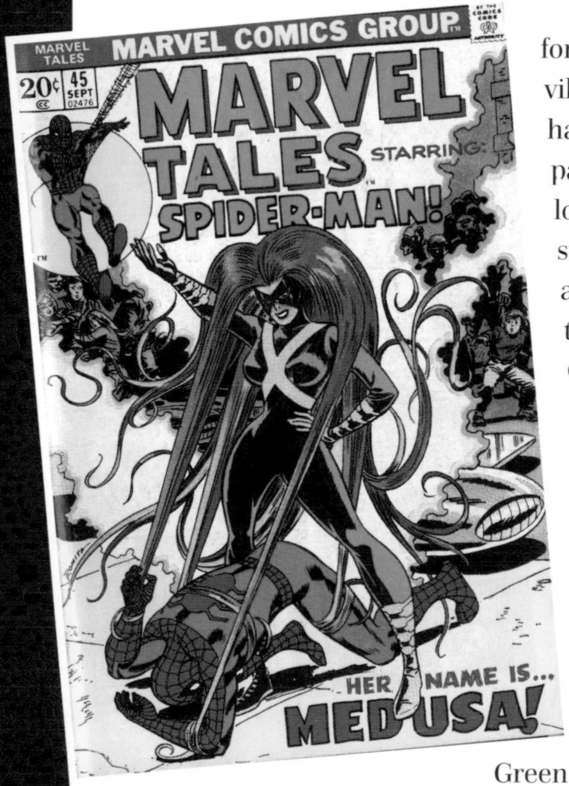
MARVEL COMICS GROUP
MARVEL TALES
20¢
45 SEPT 02476
MARVEL TALES STARRING: SPIDER-MAN!
HER NAME IS... MEDUSA!

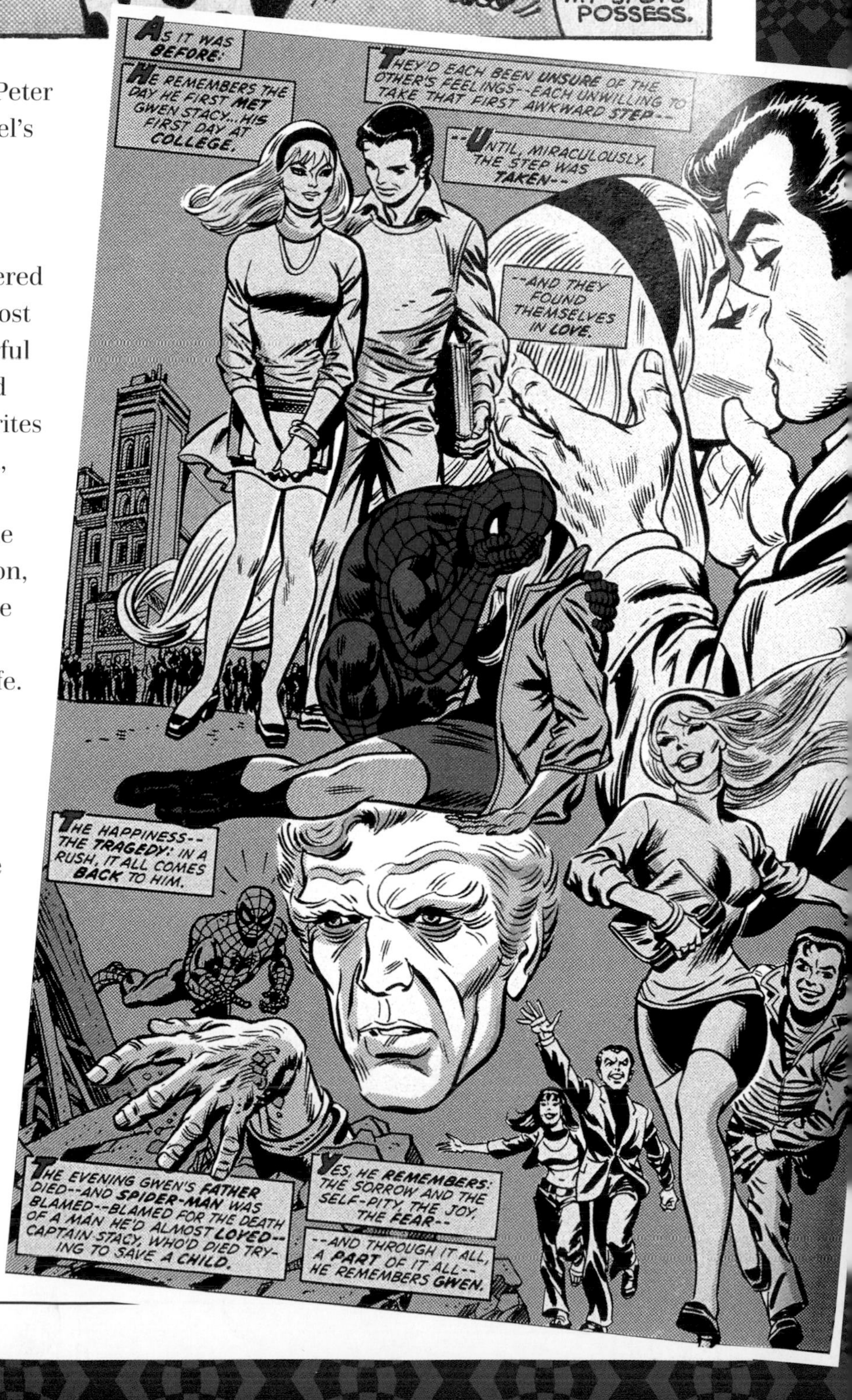
AS IT WAS BEFORE:
HE REMEMBERS THE DAY HE FIRST MET GWEN STACY...HIS FIRST DAY AT COLLEGE.
THEY'D EACH BEEN UNSURE OF THE OTHER'S FEELINGS--EACH UNWILLING TO TAKE THAT FIRST AWKWARD STEP--
--UNTIL, MIRACULOUSLY, THE STEP WAS TAKEN--
--AND THEY FOUND THEMSELVES IN LOVE.
THE HAPPINESS--THE TRAGEDY: IN A RUSH, IT ALL COMES BACK TO HIM.
THE EVENING GWEN'S FATHER DIED--AND SPIDER-MAN WAS BLAMED--BLAMED FOR THE DEATH OF A MAN HE'D ALMOST LOVED--CAPTAIN STACY, WHO'D DIED TRYING TO SAVE A CHILD.
YES, HE REMEMBERS: THE SORROW AND THE SELF-PITY, THE JOY, THE FEAR--
--AND THROUGH IT ALL, A PART OF IT ALL--HE REMEMBERS GWEN.

Spidey has been fortunate in that the villains he's encountered have been, for the most part, a vile and colorful lot. They've included such recurring favorites as the Green Goblin, the Kingpin, Doc Octopus, Kraven the Hunter, the Scorpion, and Morbuis. There have been various ladies in Peter's life. His first true love was Gwen Stacy, but she was tragically murdered by the Green Goblin. He met Mary Jane Watson, redheaded actress and model, in the middle 1960s, and after a courtship that waxed and waned over twenty years, they were married in 1987. Marriage hasn't slowed him down or much affected his popularity. There are many fans, however, who feel the woman for Peter was Gwen Stacy and still miss her.

Among the artists who've drawn the old web-spinner have been John Buscema, Gil Kane, John Byrne, Todd McFarlane, and a host of others.

SPIEGELMAN, ART *(1948–)*

■ The only artist working in the comic-book format thus far to win a Pulitzer Prize, Spiegelman did it with an unlikely combination of funny animal drawings and a biography of his Holocaust-surviving parents. *Maus: A Survivor's Tale* appeared in book form in 1986, published by Pantheon. The material had originally appeared from 1980 to 1986 in *Raw*, a now-and-then underground comic edited by Spiegelman and his wife, Francoise Mouly.

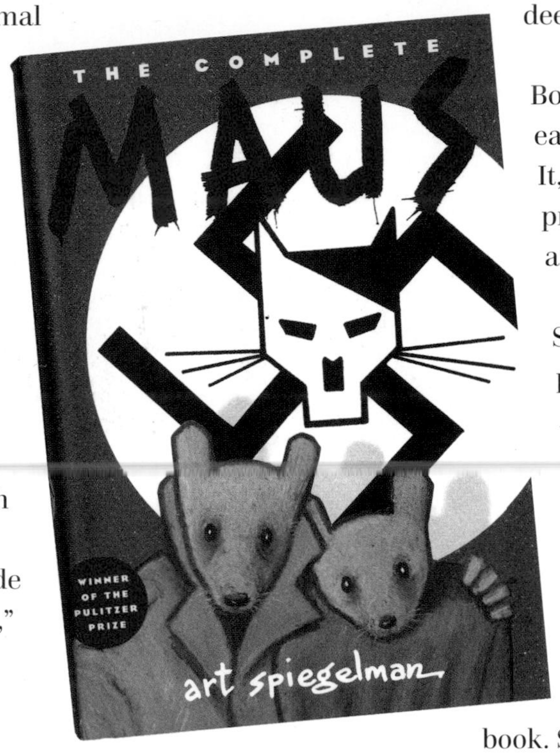
THE COMPLETE
MAUS
WINNER OF THE PULITZER PRIZE
art spiegelman

In *Maus*, the Jews are drawn as mice and the Nazis as cats. "Though some readers might have been shocked by the depiction of genocide in a traditionally frivolous medium," comics historian Dennis Wepman has observed, "the book had a profound impact on three separate audiences: comics buffs, who saw it as giving a new dimension to the medium; the Jewish community, who recognized in it a sensitive account of the most moving event of the century; and the general public, who were deeply affected by its gripping narrative."

Maus was nominated for a National Book Award and, more impressively, earned Spiegelman a Pulitzer Prize. It, along with the sequel, remains in print in America and several countries around the world.

Over the past decade or so Spiegelman has branched out, producing children's books like *Open Me . . . I'm A Dog!* and contributing to such compilations as *Little Lit: Folk & Fairy Tale Funnies*, edited by him and his wife. He also contributed quite a few attractive and often controversial covers to *The New Yorker*. His essay in that magazine on Plastic Man creator Jack Cole was later expanded into a book. Spiegelman recently parted company with *The New Yorker*, and his work has been showing up in other venues.

THE SPIRIT

■ Denny Colt began playing dead in 1940 and has continued to do so ever since. As the forties began, comic books were selling in the millions, a fact that had not gone unnoticed by newspaper syndicates. *Superman* had branched out into a newspaper strip in 1939, and by the following year ready-print comic books were being offered for insertion in Sunday newspapers. Enterprising publisher Victor Fox tried to launch one, the *Chicago Tribune* introduced a *Comic Book Magazine*, and the Register & Tribune Syndicate, a silent partner in Everett "Busy" Arnold's Quality comic-book line, brought forth a sixteen-page weekly *Spirit* booklet. The first one appeared June 2, 1940. Will Eisner wrote and drew the Spirit's adventures.

In addition to Eisner's masked hero, it featured *Lady Luck*, originally drawn by Chuck Mazoujian, and Bob

Powell's *Mr. Mystic.* Although the Spirit somewhat resembled a traditional comic-book character, he differed sharply from the brightly costumed superheroes. For one thing, he refused to take his work seriously, and his working outfit was a baggy blue suit, a slouch hat, and a domino mask. Once, the Spirit had been Denny Colt, a private eye. But after the world came to believe he'd been murdered by a villain known as Dr. Cobra, Colt went underground to become a masked avenger. He took up residence in a roomy crypt in Central City's Wildwood Cemetery and, aided by a black youth named Ebony White, he waged war on crooks, con men, criminal masterminds, and shady ladies. The grump Inspector Dolan and his lovely blond daughter Ellen both knew who the Spirit really was.

Eisner quite obviously learned on the job and had a great deal of fun doing it. His stories grew better, trickier, and less melodramatic. His layouts moved further and further away from the traditional. Nobody has equaled him in incorporating his logo into the splash panel in a variety of ways, and few have come close to capturing the look and feel, the shadows and smells, of big-city life.

Eisner entered the service in 1942, turning the weekly Spirit story over to others, chiefly Lou Fine. He returned in 1945 and, aided by such artists as John Spranger, Jerry Grandenetti, Wally Wood, and Jules Feiffer, produced six more years of *The Spirit.*

Arnold's *Police Comics*, which starred Plastic Man, started reprinting a Spirit story in each issue from #11 (September 1942) onward, and the rumpled crimefighter remained in the magazine until #93 (November 1950). A separate title devoted exclusively to *Spirit* reprints began in 1944 and continued until 1950. The stories, which Eisner owns, have been reprinted regularly in the United States and around the world ever since. In this country Fiction House, Harvey, Warren, and Kitchen Sink have all reprinted them. Recently DC initiated a hardcover series to reprint the entire run. And in 1997 Kitchen Sink introduced a limited series titled *The Spirit: The New Adventures*, which used stories by such writers and artists as Alan Moore, Brian Bolland, and Mike Allred.

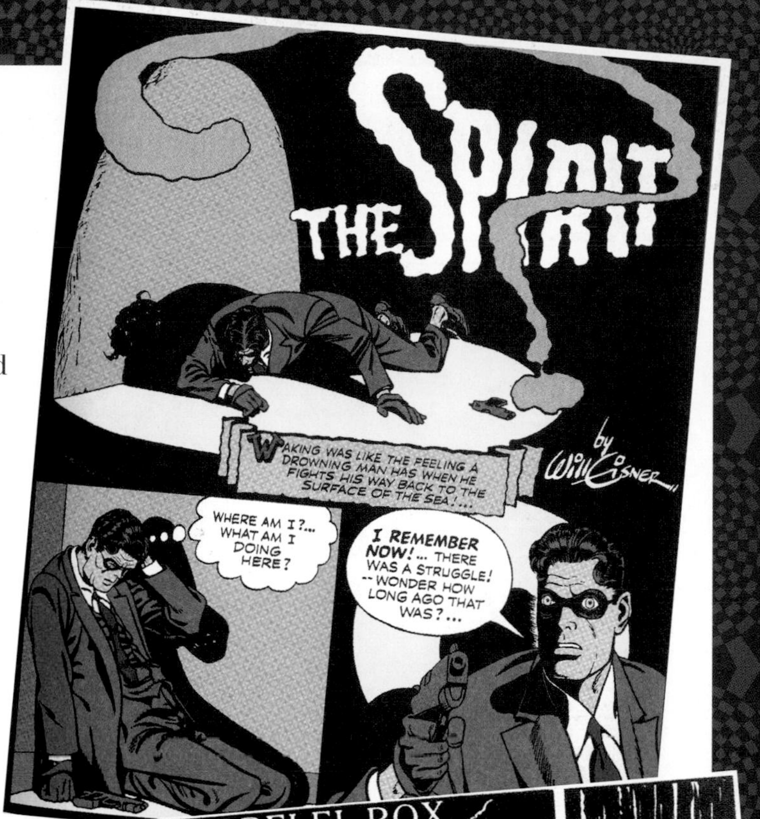
THE SPIRIT
WAKING WAS LIKE THE FEELING A DROWNING MAN HAS WHEN HE FIGHTS HIS WAY BACK TO THE SURFACE OF THE SEA...
by Will Eisner
WHERE AM I?... WHAT AM I DOING HERE?
I REMEMBER NOW!... THERE WAS A STRUGGLE! --WONDER HOW LONG AGO THAT WAS?...

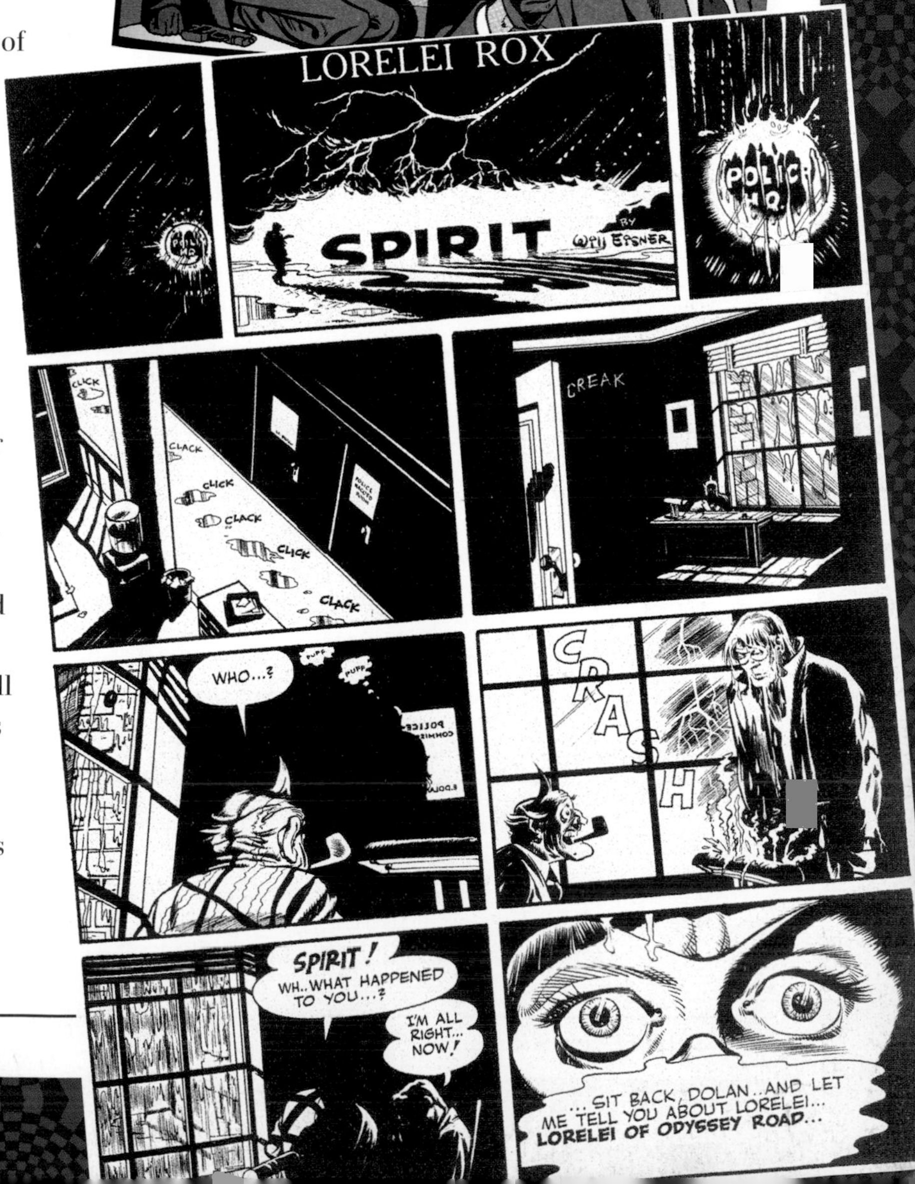
LORELEI ROX
SPIRIT
BY WILL EISNER
POLICE H.Q.
CLICK
CLACK
CLICK
CLACK
CLICK
CLACK
CREAK
WHO...?
PUFF
PUFF
CRASH
SPIRIT!
WH..WHAT HAPPENED TO YOU...?
I'M ALL RIGHT... NOW!
...SIT BACK, DOLAN...AND LET ME TELL YOU ABOUT LORELEI... LORELEI OF ODYSSEY ROAD...

STANLEY, JOHN

■ See LITTLE LULU.

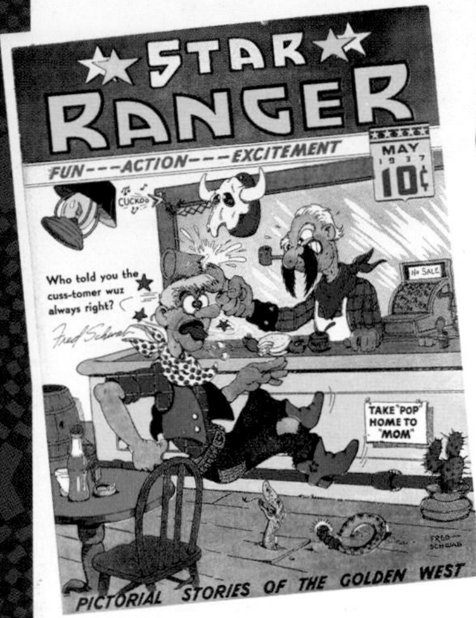
STAR RANGER
FUN---ACTION---EXCITEMENT
MAY 1937
10¢
Who told you the cuss-tomer wuz always right?
TAKE 'POP' HOME TO 'MOM'
PICTORIAL STORIES OF THE GOLDEN WEST

STAR RANGER COMICS

■ Tied with *Western Picture Stories* for the title of the first Western comic book, *Star Ranger* bore the cover date of February 1937 and was published and packaged by Harry "A" Chesler. By the tenth issue (March 1938), Centaur Publications had taken over the magazine, and with the thirteenth it became *Cowboy Comics.* Shortly thereafter it was *Star Ranger Funnies.*

The book contained a large number of short features, ranging from one to four pages. There were serious cowboy yarns and comedy fillers. Among the artists who later moved on to successful careers in comic books were Fred Guardineer, Fred Schwab, Paul Gustavson, Craig Flessel, Jack Cole, and Charles Biro. At that period Biro hadn't entered his serious, hard-boiled period and was drawing a cute kid strip about Wild West, Jr.

Despite its pioneer status, the magazine didn't last beyond the fall of 1939.

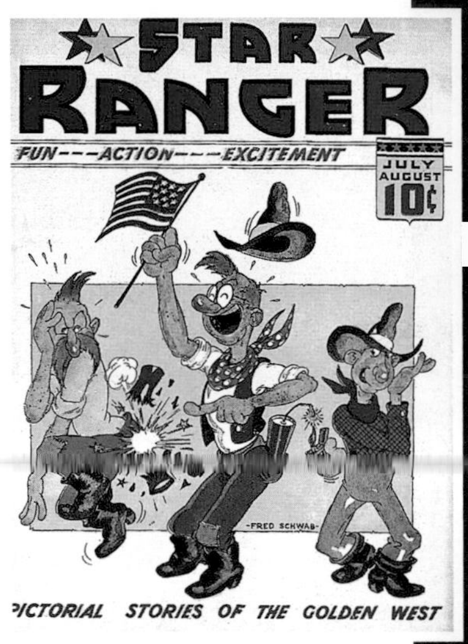
STAR RANGER
FUN---ACTION---EXCITEMENT
JULY AUGUST
10¢
FRED SCHWAB
PICTORIAL STORIES OF THE GOLDEN WEST

STAR SPANGLED COMICS

■ DC's eighth monthly title went on sale on August 6, 1941, "the result of months of careful research into just what sort of features you readers DEMAND!" What the company thought potential readers of *Star Spangled Comics* wanted were two separate stories about the Star Spangled Kid and Stripesy, totaling thirty-four pages, plus stories about three other acceptable but far from outstanding characters. Obviously editor Whit Ellsworth was banking on the Kid and his husky sidekick, who'd been described in a three-page ad in *Action Comics* as "arch-foes of hate and intolerance, champions of LIBERTY and JUSTICE, the embodiment of the TRUE AMERICAN SPIRT! In other words, they are . . . YOU!" And on top of that, the script writer was Jerry Siegel, "creator of SUPERMAN."

In civilian life the Kid was mild-mannered and wealthy young Sylvester Pemberton and Stripesy was his chauffer Pat Dugan, which relationship reversed the usual formula and gave the small kid a large, muscular companion. Being an ace mechanic, Stripesy had redesigned Sylvester's limo so that at the flip of a switch it turned into the Star-Rocket Racer and took to the air. The artist was Hal Sherman, up until then a gag cartoonist who drew occasional comedy fillers for comics. His serious style was still a mite too cartoony for this sort of fare. For whatever reasons, the Kid and

Stripesy's battle with strange villains, spies, and saboteurs didn't win a massive audience.

With the seventh issue (April 1942) there was a major overhaul. Joe Simon and Jack Kirby, recently hired away from Martin Goodman's *Captain America*, came to the rescue with *The Newsboy Legion*. This was not only another kid gang, they had a costumed crimefighter looking out for them in the person of the Guardian. They took the starring spot in the book and the cover for the next several years. The Star Spangled Kid and Stripesy, reduced to thirteen pages and then ten, were moved further back.

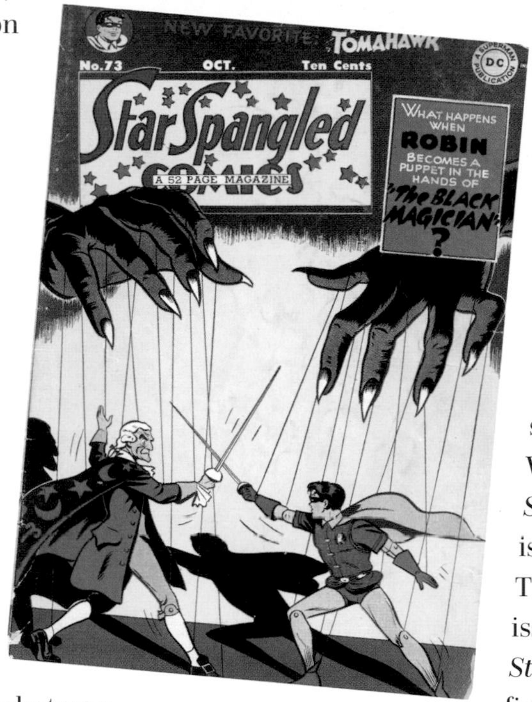
NEW FAVORITE: TOMAHAWK
No.73
OCT.
Ten Cents
DC
Star Spangled
COMICS
A 52 PAGE MAGAZINE
WHAT HAPPENS WHEN
ROBIN
BECOMES A PUPPET IN THE HANDS OF
"The BLACK MAGICIAN"?

Other new characters added were TNT and Dan the Dyna-Mite, Penniless Palmer (who returned in #8 after having debuted in #6), and Robotman, originally a product of the Siegel and Shuster studio, though uncredited. As the years passed, a patriotic blonde known as Liberty Belle joined the lineup. Robotman's finest hour came in the middle 1940s, when Jimmy Thompson, who added a needed touch of humor, took over the feature and gave the metallic hero a feisty robot dog for a sidekick.

Tomahawk, somewhat in the James Fennimore Cooper tradition, was added in 1947, drawn by Edmond Good and then Fred Ray. The next year Merry the Girl of 1000 Gimmicks supported the Star Spangled Kid. Robin, billed as "Batman's two-fisted partner," soloed for the first time in a series of stories signed by Bob Kane, yet ghosted by Win Mortimer and later Jim Mooney. *Star Spangled* lasted unto its 130th issue (July 1952), with Robin and Tomahawk still aboard. The following issue was renamed *Star Spangled War Stories*, and under that banner it kept fighting until 1977.

The Star Spangled Kid, despite his less than auspicious early days, has been revived on several occasions by DC, once even as a young woman.

THE STAR SPANGLED KID

■ See STAR SPANGLED COMICS.

STEEL STERLING

■ See ZIP COMICS.

STERANKO, JAMES

■ See NICK FURY.

STRANGERS IN PARADISE

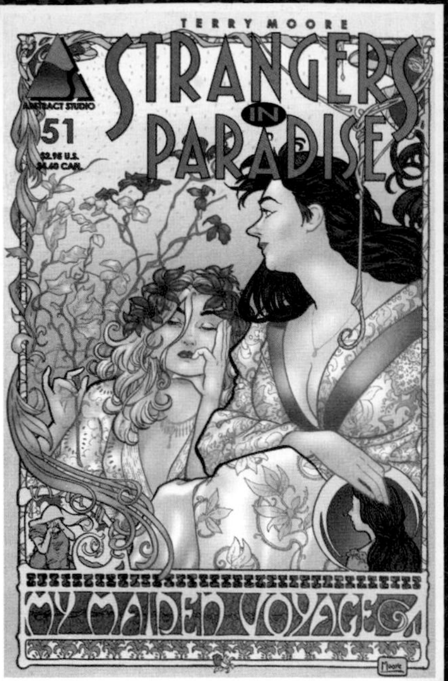
TERRY MOORE
STRANGERS IN PARADISE
ABSTRACT STUDIO
51
MY MAIDEN VOYAGE

■ *Strangers in Paradise,* which mixes the mundane with the melodramatic, has been in business for over a decade. Written, drawn, and published by Terry Moore, *SIP* is yet another example of a successful independent comic book.

It chronicles the lives of two somewhat exceptional young women—Katina "Katchoo" Choovanski and Francine Peters–Silver—and their assorted friends, lovers, relatives, and homicidal enemies. In his work Moore blends accounts of everyday life—he's especially fond of conversations in diners—with complex conspiracies involving crime lords, rings of elusive hooker/assassins, and undercover FBI agents.

SIP includes all sorts of sexual encounters, both heterosexual and homosexual. Katchoo, the main focal character, is a painter and was an abused child, a call girl, and a target of mob killers. Francine, who is intermittently Katchoo's best friend, has led a somewhat less adventuresome life. Yet she's had enough emotional ups and downs to keep a soap opera heroine busy for several seasons. A full-figured woman, she also has problems with her weight.

Moore, who draws in an attractive black-and-white style, turns out nine issues of *Strangers in Paradise* a year and six of a companion comic book titled *Paradise Too.*

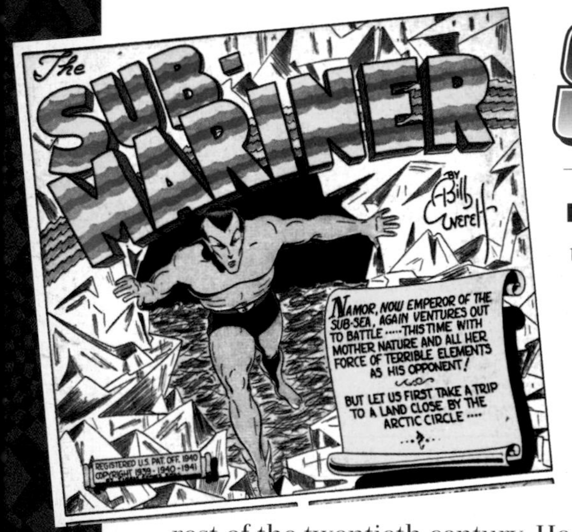
The SUB-MARINER
BY Bill Everett
NAMOR, NOW EMPEROR OF THE SUB-SEA, AGAIN VENTURES OUT TO BATTLE..... THIS TIME WITH MOTHER NATURE AND ALL HER FORCE OF TERRIBLE ELEMENTS AS HIS OPPONENT!
BUT LET US FIRST TAKE A TRIP TO A LAND CLOSE BY THE ARCTIC CIRCLE.....

SUB-MARINER

■ The Sub-Mariner, the prince of aquatic superheroes, first emerged from the briny deep in 1939 and hung around in one magazine or other for most of the rest of the twentieth century. He was the creation of artist/writer Bill Everett, and, after a single appearance in the short-lived *Motion Picture Weekly,* Sub-Mariner was reintroduced in *Marvel Comics* #1 in the autumn of 1939.

Prince Namor was born in an undersea kingdom (identified some years later as Atlantis), the result of a misalliance between his mother and an explorer named McKenzie. Because of his mixed genetic code, he was able to live on both land and in the sea. For good measure, he was incredibly strong and could fly. An angry young man, the pointy-eared Namor arrived in Manhattan from his decimated undersea home in the second issue of *Marvel.* He was bent on revenge. "You white devils have persecuted and tormented my people for years," he explained to policewoman Betty Dean, who eventually became his closest friend. Once in Manhattan, he went on a rampage of destruction.

With Sub-Mariner cutting up in New York City and the Human Torch freshly arrived in the Apple to work as a cop, a confrontation was inevitable. What happened was a battle royal that raged through #8 and #9 before winding up in a standoff in #10, when Betty Dean was able to arrange a truce. When next the representatives of fire and water met, they were "fighting side by side!" As a caption in the twenty-six-page teamup saga in *Marvel* #17 (March 1941) explained, "The Human Torch and the Sub-Mariner are together again. Not to destroy each other but to form an alliance that will stop the gigantic plans for an invasion of the United States!"

The prince calmed down somewhat after that, and with Betty often acting as his conscience, he concentrated on quieter capers. In addition to frequent fantasy elements and pretty women, Everett's stories always provided readers with numerous examples of Sub-Mariner's colorful aquatic expletives. Namor's favorite, spoken in times of stress, surprise or amazement was "Sufferin' shad!" He was also fond of "Jumpin' jellyfish!" and "Great pickled penguins!"

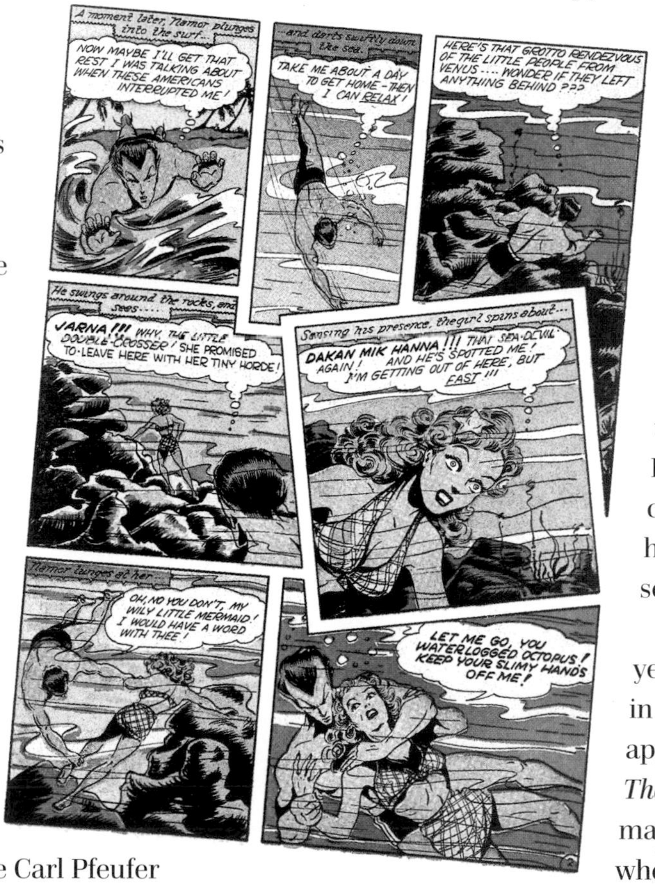
A moment later, Namor plunges into the surf...
NOW MAYBE I'LL GET THAT REST I WAS TALKING ABOUT WHEN THESE AMERICANS INTERRUPTED ME!
...and darts swiftly down the sea.
TAKE ME ABOUT A DAY TO GET HOME – THEN I CAN RELAX!
HERE'S THAT GROTTO RENDEZVOUS OF THE LITTLE PEOPLE FROM VENUS .... WONDER IF THEY LEFT ANYTHING BEHIND ???
He swings around the rocks, and sees....
JARNA!!! WHY, THE LITTLE DOUBLE-CROSSER! SHE PROMISED TO·LEAVE HERE WITH HER TINY HORDE!
Sensing his presence, the girl spins about...
DAKAN MIK HANNA!!! THAT SEA-DEVIL AGAIN! AND HE'S SPOTTED ME! I'M GETTING OUT OF HERE, BUT FAST!!!
Namor lunges at her...
OH, NO YOU DON'T, MY WILY LITTLE MERMAID! I WOULD HAVE A WORD WITH THEE!
LET ME GO, YOU WATERLOGGED OCTOPUS! KEEP YOUR SLIMY HANDS OFF ME!

A popular character, Sub-Mariner also appeared as a backup in the *Human Torch* comic book that started in 1940 and got a book of his own in 1941. He showed up as well in *All Winners* and assorted other Marvel titles. When Everett entered the service, a succession of artists carried on the feature. The best of them were Carl Pfeufer and Jimmy Thompson. Namor was very active during World War II, fighting both the Nazis and the Japanese.

Everett returned in 1947 to remain with Namor until the prince sank from sight in 1949. Betty Dean became a newspaper reporter in those postwar years, and Sub-Mariner's cousin Namora surfaced. One of several superwomen introduced by Marvel at the time, she aided her quick-tempered cousin and soloed briefly in a magazine of her own. The Prince with the Human Torch and Captain America was one of the three 1940s heroes that Marvel resurrected and attempted to reestablish in the middle 1950s. The trio first showed up in separate yarns in *Young Men* #24 in 1953. Early the following year, *Sub-Mariner* magazine returned, picking up with #33. Like his colleagues, Namor now added the Red Menace to his list of targets. His anti-communist stand was especially noticeable on the covers of most issues, where his opponents prominently displayed the hammer and sickle and such copy lines as "The Commie Frogmen vs. Sub-Mariner!" and "Sub-Mariner Fights Commies and Crooks!" were writ large. Namor fared somewhat better than the other returned heroes, and his magazine held on for ten issues before ceasing late in 1955. Everett wrote and drew most of the new adventures of his underwater avenger. Betty Dean, who now seemed to be cohabiting with Namor, was on hand, and Namora returned in several of the stories.

After an absence of several years, Sub-Mariner rose again in 1962. After assorted guest appearances, including some in *The Avengers*, he settled into his own magazine in 1968. Among the artists who drew the new series stories were John Byrne, Marie Severin, and Gene Colan. Everett drew him again in 1972 and 1973. During that period Betty Dean, now a plump, gray-haired matron, appeared again, and Namora's daughter, Namorita, was introduced. The prince surfaced several times since, serving as part of the Invaders team early on. He's spouted the Marvel version of Shakespearean dialogue at times, gone through a period where he sported a handsome ponytail and undergone other departures from his earlier persona. In the early 1990s he was billed as "Marvel's first and mightiest mutant." Namor apparently retired in the late 1990s.

SUGAR AND SPIKE

■ Another notable creation of the inventive Sheldon Mayer, they were introduced in DC's *Sugar and Spike* #1 in the spring of 1956. Its team of toddlers, who seemed as meant for each other as Romeo and Juliet or Nick and Nora, hadn't reached the age where they could communicate with grown-ups. They could talk to each other with ease, however, and together they participated in a decade and a half of wild and woolly adventures that ranged from the domestic to the fantastic. Mayer kidded not only middle-class suburban life, but, being a man who wasn't reluctant to bite the hand that fed him, many of the characters who were being treated seriously in the other DC titles of the day.

At first Mayer devoted the magazine to a series of short episodes about the two preschool next-door neighbors. The blond Sugar Plum was the dominant member of the pair, continually dragging the hapless red-haired Spike Wilson into trouble. The adventures that unfolded as Sugar and Spike explored the wonders of the everyday world were shot at kid level. Parents and other obtuse adults were usually shown from the waist down. Intended originally for a young audience, *Sugar and Spike* began to reach a somewhat wider readership.

Mayer eventually began doing "complete novel-length" stories that ran twenty or more pages. He allowed adults to appear fully, and his plots made fun of everything from superheroes to South American dictators. In #72, he introduced a toddler named Bernie the Brain, a scientific genius whose precocious inventions unfailingly got Sugar and Spike and him into complex messes with alien invaders, giant robots, growth elixirs, and other sci-fi annoyances. Mayer had always had a vigorous, appealing style, and in the longer epics he did some of his best work.

Sugar and Spike ended with #98 in the fall of 1971. Mayer continued doing the feature in the 1980s for overseas publication. Some of that material, with new covers by him, was recycled in a series of DC digests. And recently the first issue was reprinted.

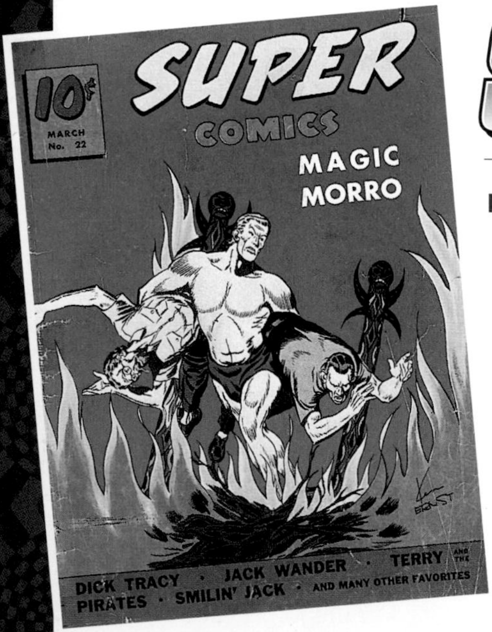
10¢
SUPER
COMICS
MARCH No. 22
MAGIC MORRO
DICK TRACY · JACK WANDER · TERRY AND THE PIRATES · SMILIN' JACK · AND MANY OTHER FAVORITES

SUPER COMICS

■ Whitman Publishing's entry into the *Famous Funnies* derby, it was introduced early in 1938 and reprinted Chicago Tribune–New York News Syndicate strips exclusively—*Dick Tracy*, *Little Orphan Annie*, *Smilin' Jack*, *Terry & the Pirates*, etc. The magazine underwent some changes during its eleven-year run, ending with its 121st issue in 1949.

Super began adding original adventure features with the twenty-first issue (February 1940). *Magic Morro* by Ken Ernst, *Jack Wander, War Correspondent* by Ed Moore, and *Jim Ellis, Adventurer*, drawn by Richard M. Fletcher and written by Moore, were added. Over the next year and a half both Morro and Jim Ellis were featured on covers. By 1948 the new adventure stuff was gone, and *Super* was basically back to reprints for the rest of its days.

SUPER MAGICIAN COMICS

■ The first comic book offering the fictitious adventures of a real-life personality who wasn't a movie cowboy, the magazine got started in the spring of 1941. The personality in question was famous stage magician Harry Blackstone, and the writer/entrepreneur who came up with the idea was Walter B. Gibson, creator of the Shadow.

Gibson had started ghosting Blackstone's magic books in the late 1920s. In 1941 he approached Street & Smith, publishers of both the Shadow pulp magazine and the comic book, and suggested a Blackstone comic. What made the deal especially appealing to S&S was the fact that Gibson guaranteed them that the magician would purchase half of each issue's print run to give away at his stage shows. The first issue (May 1941) was titled *Super-Magic Comics*. With the second, it became *Super Magician*. Blackstone grew younger and handsomer for his comic-book appearances and also acquired a pretty assistant named Rhoda. On the covers he was frequently called the "World's Greatest Living Magician."

Gibson wrote all the Blackstone stories, which usually dealt with the magician touring exotic locales with his stage show and running into spurious wizards and warlocks whom he proceeded to outwit and debunk. Another dependable plot element was Rhoda's changing into a scanty costume. Typical story titles were "Blackstone in Voodoo Valley" and "Blackstone Meets the Pirates of Twin Island."

The early artwork, mediocre at best, was provided by the Jack Binder shop. Gibson later brought in some of his cronies, including James Hammon and Kemp Starrett, and the look of the feature improved greatly. Both men, along with Gibson, had been associated with the Ledger Syndicate in Philadelphia.

When Blackstone's agreement with Street & Smith came to an end early in 1946, he ceased to be the star of *Super Magician*. He was replaced by Nigel Elliman, a fictitious magician. Gibson wrote the Elliman scripts until the magazine folded in 1947. In addition to a couple of adventures of the lead magician each issue, Gibson also ghosted a column that taught young readers magic tricks, most of them involving cards.

A variety of other characters, not scripted by Gibson, came and went in the magazine. These included Tao Anwar, a boy magician, and the Red Dragon, who possessed real magic powers. There was also Rex King, a mystery man who palled around with a black panther, and Tigerman, a fellow who could change into a tiger. Bios of famous magicians of the past, such as Houdini, were used as well. In the later issues noted pulp illustrator Edd Cartier was a contributor, as was Joe Maneely in the days before he became Marvel's premier cover artist.

As did a few other publishers, Street & Smith used a volume system for numbering the magazine. The final issue, therefore, was Volume 5, Number 8. That was the fifty-sixth issue, and it bore the cover date of February–March 1947.

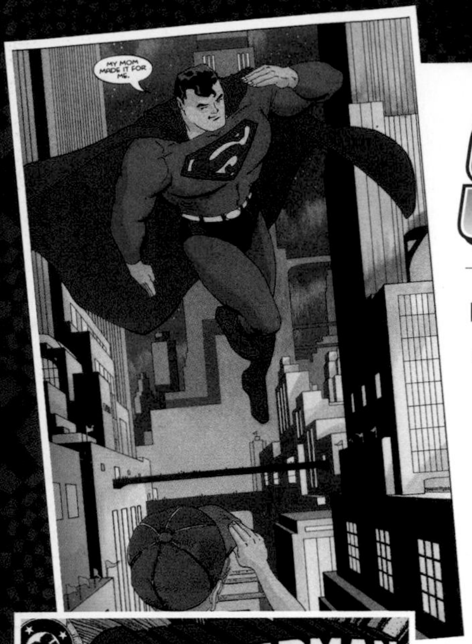
MY MOM MADE IT FOR ME.

SUPERMAN

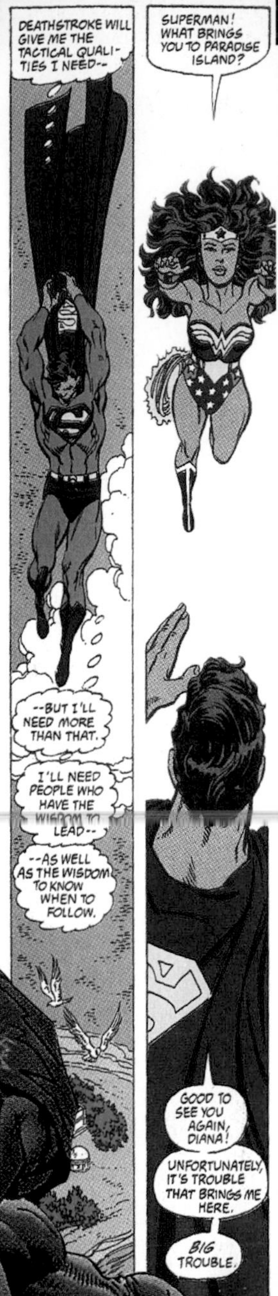
DEATHSTROKE WILL GIVE ME THE TACTICAL QUALI-TIES I NEED--
--BUT I'LL NEED MORE THAN THAT.
I'LL NEED PEOPLE WHO HAVE THE WISDOM TO LEAD--
--AS WELL AS THE WISDOM TO KNOW WHEN TO FOLLOW.
SUPERMAN! WHAT BRINGS YOU TO PARADISE ISLAND?
GOOD TO SEE YOU AGAIN, DIANA!
UNFORTUNATELY, IT'S TROUBLE THAT BRINGS ME HERE.
BIG TROUBLE.

■ The most important comic-book character of the twentieth century and the very first superhero, he was conceived in Cleveland in the early 1930s by author Jerry Siegel and artist Joe Shuster. They'd met in high school, and it took them several years to find anybody to take an interest in *Superman.* Finally in 1938, they got a break and their hero started appearing in DC's *Action Comics.* Single-handedly Superman turned the fledgling comic-book business into a major industry, changing the look and content of the four-color magazines forever. He made several people associated with him impressively rich and for nearly a decade even his creators prospered.

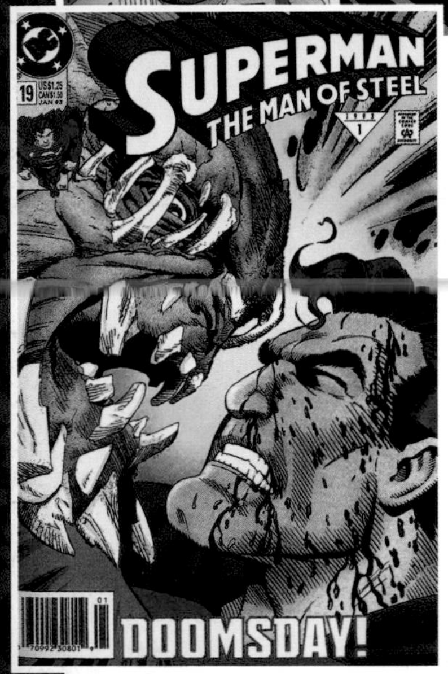
19
SUPERMAN
THE MAN OF STEEL
DOOMSDAY!

The thirteen-page story that introduced the Man of Steel in *Action* #1 (June 1938) was mostly cobbled together from Siegel and Shuster's unsold *Superman* newspaper strip. It offered a one-page introduction to the new hero, listing his birthplace only as "a distant planet" and making no mention of his real or adoptive parents. Page two began in the middle of the story, with the costumed Superman carrying a pretty nightclub singer through the air. It managed to introduce that mild-mannered Clark Kent and his newspaper coworker, Lois Lane, who was already giving him the cold shoulder.

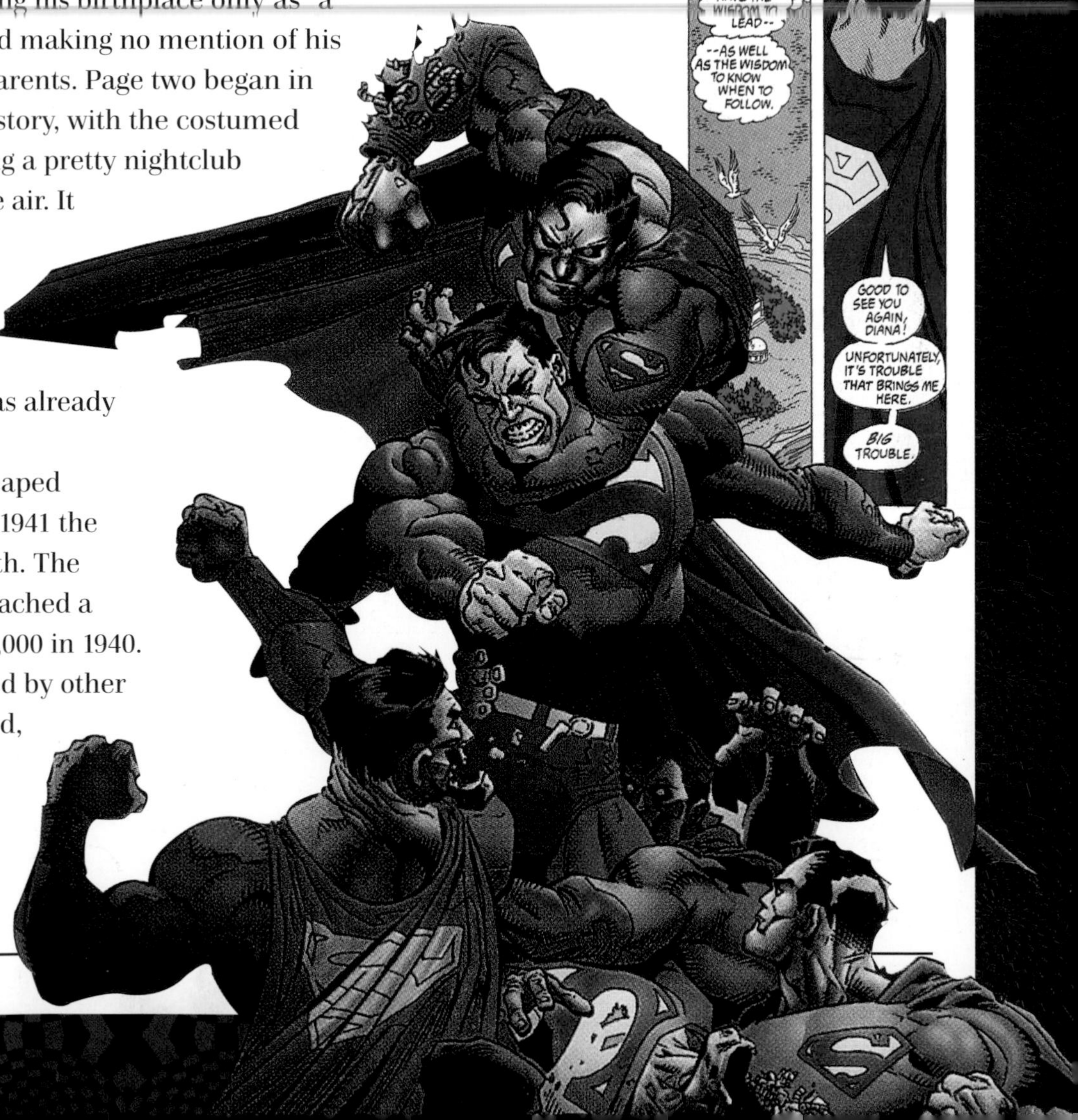

By the fourth issue, *Action*'s sales had leaped forward. They quickly rose 500,000, and by 1941 the magazine was selling 900,000 copies a month. The *Superman* magazine, begun in 1939, soon reached a circulation of 1.25 million and grossed $950,000 in 1940. These impressive figures didn't go unnoticed by other publishers, and by the time the 1940s started, a full-scale superhero book was under way.

When DC bought *Superman,* business manager Jack Liebowitz had explained that Siegel and Shuster had to sign a release

NEW YORK 15¢
WORLD'S FAIR
COMICS
1940 ISSUE
96 THRILLING PAGES IN FULL COLOR!

giving all rights to the feature to the publisher. "It is customary for all our contributors to release all rights to us," he wrote. "This is the business-like way of doing things." As the years passed and the kid from Krypton continued to pile up profits, the team grew increasingly unhappy. In 1947, when their joint income dropped to $46,000, they decided to go to court. "In New York Supreme Court in Westchester County they had filed suit seeking (1) to regain rights to their brainchild, (2) to cancel their newspaper contract with McClure [who distributed the *Superman* comic strip] and their contract with [DC publisher Harry] Donenfeld," reported the April 14, 1947, issue of *Newsweek*, "on the grounds that they had been violated, and (3) to recover about $5,000,000 they say *Superman* should have brought them over a nine-year period." There was also a conflict over the Superboy character. "When Siegel was in the army, Superboy made his debut under the double byline. Siegel claims that he never authorized the use of his name and has never received a cent for the strip." The partners did not do well. While the court ruled that "DC Comics, Inc. had acted illegally" as far as *Superboy* was concerned, DC did indeed own *Superman*. Siegel and Shuster were paid for *Superboy* in a settlement rumored to be around $50,000, but they were fired by Donenfeld. Superman was no longer theirs. It would be almost thirty years before they would see any compensation for having created one of the most valuable characters of the century.

Poison Ivy used Catwoman in those Gotham City crimes.
She felt violated being controlled by Ivy.
It's made the hunt personal for Selina.
THOUGHTLESS.
WORTHLESS.
STUPID.
MAN.

Superman continued, drawn by former Shuster ghost Wayne Boring and several others. Editor Mort Weisinger, who felt that Superman was "invulnerable, he's immortal. Even bad scripts can't hurt him," oversaw the Man of Steel in the 1950s and the 1960s. Weisinger seemed determined to test his theory about bad scripts, and during his era Superman suffered through innumerable strange, bizarre, and downright silly adventures. In addition to Superboy and Supergirl (introduced in 1959), DC made considerable use of other super things, including Krypto the Super Dog. When Weisinger departed DC in 1970, the immortal hero wasn't nearly as popular as he had once been.

SUPERMAN
66
BY DAN JURGENS AND BRETT BREEDING
PANIC IN THE SKY!
FINAL STRIKE

In the years since, DC has worked to boost Superman's popularity. In the middle 1980s, they brought in John Byrne to rejuvenate the hero. That didn't especially work. A while later Lois Lane, after a half century of conspicuous density, was finally informed by Clark Kent that he was Superman. In some venues this led to wedding bells.

By the early 1990s, there were four monthly titles featuring *Superman*. They were *Action Comics*, *Superman*, *The Adventures of Superman*, and *Superman: The Man of Steel*. A new Superman book went on sale every week, and each sold roughly 100,000 copies. At the time, those figures didn't come near matching those of Marvel hits like *X-Men*. Mike Carlin, a former Marvel editor, was in charge of the Man of Steel. "[Superman] is kind of old fashioned in that he doesn't go around killing everybody," he told an interviewer. "There are several

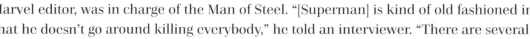

tricks you can use to boost sales." The specific trick Carlin had in mind was knocking off Superman.

Late in 1992, in the four *Superman* titles as well as *Justice League of America*, a new villain named appropriately Doomsday (and looking very much like a clone of many a Marvel monster) began slouching his way toward Metropolis. Considerable DC-generated publicity had appeared before *Superman* #75 appeared in November. The fateful issue was published in two different editions. One came sealed in a black plastic bag and included Superman's *Daily Planet* obit. A multitude of buyers, people who couldn't care less about comic books or Superman, flocked to comic shops to grab up multiple copies of what they assumed would be a valuable collector's item. Almost everybody had heard that early copies of *Superman* and *Action Comics* had sold for thousands of dollars.

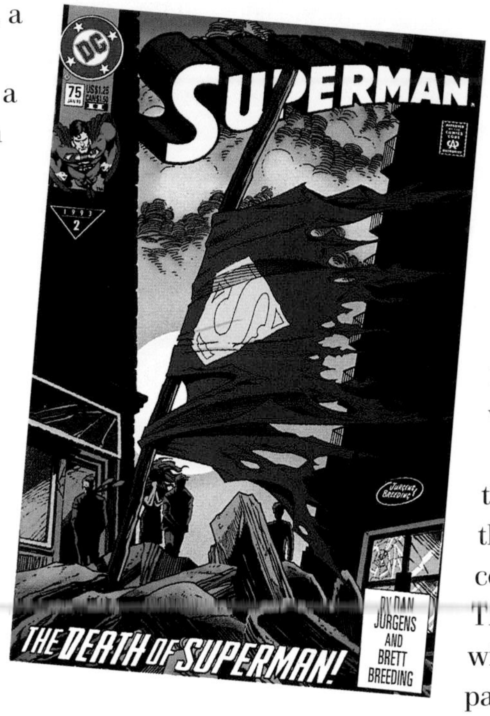
THE DEATH OF SUPERMAN!
BY DAN JURGENS AND BRETT BREEDING

DC accomplished a massive commercial success and sold over 6 million copies of the two editions of *Superman* #75. The reaction of comics fans and critics was far from positive. It was felt that Doomsday was a pretty stupid opponent to kill even an over-the-hill Superman. The event that killed the Man of Steel was a brutal hand-to-hand slugfest, dubbed "a big, brainless fistfight." The advance publicity had implied that Superman would be seen no more, and DC even held a funeral in their Superman titles. For a time some imitation Supermen carried on, including an African-American Superman and a robot version. Then a scant nine months after his death, Superman was born again in *Superman* #81.

This delighted longtime fans, but ticked off all those speculators. They thought they owned mint unopened copies of the famous hero's last go-round. They also hadn't taken into account the wisdom that several comics dealers soon passed along. Collectors' items increase in value only if there are more collectors than collectibles. Such was not the case here.

Superman has held on, though his sales have never matched those that the greatly exaggerated rumors of his death inspired.

SUPER-MYSTERY COMICS

■ Ace Magazines' second entry in the comic field, *Super-Mystery* was launched in the spring of 1940. Robert Turner, the first editor, also wrote most of the scripts. The featured superhero was Magno the Magnetic Man, drawn in the early issues by Harry Lucey. There was also a superhuman fellow named Vulcan the Volcanic Man who'd been living deep inside a volcano in the South Seas until he decided to "help the oppressed and fight evil" and moved to America.

Among the other characters who resided in the magazine during its nine-year run were the Black Spider, Dr. Nemesis, Buckskin, "Sky" Smith, Capt. Gallant and his Mini-Sub, Mr. Risk, and the Sword. After dropping many of its characters in 1947, a Nick and Nora–type detective team became the headliners in *The Adventures of Bert and Sue.*

There was considerable turnover in artists, and the list included Jim Mooney, Jack Alderman, Harry Anderson, Joe Gallagher, Dave Berg, Adolphe Barreaux, Harvey Kurtzman, Rudy Palais, and the incomparable Lou Ferstadt.

SUPERKATT

■ See GIGGLE COMICS.

SUPERSNIPE

■ Even during the heyday of superheroes not everybody took the concept seriously. For example, there was Supersnipe. Koppy McFad, also known as the Boy with the Most Comic Books in America, was an imaginative, well-meaning lad. Driven by dreams of glory that were fueled by the enormous quantities of comic books he ingested, Koppy longed to be a superhero. Undaunted by reality, he put together a costume from his father's lodge cape, his grandfather's red-flannel long johns, and his own tennis shoes. Thus attired, he set out to combat crime as Supersnipe. Sometimes he traveled by way of his bicycle.

Supersnipe was written by Ed Gruskin and drawn by George Marcoux, who'd been an assistant on the *Skippy* newspaper strip and later drawn a kid strip of his own called *Toddy*. Their feature had trial runs in Street & Smith's *Shadow Comics* and *Doc Savage Comics* before graduating to a bimonthly title of its own in the autumn of 1942.

The feature poked fun at the whole notion of costumed heroes and youthful aspirations toward adventure. Often the situations Koppy perceived to be dire crimes turned out to be far less than sinister, and when he did encounter real crooks, they were small-timers far removed from the evil masterminds of his imagination. Most of the stories had a folksy small-town America feel to them. Now and then Koppy would have

SUPERSNIPE
THE BOY WITH THE MOST COMIC BOOKS IN AMERICA
IN
"DOUBLE" "DANGER"!!
THERE WAS THE DAY KOPPY (SUPER-SNIPE) MCFAD WAS CATCHING UP ON SOME CURRENT COMIC BOOK LITERA-TURE, WHEN.......
...FROM WITHOUT CAME A DESPERATE CRY!
?!
NO...NO!-HAAALP!!

a dream sequence adventure in which Supersnipe was a real, grown-up hero, complete with rippling muscles, skin-tight costume, and flowing cape. These sequences were usually illustrated by C. M. Payne, another newspaper veteran. *Supersnipe* enjoyed a respectable run of forty-four issues before ceasing publication in 1949.

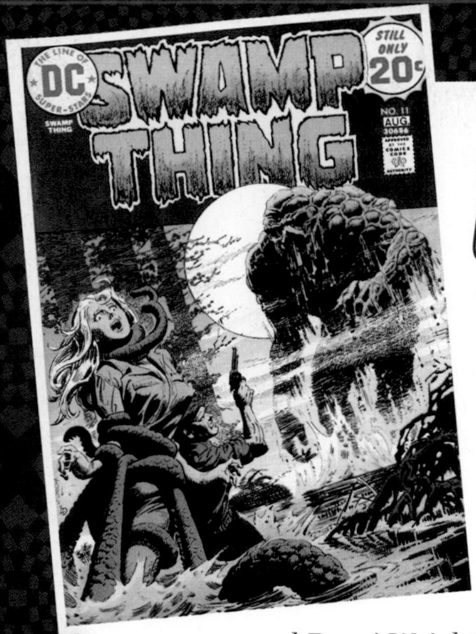
DC
SWAMP THING
STILL ONLY 20¢

SWAMP THING

■ The most successful animated compost heap in comics, he first emerged from the bog in the summer of 1972 to make his muddy debut in DC's *Swamp Thing* #1. Len Wein was the writer and Berni Wrightson, a disciple of both Frank Frazetta and Graham "Ghastly" Ingels, was the artist.

The folk belief in spontaneous generation, the notion that a living organism can form from nonliving matter, is many centuries old. It became a favorite of comic books from the 1940s onward, providing such Swamp Thing precursors as the Heap and Solomon Grundy and such contemporaries as Marvel's Man-Thing.

An earlier prototype had appeared in *House of Secrets* in the summer of 1971. Revamped, he became Swamp Thing and got his own book a year later. Never a major hit despite two movies and a television series, he has managed to hold on in comics. Wein and Wrightson concocted sentimental horror tales about a scientist who was transformed into a muck-encrusted horror after being doused by chemicals when his bayou lab was destroyed by criminals. Swamp Thing was a caring monster, and Wein's scripts worked at being touching, even philosophical, but the real attraction of the early issues was the spidery, vaguely disturbing Wrightson artwork.

Another series devoted to the forlorn bayou monster began in 1982 as *Saga of the Swamp Thing* and later became simply *Swamp Thing*. The team of Alan Moore and Steve Bissette, who worked on the newer version, earned the title considerable attention. That second series ended in 1996, and Swamp Thing returned under the Vertigo banner for twenty issues from 2000 to 2001. Mike Kaluta provided some of the drawing.

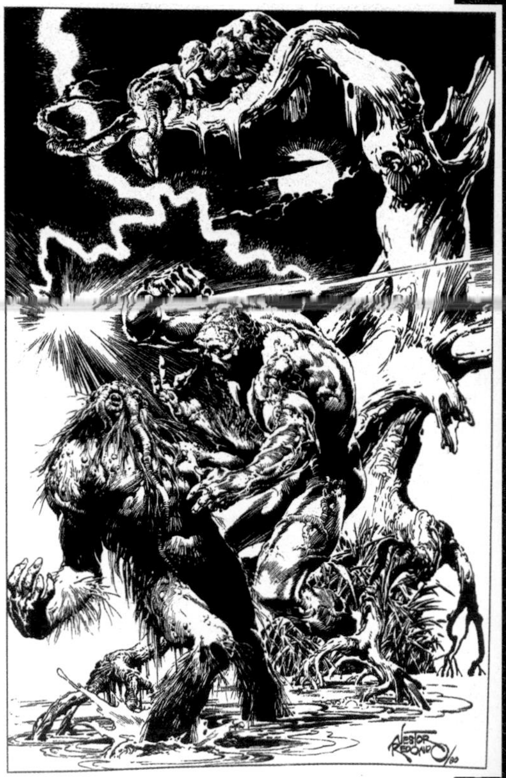

SWAN, CURT

(1920–1996)

■ To many longtime readers, Curt Swan is *the* artist on *Superman*. He drew the Man of Steel for close to forty years, developing a style that was attractive and seemed highly suitable for depicting the residents of Metropolis.

Curtis Douglas Swan studied art at the Pratt Institute and was a staff artist on *Stars & Stripes* during World War II. After the war, he signed on with DC and remained there from then on. His early work, on such features as *The Boy Commandos* and *Tommy Tomorrow*, was stiff and rather bland. Gradually, however, Swan developed an effective and forceful style. He first drew *Superman* in 1951, remaining with him until 1986. He returned in 1988 to draw him for three more years. He worked on other characters while with DC, but Superman remained his favorite.

In his final years personal problems curtailed his production in comics.

SWING SISSON

■ The only leader of a big band in forties comic books, Swing Sisson played in *Feature Comics* from #49 (October 1941) to #144 (May 1950). The original artist was Phil Martin, the original writer Robert Turner.

In addition to Swing, also known as "The Ace of the Bandstand," the featured performers were blonde vocalist Bonnie Baxter and sax player Toby Tucker. Since the band toured the country, Swing, Bonnie, and Toby were able to encounter racketeers, Japanese spies, bank robbers, and even a madman who was out to destroy "foul boogie-woogie and idiotic jitterbugging!!"

Artist Vernon Henkel took over the baton after Martin and was followed by a succession of lesser artists. In the postwar years, Swing and "his jive crew" became the house band at Manhattan's Clover Club, where they'd played their first gig back in 1941.

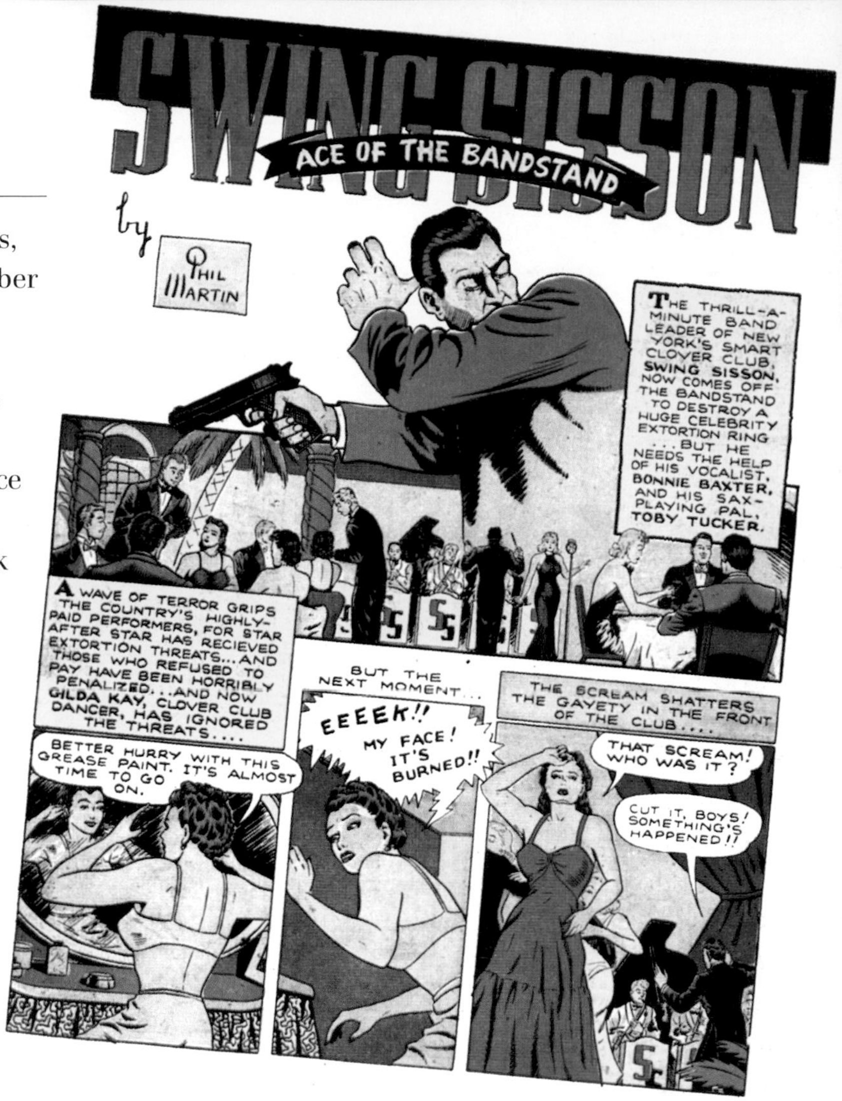
SWING SISSON
ACE OF THE BANDSTAND
by Phil Martin
THE THRILL-A-MINUTE BAND LEADER OF NEW YORK'S SMART CLOVER CLUB, SWING SISSON, NOW COMES OFF THE BANDSTAND TO DESTROY A HUGE CELEBRITY EXTORTION RING . . . BUT HE NEEDS THE HELP OF HIS VOCALIST, BONNIE BAXTER, AND HIS SAX-PLAYING PAL, TOBY TUCKER.
A WAVE OF TERROR GRIPS THE COUNTRY'S HIGHLY-PAID PERFORMERS, FOR STAR AFTER STAR HAS RECIEVED EXTORTION THREATS...AND THOSE WHO REFUSED TO PAY HAVE BEEN HORRIBLY PENALIZED...AND NOW GILDA KAY, CLOVER CLUB DANCER, HAS IGNORED THE THREATS....
BETTER HURRY WITH THIS GREASE PAINT. IT'S ALMOST TIME TO GO ON.
BUT THE NEXT MOMENT...
EEEEK!!
MY FACE! IT'S BURNED!!
THE SCREAM SHATTERS THE GAYETY IN THE FRONT OF THE CLUB....
THAT SCREAM! WHO WAS IT?
CUT IT, BOYS! SOMETHING'S HAPPENED!!

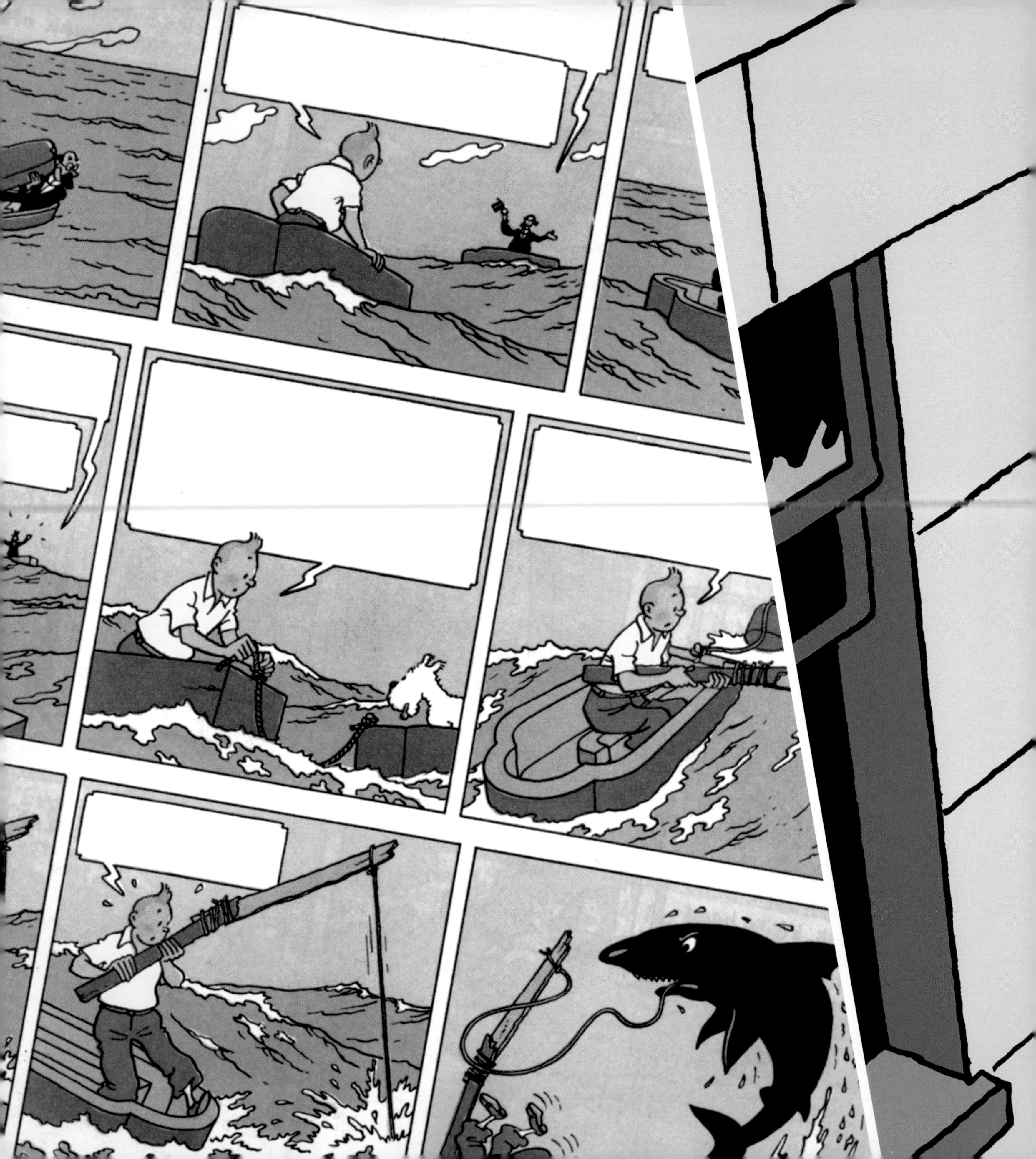

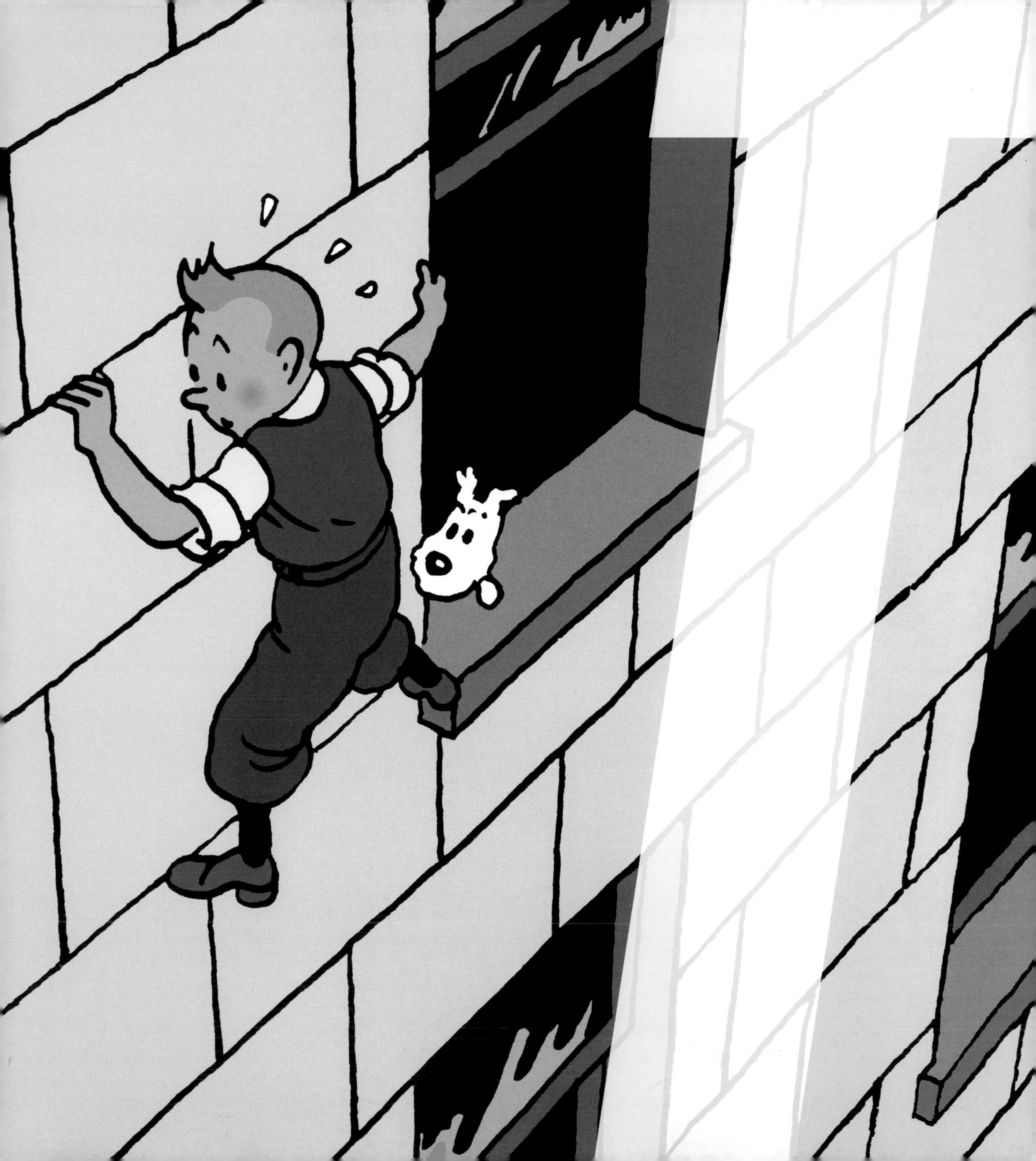

TALES OF SUSPENSE

■ Yet another anthology of fantasy and horror from Marvel, *Tales of Suspense* began late in 1959. For the first four years of its existence, the magazine showcased yet another batch of Stan Lee–Jack Kirby gigantic rampaging monsters. They included Kraa, Sporr, Goom, Googam, and the Green Thing. But then, early in 1963, the magazine presented not one more destructive demon but a brand-new superhero.

The thirty-ninth issue (March 1963) introduced "The Newest, Most Breath-Taking, Most Sensational Super Hero of All . . . IRON MAN!" The plot was credited to Lee, the script to Larry Lieber, and the art to Don Heck. After debuting in a thirteen-page original story, Iron Man pushed the monsters aside to become the star of *Tales of Suspense.* Other heroes who later showed up included Hawkeye and Captain America. From #59 (November 1964) onward, Cap and Iron Man appeared in separate stories each issue. With #100 (April 1968), the magazine became *Captain America.* Iron Man moved into a new title, *Iron Man and Sub-Mariner*, for one issue and then *Iron Man* #1 (May 1968) appeared.

Marvel reused the *Tales of Suspense* title for a one-shot in 1995.

TALES TO ASTONISH

■ Just one more Marvel bestiary when it arrived on newsstands at the end of 1958, by the summer of 1962 it was turning into another hangout for superheroes. The first thirty-some issues were dominated by assorted Stan Lee–Jack Kirby rampaging monsters, such as Titano, Droom, Mummex, the Blip, Vandoom, and Gorgilla (who struck twice). With #36 (October 1962) Ant-Man became a featured player, and with #49 (November 1963) he, possibly tired of being stepped on, turned himself into Giant Man. Less than a year later the Hulk moved into the magazine. Early in 1968 the title was changed to *The Incredible Hulk.*

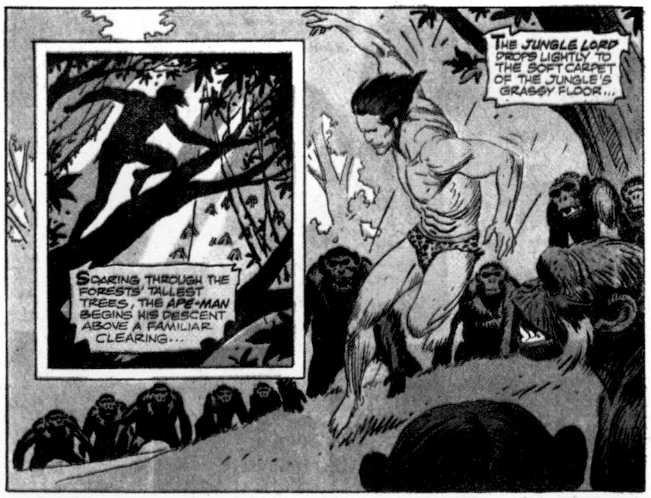
SOARING THROUGH THE FORESTS' TALLEST TREES, THE APE-MAN BEGINS HIS DESCENT ABOVE A FAMILIAR CLEARING...
THE JUNGLE LORD DROPS LIGHTLY TO THE SOFT CARPET OF THE JUNGLE'S GRASSY FLOOR...

TARZAN

■ The most famous jungle man in the world, he first swung through the trees way back in 1912 in the pages of *All-Story.* The pulp novel was by Edgar Rice Burroughs, who was fast approaching forty and had yet to settle on a profession. The success of the ape-man changed that, and from then on Burroughs was a writer of adventure yarns. When *Tarzan of the Apes* was published in hardcover in 1917, Burroughs had already written, among other things, four more Tarzan pulp novels.

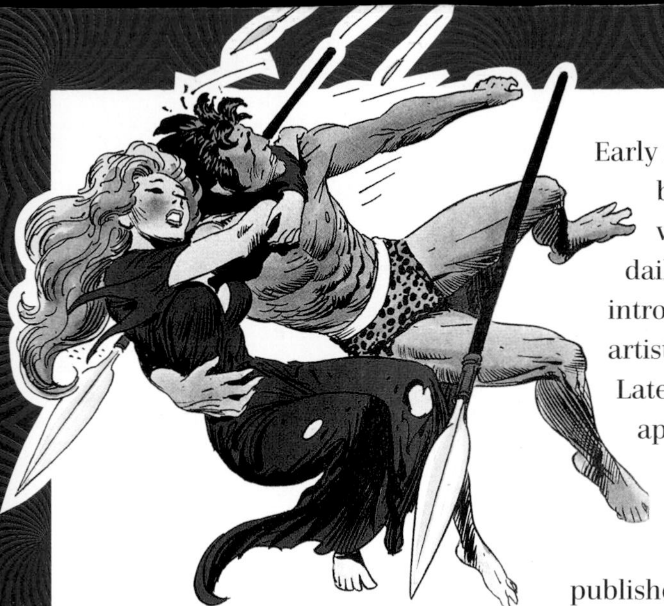

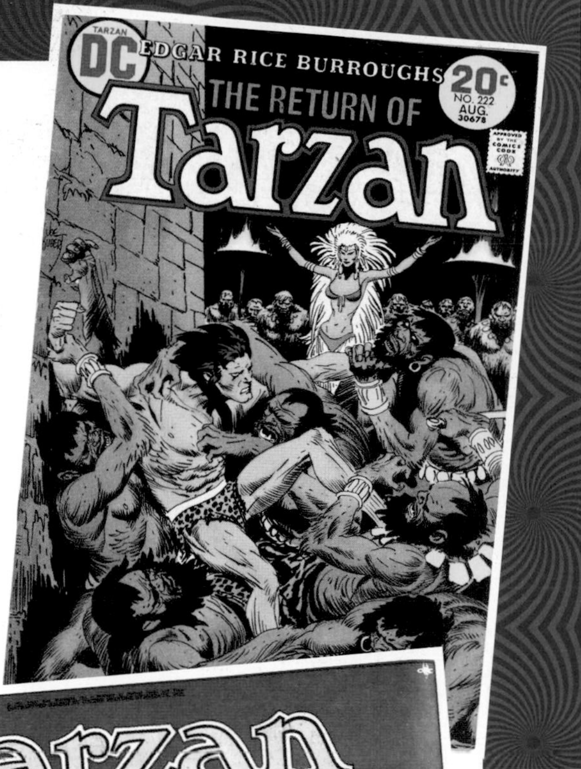
DC
EDGAR RICE BURROUGHS
THE RETURN OF
Tarzan
20¢
NO. 222
AUG.

Early in 1918, the first *Tarzan* movie, with barrel-chested Elmo Lincoln starring, was released. Finally, early in 1929 a daily *Tarzan* newspaper strip was introduced. Hal Foster, an advertising artist from Canada, did the drawing. Later that year Tarzan made his first appearance in a comic book, albeit a hardcover black-and-white comic book that reprinted the run of Foster dailies. In 1933 Whitman published a *Tarzan of the Apes* Big Little Book, again using the Hal Foster material. United Feature, which syndicated the newspaper strip and added the Sunday page by Foster in 1931, ventured into comic-book publishing in 1936. Their *Tip Top Comics* reprinted several Foster *Tarzan* Sunday pages, greatly reduced in size, each issue. Even reduced, Foster's work was impressive and influenced many a later comic artist. The colored *Tarzan* dailies ran in United's other monthly, *Comics on Parade*, launched in 1938. United also issued a complete *Tarzan* comic book in 1940. The next year the Sunday pages by Burne Hogarth were reprinted as part of United's new title, *Sparkler Comics*. In addition Dell had run Tarzan text stories in *Crackajack Funnies*, with spot drawings by such artists as Bill Ely. And in 1947 it was Dell that introduced an original-material comic book devoted to the jungle lord.

Dell's first book, *Tarzan and the Devil Ogre*, was written by Gaylord Dubois and drawn by Jesse Marsh. It appeared in 1947 and was followed a few months later by *Tarzan and the Fires of Tor*. In 1948 Dell began a regular bimonthly, with scripts by Dubois and the majority of the artwork by Marsh. Marsh, though an excellent artist, was an unconventional choice to illustrate the jungle man saga, since he worked in the lushly inked realistic style developed by Milton Caniff and Noel Sickles rather than the heroic, larger-than-life

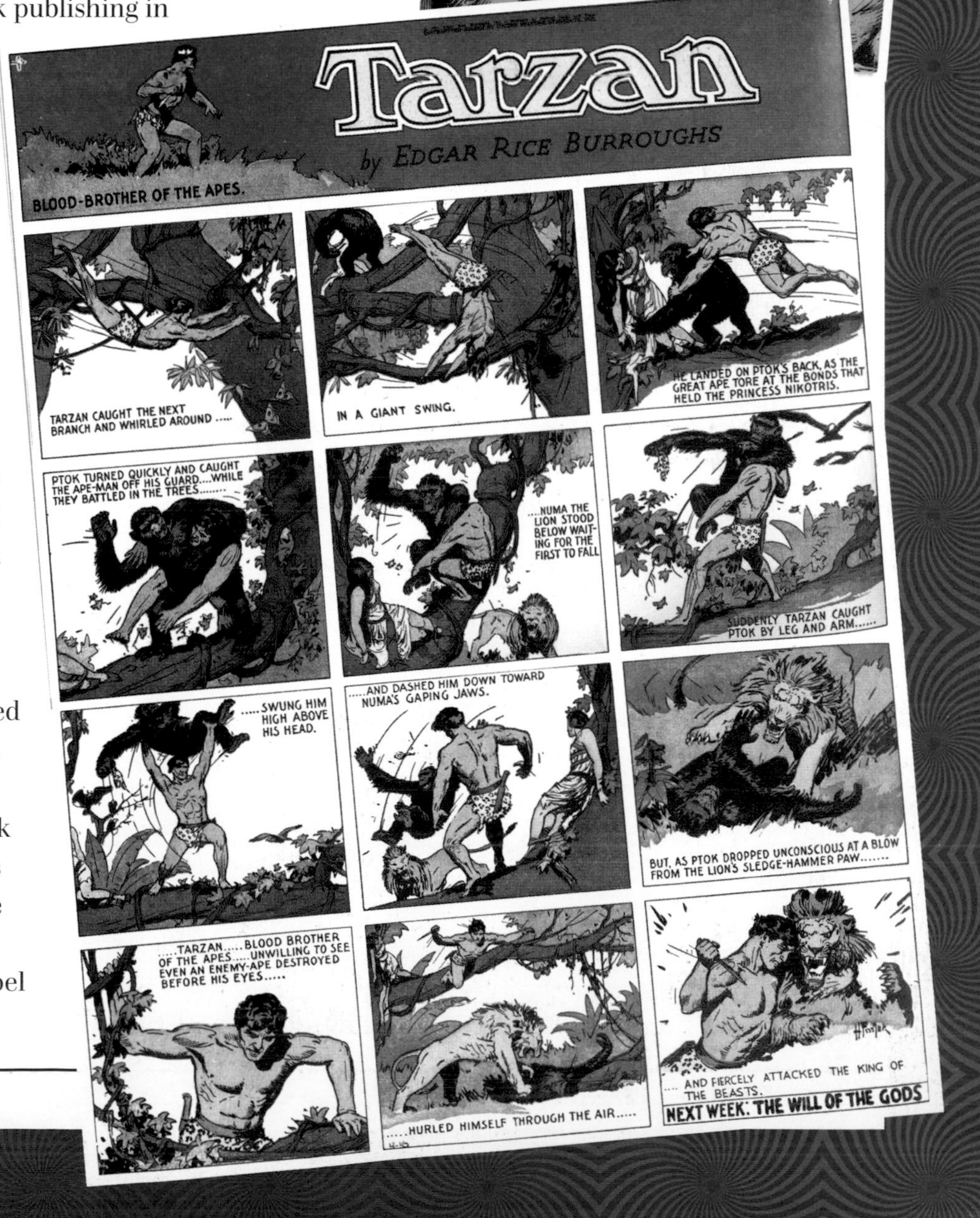
Tarzan
by EDGAR RICE BURROUGHS
BLOOD-BROTHER OF THE APES.
TARZAN CAUGHT THE NEXT BRANCH AND WHIRLED AROUND .....
IN A GIANT SWING.
HE LANDED ON PTOK'S BACK, AS THE GREAT APE TORE AT THE BONDS THAT HELD THE PRINCESS NIKOTRIS.
PTOK TURNED QUICKLY AND CAUGHT THE APE-MAN OFF HIS GUARD....WHILE THEY BATTLED IN THE TREES.......
...NUMA THE LION STOOD BELOW WAITING FOR THE FIRST TO FALL
SUDDENLY TARZAN CAUGHT PTOK BY LEG AND ARM......
.....SWUNG HIM HIGH ABOVE HIS HEAD.
.....AND DASHED HIM DOWN TOWARD NUMA'S GAPING JAWS.
BUT, AS PTOK DROPPED UNCONSCIOUS AT A BLOW FROM THE LION'S SLEDGE-HAMMER PAW.......
.....TARZAN.....BLOOD BROTHER OF THE APES.....UNWILLING TO SEE EVEN AN ENEMY-APE DESTROYED BEFORE HIS EYES.....
.....HURLED HIMSELF THROUGH THE AIR.....
... AND FIERCELY ATTACKED THE KING OF THE BEASTS.
NEXT WEEK: THE WILL OF THE GODS

manner used by the likes of Hogarth. Comic-book readers accepted him, however, and he remained with the project for more than 150 issues.

The Dell/Gold Key *Tarzan* continued until 1972. Dubois remained the chief scriptwriter. Among the other artists were Doug Wildey, Paul Norris, and Russ Manning. In 1972 DC licensed the property from Edgar Rice Burroughs, Inc., and brought out its comic-book version. Getting back to basics, their first issues featured an adaptation of *Tarzan of the Apes*. Joe Kubert, who also edited, did much of the early drawing. By late 1976, DC had given up and next Marvel took a turn. Its first issue of *Tarzan, Lord of the Jungle* had a cover date of June 1977. John Buscema, working in the Marvel house style, was the first artist. Marvel called it quits after only two years, but did return

to the jungle in 1984 with a two-issue adaptation of the latest *Tarzan of the Apes* movie. In the early 1990s Malibu Comics took a crack at a *Tarzan* comic book. In the later 1990s Dark Horse published several *Tarzan* miniseries, once even teaming him up with Predator. And in 2001 they teamed him up with Superman.

Tarzan's son made his earliest appearance in comic books in 1940, when *Comics on Parade* began serializing the newspaper-strip adaptation of Burroughs's *The Son of Tarzan*. Nearly two and a half decades later, Dell got around to publishing a *Korak, Son of Tarzan* comic book. Art was by Manning and Warren Tufts. That was published between 1964 and 1972. DC took over the title but stuck with it for only fourteen issues. Kubert provided all the covers, and Frank Thorne was the first artist.

TEEN-AGE DOPE SLAVES

■ A provocative title and cover, with an overline promising "Shocking Dope Exposé," front this 1952 comic-book reprint of a fairly polite public service sequence from the widely syndicated *Rex Morgan, M.D.* newspaper strip.

While the inventive packaging provided by Harvey Publications may not have aided sales, it did attract the attention of anti-comics crusaders, notably Dr. Fredric Wertham, who said in his *Seduction of the Innocent*, "When adolescent drug addiction had finally come to public attention, it led to publication of lurid new comic books devoted to the subject, like the one with the title, *Teen-Age Dope Slaves*. This is nothing but another variety of crime comic of a particularly deplorable character."

Clearly the crusading psychiatrist had judged the book by its cover. Nor had he apparently noticed the back cover with its message from Dr. Morgan headlined "WARNING! Dope Leads to Death!" Hardly a deplorable stand on the subject.

Earlier this sequence—written by psychiatrist Nicholas Dallis, drawn by Marvin Bradley and Frank Edginton, and dealing with the decline and then rehabilitation of a young addict—had run in hundreds of newspapers across the country without arousing much in the way of complaints. Over the years, however, because of the notoriety of *Teen-Age Dope Slaves*, collectors have paid ten to twenty times more for it than for any other *Rex Morgan, M.D.* reprint.

TEEN TITANS

■ They've been around so long that they probably should be called Middle-Aged Titans. They were introduced by DC in 1964. Originally Robin, Kid Flash, and Aqualad, three teen sidekicks of grown-up heroes, made up the first group. The membership changed and expanded over the years. In the 1980s, as the New Teen Titans, they became one of the most popular groups in comics. Writer Bob Haney and artist Bruno Premiani were responsible for the original team, Marv Wolfman and George Perez for the new, improved bunch.

When the trio of sidekicks first teamed up in *The Brave and the Bold* #54 (June–July 1964), they didn't have a group name. They got together to help some small-town teenagers who'd run afoul of a supervillain named Mr. Twister while trying to get the stodgy town adults to build them a clubhouse. The heroic trio returned in *B&B* a year later as the Teen Titans, with Wonder Girl added. After an appearance in *Showcase*, the group was promoted to a book of its own. Haney continued as scripter, but the excellent Nick Cardy took over as artist, providing striking interior art and a series of first-rate covers.

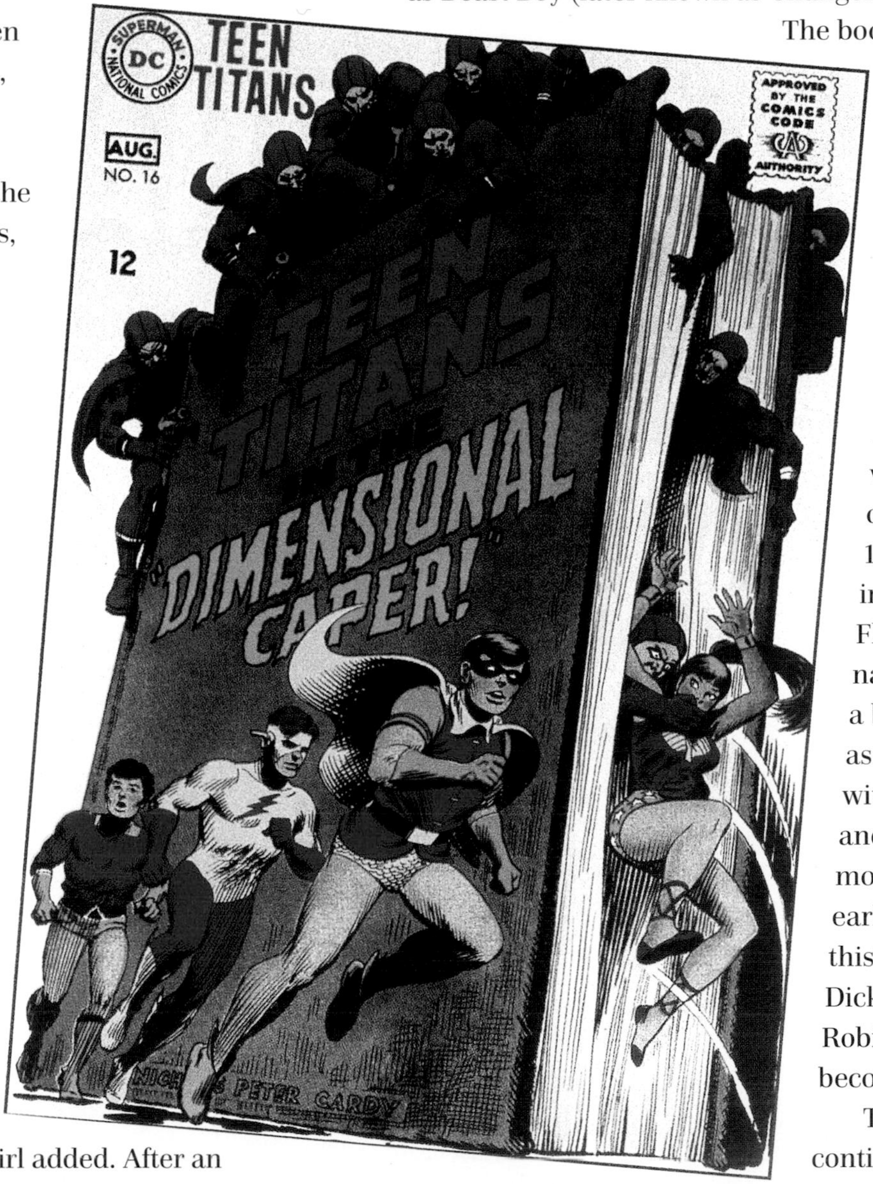

SUPERMAN DC NATIONAL COMICS
TEEN TITANS
APPROVED BY THE COMICS CODE AUTHORITY
AUG. NO. 16
12
TEEN TITANS
DIMENSIONAL CAPER!

The membership fluctuated, with Green Arrow's Speedy joining in some issues and new characters such as Beast Boy (later known as Changeling) being added. The book halted with the forty-third issue in 1973, then returned for another ten issues from 1976 to 1978.

The New Teen Titans were introduced in *DC Presents* #26 and were given their own title late in 1980. The new group included Robin, Kid Flash, an alien girl named Starfire, and a black youth known as Cyborg. This title, with Wolfman scripts and Perez art, proved more popular than the earlier ones. It was in this book in 1984 that Dick Grayson shed his Robin identity to become Nightwing.

The magazine continued until early in 1984. Late in 1988, it changed its name to simply *The New Titans*. In later incarnations it has been called *Team Titans*, *The Titans*, and *Teen Titans*.

THOR

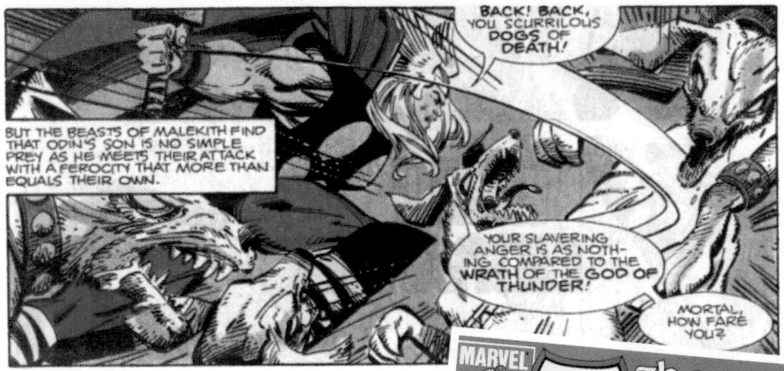
BUT THE BEASTS OF MALEKITH FIND THAT ODIN'S SON IS NO SIMPLE PREY AS HE MEETS THEIR ATTACK WITH A FEROCITY THAT MORE THAN EQUALS THEIR OWN.
BACK! BACK, YOU SCURRILOUS DOGS OF DEATH!
YOUR SLAVERING ANGER IS AS NOTHING COMPARED TO THE WRATH OF THE GOD OF THUNDER!
MORTAL, HOW FARE YOU?

■ Long fascinated by Norse mythology, Jack Kirby returned to it in 1962 when he and Stan Lee got together to invent yet another Marvel superhero. The helmeted and golden-haired Thor was introduced in *Journey into Mystery* #83 (August 1962). Lee's brother Larry Lieber wrote the scripts. Thor soon won a following and dominated the magazine. Early in 1966, with the 126th issue, the magazine changed its name to *Thor*.

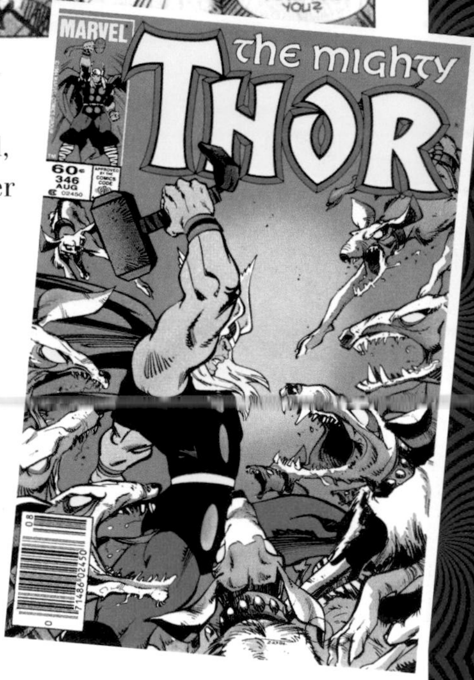
MARVEL
the mighty THOR
60¢
346
AUG

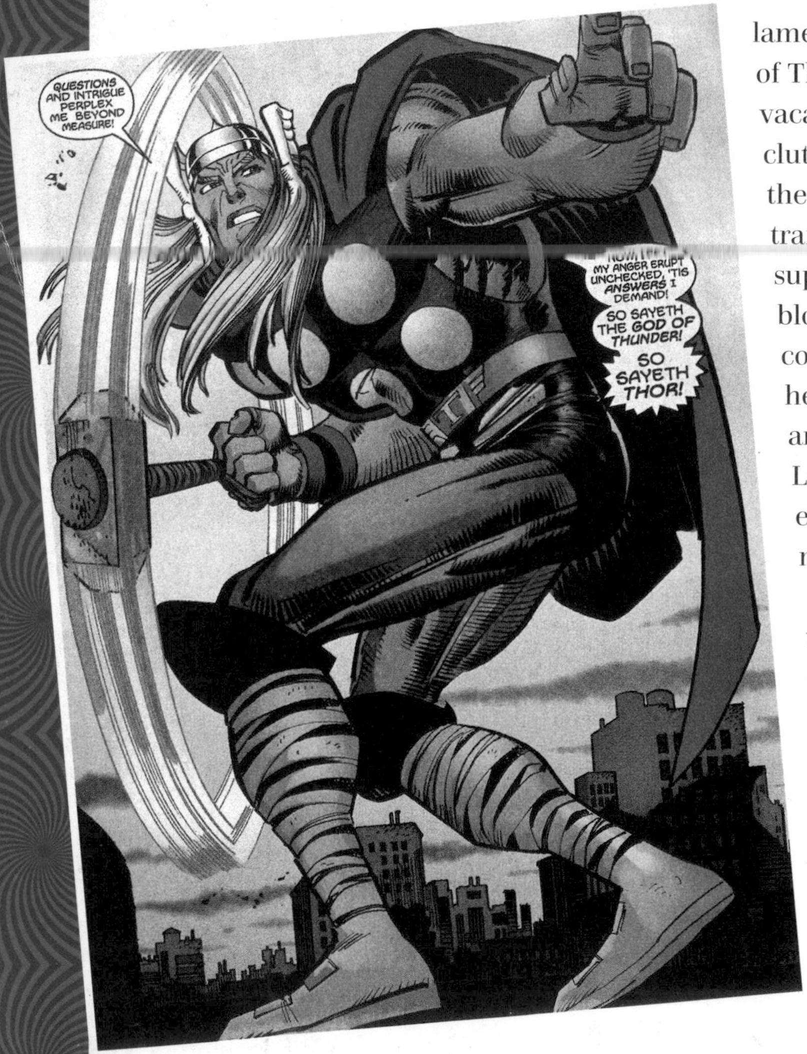
QUESTIONS AND INTRIGUE PERPLEX ME BEYOND MEASURE!
MY ANGER ERUPT UNCHECKED, 'TIS ANSWERS I DEMAND!
SO SAYETH THE GOD OF THUNDER!
SO SAYETH THOR!

The first adventure told how frail, lame Dr. Don Blake found the hammer of Thor in a secret cave while vacationing in Norway. As soon as he clutched the legendary implement, the spindly doctor was miraculously transformed into a muscular superman with shoulder-length blond hair and a form-fitting Norse costume, complete with winged helmet. In subsequent stories the amount of mythology increased. Lee, who'd taken over the writing early on, added Thor's traditional nemesis, Loki, and also tossed in Balder and Odin.

Lee has said that when he started scripting, "Thor became the first regularly published superhero to speak in a consistently archaic manner. Call it Biblical style—call it neo-Shakespearean." Kirby departed the feature in 1970, and Lee stopped writing in 1972. Roy Thomas and John Buscema carried on for some time. Then Walt Simonson took over the writing and the editing. *Thor* #337 (November 1983), the first written and drawn by Simonson, sold out in comic shops. Simonson remained with the character until the summer of 1987, and Thor has continued, though with diminished popularity, under the hands of various writers and artists.

THRILLING COMICS

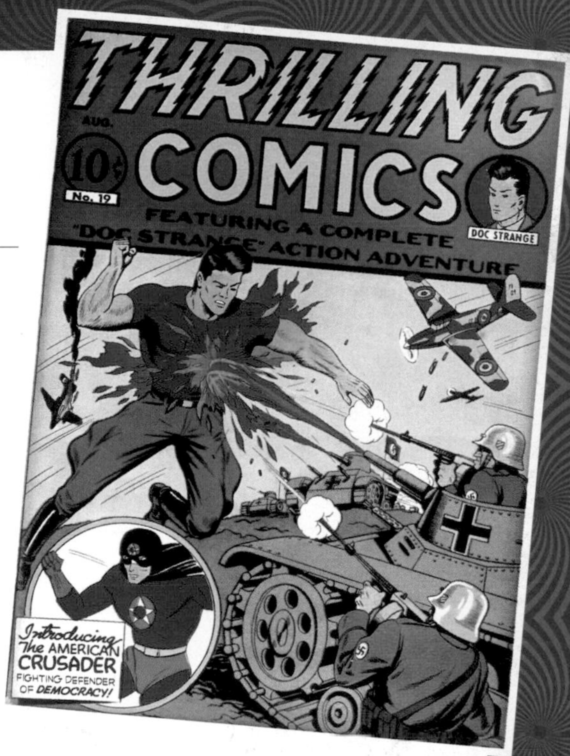
THRILLING COMICS
AUG.
10¢
No. 19
FEATURING A COMPLETE "DOC STRANGE" ACTION ADVENTURE
DOC STRANGE
Introducing The AMERICAN CRUSADER
FIGHTING DEFENDER OF DEMOCRACY!

■ It was inevitable that the man who published such pulp-fiction magazines as *Thrilling Wonder Stories*, *Thrilling Detective*, *Thrilling Love*, and *Thrilling Adventure* would eventually publish *Thrilling Comics*. And that's exactly what Ned Pines did at the end of 1939. The magazine introduced Doc Strange and the Woman in Red as well as adaptations of such pulp heroes as the Rio Kid and the Lone Eagle.

Later on came the Ghost and the American Crusaders. During the years of World War II most of the artwork was mediocre, except for the handsome covers by Alex Schomburg and interior stories by Bob Oksner and the eccentric Max Plaisted. In the postwar period the looks of *Thrilling* improved, with such artists as Frank Frazetta, Edmond Good, Artie Saaf, and John Celardo contributing. The magazine ended with its eightieth issue in 1951.

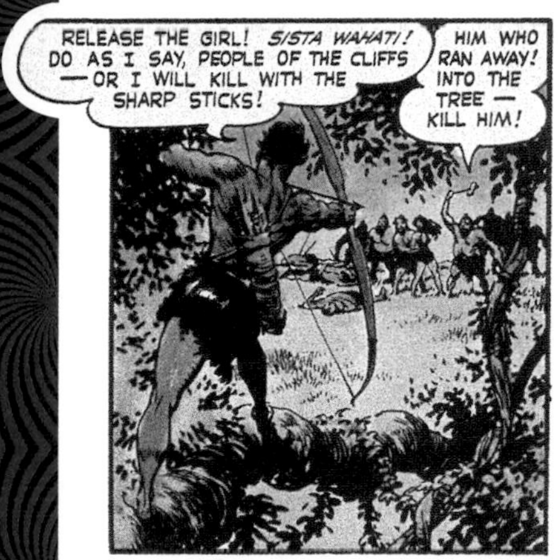
RELEASE THE GIRL! SISTA WAHATI! DO AS I SAY, PEOPLE OF THE CLIFFS — OR I WILL KILL WITH THE SHARP STICKS!
HIM WHO RAN AWAY! INTO THE TREE — KILL HIM!

THUN'DA

■ A late arrival among jungle men, he didn't reach the newsstands until 1952, well over a decade after Kaanga, Ka-Zar, and sundry other Tarzan impersonators. The first issue of *Thun'da*, drawn by Frank Frazetta, is an impressive homage to his idol Hal Foster. Bob Powell drew Thun'da in the remaining five issues of the ME title. The ubiquitous Gardner Fox scripted all six.

TIGER GIRL

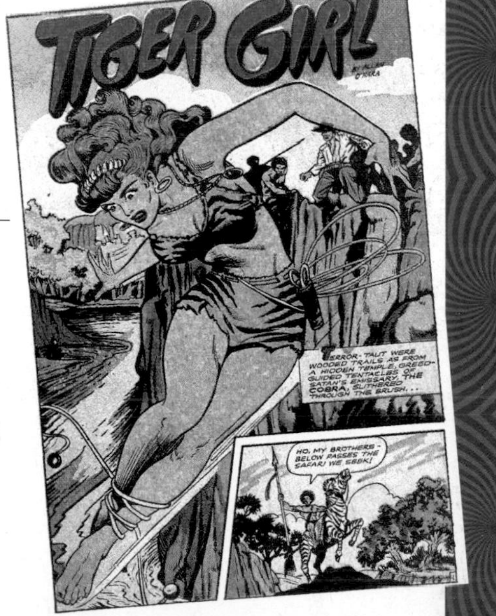
TIGER GIRL
TERROR-TAUT WERE WOODED TRAILS AS FROM A HIDDEN TEMPLE, GREED-GUIDED TENTACLES OF SATAN'S EMISSARY, THE COBRA, SLITHERED THROUGH THE BRUSH...
HO, MY BROTHERS - BELOW PASSES THE SAFARI WE SEEK!

■ Another product of the Iger shop and another rival to Sheena, she was introduced in *Fight Comics* #32 (June 1944). The formidable Matt Baker was the artist. Tiger Girl reigned in *Fight* until 1952.

She became the cover girl from #49 (April 1947), appearing thereafter on every *Fight* cover until #81 (July 1952). Like Sheena, she was rarely seen in jeopardy. Instead, wielding knife, spear, bow, or club, Tiger Girl was depicted battling slave traders, gorillas, lions, or evil hunters. She was usually accompanied by a tiger, who didn't seem to mind the fact that she wore a tiger-skin bikini. Unlike many another jungle girl, her base of operations was India and not Africa.

TINTIN

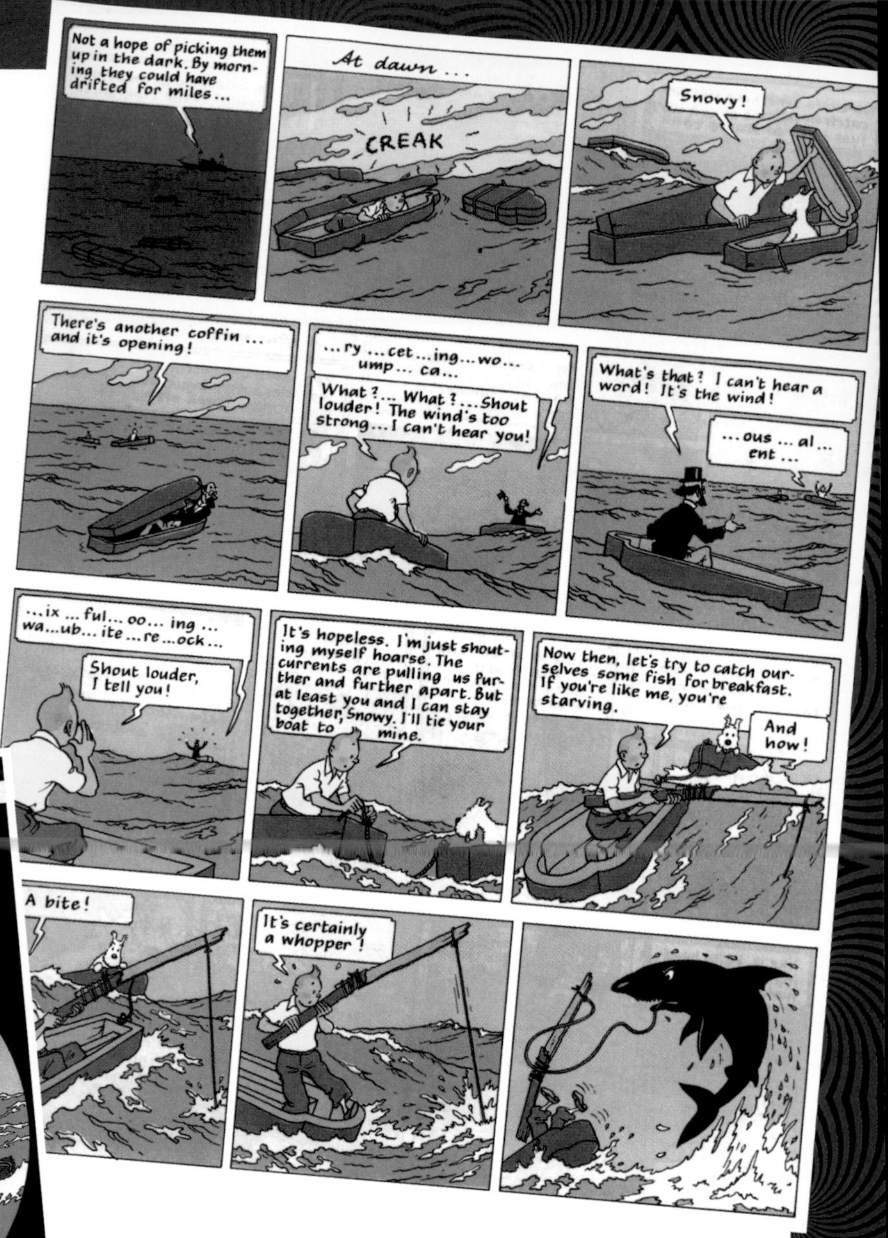

Not a hope of picking them up in the dark. By morning they could have drifted for miles...
At dawn...
CREAK
Snowy!
There's another coffin ... and it's opening!
...ry ...cet...ing...wo... ump... ca...
What?... What?... Shout louder! The wind's too strong... I can't hear you!
What's that? I can't hear a word! It's the wind!
...ous ... al... ent ...
...ix ... ful... oo... ing ... wa...ub... ite ... re ...ock...
Shout louder, I tell you!
It's hopeless. I'm just shouting myself hoarse. The currents are pulling us further and further apart. But at least you and I can stay together, Snowy. I'll tie your boat to mine.
Now then, let's try to catch ourselves some fish for breakfast. If you're like me, you're starving.
And how!
A bite!
It's certainly a whopper!

■ An international comic-book favorite, Tintin's adventures have appeared in nearly forty languages around the world. He was created in 1929 by Georges Remi (1907–1983), who used the pen name Herge. The blond boy reporter/adventurer was first seen in a weekly kids' supplement to a Belgian Catholic newspaper called *Le Vingtieme Siecle*. The adventures of Tintin and his loyal fox terrier Snowy (Milou in French) ran as black-and-white comic strips initially. His first reporting job took him to the Soviet Union; next he journeyed to the Belgian Congo. By the early 1930s, the stories were being collected and reprinted in a series of albums. Other early adventures included *Tintin in America*, *The Blue Lotus*, *The Black Island*, and *King Ottokar's Sceptre*.

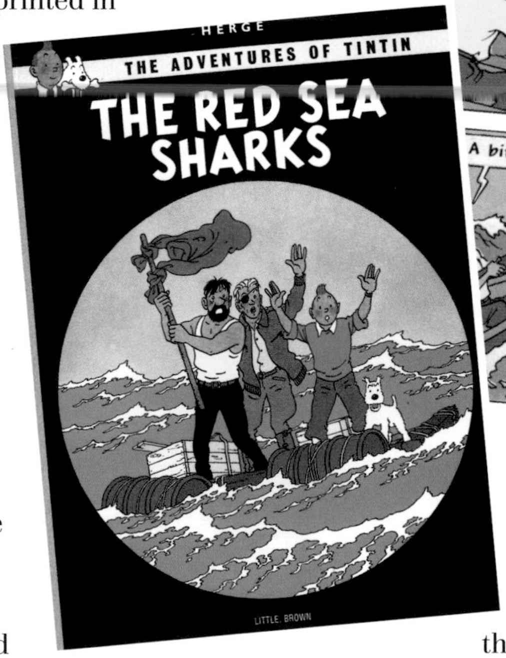

HERGE
THE ADVENTURES OF TINTIN
THE RED SEA SHARKS
LITTLE, BROWN

Herge's yarns were an appealing blend of boys' adventure elements, comedy, and some quiet satire. They were drawn in a simple, direct cartoon style. In addition to the boy and his dog, the recurring regulars included Thompson and Thomson, nearly identical mustached detectives whose chief accomplishment was bumbling; Captain Haddock, a hard-drinking seadog who served an avuncular function; and Professor Calculus, an aggressively absentminded inventor.

In the middle 1940s, Herge and the members of his staff started redrawing and revising the earlier albums. The artwork improved and color was added. A weekly *Tintin* magazine, originating in Belgium, began in 1946 and the new adventures first appeared there in short installments. Herge's most accomplished assistant/ghost was Bob DeMoor.

The final graphic novel, *Tintin and the Picaros*, appeared in the late 1970s. There have also been *Tintin* movies and several animated TV series. Despite the many millions of *Tintin* books sold worldwide, the character has never been as popular in the United States as elsewhere. Nevertheless, various American publishers continue to give him a try.

TIP TOP COMICS

■ In 1936 several publishers decided to follow in the wake of *Famous Funnies*. Dell began reprinting newspaper strips in *Popular Comics*, David McKay Publications (in collaboration with Hearst's King Features Syndicate) did the same with *King Comics*, and the United Feature Syndicate started *Tip Top Comics* to reprint most of the strips on its roster. Included in #1 (April 1936) were recycled Sunday pages of *Tarzan*, *Li'l Abner*, *Ella Cinders*, *The Captain and the Kids*, *Fritzi Ritz*, and over a dozen others. The new comic book brought the work of such artists as Hal Foster, Al Capp, and Ernie Bushmiller to a newsstand audience. Lev Gleason, who'd worked for the publishers of *Famous Funnies*, was the editor.

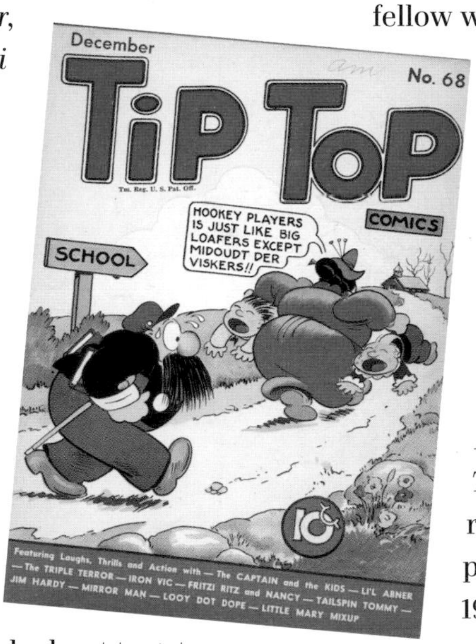
December
No. 68
Tip Top
COMICS
HOOKEY PLAYERS IS JUST LIKE BIG LOAFERS EXCEPT MIDOUDT DER VISKERS!!
SCHOOL
10¢
Featuring Laughs, Thrills and Action with — The CAPTAIN and the KIDS — LI'L ABNER — The TRIPLE TERROR — IRON VIC — FRITZI RITZ and NANCY — TAILSPIN TOMMY — JIM HARDY — MIRROR MAN — LOOY DOT DOPE — LITTLE MARY MIXUP

In addition to comics and adventuresome three-page fiction yarns by Lt. Fred Methot, there was also the *Tip Top Cartoon Club*. Budding cartoonists could submit comic strips of their own or their solutions to the Buffalo Bob Problem. Each month there was a one-panel drawing showing Bob about to get into trouble. Young artists had to draw their solutions. Each issue the five winning solutions were printed along with four amateur comic strips—"Each winner will receive the prize of one dollar." Among the youths who won a buck were Mort Walker, Jack Davis, Harvey Kurtzman, Dan Heilman, Sam Glanzman, and Warren Tufts. Tufts grew up to draw *Casey Ruggles*, a historical Western strip that he sold to United Feature. The Cartoon Club was disbanded after *Tip Top* #48 (April 1940).

A few months later, possibly concerned by the increasing popularity of superheroes, *Tip Top* made room for more original material and added a bunch of them—three in one feature. *The Triple Terror*, written by Lt. Methot and drawn by Reg Greenwood, dealt with the Brandon triplets who, in costume, became Menta the master of hypnosis, Lectra the wizard of electricity, and Chemex the chemical genius. "Fighting for humanity, the Triple Terror is invincible." Added that same month was *Mirror Man*. Also written by Methot and drawn, from the fourth appearance on, by Greenwood, it dealt with a fellow who picked up the ability to become invisible while visiting Tibet. All he had to do to switch back and forth was walk through a mirror.

Mirror Man remained in the magazine until the summer of 1944, and the Triple Terror managed to hang on until the spring of 1946. Eventually *Tip Top Comics* returned to its original format of reprints only. In addition to *Nancy*, *Curly Kayoe*, *Abbie an' Slats*, and *The Captain and the Kids*, later issues also reprinted *Peanuts*. St. John took over publication in the middle 1950s. Late in 1957, Dell was issuing *Tip Top*. This final version featured original episodes of *Nancy*, *The Captain and the Kids*, and *Peanuts*, drawn by John Stanley, Pete Wells, and such Charles Schulz assistants as Frank Hill. Although *Tip Top Comics* left the newsstands in 1961, United still uses the title on the weekly set of syndicate proofs it sends out.

Comics on Parade, a companion monthly, was introduced in the spring of 1938 by United to feature the daily strips, colored for the occasion, featuring most of the characters in *Tip Top*. From the thirtieth issue *Comics on Parade* converted to entire issues devoted to one feature. *Li'l Abner*, *The Captain and the Kids*, and *Nancy* alternated issues, and eventually little Nancy, accompanied by her Aunt Fritzi and Sluggo, took over the title.

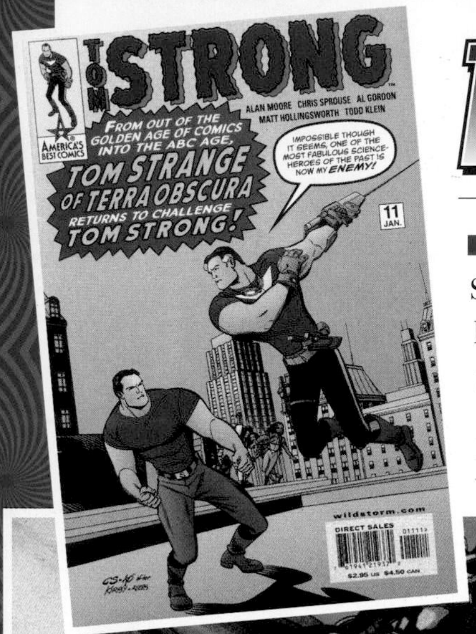
TOM STRONG
ALAN MOORE CHRIS SPROUSE AL GORDON MATT HOLLINGSWORTH TODD KLEIN
FROM OUT OF THE GOLDEN AGE OF COMICS INTO THE ABC AGE,
TOM STRANGE OF TERRA OBSCURA RETURNS TO CHALLENGE TOM STRONG!
IMPOSSIBLE THOUGH IT SEEMS, ONE OF THE MOST FABULOUS SCIENCE-HEROES OF THE PAST IS NOW MY ENEMY!
11 JAN.

TOM STRONG

■ A retro superhero, Tom Strong is a sort of homage by writer Alan Moore and artist Chris Sprouse to the kinder, gentler—relatively speaking—heroes of 1940s comic books. He made his debut in 1999, when the first issue of *Tom Strong* was released. By this time Moore had mellowed some from the days when he was scripting *Swamp Thing.*

Moore has said he was also looking back to the adventure fiction and pulp tradition—"characters like Doc Savage and so on"—for his inspiration. "What I was to do was take the most appealing elements of these things, and try to squeeze them all together into some archetypal figure that would almost become the way the superheroes could've gone if Superman and all the traditions and clichés that he brought with him hadn't come out."

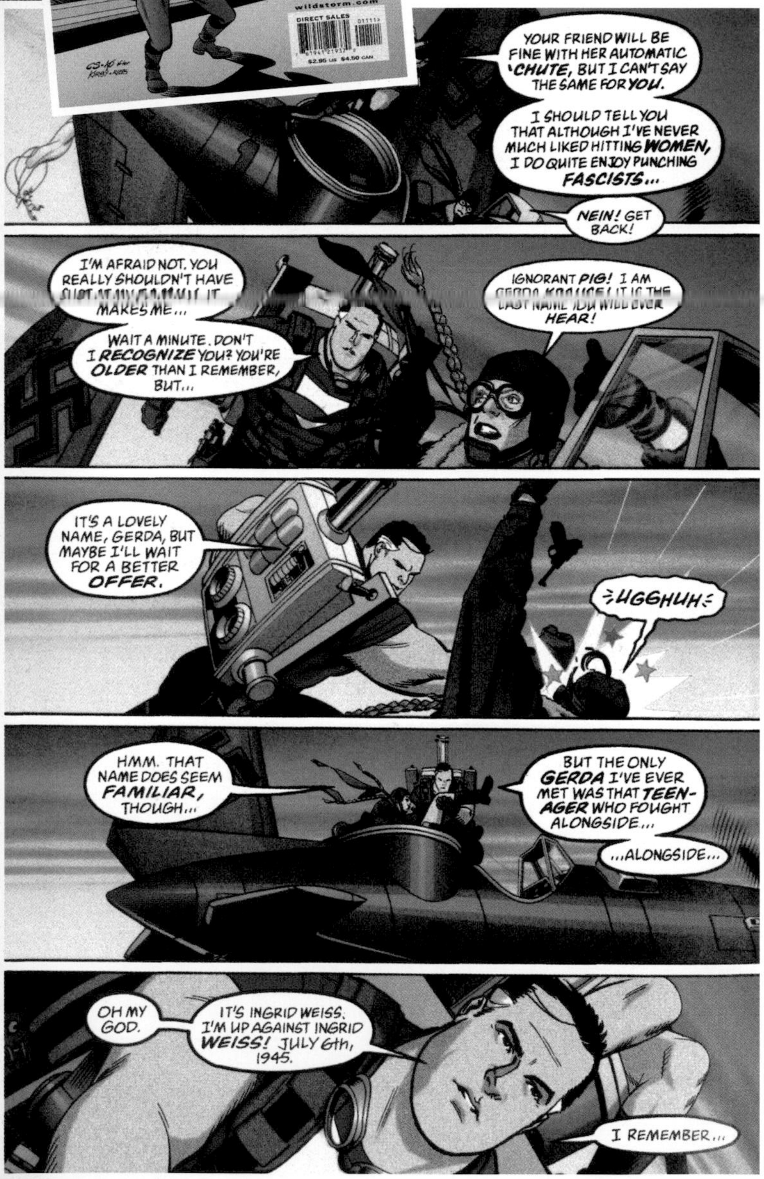
YOUR FRIEND WILL BE FINE WITH HER AUTOMATIC 'CHUTE, BUT I CAN'T SAY THE SAME FOR YOU.
I SHOULD TELL YOU THAT ALTHOUGH I'VE NEVER MUCH LIKED HITTING WOMEN, I DO QUITE ENJOY PUNCHING FASCISTS...
NEIN! GET BACK!
I'M AFRAID NOT. YOU REALLY SHOULDN'T HAVE
MAKES ME...
IGNORANT PIG! I AM
HEAR!
WAIT A MINUTE. DON'T I RECOGNIZE YOU? YOU'RE OLDER THAN I REMEMBER, BUT...
IT'S A LOVELY NAME, GERDA, BUT MAYBE I'LL WAIT FOR A BETTER OFFER.
UGGHUH
HMM. THAT NAME DOES SEEM FAMILIAR, THOUGH...
BUT THE ONLY GERDA I'VE EVER MET WAS THAT TEEN-AGER WHO FOUGHT ALONGSIDE...
...ALONGSIDE...
OH MY GOD.
IT'S INGRID WEISS. I'M UP AGAINST INGRID WEISS! JULY 6th, 1945.
I REMEMBER...

Strong is a large, muscular fellow, but not in the steroid-enhanced fashion of many contemporary supermen. His costume consists of a red T-shirt, black trousers with a gold stripe down the side, and boots. His hair is graying at the temples, possibly because he is over one hundred years old. His outfit resembles that of the original Doc Strange, who appeared in *Thrilling Comics* during the Golden Age. Moore has commented on the fact in his scripts. Strong's intelligence and longevity, readers are told, have been enhanced by the ingestion of the rare golonka root. The stories take place in an alternate world where things haven't gone exactly as they did in the world Moore inhabits.

Most of Tom Strong's adventures have been handsomely illustrated by Chris Sprouse, a sometime DC artist, invited by Moore to draw *Tom Strong.* "Alan asked me what I enjoyed drawing," he has said. "I told him I loved drawing gadgets and machinery (planes, spaceships, etc.), and Tom became a much more gadget-happy guy than he was in the original proposal." Strong's circle includes his wife, Dahlia, his daughter, Tesla, a robot named Pneuman, and an articulate and snappily dressed gorilla known as King Solomon. Both Arthur Adams and Jerry Ordway have also drawn some of Tom's adventures.

TORCHY

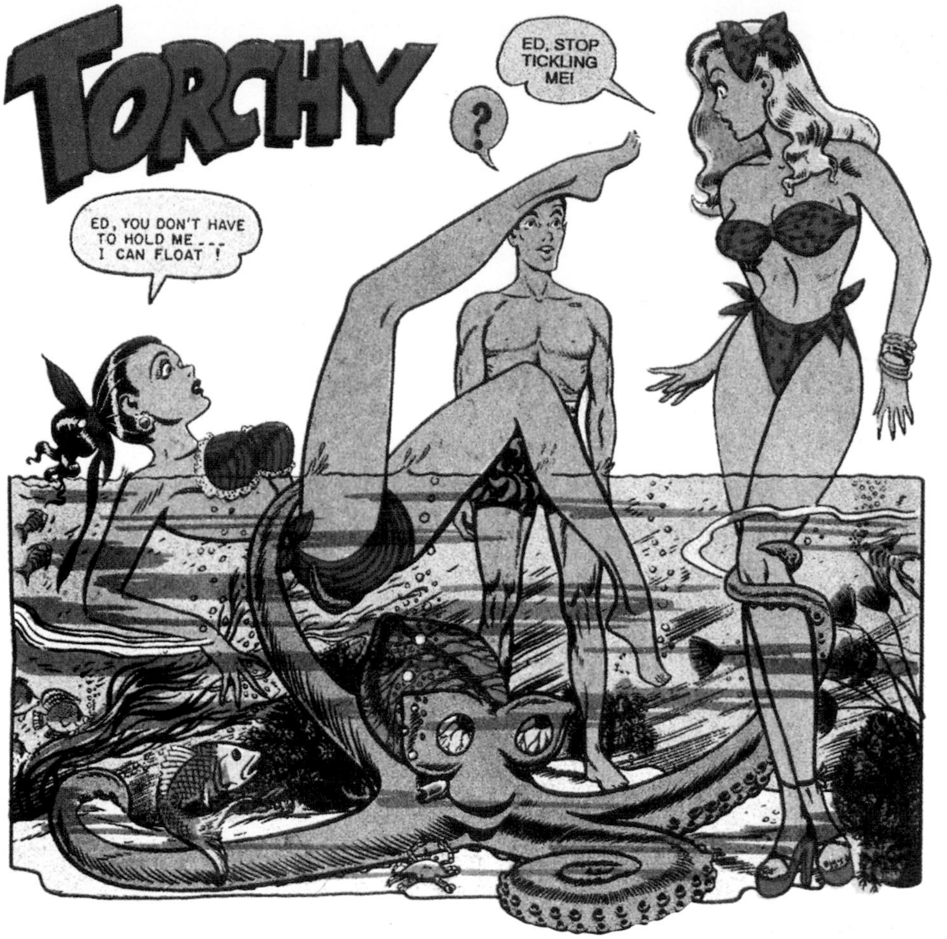
TORCHY
ED, STOP TICKLING ME!
?
ED, YOU DON'T HAVE TO HOLD ME... I CAN FLOAT!

■ Whereas most of the pretty girl comedy characters who started showing up in comic books after World War II were to be found in magazines devoted to humor, Torchy made her debut in a serious superhero comic. She then popped up in the same book that housed the serious paramilitary Blackhawk. Torchy, a "tall, whistle-provoking blonde" who was frequently to be seen wearing nothing more than frilly black lingerie, moved into *Modern Comics* in the summer of 1946. Formerly *Military Comics*, the magazine was still the home of Blackhawk and his gang. Torchy, created by cartoonist Bill Ward, remained in *Modern* until its final issue in 1950 and appeared in *Doll Man*, where she was first seen, from the spring of 1946 to the fall of 1953. She also soloed in six issues of her own title.

Ward, a graduate of both the Pratt Institute and the Jack Binder art shop, had drawn *Blackhawk* before entering the service. When he returned, he again drew the uniformed hero in the *Blackhawk* comic book. For *Modern*, however, he turned out *Torchy*, based on a comic strip he'd drawn for camp newspapers during the war. The six-page stories that ran in *Doll Man* and *Modern* somewhat resembled storyboards for a sexy sitcom. Torchy and her girlfriend would become involved with the likes of gangsters, ghosts, and eccentric millionaires. While the plot unfolded, there would arise several opportunities for Torchy to appear in her underwear, in a negligee, or with the tops of stockings showing. Like many cheesecake models of the era, she favored black spike-heel shoes.

The bimonthly *Torchy* magazine began late in 1949. Ward contributed the covers for two of the issues and drew one of the three stories in the fifth. The publisher, Everett "Busy" Arnold of Quality, assigned Ward to the nascent line of romance comics, and all the rest of the Torchy work was handled by his capable colleague Gill Fox.

TOTH, ALEX

(1928-)

■ A gifted and creative artist who has yet to get into a stylistic rut, Toth broke into comic books in 1947. Among the many features he's drawn in his long and varied career are *The Green Lantern, Rip Hunter: Time Master, Batman, The Black Canary, Zorro, Bravo for Adventure,* and *Torpedo 1936.* Toth was also a frequent contributor to such Warren black-and-white comics as *Eerie* and *Creepy.* Active in animation as well, he worked on such TV cartoon shows as *Space Angel, Space Ghost,* and *Super Friends.* In addition, he appeared regularly in *CARtoons, Drag Cartoons,* and *Hot Rod Cartoons.*

the Crushed
GARDENIA
ALEXANDER TOTH

Born in New York City, Toth sold his first work to *Heroic Comics* in 1947. Moving from nonfiction to superhero fantasy, he went to work for editor Sheldon Mayer at the All-American branch of DC. He became the regular artist on *The Green Lantern* and also drew *Dr. Mid-Nite* and *The Atom.* When *GL* was phased out of *All-American Comics,* Toth illustrated the Wild West adventures of his successor, Johnny Thunder. At this point in his development, he was somewhat under the influence of such comic-strip artists as Milton Caniff, Noel Sickles, and Frank Robbins.

Gradually, he developed a simpler, more forceful style of his own. After he moved to California to ghost Warren Tufts's *Casey Ruggles* newspaper strip, Toth signed on with Dell-Western and that led to *Zorro* as well as comic-book adaptations of other television series like *77 Sunset Strip* and *Sea Hunt* and movies like *Rio Bravo.* He did his earliest animation stint in the early 1960s, working for Clark Haas's Cambria outfit on *Space Angel.*

OBEYING ORDERS, PETE ACCELERATES THE HEAVY TOURING CAR TO HIGHER, MORE DANGEROUS SPEEDS!
70
80
90
100
MINUTES OF HARD, FAST DRIVING PASS...!
SUDDENLY...!
PETE...! WHAT'S THAT UP AHEAD OF US...? IT--!
NO! IT CAN'T BE!!
HIT THE BRAKES, PETE!
I AM! BUT IT'S...
SSSSKREEEEEEEE
...TOO LATE!!
NOOOO!

Always experimenting, Toth continued to change and modify his style, striving for clarity and force. Over the years, unlike some of his contemporaries who settled on a style early on and stuck with it, Toth experimented. His inventiveness has kept his work distinctive, but it hasn't always endeared him to editors. However, a great many comic-book artists, past and present, list him as a major influence. Semi-retired, Toth lives a quiet life in Southern California. A prolific letter writer (actually his communications are hand-lettered), his comments on comic books and his peers frequently show up in such comics-oriented magazines as *Alter Ego.*

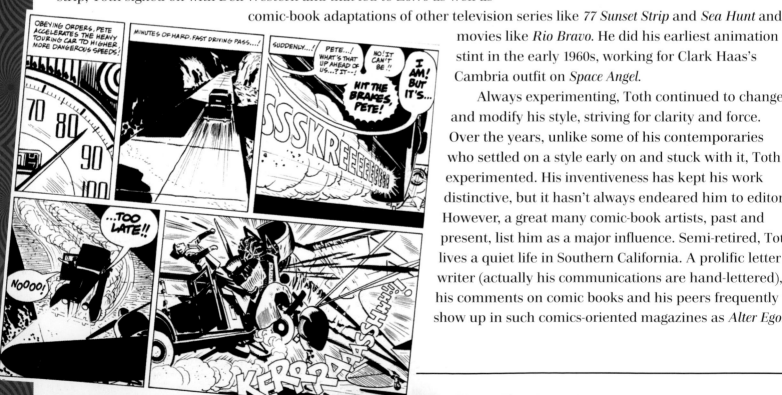

TRUE COMICS

■ By 1940, as wild and wooly comic books continued to multiply on newsstands across the nation, criticism of the increasingly popular medium also multiplied. One widely circulated critique warned, "Unless we want a coming generation even more ferocious than the present one, parents and teachers throughout America must band together to break the 'comic magazine.'"

While many parents, teachers, and librarians worked to get children away from *Superman* and back to *Robinson Crusoe*, George Hecht, the publisher of *Parents Magazine*, decided to create a wholesome comic book. One that was "attractive, intelligent and worthwhile." It would contain not superheroes, criminal masterminds, and pretty, endangered women, but rather "past and present history," offering nothing but the truth. The premier issue of Hecht's *True Comics*, which included stories about Winston Churchill, Simón Bolívar, and Indian fighters of the Old West, had a cover date of April 1941.

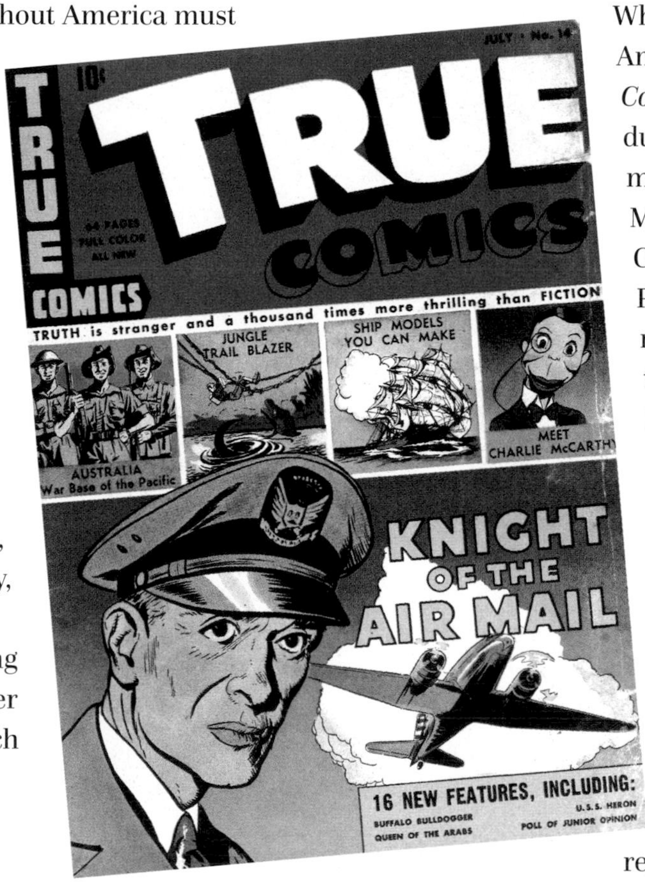
JULY · No. 14
10¢
TRUE COMICS
TRUE
COMICS
64 PAGES FULL COLOR ALL NEW
TRUTH is stranger and a thousand times more thrilling than FICTION
JUNGLE TRAIL BLAZER
SHIP MODELS YOU CAN MAKE
MEET CHARLIE McCARTHY
AUSTRALIA War Base of the Pacific
KNIGHT OF THE AIR MAIL
16 NEW FEATURES, INCLUDING:
BUFFALO BULLDOGGER
QUEEN OF THE ARABS
U.S.S. HERON
POLL OF JUNIOR OPINION

Although *Parents* didn't mention the fact in their publicity releases about *True*, the first batch of issues was packaged by Funnies, Inc. This was the same outfit that had put together *Marvel Mystery Comics* and *Blue Bolt*, comics introducing kid readers to the Human Torch, the Sub-Mariner, the Blue Bolt, and Sub-Zero Man. Despite its blandness, *True*'s maiden issue sold out its entire print run of 300,000 copies so rapidly that it had to go back to press for an additional 10,000. Gratified by this, Hecht changed the magazine from a bimonthly to a monthly. While continuing to delve into American and world history, *True Comics* gave considerable space during World War II to such military figures as Douglas MacArthur, Dwight Eisenhower, Charles de Gaulle, and George S. Patton, as well as commandos, navy aviators, the Chinese army, the Doolittle raid on Tokyo, U-boats, and the Flying Tigers.

Hecht followed *True* five months later with *True Heroes*, where there was even more emphasis on military and political figures. The next year came *True Aviation Picture-Stories*. While these spin-offs lasted but a few years, *True* survived until 1950. In the postwar issues warriors were replaced by explorers, pirates, cowboys, scientists, and sports heroes. The final newsstand issues featured "true FBI adventures." After issue #79 (October 1949), *True* left the stands. The final five issues went out to subscribers only. *True* returned for one issue in 1965, with the leading story about a "Fighting Hero of Viet Nam," and then was gone for good.

TUROK

■ Instead of cowboys and Indians, the Turok comic book gave readers dinosaurs and Indians. The Indians—Turok and his boy sidekick Andar—lived in the ancient America that existed before the intrusion of Columbus. The dinosaurs, along with other prehistoric creatures, dwelt in the Lost Valley. Turok and Andar stumbled into the place, then spent nearly three decades trying to find their way out again. Dell introduced *Turok, Son of Stone* in 1954. After two more trial issues, it became a regular title in 1956.

Turok was invented by editor Matthew Murphy. The prolific Paul S. Newman was brought in to do the writing and Rex Maxon, who'd drawn the daily *Tarzan* newspaper strip in the 1930s and 1940s, was the initial artist. In 1961,

Alberto Giolitti, based in Italy, became the artist and stayed on for roughly the next twenty years.

Newman was able to concoct a great number of stories built around the goings-on in the Lost Valley and involving Turok with various prehistoric creatures and assorted primitive men. For some reason, Turok and his boy companion called all the assorted dinosaurs Honkers, a word that apparently had a different meaning in pre-Columbian days than it does today.

The youthful fascination with dinosaurs kept Turok on the newsstands until early in 1982. From 1995 to 2000 Valiant/Acclaim tried unsuccessfully several times to market a new, upgraded version called *Turok the Hunted.*

"TWIST" TURNER

■ He has the distinction of being the only comic-book hero whose adventures were turned out by a team of four gag cartoonists. Created by the Four Roth Bros., Twist appeared in *Prize Comics* from late in 1940 until late in 1941. The Roth Brothers, however, splitting up and using the names Ben Roth, Irving Roir, Al Ross, and Salo went on to hit all the major slick magazines, from *The Saturday Evening Post* to *The New Yorker*, with their cartoons.

The *"Twist" Turner* feature was drawn in a straight style, and it's difficult to determine which brother did what. The world's greatest acrobat, Twist desired more than anything to become a member of the exclusive 99 Club, "composed of the world's champions of sports and adventure." The initiation was formidable—in order to

become the hundredth member, "[Twist] must accomplish 99 tasks given him by the club." At the rate of one challenge a month, it would've taken Twist over eight years to make the grade.

A blond fellow, Twist dressed not like an acrobat but a stage magician—evening clothes, sash, and cape. Each month he received a letter explaining his latest task. For example, "Solve the mystery behind the series of accidents at the Baylum and Barney Circus." No sooner did he clear up one job than an envelope containing the next challenge was slipped under his door or handed him by a stranger. Doggedly, he kept on and was looking forward to his tenth task when he was dropped from *Prize.*

TWO-FISTED TALES

■ Inspired by the start of the Korean conflict in June of 1950, war comics began multiplying on the newsstands in the early 1950s. The first comic book to take advantage of this new trend was EC's *Two-Fisted Tales*, edited by Harvey Kurtzman. A well-drawn, well-written, and well-researched comic, it was the least gung-ho of the combat comics of the decade.

Initially the bimonthly was intended to be simply a collection of adventure yarns. The first issue, dated November–December 1950, was not war-oriented. "When we originally started," Kurtzman once said, "we were going to do blood and thunder tales and rip-roaring adventure." By the time the magazine hit the stands, the war in Korea was in full swing. The second issue had a war cover drawn by Kurtzman, and the contents reflected his new preoccupation. He drew the next ten covers, all of them forceful, violent, and downbeat, all devoted to servicemen in the Korean War. Not all the stories in each issue dealt with that war, since Kurtzman tried for a balance between the present and the past.

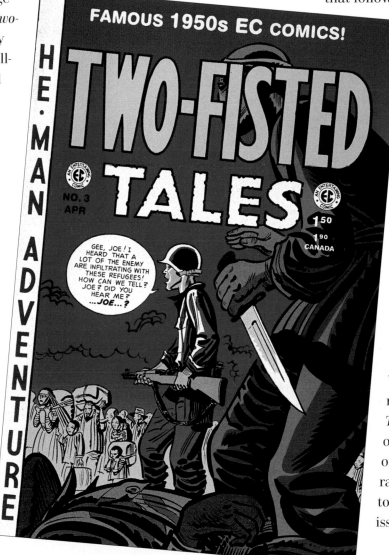

FAMOUS 1950s EC COMICS!

HE·MAN ADVENTURE

TWO-FISTED TALES

NO. 3 APR

1 50
1 90 CANADA

GEE, JOE! I HEARD THAT A LOT OF THE ENEMY ARE INFILTRATING WITH THESE REFUGEES! HOW CAN WE TELL? JOE? DID YOU HEAR ME? ...JOE...?

He did most of the writing and layout. The chief artists were Jack Davis, Wally Wood, George Evans, John Severin, and Kurtzman. Unlike many of the war comics that followed, this one never went in for flag-waving or glorifying war and combat. Kurtzman once said, "All our stories really protested war. The whole mood of our stories was that war wasn't a good thing. . . . You got killed suddenly for no reason."

Kurtzman also had an abiding interest in the Civil War and devoted two complete issues, #31 (January–February 1953) and #35 (October 1953), to it. By the time the second one appeared, the Korean War was over and the remaining six issues of *Two-Fisted* turned to tales of combat and intrigue in other climes and times, ranging from the Old West to Victorian India. The final issue came out early in 1955.

EC's other war book was *Frontline Combat*, which went through fifteen issues from 1951 to 1954. Kurtzman edited that one too, and devoted considerable space to Korea.

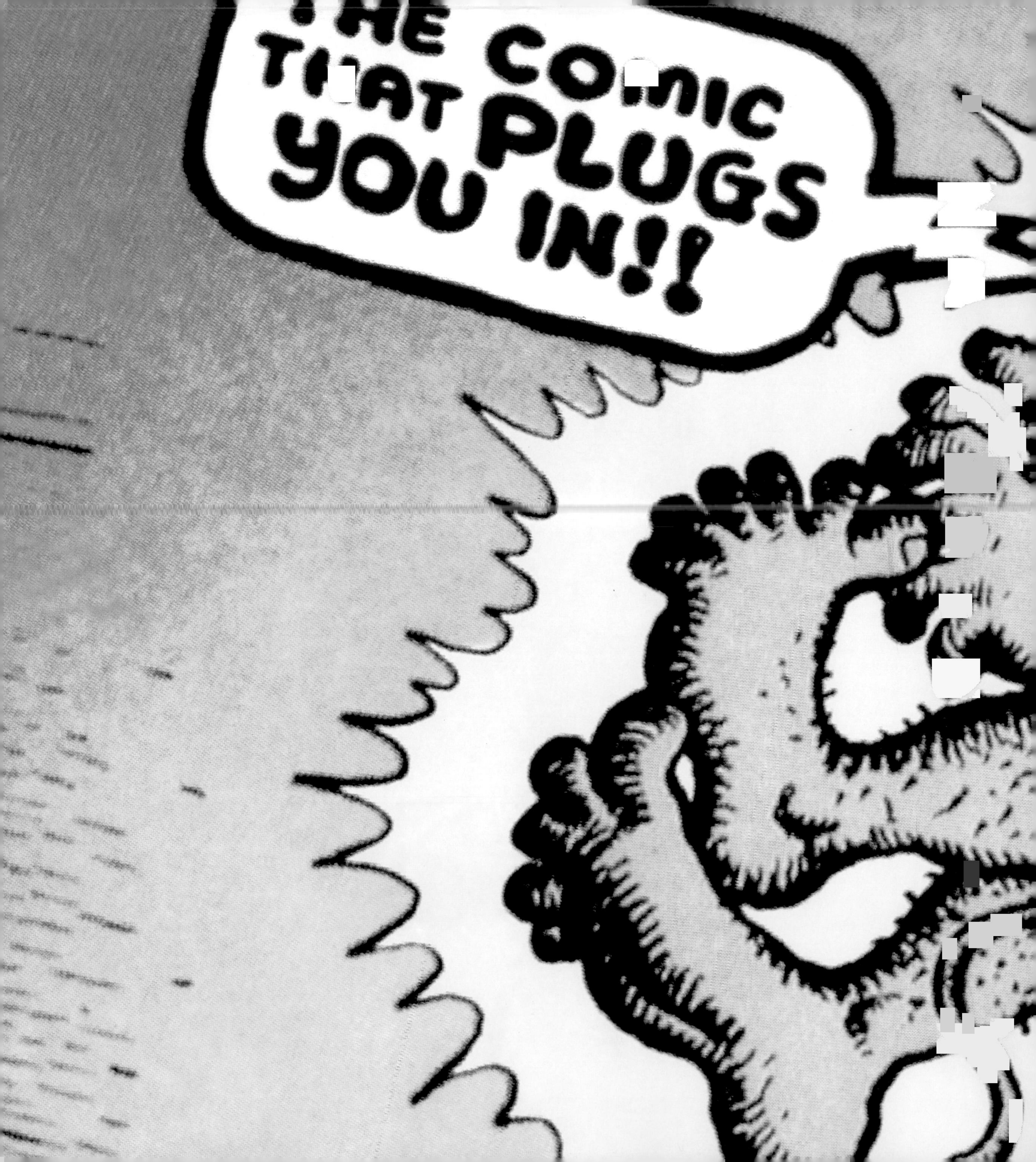
THE COMIC THAT PLUGS YOU IN!!

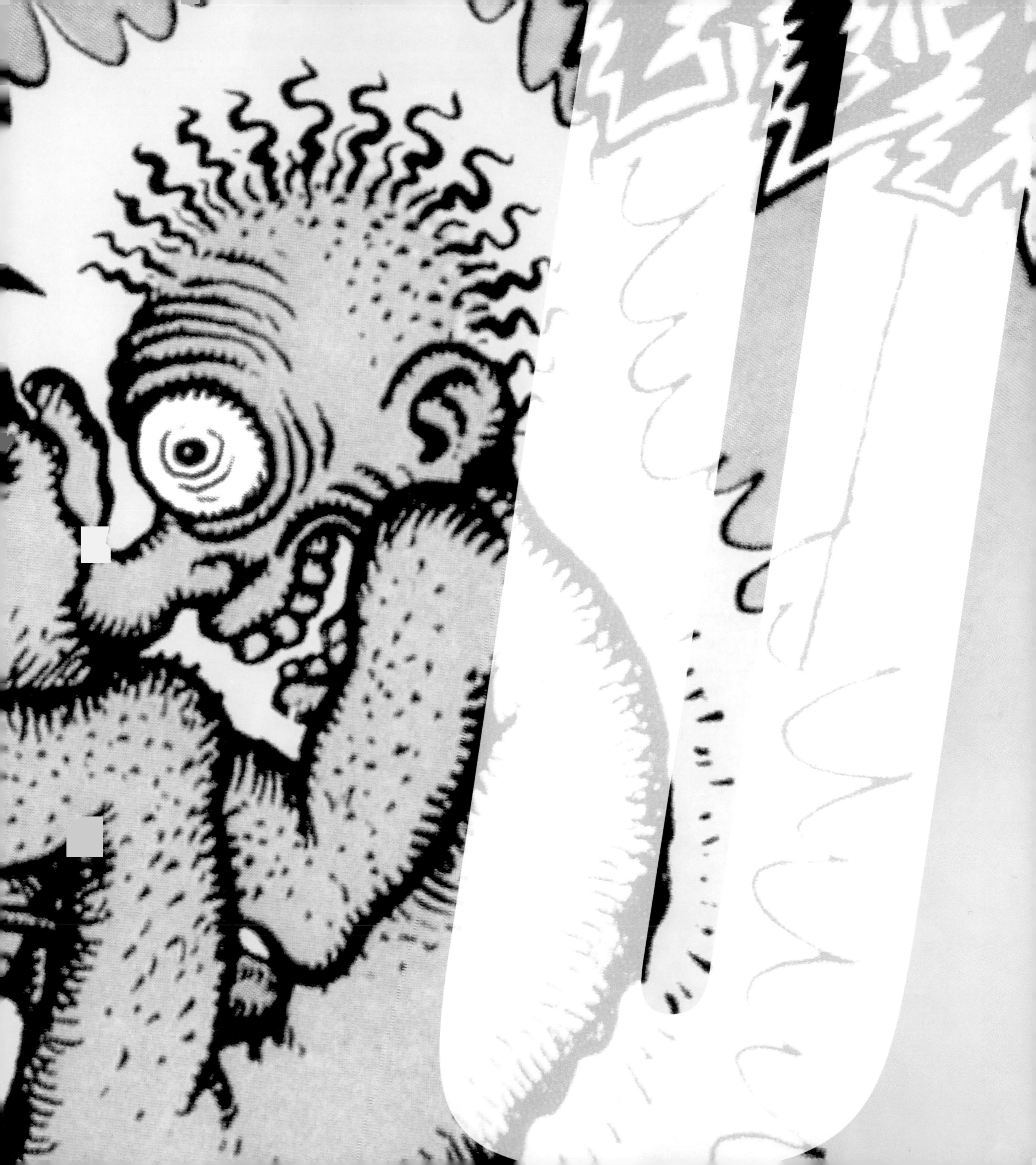

UNDERCOVER GIRL

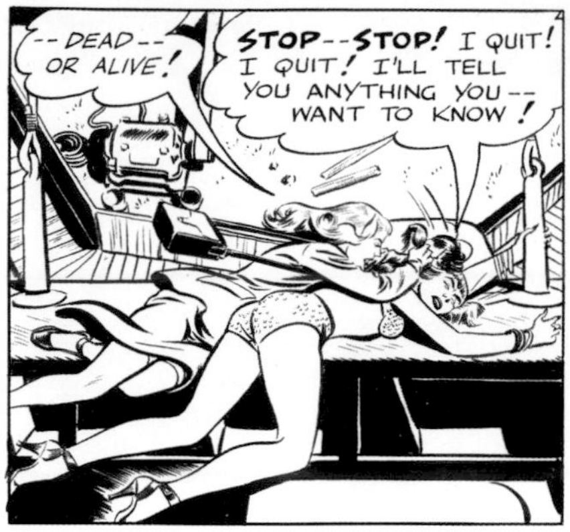
-- DEAD -- OR ALIVE!
STOP--STOP! I QUIT! I QUIT! I'LL TELL YOU ANYTHING YOU -- WANT TO KNOW!

■ Mixing Good Girl Art with foreign intrigue, artist Ogden Whitney and writer Gardner Fox came up with Starr Flagg, Undercover Girl. She was a regular in Magazine Enterprises' *Manhunt* from the first issue (October 1947). Fashionably clad, and more often fashionably unclad, she plied her trade in exotic climes in South America, Europe, and the South Seas. She did her undercover work for a United States intelligence agency, taking care of her fair share of spies, saboteurs, and assassins. Her assignments always seemed to involve frequent changes of clothes, considerable bathing, and a lot of swimming.

She closely resembled the then popular film noir movie actress Lizbeth Scott, though she was a bit huskier. After *Manhunt* folded in the summer of 1948, Starr Flagg returned, by way of reprints, in three issues of her own *Undercover Girl* comic book in the early 1950s.

UNDERGROUND COMIX

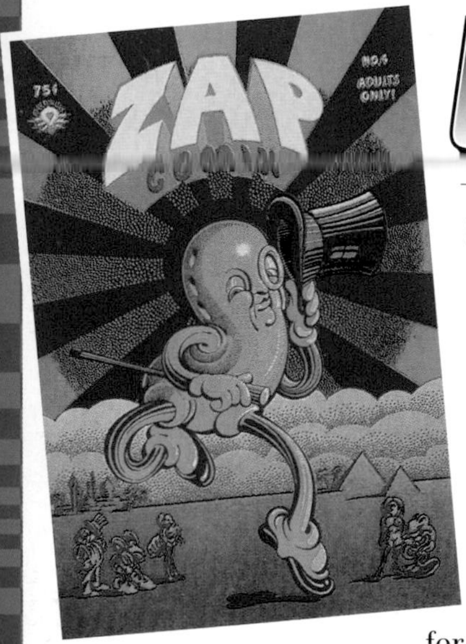
ZAP
75¢
NO.4
ADULTS ONLY!

■ A little over a decade after the triumphant return of the superheroes to mainstream comics, underground comix were born. Irreverent, iconoclastic, independent, bawdy, and vigorously drawn, this new wave of comic books spoke to, and for, a lot of young people who were coming of age in the turbulent decade of the 1960s. Hip young readers who weren't especially interested in the fortunes of the *Fantastic Four* or the latest incarnation of the Green Lantern.

Unhampered by allegiance to the Comics Code, titles such as *Bijou Funnies, Zap Comix, Corporate Crimes Comics, Gay Comix,* and *The Fabulous Furry Freak Brothers* dealt with sex, drugs, business and government corruption, the Vietnam War, women's rights, gay and lesbian issues, and other taboo topics to cause quite a few official attempts at censorship and suppression.

The acknowledged patron saint of the underground movement was Harvey Kurtzman who'd championed a more polite antiestablishment worldview in *Mad* and then *Humbug*. He also, in *Help*, published the early work of such founding fathers of comix as Robert Crumb and Gilbert Shelton. Another influence was Basil Wolverton, not only for his many bizarre 1940s comic-book burlesques such as *Powerhouse Pepper* but for his later grotesque style of drawing as seen in *Mad*.

Crumb, inventor of Zap, was the leading practitioner and the one who got the most national attention. Others who were important to the movement were Shelton, creator of *Wonder Warthog* and the *Freak Brothers*, Denis Kitchen, Kim Deitch, Rick Griffin, Trina Robbins, Bobby London, Skip Williamson, Vaughn Bode, and Shary Flenniken. The undergrounds, for the most part, flourished for only a few years. They did, however, pave the way for the independent comics and the creation of such varied titles as *Love and Rockets, Elfquest, Cerebus,* and *Teenage Ninja Turtles*.

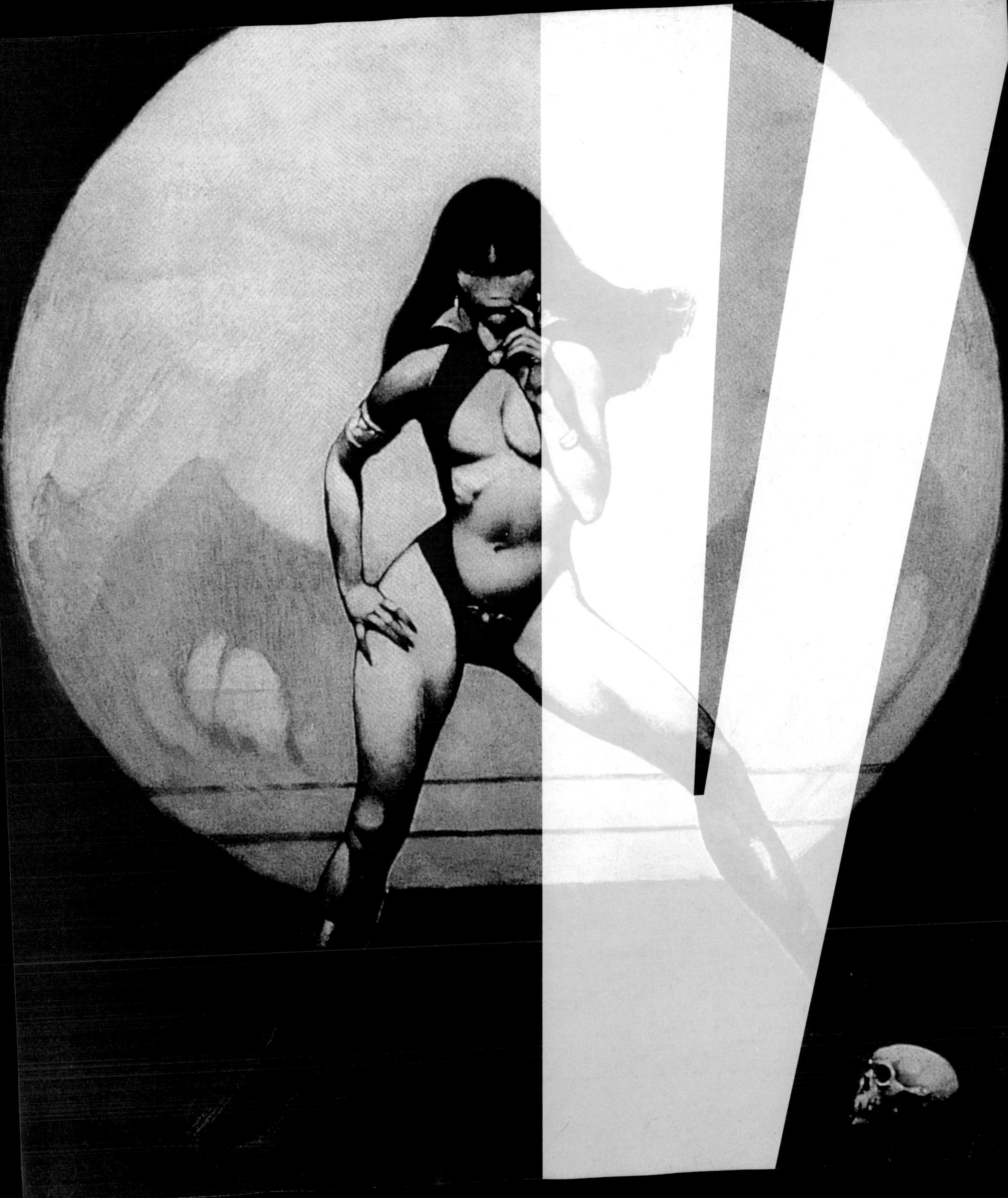

VALLELY, HENRY E. *(1881–1950)*

■ He was the foremost artist to do original work for Big Little Books, those small thick rivals of comic books. Vallely's art was also adapted for the very first Lone Ranger comic book, and he also illustrated the adventures of two superheroes created expressly for BLBs. In addition to dozens of Big and Better Little Books, the Chicago-based Vallely illustrated a great many juvenile novels for Whitman, including a series of 1940s mysteries featuring fictitious adventures of such popular movie stars as Dorothy Lamour, Ginger Rogers, John Payne, and Judy Garland.

Vallely drew in a manner that was both realistic and stylized. He was chiefly a black-and-white artist, using a uniform line and stark black shadows and having some affinities to the art nouveau style of the late nineteenth century. In the early 1940s, he illustrated two BLBs dealing with Maximo the Amazing Superman and one of the Ghost Avenger, an invisible crimebuster. He continued to work for Whitman until the late 1940s.

Henry Vallely, according to research done by Big Little Book authority John Pansmith, was born in Ireland. He arrived in America at the end of the nineteenth century and was soon working as a commercial artist. He did fashion drawing, illustrations for the *Chicago Tribune*, and eventually drifted into children's books. He worked for Whitman from the middle 1930s onward, illustrating titles ranging from *Jack Armstrong and the Ivory Treasure* to *Peggy Brown and the Big Haunted House*. He died in Evanston, Illinois, on November 25, 1950.

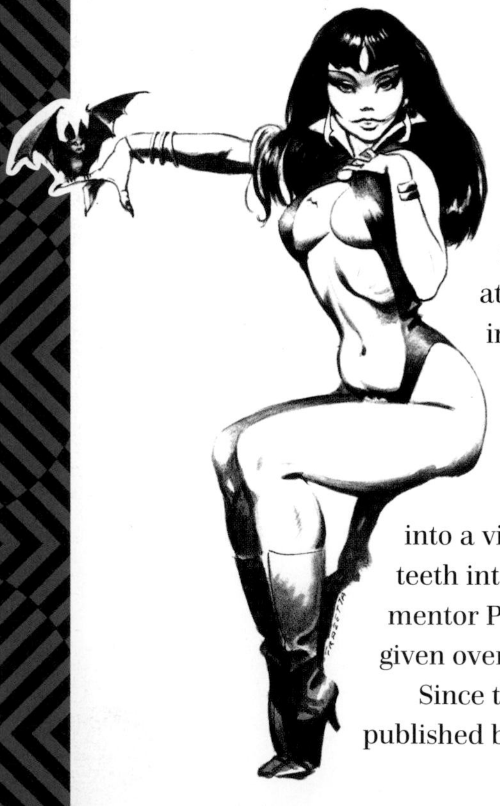

VAMPIRELLA

■ The Bettie Page of the vampire world, she was introduced by Warren Publishing in 1969. The *Vampirella* magazine, like Warren's *Creepy*, was black-and-white, aimed at a somewhat older audience, and sold for fifty cents. A Frank Frazetta color cover introduced Vampi to readers, showing her in her terse crimson costume, posing with one spike-heeled foot resting on a human skull. Sci-fi maven Forrest J. Ackerman, who was editing *Famous Monsters* for Warren, came up with the name, and in the early issues Vampi was played for laughs. When Tom Sutton became the artist with the eighth issue things got serious. Scripts by Archie Goodwin helped convert Vampirella into a viable vampire. A typical good/bad girl, she sometimes gave in to the urge to sink her teeth into somebody's throat, but she also built a career as a sexy ghostbuster, aided by her mentor Pendragon. Vampi usually appeared in the opening story with the rest of the issue given over to assorted horror tales. The magazine ended in 1983.

Since then the virtuous vampire has been brought back to life several times and is now published by Harris Publications. The most recent series commenced in 2001 and continues.

THE VIKING PRINCE

■ See THE BRAVE AND THE BOLD.

VENUS

■ The changes that comic books underwent in the years after the end of World War II are reflected in *Venus*. When the magazine first appeared in the summer of 1948, it was a mixture of romance and light fantasy. Venus, the goddess of love, returned to earth, got a job on *Beauty Magazine*, and proceeded to find out the current state of love. Venus had also recently returned to earth—by way of a statue that came back to life—in a Broadway musical called *One Touch of Venus*. The musical reached the screen in 1948 with Ava Gardner as the goddess. Marvel's Venus was a blonde.

After a few issues the tag "A Lover's Magazine" was added to the cover. By #9 (May 1950) fantasy predominated, and by #11 Venus was involved in science-fiction situations.

Bill Everett began drawing *Venus* with #13 (April 1951) and the emphasis from then on was horror. The slogan "Strange Stories of the Supernatural" had been added to the covers. The blonde goddess encountered gargoyles, grave robbers, monsters, ghouls, and a varied selection of walking skeletons. During most of the issues Venus also had many aspects of a superhero—including the ability to fly—and, like many a later Marvel character, she hung around with mythological characters that included Apollo, Loki, Mars, Thor, and, for good measure, the biblical hero Samson.

Even with its infinite variety, the magazine lasted for only nineteen issues, ending in 1952. Some of the Everett *Venus* stories were reprinted in *Weird Wonder Tales* in the middle 1970s.

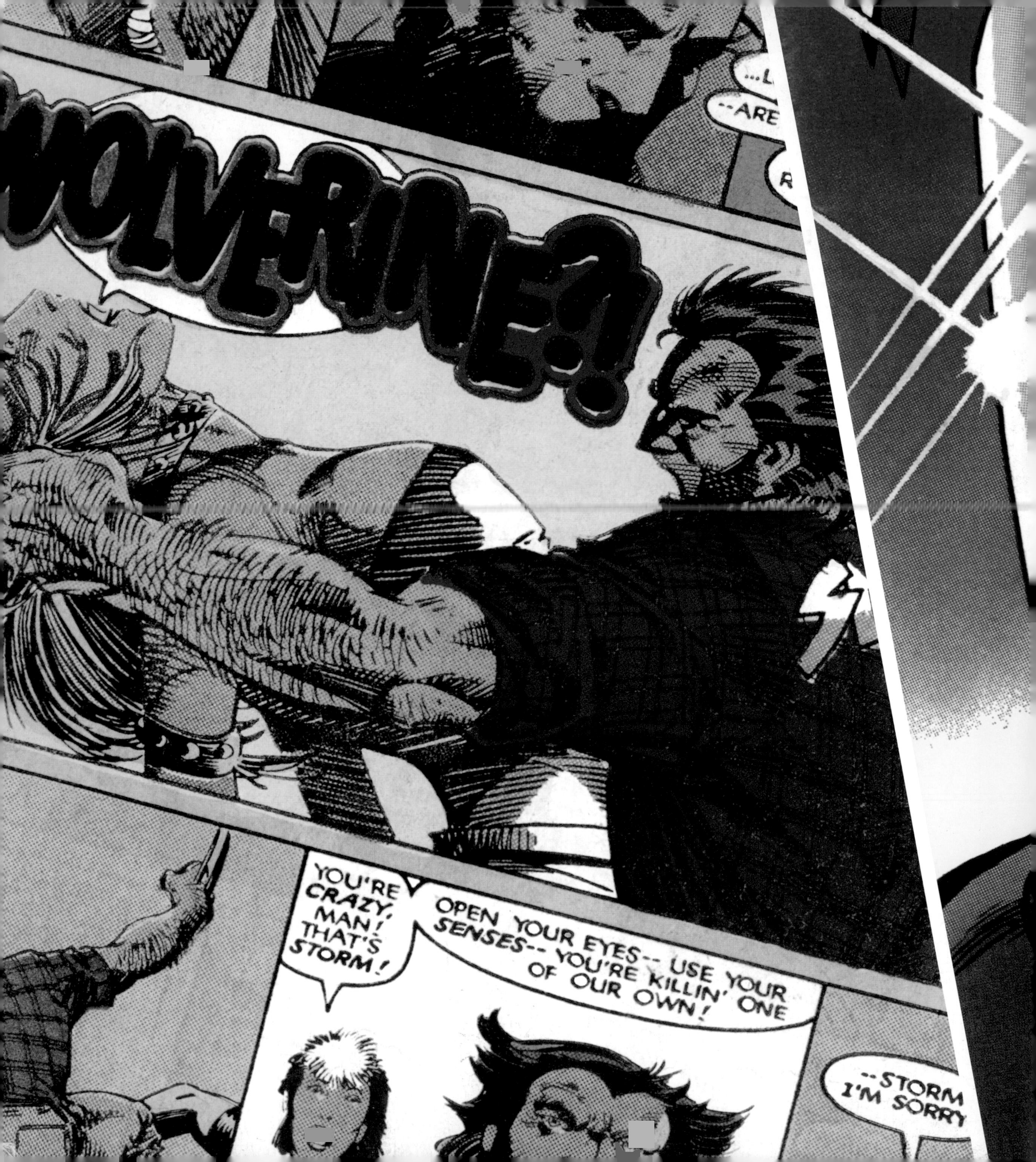
WOLVERINE?!
YOU'RE CRAZY, MAN! THAT'S STORM!
OPEN YOUR EYES-- USE YOUR SENSES-- YOU'RE KILLIN' ONE OF OUR OWN!
--STORM I'M SORRY

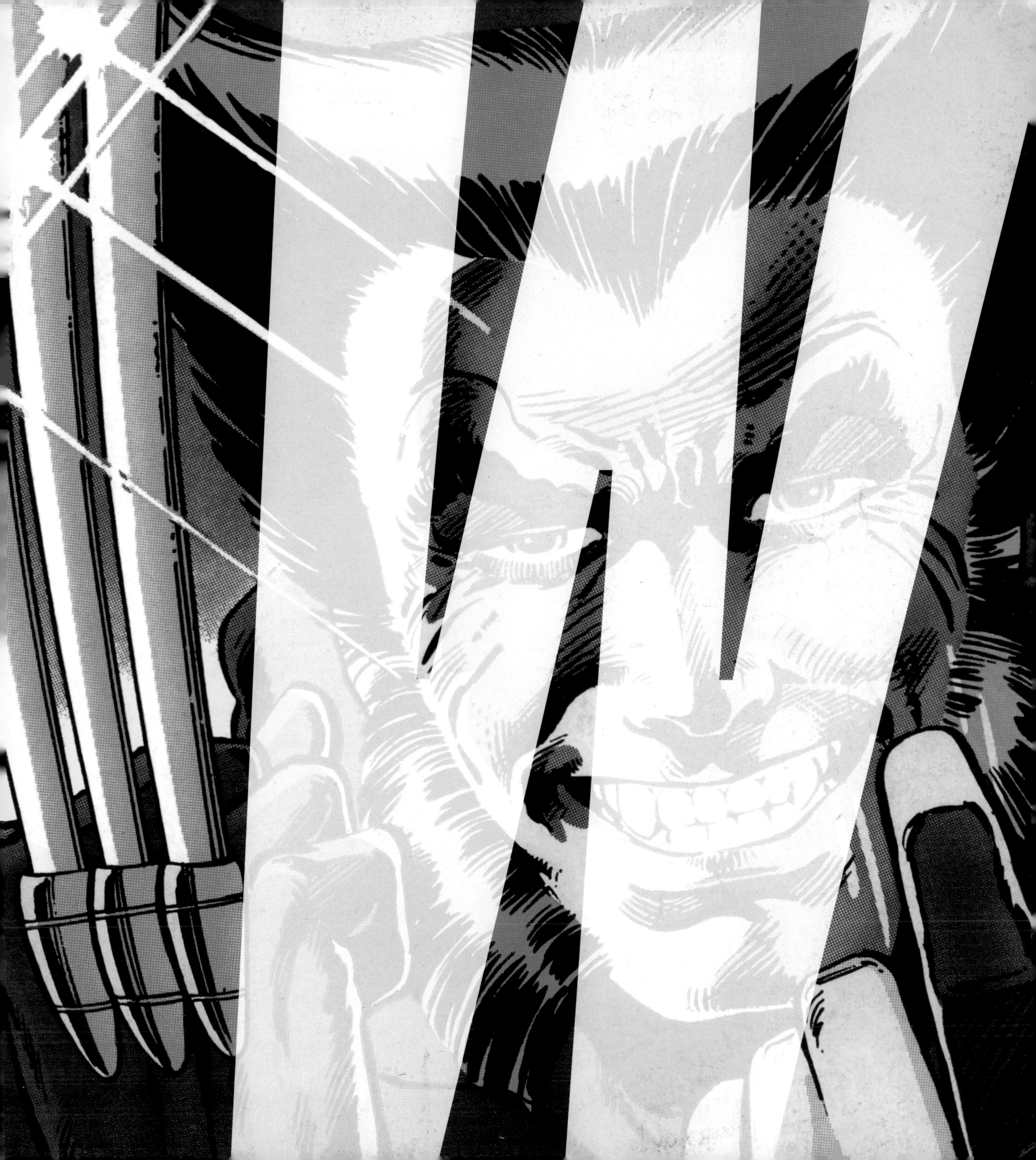

WARD, BILL

■ See TORCHY.

WARE, CHRIS

(1967–)

■ Chris Ware has created what amounts to an entire world of his own and periodically reports on it in the publications of his Acme Novelty Library, which are conveyed to the public by way of Fantagraphic Books. For one thing, time is out of joint in his world, and the past and present coexist. It's people with such characters as a paunchy hero called Super-Man, a mouse named Quimby, who seems to suffer from existential malaise, a robot, and, first and foremost, Jimmy Corrigan. Billed as "The Smartest Kid in the World," Jimmy shows up as a depressed and lonely little boy at times and at others as a melancholy middle-aged man. In whatever mode, his beautifully rendered adventures are among the saddest to be found in any comic book, past or present.

Ware is an exceptional artist with a clear, concise style that is in the tradition of such European artists as Herge and the American comic-strip master Frank King, whose Sunday *Gasoline Alley* pages are favorites of Ware. Ware is good with backgrounds as well as people, and his work is filled with splendid scenes of cities in the winter, bleak rural locales, and, one of his favorites, mammoth fairs and expositions of the past. He is also caught up in typography and seems to have as much fun designing the assorted columns of type that festoon the issues of the Library—which, by the way, vary from tiny to tabloid size, depending on his mood. Several issues also include

$3.95
The Acme Novelty Library
Beginning with This Issue
Presents
An Indefensible Attempt to Justify the Despair of Those Who Have Never Known Real Tragedy.
Featuring One of Our Most Amusing and Celebrated Personalities~
The Smartest Kid on Earth.
Jimmy Corrigan
Souvenir Book of Views.
Filled With a Variety of Fancy Fully-Colored Pictures & Scenes.
759 to Choose From.
A Guaranteed Solace for the Economically Privileged.
Fantagraphics Books
Acme Novelty Company

plans on how to build such things as a robot or a moveable cat's head as well as cutouts that turn into strange buildings.

All in all, Ware is one of the few certifiable geniuses who's come into comics in the past decade, moving up from drawing for his college newspaper to producing huge books that reprint his work.

WATCHMEN

■ See MOORE, ALAN.

WHAT IF...?

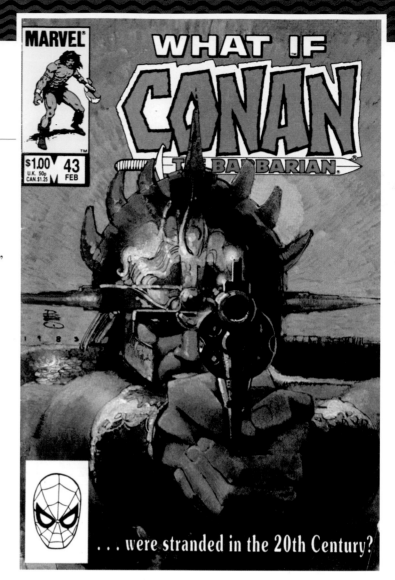

MARVEL
WHAT IF
CONAN
THE BARBARIAN
$1.00
U.K. 50p
CAN.$1.25
43
FEB
. . . were stranded in the 20th Century?

■ Aimed at fans of alternate worlds and parallel universes, Marvel's *What If . . . ?* was introduced in 1977. Among the questions contrary to the basic facts of the Marvel Universe that the magazine answered over the years were "What if Elektra had lived?" "What if Ghost Rider, Spider Woman, and Captain Marvel were villains?" and "What if the Avengers had never been?" The contributing artists included Steve Ditko, Gil Kane, Jack Kirby, John Buscema, and John Byrne. The first series ended with the forty-seventh issue in 1985.

The title was revived in 1989. DC also toyed with alternative scenarios as far back as the imaginary Superman tales and later in an ongoing series of Elseworld books wherein, for example, Batman operated during the French Revolution.

WILLIAMSON, AL (1931-)

■ The leading exponent of the heroic adventure style introduced by Alex Raymond in *Flash Gordon*, Williamson started in comic books when he was seventeen. He moved from *Heroic Comics* to Toby Press's *John Wayne* in 1950 and had Frank Frazetta inking some of his pages. He next drew some very imaginative fantasy and science-fiction stories for such titles as *Forbidden Worlds* and *Out of the Night*. In 1952 he went to work for EC.

Williamson drew for a range of EC titles, including *Weird Fantasy*, *Valor*, and *Piracy*. In the middle 1960s he actually got to draw *Flash Gordon*, when King Features ventured into comic books. In addition, he drew the *Secret Agent Corrigan* strip for King from 1967 to 1980. The first artist on the strip, when it was titled *Secret Agent X-9*, was Williamson's idol Alex Raymond.

Over the past ten or so years Williamson has concentrated on inking, chiefly for Marvel. A recent hardcover, *All Williamson Adventures*, collects some of his best earlier comic-book work.

WHIZ COMICS

■ See CAPTAIN MARVEL: I.

WINGS COMICS

■ One of the few comic books devoted entirely to aviation—well, aviation and pretty girls—*Wings Comics* remained airborne for nearly fourteen years. Published by Fiction House and borrowing its name from their aviation pulp, *Wings*, the first issue was cover-dated September 1940. The content was provided by the Eisner-Iger shop and then, after the partners had split, by the Iger shop. Most of the early covers were by Gene Fawcette, whose specialty was drawing airplanes in fiery and explosive combat.

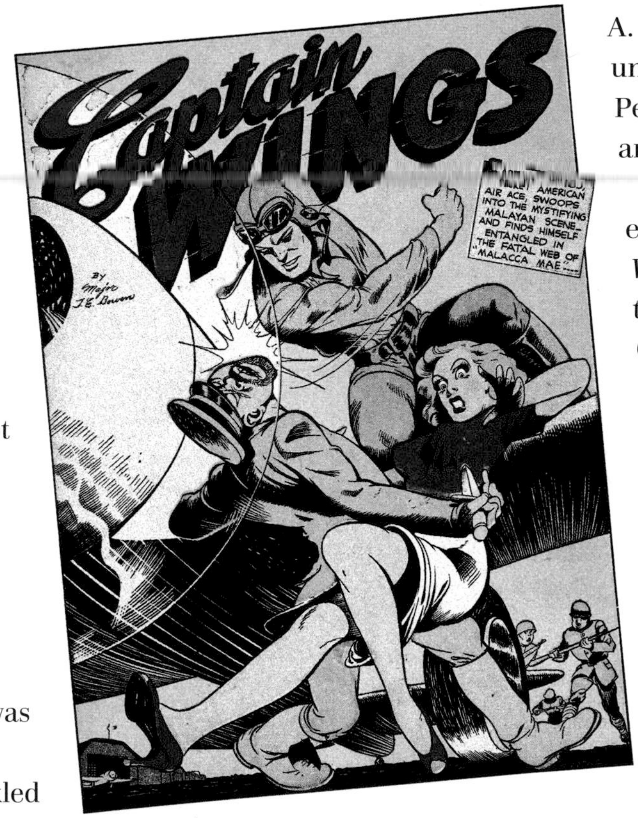
Captain WINGS
AIR ACE, SWOOPS INTO THE MYSTIFYING MALAYAN SCENE... AND FINDS HIMSELF ENTANGLED IN "THE FATAL WEB OF MALACCA MAE"....

The magazine's characters were all involved in World War II, but since the United States was not yet officially at war, they were mostly British. The Skull Squad featured three comrades in the RAF; the Parachute Patrol was made up of three English Boy Scouts who were "already experienced fliers"; Clipper Kirk was an experienced British navy flier; Grease Monkey Griffin was a freckled young English RAF mechanic. *Wings Comics* also gave room to Jane Martin, a war nurse with a pilot's license and "Powder" Burns, a freelance aviator "footloose in battle-scarred Europe."

For the first couple of years the stories concentrated on aerial combat, bombing raids, and occasional espionage. Most of the aircraft was identified specifically—"The Spitfire is brought to a skillful landing," "The Messerschmitt is squarely in his gun sights," etc. The scripts were credited to dashing pen names such as Capt. Derek West, Ace Atkins, and Capt. A. E. Carruthers. Among the mostly uncredited artists were Arthur Peddy, Klaus Nordling, Al Gabriele, and George Tuska.

By 1943, with considerable enlisted men among its readership, *Wings* was adding young women to the yarns. For example, Nick Cardy took over *Jane Martin* and streamlined the flying nurse considerably. It wasn't until 1946 that women started appearing regularly on the covers, always in the company of an airplane. Bob Lubbers, an expert on both airplanes and sparsely clad women, provided dozens of these covers. Both he and Cardy drew the adventures of Captain Wings, who showed up back in #16. Wings was a dual identity American aviator.

During its final years in the early 1950s, *Wings Comics* turned away from Good Girl Art and adventurous aviators to go back to war. This time the air war was in Korea. After its 159th issue, the magazine ceased publication.

WITCHBLADE

TOP COW
WITCHBLADE
25
AUG
$2.95
Z.
WOHL
TURNER
D-TRON
SMITH

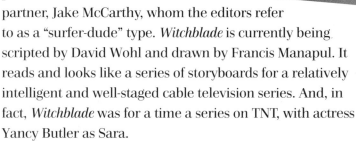

■ A blend of urban police procedural and weird fantasy, with plenty of sensuous women tossed in, *Witchblade* was first seen in comic shops in 1995. The book was a product of the Top Cow Productions division of Image Comics and Top Cow founder and CEO Marc Silvestri was its cocreator and initial artist.

The Witchblade is an ancient "mystical artifact," a metal gauntlet that grants formidable powers to the one person deemed qualified to use it in each generation. At the moment New York City police officer Sara Pezzini is that person. As is pointed out each issue, she is "the reluctant bearer of the Witchblade . . . that has bonded itself to her. [She] must resist the gauntlet's all consuming thirst for battle." The gauntlet can discourage bullets, grant Sara psychic abilities, turn into a lethal sword, and give her advice in a rather hectoring manner.

While working on gritty big-city police matters, Sara is also frequently entangled with monsters, mystical beings, and some very strange denizens of Manhattan. There is, for instance, business tycoon Kenneth Irons, who's several hundred years old (but sure doesn't look it) and determined eventually to control "the bearer of the Witchblade." Ian Nottingham is a very effective assassin who looks, dresses, and acts like a depressed rock star. He and Sara have an ambiguous relationship, and he has both tried to kill her and save her life. Nottingham has been a frequent turncoat in the battle between good and evil and is now the owner of his own witchblade. It's called Excalibur and provides incredible powers, but it hasn't seemed to lift his gloom. Sara's younger sister, Julie, is a model and is not a paragon of sisterly love. She's having an affair with Sara's erstwhile police partner, Jake McCarthy, whom the editors refer to as a "surfer-dude" type. *Witchblade* is currently being scripted by David Wohl and drawn by Francis Manapul. It reads and looks like a series of storyboards for a relatively intelligent and well-staged cable television series. And, in fact, *Witchblade* was for a time a series on TNT, with actress Yancy Butler as Sara.

Toward the end of 2003 the magazine began a "Death Pool" series and invited readers to vote on which characters should survive and which should be killed off. So there will obviously be some changes made in the basic cast of this successful title.

WOLVERINE

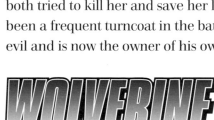

■ See X-MEN.

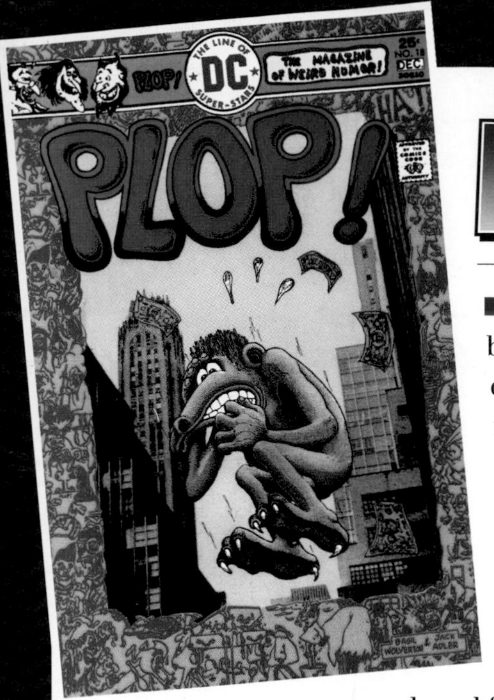
DC
THE MAGAZINE OF WEIRD HUMOR!
25¢
DEC
PLOP!

WOLVERTON, BASIL

(1909–1979)

■ One of the few comic-book artists whose work can legitimately be called unique, Wolverton entered the field in the late 1930s. Although he created such relatively serious adventure features such as *Spacehawk*, he's best remembered for such nonserious and nonsensical inventions as *Powerhouse Pepper*, *Scoop Scuttle*, *Mystic Moot and His Magic Snoot*, and the grotesqueries he later drew for *Mad* and *Plop*.

Something of a loner, Wolverton produced the majority of his comic-book work not in the New York area but from the Pacific Northwest. Contributing chiefly through the mail, he first sold to such pioneering titles as *Circus Comics* and *Amazing Mystery Funnies*. In 1940 he hooked up with *Target Comics* (published by the same folks who published *The Saturday Evening Post*) to produce his major and longest-running serious character. Wolverton, starting in the June 1940 issue, wrote and drew thirty planet-hopping adventures of Spacehawk, who wore a bulky green spacesuit and was also known as "the Lone Wolf of the Void."

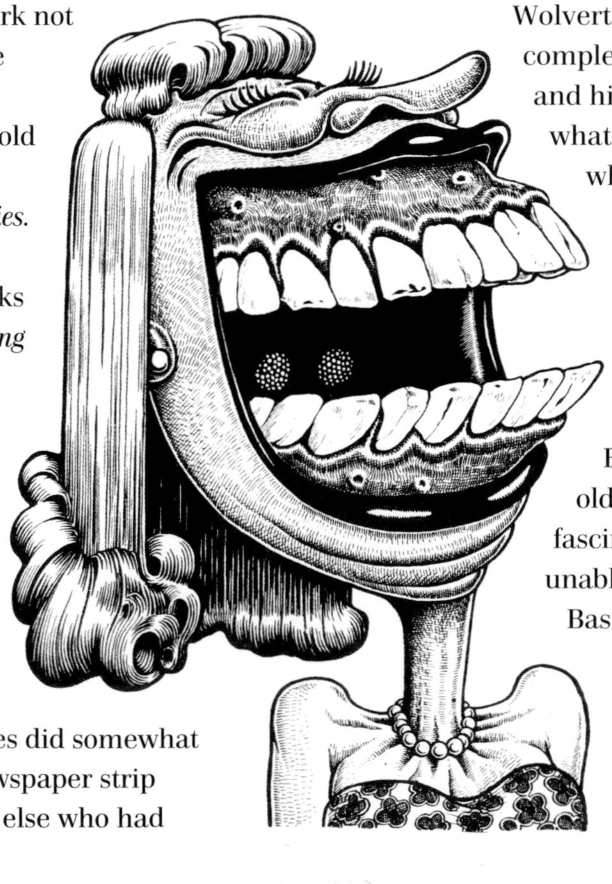

While Spacehawk's adventures did somewhat parallel those of the pulp and newspaper strip science fiction, there was nobody else who had encounters quite like his. He met the oddest aliens and creatures and experienced some of the strangest interplanetary adventures of any spaceman. On Mars he prevented a sore-loser green political candidate from smashing a moon into the planet, and once on Uranus he transplanted the brain of a dying friend into the gigantic body of a warty green hornosaur. One of the major appeals of Wolverton's space opera was the artwork. He was very good at gadgets, especially the kind that require lots of nuts and bolts. His spaceships had the bulk and feel of ocean liners, the control rooms were as cluttered with pipes and dials as an apartment-house basement. What was lurking in all of the *Spacehawk* adventures, hiding behind the asparagus-like trees and crouching behind the massive piles of rock candy, was Wolverton's sense of humor. That never completely suppressed sense of humor and his one-of-a-kind imagination were what gave a particular charm to the whole *Spacehawk* saga.

Powerhouse Pepper was Wolverton's major funny opus, a regular in *Joker Comics* and very much in tune with the baggy pants comedy that flourished in America during World War II. Before Powerhouse was many issues old, Wolverton had given in to his fascination with alliteration and was unable even to sign his name straight—by Basil Baboonbrain Wolverton, by Basil Weirdwit Wolverton, by Basil Bleakbrain Wolverton, etc. He was equally fond of internal rhyme, and his dialogue as well as the numerous signs and posters that cluttered almost every inch of wall (and often floor and ceiling) space were full of the stuff. "Zounds! Your snappers are as sound as a hound's," said one of the physicians who gave Powerhouse his army physical. He was rejected because of the shape of his head—"It's too lean, if you know what I mean. A helmet teeters over your cheaters and there's no way to clap a strap under your map!" A restaurant that was named simply Crude Food offered such delights as blue blackbirds broiled in brown bovine butter and buzz bugs basted in bilgewater. Wolverton also tossed a great deal of slapstick and satire into the feature, kidding just about every fad and foible of the day.

During the 1940s he turned on a wide range of other funny features, including *Flap Flipflop the Flying Flash*, *Bingbang Buster and His Horse Hedy*, and assorted one-page fillers. In the early 1950s he returned to serious science fiction, drawing for comic books like *Marvel Tales* and *Weird Tales of the Future*. Later on he returned to humor, now putting more emphasis on the ugly and grotesque aspects of his work, and turning out greeting cards and humor books. He also contributed to *Mad* and *Plop*. Among his last work were a series of biblical illustrations and some very unsettling drawings on nuclear war.

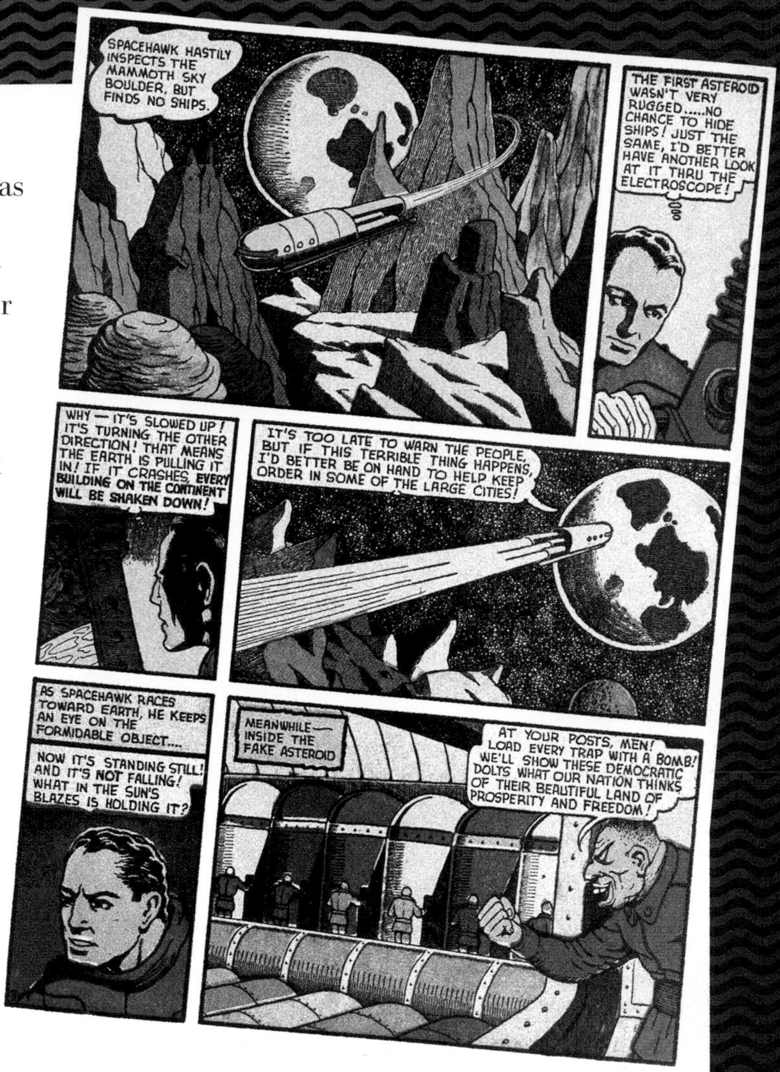
SPACEHAWK HASTILY INSPECTS THE MAMMOTH SKY BOULDER, BUT FINDS NO SHIPS.
THE FIRST ASTEROID WASN'T VERY RUGGED.....NO CHANCE TO HIDE SHIPS! JUST THE SAME, I'D BETTER HAVE ANOTHER LOOK AT IT THRU THE ELECTROSCOPE!
WHY — IT'S SLOWED UP! IT'S TURNING THE OTHER DIRECTION! THAT MEANS THE EARTH IS PULLING IT IN! IF IT CRASHES, EVERY BUILDING ON THE CONTINENT WILL BE SHAKEN DOWN!
IT'S TOO LATE TO WARN THE PEOPLE, BUT IF THIS TERRIBLE THING HAPPENS, I'D BETTER BE ON HAND TO HELP KEEP ORDER IN SOME OF THE LARGE CITIES!
AS SPACEHAWK RACES TOWARD EARTH, HE KEEPS AN EYE ON THE FORMIDABLE OBJECT....
NOW IT'S STANDING STILL! AND IT'S NOT FALLING! WHAT IN THE SUN'S BLAZES IS HOLDING IT?
MEANWHILE— INSIDE THE FAKE ASTEROID
AT YOUR POSTS, MEN! LOAD EVERY TRAP WITH A BOMB! WE'LL SHOW THESE DEMOCRATIC DOLTS WHAT OUR NATION THINKS OF THEIR BEAUTIFUL LAND OF PROSPERITY AND FREEDOM!

THE WOMAN IN RED

■ The earliest masked woman in comic books appeared as a backup character in *Thrilling Comics*, which starred Doc Strange. Known as the Woman in Red, she functioned as a sort of phantom detective and debuted in issue #2 (March 1940). George Mandel illustrated her first batch of cases.

Like many of her male counterparts, she was a law officer by profession. Peggy Allen served as an undercover agent for a large metropolitan police force. While out on a case, posing as a nurse or a maid, for example, in the mansion of a wealthy potential crime victim, she'd slip into her outfit and prowl around as "the famous Woman in Red." This outfit consisted of a long red garment, closely resembling what was then known as a housecoat, plus a red hood and a red domino mask. In addition to being a first-rate investigator and a crack shot, Peggy Allen was also an expert at jujitsu. Her cases usually combined patient searching for clues with plenty of gunplay and brawling. She left *Thrilling* early in 1945.

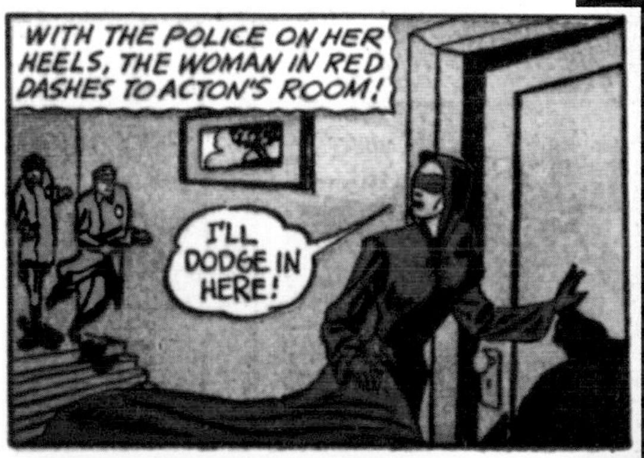
WITH THE POLICE ON HER HEELS, THE WOMAN IN RED DASHES TO ACTON'S ROOM!
I'LL DODGE IN HERE!

WONDER MAN

■ The first imitator of Superman, he appeared exactly once, in the spring of 1939. That was in the enterprising Victor Fox's *Wonder Comics.* Fox, a former accountant at DC, was one of the first to realize the financial possibilities of comic-book superheroes. He formed his own company and hired the Will Eisner–Jerry Iger shop to provide material. The one character he insisted on was Wonder Man.

Using the pen name Willis, Eisner wrote and drew the first and only adventure. In everyday life, Wonder Man was a mild-mannered blond newsman named Fred Carson and the superpowers he picked up in Tibet were fairly close to those enjoyed by the Man of Steel. As soon as DC got wind of the new character, they called in attorneys. Fox, not waiting for the courts to decide the case, retired his pioneering character. He also changed the name of the magazine to *Wonderworld Comics.*

WONDER WOMAN

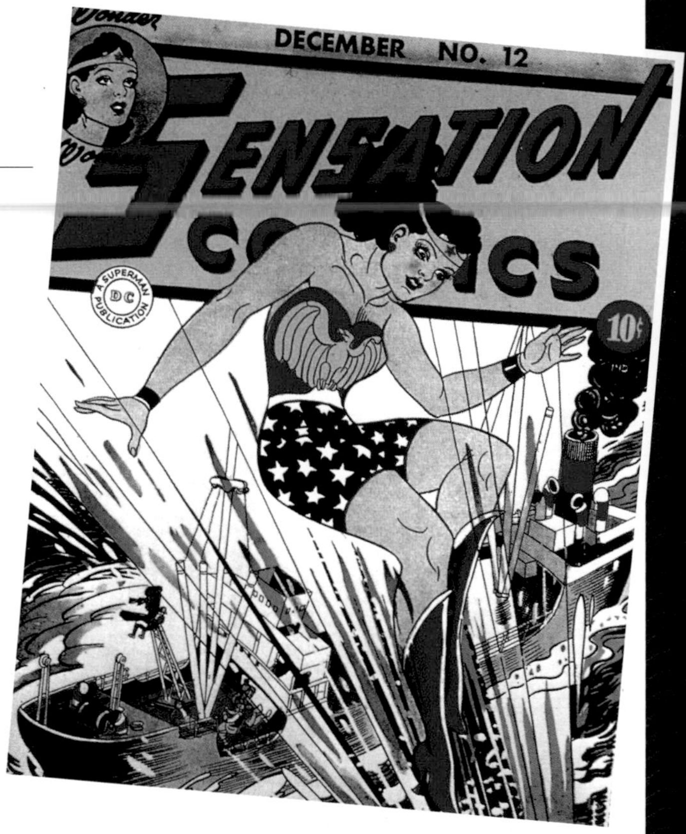
DECEMBER NO. 12
SENSATION COMICS
A SUPERMAN DC PUBLICATION
10¢

■ Unsinkable and the preeminent female superhero, Wonder Woman has been defending the nation for over three-score years. Introduced in *All Star Comics* at the tail end of 1941, she was then installed as the leading light of *Sensation Comics* a few weeks later. Psychologist William Moulton Marston, who harbored some odd notions about the relationships between men and women, more or less thought up *Wonder Woman.* He came up with the pen name Charles Moulton by combining the middle name of publisher M. C. Gaines with his middle name. For the artist, Marston selected veteran Harry G. Peter. Sheldon Mayer, who was the editor of *Sensation,* never thought much of the Amazon heroine. He also wasn't fond of Marston and had frequent battles with the author about the amount of bondage and domination elements that played an important part in the stories.

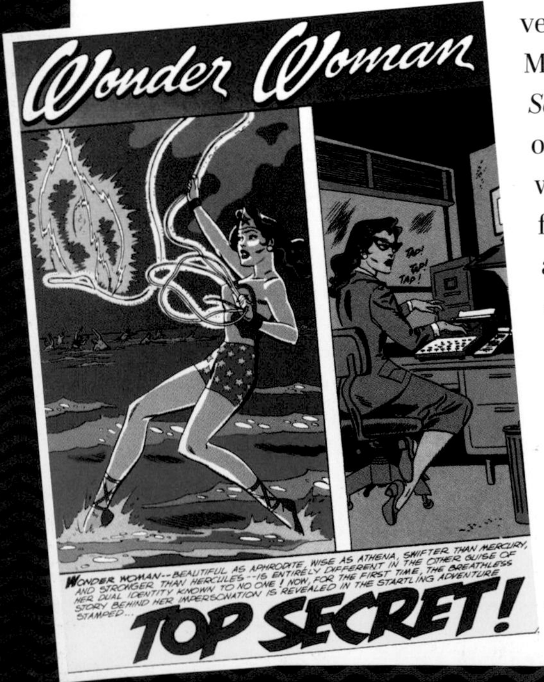
Wonder Woman
WONDER WOMAN--BEAUTIFUL AS APHRODITE, WISE AS ATHENA, SWIFTER THAN MERCURY, AND STRONGER THAN HERCULES--IS ENTIRELY DIFFERENT IN THE OTHER GUISE OF HER DUAL IDENTITY KNOWN TO NO ONE! NOW, FOR THE FIRST TIME, THE BREATHLESS STORY BEHIND HER IMPERSONATION IS REVEALED IN THE STARTLING ADVENTURE STAMPED...
TOP SECRET!

The nine-page story that introduced the character began in the manner of a Dorothy Lamour sarong epic from the late 1930s, a handsome blond aviator crashed on the "shores of an uncharted isle set in the midst of a vast expanse of ocean." Captain Steve Trevor was seriously hurt and was nursed back to health by Princess Diana, the daughter of the queen of Paradise Island. The island was an all-female enclave, and the Amazons had been living there, immortal, since before the Christian era. Because of unfortunate past experiences, they were dedicated to keeping "aloof from men." But the power of love proved too much for Princess Di, and she left her island, forsaking immortality, to escort Steve back to America.

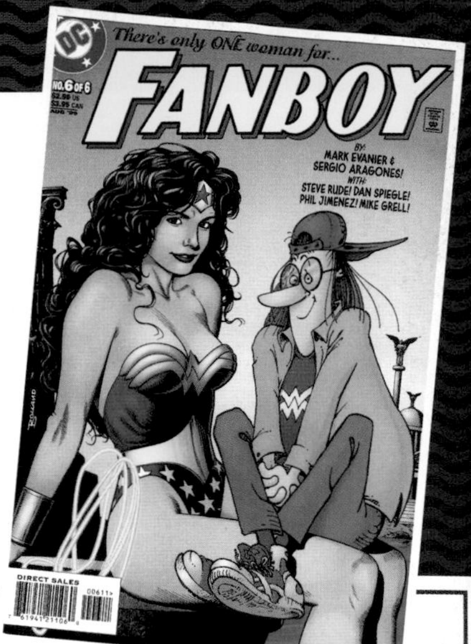
DC
There's only ONE woman for...
NO.6 OF 6
FANBOY
BY: MARK EVANIER & SERGIO ARAGONES!
WITH STEVE RUDE! DAN SPIEGLE! PHIL JIMENEZ! MIKE GRELL!
DIRECT SALES

In the initial issue of *Sensation* Wonder Woman arrived in the United States with Steve, flying her transparent airplane. Nobody ever explained the advantage of an invisible plane in which the pilot remains visible. She assumed the identity of a lovelorn nurse conveniently named Diana Prince so that she could be close to Steve while he convalesced. As with most dual-identity situations in comics, Captain Trevor never paid much attention to Diana Prince but was enamored of Wonder Woman, whom he persisted in calling "my beautiful angel." In the second issue of *Sensation*, readers met the chubby, sweets-loving Etta Candy and the other girls of the Holliday College for Women. The students all attended class wearing sweaters and shorts. Aided by Etta and the girls, Wonder Woman went on to wage war on spies, crooks, and assorted bizarre villains. There was hardly a story in which women weren't tied up with ropes, manacled with chains, and spanked. In explaining his character, Marston said that boys would go for a strong woman—"Give them an alluring woman stronger than themselves to submit to and they'll be proud to become her willing slaves!"

The early *Wonder Woman* stories were rich with the sort of bondage-submission fantasies that had hitherto been seen only in under-the-counter publications. The Moulton scripts offered some of the wackiest continuities to be found in funny books, a heady brew of whips, chains, domination, and cockeyed mythology. After the feature had been running for a while, Gaines wrote to Marston and told him to tie women up with something other than chains, as they were getting complaints. H. G. Peter, who'd been a professional cartoonist since early in the century, gave the feature a slightly decadent and entertainingly unsavory feel.

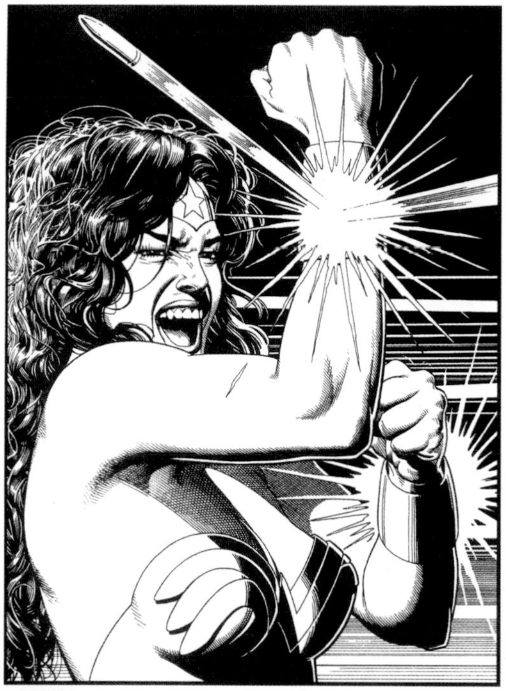

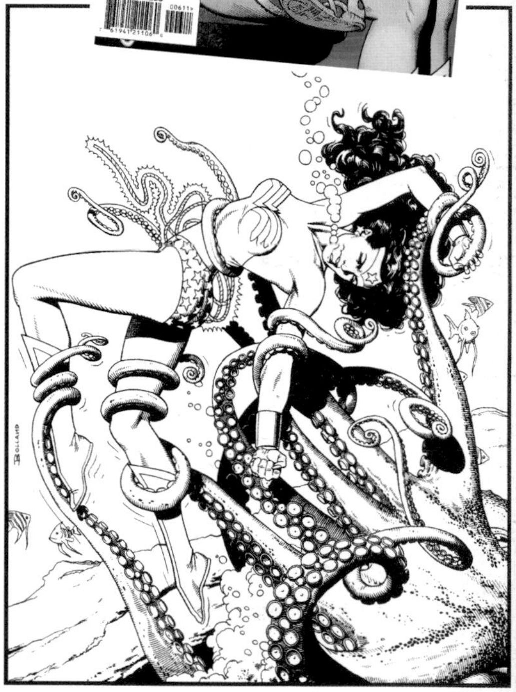

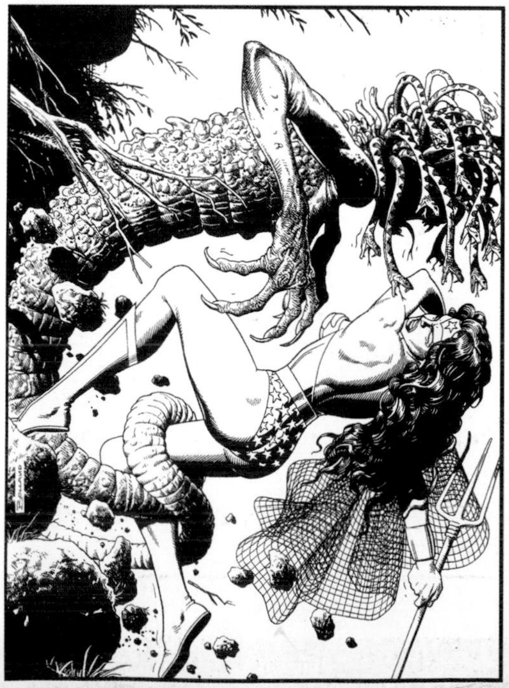

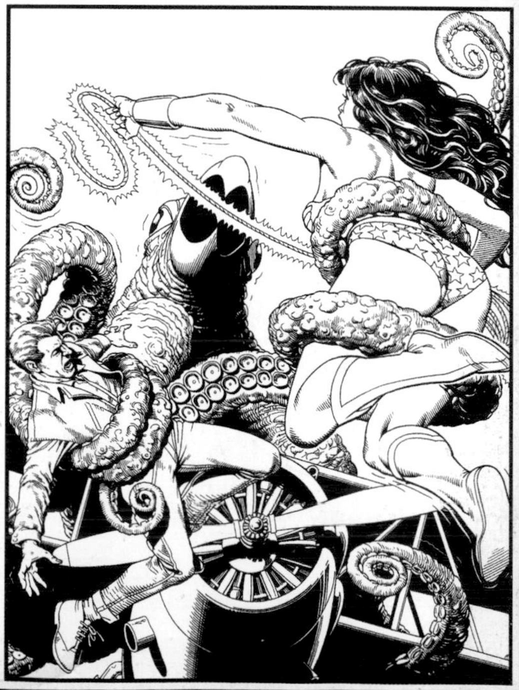

Marston died in 1947 and Peter was fired late in 1949. With editor Robert Kanigher providing scripts and the team of Ross Andru and Mike Esposito doing the drawing, *Wonder Woman* became a slicker and less eccentric feature, and the Amazon princess took to looking like the heroine of a romance comic. Affected by the waning interest in superheroics, she was dumped from *Sensation* late in 1951. The *Wonder Woman* magazine, begun in 1942, survived and served to keep the character alive. In 1968 Wonder Woman was revised by artist/writer Mike Sekowsky, given a new costume, and converted to a comic-book version of Emma Peel of *The Avengers*; a British television show. For good measure, she worked with a wise Chinese mentor who called himself I Ching.

By the early 1970s, Wonder Woman was her old self again, decked out in red, white, and blue. The *Wonder Woman* title was suspended in 1986, then revived a year later. George Perez produced the new book, returning to the earlier mythological elements and creating a livelier Princess Diana than had been seen in many a year. Wonder Woman has undergone several more makeovers in the years since then, being drawn by artists as diverse as Arthur Adams and Trina Robbins. Early in 2003, with scripts by Walt Simonson and art by Jerry Ordway, she seemed to have been born again as a young black woman.

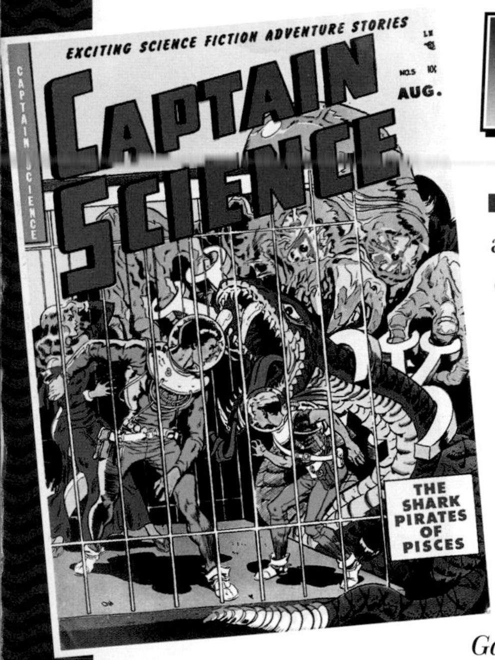
EXCITING SCIENCE FICTION ADVENTURE STORIES
AUG.
CAPTAIN SCIENCE
THE SHARK PIRATES OF PISCES

WOOD, WALLY (1927–1981)

■ A gifted but self-destructive artist, Wood's heyday occurred during the 1950s. In that decade he was one of the stars of the innovative EC Comics line and also ghosted *The Spirit*, worked with Jack Kirby on an SF comic strip called *Sky Masters*, drew illustrations for the SF magazine *Galaxy*, worked for both Marvel and DC, and handled some advertising accounts.

Wood, born in Minnesota and basically untutored in art, moved east and began working in comic books in the late 1940s. Some of his earliest work was done in collaboration with writer/artist Harry Harrison. He signed on with EC in 1949 and was soon a major contributor to most of their titles, from *Weird Fantasy* to *Mad*. Wood was good at drawing people, especially pretty girls, but he also excelled at things mechanical—whether WWII submarines or twenty-fifth century rocket ships. At the end of a story in *Weird Science* he addressed the reader directly, explaining, "My world is the world of science fiction." The alien worlds and spacecraft that Wood invented for his stories were much copied by later and less gifted artists. For *Mad* he used an informal, cartoony style that was influenced by one of his idols, Walt Kelly. In later years Wood also worked with erstwhile *Mad* editor Harvey Kurtzman on such humor magazines as *Trump* and *Humbug*.

As the demand for his stuff increased, Wood set up a sort of free-form shop. He worked a lot and apparently drank a lot. Initially his drawing didn't suffer much. He created *The T.H.U.N.D.E.R. Agents* for the short-lived Tower line of comic books and drew *Daredevil* for Marvel. For armed forces publications he produced raunchier material, such as *Sally Forth*, about a young lady who frequently shed her clothes. And he inked Jack Kirby's *Challengers of the Unknown.*

His work seriously deteriorated in the 1970s. His health deteriorated, too, and he suffered kidney failure. His last professional work consisted of some crude and badly drawn pornographic comics. Wood ended his life as the 1980s began.

WOODY WOODPECKER

■ See NEW FUNNIES.

WORLD'S FINEST COMICS

■ The first regularly issued comic book featuring both Superman and Batman, it was inspired by *New York World's Fair Comics*, which came out once in 1939 and once in 1940. DC introduced this fifteen-cent ninety-six-page comic book in the early spring of 1941. The first issue was called *World's Best Comics* and from the second on the title was *World's Finest*. What this fat, cardboard-covered anthology offered was new adventures of DC's most popular characters and, and in addition to Superman and Batman, there were new stories featuring Zatara, Johnny Thunder, and the Sandman, plus characters created just for the magazine.

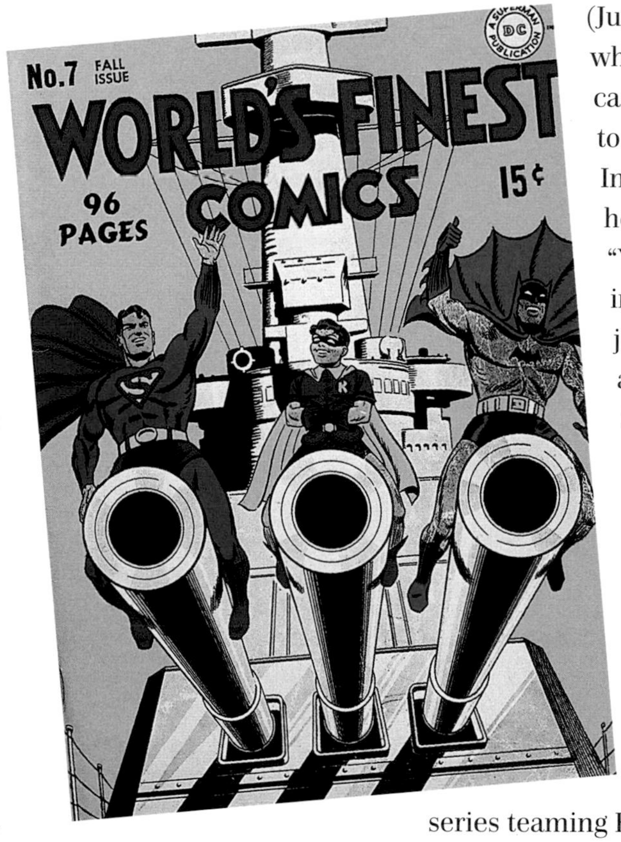
No.7 FALL ISSUE
A SUPERMAN DC PUBLICATION
WORLD'S FINEST COMICS
96 PAGES
15¢

Among the new heroes introduced were Lando, yet another magician, and Drafty, a humorous soldier, drawn first by Ed Moore and then by Stan Kaye. Henry Boltinoff did just about his only serious comic-book work on *Young Doctor Davis*. Others who frequented *World's Finest* in its early years were the Star Spangled Kid, the Green Arrow, the Boy Commandos, the Wyoming Kid, and Tommy Tomorrow.

With the seventy-first issue (July–August 1954) the magazine, which had long since shed its cardboard covers, dropped its price to ten cents and cut its page count. In another innovation, it teamed its headliners, Batman and Superman—"Your two favorite heroes together in one adventure!" Robin also joined in. The initial artist for these amalgamated yarns was Dick Sprang, who held on until 1963.

World's Finest continued until its 323rd issue (January 1986), fluctuating in price, page count, and lineup. As the magazine grew older, the Superman-Batman combo did not always appear, and considerable reprint material was used. In 1990 DC used the title for a three-issue series teaming Batman and Superman once again. This was written by Dave Gibbons, illustrated by Karl Kesel and Steve Rude. There was also a *World's Finest* one-shot published in 2001.

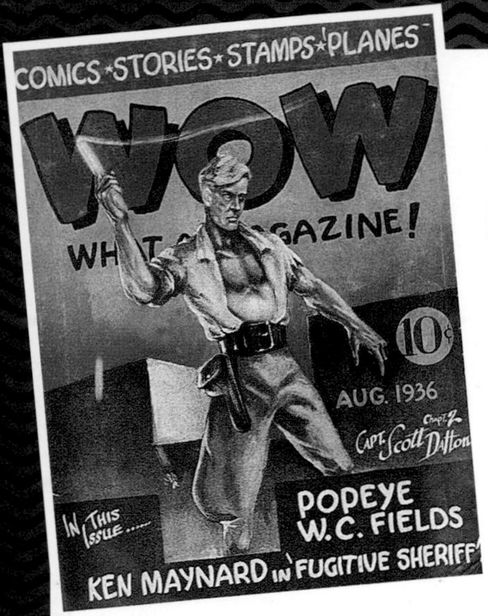
COMICS * STORIES * STAMPS * PLANES
WOW
WHAT A MAGAZINE!
10¢
AUG. 1936
Capt. Scott Dalton
IN THIS ISSUE.....
POPEYE
W.C. FIELDS
KEN MAYNARD IN FUGITIVE SHERIFF

WOW

■ Subtitled *What a Magazine!*, this ephemeral comic book is chiefly noteworthy because it published Will Eisner's first work in the field. *Wow* also brought together Eisner and its editor Jerry Iger, who went on to form one of the earliest shops to package comic books for publishers. A mixture of reprint and original material, *Wow* also ran the first professional work of Bob Kane and Dick Briefer. Both of them would join the Eisner-Iger shop in 1937. The magazine's four issues appeared in the summer and fall of 1936. Newspaper strip reprints included *Flash Gordon*, *Popeye*, *The Little King*, and *Mandrake*.

WOW COMICS

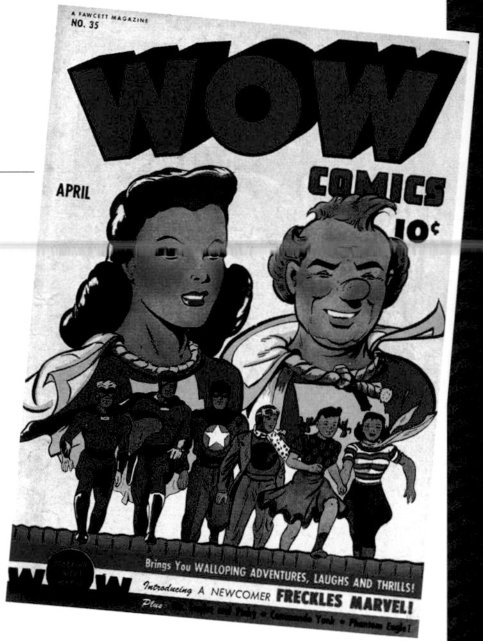
A FAWCETT MAGAZINE
NO. 35
WOW
APRIL
COMICS
10¢
Brings You WALLOPING ADVENTURES, LAUGHS AND THRILLS!
Introducing A NEWCOMER FRECKLES MARVEL!

■ You can't keep a good title down, and it was Fawcett Publications that next christened a magazine *Wow*. That was late in 1940, after they'd already issued the highly successful *Whiz Comics*, the barely hanging on *Master Comics*, and the out-and-out flops *Slam-Bang Comics* and *Nickel Comics*. Initially, Fawcett made the same mistake with *Wow Comics* that they'd made with all their unsuccessful titles. That was to rely on the unimaginative Harry "A" Chesler shop to produce most of the content.

With the exception of the costumed Mr. Scarlet, drawn by Jack Kirby, all of the other features were from the Chesler sweat shop, and several had already failed in other Fawcett comics. *Wow* struggled along as a quarterly until 1942, then late in that year the Chesler product was dumped and the magazine given an overhaul. Mr. Scarlet was retained, drawn now by Jack Binder, and some livelier characters were added. These included a masked soldier known as Commando Yank and a masked pilot known as the Phantom Eagle, this latter written and drawn by Bert Whitman. Dave Berg contributed a funny fantasy called *Spooks*.

Then with #9 (January 1943) *Wow* became a monthly and the newest member of the Shazam Family, Mary Marvel, was starred. C. C. Beck drew the introductory cover, which also showed Captain Marvel, Captain Marvel, Jr., and wise old Shazam himself. Mary, drawn by Binder, was the leading character for the next four years. The backup crew eventually narrowed down to Mr. Scarlet and his boy companion Pinky, the Commando Yank, and the Phantom Eagle. There was a detective spoof titled *Richard Richard, Private Dick*, drawn initially by Dick McKay. Marc Swayze, who'd drawn Mary Marvel when she appeared in *Captain Marvel Adventures*, drew *Phantom Eagle* for a good part of its run. Dan Barry and then Carl Pfeufer drew *Commando Yank*.

The decline in popularity of superheroes that began in the later 1940s affected Mary Marvel, and in the summer of 1947 she was dropped from *Wow*. She was replaced by an Archie surrogate named Ozzie. *Wow Comics* continued until the summer of the following year and its sixty-ninth issue.

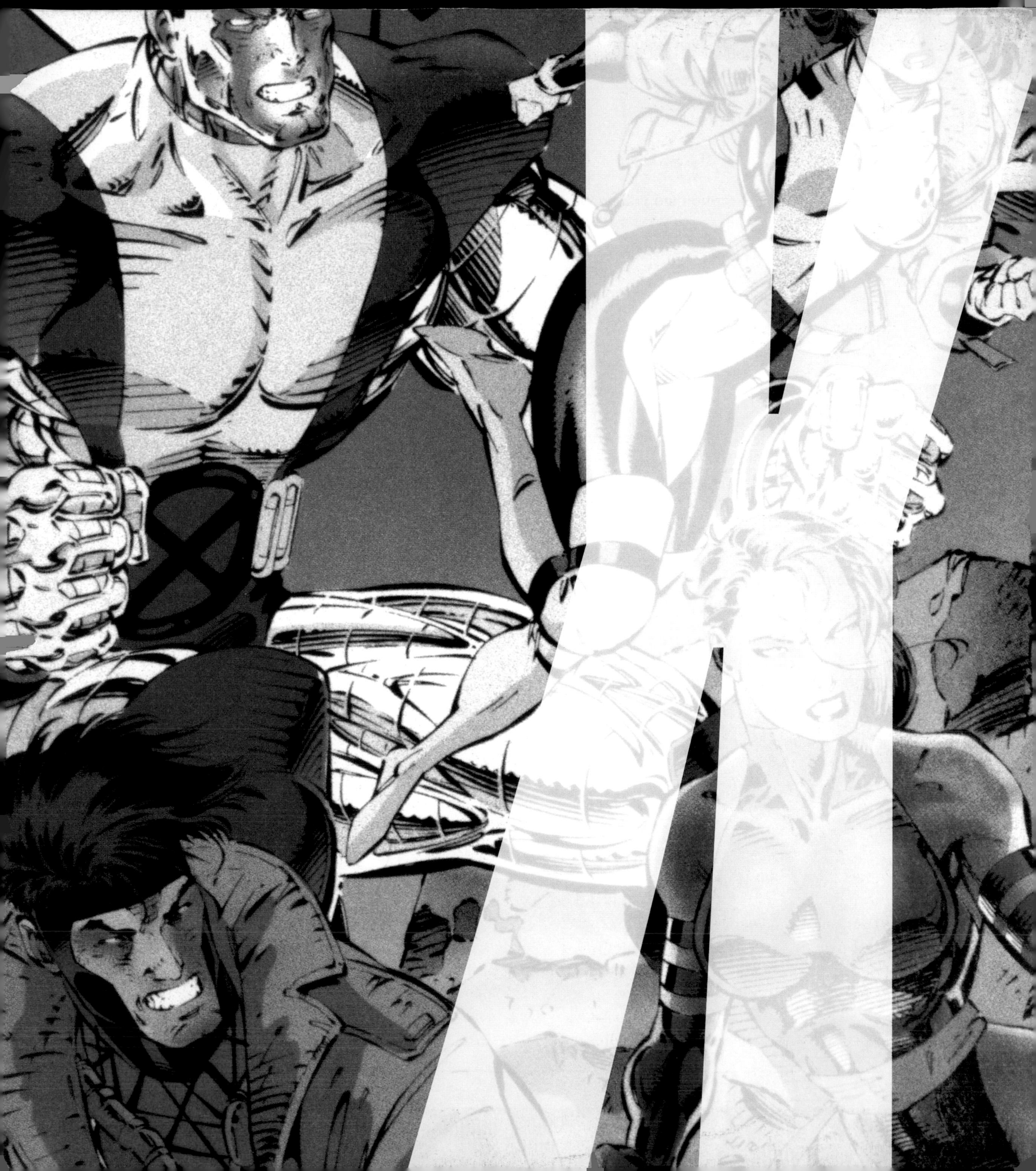

X-MEN

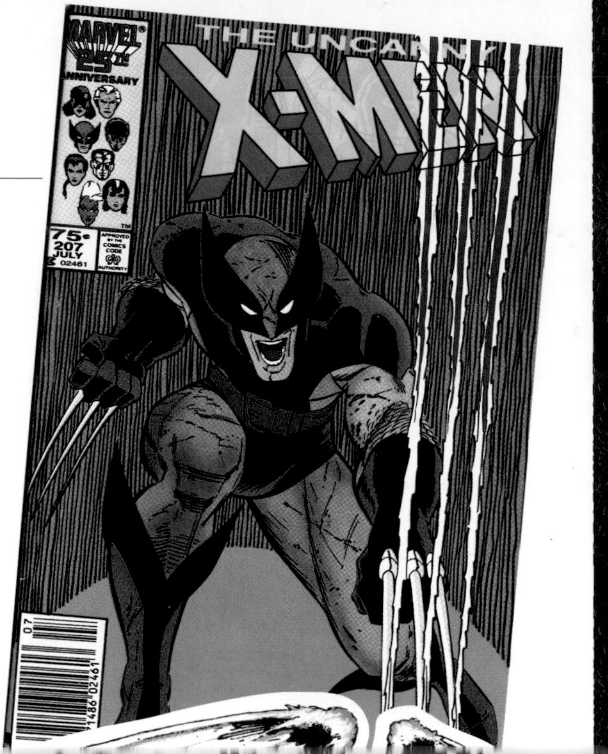
THE UNCANNY
X-MEN
MARVEL
25TH ANNIVERSARY
75¢
207
JULY

■ The X-Men, the epitome of mutant groups, began their long and highly profitable career in the summer of 1963. The cover of the first issue displayed the five charter members as well as the fellow destined to be their most persistent foe. They were the Angel, Cyclops, the Beast, Iceman, Marvel Girl, and Magneto, "Earth's Most Powerful Super Villain!!" The X-Men themselves were touted as "The Strangest Super Heroes of All!" Not depicted on the cover was the bald, wheelchair bound Professor Xavier, who had founded a mutant academy in New York's fashionable Westchester County.

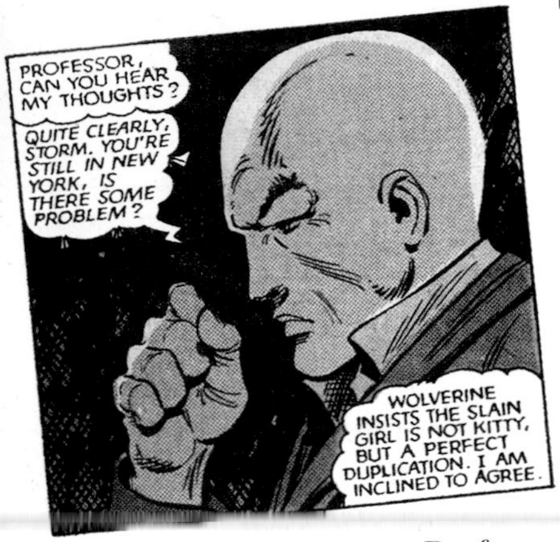
PROFESSOR, CAN YOU HEAR MY THOUGHTS?
QUITE CLEARLY, STORM. YOU'RE STILL IN NEW YORK, IS THERE SOME PROBLEM?
WOLVERINE INSISTS THE SLAIN GIRL IS NOT KITTY, BUT A PERFECT DUPLICATION. I AM INCLINED TO AGREE.

Professor Charles Xavier possessed numerous psionic powers himself, including the ability to read minds and project his thoughts within a radius of 250 miles. He could make others think he was invisible, sense the presence of another mutant, project his astral body, and control matter psychokinetically. For good measure, he studied "genetics and other sciences."

Professor X gathered together his team of good mutants "to protect mankind from . . . evil mutants." The first evil mutant they tackled was the red-armored Magneto. The initial X-Men consisted of "Hank McCoy, known to us as the Beast! Bobby Drake, nicknamed Iceman! Slim Summers, our human Cylcops! . . . Warren Worthington the Third, who is called the Angel . . . Miss Jean Grey . . . Marvel Girl!" The Beast was an apelike version of the Thing;

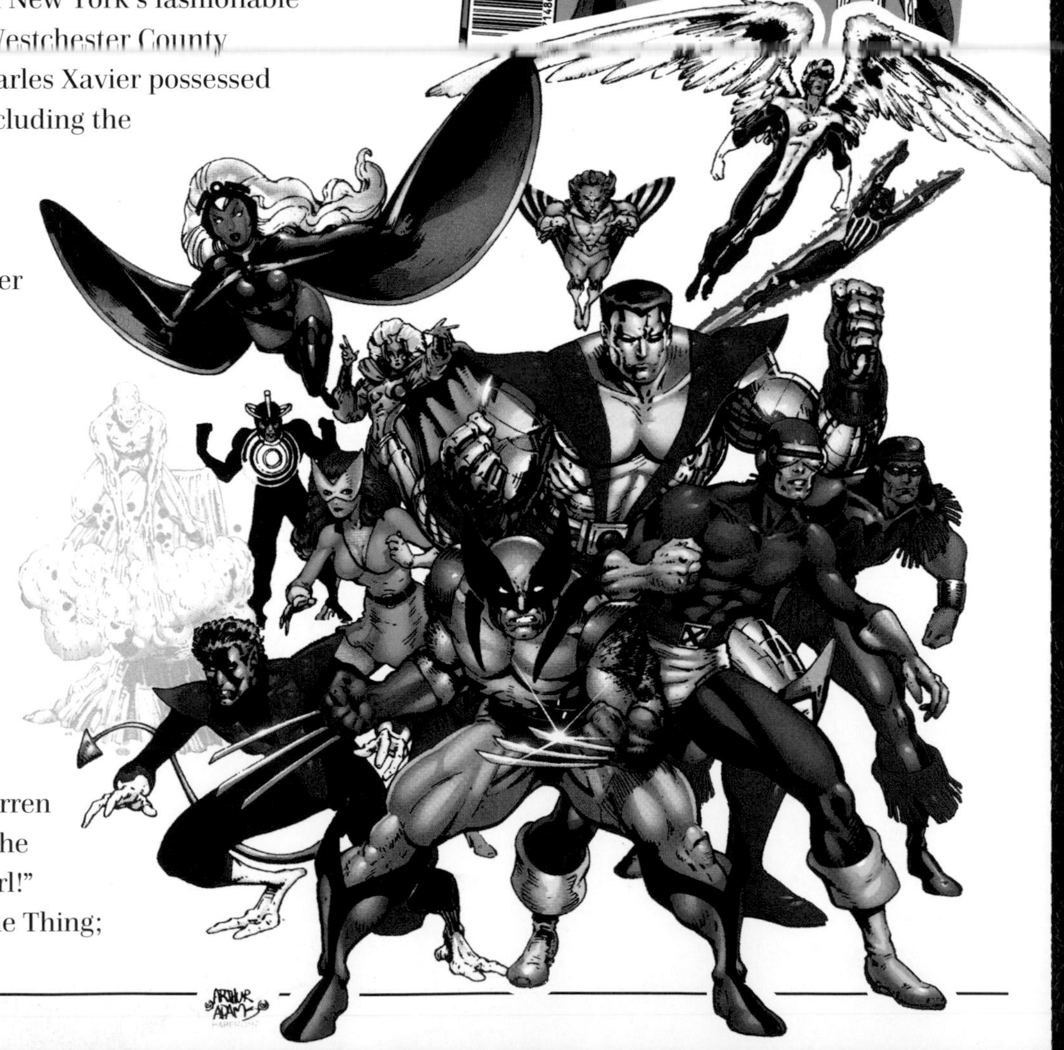

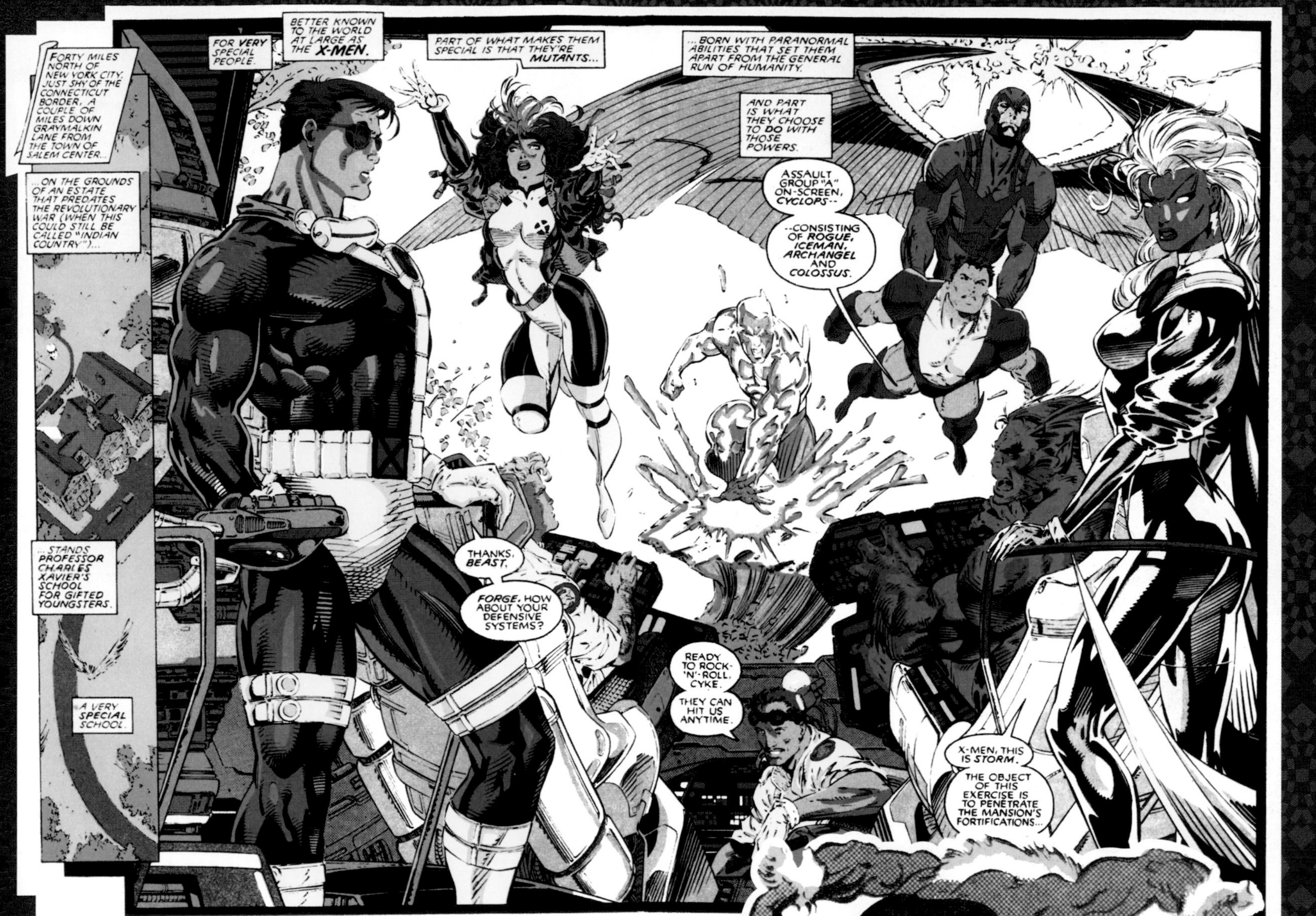
FORTY MILES NORTH OF NEW YORK CITY, JUST SHY OF THE CONNECTICUT BORDER, A COUPLE OF MILES DOWN GRAYMALKIN LANE FROM THE TOWN OF SALEM CENTER...
...ON THE GROUNDS OF AN ESTATE THAT PREDATES THE REVOLUTIONARY WAR (WHEN THIS COULD STILL BE CALLED "INDIAN COUNTRY")...
...STANDS PROFESSOR CHARLES XAVIER'S SCHOOL FOR GIFTED YOUNGSTERS.
A VERY SPECIAL SCHOOL.
FOR VERY SPECIAL PEOPLE.
BETTER KNOWN TO THE WORLD AT LARGE AS THE X-MEN.
PART OF WHAT MAKES THEM SPECIAL IS THAT THEY'RE MUTANTS...
...BORN WITH PARANORMAL ABILITIES THAT SET THEM APART FROM THE GENERAL RUN OF HUMANITY.
AND PART IS WHAT THEY CHOOSE TO DO WITH THOSE POWERS.
ASSAULT GROUP "A" ON-SCREEN, CYCLOPS--
--CONSISTING OF ROGUE, ICEMAN, ARCHANGEL AND COLOSSUS.
THANKS, BEAST.
FORGE, HOW ABOUT YOUR DEFENSIVE SYSTEMS?
READY TO ROCK-'N'-ROLL, CYKE.
THEY CAN HIT US ANYTIME.
X-MEN, THIS IS STORM.
THE OBJECT OF THIS EXERCISE IS TO PENETRATE THE MANSION'S FORTIFICATIONS...

Iceman could turn himself into a human icicle and toss deadly snowballs; Cyclops, who had two eyes, could send powerful rays out of them; the Angel had real wings growing out of his back and could fly; and Marvel Girl had powerful telekinetic powers. This collection of misunderstood misfits appealed to teenagers. After an initial success, however, *X-Men* began to fade and the original material was halted in 1970.

After the original X-Men had been in limbo for several years, existing only in reprints, Marvel issued an annual titled *Giant-Size X-Men.* This introduced a new batch of teenage mutant heroes. They included Colossus, Nightcrawler, Thunderbird, Storm, Banshee, and the chronically short-tempered and pathologically

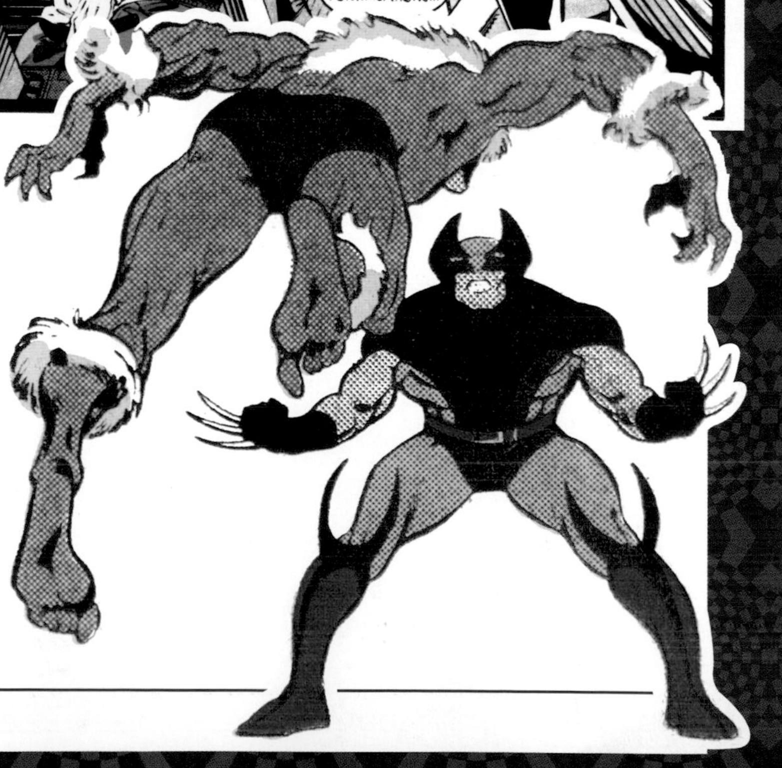

violent Wolverine. Len Wein was the writer, Dave Cockrum the artist. Starting with *X-Men* #94 (August 1975), the group began appearing in brand-new adventures in their own, revived magazine. Very shortly Chris Claremont took over as writer and made the X-Men his own. His intricate plots, ranging over many issues and mixing fantasy, science fiction, physical transmutation, adolescent anguish, identity crises, and topics of the day won an increasing readership.

The X-Men have remained popular, appearing in various graphic novel collections like *Wolverine*, *The Phoenix Saga*, and *Mutant Massacre*, and in alternate titles such as *Uncanny X-Men* and *Ultimate X-Men*. A new *X-Men*, written by Claremont and drawn by the popular Jim Lee, appeared in 1991. It sold 8 million copies to become the best-selling comic book of all time. The X-Men have in the past few years also become the stars of blockbuster movies.

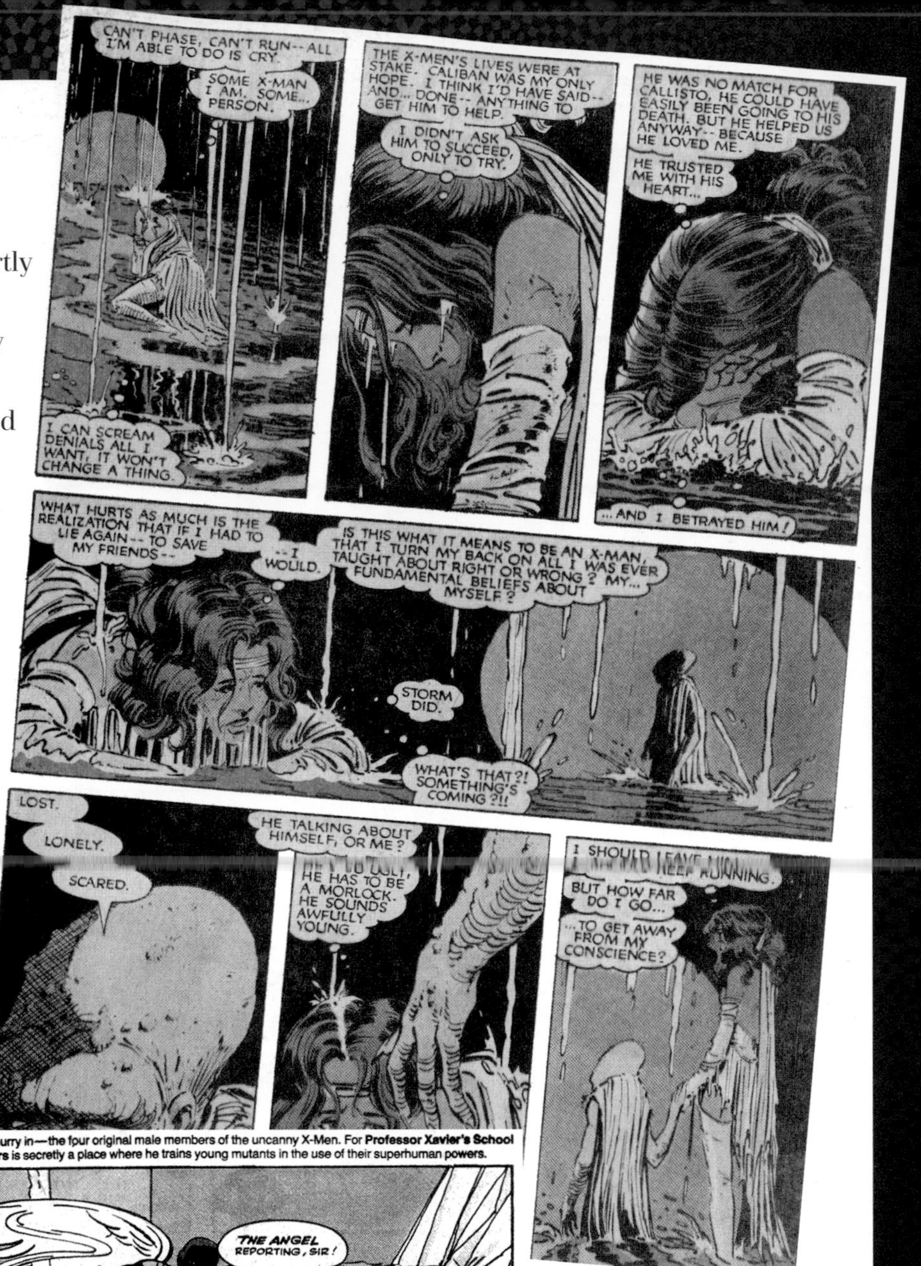
CAN'T PHASE, CAN'T RUN-- ALL I'M ABLE TO DO IS CRY.
SOME X-MAN I AM. SOME... PERSON.
I CAN SCREAM DENIALS ALL I WANT, IT WON'T CHANGE A THING.
THE X-MEN'S LIVES WERE AT STAKE. CALIBAN WAS MY ONLY HOPE. I THINK I'D HAVE SAID-- AND... DONE-- ANYTHING TO GET HIM TO HELP.
I DIDN'T ASK HIM TO SUCCEED, ONLY TO TRY.
HE WAS NO MATCH FOR CALLISTO. HE COULD HAVE EASILY BEEN GOING TO HIS DEATH. BUT HE HELPED US ANYWAY-- BECAUSE HE LOVED ME.
HE TRUSTED ME WITH HIS HEART...
...AND I BETRAYED HIM!
WHAT HURTS AS MUCH IS THE REALIZATION THAT IF I HAD TO LIE AGAIN -- TO SAVE MY FRIENDS --
-- I WOULD.
IS THIS WHAT IT MEANS TO BE AN X-MAN, THAT I TURN MY BACK ON ALL I WAS EVER TAUGHT ABOUT RIGHT OR WRONG? MY... FUNDAMENTAL BELIEFS ABOUT MYSELF?
STORM DID.
WHAT'S THAT?! SOMETHING'S COMING?!!
LOST.
LONELY.
SCARED.
HE TALKING ABOUT HIMSELF, OR ME?
HE HAS TO BE A MORLOCK. HE SOUNDS AWFULLY YOUNG.
BUT HOW FAR DO I GO...
...TO GET AWAY FROM MY CONSCIENCE?

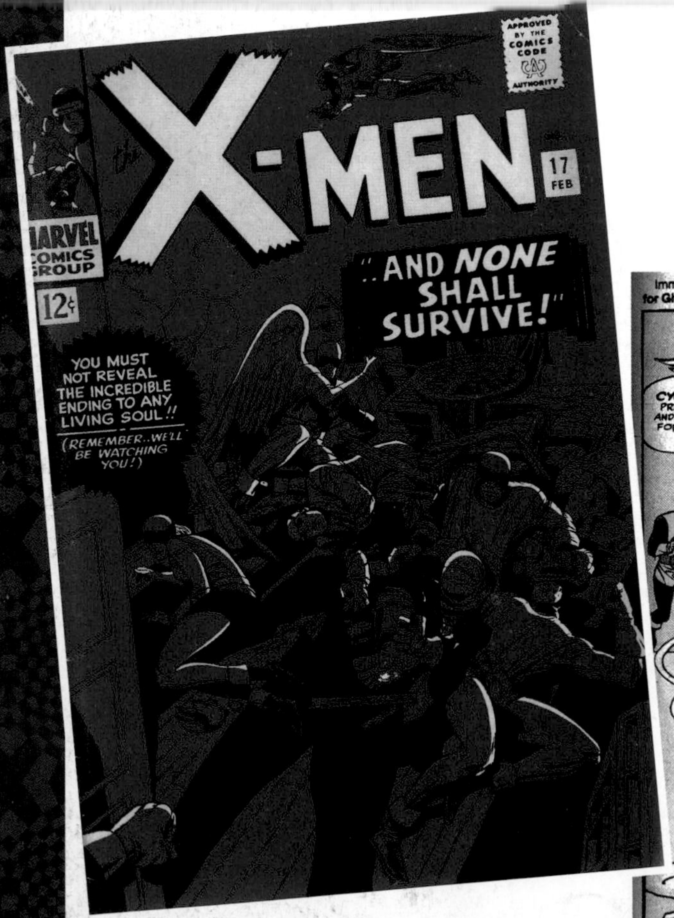
APPROVED BY THE COMICS CODE AUTHORITY
X-MEN
17 FEB
MARVEL COMICS GROUP
12¢
"...AND NONE SHALL SURVIVE!"
YOU MUST NOT REVEAL THE INCREDIBLE ENDING TO ANY LIVING SOUL!!
(REMEMBER.. WE'LL BE WATCHING YOU!)

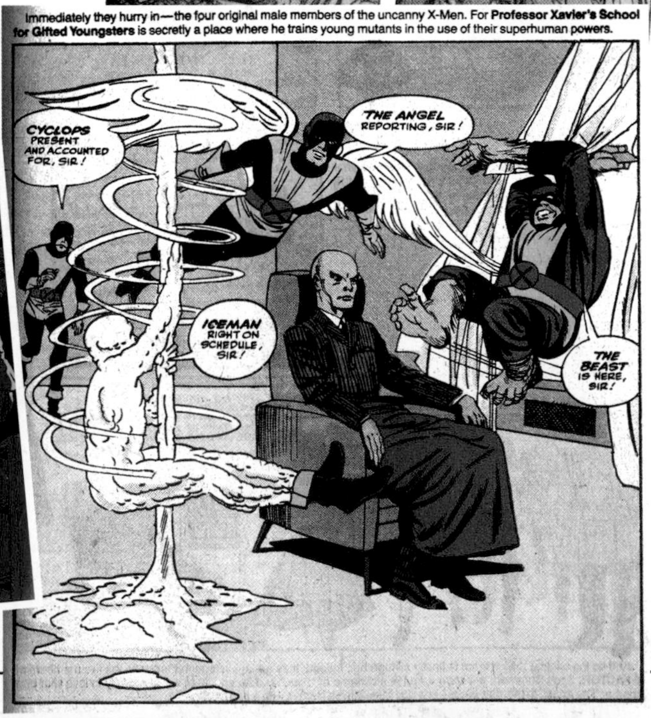
Immediately they hurry in—the four original male members of the uncanny X-Men. For Professor Xavier's School for Gifted Youngsters is secretly a place where he trains young mutants in the use of their superhuman powers.
CYCLOPS PRESENT AND ACCOUNTED FOR, SIR!
THE ANGEL REPORTING, SIR!
ICEMAN RIGHT ON SCHEDULE, SIR!
THE BEAST IS HERE, SIR!

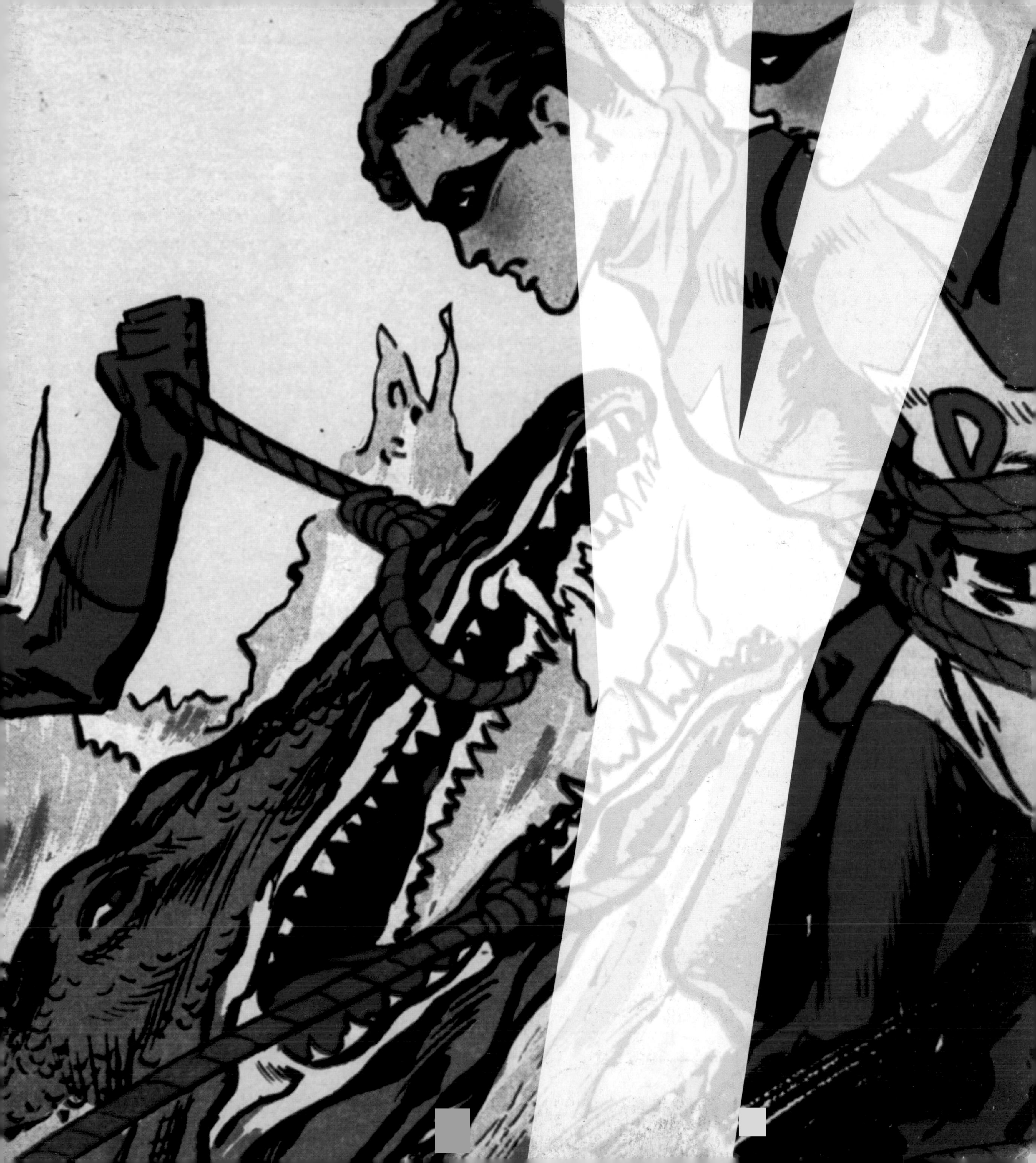

YANK AND DOODLE

■ See PRIZE COMICS.

THE YOUNG ALLIES

■ Several kid gangs got going in comic books in the early forties, but this was the only bunch that had a superpowered youth and a costumed youth among its membership. Masterminded by Joe Simon and Jack Kirby but written and drawn by others, the Young Allies were introduced by way of their own magazine in the summer of 1941. They roamed the war-torn world, battling the Nazis, the Japanese, and other enemies of America. Although they never quite adjusted to civilian life, they remained in business until the summer of 1947.

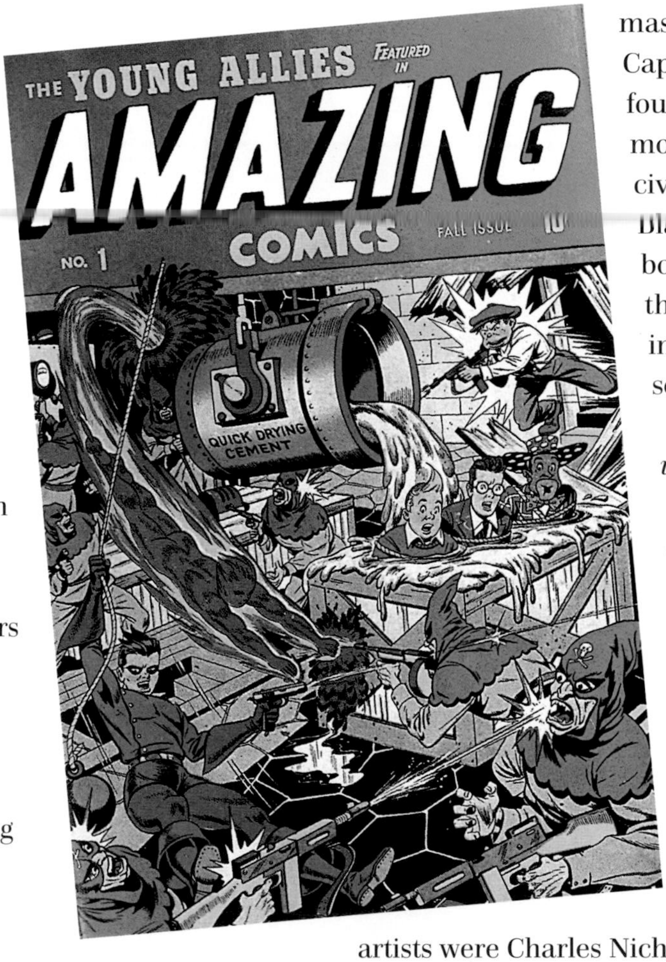
THE YOUNG ALLIES FEATURED IN
AMAZING
COMICS
NO. 1
FALL ISSUE
QUICK DRYING CEMENT

The stars of the group were Toro, the flaming boy companion of the Human Torch, and Bucky, the scrappy sidekick of Captain America. The other four members were Jeff, the brainy one who wore glasses; Tubby, the fat one; Knuckles, the Dead End Kid surrogate; and Whitewash, the zoot-suited black, who, in keeping with the stereotypes of the day, played the harmonica and was passionate about watermelon.

Simon once said that he got the name for the gang from a series of juvenile novels about the Boy Allies that he'd read as a youth. Each adventure took up nearly an entire issue, something that wasn't much done at the time. In their first outing, the new team battled Nazi spies as well as the evil Red Skull, a master villain borrowed from Captain America. The second issue found them fighting Nazis once more while discovering a lost civilization and tangling with the Black Talon, another bad guy borrowed from the captain. In that issue the boy buddies introduced their very own fight song—

We fight together thru stormy weather—
We're out to lick both crooks and spies!
We won't be stopped—and we can't be topped—
We are the Young Allies!

In addition to twenty issues of their own magazine, the lads also appeared in Timely's *Kid Comics*, *Amazing*, *Complete*, *Marvel Mystery*, *Mystic*, and *Sub-Mariner*. Among the artists were Charles Nicholas and Al Gabriele, among the writers Stan Lee and Otto Binder. The dependable Alex Schomburg supplied the majority of covers.

YOUNG ROMANCE

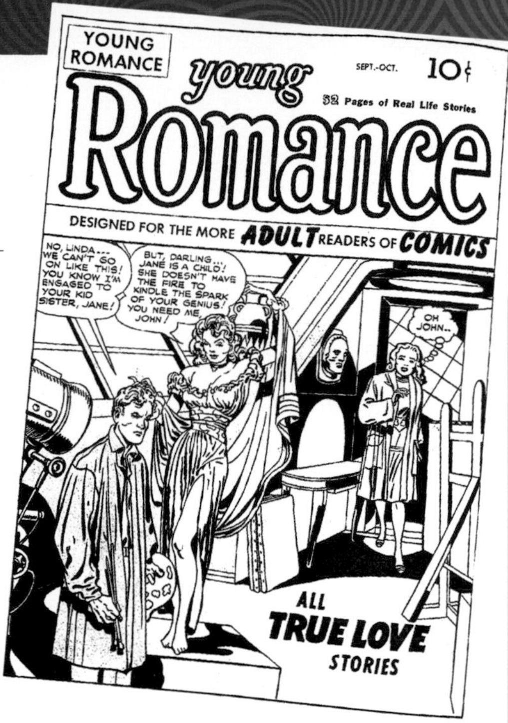

YOUNG ROMANCE
young Romance
SEPT.-OCT.
10¢
52 Pages of Real Life Stories
DESIGNED FOR THE MORE ADULT READERS OF COMICS
NO, LINDA... WE CAN'T GO ON LIKE THIS! YOU KNOW I'M ENGAGED TO YOUR KID SISTER, JANE!
BUT, DARLING... JANE IS A CHILD! SHE DOESN'T HAVE THE FIRE TO KINDLE THE SPARK OF YOUR GENIUS! YOU NEED ME, JOHN!
OH JOHN..
ALL TRUE LOVE STORIES

■ This was the publication that brought love to the newsstands, introduced the romance genre, and converted millions of girls into comic-book readers. It also inspired one of the most lucrative trends in post–World War II publishing. *Young Romance* was invented by Joe Simon and packaged and produced by him and his longtime partner Jack Kirby. Published by the Prize Group, the first issue arrived in the summer of 1947.

Although the book initially ran the slogan "For the More ADULT Readers of COMICS" on the covers, what it offered was easier-to-digest versions of the type of material that had long been available in confession magazines like *True Story*. While the audience for *Young Romance* did include older readers, the majority of the customers were teenage and preteen girls, an audience that had never supported the now-fading superheroes in any great numbers. The first issue of *Young Romance* sold out a printing of 500,000 and soon the circulation climbed to a million per issue.

Simon recruited artists such as Bill Draut and Mort Meskin and has said that he and Kirby turned out the early scripts themselves. "We wrote the whole thing. We couldn't afford writers." Later, since they were getting 50 percent of the profits, they did hire writers. "All the stories were shamelessly billed as true confessions by young women and girls," Simon later confessed, "when in actuality they were authored by men." Typical story titles were "I Was a Gangster's Moll" and "They Called Me Boy Crazy." The team followed their hit invention with *Young Love* late in 1948, and it, too, became a million-copy best-seller.

Other publishers began getting into the romance business and, according to comics historian John Benson, "at the height of the phenomenon there were nearly one hundred and fifty titles being published simultaneously." Simon and Kirby eventually moved on to other things, but *Young Romance*, which was taken over by DC in 1963, survived until its 208th issue in 1975.

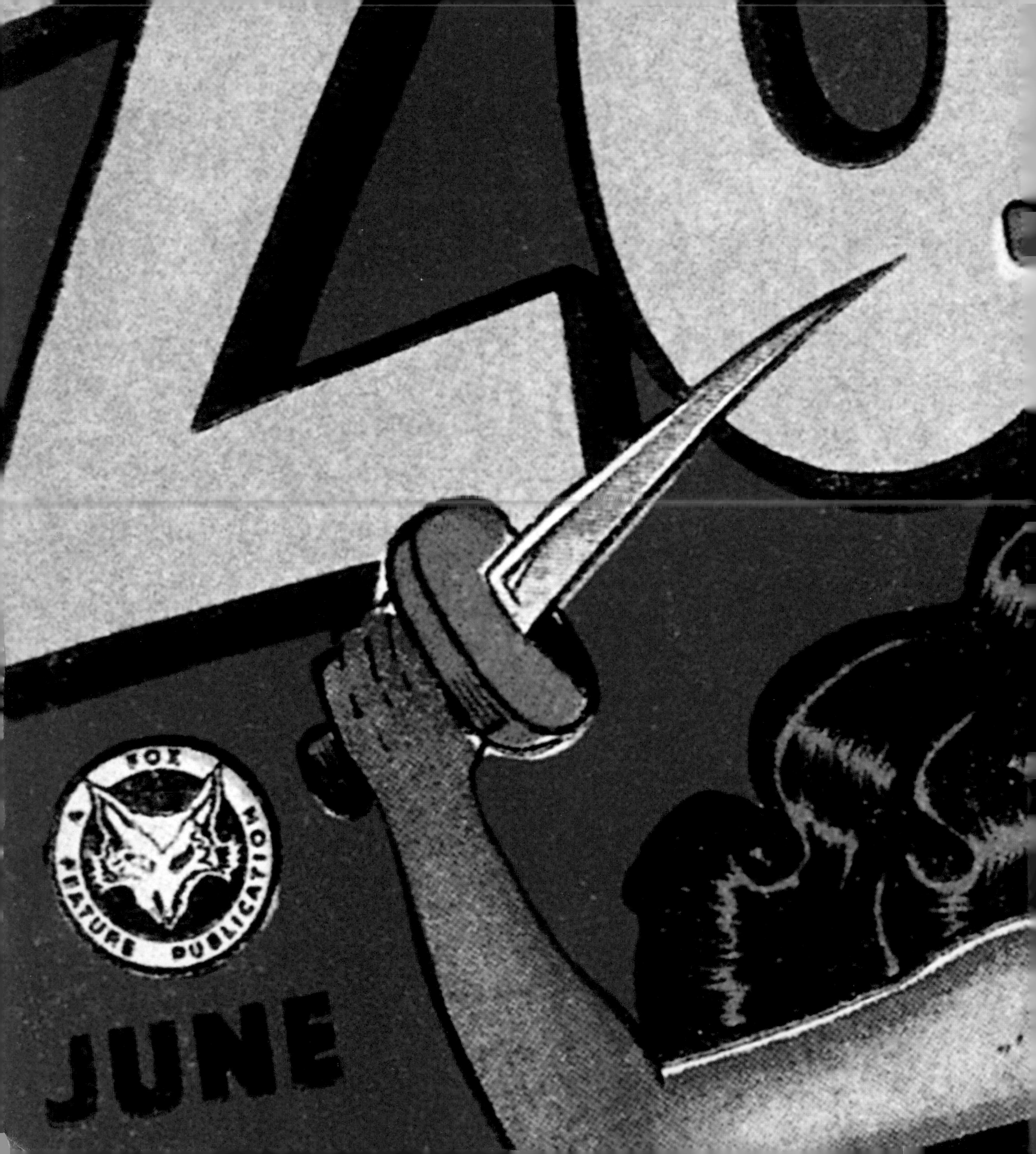
A FOX FEATURE PUBLICATION
JUNE

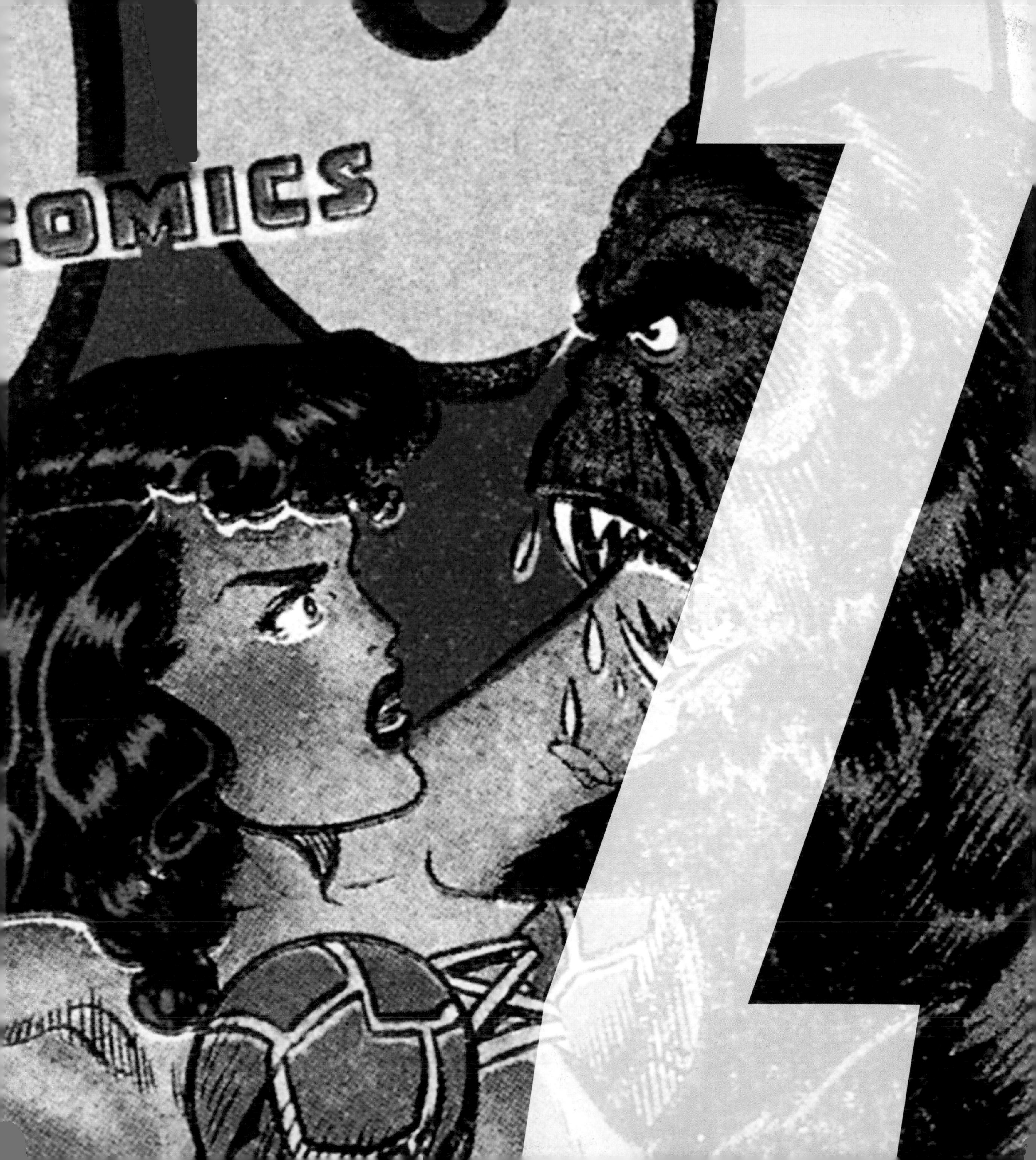
COMICS

ZATANNA

■ Daughter of magician Zatara, she was the creation of Gardner Fox, with an assist from DC editor Julius Schwartz. She first appeared as a guest in *Hawkman* #4 in the summer of 1964 and was drawn by Murphy Anderson. The notion was that she was looking for her long-lost father. This quest took her through various other titles, including *The Atom* and *Green Lantern*, until she finally found him in *Justice League* #51. Zatara was allegedly later killed in a continuity that appeared in *Swamp Thing*, but he resurfaced in the late 1980s in *Young All Stars*. These stories were set in the 1940s and didn't require resurrection.

Usually Zatanna wore a stage magician's outfit, complete with black net stockings. She became a member of the Justice League and for a time adopted a red-and-blue crimefighter costume. She has soloed on several occasions in one-shots and limited series of her own. Gray Morrow drew one of her miniseries and Esteban Maroto, with scripts by Lee Marrs, produced a very handsome four-issue run. More recently Zatanna returned in a one-shot

ZATARA

■ The founding father of what may become a dynasty of magicians, Zatara cast his first spell in *Action Comics* #1 (June 1938). The maiden adventure was written and drawn by Fred Guardineer, and in that one the magician appeared without his familiar moustache. From the second issue onward, with scripts by Gardner Fox, his resemblance to Mandrake the Magician increased by his assuming a moustache. He also had a giant sidekick named Tong to act as a Lothar surrogate. Zatara could do just about anything and there was no pretending that his tricks were merely hypnotic illusions. He really could move buildings, turn crooks' guns into snakes, turn the crooks themselves into pigs, and then project his astral body to the moon.

ZATARA
THE MASTER MAGICIAN
AND THE
TERROR FROM SATURN
BY FRED GUARDINEER

His immense mystical powers stemmed from his discovery that words said backward had unfailing effect. "Emoc nwod!" he'd command, and something or somebody would come down. Once, annoyed with some unruly gorillas, he instructed them, "Sallirog llaf ot ruoy htaed!" Zatara left *Action* in 1950 and took what seemed to be his final bow in *World's Finest* #51. Among the other artists to draw the feature were Joseph Sulman, W. F. White, and Joe Kubert.

Although his death was reported some years ago, he still appears occasionally in DC titles.

THE ZEBRA

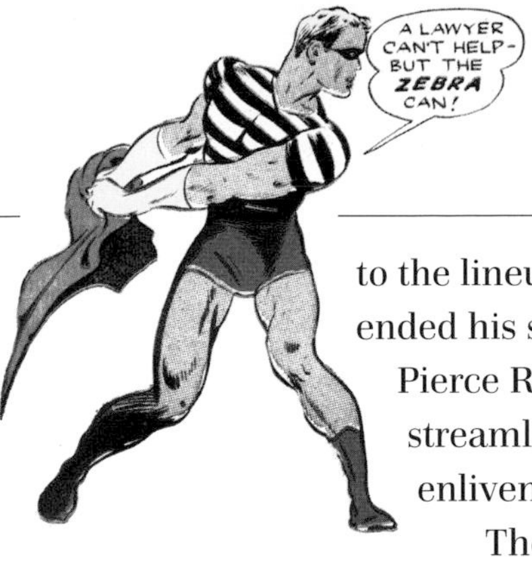
A LAWYER CAN'T HELP– BUT THE ZEBRA CAN!

■ "Sent up the river for a crime he did not commit," explained a caption in *Pocket Comics* in 1941, "John Doyle escaped and proved his innocence. . . . Now as the Zebra, he battles criminals outside the law." After concocting a black-and-white striped costume based on his prison outfit, Doyle decided that the Zebra was an apt name for his alter ego. His reputation cleared, he resumed his legal practice, making "a brilliant name for himself in criminal law."

The Zebra appeared in all four issues of Alfred Harvey's *Pocket Comics*, a ninety-six-page digest that didn't catch on. When the Harvey Brothers assumed the publishing of *Green Hornet Comics* in the spring of 1942, they revamped the magazine, adding several characters to the lineup. One of them was the Zebra, which ended his several months of unemployment. Pierce Rice drew the new adventures, streamlining the hero's costume as well as enlivening the page breakdowns.

The Zebra, having no superpowers, was vulnerable, especially to blows on the head. Once a villainous sign painter knocked him silly by dropping a bucket of red paint on his noggin, once a two-by-four did the trick. After that latter cold cocking, the Zebra awakened to find he'd been tossed in the city dump. Despite such indignities, he always rallied to bring that issue's evildoer to justice.

The Zebra, later drawn by the likes of Joe Kubert and Bob Fujitani, remained in *Green Hornet* until 1946.

ZERO

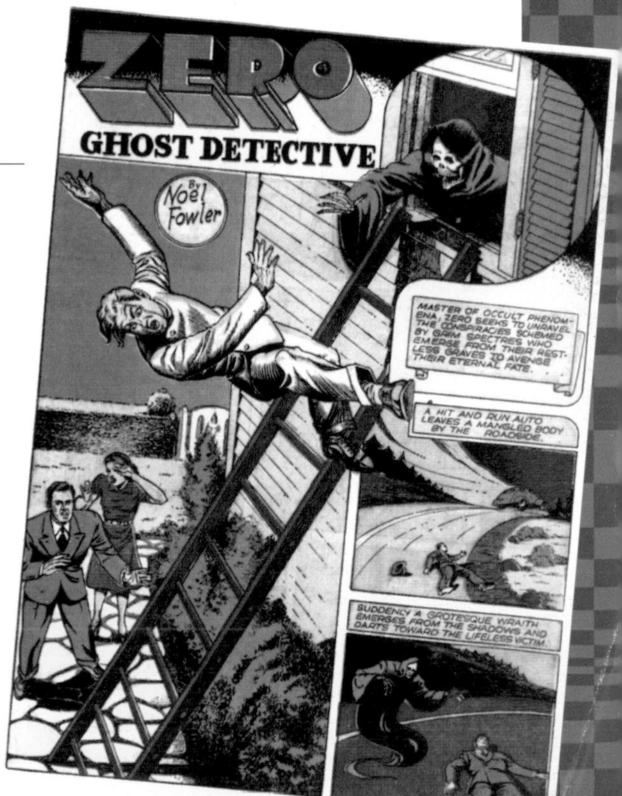
ZERO
GHOST DETECTIVE
By Noel Fowler
MASTER OF OCCULT PHENOMENA, ZERO SEEKS TO UNRAVEL THE CONSPIRACIES SCHEMED BY GRIM SPECTRES WHO EMERGE FROM THEIR RESTLESS GRAVES TO AVENGE THEIR ETERNAL FATE.
A HIT AND RUN AUTO LEAVES A MANGLED BODY BY THE ROADSIDE.
SUDDENLY A GROTESQUE WRAITH EMERGES FROM THE SHADOWS AND DARTS TOWARD THE LIFELESS VICTIM.

■ Despite his nonachievers name, Zero had a thriving practice as an occult investigator from 1940 through 1943 in the back pages of *Feature Comics*. He got going in #32 (May 1940) and ghost-detected his way through two-score issues of the magazine before closing up shop.

Zero was a handsome fellow with an Errol Flynn moustache, and he didn't handle mundane cases—"I don't handle any case unless it has to do with the supernatural." His fearless labor policy caused the dapper sleuth to undertake some fairly grim jobs. During his stay in *Feature*, Zero, billed as "the only mortal who communes with the supernatural on equal terms," tangled with such things as a three-fingered ogre, a skeleton fiddler who was staging midnight jam sessions in the local graveyard, a ghostly galleon crewed by spectral pirates, and a ghost hand that went around rapping on its victims' heads.

The Zero ambience was unremittingly gloomy. Wherever he went the weather was always bad, hardly a mansion he dropped in on that wasn't decaying and located in a patch of real estate described as "dark countryside." Not an issue went by without the occult gumshoe meeting up with at least one walking skeleton and/or shrouded ghoul. He couldn't go whistling by a cemetery without a few graves opening up to release some perturbed, and usually green, spirits. All the *Zero* scripts were credited to the pen name Noel Fowler and the artwork was provided by such as Dan Zolnerowich, Charles Sultan, and John Celardo.

Zero was the product of the Jerry Iger shop. While that establishment was noted for its mass production of Good Girl Art, it also had a flourishing sideline in spooky stuff. In addition to *Zero*, the Iger staff produced such gloomy features as *Ghost Gallery* and *The Werewolf Hunter*.

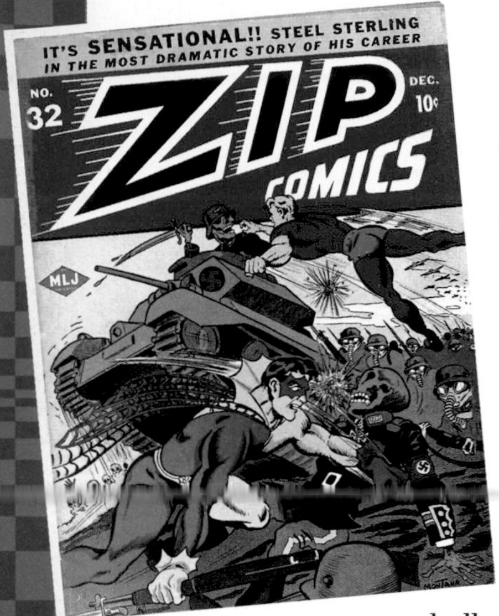
IT'S SENSATIONAL!! STEEL STERLING IN THE MOST DRAMATIC STORY OF HIS CAREER
NO. 32
DEC. 10¢
ZIP COMICS
MLJ

ZIP COMICS

■ Begun as yet another haven for superheroes and crimebusters, *Zip* ended its days chock full of comedy features. The fourth of the recently formed MLJ Magazines' monthlies, the #1 issue was cover-dated February 1940. Its main challenge to DC's Man of Steel was Steel Sterling, the Man of Steel. He became a superhero in an extremely traumatic manner. "To avenge the death of his father, who was murdered and robbed of all his wealth by gangsters, and to avoid a similar end for himself," explained an early caption, "John Sterling . . . hurled himself into a tank of molten steel and fiery chemicals! The test realized his life ambition. He emerged as 'Steel Sterling' with the attributes of this sturdiest of metals!!"

Charles Biro was the artist, and Abner Sundell, the magazine's editor, wrote the scripts. To live up to the book's title, Steel usually produced a *zip* sound while speeding into action. Biro also drew the covers through #17 (August 1941), all of them showing Steel in action and over half of them showing the blond, red-clad hero saving young women from being buried alive, decapitated, or hanged. The team of penciler Pierce Rice and Inker Irv Novick were the next to take over the job of drawing *Steel Sterling*.

Among the other characters introduced were the Scarlet Avenger, a masked cowboy on a white horse, twin daredevil aviators, and a magician. *Zip* introduced Wilbur, MLJ's first teenage character, in #18 (September 1941). Black Jack arrived two issues later, a violent fellow in a red costume with the ace of spades on its chest. Stabbing was the favorite mode of murder practiced by most of his opponents. Even bloodier were the adventures of the Web, who debuted in #27 the following year. He wore a green-and-yellow costume and a cape that resembled a spiderweb. When not thusly tricked out, he was a mild-mannered criminology professor. He operated in war-torn Europe and seemed to run into a lot of victims who'd been decapitated. This feature, a product of the Jerry Iger shop, was initially illustrated by Mort Leav.

Early in 1944, because of MLJ's conversion to a devout belief in humor brought about by the impressive success of Archie, *Zip Comics* was abruptly changed. Just about everybody except Steel, the Web, and Wilbur was dropped, replaced by "brand new funny features." These included *Ginger*, *Senor Banana*, and *The Slaphappy Applejacks*. *Zip* also tried a feeble superhero parody titled *Red Rube*. With issue #47 (Summer 1944) *Zip* ceased to be. Steel Sterling managed to hold on until the end.

The Web and Steel Sterling have returned over the years, most recently in DC's ill-fated Impact line in the early 1990s.

ZOOT COMICS

■ A Victor Fox title, the magazine started in 1946 as a showcase for "ribtickling humor." That was provided by a parrot named Red Kamphor and "your old friends the Joy Family." Soon, however, Fox and packager Jerry Iger were up to their old tricks and with #7 (June 1947) *Zoot* was given over to the adventures of Rulah, Jungle Goddess. A dark-haired young lady, who somewhat resembled cheesecake model Bettie Page, Rulah wore a bikini that appeared to be fashioned from giraffe skin. The art, in the Iger house style, contained elements of both Matt Baker and Jack Kamen.

With issue #17 (July 1948) Zoot became *Rulah*. The jungle goddess remained in charge until the twenty-ninth issue. Next time around the book was called *I Loved* and was full of "true-to-life love stories." During this same period Rulah could also be found in Fox's *All Top*.

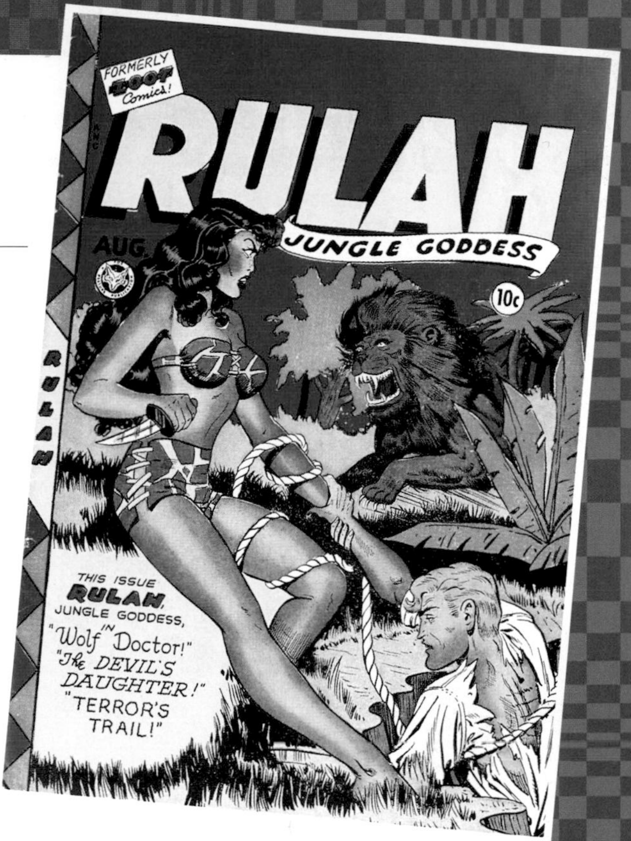
FORMERLY ZOOT Comics!
RULAH
JUNGLE GODDESS
AUG.
10¢
THIS ISSUE RULAH JUNGLE GODDESS, IN
"Wolf Doctor!"
"The DEVIL'S DAUGHTER!"
"TERROR'S TRAIL!"

ZORRO

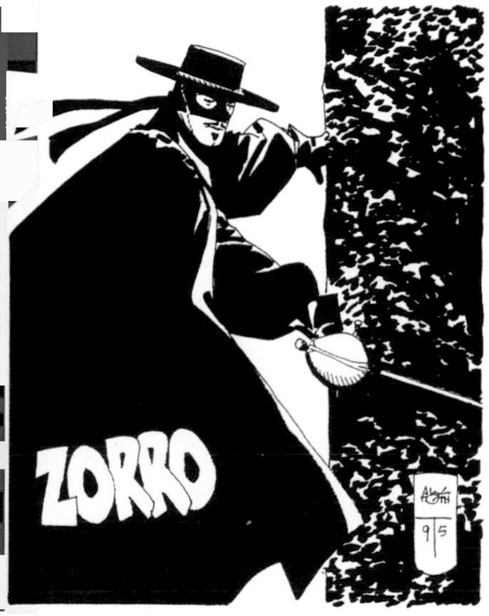
ZORRO

■ One of the best-known masked heroes of the twentieth century and an inspiration to the creators of *Batman*, Zorro started out in the pages of a pulp-fiction magazine in 1919. The following year, he jumped into silent films, and in the 1930s and 1940s he fenced his way through both serials and feature films. Zorro first appeared in a comic book in 1949. Disney got hold of the masked swordsman of Old California in 1957 and made him into a television star. More comic books resulted from that. A 1990 cable TV series brought Zorro back into public view and, briefly, into the comic shops. A 1998 feature film had a similar result.

Johnston McCulley, a one-time newspaper man from the Midwest, created Zorro in a serial that appeared in Munsey's *All-Story Weekly* in 1919. Eventually McCulley would write more than sixty novels and stories about the mild-mannered, foppish young Don Diego who donned a mask to become a fearless avenger and champion of the underdog. In 1920 the story served as the basis for Douglas Fairbanks, Sr.'s *The Mark of Zorro*. It was remade by 20th Century Fox in 1940 with Tyrone Power as the dueling hero. Republic Pictures also bought partial rights to the character and that resulted in a 1936 movie titled *The Bold Caballero* and such chapter plays as *Zorro Rides Again* in 1937 and *Zorro's Fighting Legion* in 1939.

Dell issued the first Zorro comic book in 1949, a one-shot titled *The Mark of Zorro*, with artwork by Bill Ely. Dell returned to the character several times in the early and middle 1950s, offering such titles as *The Return of Zorro* and *The Challenge of Zorro* as part of its Four Color series. Early in 1958, Dell released a new series of comic books based on the Disney TV show. These used photos of actor Guy Williams, in costume, on the covers. The interior artwork was first done by Alex Toth. Warren Tufts later drew the character.

The magazine outlasted the show, which went off the air in 1959, and didn't cease until 1961. Between 1966 and 1968, Gold Key offered a nine-issue series that reprinted from the earlier Dell issues. In 1990, to tie in with the new Family Channel *Zorro*, Marvel published a short-lived series of comic books. Toth drew some of the covers. Topps, during their brief fling with comics, published eleven issues of *Zorro* in 1993 and 1994. In 1998 Image put forth a four-issue series adapted from the Antonio Banderas film, *The Mask of Zorro*.

ART CREDITS

Blue Beetle, Fantastic Comics, Mystery Men, Rex Dexter of Mars © 1939, 1940, 1941 by Fox Publications, Inc.

All Top, Phantom Lady, Rulah, Zoot © 1948 by Fox Features Syndicate.

Captain Wings, Firehair, Jumbo Comics, Jungle Comics, Tiger Girl © 1940, 1942, 1945, 1947 by Fiction House Magazines.

Famous Funnies, Hyaroman, Jingle Jangle © 1936, 1937, 1938, 1941, 1942, 1953 by Famous Funnies, Inc.

Action Comics, Adventure Comics, All-American Comics, All Funny, All-Flash, Amethyst, Aquaman, The Atom, Atomic Knights, Barry O'Neill, Bat Lash, Batman, Beware the Creeper, Black Canary, Blue Devil, Boy Commandos, Catwoman, Challengers of the Unknown, The Crimson Avenger, A Date with Judy, Danger Girl, Deadman, Death, Detective Comics, Dr. Occult, Doom Patrol Eclipso, Elongated Man, The Flash, Green Lantern, Harley Quinn, Hellblazer, Johnny Thunder, Justice League, More Fun Comics, 100 Bullets, Pinhead, Plop, Rex the Wonder Dog, Ronin, Sandman, Scribbly, Secret Origins, Sensation Comics, Sgt. Rock, Slam Bradley, The Spectre, Star Spangled Comics, Superman, Swamp Thing, Teen Titans, Tom Strong, Watchmen, Wildcat, Wonder Woman, World's Finest Comics, Zatanna, Zatara © 2004 by DC Comics, Inc.

John Carter of Mars, Tarzan © 2004 by Edgar Rice Burroughs, Inc.

Blondie, Flash Gordon, Jungle Jim, The Katzenjammer Kids © 2004 by King Features Syndicate.

Hate Annual © 2002 by Peter Bagge.

The Spirit © 2004 by Will Eisner.

Fighting American © 2004 by Joe Simon.

Eerie Comics © 1947 by Avon Periodicals.

Archie, Bats, Blue Ribbon Comics, The Comet, The Fly, Hangman, Madam Satan, Top-Notch Comics, Zip Comics © 2004 by Archie Comics, Inc.

The Lone Ranger © 1939, 1944 by The Lone Ranger, Inc.

Captain Midnight © 1942 by The Wander Company.

Black Condor, Blackhawk, Candy, The Clock, Feature Comics, Hit Comics, Madam Fatal, Midnight, Plastic Man, The Ray, Zero-Ghost Detective © 1940, 1941, 1942, 1948 by Quality Comics Group.

Concrete, Dark Horse Presents, Ghost, Lone Wolf and Cub, Monkeyman & O'Brien © 2004 by Dark Horse Comics.

Hellboy © 2004 by Mike Mignola.

Bone © 2004 by Jeff Smith.

Gen 13, Witchblade © 2004 by Image Comics, Inc.

Lt. Blueberry © by Dargaud Editeur.

Giggle Comics, Herbie, Hi-Jinx © 1945, 1946, 1947 by American Comics Group.

Dick Tracy © by Tribune-Media Syndicate, Inc.

Casper © by Harvey Famous Cartoons.

Richie Rich © by Harvey Features.

Dennis the Menace © 1968 by Publishers-Hall Syndicate.

Undersea Agent © 1966 by Tower Comics, Inc.

Donald Duck, Mickey Mouse © by The Walt Disney Company.

Captain Marvel, Captain Marvel, Jr., Doctor Voodoo, Master Comics, Nickel Comics, Nyoka, Wow Comics © 1940, 1941, 1942, 1943, 1946 by Fawcett Publications, Inc.

Devil Girl, Mr. Natural, and other *Robert Crumb* images © 2004 by Robert Crumb.

Classic Comics, Classics Illustrated © by Gilberton Company, Inc.

Airboy, The Heap © 1944, 1946 by Hillman Periodicals, Inc.

Looney Tunes and Merrie Melodies © 1942 by Leon Schlesinger Productions.

Vampirella © 2004 by Frank Frazetta.

Charlie Chan, Prize Comics, Yank and Doodle © 1943, 1949 by Crestwood Publishing Co., Inc.

Tip Top Comics © 1941 by United Feature Syndicate, Inc.

It's a Good Life If You Don't Weaken © 2003 by Seth (G. Gallant).

Cerebus © 2004 by Dave Sim.

Little Lulu © 1969 by Marjorie Henderson Buell.

Spawn © 2004 by Todd McFarlane Productions, Inc.

American Flagg © 1985 by First Comics, Inc., and Howard Chaykin, Inc.

The Avengers, Alpha Flight, Amazing Fantasy, Black Cat, Black Panther, Blonde Phantom, Captain America, Daredevil, Dazzler, Dr. Strange, Fantastic Four, The Ghost Rider, Howard the Duck, The Hulk, The Human Torch, Ka-Zar, Marvel Mystery Comics, New Mutants, Nick Fury, Powerhouse Pepper , Sgt. Fury, She-Hulk, Spider-Man, Sub-Mariner, Thor, Tomb of Dracula, Wolverine, What If...?, X-Men, Conan, Falcon, Iron Man © 2004 by Marvel Characters, Inc. Used with permission.

Liberty Meadows © 2004 by Frank Cho.

Jimmy Corrigan © 2004 by Chris Ware.

Tintin © 2004 by Hergé/Moulinsart.

Felix the Cat © 2004 by Felix the Cat Productions, Inc.

Strangers in Paradise © 2004 by Terry Moore.

INDEX

TIME LINE (continued)

1956 The Silver Age begins modestly when DC editor Julius Schwartz introduces a new Flash in Showcase #4.

1959 Destined to become the biggest hero group of them all, the Legion of Superheroes gets going in Adventure Comics #247. ■ A new Green Lantern joins the new Flash on the stands.

1960 The Justice League, an updated Justice Society, goes into business in DC's Showcase #28 and gets its own title later in the year.

1978 Spirit creator Will Eisner makes his first venture into the field of Graphic novels with A Contract with God.

1980 Updating some older characters, Marv Wolfman and George Perez have a hit with The New Teen Titans.

1984 Teenage Mutant Ninja Turtles appear, soon proving that it's possible for a low-budget independent to became a palpable hit. ■ Blue Devil, an unusual and reluctant superhero, makes his DC debut.

1986 Art Spiegelman's Maus appears, later becoming the first, and only, comic book to win a Pulitzer Prize.

1987 Alan Moore and Dave Gibbons produce Watchmen for DC, taking a more realistic and cynical approach to superheroes. The popular twelve-issue series is later issued as a graphic novel.

2000 Florida-based Mark Alessi founds his CrossGeneration Comics Company and introduces a Cross Gen universe in which all titles initially operate. He hires the likes of George Perez, Barbara Kessel, and Mark Waid, and they produce such titles as CrossGenChronicles, Meridian, Mystic, Scion, and Sojourn. ■ Marvel tries another successful variation on its basic stable with its Ultimate series, including Ultimate Spider-Man, etc. ■ Image publishes Powers.

2002 An alternate 1940s Captain America, an African-American soldier, is introduced in a miniseries titled Truth: Red, White & Black.

2003 Marvel revives Conan, with Kurt Busiek scripting and also reintroduces a grey-complexioned Hulk. ■ DC brings back Sgt. Rock in a hardcover graphic novel. ■ Image offers a new variation on an old monster with Frankenstein Mobster.

2004 DC starts a Focus line, featuring titles that take place outside the regular DC universe.

?